Advances in Economics and Econometrics

This is the third of three volumes containing edited versions of papers and a commentary presented at invited symposium sessions of the Ninth World Congress of the Econometric Society, held in London in August 2005. The papers summarize and interpret key developments, and they discuss future directions for a wide variety of topics in economics and econometrics. The papers cover both theory and applications. Written by leading specialists in their fields, these volumes provide a unique survey of progress in the discipline.

Richard Blundell, CBE FBA, holds the David Ricardo Chair in Political Economy at University College London and is Research Director of the Institute for Fiscal Studies, London. He is also Director of the Economic and Social Research Council's Centre for the Microeconomic Analysis of Public Policy. Professor Blundell served as President of the Econometric Society for 2006.

Whitney K. Newey is Professor of Economics at the Massachusetts Institute of Technology. A 2000–2001 Fellow at the Center for Advanced Study in the Behavioral Sciences in Palo Alto, he is associate editor of *Econometrica* and the *Journal of Statistical Planning and Inference*, and he formerly served as associate editor of *Econometric Theory*.

Torsten Persson is Professor and Director of the Institute for International Economic Studies at Stockholm University and Centennial Professor of Economics at the London School of Economics. He was elected a Foreign Honorary Member of the American Academy of Arts and Sciences in 2001 and served as President of the European Economic Association in 2003.

Econometric Society Monographs No. 43

Editors:

Andrew Chesher, University College London
Matthew Jackson, Stanford University

The Econometric Society is an international society for the advancement of economic theory in relation to statistics and mathematics. The Econometric Society Monographs series is designed to promote the publication of original research contributions of high quality in mathematical economics and theoretical and applied econometrics.

Other titles in the series:

G. S. Maddala, *Limited dependent and qualitative variables in econometrics*, 0 521 33825 5
Gerard Debreu, *Mathematical economics: Twenty papers of Gerard Debreu*, 0 521 33561 2
Jean-Michel, Grandmont *Money and value: A reconsideration of classical and neoclassical monetary economics*, 0 521 31364 3
Franklin M. Fisher, *Disequilibrium foundations of equilibrium economics*, 0 521 37856 7
Andreu Mas-Colell, *The theory of general equilibrium: A differentiable approach*, 0 521 26514 2, 0 521 38870 8
Truman F. Bewley, Editor, *Advances in econometrics – Fifth World Congress* (Volume I), 0 521 46726 8
Truman F. Bewley, Editor, *Advances in econometrics – Fifth World Congress* (Volume II), 0 521 46725 X
Herve Moulin, *Axioms of cooperative decision making*, 0 521 36055 2, 0 521 42458 5
L. G. Godfrey, *Misspecification tests in econometrics: The Lagrange multiplier principle and other approaches*, 0 521 42459 3
Tony Lancaster, *The econometric analysis of transition data*, 0 521 43789 X
Alvin E. Roth and Marilda A. Oliviera Sotomayor, Editors, *Two-sided matching: A study in game-theoretic modeling and analysis*, 0 521 43788 1
Wolfgang Härdle, *Applied nonparametric regression*, 0 521 42950 1
Jean-Jacques Laffont, Editor, *Advances in economic theory – Sixth World Congress* (Volume I), 0 521 56610 X
Jean-Jacques Laffont, Editor, *Advances in economic theory – Sixth World Congress* (Volume II), 0 521 48460 X
Halbert White, *Estimation, inference and specification*, 0 521 25280 6, 0 521 57446 3
Christopher Sims, Editor, *Advances in econometrics – Sixth World Congress* (Volume I), 0 521 56610 X
Christopher Sims, Editor, *Advances in econometrics – Sixth World Congress* (Volume II), 0 521 56609 6
Roger Guesnerie, *A contribution to the pure theory of taxation*, 0 521 23689 4, 0 521 62956 X
David M. Kreps and Kenneth F. Wallis, Editors, *Advances in economics and econometrics – Seventh World Congress* (Volume I), 0 521 58011 0, 0 521 58983 5
David M. Kreps and Kenneth F. Wallis, Editors, *Advances in economics and econometrics – Seventh World Congress* (Volume II), 0 521 58012 9, 0 521 58982 9
David M. Kreps and Kenneth F. Wallis, Editors, *Advances in economics and econometrics – Seventh World Congress* (Volume III), 0 521 58013 7, 0 521 58981 9
Donald P. Jacobs, Ehud Kalai, and Morton I. Kamien, Editors, *Frontiers of research in economic theory: The Nancy L. Schwartz Memorial Lectures, 1983–1997*, 0 521 63222 6, 0 521 63538 1
A. Colin Cameron and Pravin K. Trivedi, *Regression analysis of count data*, 0 521 63201 3, 0 521 63567 5
Steinar Strom, Editor, *Econometrics and economic theory in the 20th century: The Ragnar Frisch Centennial Symposium*, 0 521 63323 0, 0 521 63365 6
Eric Ghysels, Norman R. Swanson, and Mark Watson, Editors, *Essays in econometrics: Collected papers of Clive W. J. Granger* (Volume I), 0 521 77297 4, 0 521 80407 8, 0 521 77496 9, 0 521 79697 0

Continued on page following the index

Advances in Economics and Econometrics

Theory and Applications, Ninth World Congress, Volume III

Edited by

Richard Blundell
University College London

Whitney K. Newey
Massachusetts Institute of Technology

Torsten Persson
Stockholm University

CAMBRIDGE
UNIVERSITY PRESS

CAMBRIDGE UNIVERSITY PRESS
Cambridge, New York, Melbourne, Madrid, Cape Town, Singapore, São Paulo

Cambridge University Press
32 Avenue of the Americas, New York, NY 10013-2473, USA

www.cambridge.org
Information on this title: www.cambridge.org/9780521871549

First published 2007

Printed in the United States of America

A catalog record for this publication is available from the British Library.

Library of Congress Cataloging in Publication Data

Advances in economics and econometrics : theory and applications, Ninth World
Congress / edited by Richard Blundell, Whitney K. Newey, Torsten Persson.
   p. cm. – (Econometric Society monographs; no. 43)
Edited versions of papers and a commentary presented at invited symposium sessions
of the ninth World Congress of the Econometric Society, held in London in 2005.
Includes bibliographical references and index.
ISBN 0-521-87152-2 (hardback: v.1) – ISBN 0-521-69208-3 (pbk.: v.1)
ISBN 0-521-87153-0 (hardback: v.2) – ISBN 0-521-69209-1 (pbk.: v.2)
1. Econometrics – Congresses. 2. Economics – Congresses. I. Blundell, Richard.
II. Newey, Whitney K. III. Persson, Torsten. IV. Econometric Society. World
Congress (9th : 2005 : London, England) V. Title. VI. Series.
HB139.A35   2005
330 – dc22   2006014485

ISBN   978-0-521-87154-9 hardback
ISBN   978-0-521-69210-6 paperback

1005 33 8010

Contents

Contributors

Yacine Aït-Sahalia
Princeton University

Donald W. K. Andrews
Yale University

Manuel Arellano
CEMFI, Spain

Ole E. Barndorff-Nielsen
University of Aarhus, Denmark

Martin Browning
University of Copenhagen

Jesus Carro
Universidad Carlos III de Madrid

Andrew Chesher
University College London

Jinyong Hahn
UCLA

Guido W. Imbens
Harvard University

Ilze Kalnina
London School of Economics

Yuichi Kitamura
Yale University

Arthur Lewbel
Boston College

Oliver Linton
London School of Economics

Rosa L. Matzkin
Northwestern University

Neil Shephard
Nuffield College, Oxford

Richard J. Smith
University College London

James H. Stock
Harvard University

Tiemen M. Woutersen
Johns Hopkins University

Introduction by the Editors

These volumes constitute the invited proceedings from the Ninth World Congress of the Econometric Society held on the campus of University College London on August 19–24, 2005.

As co-chairs of the Program Committee for the Congress, one of our most pleasant tasks was to select topics and authors for fifteen invited symposia – each organized around two papers. We chose topics for these invited papers that we thought were important, of current research interest, and showed a prospective long-run impact on the profession. All of the scholars that we first contacted agreed to contribute a paper. We encouraged them to write papers that would be of broad interest but would not necessarily be comprehensive literature surveys.

In the event, all symposia ran for two hours, during which the authors presented their papers and an invited discussant made comments on both of them. This book collects revised versions of the thirty papers presented in the fifteen invited symposia, as well as some of the comments by the discussants.

In all but one day of the congress, three invited symposia were run in parallel: one in economic theory, one in an applied field, and one in econometrics. The three volumes making up the book are organized by the same principle.

Volume I contains the papers on economic theory, broadly defined. In Chapter 1, "The Economics of Social Networks," Matthew Jackson discusses a central field of sociological study, a major application of random graph theory, and an emerging area of study by economists, statistical physicists, and computer scientists. The chapter provides an illuminating perspective on these literatures, with a focus on formal models of social networks, especially those based on random graphs and those based on game-theoretic reasoning. Jackson highlights some of the strengths, weaknesses, and potential synergies between these two network modeling approaches.

Chapter 2, "Multi-Contracting Mechanism Design" by David Martimort, surveys the literature on common agency. Martimort describes the features that make common-agency games special, reviews the tools needed to describe equilibrium allocations under common agency, and uses a set of simple examples to illustrate such equilibrium allocations – under complete as well as asymmetric information – and their efficiency properties. The chapter concludes that common agency might perform quite well, especially in the presence of collusion or limited commitment.

Chapter 3, by Philippe Jehiel and Benny Moldovanu, is entitled "Allocative and Informational Externalities in Auctions and Related Mechanisms." Such externalities arise naturally in models embedding (multi-object) auctions in larger economic contexts, for example, when bidders interact downstream once the auction has closed. In such settings, traditional auction formats need no longer be efficient, and may give rise to multiple equilibria and strategic non-participation. Jehiel and Moldovanu discuss which allocations are possible and impossible to achieve under different approaches to implementation and in different information environments.

In Chapter 4, "The Economics of Relationships," Larry Samuelson discusses recent work in the theory of repeated games, which provides the tools for studying long-run relationships. He examines folk theorems for games with imperfect public and private monitoring, and new techniques for studying equilibria when folk theorems are not helpful because players are not sufficiently patient or well informed. The chapter illustrates a number of recent applications that have moved the literature on repeated games from technical questions to findings of economic relevance. It concludes with a discussion of outstanding problems.

Following these chapters on game theory are two chapters on economic design. Chapter 5, "Information in Mechanism Design," written by Dirk Bergemann and Juuso Välimäki, examines endogeneity of private information, and robustness to private information in mechanism design. The authors view information acquisition and robustness to private information as two distinct but related aspects of information management, which are important in many design settings. The chapter not only surveys the existing literature, but also points out directions for future work.

In Chapter 6, "Computational Issues in Economic Design," Ilya Segal argues that full revelation of privately held information about preferences may often be impractical or undesirable. He then asks what minimal information must be elicited from agents to achieve the social goals of the mechanism designer. Segal relates this question to the work on communication complexity in computer science and dimensionality of message space in economics, where communication is measured in bits and real numbers, respectively. He outlines existing results on the topic, a substantial body of related work, and some extensions.

The next two chapters deal with macroeconomic theory. Chapter 7, by Naryana Kocherlakota, is entitled "Advances in Dynamic Optimal Taxation." It surveys the recent literature concerning the structure of optimal taxes in dynamic economies. As in the literature following Mirrlee's path-breaking work on optimal static taxation, there are no restrictions on the available policy instruments, and the optimal tax schedules are designed subject only to the private information held by private agents about skills and effort. Kocherlakota illustrates and explains the major results achieved so far and suggests where the literature may go next.

In Chapter 8, "Quantitative Macroeconomic Models with Heterogeneous Agents," Per Krusell and Tony Smith review recent work on dynamic stochastic macroeconomic models with individual heterogeneity in income, employment status, and wealth, to approximate empirical models in the applied consumption and labor literatures. They focus on the properties of such models – especially so-called approximate aggregation – and the computational methods for analyzing them. The chapter also presents a simple two-period setting that serves as a useful laboratory to examine the implications of the distribution of income in different economic settings.

The final section of the volume concerns political economy. In Chapter 9, "Modeling Inefficient Institutions," Daron Acemoglu asks why inefficient institutions emerge and persist, and he develops a simple framework to provide some answers to this question. He illustrates how a group may want to pursue inefficient policies so as to increase their income and to directly or indirectly transfer resources from the rest of the society to themselves, and how the preferences over inefficient policies may translate into inefficient economic institutions. The chapter also provides a framework for the analysis of institutional change and institutional persistence.

While Acemoglu emphasizes the macro side of political economy, Chapter 10, "Whither Political Economy? Theories, Facts, and Issues," by Antonio Merlo emphasizes the micro side. Merlo reviews current research on four of the fundamental institutions of a political economy: voters, politicians, parties, and governments. He identifies and discusses salient questions posed in the literature, presents some stylized models and examples, and summarizes the main theoretical findings. Moreover, the chapter describes available data, reviews relevant empirical evidence, and discusses challenges for empirical research in political economy.

Volume I ends with a discussion of Chapters 9 and 10, by Tim Besley.

Volume II contains papers on applied economics and applied econometrics, again broadly defined. For example, the first six chapters present a broad review and evaluation of developments in modern industrial economics. There is then an assessment of behavioral economics. This is followed by a detailed review of progress in dynamic labor economics. The volume rounds up with two insightful chapters on progress and new ideas in empirical development economics.

In Chapter 1 of Volume II, "Empirical Models of Auctions," Susan Athey and Phil Haile review some of the most innovative of the recent empirical applications and present three key insights that underlie much of the progress in the econometrics of auction models. The first is the usefulness of casting the identification problem as one of learning about latent distribution functions based on observation of certain order statistics. The second is the observation that equilibrium can be thought of as a state of mutual best responses. The third is the value of additional variation in the data beyond the realizations of bids. Although observable variation in auction characteristics might initially seem to be minor nuisances to be dealt with, they argue that these kinds of variation often can be exploited to aid identification. Chapter 2, "Identification in Models of Oligopoly Entry" by Steve Berry and Elie Tamer, reviews and extends a number of results on the identification of models that are used in the empirical literature. They present simple versions of both static and dynamic entry models. For simple static models, they show how natural shape restrictions can be used to identify competition effects. In the case of dynamic models, they examine existing results on the model with i.i.d. linear errors, and then consider more realistic cases, such as when the distribution of fixed costs is unknown. Chapter 3, "Empirical Models of Imperfect Competition: A Discussion," by Liran Einav and Aviv Nevo, discusses the first two chapters of this volume. They note that in the empirical IO literature much progress has been made on identification and estimation of many different dimensions of firms' decisions. There are more flexible models of consumer demand and better methods to nonparametrically estimate bidder valuation in auctions, and significant progress has been made on estimating entry and dynamic games.

Chapter 4, "Recent Developments in the Economics of Price Discrimination" by Mark Armstrong, surveys the recent literature on price discrimination. The focus is on three aspects of pricing decisions: the information about customers available to firms; the instruments firms can use in the design of their tariffs; and the ability of firms to commit to their pricing plans. Armstrong notes that developments in marketing technology mean that firms often have access to more information about individual customers than was previously the case. The use of this information might be restricted by public policy toward customer privacy. Where it is not restricted, firms may be unable to commit to how they use the information. With monopoly supply, an increased ability to engage in price discrimination will boost profit unless the firm cannot commit to its pricing policy. Likewise, an enhanced ability to commit to prices will benefit a monopolist. With competition, the effects of price discrimination on profit, consumer surplus, and overall welfare depend on the kinds of information and/or tariff instruments available to firms. The paper shows that the ability to commit to prices may damage industry profit. Chapter 5, "Bounded Rationality in Industrial Organization" by Glenn Ellison, notes that three main approaches are found in the recent literature: rule-of thumb papers specify simple rules for behavior; explicit bounds papers consider agents who maximize payoffs net of cognitive costs; and the psychology and economics approach typically cites experimental evidence to motivate utility-like frameworks. Common to each recent literature is a focus on consumer irrationalities that firms might exploit. The paper then discusses several new topics that have been opened up by the consideration of bounded rationality and new perspectives that have been provided on traditional topics. Chapter 6, "Price Discrimination and Irrational Consumers: A Discussion of Armstrong and Ellison" by Ken Hendricks, presents a discussion of these two chapters. In relation to the Armstrong paper he argues that one of the roles of theory is to classify the kinds of oligopoly markets where price discrimination is likely to occur, the form that it is likely to take, and the impact that it is likely to have on profits and welfare. He notes that the theme of firms exploiting consumers is also present in Ellison's chapter, which focuses primarily on irrational consumers. However, the main issues there are methodological, challenging the field to reexamine its traditional approach.

Chapters 7 to 9 turn to the field of behavioral economics. In Chapter 7, Colin Camerer shows how evidence from psychology and other disciplines has been used in behavioral economics to create models of limits on rationality, willpower, and self-interest and explores their implications in economic aggregates. The paper reviews the basic themes of behavioral economics: sensitivity of revealed preferences to descriptions of goods and procedures; generalizations of models of choice over risk, ambiguity, and time; fairness and reciprocity; non-Bayesian judgment; and stochastic equilibrium and learning. He argues that a central concern is what happens in equilibrium when agents are imperfect but heterogeneous. Camerer argues that neuroeconomics extends the psychological data use and suggests that it is likely to support rational choice theory in some cases, to buttress behavioral economics in some cases, and to suggest different constructs as well. In Chapter 8, "Incentives and Self-Control," Ted O'Donoghue and Matthew Rabin investigate the design of incentives for people subject to self-control problems in the form of a time-inconsistent taste for immediate gratification. They argue that because such present-biased people may not behave in their own long-run best interests, there is scope for firms, policymakers, friends and family, and the people themselves to create incentives for "better" behavior. They note that optimal incentive design, therefore, will attend to details that the conventional model would say are essentially irrelevant. The paper goes on to describe some general principles that have emerged in recent and ongoing research on incentives, highlighting the importance of heterogeneity among agents and providing for flexibility, and illustrating these principles with some simple examples. In his discussion presented in Chapter 9, Ariel Rubinstein argues that although there is no reason for economics to hide behind the traditional barriers, for behavioral economics to be a revolutionary program of research rather than a passing episode, it must become more open-minded and much more self-critical.

Turning to dynamic labor economics, in Chapter 10, "Dynamic Models for Policy Evaluation," Costas Meghir shows that the evaluation of interventions has become a commonly used policy tool, which is frequently adopted to improve the transparency and effectiveness of public policy. However, he argues that evaluation methods based on comparing treatment and control groups in small-scale trials are not capable of providing a complete picture of the likely effects of a policy and do not provide a framework that allows issues relating to the design of the program to be addressed. Meghir shows how experimental data from field trials can be used to enhance the evaluation of interventions and also illustrates the potential importance of allowing for longer-term incentive and general equilibrium effects. In Chapter 11, "Microeconometric Search-Matching Models and Matched Employer–Employee Data," Jean-Marc Robin suggests that the recent advent of matched employer–employee data has allowed significant progress in our understanding of individual labor earnings. He argues that viewing these empirical analyses through the lens of structural job search models can help clarify and unify some of its recurring findings. Among other things he shows how search frictions combined with a theoretically founded wage formation rule based on renegotiation by mutual consent can account for the widely documented dynamic persistence of individual wages. In his discussion of these two papers in Chapter 12, Joe Altonji argues that they provide useful analyses of developments in two important areas in labor economics and public finance. He examines the potential to utilize a continuum of models between a simple experimental or quasi-experimental analysis on the one hand and a dynamic structural model on the other, even in complicated dynamic settings in which reduced form analysis is difficult. He also supplements the research agenda in search/matching models and the application using matched employer–employee data.

Volume II concludes with two key papers on advances in development economics. Chapter 13, "Field Experiments in Development Economics" by Esther Duflo, observes that over the last decade, the long tradition in development economics of collecting original data to test specific hypotheses has merged with an expertise in setting up randomized field experiments. This in turn has resulted in an increasingly large number of studies in which an original experiment has been set up to test economic theories and hypotheses. The paper extracts some substantive and methodological lessons from such studies in three domains: incentives, social learning, and time-inconsistent preferences. It makes the case that we need both to continue testing existing theories and to start thinking of how the theories may be adapted to make sense of the field experiment results, many of which are starting to challenge them. In Chapter 14, "Institutions and Development: A View from Below," Rohini Pande and Christopher Udry argue the case for greater exploitation of synergies between research on specific institutions based on micro-data and the big questions posed by the institutions and growth literature. They suggest two research programs based on micro-data that have significant potential. The first uses policy-induced variation in specific institutions within countries to understand how these institutions influence economic activity. The second exploits the fact that the incentives provided by a given institutional context often vary with individuals' economic and political status. The chapter analyzes the way variations in individual responses to the same institution can be used to both identify how institutions affect economic outcomes and to understand how institutional change arises in response to changing economic and demographic pressures.

Volume III contains papers on econometrics. The first five chapters are about identification and estimation when unobserved heterogeneity has nonlinear effects. This work is motivated by economic models in which the common assumption of additive disturbances is not satisfied. The three chapters that follow concern weak instruments and empirical likelihood. These methods provide alternatives to classical instrumental variables inference, which can be important in applications. The next three chapters are about econometrics for financial markets. They summarize powerful approaches to analyzing the time series behavior of asset markets. The last two chapters return to the subject of unobserved heterogeneity, now in the context of nonlinear models for panel data. They consider bias correction methods for fixed effects estimation, a promising method of controlling for unobserved heterogeneity in panel data.

In Chapter 1 of Volume III, "Identification of Nonadditive Structural Functions," Andrew Chesher reviews recent work on identification of structural models with disturbances that are not additively separable. This chapter focuses on the case in which there are no more disturbances than endogenous variables. In the one-disturbance-per-equation case, independence of the instrument and a conditional quantile of the disturbance can suffice for identification of the structural equation at a particular value of the disturbance. In the triangular model case, in which the number of disturbances entering each equation is equal to the number of endogenous variables in that equation, local independence of instruments and disturbances suffices for identification of structural derivatives. Bounds are also given for the case with a discrete endogenous variable. In Chapter 2, "Nonadditive Models with Endogenous Regressors," Guido Imbens considers the case in which the disturbance in the equation of interest can have any dimension. Identification and estimation with control functions are discussed, a control function being a variable that when conditioned on gives exogeneity. A control function for the triangular system is provided. Identification of certain policy effects is considered.

In Chapter 3, "Heterogeneity and Microeconometric Modeling," Martin Browning and Jesus Carro suggest that heterogeneity is more common in applications than usually allowed for, that how it is allowed for can often have large effects on results, and that it is difficult to allow for in a general way. They illustrate these suggestions with applied and theoretical examples. In particular, they consider a stationary first-order Markov chain model that allows for general heterogeneity, where they propose estimators and analyze their properties. Chapter 4, "Heterogenous Choice" by Rosa Matzkin, gives identification results for nonparametric choice models in which disturbances enter nonlinearly. For models in which choices are dependent variables, this paper describes very recent results on identification of demand models and discrete choice models that are important for understanding revealed preference with unobserved heterogeneity. For models in which the choices are regressors, the paper gives control function and other identification results for structural effects. In Chapter 5, "Modeling Heterogeneity," Arthur Lewbel discusses the results from Chapters 3 and 4, showing that model interpretation depends critically on how the nonseparable disturbance enters.

Chapter 6, "Inference with Weak Instruments" by Donald Andrews and James Stock, reviews recent developments in methods for dealing with weak instruments (IVs) in IV regression models. The focus is more on tests (and confidence intervals derived from tests) than estimators. Power comparisons of the conditional likelihood ratio (CLR), Anderson-Rubin, and Lagrange multiplier tests are made. The paper also presents new testing results under "many weak IV asymptotics." Chapter 7, "Empirical Likelihood Methods in Econometrics: Theory and Practice" by Yuichi Kitamura, gives nonparametric maximum likelihood and generalized minimum contrast interpretations of the empirical likelihood estimator. This chapter presents an asymptotic optimality result for empirical likelihood under a large deviations optimality criterion. Monte Carlo results are given, illustrating substantial gains that can result. Also, the literature on higher-order properties of empirical likelihood is reviewed. Chapter 8, "Weak Instruments and Empirical Likelihood: A Discussion of Papers by D. W. K. Andrews and J. H. Stock and Yuichi Kitamura" by Richard Smith, considers inference for GMM with weak identification based on generalized empirical likelihood. It provides an asymptotic analysis for GMM that is a direct extension of the Andrews and Stock small sample analysis for IV. This chapter proposes a version of the CLR for GMM that is a precise analog to the IV case.

Chapter 9, "Estimating Continuous Time Models with Discretely Sampled Data" by Yacine Ait-Sahalia, starts with a familiar model and describes many of the most recent developments. It begins with identification and estimation of a univariate diffusion. This model is then progressively generalized to allow for different data generating processes (such as multivariate diffusions or jump processes), different observation schemes (such as incorporating market microstructure noise), and different sampling schemes (such as allowing for random time intervals). Chapter 10, "Variation, Jumps, and High-Frequency Data in Financial Econometrics" by Neil Shephard and Ole Barndorff-Nielsen, describes the econometrics of realized volatility. This chapter focuses on quadratic variation and considers the detection of jumps. The impact of market frictions is considered. Chapter 11, "Discussion of Ait-Sahalia and Barndorff-Nielsen and Shephard" by Oliver Linton and Ilze Kalnina, considers an approach to allowing for market microstructure noise. It presents consistency results for estimation of quadratic variation in the presence of small measurement errors.

Chapter 12, "Understanding Bias in Nonlinear Panel Models: Some Recent Developments" by Manuel Arellano and Jinyong Hahn, describes and discusses the relationship among recently developed bias adjustments for nonlinear panel data models with fixed effects. These bias adjustments are used to reduce the bias order of fixed effect parameter and marginal effects as the number of time series observations grows with the number of cross-section observations. The paper shows that a wide variety of bias adjustments lead to similar results, including those based on profile likelihoods and those based on moment conditions. In Chapter 13, "Fixed and Random Effects in Nonlinear Panels: A Discussion of Arellano and Hahn" by Tiemen Woutersen, an alternative bias reduction approach is discussed. This approach, which predates many of the others, involves integrating the fixed effect over a prior distribution and produces bias reductions equivalent to the other methods.

We are grateful to Christina Lönnblad, Emma Hyman, and Emily Gallagher for assisting us in our work with putting the papers together into books.

We would also like to thank all the authors, not only for writing such excellent papers, but also for delivering them in time for these books to appear promptly after the Congress. Such prompt publication would, of course, not have possible without the keen support of our Cambridge editor, Scott Parris.

London, Cambridge, and Stockholm, May 2006

Richard Blundell, Whitney Newey, and Torsten Persson

CHAPTER 1

Identification of Nonadditive
Structural Functions*
Andrew Chesher[†]

1 INTRODUCTION

When latent variates appear nonadditively in a structural function the effect of
a *ceteris paribus* change in an observable argument of the function can vary
across people measured as identical. Models that admit nonadditive structural
functions permit responses to policy interventions to have probability distributions. Knowledge of the distributions of responses is important for welfare
analysis and it is good to know what conditions secure identification of these
distributions. This lecture examines some aspects of this problem.

Early studies of identification in econometrics dealt almost exclusively with
linear additive "error" models. The subsequent study of identification in nonlinear models was heavily focused on additive error models until quite recently[1]
and only within the last ten years has there has been extensive study of identification in nonadditive error models. This lecture examines some of these recent
results, concentrating on models which admit no more sources of stochastic variation than there are observable stochastic outcomes. Models with this property
are interesting because they are direct generalizations of additive error models
and of the classical linear simultaneous equation models associated with the
work of the Cowles Commission, and because the addition of relatively weak
nonparametric restrictions results in models which identify complete structural
functions or specific local features of them.

Nonparametric restrictions are interesting because they are consonant with
the information content of economic theory. Even if parametric or semiparametric restrictions are imposed when estimation and inference are done, it is
good to know nonparametric identification conditions because they tell us what
core elements of the model are essential for identification and which are in

* I thank Lars Nesheim and Whitney Newey for helpful comments. I am grateful for generous
support from the Leverhulme Trust through their funding of the Centre for Microdata Methods
and Practice and the research project "Evidence, Inference and Enquiry."
† Centre for Microdata Methods and Practice, IFS and UCL.
1 See, for example, the review in Blundell and Powell (2003).

principle falsifiable. If just-identifying conditions can be found then we know what must be believed if the result of econometric analysis is to be given economic meaning.

Nonadditive error models permit covariates to influence many aspects of the distributions of outcomes. Koenker (2005), motivating the study of estimation of quantile regression functions, argues persuasively for consideration of models more general than the classical location shift, additive error model, that took center stage in the early history of econometrics. Models for discrete outcomes have a natural expression in terms of nonadditive structural functions as do many microeconometric models for continuous outcomes, for example, the following model for durations with heterogeneity.

Example 1 *In the analysis of a continuous duration, Y_1, with distribution function $F_{Y_1|X}$ conditional on X, it is common to use a proportionate hazard model in which the hazard function:*

$$h(y, x) \equiv -\nabla_y \log(1 - F_{Y_1|X}(y|x))$$

is restricted to have the multiplicatively separable form $\lambda(y)g(x)$. With $U_1|X \sim Unif(0, 1)$ values of Y_1 with conditional distribution function $F_{Y_1|X}$ are generated by:

$$Y_1 = \Lambda^{-1}(-\log(1 - U_1)/g(X))$$

in which the structural function is generally nonadditive. Here Λ^{-1} is the inverse of the integrated hazard function: $\Lambda(y) \equiv \int_0^y \lambda(s)ds$. Classical censoring nests the function Λ^{-1} inside a step function. In the mixed, or heterogeneous, proportionate hazard model the hazard function conditional on X and unobserved U_2 is specified as multiplicatively separable: $\lambda(y)g(x)U_2$ and there is the structural equation:

$$Y_1 = \Lambda^{-1}(-U_2^{-1}\log(1 - U_1)/g(X))$$

in which, note, there is effectively just one stochastic term: $V \equiv U_2^{-1} \log(1 - U_1)$. Endogeneity can be introduced by allowing U_2 and elements of X to be jointly dependent.

Imbens and Newey (2003) provide examples of economic contexts in which nonadditive structural functions arise naturally and are an essential feature of an economic problem if endogeneity is to be present. Card (2001) provides a parametric example.

As set out below, identification conditions in nonadditive models are rather natural extensions of those employed in additive models involving, on the one hand, conditions on the sensitivity of structural functions to variation in certain variables and, on the other, restrictions on the dependence of those variables and the latent variables. Local quantile independence conditions are helpful in identifying certain local features of structural functions. Full independence is commonly imposed in order to identify complete structural functions.

The precise form of the independence condition employed has significant implications for the way in which identification is *achieved*, by which I mean the way in which information about a structural function is carried in the distribution of outcomes about which data is informative. That in turn has implications for the challenges to be faced when developing estimators and conducting inference.

In the context of identification of a single structural function involving two jointly dependent outcomes the two contrasting cases considered here involve an independence restriction involving (i) a single latent variable and (ii) two latent variables. The latter conveys more information, is more tolerant of limitations in the support of instruments, facilitates identification of local structural features when global features may not be identifiable and motivates more benign estimation and inference. However, these benefits come at the cost of a more restrictive model whose conditions are difficult to justify in some economic problems.

Sections 2 and 3 consider identification of nonadditive structural functions under the two types of condition. Section 4 concludes.

2 MARGINAL INDEPENDENCE

In the first class of models considered the structural function delivering the value of an outcome Y_1 involves a single latent random variable.

$$Y_1 = h(Y_2, X, U_1)$$

The function h is restricted to be strictly monotonic in U_1 and is normalized increasing. There are covariates, X, whose appearance in h will be subject to exclusion-type restrictions that limit the sensitivity of h to variations in X. The variable Y_2 is an observed outcome which may be jointly dependent with U_1 and thus "endogenous."

The latent variable, U_1, and X are restricted to be independently distributed. The independence condition can be weakened to τ-quantile independence, that is, that $q_\tau \equiv Q_{U_1|X}(\tau|x)$ be independent of x for some value of τ. Then there can be identification of $h(Y_2, X, q_\tau)$. In all cases of econometric interest U_1 will be continuously distributed and the strict monotonicity condition on h then implies that Y_1 given X is continuously distributed.

This is in the family of models studied in Chernozhukov and Hansen (2005), and is essentially the model studied in Chernozhukov, Imbens, and Newey (2007). Matzkin (2003) studies the special case in which Y_2 is "exogenous," independent of U_1.

There is, using the independence condition at the first step, and the monotonicity restriction at the second, for all x:

$$\begin{aligned}
\tau &= P[U_1 \le q_\tau | X = x] \\
&= P[h(Y_2, X, U_1) \le h(Y_2, X, q_\tau) | X = x] \\
&= P[Y_1 \le h(Y_2, X, q_\tau) | X = x].
\end{aligned}$$

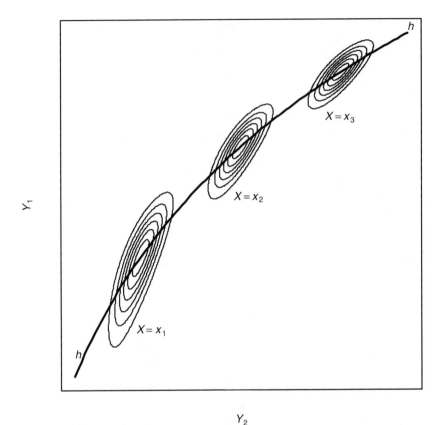

Figure 1.1. Contours of a joint density function of Y_1 and Y_2 conditional on X at three values of X. The line marked hh is the structural function $h(Y_2, X, q_\tau)$, not varying across $X \in \{x_1, x_2, x_3\}$, drawn with $q_\tau = 0.5$.

So the function $h(Y_2, X, q_\tau)$ is such that the moment condition:

$$E_{Y_1 Y_2 | X}[\mathbf{1}[Y_1 \leq h(Y_2, x, q_\tau)] - \tau | x] = 0 \qquad (1.1)$$

is satisfied for all x.

The structural function $h(\cdot, \cdot, q_\tau)$ satisfies (1.1) for all x in the support of X. It is identified if there are restrictions on the structural function, h, the joint distribution of U_1 and Y_2 given X and the support of X sufficient to ensure that no function distinct from h satisfies this condition for all x. Chernozhukov, Imbens, and Newey (2007) show that with a joint normality restriction there is an identification condition like the classical rank condition. In the absence of some parametric restrictions it is difficult to find primitive identification conditions which can be entirely motivated by economic considerations.

Figure 1.1 illustrates the situation. It shows contours of a joint distribution of Y_1 and Y_2, conditional on X, at three values of X: $\{x_1, x_2, x_3\}$. The joint distribution does vary with X and there is an exclusion restriction so that the structural function $h(\cdot, x, q_\tau)$, marked hh, is unaffected by variation in X across $x \in \{x_1, x_2, x_3\}$. The value q_τ is the τ-quantile of U_1 given X which is restricted to be invariant with respect to $x \in \{x_1, x_2, x_3\}$ and the result is that at each value of x there is the same probability mass (τ) falling below the structural function. In the case illustrated here $\tau = 0.5$. If the structural function h is the only function which has that property then h is identified.

Clearly, there could be many functions with this property, and so no identification of h, if there were, as illustrated, only three values of X at which the various conditions hold. It is evident that identification of h (in the absence of parametric restrictions) is critically dependent on the nature of the support of X which must be at least as rich as the support of the endogenous Y_2. If Y_2 is binary then binary X may suffice for identification and if X has richer support there can be nonparametric overidentification. If Y_2 is continuous then X must be continuous if h is to be identified.

The role in identification of the support of instruments is easily appreciated in the case in which there is discrete $Y_2 \in \{y_2^1, \ldots, y_2^M\}$ and discrete $X \in \{x_1, \ldots, x_J\}$ and X does not feature in h. The values of h at the M points of support of Y_2 and at $U_1 = q_\tau$ are denoted by $\theta_\tau^m \equiv h(y_2^m, q_\tau), m \in \{1, \ldots, M\}$. The J values of X yield equations which are *nonlinear* in the terms θ_τ^m

$$\sum_{m=1}^{M} G(\theta_\tau^m, y_2^m | x_j) = \tau \quad j \in \{1, \ldots, J\} \tag{1.2}$$

where G is a conditional probability distribution – probability mass function defined as follows.

$$G(a, b | x) \equiv P[Y_1 \leq a \cap Y_2 = b | X = x]$$

The M values of the θ_τ^m's do satisfy (1.2) because those values are instrumental in determining the function G. However, without further restriction there can be other solutions to these nonlinear simultaneous equations and the θ_τ^m's will not be identified. Without further restriction there must be as many equations as unknowns and so the requirement that the support of X is at least as rich as the support of discrete Y_2. The J equations must be distinct which requires that X does have influence on the distribution of Y_2 given X. Conditions like the classical instrumental variables inclusion and exclusion restrictions are necessary. Chernozhukov and Hansen (2005) give a rank condition sufficient for local identification.

When X has sparse support relative to Y_2 and $P[Y_2 = y_2^m | x] \in (0, 1)$ for all x then no value of h is point identified. Parametric restrictions on h can lead to point identification in this case. When Y_2 is continuous there is generally point identification of the structural function nowhere unless instruments have continuous variation.

In the additive error model $Y_1 = h(Y_2, X) + U_1$ with the conditional expectation restriction: $E[U_1 | X = x] = 0$ the moment condition corresponding to (1.1) is

$$E_{Y_1 Y_2 | X}[Y_1 - h(Y_2, x, q_\tau) | x] = 0$$

which reduces to

$$E_{Y_1|X}[Y_1|x] - E_{Y_2|X}[h(Y_2, x)]|x] = 0$$

and to *linear* equations in the values of h when Y_2 is discrete, a case studied in Das (2005) and Florens and Malavolti (2003). When Y_2 is continuous the structural function h is the solution to an integral equation which constitutes an ill-posed *linear* inverse problem and leads to challenging problems in estimation and inference studied in, for example, Darolles, Florens, and Renault (2003), Florens (2003), Blundell and Powell (2003), Hall and Horowitz (2005).

In the nonadditive case with continuous Y_2 the structural function h is a solution to the integral equation

$$\int_{-\infty}^{\infty} G(h(y_2, x, q_\tau), y_2|x)dy_2 = \tau \tag{1.3}$$

which constitutes an ill-posed *nonlinear* inverse problem with significant challenges for estimation and inference studied in Chernozhukov, Imbens, and Newey (2007), Chernozhukov and Hong (2003), and Chernozhukov and Hansen (2005).

The inverse problem (1.3) is nonlinear because of the use of quantile independence conditions and arises in the additive error case as well if a quantile independence rather than a mean independence condition is employed. In the additive error model there is, with quantile independence:

$$\int_{-\infty}^{\infty} G(h(y_2, x) + q_\tau, y_2|x)dy_2 = \tau$$

and there can be overidentification because $h(y_2, x)$ may be identified up to an additive constant at any value of τ.

3   JOINT INDEPENDENCE

In the second class of models considered here the structural function delivering the value of an outcome Y_1 involves one or two latent random variables.

$$Y_1 = h(Y_2, X, U_1, U_2)$$

The function h is restricted to be monotonic in U_1 and is normalized increasing. There are covariates, X, whose appearance in h will be subject to exclusion-type restrictions and the variable Y_2 is an observed outcome which may be jointly dependent with U_1 and thus "endogenous."

In this model the latent variable U_2 is the *sole* source of stochastic variation in Y_2 given X and there is the equation

$$Y_2 = g(X, U_2)$$

with g strictly monotonic in U_2, normalized increasing. If U_2 is specified as uniformly distributed on $[0, 1]$ independent of X then $g(X, U_2) = Q_{Y_2|X}(U_2|X)$. In all cases of econometric interest the latent variables are continuously distributed and the strict monotonicity restriction on g means that Y_2 is continuously distributed given X which is not required by the model of Section 2. However, in this model Y_1 can have a discrete distribution which is not permitted in the model of Section 2.

For global identification of h the latent variables (U_1, U_2) and X are restricted to be independently distributed. Note this is more general than the pair of marginal independence conditions: $U_1 \perp X$ and $U_2 \perp X$.[2] This can be substantially weakened to a local quantile independence condition with $Q_{U_1|U_2X}(\tau_1|\tau_2, x) = a(\tau_1, \tau_2)$ a function constant with respect to variation in x for some τ_1 and τ_2.[3] Then there can be identification of h when $U_1 = a(\tau_1, \tau_2)$ and $U_2 = \tau_2$. This is similar to the model studied by Imbens and Newey (2003) and Chesher (2003).

3.1　Continuous Y_2

An argument leading to identification in the continuous Y_2 case is as follows. Holding $U_2 = \tau_2$ and setting U_1 equal to its τ_1-quantile given $U_2 = \tau_2$, there is, in view of the monotonicity restriction on h and the equivariance property of quantiles, the following conditional quantile of Y_1 given U_2 and X.

$$Q_{Y_1|U_2X}(\tau_1|\tau_2, x) = h(g(x, \tau_2), x, a(\tau_1, \tau_2), \tau_2)$$

Because of the strict monotonicity restriction on g, which ensures a one-to-one correspondence between U_2 and Y_2 given X, there is the conditional quantile of Y_1 given Y_2 and X:

$$Q_{Y_1|Y_2X}(\tau_1|Q_{Y_2|X}(\tau_2|x), x) = h(y_2, x, a(\tau_1, \tau_2), \tau_2) \tag{1.4}$$

where on the right-hand side: $y_2 \equiv Q_{Y_2|X}(\tau_2|x)$. This identifies the *value* of the structural function at the indicated arguments of h. Note that this step involving a change in conditioning (from U_2 to Y_2) could not be taken if Y_2 were discrete, a case returned to shortly.

Now suppose that h is insensitive through its X-argument to a movement in X from x' to x'', which is in the nature of an exclusion restriction. Define $y_2' \equiv Q_{Y_2|X}(\tau_2|x')$ and $y_2'' \equiv Q_{Y_2|X}(\tau_2|x'')$. Then for $x^* \in \{x', x''\}$

$$Q_{Y_1|Y_2X}(\tau_1|Q_{Y_2|X}(\tau_2|x'), x') = h(y_2', x^*, a(\tau_1, \tau_2), \tau_2)$$
$$Q_{Y_1|Y_2X}(\tau_1|Q_{Y_2|X}(\tau_2|x''), x'') = h(y_2'', x^*, a(\tau_1, \tau_2), \tau_2)$$

and the difference in the iterated conditional quantiles

$$Q_{Y_1|Y_2X}(\tau_1|Q_{Y_2|X}(\tau_2|x'), x') - Q_{Y_1|Y_2X}(\tau_1|Q_{Y_2|X}(\tau_2|x''), x'') \tag{1.5}$$

---

[2] The notation $A \perp B$ indicates that the random variables A and B are statistically independent.
[3] There is $Q_{U_1|X}(\tau_2|x) = \tau_2$ by virtue of the definition of U_2.

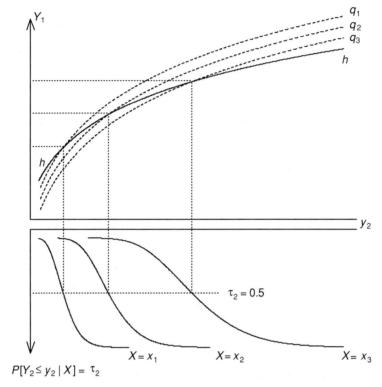

Figure 1.2. Identification of partial differences. Upper graph – q_1, q_2, q_3 are conditional τ_1-quantiles of Y_1 given Y_2 and X at $x \in \{x_1, x_2, x_3\}$ and hh is the structural function $h(y_2, x, a(\tau_1, \tau_2), \tau_2)$. Lower graph – conditional quantiles of Y_2 given $X = x$ for $x \in \{x_1, x_2, x_3\}$ with conditional medians displayed.

identifies the partial difference of the structural function

$$h(y_2', x^*, a(\tau_1, \tau_2), \tau_2) - h(y_2'', x^*, a(\tau_1, \tau_2), \tau_2) \tag{1.6}$$

and so the *ceteris paribus* effect on h of a change in Y_2 from y_2' to y_2''.

Under the iterated covariation condition considered here there is identification of values delivered by the structural function however limited the support of X. However, the locations at which identification can be achieved is critically dependent on the support of X and on the dependence of the distribution of Y_2 on X.[4] When this dependence is weak it may only be possible to identify the structural function over a very limited range of values of Y_2. In this case parametric restrictions have substantial identifying power allowing extrapolation away from the locations at which nonparametric identification can be achieved.

---

[4] Identification of partial differences using discrete instruments is discussed in Chesher (2007).

Figure 1.2 illustrates the situation. In the upper and lower parts of Figure 1.2 values of Y_2 are measured along the horizontal axes. The vertical axis in the upper part of Figure 1.2 measures values of Y_1. In the lower part of Figure 1.2 the vertical axis measures values of the distribution function of Y_2 given X.

In the upper part of Figure 1.2 the three dashed curves marked q_1, q_2, q_3 are conditional τ_1-quantiles of Y_1 given $Y_2 = y_2$ and $X = x$ drawn for some value of τ_1 as functions of y_2 for $x \in \{x_1, x_2, x_3\}$. In the upper part of the picture the solid curve (marked hh) is the structural function $h(y_2, x, U_1, U_2)$ drawn as a function of y_2 with $U_1 = a(\tau_1, \tau_2)$ and $U_2 = \tau_2$ for the same value τ_1 that determines the dashed conditional quantile functions and for $\tau_2 = 0.5$. There is an exclusion-type restriction so that the structural function remains fixed as x varies across $\{x_1, x_2, x_3\}$.

The three curves in the lower part of Figure 1.2 are conditional distribution (viewed another way, quantile) functions of Y_2 given X for $x \in \{x_1, x_2, x_3\}$ – the *same* values that generate the conditional quantile functions of Y_1 shown in the upper part of the picture. The median ($\tau_2 = 0.5$) values of Y_2 given $X \in \{x_1, x_2, x_3\}$ are marked off on the horizontal axes and, in consequence of equation (1.4), it is at these values that the iterated conditional quantile functions of Y_1 given Y_2 and X intersect with the structural function in the upper part of Figure 1.2 which as noted has been drawn for the case $\tau_2 = 0.5$. Differences of values of Y_1 at these intersections, as given in equation (1.5), identify partial differences of the structural function as given in equation (1.6). The number of feasible comparisons is clearly constrained by the support of X.

When X varies continuously there is the possibility of identification of derivatives of the structural function. In (1.5) and (1.6) divide by $\Delta x \equiv x' - x''$ (X is now assumed scalar), consider $\Delta x \to 0$ and suppose the required derivatives exist. From (1.5) there is, noting that x affects $Q_{Y_1|Y_2 X}$ through its X argument and via $Q_{Y_2|X}$ though its Y_2 argument:

$$\nabla_{y_2} Q_{Y_1|Y_2 X}(\tau_1|y_2, x)|_{y_2 = Q_{Y_2|X}(\tau_2|x)} \nabla_x Q_{Y_2|X}(\tau_2|x)$$
$$+ \nabla_x Q_{Y_1|Y_2 X}(\tau_1|y_2, x)|_{y_2 = Q_{Y_2|X}(\tau_2|x)}$$

and from (1.6) there is, on using $y_2 \equiv Q_{Y_2|X}(\tau_2|x)$ and assuming that h does not vary with x:

$$\nabla_{y_2} h(y_2, x^*, a(\tau_1, \tau_2), \tau_2)|_{y_2 = Q_{Y_2|X}(\tau_2|x)} \nabla_x Q_{Y_2|X}(\tau_2|x)$$

and so the following correspondence identifying the y_2-derivative of h.

$$\nabla_{y_2} h(y_2, x^*, a(\tau_1, \tau_2), \tau_2)|_{y_2 = Q_{Y_2|X}(\tau_2|x)}$$
$$= \nabla_{y_2} Q_{Y_1|Y_2 X}(\tau_1|y_2, x)|_{y_2 = Q_{Y_2|X}(\tau_2|x)}$$
$$+ \frac{\nabla_x Q_{Y_1|Y_2 X}(\tau_1|y_2, x)|_{y_2 = Q_{Y_2|X}(\tau_2|x)}}{\nabla_x Q_{Y_2|X}(\tau_2|x)}$$

Imbens and Newey (2003) propose a two-step estimation procedure for estimating h by nonparametric quantile regression of Y_1 on X and a first step estimate of the conditional distribution function of Y_2 given X, the latter serving as a control variate. Ma and Koenker (2006) and Lee (2004) consider control variate estimation procedures under parametric and semiparametric restrictions. Chesher (2003) suggests estimating derivatives and differences of h by plugging unrestricted estimates of the quantile regressions of Y_1 on Y_2 and X and of Y_2 on X into expressions like that given above. Ma and Koenker (2006) study a weighted average version of this estimator in a semiparametric model.

3.2   Discrete Y_2

The joint independence model is useful when X is discrete because, unlike the marginal independence model, it can identify the *ceteris paribus* effect of continuous Y_2 on h. This advantage apparently vanishes once Y_2 is discrete.

The difficulty is that when Y_2 is discrete the conditional independence model does not point identify the structural function without further restriction. This is so however rich the support of discrete Y_2. The reason is that holding discrete Y_2 at a particular quantile does *not* hold U_2 at a quantile of its distribution. In Figure 1.2 the quantile functions in the lower graph are step functions when Y_2 is discrete and so there is a *range* of values of U_2 associated with any particular conditional quantile of Y_2. With U_2 uniformly distributed on $(0, 1)$, when $Y_2 = y_2^m$ and $X = x$ the value of U_2 must lie in the interval $(F_{Y_2|X}(y_2^{m-1}|x), F_{Y_2|X}(y_2^m|x)]$ which, note, may be narrow when Y_2 has many points of support.

If the dependence of U_1 on U_2 can be restricted then this interval restriction on U_2 can imply an interval restriction on the quantiles of the distribution of Y_1 given Y_2 and X and interval identification of the structural function.

The effect of restricting the conditional quantile function of U_1 given U_2 to be a monotonic function of U_2 is studied in Chesher (2005a). The case in which U_2 does not appear in h in its own right is considered here. If there exist values of X, $\tilde{x}_m \equiv \{x_{m-1}, x_m\}$ such that

$$F_{Y_2|X}[y_2^m|x_m] \leq \tau_2 \leq F_{Y_2|X}[y_2^{m-1}|x_{m-1}] \tag{1.7}$$

then $Q_{Y_1|Y_2X}(\tau_1|y_2^m, x_m)$ and $Q_{Y_1|Y_2X}(\tau_1|y_2^m, x_{m-1})$ bound the value of $h(y_2^m, x, a(\tau_1, \tau_2))$ where $x \in \tilde{x}_m$. It is necessary that h is insensitive to changes in x within $\tilde{x}_m$. Specifically, with:

$$q^L(y_2^m, \tilde{x}_m) \equiv \min \left(Q_{Y_1|Y_2X}(\tau_1|y_2^m, x^{m-1}), Q_{Y_1|Y_2X}(\tau_1|y_2^m, x^m) \right)$$

$$q^U(y_2^m, \tilde{x}_m) \equiv \max \left(Q_{Y_1|Y_2X}(\tau_1|y_2^m, x^{m-1}), Q_{Y_1|Y_2X}(\tau_1|y_2^m, x^m) \right)$$

there is the bound:

$$q^L(y_2^m, \tilde{x}_m) \leq h_1(y_2^m, x, a(\tau_1, \tau_2)) \leq q^U(y_2^m, \tilde{x}_m).$$

A bound on the *ceteris paribus* effect of *changing* Y_2 from y_2^m to y^n is available if for the *same* value τ_2 there exist $\tilde{x}_n \equiv \{x_{n-1}, x_n\}$ such that

$$F_{Y_2|X}[y_2^n|x_n] \leq \tau_2 \leq F_{Y_2|X}[y_2^{n-1}|x_{n-1}] \tag{1.8}$$

and there is then the following bound.

$$q^L(y_2^m, \tilde{x}_m) - q^U(y_2^n, \tilde{x}_n)$$
$$\leq h_1(y_2^m, x, a(\tau_1, \tau_2)) - h_1(y_2^n, x, a(\tau_1, \tau_2))$$
$$\leq q^U(y_2^m, \tilde{x}_m) - q^L(y_2^n, \tilde{x}_n)$$

where $x \in \tilde{x}_{mn} \equiv \tilde{x}_m \cup \tilde{x}_n$ and h is restricted to be insensitive to variations in x within $\tilde{x}_{mn}$.

Even when X has limited support relative to Y_2 intervals like this can provide information about the *ceteris paribus* effect of Y_2 on h if the effect of X on the distribution of Y_2 is strong enough. However, if the effect of X on the distribution of Y_2 is weak it may not be possible to find values of X such that inequalities like (1.7) and (1.8) hold. In this case parametric restrictions may hold the key to identification. Chesher (2005a) discusses this in the context of the returns-to-schooling study of Angrist and Krueger (1991).[5]

These results for discrete Y_2 are not useful when Y_2 is binary because in that case the inequalities (1.7) and (1.8) cannot be satisfied for any τ_2 within the unit interval. However, when Y_1 is continuous the marginal independence model can identify h when Y_2 is binary if X has at least two points of support. This is the leading case considered in Chernozhukov and Hansen (2005).

4 DISCUSSION

Structural functions in which latent variables appear nonadditively are of interest because they permit responses to policy interventions to have stochastic variation among people measured as identical. Knowing about the distributions of responses is important for welfare analysis and it is good to know what conditions must hold if these distributions are to be identified.

The focus here has been on models in which the same number of sources of stochastic variation is the same as the number of observed stochastic outcomes. These models are nonadditive extensions of the classic Cowles Commission simultaneous equation models and the conditions under which they identify a structural function are quite similar. There are two types of condition.

1. Conditions which limit the sensitivity of a structural function to variation in certain covariates, and require those covariates to have impact on the conditional distribution of endogenous variables.
2. Conditions on the degree of dependence permitted between latent variates and covariates. In nonadditive models strong independence conditions are required though a kind of local independence (e.g., median

---

[5] Chesher (2004) considers interval identification in additive error discrete endogenous variable models.

independence) can suffice for identification of local features of structural functions.

The precise nature of the independence condition has a substantial effect on the way in which identification is achieved, and consequences for estimation and inference. Models employing marginal independence and conditional independence restrictions have been considered.

In the *marginal independence* (MI) model

$$Y_1 = h(Y_2, X, U_1) \qquad U_1 \perp X$$

there can be exact identification of h only if the support of X is as rich as the support of Y_2. The variable Y_1 must be continuous. The variable Y_2 may be continuous or discrete. When Y_2 is discrete the values of the structural function at the points of support of Y_2 are the solution to sets of nonlinear simultaneous equations. When Y_2 is continuous the structural function at each value of U_1 is the solution to an integral equation. This is an "ill posed inverse problem." One consequence is that an identifying model has to include completeness conditions ruling out certain joint distributions of outcomes. Another consequence is that estimation and inference are relatively difficult. Without further restriction h is point identified either everywhere or nowhere.

Adding an equation for Y_2

$$Y_2 = g(X, U_2)$$

with $U_2 \perp X$, and replacing the condition $U_1 \perp X$ by the condition $U_1 \perp X|U_2$ implying $(U_1, U_2) \perp X$ gives a *joint independence* (JI) model.

In this model there can be point identification of features of h when X has sparse support relative to Y_2. The variable Y_1 can be continuous or discrete. The variable Y_2 must be continuous. However, if it is discrete then there can be interval identification of features of h if the dependence of U_1 on U_2 is restricted. The value of h at any set of values of its arguments is an explicit functional of quantile regressions associated with the joint distribution of Y_1 and Y_2 given X. There is no ill-posed inverse problem and estimation and inference are relatively simple. The latent variable U_2 can appear as an argument of h.

The joint independence condition implies the marginal independence conditions: $U_1 \perp X$ and $U_2 \perp X$. It is a stronger restriction and so can have greater identifying power. In the continuous endogenous variable case it removes the requirement for a completeness condition. However, it does not necessarily have greater identifying power for the structural function.

Chesher (2004) considers additive error models with a discrete endogenous variable and alternative marginal and joint independence conditions. When covariates have rich support the stronger joint independence condition enables identification of features of the joint distribution of the latent variables but has no additional identifying power for the structural function. When the joint independence condition overidentifies the structural function there is the possibility of detecting failure of the condition, for example, by comparing the IV type estimators which marginal independence motivates with control function estimators which joint independence motivates.

In view of the advantages that come with the joint independence condition it is worth asking whether for the purpose of *single equation* identification a simultaneous equations model

$$Y_1 = h(Y_2, X, U_1) \tag{1.9a}$$
$$Y_2 = g(Y_1, X, U_2) \tag{1.9b}$$

with the joint independence condition $(U_1, U_2) \perp X$ can be expressed as

$$Y_1 = h(Y_2, X, U_1) \tag{1.10a}$$
$$Y_2 = s(X, V) \tag{1.10b}$$

with $(U_1, V) \perp X$. This can be done when h and g are linear but not in general. There is always a representation of (1.9) like (1.10) that satisfies *marginal* independence: $U_1 \perp X$, $V \perp X$ because there is the representation $Y_2 = Q_{Y_2|X}(V|X)$ where $V|X \sim Unif(0, 1)$, but without further restriction *joint* independence: $(U_1, V) \perp X$ does not hold.

The triangular form of the equations together with the joint independence condition is a substantive restriction entailing an essential recursiveness in the determination of the outcomes that can be aligned with an iterated decomposition of the joint distribution of outcomes given covariates. Recursiveness could arise because outcomes are ordered in time as in the classical returns-to-schooling models where wage determination occurs after schooling choice and in other cases in which a causal mechanism is postulated. Koenker (2005) describes the nonadditive triangular form as an extension of the recursive causal chain models discussed in Strotz and Wold (1960).

The nontriangular form (1.9) with joint independence was studied in Roehrig (1988). The identification conditions given there have been called into question by Benkard and Berry (2004). Matzkin (2005) proposes alternative identification conditions for the structural functions.

Up to this point the focus has been on models in which there are the same number of sources of stochastic variation as there are stochastic outcomes. This restriction on the dimensionality of the stochastic variation driving the data generating process is important. In the triangular model with joint independence the values of the latent variables can be held fixed by holding outcomes at quantiles of conditional distributions of outcomes given covariates. When there are more sources of stochastic variation than outcomes, this tight control of latent variates is not possible without further restriction.

One option in this circumstance is to seek to identify some average structural function a possibility that has generated a large literature not addressed here at all.[6] Another option is to impose restrictions which reduce the number of

---

[6] See Blundell and Powell (2003) for an account of recent work on estimation of Average Structural Functions. Heckman and Vytlacil (2005) give a synthesis of work in the treatment effects literature.

effective sources of variation. The mixed proportionate hazard model sketched in Section 1 is an example of this in action.[7] This sort of reduction occurs in linear but not nonlinear measurement error models. A further option is entertain restrictions which leave some structural features constant with respect to certain sources of random variation, for example, by imposing index restrictions and not admitting stochastic variation within indexes.[8]

Many significant challenges remain in many latent variable cases when none of these options is attractive. Typically, these must be addressed on a case by case basis as has been done in, for example, the notable contributions of Schennach (2004, 2007) to nonparametric identification in nonlinear measurement error models and Altonji and Matzkin (2005) to nonparametric identification in panel data models.

References

ALTONJI, JOSEPH AND ROSA L. MATZKIN (2005): "Cross Section and Panel Data Estimators for Nonseparable Models with Endogenous Regressors," *Econometrica*, 73, 1053–1102.

ANGRIST, JOSHUA D. AND ALAN B. KRUEGER (1991): "Does Compulsory Schooling Attendance Affect Schooling and Earnings?" *Quarterly Journal of Economics*, 106, 979–1014.

BENKARD, C. LANIER AND STEVEN BERRY (2004): "On the Nonparametric Identification of Nonlinear Simultaneous Equations Models: Comment on B. Brown (1983) and Roehrig (1988)," *Econometrica*, 74(5), 1429–1440.

BLUNDELL, RICHARD AND JAMES L. POWELL (2003): "Endogeneity in Nonparametric and Semiparametric Regression Models," in *Advances in Economics and Econometrics, Theory and Applications,* Vol. II, edited by Mathias Dewatripont, Lars Peter Hansen, and Steven Turnovsky, Cambridge: Cambridge University Press.

CARD, DAVID (2001): "Estimating the Returns to Schooling: Progress on Some Persistent Econometric Problems," *Econometrica*, 69, 1127–1160.

CHERNOZHUKOV, VICTOR AND CHRISTIAN HANSEN (2005): "An IV Model of Quantile Treatment Effects," *Econometrica*, 73, 245–261.

——— (2006): "Instrumental Quantile Regression Inference for Structural and Treatment Effect Models," *Journal of Econometrics*, 132(2), 491–525.

CHERNOZHUKOV, VICTOR AND HAN HONG (2003): "An MCMC Approach to Classical Estimation," *Journal of Econometrics*, 115, 293–346.

CHERNOZHUKOV, VICTOR, GUIDO W. IMBENS, AND WHITNEY K. NEWEY (2007): "Instrumental Variable Estimation of Nonseparable Models," *Journal of Econometrics*, forthcoming.

CHESHER, ANDREW (2002): "Semiparametric Identification in Duration Models," Centre for Microdata Methods and Practice Working Paper CWP 20/02.

---

[7] This example is worked through in more detail in Chesher (2002).

[8] This is considered in Chesher (2005b) and related joint work with Whitney Newey and Frank Vella.

CHESHER, ANDREW (2003): "Identification in Nonseparable Models," *Econometrica*, 71, 1405–1441.

——— (2004): "Identification in Additive Error Models with Discrete Endogenous Variables," Centre for Microdata Methods and Practice Working Paper CWP 11/04.

——— (2005a): "Nonparametric Identification Under Discrete Variation," *Econometrica*, 73, 1525–1550.

——— (2005b): "Identification with Excess Heterogeneity," Centre for Microdata Methods and Practice Working Paper CWP 19/05.

——— (2007): "Instrumental Values," Centre for Microdata Methods and Practice Working Paper CWP 17/02, revised paper, *Journal of Econometrics*, forthcoming.

DAROLLES, S., JEAN-PIERRE FLORENS, AND ERIC RENAULT (2003): "Nonparametric Instrumental Regression," Working Paper CREST 2000-17, 2000.

DAS, M. (2005): "Instrumental Variables Estimation of Nonparametric Models with Discrete Endogenous Variables," *Journal of Econometrics*, 124, 335–361.

FLORENS, JEAN-PIERRE (2003): "Inverse Problems and Structural Econometrics: The Example of Instrumental *Variables*," in *Advances in Economics and Econometrics, Theory and Applications,* Vol. II, edited by Mathias Dewatripont, Lars Peter Hansen, and Steven Turnovsky, Cambridge: Cambridge University Press.

FLORENS, JEAN-PIERRE AND LAETITIA MALAVOLTI (2003): "Instrumental Regression with Discrete Variables," Paper presented at the 2003 European Meeting of the Econometric Society, Stockholm.2

HALL, PETER AND JOEL L. HOROWITZ (2005): "Nonparametric Methods for Inference in the Presence of Instrumental Variables," *Annals of Statistics*, 33, 2904–2929.

HECKMAN, JAMES J. AND EDWARD VYTLACIL (2005): "Structural Equations, Treatment Effects, and Econometric Policy Evaluation," *Econometrica*, 73, 669–738.

IMBENS, GUIDO W. AND WHITNEY K. NEWEY (2003): "Identification and Estimation of Triangular Simultaneous Equations Models Without Additivity," Paper presented at the 14th EC^2 Meeting, cemmap, London, December 12th–13th, 2003.

KOENKER, ROGER (2005): *Quantile Regression*, Econometric Society Monograph Series, Cambridge: Cambridge University Press.

LEE, SOKBAE (2004): "Endogeneity in Quantile Regression Models: A Control Function Approach," Centre for Microdata Methods and Practice Working Paper 08/04.

MA, LINGJAE AND R. W. KOENKER (2006): "Quantile Regression Methods for Recursive Structural Equation Models," *Journal of Econometrics*, 134(2), 471–506.

MATZKIN, ROSA L. (2003): "Nonparametric Estimation of Nonadditive Random Functions," *Econometrica*, 71, 1339–1376.

——— (2005): "Nonparametric Simultaneous Equations," manuscript.

ROEHRIG, CHARLES S. (1988): "Conditions for Identification in Nonparametric and Parametric Models,"*Econometrica*, 56, 433–447.

SCHENNACH, M. SUSANNE (2004): "Estimation of Nonlinear Models with Measurement Error," *Econometrica*, 72, 33–75.

———— (2007): "Instrumental Variable Estimation of Nonlinear Errors-in-Variables Models," Econometrica, 75, 201–239.

STROTZ, ROBERT H. AND HERMAN O. A. WOLD (1960): "Recursive vs Nonrecursive Systems: An Attempt at Synthesis (Part 1 of a Triptych on Causal Systems)," *Econometrica*, 28, 417–463.

CHAPTER 2

Nonaddithe Models with Endogenous Regressors[*]

Guido W. Imbens[†]

1 INTRODUCTION

In the last fifteen years there has been much work on identification of causal effects under weak conditions in settings with endogeneity. Earlier, researchers focused on linear systems with additive residuals. However, such systems are often difficult to motivate by economic theory. In many cases it is the nonlinearity of the system and the presence of unobserved heterogeneity in returns (and thus nonadditivity in the residuals) that leads to the type of endogeneity problems that economists are concerned with. In the more recent literature researchers have attempted to characterize conditions for identification that do not rely on such functional form or homogeneity assumptions, instead relying solely on assumptions that are more tightly linked to economic theory. Such assumptions typically include exclusion and monotonicity restrictions and (conditional) independence assumptions.

In this paper I will discuss part of this literature. I will focus on a two-equation triangular (recursive) system of simultaneous equations with a single endogenous regressor and a single instrument. Although much of the earlier literature on simultaneous equations focused on larger systems (in fact, much of the theoretical literature studied systems with an arbitrary number of endogenous regressors and an arbitrary number of instruments despite the rare occurrence of systems with more than two endogenous variables in empirical work and the practical difficulty of even finding a single credible instrument), many applications have this two-equation form and the framework is sufficiently rich for discussing the nature of the identification problems that are studied here. I focus on identification of the outcome equation relating the outcome to the

[*] This paper was presented as an invited lecture at the Econometric Society World Congress held in London, August 2005. Financial support for this research was generously provided through NSF grants SES 0136789 and SES 0452590. I am grateful for comments by Richard Crump, Whitney Newey, and Edward Vytlacil.

[†] Department of Economics, Harvard University, M-24 Littauer Center, 1830 Cambridge Street, Cambridge, MA 02138, and NBER. Electronic correspondence: imbens@harvard.edu, http://www.economics.harvard.edu/faculty/imbens/imbens.html

regressor of interest. The latter is potentially endogenous. It is itself determined in the second equation, the choice equation, partly by a set of instruments and partly by unobserved residuals. The endogeneity of the regressor arises from the correlation between the residuals in the outcome and choice equations. A natural setting for such models is one where an economic agent chooses an action to optimize some objective function with incomplete information regarding the objective function. The discussion will include settings with binary endogenous variables (see, among others, Abadie, Angrist, and Imbens, 2002; Angrist and Krueger, 1999; Blundell and Powell, 2003; Heckman and Robb, 1984; Imbens and Angrist, 1994; Manski, 1990; Vytlacil, 2002), continuous endogenous regressors (Altonji and Matzkin, 2005; Angrist, Graddy, and Imbens 2000; Chernozhukov and Hansen, 2005; Chesher, 2003; Darolles, Florens, and Renault, 2001; Imbens and Newey, 2002; Newey, Powell, and Vella, 1999; Roehrig 1988), and discrete regressors (Angrist and Imbens, 1995; Chesher, 2005; Das, 2005; Vytlacil, 2006).

Such a triangular system corresponds to a special and potentially restrictive form of endogeneity, especially with a single unobserved component combined with monotonicity in the choice equation. It contrasts with a part of the literature on endogeneity where researchers have refrained from imposing any restrictions on the form of the relationship between the endogenous regressor and the instruments beyond assuming there is one, and instead merely assume independence of the instrument and the unobserved component in the outcome equation (e.g., Chernozhukov, Imbens and Newey, 2005; Chernozhukov and Hansen, 2005; Darolles, Florens, and Renault, 2001; Hall and Horowitz, 2003; Newey and Powell, 2003; Newey, Powell, and Vella, 1999). There has been little discussion regarding tradeoff between the benefit in terms of identification of making such assumptions and the cost in terms of potential misspecification.

It is also important to note that the motivation for the endogeneity considered here differs from that arising from equilibrium conditions. I will refer to the latter as *intrinsically simultaneous* models, in contrast to the *recursive* or triangular models considered here. In the leading case of the intrinsically simultaneous equations model, the supply and demand model, there are two (sets of) agents, characterized by a relation describing quantities supplied and demanded as a function of prices. Endogeneity of prices arises by the equilibrium condition that quantities supplied and demanded are equal. Although in linear cases the models corresponding to this type of endogeneity are essentially the same as those for the recursive models considered here, some of the assumptions considered in the current paper are more plausible in the recursive system than in the intrinsically simultaneous setup, as will be discussed in more detail below.

The form of the endogeneity I consider in this paper implies that conditioning on some unobserved variable would suffice to remove the endogeneity. One possibility is to condition directly on the unobserved component from the choice equation, but more generally there can be functions of the unobserved component that suffice to eliminate endogeneity. This approach is not directly feasible because these variables are not observed. However, in some cases it is possible to indirectly adjust for differences in these variables. Methods developed for doing so depend critically on the nature of the system, that is, whether the endogenous regressor is binary, discrete, or continuous. A benefit of this approach is that the identification results I will discuss here are constructive, and so they are closely tied to the actual methods for adjusting for endogeneity.

A major theme of the current paper, and of my work in this area more generally, is the choice of estimands. In settings with heterogeneous effects and endogenous regressors it can often be difficult to infer the effects of policies that affect all agents, or that move some agents far from their current choices. Instead it can be much easier to evaluate policies that move agents locally by eliminating endogeneity problems for some subpopulations even when the instruments are not useful for eliminating endogeneity problems for other subpopulations. For these subpopulations the instruments induce exogenous variation in the regressor that allows the researcher to infer *local* causal effects over some range of the regressor. However, the amount of variation in the instruments and the strength of their correlation with the endogenous regressor defines these subpopulations. This has led to some concern that such local effects are in general of limited interest as they do not directly correspond to specific policy parameters. However, it is important to keep in mind that if the endogeneity problem were entirely eliminated by observing the residuals that lead to the endogeneity this would not lead to additional variation in the exogenous regressors and would therefore still limit the ability to make precise inferences about the causal effects for the entire population. These limits on the identification can be addressed in two ways. One is to acknowledge the lack of identification and report ranges of values of the estimand of primary interest in a bounds approach (e.g., Manski, 1990, 2003). Alternatively, one can impose additional restrictions on the outcome equation that would allow for extrapolation. Before doing so, or in addition to doing so, it may be useful, however, to study the subpopulations for which one can (point) identify causal effects. These subpopulations will be defined in terms of the instruments and the individual's responses to them. They need not be the most interesting subpopulations from the researcher's perspective, but it is important to understand the share of these subpopulations in the population and how they differ from other subpopulations in terms of outcome distributions that can be compared. This strategy is similar in spirit to the focus on internal validity in biomedical trials where typically the stress is on conducting careful clinical trials without requiring that these equally satisfy external validity concerns.

In the next section I will set up the basic framework. I will discuss both the potential outcome framework popularized by Rubin (1974) that is now standard in the program evaluation literature for the binary regressor case as well as the equation-based framework traditionally used in the simultaneous equations literature in econometrics following the Cowles foundation work (see Hendry and Morgan (1997) for a historical perspective on this). In Section 3, I will discuss in some detail two economic examples that lead to the type of structure that is studied in this paper. This will illustrate how the models discussed in the current paper can arise in economic settings with agents in an environment with incomplete information.

I will then discuss the role of multi-valued endogenous regressors and multi-valued instruments. I will discuss separately three cases. First, the setting with a binary endogenous regressor. In that case Imbens and Angrist (1994) show that the average effect of the regressor is identified only for a subpopulation they call compliers. I then discuss the case with a continuous endogenous regressor. This case is studied in Imbens and Newey (2002) who present conditions for identification of what they call the average conditional response function in the nonadditive case. Finally, I discuss the case with a discrete endogenous regressor. Here I build on the work by Angrist and Imbens (1995). (A different approach to the discrete case is taken by Chesher (2005) who combines assumptions about the outcome equation with assumptions on the choice equation and focuses on local aspects of the regression function.) In the current literature these three cases have received separate treatment, often with distinct assumptions (e.g., weak monotonicity in the binary regressor case versus strict monotonicity and continuity in the continuous regressor case). I will provide some comments linking the three cases more closely, and discuss formulations of the key assumptions that underly all three. These assumptions include monotonicity-type assumptions in both observables and unobservables, as well as smoothness assumptions. I will also discuss the role of binary versus multi-valued and continuous instruments in all three cases.

2   THE MODEL

The basic setup I consider in this paper is the following two-equation structural model:

$$Y_i = g(X_i, \varepsilon_i), \tag{2.1}$$

$$X_i = h(Z_i, \eta_i). \tag{2.2}$$

Both equations are structural equations, describing causal relations between the right-hand side and left-hand side variables. The system is triangular or recursive rather than simultaneous, with X entering the equation determining Y, but not the other way around. This differs from the recursive form of the general simultaneous equations model (e.g., Hausman, 1983), where the recursive nature is by construction. The unobserved components in (2.1) and (2.2) are potentially correlated.

The first equation, (2.1), is the equation of primary interest. I will refer to it as the *outcome* equation. It is a primitive of the model and describes the causal or behavioral relation between a scalar outcome Y_i and the scalar regressor of primary interest X_i. In the examples I consider this is a mechanical relation such as a production function, not under the control of the agent. The two arguments of this production function are the regressor of interest X_i and an unobserved component denoted by ε_i. This unobserved component can be a vector or a scalar. We will largely refrain from making assumptions concerning the dependence of this function on its arguments.

The second equation, (2.2), describes the behavioral relation between the potentially endogenous regressor X_i and a single, or set of, instruments Z_i. In the case with a binary endogenous regressor this relation is often referred to as the *participation* or *selection* equation. With a potentially multi-valued regressor that is less appropriate and here I will generally refer to it as the *choice* equation. In part this terminology makes the point that this equation often describes a choice made by an economic agent, in contrast to the outcome equation which typically describes a mechanical relation such as a production function. The endogenous regressor also depends on an unobserved component η_i. Again this unobserved component can be a vector, although I will often make assumptions that essentially reduce the dimension of η_i to one.

This type of triangular structural model, in particular in combination with the scalar η assumption, is less appropriate for settings where the endogeneity arises from equilibrium conditions. Such intrinsically simultaneous settings often have more than one unobserved component in the second equation that would result from the equilibrium. For example, consider a demand and supply system with the demand function

$$Q_i = q^d(P_i, X_i, \varepsilon_i), \tag{2.3}$$

and the supply function

$$Q_i = q^s(P_i, Z_i, v_i). \tag{2.4}$$

The reduced form for the equilibrium price depends on both unobserved components in addition to the potential instruments,

$$P_i^e = g(X_i, Z_i, \varepsilon_i, v_i). \tag{2.5}$$

If both supply and demand are additive in the unobserved component then the equilibrium price can be written in terms of a scalar unobserved component, and the model is similar to the setting in (2.1)–(2.2) that is the primary focus of this paper. Outside of such additive models it is generally impossible to write the equilibrium price in terms of a single unobserved component. See for a more detailed discussion of such models that are intrinsically simultaneous in a nonadditive setting the recent work by Chernozhukov and Hansen (2005), Chernozhukov, Imbens, and Newey (2005), Benkard and Berry (2005), and Matzkin (2005).

The formulation of the model in equations (2.1) and (2.2) is common in the econometric literature on simultaneous equations with continuous endogenous regressors. In the modern literature on the binary endogenous regressor case a slightly different setup is typically used based on the potential outcomes framework developed by Rubin (1974). This amounts to writing the outcome for unit i as a function of the regressor x as $Y_i(x)$. In the equation-based model this equals $Y_i(x) = g(x, \varepsilon_i)$, with the observed outcome $Y_i = Y_i(X_i)$. (It is interesting to note that Haavelmo uses the same potential outcomes notation with the explicit distinction between x as the argument in the function and the observed value X_i in his early work on simultaneous equations, e.g., Haavelmo, 1943.) Similar to the outcome function $Y_i(x)$ the value of the regressor X would be written in this framework as a function of the instrument z as $X_i(z) = h(z, \eta_i)$, with the observed outcome equal to $X_i = X_i(Z_i)$. If we do not restrict ε_i and η_i to be scalars, there is no essential loss of generality in writing the model as (2.1) and (2.2). However, restricting either ε_i or η_i to be scalar, in particular in combination with the assumption of monotonicity would be restrictive. I will return to this issue later.

I maintain the following assumption throughout the discussion.

Assumption 2.1 (INDEPENDENCE) *The instrument Z_i is independent of the pair of unobserved components (ε_i, η_i).*

In the potential outcome formulation this amounts to assumption that $\{(Y_i(x), X_i(z))\}_{z,x}$ are jointly independent of Z_i.

This assumption embodies two notions. First, and this is somewhat implicit in the formulation of the model with z not an argument of $(g\cdot)$ in (2.1), there is no direct causal effect of Z on Y. This is typically referred to as an exclusion restriction. Second, Z is exogenous with respect to X and Y so that the causal effect of Z on X and Y can be estimated by comparing units with different values of Z. This is like a random assignment assumption. It can be weakened by allowing for additional exogenous covariates. In the binary case Angrist, Imbens, and Rubin (1996) discuss the distinctions between the two components of this assumption in more detail.

Assumption 2.1 is a strong assumption. It is common in much of the recent identification literature that considers models with nonadditive unobserved components, including both settings with binary regressors (Imbens and Angrist, 1994), and with continuous regressors (Chernozhukov and Hansen, 2005; Chernozhukov, Imbens, and Newey, 2005; Imbens and Newey, 2002; Matzkin, 2003).

In the next section I will discuss some examples that show this assumption can arise in economic models. Various weaker versions have been considered in the literature. Three of those deserve special mention. First, researchers have often assumed mean independence $\mathbb{E}[\varepsilon_i | Z_i] = 0$ and $\mathbb{E}[\eta_i | Z_i] = 0$, instead of full independence (Darolles, Florens, and Renault, 2001; Newey, Powell, and Vella, 1999). Unless the model is additive in η and ε, this is generally not sufficient for identification. A second potential disadvantage of the mean-independence assumption is that it ties the identifying assumptions to the functional form of the model. Second, in a very different approach Manski and Pepper (2000) discuss one-sided versions of the exclusion restriction where the instrument may increase but not decrease the outcome. Such assumptions may be more justified in specific economic models than the full independence assumption. Third, more recently Chesher (2003, 2005) has suggested local versions of the independence assumption where at a particular value x specific quantiles of the distribution of $Y(x)$ do not vary with Z.

Endogeneity of X arises in this system of equations through the correlation of the two unobserved components ε and η. This correlation implies that X and ε are potentially correlated and therefore methods that treat X as exogenous are in general not appropriate. The exogeneity of the instrument embodied in Assumption 2.1 implies that although X and ε are potentially correlated, the correlation arises solely from their joint dependence on η. Hence conditional on η, the regressor X and ε are independent, and X is exogenous. An alternative way of formulating the endogeneity problem in this model is therefore that X is exogenous only conditional on an unobserved covariate. A similar setup occurs in Chamberlain (1983) where conditional on an unobserved permanent component regressors are exogenous in a panel data setting. This argument illustrates some limits to the type of identification results we can hope for. Even if we were to infer the value of η for each individual, either through direct observation or through estimation, we could not hope to learn about the relation between Y and X other than conditional on η. In other words, given knowledge of η we could identify the conditional mean $\mathbb{E}[Y|X, \eta]$ on the joint support of (η, X). This gives a causal relation between Y and X on this joint support, but in general it will not be informative outside this support. In particular, if the conditional support of $X|\eta$ varies by η we will not be able to integrate over the marginal distribution of η, and in that case we will not be able to infer variation in the conditional distribution of $Y(x)$ by x alone. There are a number of directions one can take in that case. First, one can focus on questions that do not require integration over the marginal distribution of η. This may take the form of focusing on subpopulations with overlap in the distributions of η and X, or focusing on quantiles. Second, one can obtain bounds on the effects of interest. Third, one can make additional assumptions on the conditional distribution of the outcomes given η and X that allow for the extrapolation necessary to obtain point identification.

As this discussion illustrates, this unobserved component η plays an important role in the analysis. Conditional on this variable the regressor of interest is exogenous, and this motivates two approaches to identification and estimation. First, in some cases η can be estimated consistently. The leading case of this arises in settings with X continuous and $h(z, \eta)$ strictly monotone in η (Blundell and Powell, 2003; Imbens and Newey, 2002). Given a consistent estimator for η one can then in the second stage regress Y on X controlling for $\hat{\eta}$. This is a generalization of the control function approach (e.g., Blundell and Powell, 2004; Heckman and Robb, 1984).

In other cases, however, one cannot estimate η consistently. Even in that case the conditional distribution of Y given X and Z can be interpreted as a mixture of conditional distributions of Y given X and η. The second approach to identification and estimation exploits the fact that in some cases these mixtures can be disentangled, often requiring additional assumptions. The leading case here is the binary case where a weak monotonicity condition is sufficient to identify the local average treatment effect (Imbens and Angrist, 1994). In both cases it is important that η is a scalar with $h(z, \eta)$ (weakly) monotone in η. The first step in understanding these cases is to note that one need not condition on η itself. It may be sufficient to condition on a function of η in order to eliminate endogeneity of the covariate. Especially when η is continuous and X takes on only few values this may simplify the problem considerably. I will call this function the *type* of a unit. It will be denoted by $T_i = T(\eta_i)$ for unit i. By conditioning on the type of a unit the endogeneity of the regressor can be eliminated. Formally,

Definition 2.1 *The type of a unit is a function $T(\eta)$ such that*

$$\varepsilon \perp X \mid T(\eta).$$

Let $\mathbb{T}$ be the set of values that T takes on. If X and Z are discrete there are choices for the type function T that take on only a finite number of values even if η is continuous. With either Z or X continuous there may be an uncountable infinite number of types, with in the worst case $T(\eta) = \eta$. The type of a unit has some similarities to the notion of the balancing score in settings with unconfoundedness or selection on observables (e.g., Rosenbaum and Rubin, 1983). Like the propensity score the definition of a type is not unique. Under the independence assumption the unobserved component η itself satisfies this definition and so does any strictly monotone transformation of η. It is useful to look for the choice of type that has the least variation, the same way in the treatment evaluation literature we look for the balancing score that is the coarsest function among all possible balancing scores. In the program evaluation setting with selection on observables the solution is the propensity score. Here the optimal (coarsest) choice of the type function is any function that is constant on sets of values of η that for all z lead to the same value of X:

$$T(\eta) = T(\eta') \quad \text{if } h(z, \eta) = h(z, \eta') \; \forall \, z \in \mathbb{Z}.$$

This implies that we can write the choice equation in terms of the type as $X_i = \tilde{h}(Z_i, T_i)$.

Much of the identification discussion in this paper will therefore focus on identification of

$$\beta(x, t) = \mathbb{E}[Y \mid X = x, T = t], \tag{2.6}$$

the conditional expectation of the outcome given the regressor of interest and the type, on the joint support of (X, T). Because conditional on the type the regressor is exogenous, this conditional expectation has a causal interpretation as a function of x. The main issue in identification will be whether one can either infer (and estimate) the type directly and estimate $\beta(x, t)$ by regressing Y on X and the estimated type $\hat{T}$, or indirectly infer $\beta(x, t)$ for some values of x and some types from the joint distribution of (Z, X, Y). There will also be some discussion relating the function $\beta(x, t)$ to policy parameters. Here the limits on the identification stemming from the restriction of the identification to the joint support of (X, T) will be important. Many policy questions will involve values of $\beta(x, t)$ outside the support of (X, T). Such questions are only partially identified under the assumptions considered in the current discussion. To obtain point identification the researcher has to extrapolate $\beta(x, t)$ from the joint support of (X, T) to other areas. This may be more credible in some cases (e.g., if $\beta(x, t)$ is flat in t and the additional values of $\beta(x, t)$ required involve extrapolation only over t) than in others.

I will consider a couple of assumptions beyond the independence assumption that involve monotonicity of some form. The role of monotonicity assumptions in identification has recently been stressed by Imbens and Angrist (1994), Matzkin (2003), Altonji and Matzkin (2005), Athey and Imbens (2006), Chernozhukov and Hansen (2005), Chesher (2003), Imbens and Newey (2002), and others. First, I consider two monotonicity assumptions on the choice equation. These assumptions are closely related to separability conditions (e.g., Goldman and Uzawa, 1964; Pinkse, 2001).

Assumption 2.2 (WEAK MONOTONICITY IN THE INSTRUMENT) *If $h(z, \eta) > h(z', \eta)$ for some (z, z', η), then $h(z, \eta') \geq h(z', \eta')$ for all η'.*

The second monotonicity condition concerns monotonicity in the unobserved component of the choice function.

Assumption 2.3 (WEAK MONOTONICITY IN THE UNOBSERVED COMPONENT) *If $h(z, \eta) > h(z, \eta')$ for some (z, η, η'), then $h(z', \eta) \geq h(z', \eta')$ for all z'.*

Sufficient, but not necessary, for the second monotonicity assumption is that η is a scalar and that $h(z, \eta)$ is nondecreasing in η. The two monotonicity assumptions are substantively very different, although closely related in some cases. Both can aid in identifying the average causal effect of changes in the covariate. Neither is directly testable.

I will also consider strict monotonicity versions of both assumptions.

Assumption 2.4 (STRICT MONOTONICITY IN THE INSTRUMENT) *If $h(z, \eta) > h(z', \eta)$ for some (z, z', η), then $h(z, \eta') > h(z', \eta')$ for all η'.*

Assumption 2.5 (STRICT MONOTONICITY IN THE UNOBSERVED COMPONENT) *If $h(z, \eta) > h(z, \eta')$ for some (z, η, η'), then $h(z', \eta) > h(z', \eta')$ for all z'.*

The strict monotonicity assumptions are particularly restrictive in settings with discrete choices where they restrict the number of support points for the instrument or the unobserved component to be equal to the number of values that the choice can take on. Additivity of the choice equation in the instruments and the unobserved component directly implies assumptions 2.4 and 2.5, but the combination of these two assumptions is still much weaker than additive separability.

These monotonicity assumptions 2.3 and 2.5 are much less plausible in settings where the endogeneity arises from equilibrium conditions. As equation (2.5) shows, with nonadditive demand and supply functions the reduced form for the price is generally a nonseparable function of the two unobserved components.

3   TWO ECONOMIC EXAMPLES AND SOME POLICIES OF INTEREST

In this section I discuss two economic examples where the type of triangular systems studied in the current paper can arise. In both examples an economic agent faces a decision with the payoff depending partly on the production function that is the primary object of interest in our analysis. In the first example the agent faces a binary decision. In the second example the decision is a continuous one. There are two critical features of the examples. First, the payoff function of the agents differs from the production function that the econometrician is interested in. This difference generates exogenous variation in the regressor. Second, the production function is nonadditive in the unobserved component. It is the unobserved heterogeneity in returns that follows from this nonadditivity that leads agents with identical values of observed characteristics to respond differently to the same incentives. This important role of nonadditivity is highlighted by Athey and Stern (1998) in their discussion of complementarity. Again, it is important to note that the role of nonadditivity in these models is different from that in supply and demand models. In supply and demand models endogeneity of prices arises from equilibrium conditions. It requires neither nonlinearity nor nonadditivity. In the current setting endogeneity arises in a way similar to the endogeneity in the binary selection models developed by Heckman (1978).

I will also discuss some estimands that may be of interest in these settings and how they relate to the model specified in equations (2.1) and (2.2). Traditionally, researchers have focused on estimation of the function $g(x, \varepsilon)$ itself. This can be unwieldy when the regressor takes on a large number of values. The estimands I consider here fall into two categories. The first category consists of summary measures of the effect of the endogenous regressor on the outcome of interest. These include average differences or average derivatives, for the population as a whole or for subpopulations. The second set consists of the effects of specific policies that change the incentives for individuals in choosing the value of the potentially endogenous regressor.

3.1   Two Economic Examples

Example 1 (JOB TRAINING PROGRAM) *Suppose an individual faces a decision whether or not to enroll in a job training program. Life-time discounted*

*earnings y is a function of participation in the program $x \in \{0, 1\}$ and ability ε:
$y = g(x, \varepsilon)$. Ability ε is not under the control of the individual, and not observed
directly by either the individual or the econometrician. The individual chooses
whether to participate by maximizing expected life-time discounted earnings
minus costs associated with entering the program conditional on her information set. This information set includes a noisy signal of ability, denoted by η,
and a cost shifter z. The signal for ability could be a predictor such as prior
labor market history. The cost of entering the program depends on an observed
cost shifter z such as the availability of training facilities nearby. Although I
do not explicitly allow for this, the costs could also depend on the signal η, if
merit-based financial aid is available. Hence, utility is*

$$U(x, z, \varepsilon) = g(x, \varepsilon) - c(x, z),$$

and the optimal choice satisfies

$$X = \mathrm{argmax}_{x \in \{0,1\}} \mathbb{E}\left[U(x, Z, \varepsilon)\Big| \eta, Z\right]$$

$$= \mathrm{argmax}_{x \in \{0,1\}}\left[\mathbb{E}\left[g(x, \varepsilon)\Big| \eta, Z\right] - c(x, Z)\right].$$

$$= \begin{cases} 1 & \text{if } \mathbb{E}[g(1, \varepsilon)|\eta, Z] - c(1, z) \geq \mathbb{E}[g(0, \varepsilon)|\eta, Z] - c(0, z) \\ 0 & \text{otherwise.} \end{cases}$$

Thus, $X = h(Z, \eta)$, so that equations (2.1) and (2.2) are satisfied.

*Let us return to the two crucial features of the setup. The first point concerns
the importance of the distinction between the payoff function of the individual
$(U(x, z, \varepsilon) = g(x, \varepsilon) - c(x, z))$ and the production function that is the focus of
the researcher $(g(x, \varepsilon))$. Suppose the individual were interested in maximizing
$g(x, \varepsilon)$ without subtracting the cost $c(x, z)$. In that case Z would not be a
valid instrument since it would not affect the choice. On the other hand, if the
researcher is interested in the causal effect of X on the objective function of
the individual, $U(x, z, \varepsilon)$, then Z is not a valid instrument because it cannot
be excluded from the objective function. Validity of an instrument requires it to
shift the objective function without entering the production function.*

*The second point is the nonadditivity of the production function in its un-
observed component. If the production function $g(x, \varepsilon)$ were additive in ε, the
participation decision would be the solution to $\max_x g(x) - c(x, Z)$. In that
case the optimal solution $X = h(Z, \eta)$ would not depend on the signal for ability η. As a result all individuals with the same level of the instrument Z would
make the same choice and the instrument and regressor would be perfectly
correlated. To generate individual variation in the endogenous regressor conditional on the instrument it is essential to have unobserved heterogeneity in
the returns, that is, nonadditivity of the production function in the unobserved
component.*

*Consider now the assumptions introduced in Section 2. The independence
assumption could be plausible in this case if there is individual-level variation*

*in the costs associated with attending the training program that are unrelated
to individual characteristics that affect earnings. This may be plausible if the
costs are determined by decisions taken by different agents. For example, the
costs could be determined by location decisions taken by administrative units.
The monotonicity conditions can both be plausible in this example. Suppose the
costs are monotone in the instrument. This implies that the choice function is
monotone in Z. Das (2001) discusses a number of examples where monotonicity
of the choice function in the unobserved component is implied by conditions
on the economic primitives using monotone comparative statics results (e.g.,
Athey, 2002; Milgrom and Shannon, 1994).*

*One could generalize this model to allow for multi-valued X, for example,
education. In that case this model is closely related to the models for educational
choices such as those used by Card (2001). See also Das (2001) for a discussion
of a similar model.*   □

Example 2 (PRODUCTION FUNCTION) *This is a nonadditive extension of
the classical problem in the estimation of production functions, for example,
Mundlak (1963). Consider a production function that depends on three inputs.
The first input is observable to both the firm and the econometrician, and is
variable in the short run (e.g., labor). It will be denoted by x. The second input is observed only by the firm and is fixed in the short run (e.g., capital or
management). It will be denoted by η. Finally, the third input is unobserved
by the econometrician and unknown to the firm at the time the labor input is
chosen, for example, weather. It will be denoted by v: thus $y = g(x, \eta, v)$. Note
that now the unobserved component in the outcome equation, ε, consists of two
elements, η and v.*

*The level of the input x is chosen optimally by the firm to maximize expected
profits. At the time the level of the input is chosen the firm knows the form of
the production function, the level of the capital input η and the value of a cost
shifter for the labor input, for example, an indicator of the cost of labor inputs.
This cost shifter is denoted by z. Profits are the difference between production
times price (normalized to equal one), and costs, which depend on the level of
the input and the observed cost shifter z:*

$$\pi(x, z, \eta, v) = g(x, \eta, v) - c(x, z),$$

so that the firm solves the problem

$$X = \text{argmax}_x \mathbb{E}\left[\pi(x, Z, \eta, v)\middle| \eta, Z\right] = \text{argmax}_x\left[\mathbb{E}\left[g(x, \eta, v)\middle| \eta\right] - c(x, Z)\right].$$

Thus, $X = h(Z, \eta)$, so that equations (2.1) and (2.2) are satisfied.

*Again, it is crucial that there is a difference between the payoff function
for the agent and the production function that is the object of interest for the
researcher, and that the production function is nonadditive in the unobserved
component. If, for example, $g(x, \eta, v)$ were additive in η, the optimal level of the*

input would be the solution to $\max_x g(x, v) - c(x, Z)$. *In that case the optimal solution* $X = h(Z, \eta)$ *would not depend on* η *and all firms with the same level of the instrument* Z *would choose the same level of the labor input irrespective of the amount of capital.*　　　　　　　　　　　　　　　　　　　□

3.2   Policies of Interest

Next, I want to discuss some specific policies that may be of interest and how they relate to the model specified in equations (2.1) and (2.2). Traditionally, researchers have focused on identification and estimation of the production function $g(x, \varepsilon)$ itself. There is two concerns with this focus. First, it may not be enough. Evaluation of specific policies often requires knowledge of the joint distribution of X and ε in addition to knowledge of $g(x, \varepsilon)$. Second, it may be too much. Identification of the entire function $g(x, \varepsilon)$ can require very strong support conditions. To avoid the second problem researchers have often reported summary statistics of the production function. A leading example of such a summary statistic in the binary regressor case is the difference in the average value of the function at the two values of the regressor, in that setting referred to as the average treatment effect, $\mathbb{E}[g(1, \varepsilon) - g(0, \varepsilon)]$. Another approach is to report average derivatives (e.g., Powell, Stock, Stoker, 1989). Such statistics are very useful ways of summarizing the typical (e.g., some average) effect of the regressor even though they rarely correspond to the effect of a policy that may actually be considered for implementation. Such policies typically involve changing the incentives for individuals to make particular choices. Only as a limit does this involve mandating a specific level of the choice variable for all individuals. In general, policies changing the incentives require researchers to estimate both the outcome equation and the choice equation. Since the choice behavior of an individual or unit is wholly determined by the value of the instrument and the type of the unit, these policy effects can often be expressed in terms of two objects, first the expected production function given the agent type,

$$\beta(x, t) = \mathbb{E}[g(x, \varepsilon)|T],$$

and second the joint distribution of the type and regressor, $f_{XT}(x, t)$.

Here I want to mention briefly three examples of parameters that may be of interest to report in such an analysis. The first two are of the summary statistic type, and the last one corresponds to a more specific policy. Blundell and Powell (2003) focus on the identification and estimation of what they label the *average structural function* (ASF, see also Chamberlain, 1983), the average of the structural function $g(x, \varepsilon)$ over the marginal distribution of ε,

$$\mu(x) = \int g(x, \varepsilon) F_\varepsilon(d\varepsilon). \tag{3.7}$$

This is an attractive way of summarizing the effect of the regressor, although it does not correspond to a particular policy. By iterated expectations the average structural function can also be characterized in terms of the conditional average response function:

$$\mu(x) = \int \beta(x, t) F_T(dt).$$

A second summary measure corresponds to increasing for all units the value of the input by a small amount. In the continuous regressor case the per-unit effect of such a change on average output is

$$\mathbb{E}\left[\frac{\partial g}{\partial x}(X, \varepsilon)\right] = \int \int \frac{\partial g}{\partial x}(x, \varepsilon) F_{\varepsilon|X}(d\varepsilon|x) F_X(dx)$$

$$= \mathbb{E}\left[\frac{\partial \beta}{\partial x}(X, T)\right], \tag{3.8}$$

where the last equality holds by changing the order of differentiation and integration. This average derivative parameter is analogous to the average derivatives studied in Powell, Stock, and Stoker (1989) in the context of exogenous regressors. Note that this average derivative is generally *not* equal to the average derivative of the average structural function,

$$\mathbb{E}\left[\frac{\partial \mu}{\partial x}(X)\right] = \int \int \frac{\partial g}{\partial x}(x, \varepsilon) F_{\varepsilon}(d\varepsilon) F_X(dx),$$

where the derivative of the production function is averaged over the product of the marginal distributions of ε and X rather than over their joint distribution. Equality holds if X and ε are independent ($F_{\varepsilon|X}(\varepsilon|x) = F_{\varepsilon}(\varepsilon)$, and thus X is exogenous), or if the derivative is constant (e.g., in the linear model).

An example of a more specific policy is the implementation of a ceiling on the value of the input at $\bar{x}$. This changes the optimization problem of the firm in the production function example (Example 2) to

$$X = \operatorname{argmax}_{x \leq \bar{x}} \mathbb{E}\left[\pi(x, Z, \eta, \nu)|\eta, Z\right]$$
$$= \operatorname{argmax}_{x \leq \bar{x}} \left[\mathbb{E}\left[g(x, \eta, \nu)|\eta\right] - c(x, Z)\right].$$

Those firms who in the absence of this restriction would choose a value for the input that is outside the limit now choose the limit $\bar{x}$ (under some conditions on the production and cost functions), and those firms whose optimal choice is within the limit are not affected by the policy, so that under these conditions the new input is $\ell(X) = \min(X, \bar{x})$, and the resulting average production is

$$\mathbb{E}\left[g(\ell(X), \eta, \nu)\right] = \mathbb{E}\left[\beta(\ell(X), T)\right]. \tag{3.9}$$

One example of such a policy would arise if the input is causing pollution, and the government is interested in restricting its use. Another example of such a policy is the compulsory schooling age, with the government interested in the effect such a policy would have on average earnings.

More generally, one may be interested in policies that change the incentives in a way that leads all agents who currently make the choice X to make the same new choice $\ell(X)$. The average outcome that is the result from such a policy has the form $\mathbb{E}[g(\ell(X), \eta, \nu)]$. Note that even in the context of standard additive linear simultaneous equation models knowledge of the regression coefficients and knowledge of the function $\ell(X)$ would not be sufficient for the evaluation of such policies – unless X is exogenous this would also require knowledge of the joint distribution of (X, η), not just the effect of a unit increase in X on Y.

The identification of the average effects of policies of this type can be difficult compared to (3.8) partly because the policy does not correspond to a marginal change: for some individuals the value under the new policy can be far away from the value in the current environment. It can therefore be useful to define a local version of such a policy. Consider a parametrization of the policy by a parameter γ, so that under the new policy the value of the regressor for an individual whose current value is x is $\ell(x, \gamma)$, with $\ell(x, 0) = x$ corresponding to the current environment. Assuming $\ell(x, \gamma)$ is sufficiently smooth, we can focus on

$$\mathbb{E}\left[\frac{\partial g}{\partial \gamma}(\ell(X, \gamma), \eta, \nu)\right]\Bigg|_{\gamma=0} = \mathbb{E}\left[\frac{\partial \beta}{\partial \gamma}(\ell(X, \gamma), T)\right]\Bigg|_{\gamma=0}, \qquad (3.10)$$

the average effect of a marginal change in the incentives. For example, one may be interested in the effect of a new tax on the quantity traded in a particular market. Rather than attempt to estimate the effect of the new tax at its proposed level, it may be more credible to estimate the derivative of the quantity traded with respect to the new tax, evaluated at the current level of the tax.

4 A BINARY ENDOGENOUS REGRESSOR: LOCAL AVERAGE TREATMENT EFFECTS

In this section I discuss the case with a binary endogenous regressor. First, I focus on the case where the instrument is also binary. Next, I will consider the case with Z multi-valued or even continuous. This section relies heavily on the discussion in Imbens and Angrist (1994) and Angrist, Imbens, and Rubin (1996).

4.1 A Binary Instrument

With both the regressor and instrument binary the four types can fully describe the set of responses to all levels of the instrument, irrespective of the cardinality of η. It is useful to list them explicitly:

$$T_i = \begin{cases} (0, 0) \text{ (nevertaker)} & \text{if } h(0, \eta_i) = h(1, \eta_i) = 0, \\ (0, 1) \text{ (complier)} & \text{if } h(0, \eta_i) = 0, h(1, \eta_i) = 1, \\ (1, 0) \text{ (defier)} & \text{if } h(0, \eta_i) = 1, h(1, \eta_i) = 0, \\ (1, 1) \text{ (alwaystaker)} & \text{if } h(0, \eta_i) = h(1, \eta_i) = 1. \end{cases}$$

The labels nevertaker, complier, defier, and alwaystaker (Angrist, Imbens, and Rubin, 1996) refer to the setting of a randomized experiment with noncompliance, where the instrument is the (random) assignment to the treatment and

Table 2.1. *Type by observed variables*

		Z_i	
		0	1
$X_i = h(Z_i, \eta_i)$	0	Nevertaker/Complier	Nevertaker/Defier
	1	Alwaystaker/Defier	Alwaystaker/Complier

the endogenous regressor is an indicator for the actual receipt of the treatment. Compliers are in that case individuals who (always) comply with their assignment, that is, take the treatment if assigned to it and not take it if assigned to the control group.

In this case we cannot infer the type of a unit from the observed variables of Y_i, X_i, and Z_i. To see this, consider Table 2.1. Each pair of observed values (Z, X) is consistent with two of the four types.

This changes if one is willing to assume monotonicity. This can be done in two ways, monotonicity in the observed (Assumption 2.2) or monotonicity in the unobserved component (Assumption 2.3) of the choice function. In the case with Z and X binary these two assumptions are both equivalent to ruling out the presence of both compliers and defiers, and it is therefore sometimes referred to as the "no-defiance" assumption (Balke and Pearl, 1994; Pearl, 2000). Suppose Assumption 2.2 holds and $h(z, \eta)$ is nondecreasing in z. Then if $h(0, \eta) = 1$, it must be that $h(1, \eta) = 1$ because $h(1, \eta) \geq h(0, \eta)$. Hence there can be no defiers. (Similarly, if $h(z, \eta)$ is nonincreasing in z the presence of compliers would be ruled out.) Now suppose Assumption 2.3 holds. Suppose that there is a complier with η_0 such that $h(0, \eta_0) = 0$ and $h(1, \eta_0) = 1$. Now consider an individual with $\eta_1 > \eta_0$. Then $h(1, \eta_1) = 1$ because $h(1, \eta_1) \geq h(1, \eta_0) = 1$. For an individual with $\eta_1 < \eta_0$ it must be that $h(0, \eta_1) = 0$ because $h(0, \eta_1) \leq h(0, \eta_0) = 0$. Hence no individual can be a defier. So, again the assumption is equivalent to ruling out the presence of either compliers or defiers. Vytlacil (2002), discussing the relation between this model and the selection type models developed by Heckman (e.g., Heckman, 1978; Heckman and Robb, 1984), shows that this assumption is also equivalent to the existence of an additive latent index representation of the choice function, $h(z, \eta) = 1\{m(z) + \eta \geq 0\}$. Note that monotonicity is not a testable assumption based on the joint distribution of (Z_i, X_i). Obviously, if we specified the assumption as requiring that $h(z, \eta)$ is nondecreasing in z, there would a testable implication, but simply requiring monotonicity does not impose any restrictions on the distribution of (Z_i, X_i). It does impose some fairly weak conditions on the conditional distribution of Y_i given (Z_i, X_i) that stem from the mixture implications of the model. See Imbens and Rubin (1997) and Balke and Pearl (1994).

Monotonicity is not sufficient to identify the type of an individual given the value of Z and X. Although it rules out the presence of defiers, it does not eliminate all mixtures. Table 2.2 shows the additional information from the

Table 2.2. *Type by observed variables*

		Z_i	
		0	1
$X_i = h(Z_i, \eta_i)$	0	Nevertaker/Complier	Nevertaker
	1	Alwaystaker	Alwaystaker/Complier

monotonicity assumption. Consider individuals with $(Z_i, X_i) = (1, 0)$. Because of monotonicity such individuals can only be nevertakers. However, consider now individuals with $(Z_i, X_i) = (0, 0)$. Such individuals can be either compliers or alwaystakers. We cannot infer the type of such individuals from the observed data alone. Hence, a control function approach (Blundell and Powell, 2003; Heckman and Robb, 1984; Imbens and Newey, 2002) is not feasible. Even though we cannot identify the type of some units, we can indirectly adjust for differences in types. Imbens and Angrist (1994) show how the mixtures can be decomposed to obtain the average difference between $g(1, \varepsilon)$ and $g(0, \varepsilon)$ for compliers, that is units with η such that $h(1, \eta) = 1$ and $h(0, \eta) = 0$. More generally, we can identify the outcome distributions for units in this subpopulation.

The intuition is as follows. The first step is to see that we can infer the population proportions of the three remaining subpopulations, nevertakers, alwaystakers, and compliers (using the fact that the monotonicity assumption rules out the presence of defiers). Call these population shares P_t, for $t = (0, 0), (0, 1), (1, 1)$. Consider the subpopulation with $Z_i = 0$. Within this subpopulation we observe $X_i = 1$ only for alwaystakers. Hence, the conditional probability of $X_i = 1$ given $Z_i = 0$ is equal to the population share of alwaystakers: $P_{(1,1)} = \Pr(X = 1 | Z = 0)$. Similarly, in the subpopulation with $Z_i = 1$ we observe $X_i = 0$ only for nevertakers. Hence, the population share of nevertakers is equal to the conditional probability of $X_i = 0$ given $Z_i = 1$: $P_{(0,0)} = \Pr(X = 0 | Z = 1)$. The population share of compliers is then obtained by subtracting the population shares of nevertakers and alwaystakers from one. The second step uses the distribution of Y given (Z, X). We can infer the distribution of $Y_i | X_i = 0, T_i = (0, 0)$ from the subpopulation with $(Z_i, X_i) = (1, 0)$ since all these individuals are known to be nevertakers. Then we use the distribution of $Y_i | Z_i = 0, X_i = 0$. This is a mixture of the distribution of $Y_i | X_i = 0, T_i = (0, 0)$ and the distribution of $Y_i | X_i = 0, T_i = (0, 1)$, with mixture probabilities equal to the relative population shares. Since we already inferred the population shares of the nevertakers and compliers as well as the distribution of $Y_i | X_i = 0, T_i = (0, 0)$, we can obtain the conditional distribution of $Y_i | X_i = 0, T_i = (0, 1)$. Similarly, we can infer the conditional distribution of $Y_i | X_i = 1, T_i = (0, 1)$. The average difference between these two conditional distributions is the Local Average Treatment Effect or LATE introduced by Imbens and Angrist (1994):

$$\tau^{\text{LATE}} = \mathbb{E}[g(1, \varepsilon) - g(0, \varepsilon) | h(0, \eta) = 0, h(1, \eta) = 1].$$

This implies that in this setting we can under the independence and monotonicity assumptions identify the conditional average response function $\beta(x, t)$ on the joint support of (X, T). However, because this support is not the Cartesian product of the support of X and the support of T we cannot necessarily identify the effects of all policies of interest. Specifically, $(X, T) = (0, (1, 1))$ and $(X, T) = (1, (0, 0))$ are not in the joint support of (X, T). As a consequence, we cannot identify the average effect of the regressor $\mathbb{E}[(g(1, \varepsilon) - g(0, \varepsilon)]$, the average of $\beta(x, t)$ over the distribution of T at all values of x, nor can we generally identify the average effect for those with $X = 1$, the average effect for the treated.

4.2   A Multi-Valued Instrument

Now suppose the instrument Z_i takes on values in a set $\mathbb{Z}$. This improves our ability to identify the causal effects of interest by providing us with additional information to infer the type of a unit. Compared to the examples with a binary instrument one can think of the multiple instrument case as arising in two ways. First, it could be that incentives are allocated more finely. Specifically, in terms of the first example in Section 3, a binary instrument could correspond to participation costs of $Z = 10$ and $Z = 20$. A multi-valued instrument could correspond to $Z \in \{10, 12.5, 15, 17.5, 20\}$. Alternatively, we can add more extreme values of the incentives, for example, $Z \in \{0, 10, 20, 30\}$. This will have different implications for the identification results. With the former we will be able to make finer distinctions between different types of compliers, and estimate the extent of variation in the effect of the regressor for these subpopulations. With the latter, we will be able to expand the subpopulation of compliers and obtain estimates for more representative subpopulations.

First, consider the case with finite set of value, or $\mathbb{Z} = \{z_1, \ldots, z_K\}$. The type of a unit now consists of the set of values $T_i = (X_i(z_0), \ldots, X_i(z_K))$. Without the monotonicity assumption there are now 2^K different types. Monotonicity in η reduces this to $K + 1$ different types, all of the form $T_i = (0, \ldots, 0, 1, \ldots, 1)$, characterized by a unique value of the instrument where the type switches from $h(z, \eta) = 0$ to $h(z, \eta) = 1$ (this transition can occur after $Z = z_K$, leading to the 1 in the $K + 1$ types). The second form of monotonicity in the instrument (Assumption 2.2) is again equivalent to monotonicity in η. To see this, suppose that monotonicity in z holds, and that there is a η_0 and $z < z'$ such that $h(z, \eta_0) = 0$ and $h(z', \eta_0) = 1$. To show that monotonicity in η holds one just needs to show that there are no η_1 such that $h(z, \eta_1) = 1$ and $h(z', \eta_1) = 1$. This follows directly from monotonicity in z. The assertion in the other direction is trivial.

Let us consider the case with a three-valued instrument under monotonicity. In that case we have four types, $T_i \in \{(0, 0, 0), (0, 0, 1), (0, 1, 1), (1, 1, 1)\}$. A simple extension of the argument for the binary instrument case shows that one can infer the population shares for the four types (see Table 2.3). Using that we can infer the distribution of $Y(0)$ for the types $(0, 0, 0), (0, 0, 1)$, and $(0, 1, 1)$, and the distribution of $Y(1)$ for the types $(0, 0, 1), (0, 1, 1)$, and $(1, 1, 1)$. Hence,

Table 2.3. *Type by observed variables*

		Z_i		
		Z_1	Z_2	Z_3
X_i	0	(0,0,0),(0,0,1),(0,1,1)	(0,0,0),(0,0,1)	(0,0,0)
	1	(1,1,1)	(0,1,1),(1,1,1)	(0,0,1),(0,1,1),(1,1,1)

we can infer the causal effects for the two types $(0, 0, 1)$ and $(0, 1, 1)$. Both are compliers in the sense that with sufficient incentives they are willing to switch from $X = 0$ to $X = 1$. These two types of compliers differ in the amount of incentives required to participate. Another way of understanding this case with a binary regressor and a multi-valued instrument is as a set of local average treatment effects. Suppose we focus on the subpopulation with $Z \in \{z, z'\}$. Within this subpopulation the basic assumption (independence and monotonicity in the unobserved component) are satisfied if they are satisfied in the overall population. Hence, we can estimate the local average treatment effect for this pair of instrument values,

$$\mathbb{E}[g(1, \varepsilon) - g(0, \varepsilon)|h(z, \eta) = 0, h(z', \eta) = 1].$$

This holds for all pairs (z, z'), and thus this argument implies that we can estimate the local average treatment effect for any of the $K \times (K - 1)/2$ pairs of instrument values,

$$\tau_{z,z'}^{\text{LATE}} = \mathbb{E}[g(1, \varepsilon) - g(0, \varepsilon)|h(z, \eta) = 0, h(z', \eta) = 1].$$

These $K \times (K - 1)/2$ local average treatment effects are closely related since there are only $K - 1$ different types of compliers. The remaining local average treatment effects can all be written as linear combinations of the $K - 1$ basic ones. One of the most interesting of these local average treatment effects is the one corresponding to the largest set of compliers. This corresponds to the pair of instrument values with the largest effect on the regressor, (z_1, z_K) if the instrument values are ordered to satisfy monotonicity.

Having a multi-valued instrument helps in two ways if one maintains the independence and monotonicity assumptions. It allows us to estimate separate causal effects for different subpopulations, thus giving the researcher information to assess the amount of heterogeneity in the treatment effect. Second, if the multiple values reflect stronger incentives to participate or not in the activity, they will increase the size of the subpopulation for which we can identify causal effects. With a large number of values for the instrument there are more complier types. One interesting limit is the case with a scalar continuous instrument. If $h(z, \eta)$ is monotone in both z and η, and right continuous in z, we can define the limit of the local average treatment effect as

$$\mathbb{E}[g(1, \varepsilon) - g(0, \varepsilon)|h(z, \eta) = 1, \lim_{v \uparrow z} h(v, \eta) = 0],$$

the average treatment effect for units who change regressor value when the instrument equals z. In the context of additive latent index models with $h(z, \eta) = 1\{m(z) + \eta \geq 0\}$ this is equal to $\mathbb{E}[g(1, \varepsilon) - g(0, \varepsilon)|\eta = -m(z)]$. Heckman and Vytlacil (2001) refer to this limit of the local average treatment effect as the marginal treatment effect.

5   A CONTINUOUS ENDOGENOUS REGRESSOR

5.1   A Scalar Unobserved Component

In this section I will discuss the case with a continuous endogenous regressor. The discussion will lean heavily on the work by Imbens and Newey (2002). Initially, I will use Assumption 2.5, the strict version of the monotonicity-in-the-unobserved-component assumption: In the binary case (as well as in the general discrete case) strict monotonicity is extremely restrictive. In that case strict monotonicity in combination with the independence assumption would imply that η can take on only two values, and thus one can immediately identify the type of a unit because it is perfectly correlated with the endogenous regressor. Conditional on the type there is no variation in the value of the endogenous regressor and so one cannot learn about the effect of the endogenous regressor for any type. In the continuous regressor case this is very different, and strict monotonicity has no testable implications. However, this obviously does not mean that substantively strict monotonicity is not a strong assumption.

In addition to the assumptions discussed in Section 2, I will make a smoothness assumption:

Assumption 5.1 (CONTINUITY) $h(z, \eta)$ *is continuous in η and z.*

In the continuous X case the type of a unit is a one-to-one function of the unobserved component η. A convenient normalization of the distribution of the type is to fix it to be uniform on the interval $[0, 1]$. In that case one can identify for each individual the type $T(\eta)$ given the strict monotonicity assumption as a function of the value of the instrument and the value of the regressor as:

$$T_i = F_{X|Z}(X_i|Z_i).$$

One can then use the inferred value of T_i to identify the conditional expectation of Y given X and T:

$$\beta(X, T) = \mathbb{E}[Y|X, T].$$

This identifies $\beta(x, t)$ for all values of x and t in their joint support. However, this support may be very limited. Suppose that the instrument is binary, $Z \in \{0, 1\}$. In that case the argument still works, but now for each value of T there are only two values of X that can be observed, namely $h(0, \eta(T))$ and $h(1, \eta(T))$. Hence, for each type T we can infer the difference between $\mathbb{E}[g(x, \varepsilon)|T]$ at $x = x_0 = h(0, \eta(T))$ and $x = x_1 = h(1, \eta(T))$. These values x_0 and x_1 where we can evaluate this expectation generally differ by type T, so the set of identified effects is very limited.

As the range of values of the instrument increases, there are for each type more and more values of the conditional regression function that can be inferred from the data. In the limit with Z continuous we can infer the value of $\mathbb{E}[Y|X, T]$ over an interval of regressor values. This may be sufficient for some policy questions, but for others there may not be sufficient variation in the instrument. For example, it may be that the instrument generates for each type of agent variation in the endogenous regressor over a different interval, making identification of the population average effect difficult.

If there is sufficient overlap in the joint distribution of X and T one can identify the marginal effect of X on Y by integrating $\beta(x, t)$ back over T. Given that the marginal distribution of T is uniform the average structural function can be written as

$$\mu(x) = \int_t \beta(x, t)dt.$$

Typically, the support conditions that allow for identification of the average structural function are strong, and conditions for identification of local effects, either local in the sense of referring to a subpopulation as in the local average treatment effect, or local in the sense of moving agents only marginally away from their current choices, may be more plausible.

5.2 Multiple Unobserved Components in the Choice Equation

Throughout most of the discussion I have assumed that the unobserved component in the choice equation (2.2) can be summarized by the type of a unit, with ordering on the set of types that corresponds to an ordering on $h(z, t)$ for all z. Here I want to discuss some of the issues that arise when there are multiple unobserved components so that η_i is a vector and no such ordering need exist. In that case neither the LATE approach nor the generalized control function approach work. In that case it is still true that conditional on the vector η_i the regressor X_i is independent of the residual in the outcome equation ε_i. Hence, conditioning on η would still eliminate the endogeneity problem. However, even in the case with continuous instruments and regressors one can no longer infer the value of the (vector of) residuals. This can be illustrated in a simple example with a bivariate η.

Suppose

$$X = h(Z, \eta_1, \eta_2) = \eta_1 + \eta_2 \cdot Z,$$

with $Z \geq 0$. Suppose also that η_1 and η_2 are independent of each other and normally distributed with mean zero and unit variance. Finally, suppose that

$$\varepsilon|\eta_1, \eta_2 \sim \mathcal{N}(\eta_1 + \eta_2, 1),$$

and

$$Y_i = \alpha \cdot X_i + \varepsilon_i.$$

Now consider following the Imbens–Newey generalized control function strategy of calculating the generalized residual $v = F_{X|Z}(X|Z)$. The conditional distribution of $X|Z$ is normal with mean zero and variance $1 + Z^2$. Hence, the generalized residual is

$$v_i = F_{X|Z}(X_i|Z_i) = \Phi\left(\frac{X_i}{\sqrt{1 + Z_i^2}}\right).$$

Note that by construction $v \perp Z$, and by assumption $\varepsilon \perp Z$. However, it is not necessarily true that $(\varepsilon, v) \perp Z$. Rather than work with this residual itself it is easier to work with a strictly monotone transformation, $v_i = X_i/\sqrt{1 + Z_i^2}$. Now consider the conditional expectation of Y given X and v. Previously, conditioning on η removed the dependence between ε and X. Here this is not the case. To see this, consider the conditional expectation of Y given $X = x_0$ and $v = v_0$. Since Z and X are one-to-one given v, this conditional expectation is identical to the conditional expectation of Y given $Z = z_0 = \sqrt{x_0^2/v_0^2 - 1}$ and $v = v_0$:

$$\mathbb{E}[Y|X = x_0, v = v_0]$$
$$= \alpha x_0 + \mathbb{E}[\varepsilon|X = x_0, v = v_0]$$
$$= \alpha x_0 + \mathbb{E}[\varepsilon|Z = z_0, v = v_0]$$
$$= \alpha x_0 + \mathbb{E}[\eta_1 + \eta_2|Z = z_0, X/\sqrt{1 + Z^2} = v_0]$$
$$= \alpha x_0 + \mathbb{E}[\eta_1 + \eta_2|Z = z_0, (\eta_1 + \eta_2 Z)/\sqrt{1 + Z^2} = v_0].$$

Now evaluate this expectation at $(z_0 = 0, v_0, x_0 = v_0)$:

$$\mathbb{E}[Y|X = v_0, v = v_0]$$
$$= \alpha v_0 + \mathbb{E}[\eta_1 + \eta_2|Z = z_0, \eta_1 = v_0] = v_0 \cdot (1 + \alpha).$$

Next, evaluate this expectation at $(z_0 = 1, v_0, x_0 = \sqrt{2}v_0)$:

$$\mathbb{E}[Y|X = \sqrt{2}v_0, v = v_0]$$
$$= \alpha\sqrt{2}v_0 + \mathbb{E}[\eta_1 + \eta_2|Z = z_0, (\eta_1 + \eta_2)/\sqrt{2} = v_0]$$
$$= v_0 \cdot \sqrt{2} \cdot (1 + \alpha).$$

Hence, the expectation depends on X given v, and therefore X is not exogenous conditional on v.

There are two points to this example. First, it shows that the assumption of a scalar unobserved component in the choice equation that enters in a monotone way is very informative. The part of the literature that avoids specification of the choice equation potentially ignores this information if this assumption is plausible. The second point is that often economic theory has much to say about the choice equation. In many cases motivation for endogeneity comes from a specific economic model that articulates the optimization problem that the agents solve as well as specifies the components that lead to the correlation between the unobserved components in the two equations. This includes the examples in Section 3. In that case it seems useful to explore the full identifying power from the theoretical model. Even if theoretical considerations do not determine the exact functional form of the choice equation, it may suggest that it is monotone. Consider for example the two examples in Section 3. In the first case ability is the unobserved component of the outcome equation, and the signal concerning this is the unobserved component in the choice equation. It appears plausible that the choice decision is monotone in this signal.

6 A DISCRETE ENDOGENOUS REGRESSOR AND DISCRETE INSTRUMENTS

In this section I will focus on the case where both Z and X are discrete. For concreteness I will assume that $\mathbb{Z} = \{0, \dots, M\}$ and $\mathbb{X} = \{0, \dots, L\}$. The discrete case is remarkably different from both the binary and continuous cases. Neither the strategy of inferring the value of η and estimating $\beta(x, \eta)$ directly, as was effective in the continuous regressor case in Section 5, nor the strategy of undoing the mixture of outcome distributions by type as was useful in the binary regressor case analyzed in Section 4 works for this setting in general. To gain insight into, and illustrate some of the difficulties of, these issues, I largely focus on the case where the endogenous regressor takes on three values, $\mathbb{X} = \{0, 1, 2\}$. Initially, I consider the case with a binary instrument with $\mathbb{Z} = \{0, 1\}$, and then I will look at the case with a multi-valued and continuous instrument.

Without any monotonicity or separability restrictions the number of distinct types in the case with a binary instrument and three-valued regressor, that is the number of distinct pairs $(h(0, \eta), h(1, \eta))$ is nine: $T_i \in \{(0, 0),$ $(0, 1), (0, 2), (1, 0), \dots, (2, 2)\}$. For some types there is a single outcome distribution under the independence or exclusion restriction. For example, for the type $T_i = (0, 0)$, there is only $f_{Y|X,T}(y|x = 0, t = (0, 0))$. For others there are two outcome distributions, for example, for type $T_i = (0, 1)$ there are $f_{Y|X,T}(y|x = 0, t = (0, 1))$ and $f_{Y|X,T}(y|x = 1, t = (0, 1))$. This leads to a total number of outcome distributions by regressor x and type t, $f_{Y|X,T}(y|x, t)$, equal to 15. Given that one only observes data in six cells defined by observed values of (Z_i, X_i), $f_{Y|X,Z}(y|x, z)$, it is clear that one cannot identify all potential outcome distributions. In the binary regressor/binary instrument case the same problem arose. Without monotonicity there were six outcome distributions $f_{Y|X,T}(y|x, t)$ (two each for defiers and compliers, and one each for nevertakers and alwaystakers) and four outcome distributions, $f_{Y|X,Z}(y|x, z)$. In that binary regressor case monotonicity ruled out the presence of defiers, reducing the number of outcome distributions by type and regressor $f_{Y|X,T}(y|x, t)$ to four. With the four outcome distributions by regressor and instrument $f_{Y|X,Z}(y|x, z)$ this led to exact identification. In the discrete regressor case it is also useful to consider some restrictions on the number of types.

In the discrete case, as in the binary case, strict monotonicity is extremely restrictive. I therefore return to the weak monotonicity assumption in the unobserved component (Assumption 2.3). This rules out the presence of some types,

Table 2.4. *Type by observed variables*

		Z_i	
		0	1
X_i	0	(0,0),(0,1)	(0,0)
	1	(1,1),(1,2)	(0,1),(1,1)
	2	(2,2)	(1,2),(2,2)

but there are multiple sets of five types that satisfy this monotonicity assumption. Three of them are $\{(0, 0), (0, 1), (1, 1), (1, 2), (2, 2)\}$, $\{(0, 0), (0, 1), (0, 2), (1, 2), (2, 2)\}$, and $\{(0, 0), (0, 1), (1, 1), (2, 1), (2, 2)\}$. Also, requiring weak monotonicity in the instrument (Assumption 2.2) rules out the third of these sets.

To further reduce the sets of different types it may be useful to consider a smoothness assumption. In the discrete regressor case it is not meaningful to assume continuity of the choice function. Instead we assume that changing the instrument by the smallest amount possible does not lead to a jump in the response larger than the smallest jump possible. We formulate this assumption as follows: In the setting with $\mathbb{Z} = \{0, 1, \ldots, M\}$ and $\mathbb{X} = \{0, 1, \ldots, L\}$, this requires that $|h(z, \eta) - h(z + 1, \eta)| \leq 1$. In the continuous case this assumption is implied by continuity. In the binary case it is automatically satisfied as there can be no jumps larger than size one in the endogenous regressor. This is potentially a restrictive assumption and it may not be reasonable in all settings. In the three-valued regressor and binary instrument case this implies that we rule out the type $T = (0, 2)$ where an individual changes the value of the regressor by two units in response to a one unit increase in the instrument.

The three assumptions combined lead to the following set of five different types:

$$T_i \in \{(0, 0), (0, 1), (1, 1), (1, 2), (2, 2)\}.$$

From the joint distribution of (X, Z) we can infer the population shares of each of these types. For example,

$$\Pr(T = (0, 0)) = \Pr(X = 0|Z = 1),$$

and

$$\Pr(T = (0, 1)) = \Pr(X = 0|Z = 0) - \Pr(X = 0|Z = 1).$$

Similarly, one can identify $\Pr(T = (2, 2))$ and $\Pr(T = (1, 2))$ so that $\Pr(T = (1, 1))$ can be derived from the fact that the population shares add up to unity.

For these five types there are a total of seven outcome distributions, $f(y(0)|T = (0, 0))$, $f(y(0)|T = (0, 1))$, $f(y(1)|T = (0, 1))$, $f(y(1)|T = (1, 1))$, $f(y(1)|T = (1, 2))$, $f(y(2)|T = (1, 2))$, and $f(y(2)|T = (2, 2))$. We observe data in six cells, so we cannot identify all seven distributions. Table 2.4 illustrates this. It is clear that we can infer the distributions $f(y(0)|T = (0, 0))$

(from the $(Z, X) = (1, 0)$ cell), $f(y(0)|T = (0, 1))$ (from the $(Z, X) = (0, 0)$ and $(Z, X) = (1, 0)$ cells), $f(y(2)|T = (2, 2))$ (from the $(Z, X) = (0, 2)$ cell), $f(y(2)|T = (1, 2))$ (from the $(Z, X) = (0, 2)$ and $(Z, X) = (1, 2)$ cells). However, we cannot infer the distributions of $f(y(1)|T = (0, 1))$, $f(y(1)|T = (1, 1))$, and $f(y(1)|T = (1, 2))$ from the $(Z, X) = (0, 1)$ and $(Z, X) = (1, 1)$ cells. These cells give us some restrictions on these distributions in the form of mixtures with known mixture probabilities, but not point-identification.

As a result we cannot infer the average causal effect of the regressor for any level or for any subpopulation under these assumptions in this simple case. Now let us consider what happens if there are three values for the instrument as well. Without restrictions there are 27 different types $t = (x_0, x_1, x_2)$, for $x_0, x_1, x_2, \in \{0, 1, 2\}$. Assuming that $h(x, \eta)$ is monotone in both z and x, and making the smoothness assumption $|h(z, \eta) - h(z + 1, \eta)| \leq 1$ this is reduced to seven types:

$$T \in \{(0, 0, 0), (0, 0, 1), (0, 1, 1), (1, 1, 1), (1, 1, 2), (1, 2, 2), (2, 2, 2)\}.$$

This leads to eleven different outcome distributions. There are only nine cells to estimate these outcome distributions from so as before it will in general still not be possible to estimate the distribution of $Y(1)$ for any of the types $T \in \{(0, 0, 1), (0, 1, 1), (1, 1, 1), (1, 1, 2), (1, 2, 2)\}$.

There are a number of approaches to deal with this problem. First, in the spirit of the work by Manski (1990, 2003), one can focus on identifying bounds for the parameters of interest. Chesher (2005) follows this approach and obtains interval estimates for quantiles of the production function at specific values for the endogenous regressor. Second, following Angrist and Imbens (1995) one can identify weighted average of unit increases in the regressor. Here the weights are partly determined by the joint distribution of the regressor and the instrument and not under the control of the researcher. Thus, one cannot simply estimate the expected value of, say, $\mathbb{E}[g(X, \varepsilon) - g(X - 1, \varepsilon)]$ over the sample distribution of X.

6.1   Bounds on the Conditional Average Response Function

One approach to identification in the case with endogenous regressors is to focus on bounds. With endogenous regressors we cannot determine the exact type of a unit. However, we can determine a range of types consistent with the observed values of the choice and instrument. Hence, we can analyze the problem as one with a mismeasured regressor. See Manski and Tamer (2002).

To see how such an approach could work, note that under the assumption of monotonicity in the unobserved component one can normalize η as uniform on the interval $[0, 1]$. Under the smoothness assumption and the monotonicity assumption we can estimate the probabilities of each of the types. Hence, we can identify each type with a range of values of η. Now take a particular observation with values (Z_i, X_i). This implies that the value of η is between

$F_{X|Z}(X_i - 1|Z_i)$ and $F_{X|Z}(X_i|Z_i)$. Hence, we identify η up to the interval $[F_{X|Z}(X_i - 1|Z_i), F_{X|Z}(X_i|Z_i)]$. If we were to observe η we could regress Y on X and η because conditional on η X is exogenous. Now we can do the same with the provision that η is observed only to lie in an interval, fitting the Manski–Tamer framework. This would lead to an identified region for the regression function $\mathbb{E}[Y|x, \eta]$.

This approach is more likely to be useful when the endogenous regressor and the instrument take on a large number of values. In that case the type can be measured accurately and the bounds are likely to be tight. In the limit one gets to the continuous endogenous regressor case where the type can be measured without error.

6.2   Identification of Weighted Average Causal Effects

Angrist and Imbens (1995) follow a different approach. They show that under the independence assumption the standard IV estimand, the ratio of average effects of the instrument on the outcome and on the endogenous regressor,

$$\beta^{IV}(z_0, z_1) = \frac{\mathbb{E}[Y|Z = z_1] - \mathbb{E}[Y|Z = z_0]}{\mathbb{E}[X|Z = z_1] - \mathbb{E}[X|Z = z_0]},$$

can be written as a weighted average of unit-level increases in the regressor, with the weights depending on the level of the regressor and the subpopulation:

$$\beta^{IV} = \sum_{l=1}^{L} \sum_{t|h(z_1,t)\geq l, h(z_0,t)<l} \lambda_l \cdot \mathbb{E}[g(l, \varepsilon) - g(l - 1, \varepsilon)|T = t],$$

with

$$\lambda_l = \frac{\Pr(h(z_1, T) \geq l > h(z_0, T))}{\sum_{m=1}^{L} \Pr(h(z_1, T) \geq m > h(z_0, T))},$$

so that $\sum_l \lambda_l = 1$. If the effect of a unit increase in the regressor is the same for all individuals and the same across all levels of the treatment,

$$g(x, \varepsilon) - g(x - 1, \varepsilon) = \beta_0,$$

than $\beta^{IV} = \beta_0$.

Angrist and Imbens show that although the weights $\lambda_{l,t}$ add up to unity, some of them can be negative. They then show that if $h(z, \eta)$ is monotone in z, the weights will be nonnegative. Formally, if $h(z, \eta)$ is nondecreasing in z, then $\lambda_{x,t} \geq 0$.

In this approach one is not limited to a particular pair of instrument values (z_0, z_1). For each pair one can estimate the corresponding β_{z_0,z_1}^{IV}, each with its own set of weights. One can then combine these β_{z_0,z_1}^{IV} using any set of weights to get

$$\beta_{\omega}^{IV} = \sum_{z<z'} \omega(z, z')\beta^{IV}(z, z').$$

The weights $\omega(z, z')$ can be chosen to make β_ω^{IV} as close as possible to the policy parameters of interest. The variation in the weighted local average treatment effects by different choices for the weights also give some indication regarding the variation in the effect of the regressor by individual and level of the regressor. Although such effects may not be representative for large policy changes, they may be relevant for predicting the effects of small policy changes where individuals remain close to their currently optimal level of the regressor.

7 CONCLUSION

In this discussion I have described some of the identification issues arising in two-equation triangular simultaneous equation systems with endogenous variables. I have discussed the differences between the binary regressor case and the case with a continuous endogenous regressor. Both cases have been analyzed extensively and the requirements for identification are well understood at this point. Somewhat surprisingly the case with a discrete endogenous regressor is much more difficult than either the discrete or binary case. Although one can identify weighted average effects, it is difficult to identify the average effect of specific changes in the regressor for either the entire population or even for specific subpopulations unless one has instruments that take on a wider range of values than what is typically seen in practice. The identification results highlight the role of monotonicity in various forms, either strict as in the case with a continuous regressor, or weak monotonicity conditions of the type that underlie the local average treatment effect for the binary regressor case.

References

ABADIE, A., J. ANGRIST, AND G. IMBENS (2002): "Instrumental Variable Estimates of the Effect of Subsidized Training on the Quantiles of Trainee Earnings," *Econometrica*, 70(1), 91–117.

ALTONJI, J. AND R. MATZKIN (2005): "Cross Section and Panel Data Estimators for Nonseparable Models with Endogenous Regressors," *Econometrica*, 73(4), 1053–1102.

ANGRIST, J. AND G. IMBENS (1995): "Two-Stage Least Squares Estimation of Average Causal Effects in Models with Variable Treatment Intensity," *Journal of the American Statistical Association*, 90(430), 431–442.

ANGRIST, J. D., G. W. IMBENS, AND D. B. RUBIN (1996): "Identification of Causal Effects Using Instrumental Variables," *Journal of the American Statistical Association*, 91, 444–472.

ANGRIST, J., K. GRADDY, AND G. IMBENS (2000): "The Interpretation of Instrumental Variables Estimators in Simultaneous Equations Models with an Application to the Demand for Fish," *The Review of Economic Studies*, 67(July), 499–527.

ANGRIST, J. D. AND A. B. KRUEGER (1999): "Empirical Strategies in Labor Economics," in *Handbook of Labor Economics*, Vol. 3, edited by A. Ashenfelter and D. Card, New York: Elsevier Science.

ATHEY, S. (2002): "Monotone Comparative Statics Under Uncertainty" *Quarterly Journal of Economics*, 117, 187–223.

ATHEY, S. AND G. IMBENS (2006): "Identification and Inference in Nonlinear Difference-in-Difference Models," *Econometrica*, 74(2), 431–497.

ATHEY, S. AND S. STERN (1998): "An Empirical Framework for Testing Theories About Complementarity in Organizational Design," NBER Working Paper 6600.

BALKE, A. AND J. PEARL (1994): "Nonparametric Bounds of Causal Effects from Partial Compliance Data," Technical Report R–199–J, Computer Science Department, University of California, Los Angeles.

BENKARD, C. L. AND S. BERRY (2005): "On the Nonparametric Identification of Nonlinear Simultaneous Equations Models: Comment on B. Brown (1983) and Roehrig (1988)," *Econometrica*, 74(5), 1429–1440.

BLUNDELL, R. AND J. POWELL (2003): "Endogeneity in Nonparametric and Semiparametric Regression Models," Invited Lecture at the 2000 World Congress of the Econometric Society, *Advances in Economics and Econometrics, Theory and Applications*, Vol. 2, edited by Dewatripont, Hansen, and Turnovsky, Cambridge: Cambridge University Press.

——— (2004): "Endogeneity in Semiparametric Binary Response Models," *University of California, Berkeley Review of Economic Studies*, 71(3), 655–679.

CARD, D. (2001): "Estimating the Return to Schooling: Progress on Some Persistent Econometric Problems," *Econometrica*, 69(5), 1127–1160.

CHAMBERLAIN, G. (1983): "Panel Data Models," in *Handbook of Econometrics*, Vol. 2, edited by Z. Griliches and M. Intriligator, Amsterdam: North Holland, pp. 1247–1318.

CHERNOZHUKOV, V. AND C. HANSEN (2005): "An IV Model of Quantile Treatment Effects," *Econometrica*, 73(1), 245–261.

CHERNOZHUKOV, V., G. IMBENS, AND W. NEWEY (2005): "Instrumental Variable Identification and Estimation of Nonseparable Models via Quantile Conditions," Unpublished manuscript.

CHESHER, A. (2003): "Identification in Nonseparable Models," *Econometrica*, 71(5), 1405–1441.

——— (2005): "Nonparametric Identification Under Discrete Variation," *Econometrica*, 73(5), 1525–1550.

DAROLLES, S., J.-P., FLORENS, AND E. RENAULT (2001): "Nonparametric Instrumental Regression," Invited Lecture at the 2000 World Congress of the Econometric Society, *Advances in Economics and Econometrics, Theory and Applications* Vol. 2, Dewatripont, Hansen, and Turnovsky, Cambridge: Cambridge University Press.

DAS, M. (2001): "Monotone Comparative Statics and the Estimation of Behavioral Parameters," Working Paper, Department of Economics, Columbia University.

——— (2005): "Instrumental Variable Estimators of Nonparametric Models with Discrete Endogenous Regressors," *Journal of Econometrics*, 124, 335–361.

GOLDMAN, S. AND H. UZAWA (1964): "A Note on Separability in Demand Analysis," *Econometrica*, 32(3), 387–398.

HAAVELMO, T. (1943): "The Statistical Implications of a System of Simultaneous Equations," *Econometrica*, 11(1), 1–12.

HALL, P. AND J. HOROWITZ, J. (2003): "Nonparametric Methods for Inference in the Presence of Instrumental Variables," Unpublished manuscript.

HAUSMAN, J. (1983): "Specification and Estimation of Simultaneous Equations Models," in *Handbook of Econometrics*, Vol. 1, edited by Z. Griliches and M. Intriligator, Amsterdam: North Holland, pp. 391–448.

HECKMAN, J. (1978): "Sample Selection Bias as a Specification Error," *Econometrica*, 47(1), 153–162.

HECKMAN, J. AND R. ROBB (1984): "Alternative Methods for Evaluating the Impact of Interventions," in *Longitudinal Analysis of Labor Market Data*, edited by J. Heckman and B. Singer, Cambridge: Cambridge University Press.

HECKMAN, J. AND E. VYTLACIL (2001): "Local Instrumental Variables," in *Nonlinear Statistical Modeling*, edited by C. Hisao, K. Morimune, and J. Powell, Cambridge: Cambridge University Press.

HENDRY, D. AND M. MORGAN (1997): *The Foundation of Econometric Analysis*, Cambridge: Cambridge University Press.

IMBENS, G. AND J. ANGRIST (1994): "Identification and Estimation of Local Average Treatment Effects," *Econometrica*, 62(2), 467–476.

IMBENS, G. AND W. NEWEY (2002): "Identification and Estimation of Triangular Simultaneous Equations Models Without Additivity," NBER Technical Working Paper 285.

IMBENS, G. AND D. RUBIN (1997): "Estimating Outcome Distributions for Compliers in Instrumental Variable Models," *Review of Economic Studies*, 64(3), 555–574.

MANSKI, C. (1990): "Nonparametric Bounds on Treatment Effects," *American Economic Review Papers and Proceedings*, 80, 319–323.

———— (2003): *Partial Identification of Probability Distributions*, New York: Springer-Verlag.

MANSKI, C. AND J. PEPPER (2000): "Monotone Instrumental Variables: With an Application to the Returns to Schooling," *Econometrica*, 68(4), 997–1010.

MANSKI, C. AND E. TAMER (2002): "Inference on Regressions with Interval Data on a Regressor or Outcome," *Econometrica*, 70(2), 519–546.

MATZKIN, R. (2003): "Nonparametric Estimation of Nonadditive Random Functions," *Econometrica*, 71(5), 1339–1375.

MATZKIN, R. (2005): "Identification in Nonparametric Simultaneous Equations," Unpublished manuscript, Department of Economics.

MILGROM, P. AND C. SHANNON (1994): "Monotone Comparative Statics," *Econometrica*, 62(1), 1255–1312.

MUNDLAK, Y. (1963): "Estimation of Production Functions from a Combination of Cross-Section and Time-Series Data," in *Measurement in Economics, Studies in Mathematical Economics and Econometrics in Memory of Yehuda Grunfeld*, edited by C. Christ, Stanford: Stanford University Press, pp. 138–166.

NEWEY, W. AND J. POWELL (2003): "Instrumental Variable Estimation of Nonparametric Models," *Econometrica*, 71(5), 1565–1578.

NEWEY, W., J. POWELL, AND F. VELLA (1999): "Nonparametric Estimation of Triangular Simultaneous Equations Models," *Econometrica*, 67(3), 565–603.

PEARL, J. (2000): *Causality: Models, Reasoning and Inference*, Cambridge: Cambridge University Press.

PINKSE, J. (2001): "Nonparametric Regression Estimation Using Weak Separability," Unpublished manuscript, Department of Economics, Pennsylvania State University.

POWELL, J., J. STOCK, AND T. STOKER (1989): "Semiparametric Estimation of Index Coefficients," *Econometrica*, 57(6), 1403–1430.

ROEHRIG, C. (1988): "Conditions for Identification in Nonparametric and Parametric Models," *Econometrica*, 56(2), 433–447.

ROSENBAUM, P. AND D. RUBIN (1983): "The Central Role of the Propensity Score in Observational Studies for Causal Effects," *Biometrika*, 70, 41–55.

RUBIN, D. (1974): "Estimating Causal Effects of Treatments in Randomized and Non-Randomized Studies," *Journal of Educational Psychology*, 66(5), 688–701.

VYTLACIL, E. (2002): "Independence, Monotonicity, and Latent Index Models: An Equivalence Result," *Econometrica*, 70(1), 331–341.

——— (2006): "Ordered Discrete Choice Selection Models and Local Average Treatment Effects: Equivalence, Nonequivalence, and Representation Results," *Review of Economics and Statistics*, LXXXVIII(3), 578–581.

CHAPTER 3

Heterogeneity and Microeconometrics Modeling*
Martin Browning[†] and Jesus Carro[‡]

1 INTRODUCTION

There is general agreement that there is a good deal of heterogeneity in observed
behavior. Heckman in his Nobel lecture (Heckman, 2001) states: "the most
important discovery [from the widespread use of micro-data is] the evidence on
the pervasiveness of heterogeneity and diversity in economic life." This is true
but to see it in print as a "discovery" is a surprise since we have internalized it
so thoroughly and it is now second nature for anyone working with microdata
to consider heterogeneity.

We have been unable to find a consensus definition of heterogeneity. A
definition we suggest (which derives from Cunha, Heckman, and Navarro, 2005)
is that *heterogeneity* is the dispersion in factors that are relevant *and known*
to individual agents when making a particular decision. *Latent heterogeneity*
would then be those relevant factors that are known to the agent but not to the
researcher. The heterogeneity could be differences in tastes, beliefs, abilities,
skills, or constraints. Note that this definition does not impose that heterogeneity
is constant over time for a given individual nor that because something is fixed
and varies across the population that it is necessarily heterogeneous. Examples
of the former would be changing information sets and an example of the latter
would be, say, some genetic factor which impacts on outcomes but which is
unobserved by any agent. Thus a "fixed effect" in an econometric model may
or may not be consistent with heterogeneity, as defined here.

Our definition of heterogeneity distinguishes it clearly from uncertainty,
measurement error, and model misspecification that are other candidates for

* We thank Arthur Lewbel, Richard Blundell, Pedro Mira, Pedro Albarran, Manuel Arellano, and
our colleagues at CAM for comments. We also express our gratitude to the AGE RTN (contract
HPRN-CT-2002-00235) and the Danish National Research Foundation, though its grant to CAM,
for financial support.
† Center for Applied Microeconometrics (CAM), Department of Economics, University of
Copenhagen.
‡ Department of Economics, Carlos III, Madrid.

the variation we see around the predictions of a given deterministic model.[1] The conceptual distinction between heterogeneity and measurement error and model misspecification is obvious (although it may be difficult to distinguish in empirical work), so we concentrate on uncertainty. To illustrate the issue we present an example about milk consumption. Most of the world's adult population cannot drink more than one cup of milk in day without feeling quite ill (see Patterson, 2001 for details and references). This is because they lack the enzyme lactase that breaks down the sugar in milk (lactose) into usable sugars. The inability to digest milk is known as lactose intolerance but we should more properly speak of lactase persistence for those who can drink milk since this is a relatively late adaptation in our evolutionary history. The ability to drink milk as an adult seems to have arisen at least twice independently, both times among pastoralists. This happened very recently, perhaps as late as 6000 years ago. This has lead to considerable variation across the world in lactase persistence; for example, the rate is 97% in Denmark, 47% in Greece, 29% in Sicily, 8% among Han Chinese, and 5% for the San in South Africa. In early childhood no one knows their type (lactose intolerant or lactase persistent). If every child within a population has the same beliefs, then there is no heterogeneity and only uncertainty. In adulthood, everyone knows their type. Then the variation observed in the population, at age 20 for instance, is due to heterogeneity, but there is no uncertainty. If people were ignorant of their type in childhood but had different beliefs, then there would be uncertainty and heterogeneity (in beliefs, not in their ability to digest milk). Distinguishing between heterogeneity and uncertainty is an important but difficult task; see Cunha, Heckman, and Navarro (2005) for an analysis of this in the context of schooling choice.

Before going on it is necessary to mention a contrary view on heterogeneity in tastes which derives from Stigler and Becker (1977). They took the position that "tastes neither change capriciously nor differ importantly between people." Tastes for Becker and Stigler take as their domain commodities that are produced from market goods and time use or even deeper structures. Consider, for example, food. Market goods constitute the highest level of observability. Obviously, tastes over different foods differ; for example, tastes for milk as discussed in the previous paragraph. At the next level, tastes are defined over the characteristics inherent in food market goods; for example, different kinds of fats, calcium, vitamins etc. It is by no means obvious that tastes over characteristics differ significantly over time or place. The interest in this intermediate level is that we may be able to recover the food/nutrient conversion mapping from independent sources. This then makes the consumption of characteristics observable. This would allow us to test for various levels of heterogeneity. For example, does everyone in a given population have the same tastes? A weaker

---

[1] This definition has one major drawback which is that the vernacular term "heterogeneity" does not coincide with the analytical definition suggested here. In some ways it would be best to have a wholly new term for heterogeneity as defined here, but that seems impossible at this late date.

and more interesting hypothesis is that there is heterogeneity but the dispersion of tastes is the same across populations, conditional on demographic factors such as the age distribution. But even moving to characteristics may not be a deep enough level to allow us to support the hypothesis that everyone has the same tastes. People with different metabolic rates will have different tastes over second level characteristics such as nutrients. Thus saturated fat is not valued because it is saturated fat but because it provides an energy source that allows us to function in a satisfactory way. Similarly, vitamin B12 (which is not found in any vegetables) is a vital ingredient for brain functioning but vegans might be happy to have some alternative that allowed their brain to continue working once they have depleted the five-year store that the body usually keeps as a buffer stock. In this view, we may have to go to the deeper level of capabilities for the domain of common preferences.

Explicit in the Becker–Stigler view is the contention that an appeal to undefined heterogeneity in tastes is too ready an admission of ignorance. Certainly, the immediate use of "fixed effects" or other heterogeneity schemes to allow for observable differences in outcomes is an admission of failure in economics (even if it sometimes considered a triumph in econometrics). The Becker–Stigler approach leads naturally to a research program that attempts to rationalize all observable differences in behavior with no differences in tastes and only taking account of prices and incomes (or potentially observable constraints) and heterogeneity in the mapping from market goods to the domain of preferences which can potentially be identified from observable background factors. However, to assert homogeneity of tastes at the level of capabilities (as suggested in the last paragraph) is much less attractive for modeling since it seems to substitute one ignorance (of the mapping from market goods to capabilities) for another (the undifferentiated distribution of tastes over market goods).

This paper attempts to make three main points. First, we claim that there is a lot more heterogeneity about than we usually allow for in our microeconometric modeling. This first theme is covered in Section 2. The illustrations we present are from our own work but we believe that the point is a very general one. Second, in most contexts it makes a big difference for outcomes of interest whether and how we allow for heterogeneity. We shall illustrate this as we go along. Our third main point is that it is difficult to allow for heterogeneity in a general way. This is particularly the case if we want to fit the data and be consistent with economic theory. This is discussed in Section 3, which provides some examples. Our main contention there is that most schemes currently employed in applied microeconometrics are chosen more for their statistical convenience than for their fit to the data or their congruence with economic theory. We believe that heterogeneity is too important to be left to the statisticians and that we may have to sacrifice some generality for a better fit and more readily interpretable empirical estimates. In stating this we certainly do not want to suggest that all microeconometric analyses suffer from this problem. The struggle to find heterogeneity structures that also provide interpretable estimates is an old one and one that continues to inform much structural estimation to this day. A classic example is Mundlak (1961) who allows for heterogeneity in managerial ability for farmers and more recent examples are McFadden and Train (2000) for discrete choice models, Heckman, Matzkin, and Nesheim (2003) for hedonic models and Laroque (2005) for models of labor supply allowing for heterogeneity in the taste for work that is correlated with productivity.

In Section 4, we present some results from our own work on dynamic binary choice models that allow for maximal heterogeneity. Since not much is known about the properties of estimators in this context, even when we only allow for conventional "fixed effects," we choose to study in depth the simplest model, a stationary first-order Markov chain model. Working with such a simple model we can recover analytical results concerning bias, mean squared error (mse), the power of tests etc. As we shall show, this allows us to develop novel estimators that are designed with our choice criteria (bias or mse) in mind.

2   THERE IS A LOT OF HETEROGENEITY ABOUT

2.1   Earnings Processes

In many contexts the evidence points toward more heterogeneity than is usually allowed for. We hazard a conjecture that in a majority of published empirical papers there is "significantly" more heterogeneity than is allowed for in the modeling. We shall illustrate this with two examples from our own work. The first example is for a linear dynamic model for earnings processes. A close to consensus model is that once we control for common time effects, log earnings are a unit root with homogeneous short-run variances, an MA error term and no drift:

$$\Delta y_{it} = \varepsilon_{it} + \theta \varepsilon_{i,t-1} \text{ with } \varepsilon_{it} \sim iid\left(0, \sigma^2\right) \tag{1}$$

for agent i. This model has two parameters (or more if we allow an $MA(2)$ process or an error distribution with more than one parameter). This model seems to be popular because it is the reduced form for a model which has a "permanent income" component and also because it is believed that it fits the data well. Although very popular, other processes have also been considered. For example, trend stationary models which allow for a negative correlation between starting values and the trend. This captures Mincer style on the job training in which some workers trade-off initial earnings for higher earnings later on; see Rubinstein and Weiss (2005). The important point about all of these analyses is that they typically assume very little heterogeneity once we condition on the starting value. Figure 3.1 shows 10 paths for white, high school educated males from age 25 to 35, drawn from the PSID.[2] The subsample displayed is

---

[2] In line with convention in the earnings literature, these are actually the residuals from a first-round regression (on a larger sample) of log earnings on time and age dummies. The larger sample is identical to that taken in Meghir and Pistaferri (2004); it is an unbalanced panel that covers the years 1968–1993 and includes workers aged between 25 and 55.

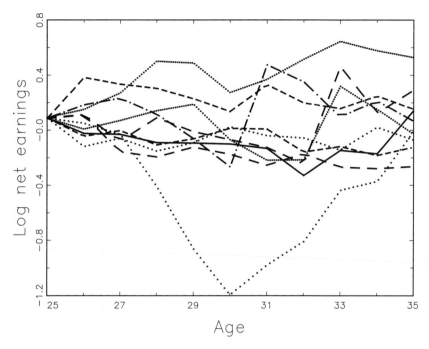

Figure 3.1. Ten earnings paths for US white male high school graduates.

chosen so that all have close to the mean earnings at age 25. This figure suggests that the consensus model may not be adequate to fit the data, even when we have the same initial observation. There seems to be clear evidence of differences in volatility and also some visual evidence of differences in trends. On the other hand, even practiced eyes may not be able to tell drift from the working out of a unit root with only 10 observations, so more formal evidence is required.

Alvarez, Browning and Ejrnaes (2002) (ABE) consider a model with lots more heterogeneity than is allowed for in previous empirical analyses. They start with a parametric model that has six parameters per worker and in which all of the parameters are heterogeneous. To overcome the curse of dimensionality for this model they use a simulated minimum distance (or indirect inference) estimation approach that requires that the final model fits *all* of the outcomes of interest that previous researchers have suggested are important (and some other data features that have not been considered before). They find that the following stable (but not stationary[3]) four parameter model gives a good fit to the data:

$$y_{it} = \delta_i \left(1 - \beta_i\right) + \beta_i y_{h,t-1} + \varepsilon_{it} + \theta_i \varepsilon_{i,t-1} \text{ with } \varepsilon_{it} \sim iiN\left(0, \sigma_i^2\right)$$
$$(2)$$

---

[3] We follow the terminology of Arellano (2003a) and say that a first-order dynamic process is *trend stable* if the AR parameter is less than unity and the initial values are unrestricted. If the initial values are restricted to be consistent with the long-run distribution then the process is stationary.

Interestingly, unit root models are decisively rejected (but models with a mixture of a unit root and a stable process do quite well). The consensus model fits very poorly, contradicting the widespread belief that it fits well. The important point in the current context is that all four parameters $(\delta, \beta, \theta, \sigma)$ are heterogeneous. ABE find that the joint distribution of these four parameters is described well by a three-factor model. One of these factors is the starting value and the other two are latent factors.[4] The preferred version of the general model has heterogeneity in all of the four parameters above (plus a parameter for an ARCH scheme).

A finding that conventional empirical models do not make adequate allowance for heterogeneity in parameters does not necessarily mean that they are significantly wrong for all outcomes of interest. To illustrate, we consider two outcomes of interest for earnings processes. The first is actually a parameter: the short-run standard deviation, σ_i. This is a crucial input in models of consumption which allow for precautionary saving. Typically, the level of precautionary saving is an increasing and strictly convex function of the standard deviation of income risk.[5] It will be clear that allowing for heterogeneity in this parameter will impact on estimates of precautionary saving. Agents who are identical in every respect except for the income risk they face will hold different levels of "buffer stocks" and the mean of the homogeneous model may be very different to that from a model with heterogeneous variances. For the consensus model (1) (with allowance for ARCH and measurement error) the estimate of the standard deviation for the zero mean Normally distributed error is 0.142; this gives that the probability of a large drop in earnings (20% or more) between any two periods is about 8%. Table 3.1 presents the distribution of the standard deviation for (1) with allowance for a heterogeneous variance and for (2). For the consensus model with heterogeneous variances (row 1) there is a great deal of heterogeneity in variances (as we would expect from Figure 3.1). Many workers face low risk and would have virtually no precautionary motive. On the other hand, about 10% of workers have a standard deviation of over 0.25, which implies a probability of a large drop of about 21%; for this group the precautionary motive would be very strong. When we move to the fully heterogeneous model (the second row of Table 3.1) the standard deviation distribution is lower (because the error terms in the consensus model with variance heterogeneity have to "mop up" the heterogeneity in the other parameters) but there is still considerable dispersion in risk. The lesson we draw from this is that if the primary interest is in the variance, then a simple model with allowance for heterogeneity in the variances would probably suffice but the homogeneous variances model is way off.

---

[4] This modeling methodology is an extension of the scheme suggested in Chamberlain (1980) in which the distribution of the individual parameters is allowed to be conditional on the starting values. See Wooldridge (2005) for post-Chamberlain references and a strong defence of this mode of modeling.

[5] The leap from the error variance in (2) to risk is a large one – there is measurement error and the changes may be anticipated or even have been chosen – but it is often made in consumption modeling.

Table 3.1. *The distribution of the standard deviation of income residuals*

Percentile	10%	25%	50%	75%	90%
Equation (1) with heterogeneous variances	0.07	0.09	0.13	0.19	0.25
Equation (2)	0.05	0.07	0.10	0.15	0.21

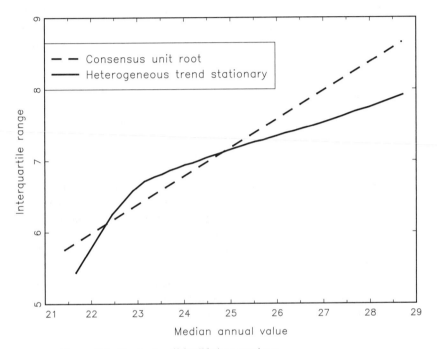

Figure 3.2. The trade-off for lifetime earnings.

Our second outcome of interest is the distribution of lifetime earnings. Cunha, Heckman, and Navarro (2005) have a discussion of the formidable problems in using empirical distributions such as these in modeling schooling decisions. In particular, they treat carefully the distinction between heterogeneity (what subjective distributions do young people have over the parameters) and uncertainty (the residual uncertainty given a model with a set of parameters) that motivated the definition of heterogeneity given in the introduction. Unlike the distribution of the error variances, the moments or quantiles of the lifetime earnings distribution are highly nonlinear function of the model parameters and it is impossible, a priori, to judge whether allowing for heterogeneity will make much difference. To generate the distribution of lifetime earnings we simulate 25,000 paths from age 25 to 55 using the model (2), add back in the age effects taken out in the first-round regressions and discount earnings back to age 25 with a discount rate of 3%. In Figure 3.2, we present estimates of the trade-off between median and interquartile range based on the consensus model with heterogeneous variances (as in the first row of Table 3.1), and the preferred model (2). As can be seen, the trade-off is very close to linear and increasing for the consensus model with heterogeneous variances but nonlinear for the preferred model. In particular, the trade-off between median and interquartile range is much steeper for those who expect a relatively low median lifetime income. Whether or not these significantly different outcomes would translate into different estimates of, say, schooling choices would depend on the exact details of how we use these estimates, but there is at least the potential for serious error if we use the consensus model rather than the preferred model which allows for significantly more heterogeneity.

2.2   Dynamic Discrete Choice

Our second example of the ubiquity of heterogeneity is for a dynamic discrete choice model for the purchase of whole (full fat) milk; see Browning and Carro (2005). The data are drawn from a Danish consumer panel which is unusual in that the panel follows a large and representative group of households over a long period. Specifically, we consider weekly purchases of different varieties of milk and we observe each household for at least 100 weeks (and some for 250 weeks). After some selection to meet various criteria (such as buying whole milk in at least 10% and at most 90% of the weeks we observe) we have a sample of 371 households. The availability of such a long panel enables us to explore with real data the effectiveness of different heterogeneity schemes suggested for small-T panels. In Section 4, we shall return to a detailed study of estimators in this context but for now we simply want to show that there is more heterogeneity in this choice than we would usually allow for. To do this, we use a dynamic Probit for each household:

$$\Pr\left(y_{it} = 1 \mid y_{i,t-1}, x_{it}\right) = \Phi\left(\eta_i + \alpha_i y_{i,t-1} + x'_{it}\beta\right) \tag{3}$$

where y_{it} is a dummy for household i buying whole milk in week t and x_{it} is a vector of covariates such as seasonal dummies, a trend and family composition variables. In this analysis we impose that the parameters for the latter are homogeneous but we could let them be idiosyncratic for each household in which case we would treat the data as a collection of 371 time series. We do, however, allow that the AR parameter may vary across households. The usual approach is to impose homogeneity on this parameter:

$$\Pr\left(y_{it} = 1 \mid y_{i,t-1}, x_{it}\right) = \Phi\left(\eta_i + \alpha y_{i,t-1} + x'_{it}\beta\right) \tag{4}$$

Our interest here is in whether the latter is a reasonable assumption.

Before presenting results it is worth considering the role of the homogeneous AR parameter assumption in dynamic models generally. If we had a linear model:

$$y_{it} = \eta_i + \alpha_i y_{i,t-1} + \varepsilon_{it} \tag{5}$$

then the most common restriction to impose is that the marginal dynamic effect, in this case α_i, is the same for everyone. This is usually assumed more for econometric convenience than for its plausibility but it has the virtue of imposing a restriction on an object of interest. When moving to a nonlinear model the letter of this restriction is usually retained but the spirit is lost. Consider, for example, the dynamic discrete choice model:

$$pr\left(y_{it} = 1 \mid y_{it-1}\right) = F\left(\eta_i + \alpha_i y_{it-1}\right) \tag{6}$$

where $F\left(.\right)$ is some parametric cdf. The marginal dynamic effect is given by:

$$M_i = F\left(\eta_i + \alpha_i\right) - F\left(\eta_i\right)$$

Imposing that the AR parameter α_i is homogeneous does not imply a homogeneous marginal dynamic effect. Furthermore, this restriction is *parametric* and depends on the chosen cdf. Thus assuming that $\alpha_i = \alpha$ for all i for one choice of $F\left(.\right)$ implies that it is heterogeneous for all other choices, unless α is zero. This emphasizes the arbitrariness in the usual homogeneity assumption since there is no reason why the homogeneity of the state dependence parameter α should be linked to the distribution of $F\left(.\right)$. In contrast, the homogeneous marginal dynamic effect assumption, $M_i = M$, that is the correct analogue of the linear restriction gives:

$$\alpha_i = F^{-1}\left(M + F\left(\eta_i\right)\right) - \eta_i \tag{7}$$

for some constant M. Thus the homogeneous AR parameter model is conceptually at odds with the same assumption for linear models. Although we believe the (7) assumption to be more interesting, we shall continue the analysis of the restriction in (4) since it is the conventional approach.

Figure 3.3 shows the marginal distributions (top panel) and the joint distribution (bottom panel) for the parameters (η, α) in equation (3). The two panels show two important features. First, both parameters display a lot of variability. Moreover, the heterogeneity in α is "significant"; the formal LR test statistic for a homogeneous AR parameter is 3058 with 370 degrees of freedom. This is very strong evidence that the AR parameter is heterogeneous as well as the "fixed effect," η. The second important feature is that the joint distribution is far from being bivariate Normal. There is evidence of bimodality and fat tails relative to the Normal. This suggests that the first resort to modeling the data, a random effects model with a joint Normal distribution, will not suffice to adequately model the heterogeneity.

Once again, we make a distinction between heterogeneity in parameters and in objects of interest. For a dynamic discrete choice model there are two natural objects of interest: the marginal dynamic effect:

$$M_i = pr\left(y_{it} = 1 \mid y_{i,t-1} = 1\right) - pr\left(y_{it} = 1 \mid y_{i,t-1} = 0\right) \tag{8}$$

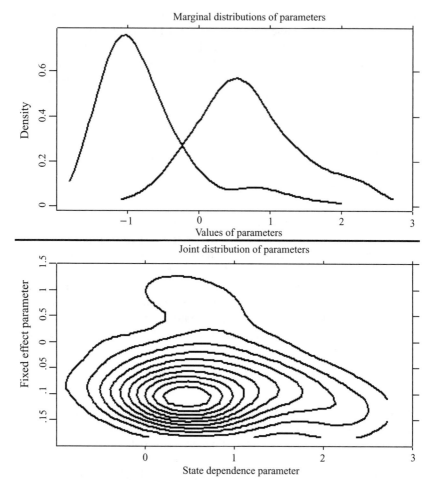

Figure 3.3. Distribution of parameters for dynamic discrete choice model.

and the long-run probability of being unity which for a first-order Markov chain is given by:

$$
\begin{aligned}
L_i &= \frac{pr\left(y_{it} = 1 \mid y_{i,t-1} = 1\right)}{\left(1 + pr\left(y_{it} = 1 \mid y_{i,t-1} = 1\right) - pr\left(y_{it} = 1 \mid y_{i,t-1} = 0\right)\right)} \\
&= \frac{pr\left(y_{it} = 1 \mid y_{i,t-1} = 1\right)}{(1 + M_i)}
\end{aligned}
\tag{9}
$$

Figure 3.4 show the marginal densities for M and L, with and without heterogeneity in the slope parameter. As can be seen, allowing for "full" heterogeneity makes a great deal of difference. Thus the heterogeneity in the AR parameter is not only statistically significant but it is also substantively significant.

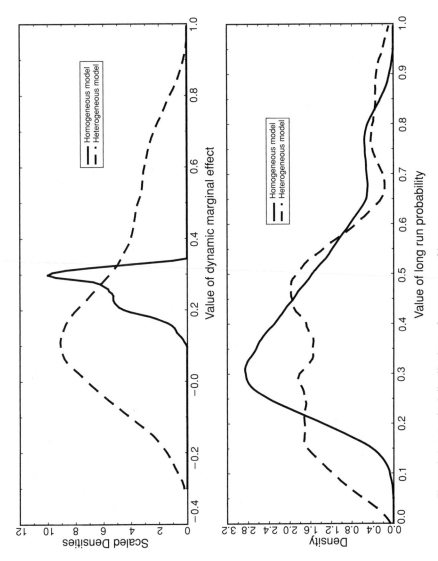

Figure 3.4. Marginal distributions of parameters of interest.

3 HETEROGENEITY IS DIFFICULT TO MODEL

3.1   The Need to Allow for Heterogeneity

The concern to allow for heterogeneity arises from one of two considerations. First, the heterogeneity may not be of interest in itself (it is a "nuisance") but ignoring it would lead to faulty inference for objects of interest. The latter could be qualitative outcomes such as the presence of state dependence in some process (see Heckman, 1981) or the presence of duration dependence in duration models (Lancaster, 1979). Even if ignoring heterogeneity did not lead to errors regarding qualitative outcomes, it might lead to inconsistency in the estimation of parameters of interest. This has been one of the traditional concerns in modeling heterogeneity. The prime example of a scheme to deal with heterogeneity in linear models with strictly exogenous covariates is to assume that only the intercept is heterogeneous so that we can first difference the heterogeneity away. This highlights the tension between the desirability for generality (we do not have to assume anything about the distribution of the fixed effect once we assume that only the slope parameter is homogeneous) and the need to fit the data (the slope parameters might also be heterogeneous).

Even in the linear case, heterogeneous panel models are difficult to deal with. In a large T framework a few solutions have been proposed, most of them in the macroeconomics literature; for example, for endogenous growth models using cross-country panels with long time periods. There, allowing for country-specific coefficients due to heterogeneity can be important, but it is out of the scope of this paper that focus on microeconometrics. Pesaran and Smith (1995) consider this problem and discuss how to estimate one of the possible parameters of interest from dynamic heterogeneous panel in that context. Once we move away from linear models or focus on outcomes other than actual parameter values, then heterogeneity becomes of importance in its own right. As a well-known example, suppose we are interested in the marginal effects of an exogenous variable in a nonlinear model; this will usually depend on the heterogeneity directly. Thus, if we have $y_{it} = G\left(\eta_i + \beta x_{it}\right)$ then the marginal effect for a change in x of Δ for any individual is given by:

$$G\left(\eta_i + \beta\left(x + \Delta\right)\right) - G\left(\eta_i + \beta x\right) \tag{10}$$

which obviously depends on the value of η_i.

It is usually impossible to model allowing for unrestricted heterogeneity "everywhere" and we have to make a priori decisions about how to include allowance for heterogeneity in our empirical models. A major disappointment in panel data modeling is that simple first differencing schemes that work for linear models do not work in nonlinear models. The classic example is limited dependent variable models, but the point is more pervasive. The result has been that we have developed a series of "tricks" which often have limited applicability. Almost always decisions on how to include allowance for heterogeneity are made using conventional schemes that have been designed by statisticians to put in the heterogeneity in such a way that we can immediately take it out again. As just stated, the leading example of this is the use of a "fixed effect" in linear panel data models. More generally, various likelihood factoring schemes have been suggested for nonlinear models; see, for example, Lindsey (2001), chapter 6. The most widely used of these is for the panel data discrete choice model, due to Andersen (1970). Our main contention is that decisions about how to incorporate heterogeneity are too important to be left to the statisticians for two major reasons. First, these schemes may not fit the data. Indeed, it is an extraordinary fact that the great majority of empirical analyses choose the heterogeneity scheme without first looking at the data. Second, conventional schemes, which are often presented as "reduced forms," implicitly impose assumptions about the structural model. Usually, it is impossible to make these assumptions explicit, so that estimated effects are effectively uninterpretable. One feature of this that will emerge in the examples below is issues of fitting the data and theory congruence arise whether or not the source of the heterogeneity is observed by the researcher.

The ideal would be to develop economic models in which the heterogeneity emerges naturally from the theory model. An alternative is look to other disciplines for structural suggestions; psychology ("personality types"); social psychology (for the effects of family background), or genetics. For example, psychologists suggest that personalities can be usefully characterized by a small number of factors. As an example, for economists looking at intertemporal allocation the relevant parameters are risk aversion, discount factor, and prudence. We might want particular dependence between all three. For example, more risk averse people may be likely to also be more prudent.[6] Information on the nature of this dependence might be found in psychological studies. To date, such attempts have not been very encouraging. Heterogeneity that arises from genetic variations is of particular interest since this is probably as deep as we wish to go (as economists) in "explaining" observed differences in behavior. We already have mentioned in the introduction one important commodity, milk, for which genetic variation explains why most of the world's adult population do not consume it. This is an important factor if we are modeling the demand for different foods, even if we use a characteristics framework with preferences defined on calcium, different fats, different vitamins etc. The mapping from market goods to characteristics depends on the lactase gene. It is now known exactly where the gene for lactase persistence resides (it is on chromosome 2) and with a DNA sample we could determine exactly whether any given individual was lactase persistent. This may be considered fanciful, but increasingly DNA samples will be collected in social surveys; see National Research Council (2001) for details on the feasibility, practicalities, possibilities, and ethics of this.

---

[6] In conventional schemes that use a simple felicity function (such as quadratic or iso-elastic utility functions) risk aversion and prudence are often deterministically dependent, but they need not be. Marshall, for example, seemed to believe that "laborers" were risk averse but imprudent whereas people like himself were both risk averse and prudent.

3.2　Examples from Economics

3.2.1　Empirical Demand Analysis

Demand theory presents many good examples of the interactions between the specification of heterogeneity, fitting the data and coherence with the theory. Here the theory is in its purest form either as the Slutsky conditions or revealed preference conditions. There is general agreement that extended versions of AI demand system are needed to fit data reasonably well (at least for the Engel curves) but for illustrative purposes, it is enough to consider the basic form. The AI functional form for the budget share for good i, w_i, given prices $(p_1, p_2, ..., p_n)$ and total outlay x is given by:

$$w_i = \alpha_i + \sum_{j=1}^{n} \gamma_{ij} \ln p_j + \beta_i \ln \left(\frac{x}{a(\mathbf{p})} \right)$$

where $a(\mathbf{p})$ is a linear homogeneous price index that depends on all the α and γ parameters. If we wish to estimate with data from many households, we have to allow for heterogeneity. The simplest approach is to assume that all of the parameters are heterogeneous with a joint distribution that is independent of the prices and total expenditure (a "random effects" approach). If we do this then we run into problems when we impose the Slutsky conditions. The homogeneity and Slutsky symmetry are OK:

$$\sum_{j=1}^{n} \gamma_{ij} = 0, \forall i$$
$$\gamma_{ij} = \gamma_{ji}, \forall i, j$$

since the restrictions are independent of the data. However, the Slutsky negativity condition does depend on the data. For example, the condition that the own price compensated effect should be nonpositive is given by:

$$\gamma_{ii} + (\beta_i)^2 \ln \left(\frac{x}{a(\mathbf{p})} \right) + w_i(w_i - 1) \leq 0$$

which clearly depends on the data. Thus the parameters and data are not variation independent[7] which is a necessary condition for stochastic independence. At present it is an open question as to the class of preferences that admit of a random effects formulation. The Cobb–Douglas restriction on the AI system ($\beta_i = \gamma_{ij} = 0$ for all i, j) shows that the class is not empty. On the other hand, although the Cobb–Douglas does well in terms of consistency with theory it does spectacularly poorly in fitting the data.

---

[7] If we have two sets of random variables $\theta \in \Theta$ and $\gamma \in \Gamma$ they are *variation independent* if their joint space is the cross product of the two spaces: $\Theta \times \Gamma$. Thus the support for one set of the random variables does not depend on the realizations of the other.

3.2.2 Duration Models

Our second example of the difficulty of finding heterogeneity that fit the data and are consistent with theory models is from duration modeling; our discussion here relies heavily on van den Berg (2005). The mixed proportional hazard (MPH) model is very widely used in duration modeling; this is given by:

$$\theta(t \mid x, \upsilon) = \psi(t)\theta_0(x)\upsilon \tag{11}$$

where $\theta(.)$ is the hazard given observables x and unobservable υ, $\psi(.)$ is a baseline hazard that is assumed common to all agents, $\theta_0(x)$ is the "systematic" component and υ captures unobserved heterogeneity. This scheme, which was initially devised by statisticians and has been refined by econometricians, has the twin virtues of being easy to estimate and of treating latent and observed heterogeneity in the same way (as multiplicative factors). There are, however, problems with both fit and theory. First, as a matter of fact, stratifying often indicates a significantly different baseline hazard for different strata. Although this can be overcome in the obvious way if we have a lot of data and we observe the variables that define the strata, it is worrying that we just happen to assume the same baseline hazard for stratification that is not observed. The second major problem with the MPH scheme is that it is often presented as reduced form analysis but it is never very clear exactly which structural models are thus ruled out. van den Berg (2005) presents an insightful discussion of this which shows that the class of structural models which have the MPH as a reduced form is relatively uninteresting and many interesting structural models do not have the MPH as a reduced form.

3.2.3 Dynamic Structural Models

Our next example is taken from Carro and Mira (2005). They propose and estimate a dynamic stochastic model of sterilization and contraception use. Couples choose between using reversible contraceptive methods, not contracepting and sterilizing. These contraceptive plans are chosen to maximize the intertemporal utility function subject to the laws of motion of the state and, in particular, to birth control "technology," $\{F_{jt}\}$, for the probability of a birth in period t given contraceptive option j. A homogenous model could not fit the data nor give sensible estimates of the parameters of the model. Two sources of heterogeneity have to be introduced. First, heterogeneity in the value of children and, second, heterogeneity in the probabilities of a birth (the ability to conceive). Heterogeneity only in preferences did not solve the problem, because in the data there were groups of people not contracepting in almost any period and also having children with much lower probability than other couples who were not contracepting. That is, some couples have lower fecundity, not just different preferences over number of children. Without unobserved heterogeneity in the probability of having a birth (ability to conceive) the model explained the data by saying that the utility cost of contracepting was not a cost; that is, it was positive and significant; and the estimated model did not fit the patterns of contraceptive use across number of children and age. Simple forms of permanent unobserved heterogeneity across couples, using mixing distributions with a small number of types, capture these features of the data. Estimating a structural model allows us to introduce separately heterogeneity in both the probability of having a birth and the value of children. It turns out that both are significant and they are stochastically dependent. A reduced form equation could not separate both sources of unobserved heterogeneity, and using only a fixed effect in a reduced form model will probably not be able to capture the complex effects of both kinds of heterogeneity over couples' choices in the life cycle.

Adding unobserved heterogeneity in $\{F_{jt}\}$ complicated the estimation procedure, since we could no longer write separate likelihoods for choices and conditional probabilities of a birth. Furthermore, with unobserved heterogeneity the dynamic structural model implied by the forward looking behavior has to be solved for each unobserved type, significantly increasing the computational costs. This is why in this literature only a small number of unobserved types are considered as forms of permanent unobserved heterogeneity, in contrast to the more general specifications considered in reduced form models.

Another example of this is Keane and Wolpin (1997). They estimate a dynamic structural model of schooling, work, and occupational choice decisions. They allow for four unobserved types. Each type of individuals differs from the other types on the initial endowments of innate talents and human capital accumulated up to the age of 16, which is taken as the start of the process in this model. The endowment is known by the individual but unobserved by the researcher. A fundamental finding in Keane and Wolpin (1997) is "that inequality in skill endowments 'explains' the bulk of the variation in lifetime utility." According to their estimates, "unobserved endowment heterogeneity, as measured at age 16, accounts for 90 percent of the variance in lifetime utility." As they say, " it is specially troublesome, given this finding, that unobserved heterogeneity is usually left as a black box." Nevertheless, they have a clear interpretation for this unobserved heterogeneity coming from the structural model, they can determine some of the correlates of the heterogeneity and compute the conditional probability distribution of the endowment types using Bayes rule. This helps to understand the source of this important unobserved factor on the lifetime well-being, and to obtain some knowledge about how inequality could be altered by policy.

3.2.4   *Returns to Schooling*

The estimation of the returns to schooling is another good example where unobserved heterogeneity has played a major role, in both the theoretical and the empirical literature. During more than three decades a vast number of research papers have tried to address this issue in a convincing and theoretically coherent way. It has proven to be a difficult task. The classical Mincer equation used in many papers to estimate the returns to schooling in practice assumed homogenous returns to schooling. Nevertheless, a model with heterogeneous returns to schooling is an integral part of the human capital literature. A recent example of such a model where heterogeneity is allowed to affect both the intercept of the earnings equation and the slope of the earnings–schooling relation can be found in Card (1999, 2001). These heterogeneous factors are in principle correlated with schooling, since they are taken into account in the schooling decisions of the individuals. A widely used solution to estimate this heterogeneous model is instrumental variables. The conditions under which this method identifies the return to schooling and the interpretation of this estimate are directly related with the treatment effects literature. The identification of the average return to schooling by IV is only possible under certain restrictive conditions. These are unlikely to be satisfied by many of the supply side instruments used since individual schooling decisions are taken depending also on the supply characteristics.[8] In the context of a dichotomous instrument, if those conditions are not satisfied, conventional IV estimates give the Local Average Treatment Effect, see Imbens and Angrist (1994). More generally, Heckman and Vytlacil (2005) show how the Marginal Treatment Effect can be used to construct and compare alternative measures or averages of the returns to schooling, including the Local Average Treatment Effect. As explained by Card (2001), the IV estimate of the returns to schooling on a heterogeneous earnings equation can be interpreted as a weighted average of the marginal returns to education in the population. The weight for each person is a function of the increment in their schooling induced by the instrument. Depending on the problem considered, this average return to schooling for those affected by the instrument could be the policy parameter of interest.

This literature has the virtue of providing a connection between the traditional IV estimator and the economic decision model. In the case we have considered here, the estimation of the classical earnings equation using as instrument a change in the supply conditions (e.g., distance to the closest college) gives an average effect for a subgroup of the population in the context of an economic model of schooling decisions with heterogeneous returns to schooling. Nonetheless, even if that is the parameter of interest, some homogeneity on the schooling choice equation is needed: the so-called "monotonicity assumption" in the treatment effects literature, see Heckman and Vytlacil (2005). In a situation where the monotonicity assumption is not satisfied, or in the case where we want to estimate the average return to schooling for the whole population we need to look for alternatives to identify and estimate the effect of interest. A possibility is estimating a structural model of earnings and schooling; Keane and Wolpin (1997) is a good example.

3.2.5 Dynamic Discrete Choice Modeling

Our final example concerns smoking; although quite specific we believe it illustrates an important general point. Vink, Willemsen, and Boomsma (2003) (VWB) present results based on smoking histories for identical twins,

---

[8] See Card (1999, 2001) for a discussion of this result and of the conditions needed for the IV to identify the average returns to schooling. See also Heckman and Vytlacil (1998).

nonidentical twins, and siblings. They conclude that the starting conditions (in late childhood or early adulthood) are homogeneous (conditional on potentially observable factors) but that persistence, once started, is largely genetic. Although we might have specific objections to the VWB analysis, let us take it as our "theory" model for now. Let y_{it} be indicator for i smoking in month t and assume a first-order Markov model. In line with the VWB hypothesis, suppose there are two types: "tough quitters" (A) and "easy quitters" (B) with:

$$pr_A (y_t = 0 \mid y_{t-1} = 1) < pr_B (y_t = 0 \mid y_{t-1} = 1) \tag{12}$$

(where, for convenience, we have dropped other covariates). The starting condition, according to VWB, is homogeneous, conditional on the variables that the researchers observe on environmental factors in late childhood (e.g., family background) denoted z_{i0}, so that:

$$pr_A (y_{i0} = 1 \mid z_{i0}) = pr_B (y_{i0} = 1 \mid z_{i0}) \tag{13}$$

What of the "resuming" transition probability: $pr (y_t = 1 \mid y_{t-1} = 0)$? We could model this as homogeneous or as heterogeneous. An obvious assumption is that the resuming probability is negatively correlated with the quitting probability so that:

$$pr_A (y_t = 1 \mid y_{t-1} = 0) > pr_B (y_t = 1 \mid y_{t-1} = 0) \tag{14}$$

For economists, however, an attractive alternative assumption is that since people are forward looking and know their own type,[9] a type A who has stopped might be much more reluctant to start again. This assumption reverses the inequality in (14). Whatever the case, we would not want an initial specification for the two transition probabilities and the starting condition that would rule out these possibilities. Now consider a conventional specification that has only one "fixed effect":

$$pr (y_{it} = 1 \mid y_{it-1}) = \mathbf{F} \left(\alpha_i + \beta y_{i,t-1} \right) \tag{15}$$

With two types, the easy/tough quitting structure (12) is:

$$1 - \mathbf{F} (\alpha_A + \beta) < 1 - \mathbf{F} (\alpha_B + \beta) \tag{16}$$

which implies $\mathbf{F} (\alpha_A) > \mathbf{F} (\alpha_B)$ which is (14). Thus the conventional formulation (15), which is often presented as an unrestricted "reduced form," rules out the interesting structure that would occur to most economists.

This concludes our brief and highly selective discussion of the difficulties of allowing for heterogeneity in a flexible enough way to capture what is in the data and to allow for a wide range of structural models. We now present some of our own recent work on dynamic discrete choice modeling that was motivated by the empirical findings on the demand for whole fat milk presented in Section 2 and by examples such as the smoking analysis presented here.

---

[9] So that the type is heterogeneous and not uncertain by our definition of heterogeneity. If those who never smoked do not know their type then we have both heterogeneity and uncertainty in types.

4 DYNAMIC DISCRETE CHOICE MODELS

4.1 A Stationary Markov Chain Model

This section presents and summarizes some results from Browning and Carro (2005) (BC) concerning heterogeneity in dynamic discrete choice models. Since very little is known about such models when we allow for lots of heterogeneity, we consider the simple model with no covariates. An additional and important advantage of considering the simple model is that we can derive exact analytical finite sample properties. The restriction on theory that we impose is that the reduced form for the structural model is a stationary first-order Markov chain. In many contexts the stationarity restriction may be untenable, but we have to start somewhere. In this simple model the approach is fully nonparametric, conditional only on that modeling choice. We focus directly on the two transition parameters:

$$G_i = pr\left(y_{it} = 1 \mid y_{i,t-1} = 0\right)$$
$$H_i = pr\left(y_{it} = 1 \mid y_{i,t-1} = 1\right) \tag{17}$$

where i is individual indicator, t is time indicator, and $t = 0, 1, \ldots, T$. This is the maximal heterogeneity we can allow in this context. For instance, in the smoking example of Subsection 3.2.5, the structure described by equations (12) and (14), correspond to $H_A > H_B$ and $G_A > G_B$ respectively. In this exposition we shall focus on the marginal dynamic effect:

$$M_i = H_i - G_i \tag{18}$$

which gives the impact on the current probability of $y_{it} = 1$ from changing the lagged value from 0 to 1. A model with homogeneous dynamic marginal effects would impose:

$$H_i = M + G_i \in [0, 1] \tag{19}$$

for some $M \in [-1, 1]$. A parametric model with a homogeneous persistence parameter would impose:

$$G_i = F\left(\alpha_i\right)$$
$$H_i = F\left(\alpha_i + \beta\right) \tag{20}$$

for some cdf $F\left(.\right)$.

4.2 Estimation with One Sequence

We begin by considering a single realization of a sequence for one person. There are 2^{T+1} possible sequences of 1's and 0's for a single chain of length $T + 1$ (or 2^T if we condition on the initial value). An estimator $\left(\hat{G}, \hat{H}\right)$ is a mapping from the 2^{T+1} realizations to sets in the unit square. If the mapping is single-valued then the parameters are point identified by that estimator. The first result in BC is that there is no unbiased estimator for G and H. With this result in mind we look for estimators that have low bias or low mse. The maximum likelihood estimator (MLE) has a simple analytical closed form:

$$\hat{G}^{\text{MLE}} = \frac{n_{01}}{n_{00}+n_{01}} \tag{21}$$

$$\hat{H}^{\text{MLE}} = \frac{n_{11}}{n_{10}+n_{11}} \tag{22}$$

where n_{01} is the number of $0 \rightarrow 1$ transitions, etc. Note that $\hat{G}^{\text{MLE}}$ is point identified iff we have a sequence that has at least one pair beginning with a zero, so point identification requires us to drop some possible observations. The second result in BC is that the MLE estimate of the marginal dynamic effect (if it exists) has a negative bias, that is:

$$E\left(\hat{H}^{\text{MLE}} - \hat{G}^{\text{MLE}}\right) < M \tag{23}$$

This result is the discrete choice analogue of the Nickell bias for linear dynamic models (see Arellano, 2003a) . The degree of bias depends on the parameter values and the length of the panel, T. As we would hope, the bias of the MLE estimator of the marginal dynamic effect diminishes as we increase the length of the panel, but even for $T = 16$ it can be high.

Based on the exact formulae for the bias of the MLE, BC construct a nonlinear bias corrected (NBC) estimator as a two-step estimator with the MLE as the first step.[10] We find that this estimator does indeed reduce the bias for most cases (as compared to MLE). For all but extreme values of negative state dependence, the NBC estimator also has a negative bias for the marginal dynamic effect. The order of bias for the MLE is approximately $O\left(T^{-1}\right)$ (the exact order depends on the parameter values) whereas the order for the NBC estimator is approximately $O\left(T^{-2}\right)$ so that the small sample bias diminishes much faster for NBC. Despite these advantages on the bias, in mse terms the NBC estimator is never much better than MLE and it is worse in some cases. A detailed examination of the MLE and NBC estimators suggested that neither can be preferred to the other.

Given the relatively poor performance of the MLE and NBC in terms of mse, BC construct an estimator that addresses the mse directly. The mse for an estimator $\hat{M}$ of the marginal dynamic effect is given by:

$$\lambda\left(\hat{M}; G, H\right) = \sum_{j=1}^{J} p_j\left(G, H\right)\left(\hat{M}_j - (H - G)\right)^2 \tag{24}$$

where j denotes a particular sequence, $J = 2^T$ (if we condition on the initial value) and p_j is the probability of sequence j given the values of G and H. Since there is no estimator that minimizes the mse for all values of (G, H), we look for the minimum for some choice of a prior distribution of (G, H), $f(G, H)$ so that the integrated mse is given by:

$$\int_0^1 \int_0^1 \lambda\left(\hat{M}; G, H\right) f(G, H) \, dG \, dH \tag{25}$$

---

[10] BC show analytically that the estimator which continues to apply bias corrections after the first does not necessarily converge, so that only the two-step estimator is considered.

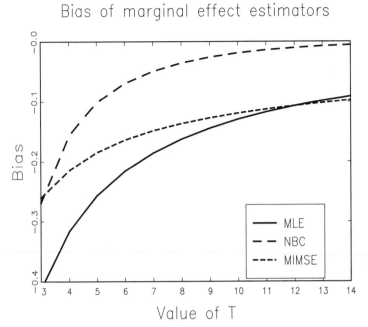

Figure 3.5. Bias of three estimators.

Given that we consider a general case in which we have no idea of the context, the obvious choice is the uniform distribution on $[0, 1]^2$, $f(G, H) = 1$. Minimizing gives the following minimum integrated mse (MIMSE) estimator:

$$\hat{M}_j^{\text{MIMSE}} = \frac{n_{11} + 1}{n_{10} + n_{11} + 2} - \frac{n_{01} + 1}{n_{00} + n_{01} + 2} \tag{26}$$

This estimator is the mean of the posterior distribution assuming a uniform prior. The attractions of the MIMSE estimator are that it is very easy to compute, it is always identified and it converges to maximum likelihood as T becomes large so that it inherits all of the desirable large sample properties of MLE. Figure 3.5 shows the small sample bias for the three estimators. The rate of convergence of the bias to zero for the MIMSE estimator is approximately $O\left(T^{-0.6}\right)$. As can be seen, the NBC estimator starts off with a relatively small bias and converges more quickly to zero. Thus the NBC estimator unequivocally dominates the other two estimators in terms of bias. When we turn to the mse, however, MIMSE is much better than either of the other two estimators, particularly when there is some positive state dependence ($M > 0$). This is shown in Figure 3.6 . As can be seen there, the MIMSE estimator starts not too far above the CR bound (for the MLE estimator) and converges relatively slowly to it. The other two estimators have a relatively high RMSE, particularly when we have short observation period.

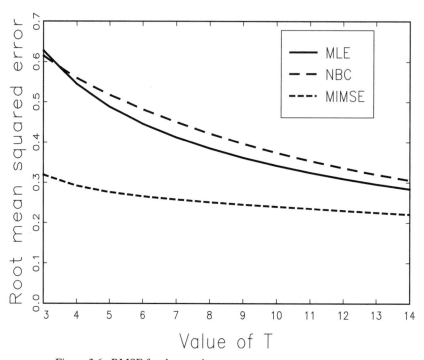

Figure 3.6. RMSE for three estimators.

4.3   Estimation with Pooled Data

In the previous subsection we considered households in isolation but in most cases the interest is not in individual households, but in the population. Thus, it may be that the distribution of M in the population is of primary interest, rather than the values for particular households. Suppose that we observe many households. We first consider the nonparametric identification of the distribution of (G, H) with fixed T. We shall assume that we are given population values for outcomes. In this case the relevant population values are the proportions of each of the 2^T possible cases. Denote the population values by π_j for $j = 1, 2...2^T$. Now suppose that (G, H) are distributed over $[0, 1]^2$ with a density $f(G, H)$. The population proportions are given by the integral equations[11]:

$$\pi_j = \int_0^1 \int_0^1 p_j(G, H) f(G, H) \, dG dH, \, j = 1, 2...2^T \qquad (27)$$

---

[11] Note that we have made an analysis conditional on the initial observation y_{i0}, so $f(G, H)$ here it is the distribution given y_{i0}. A similar result could be get about the identification of the unconditional distribution.

where, the probabilities are given by:

$$p_j(G, H) = G^{n_{01}^j} (1 - G)^{n_{00}^j} H^{n_{11}^j} (1 - H)^{n_{10}^j} \tag{28}$$

Assuming that the π_j's satisfy the conditions imposed by the model, we check the following necessary condition for identification: is there only one density $f(G, H)$ which is consistent with the set of 2^T equations (27)? The answer is negative. To show this we impose some structure on the model and show that even with these additional constraints the structure is not identified. Consider the case with $T = 3$ and in which we restrict the distribution of the G's and H's to be discrete, each with three values: $\{G_1, G_2, G_3\}$ and $\{H_1, H_2, H_3\}$. Let the probabilities of each of the nine combinations (G_k, H_l) be given by the (9×1) vector θ with values that sum to unity. Define the (8×9) matrix A by:

$$A_{jm} = (G_m)^{n_{01}^j} (1 - G_m)^{n_{00}^j} (H_m)^{n_{11}^j} (1 - H_m)^{n_{10}^j} \tag{29}$$

Then the analogue to (27) is:

$$\pi = A\theta \tag{30}$$

where π is observed and the values of $\{G_1, G_2, G_3\}$, $\{H_1, H_2, H_3\}$, and θ are to be solved for. Clearly, the latter are not uniquely determined by the former since we have 8 equations and 14 unknowns.[12] There are more than one distribution of (G, H) that generates the same observed π in (30). Thus the distribution is not nonparametrically identified. We need to either put on more structure such as a parametric model for heterogeneity, or estimate nonparametrically M_i for each unit separately and then use those estimates to define the empirical distribution of the parameters. In BC we explore the latter approach, that is, obtaining the empirical distribution from estimates for each unit. Simulations with $T = 9$ (i.e., with 10 observations, including the initial observation) suggest that the MIMSE-based estimator significantly outperforms the MLE and NBC estimators in recovering the distribution of the marginal dynamic effect. This can be seen, for instance, in Figure 3.7, that presents cdf's of the three estimators from simulations using the empirical distribution for (G, H) from the estimates reported in Section 2.

This analysis suggests that it is feasible to define reasonably well-performed estimators with maximal heterogeneity for the dynamic discrete choice model. Clearly, such an estimator will be consistent with any theory model that generates a stationary first-order Markov chains and it will also fit any generating process for the heterogeneity. In some contexts such estimators will significantly outperform (in terms of fit and congruence with theory) some version of (20) estimated using a conventional "fixed effect" scheme.

---

[12] The number of equations, 8 is equal to 2^T. As a matter of fact, two of the 2^T cases give the same equation on (30), so there are only seven different equations.

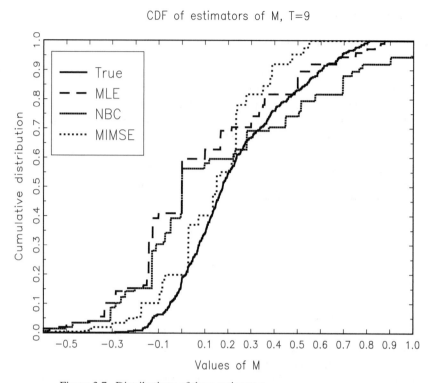

Figure 3.7. Distributions of three estimators.

4.4   Relation to Recent Developments in Estimation of Nonlinear Panel Data Models

In the recent years new methods of estimation for nonlinear panel data models have been developed. Arellano and Hahn (2005) present a review and explain and derive connections between the different solutions developed.[13] The central focus is on nonlinear models with fixed effects and the attempt to overcome the incidental parameters problem that arises from the estimation by standard MLE of common parameters in these models. Usually the specific constant intercept, the so-called fixed effect, is the only heterogeneous coefficient and the consequent incidental parameters problem may lead to severe bias in panels where T is not large. The new methods developed reduce the order of the magnitude in T of that bias, so that it may be negligible in finite samples used in practice. They remove the first-order term on the expansion of the asymptotic bias of the MLE, and consider asymptotics with both N and T going to infinity.

In BC not only the intercept but also the slope are individual specific. Given this, we have a separate model for each individual in the panel. In contrast

---

[13] The literature reviewed by Arellano and Hahn (2005) includes Arellano (2003b), Carro (2004), Fernandez-Val (2005), Hahn and Newey (2004), and Woutersen (2004) among others.

with the literature reviewed in Arellano and Hahn (2005), where the object of interest is a common parameter in the population, we first consider estimating each separate model with the T observations of each individual. In this regard our analysis is closer to the time series literature. There is no asymptotic in N given that we are estimating with one sequence. Another difference is that the NBC considered by BC is not based on a first-order reduction on the asymptotic bias. It is based on the exact finite sample properties of the MLE. So the NBC estimator is based on the exact formulae of the finite sample bias that BC derive. These differences imply that some of our conclusions diverge from the recent literature. Theoretically, the first-order reduction on the asymptotic bias reviewed in Arellano and Hahn (2005) does not increase the asymptotic variance as N and T go to infinity at the same rate. Furthermore, finite sample experiments, for example, in Carro (2004) and Fernandez-Val (2005), provide some evidence that bias reduction can lead to a better estimator in terms of mse for a panel with a moderate number of periods.[14] However, derivations of the exact mse of the NBC show that it does not dominate the MLE in this criterion since it is never much better and it is worse in some cases. This means that while NBC significantly reduces the bias, it also significantly increases the variances of the estimator in finite samples. MIMSE is a different approach in the sense that it is not derived to reduce the bias but to minimize the mse in finite samples. Given this, it is not defined as a bias correction of the MLE, but as new estimator in accordance with the chosen criterion.

There are two possible motivations for considering estimation of each individual's model with one sequence. First, we may be interested in each individual, for example, if we are analyzing the default risk of each credit applicant. Second, in the kind of models considered, having an unbiased estimator for each individual is sufficient to define a fixed-T consistent estimator of a parameter on the population of individuals. Even if is not possible to define an unbiased estimator, as shown in BC for a first-order Markov chain, having an estimator for each individual model with improved properties in finite samples could lead to an estimator of a parameter defined over the population of individuals, with good finite sample properties when pooling many households. Any parameter of interest defined as a function of the model's parameters will benefit from this. In the analysis discussed in the previous three subsections there is no parameter of the model that is common to all the individuals and the marginal effect of a variable is heterogeneous. Nevertheless, in many cases our interest is in particular moments of the distribution of the marginal effect on the population; for example, the median marginal effect of a variable. BC consider estimating the whole distribution of the marginal effect in the population with pooled data. As described in the previous subsection, BC explore using the nonparametric estimators for each unit already considered (MLE, NBC, MIMSE) and then

---

[14] Of course, simulation experiments have been done only for some specific sample sizes and binary choice models. More finite sample experiments are needed to evaluate each of those new methods.

obtaining the empirical distribution in the population from estimates of the individual marginal effects. Focusing on a moment of that distribution, in principle it could be possible to apply the ideas in Arellano and Hahn (2005), since this is a common parameter to be estimated with a not very large number of periods that suffers the incidental parameters problem. This correction, following ideas in section 8 of Arellano and Hahn (2005), would be specific to each parameter of interest one may want to consider, in contrast to the case where you have good estimates of the model's parameters. In any case, this possibility remains unexplored in practice for models where all the parameters are heterogeneous.

5 CONCLUSIONS

In this paper we have presented a selective and idiosyncratic view of the current state of allowing for heterogeneity in microeconometric modeling. Our main theme has been that there is more heterogeneity than we usually allow for and it matters for outcomes of interest. Additionally, it is difficult to allow for heterogeneity but when considering how to do it we have to keep an eye on fitting the data and on the interpretability of the estimates. Thus how we introduce heterogeneity into our empirical analysis should depend on the data to hand, the questions deemed to be of interest and the economic models under consideration. The lesson from the last thirty years seems to be that this requires case by case specifications and eschewing the use of schemes whose only virtue is that they are statistically convenient.

References

ALVAREZ, JAVIER, MARTIN BROWNING, AND METTE EJRNAES, (2002): "Modelling Income Processes with Lots of Heterogeneity," CAM WP-2002-01, University of Copenhagen.

ANDERSEN, ERLING B. (1970): "Asymptotic Properties of Conditional Maximum Likelihood Estimators," *Journal of the Royal Statistical Society*, Series B, 32, 283–301.

ARELLANO, MANUEL (2003a): *Panel Data Econometrics*, Oxford: Oxford University Press.

——— (2003b): "Discrete Choice with Panel Data," *Investigaciones Económicas*, XXVII(3), 423–458.

ARELLANO, MANUEL AND JINYONG HAHN (2005): "Understanding Bias in Nonlinear Panel Models: Some Recent Developments," CEMFI Working Paper No. 0507. Prepared for the Econometric Society World Congress, London, August 2005.

BROWNING, MARTIN AND JESUS CARRO (2005): "Heterogeneity in Dynamic Discrete Choice Models," Unpublished manuscript.

CARD, DAVID (1999): "The Causal Effect of Education on Earnings," in *Handbook of Labor Economics*, Vol. 3A, edited by Orley Ashenfelter and David Card, Amsterdam and New York: North Holland.

——— (2001): "Estimating the Return to Schooling: Progress on Some Persistent Econometric Problems," *Econometrica*, 69, 1127–1160.

CARRO, JESUS (2004): "Estimating Dynamic Panel Data Discrete Choice Models with Fixed Effects," Unpublished manuscript.

CARRO, JESUS AND PEDRO MIRA (2005): "A Dynamic Model of Contraceptive Choice of Spanish Couples," *Journal of Applied Econometrics*, 21, 955–980.

CHAMBERLAIN, G. (1980): "Analysis of Covariance with Qualitative Data," *Review of Economic Studies*, 47, 225–238.

CUNHA, FLAVIO, JAMES HECKMAN, AND SALVADOR NAVARRO (2005): "Separating Uncertainty from Heterogeneity in Life Cycle Earnings," *Oxford Economic Papers*, 57, 191–261.

FERNANDEZ-VAL, IVAN (2005): "Estimation of Structural Parameters and Marginal Effects in Binary Choice Panel Data Models with Fixed Effects," Unpublished manuscript.

HAHN, JINYONG AND WHITNEY NEWEY (2004): "Jackknife and Analytical Bias Reduction for Nonlinear Panel Models," *Econometrica*, 72, 1295–1319.

HECKMAN, JAMES (1981): "Statistical Models for Discrete Panel Data," in *Structural Analysis of Discrete Data with Econometric Applications*, edited by C. F. Manski and D. McFadden, Cambridge, MA: MIT Press.

——— (2001): "Micro Data, Heterogeneity, and the Evaluation of Public Policy: Nobel Lecture," *Journal of Political Economy*, 109, 673–748.

HECKMAN, JAMES, ROSA MATZKIN, AND LARS NESHEIM (2003): "Simulation and Estimation of Nonadditive Hedonic Models," NBER Working Papers: 9895.

HECKMAN, JAMES AND EDWARD VYTLACIL (1998): "Instrumental Variables Methods for the Correlated Random Coefficient Model: Estimating the Average Rate of Return to Schooling When the Return is Correlated with Schooling," *Journal of Human Resources*, 33, 974–987.

——— (2005): "Structural Equations, Treatment Effects, and Econometric Policy Evaluations," *Econometrica*, 73, 669–738.

IMBENS, GUIDO AND JOSHUA D. ANGRIST (1994): "Identification and Estimation of Local Average Treatment Effects," *Econometrica*, 62, 467–476.

KEANE MICHAEL P. AND KENNETH I. WOLPIN (1997): "The Career Decisions of Young Men," *Journal of Political Economy*, 105, 473–521.

LANCASTER, TONY (1979): "Econometric Methods for the Duration of Unemployment," *Econometrica*, 47, 939–956.

LAROQUE, GUY (2005): "Income Maintenance and Labor Force Participation," *Econometrica*, 73, 341–376.

LINDSEY, J. K. (2001): *Parametric Statistical Inference*, Oxford Statistical Science Series, Oxford: Clarendon Press.

MCFADDEN, DANIEL AND KENNETH TRAIN (2000): "Mixed MNL Models of Discrete Response," *Journal of Applied Econometrics*, 15, 447–470.

MEGHIR, COSTAS AND LUIGI PISTAFERRI (2004): "Income Variance Dynamics and Heterogeneity," *Econometrica*, 72, 1–32.

MUNDLAK, Y. (1961): "Empirical Production Function Free of Management Bias," *Journal of Farm Economics*, 43, 44–56.

NATIONAL RESEARCH COUNCIL (2001): *Cells and Surveys*, Washington, DC: National Academy Press.

PATTERSON, K. DAVID (2001): "Lactose Intolerance," in *The Cambridge World History of Food*, Vol. 1, edited by Kenneth Kiple and Kriemhild Conee Ornelas, Cambridge: Cambridge University Press.

PESARAN M. HASHEM AND RON SMITH (1995): "Estimating Long-run Relationships from Dynamic Heterogenous Panels, " *Journal of Econometrics*, 68, 79–113.

RUBINSTEIN, YONA AND YORAM WEISS (2005): "Post Schooling Wage Growth: Investment, Search and Learning," Mimeo, Eithan Berglas School of Economics, Tel-Aviv University.

STIGLER, GEORGE J. AND GARY S. BECKER (1977): "De Gustibus Non Est Disputandum," *American Economic Review*, 67, 76–90.

VAN DEN BERG AND J. GERARD (2001): "Duration models: specification, identification and multiple duration," in *Handbook of Econometrics*, Vol. 5, edited by J. J. Heckman and E. E. Leamer, Amsterdam: Elsevier, Chapter 55, pp. 3381–3460.

VINK, JACQUELINE, GONNEKE WILLEMSEN, AND DORRET BOOMSMA (2003): "The Association of Current Smoking Behavior with the Smoking of Parents, Siblings, Friends and Spouses," *Addiction*, 98, 923–931.

WOOLDRIDGE, JEFFREY (2005): "Simple Solutions to the Initial Conditions Problem in Dynamic, Nonlinear Panel Data Models with Unobserved Heterogeneity," *Journal of Applied Econometrics*, 20, 39–54.

WOUTERSEN, TIEMEN (2004): "Robustness Against Incidental Parameters," Unpublished manuscript.

CHAPTER 4

Heterogeneous Choice[*]

Rosa L. Matzkin[†]

1 INTRODUCTION

This paper considers nonparametric identification in models with nonadditive unobservables, where choices are either the dependent or the explanatory variables. For models where choices are dependent variables, the paper presents some of the latest developments in nonparametric identification, in the context of two popular models of consumer demand: the classical consumer demand and discrete choice. For models where choices are explanatory variables, it discusses several of the methods that have recently been developed to deal with their endogeneity.

Choice is the selection of an alternative from a set of alternatives. In many economic models, the role of economic agents is to make choices. Workers choose how to allocate their time between leisure and work-time. Consumers choose how to allocate their income between consumption and savings. Firms choose what and how much to produce. Governments choose taxes and subsidies. The usual assumption made in these economic models is that when making a choice, each economic agent has an objective function, and the choice is made so as to maximize that objective function over the set of possible alternatives.

Observable choices, made either by an agent or by different agents, are typically heterogeneous. This heterogeneity may be the result of heterogeneous choice sets, or of heterogenous objective functions. Some of this heterogeneity may be explained by different values of observable variables. Some may be explained by different values of unobservable variables. Understanding the

[*] This paper was presented as an invited lecture at the World Congress of the Econometric Society, London, August 2005. I am grateful to the National Science Foundation for financial support through grants SES-0551272, BCS 0433990, and SES 0241858. I have benefitted from discussions with and comments of Richard Blundell, Donald Brown, James Heckman, Arthur Lewbel, Daniel McFadden, Whitney Newey, Viktor Soubbotine, participants at the World Congress of the Econometric Society, and participants at the Harvard/MIT econometrics workshop and the Yale University Cowles Lunch series, where parts of this paper were presented.

[†] Department of Economics, Northwestern University.

source and shape of heterogeneity in choices is important, among other things, for accurately predicting behavior under new environments, and for evaluating the differential effect of policies over heterogeneous populations.

A usual approach in many econometric models has proceeded in the past by using economic theory to derive a relationship only between observable variables. Unobservable variables would then be added to the relationship, as an after-thought. An alternative approach proceeded by explicitly deriving the relationship between the underlying unobservable variables and the dependent variables. In these models, variables such as unobservable attributes of alternatives, unobservable taste for work, and unobservable productivity shocks were explicitly incorporated into the relationship fitted to the data. This typically resulted in models where the unobservable variables entered into the relationship in nonlinear, nonadditive ways (Heckman, 1974; Heckman and Willis, 1977; Lancaster, 1979; McFadden, 1974). While those previous studies were parametric, in the sense that the underlying functions in the model as well as the distribution of the unobservable variables were specified up to a finite-dimensional parameter, a large literature has evolved since then, following Manski (1975) and Heckman and Singer (1984), which relaxed those parametric assumptions. The present state of the literature allows us to consider models in which we can incorporate multidimensional, nonadditive unobservables in nonparametric models. [See, for example, the recent survey paper by Matzkin (2006), as well as the recent papers by Chesher (2006) and Imbens (2006).]

The outline of the paper is as follows. In the next section, we deal with the classical consumer demand model. We first consider a model with a distribution of consumers, each choosing a bundle of commodities from a linear budget set. We present conditions under which the distribution of preferences is identified, and show how one can recover the utility functions and the distribution of tastes from the distribution of demand. We then show how a large support condition on observable variables, which generate heterogeneity of tastes, can substitute for the large support condition on prices required for our first set of results. Nonlinear budget sets and situations where one observes variation in income but not in prices are also analyzed. Section 3 deals with discrete choice models. Section 4 deals with some of the latest methods that have been developed to deal with situations where explanatory variables are endogenous, in nonparametric models with nonadditive unobservables. It describes how that literature can be applied to models with heterogeneous choice. Section 5 concludes.

2   CLASSICAL CONSUMER DEMAND

Consumer behavior is arguably one of the most important elements that are taken into account when considering policies and when determining actions by firms. The analysis of changes in income tax, interest rates, the proper design of cost of living indices, the pricing decision by firms, and the evaluation of changes in the welfare of consumers due to government policies require a good understanding of consumer behavior.

The classical model of consumer behavior is typically described as one where a consumer faces either a linear or a nonlinear budget set, which is determined by prices and the consumer's income. The consumer has preferences over commodities, and chooses the bundle of commodities that maximizes his preferences. Since consumers' preferences might be different across individuals, one would like these preferences to depend on observable and on unobservable characteristics. The consumer's optimization problem can then be described as

$$
\begin{aligned}
Max_y \quad & V(y, z, \varepsilon) \\
s.t. \quad & y \in B(w)
\end{aligned}
\tag{2.1}
$$

where $V(\cdot, z, \varepsilon)$ is a utility function representing the preferences of the consumer over bundles of commodities, y; $z \in R^L$ denotes a vector of observable socioeconomic characteristics of the individual, $\varepsilon \in R^S$ denotes a vector of unobservable characteristics of the individual, and $B(w)$ denotes a subset of R^K, indexed by the observable vector w. In a standard example, w would be the vector of prices of the products and income of the consumer, z may denote age, profession, and/or level of education, and ε may denote a vector representing the different tastes of the consumer for the various products. The solution to this optimization problem, if unique, will be a vector $y = d(z, w, \varepsilon)$, such that $y \in B(w)$ and

$$
V(d(z, w, \varepsilon), z, \varepsilon) > V(y', z, \varepsilon)
$$

for all $y' \in B(w)$ such that $y' \neq y$.

The observable variables are w, z, and the choice y. The questions that one may be interested in analyzing are (i) what restrictions the optimization assumption places on the distribution of y given (z, w), (ii) given the distribution of (y, z, w), under what conditions can we recover the function V and the distribution of ε, and (iii) suppose that the conditions for identification of V and the distribution of ε are not satisfied, then, what features of V and the distribution of ε can we recover.

Suppose that, in model (2.1), preferences did not depend on the values of unobservable variables, ε. Assume that the utility function V and the budget set $B(w)$ are such that the solution to the optimization problem is always unique. Then, on each budget set, $B(w)$, and for each z, one would observe only one choice, $d(z, w)$. In this case, the distribution of y given (z, w) would be degenerate. If the budget set were linear, then, for each z, $d(z, w)$ would satisfy the Slutsky conditions. And from $d(z, w)$, one could recover the utility function $V(y, z)$ using integrability or revealed preference theory. In this deterministic model, one could make use of the extensive literature on revealed preference, integrability, and duality theories (Afriat, 1967; Epstein, 1981; Houthakker, 1950; Mas-Colell, 1977, 1978; Matzkin, 1991b; Matzkin and Richter, 1991; McFadden, 1978; Richter, 1966; Samuelson, 1938; Yatchew, 1985, among many others). These allow one to study characterizations of optimization and to infer the preferences generating the observable demand function of an individual.

When, on the other side, preferences depend on the value of unobservable variables, ε, then, on each observable budget set, $B(w)$, and for each z, one observes a distribution of choices, y, which are generated by the distribution of ε. A common approach in this situation proceeds by deriving the conditional expectation of the distribution of demand, and applying the theoretical results on consumer demand to this conditional expectation, as if it represented the deterministic demand of a representative consumer. On any budget set, any observable choice that is different from the conditional expectation of the distribution of demand on that budget set is represented by an unobservable random term that is added to that conditional expectation. However, in many situations, such a procedure might not be desirable. First, only under very strong assumptions on the preferences of all consumers one could guarantee that such representative consumer acted as if maximizing some utility function. Moreover, as pointed out and shown in McElroy (1981, 1987), Brown and Walker (1989, 1995), and Lewbel (2001), the additive unobservables tacked on to the deterministic relationship will typically be functionally dependent on the variables, w, that determine the choice set. One could alleviate these situations using parametric specifications for the utility V and/or the distribution of unobservable random terms, as suggested in those papers and their references (see, e.g., Barten, 1968). We opt, instead, for a substantially more general, nonparametric analysis, that deals explicitly with unobservable taste heterogeneity.

2.1   Linear Choice Sets, Price and Income Variation

The most common model of classical consumer demand is where the budget set is linear. In this model, w represents an observable vector, p, of K prices, and an observable variable, I, which denotes income. The choice (budget) set of the consumer is

$$B(p, I) = \left\{ y \in R_+^K \mid p \cdot y \le I \right\}.$$

For each vector of observable socioeconomic characteristics, z, and unobservable tastes, ε, the preferences of the consumer over bundles, y, are represented by a function, $V(\cdot, z, \varepsilon)$, which is strictly increasing and strictly quasiconcave in y. For simplicity, we will strengthen this to consider only preferences that admit a strictly concave, twice continuously differentiable utility function. In addition, to avoid dealing with nonnegativity constraints, we will allow consumption to be negative. Denote the choice of a consumer with utility function $V(y, z, \varepsilon)$, facing prices p and income I, by

$$y = d(p, I, z, \varepsilon)$$

then,

$$d(p, I, z, \varepsilon) = \arg \max_{\widetilde{y}} \{ V(\widetilde{y}, z, \varepsilon) \mid p \cdot \widetilde{y} \le I \}.$$

For notational simplicity we will eliminate for the moment the dependence of V on z. Moreover, for the cases that we want to deal with later on, it will be important that the dimension of the vector ε be equal to the number of commodities minus 1. Hence, we will assume that the utility function is

$$V(y_1, \ldots, y_K, \varepsilon_1, \ldots, \varepsilon_{K-1}).$$

The homogeneity of the budget constraint implies that we can normalize the value of one price. Hence, we set $p_K = 1$. The strict monotonicity of V in y guarantees that at any solution to the maximization problem, the budget constraint will be binding. Hence, we can restrict attention to those commodity bundles that satisfy the budget constraint. This allows us to substitute y_K for $y_K = I - \sum_{k=1}^{K-1} y_k p_k$, and solve for the unconstrained maximizer of

$$V\left(y_1, \ldots, y_{K-1}, I - \sum_{k=1}^{K-1} y_k p_k, \varepsilon_1, \ldots, \varepsilon_{K-1}\right).$$

The first-order conditions for such maximization are, for $k = 1, \ldots, K - 1$,

$$V_k\left(y_1, \ldots, y_{K-1}, I - \sum_{k=1}^{K-1} y_k p_k, \varepsilon_1, \ldots, \varepsilon_{K-1}\right)$$
$$- V_K\left(y_1, \ldots, y_{K-1}, I - \sum_{k=1}^{K-1} y_k p_k, \varepsilon_1, \ldots, \varepsilon_{K-1}\right) p_k = 0.$$

The second-order conditions are satisfied, for each $(\varepsilon_1, \ldots, \varepsilon_{K-1})$, by the strict concavity of the utility function V. The first-order conditions represent a system of $K - 1$ simultaneous equations, with $K - 1$ endogenous variables, $(y_1, \ldots, y_{K-1})$, and K exogenous variables, $p_1, \ldots, p_{K-1}, I$. The reduced form system can be expressed as a system of demand functions:

$$y_1 = d_1(p_1, \ldots, p_{K-1}, I, \varepsilon_1, \ldots, \varepsilon_{K-1})$$
$$y_2 = d_2(p_1, \ldots, p_{K-1}, I, \varepsilon_1, \ldots, \varepsilon_{K-1})$$
$$\cdots$$
$$y_{K-1} = d_{K-1}(p_1, \ldots, p_{K-1}, I, \varepsilon_1, \ldots, \varepsilon_{K-1}).$$

Since V is not specified parametrically, each function in this system is a non-parametric function, which possesses $K - 1$ unobservable arguments. On each budget set, characterized by a vector of prices and income (p, I), the distribution of demand is generated by the distribution of $(\varepsilon_1, \ldots, \varepsilon_{K-1})$.

2.1.1   Invertibility of Demand Functions in the Unobservables

A condition that, as we will show, will allow us to deal with a system of equations where each function depends on a vector of unobservable variables, is invertibility of the demand functions in that vector of unobservable variables. Invertibility guarantees that on each budget set, each observable choice corresponds to one and only one vector of the unobservable variables. It allows us to express the system of demand functions in terms of functions, $r_1, \ldots, r_{K-1}$, such that

$$\varepsilon_1 = r_1(y_1, \ldots, y_{K-1}, p_1, \ldots, p_{K-1}, I)$$
$$\varepsilon_2 = r_2(y_1, \ldots, y_{K-1}, p_1, \ldots, p_{K-1}, I)$$
$$\cdots$$
$$\varepsilon_{K-1} = r_{K-1}(y_1, \ldots, y_{K-1}, p_1, \ldots, p_{K-1}, I).$$

Under invertibility, this system is obtained by solving for ε the system of demand equations.

Invertibility is not an innocuous assumption. When $K = 2$, it is satisfied if the demand function is either strictly increasing or strictly decreasing in ε. The following example is considered in Matzkin (2003):

Example 1   *Suppose that the consumer's problem is to maximize the random utility function*

$$v(y_1, y_2) + w(y_1, \varepsilon)$$

$$\text{subject to } p\, y_1 + y_2 \le I.$$

Assume that the functions v and w are twice continuously differentiable, strictly increasing and strictly concave, and that $\partial^2 w(y_1, \varepsilon)/\partial y_1 \partial \varepsilon > 0$. Then, the demand function for y_1 is invertible in ε.

To see this, note that the value of y_1 that solves the maximization of

$$v(y_1, I - py_1) + w(y_1, \varepsilon)$$

satisfies

$$v_1(y_1, I - py_1) - v_2(y_1, I - py_1)\, p + w_1(y_1, \varepsilon) = 0$$

and

$$v_{11}(y_1, I - py_1) - 2\, v_{12}(y_1, I - py_1)\, p + v_{22}(y_1, I - py_1)\, p^2$$
$$+ w_{11}(y_1, \varepsilon) < 0$$

where $v_i, v_{ij}, w_i,$ and w_{ij} denote the partial derivatives of $v, v_i, w,$ and w_i with respect to the ith, jth, ith, and jth coordinate. By the Implicit Function Theorem, $y_1 = d(p, I, \varepsilon)$ that solves the first-order conditions exists and satisfies for all $p, I, \varepsilon,$

$$\frac{\partial d(p, I, \varepsilon)}{\partial \varepsilon}$$
$$= -\frac{w_{12}(y_1, \varepsilon)}{v_{11}(y_1, I - py_1) - 2\, v_{12}(y_1, I - py_1)\, p + v_{22}(y_1, I - py_1)\, p^2 + w_{11}(y_1, \varepsilon)}$$
$$> 0$$

Hence, the demand function for y_1 is invertible in ε.   ∎

Example 1 demonstrates that some utility functions can generate demand functions that are strictly increasing in ε. This example also suggests that the demand functions generated from many other utility functions will not necessarily satisfy this condition.

When $K > 2$, invertibility requires even stronger conditions. Brown and Matzkin (1998) derived invertible demand functions by specifying a utility function of the form

$$V(y_1, \ldots, y_K, \varepsilon_1, \ldots, \varepsilon_{K-1}) = U(y_1, \ldots, y_K) + \sum_{k=1}^{K-1} \varepsilon_k \, y_k + y_K$$

where U is twice differentiable and strictly concave. In this case, the first-order conditions for the maximization of V subject to the constraint that $y_K = I - \sum_{k=1}^{K-1} y_k p_k$, are

$$\varepsilon_1 = \left(U_K \left(y_1, \ldots, y_{K-1}, I - \sum_{k=1}^{K-1} y_k p_k \right) + 1 \right) p_1$$
$$- U_1 \left(y_1, \ldots, y_{K-1}, I - \sum_{k=1}^{K-1} y_k p_k \right)$$

$$\varepsilon_2 = \left(U_K \left(y_1, \ldots, y_{K-1}, I - \sum_{k=1}^{K-1} y_k p_k \right) + 1 \right) p_2$$
$$- U_2 \left(y_1, \ldots, y_{K-1}, I - \sum_{k=1}^{K-1} y_k p_k \right)$$

$$\cdots$$

$$\varepsilon_{K-1} = \left(U_K \left(y_1, \ldots, y_{K-1}, I - \sum_{k=1}^{K-1} y_k p_k \right) + 1 \right) p_{K-1}$$
$$- U_{K-1} \left(y_1, \ldots, y_{K-1}, I - \sum_{k=1}^{K-1} y_k p_k \right).$$

Hence, for each vector $(y_1, \ldots, y_{k-1})$, there exists only one value for $(\varepsilon_1, \ldots, \varepsilon_{K-1})$ satisfying the first-order conditions.

Brown and Calsamiglia (2003), considering tests for random utility maximization, specified a slightly more restrictive utility function, which differs from the one in Brown and Matzkin (1998) mainly in that the twice differentiable and strictly concave function U depends only on $(y_1, \ldots, y_{K-1})$, and not on y_K :

$$V(y_1, \ldots, y_K, \varepsilon_1, \ldots, \varepsilon_{K-1}) = U(y_1, \ldots, y_{K-1}) + \sum_{k=1}^{K-1} \varepsilon_k y_k + y_K.$$

The first-order conditions for the maximization of U subject to the constraint that $y_K = I - \sum_{k=1}^{K-1} y_k p_k$, in this case, have the much more simplified form:

$$\varepsilon_1 = p_1 - U_1(y_1, \dots, y_{K-1})$$
$$\varepsilon_2 = p_2 - U_2(y_1, \dots, y_{K-1})$$
$$\cdots$$
$$\varepsilon_{K-1} = p_{K-1} - U_{K-1}(y_1, \dots, y_{K-1}).$$

The optimal quantities of $y_1, \dots, y_{K-1}$ depend on prices, p, and unobservable tastes, $(\varepsilon_1, \dots, \varepsilon_{K-1})$, only through the vector $(p_1 - \varepsilon_1, \dots, p_{K-1} - \varepsilon_{K-1})$. The strict concavity of U imply that this system has a unique solution, which is of the form

$$y_1 = d_1(p_1 - \varepsilon_1, \dots, p_{K-1} - \varepsilon_{K-1})$$
$$y_2 = d_2(p_1 - \varepsilon_1, \dots, p_{K-1} - \varepsilon_{K-1})$$
$$\cdots$$
$$y_{K-1} = d_{K-1}(p_1 - \varepsilon_1, \dots, p_{K-1} - \varepsilon_{K-1}).$$

Beckert and Blundell (2005) consider more general utility functions, whose demands are invertible in the unobservable variables.

A very important question in demand models is whether one can recover the distribution of tastes and the utility function U, from the distribution of demand. The answer is much easier to obtain when demand depends on one unobservable taste than when it depends on many unobservable tastes. The first case typically occurs when the number of commodities is two. The latter typically occurs when this number of larger than two.

2.1.2   Identification When $K = 2$

As Example 1 illustrates, in some circumstances, when the number of commodities is 2, it is possible to restrict the utility function to guarantee that the demand function for one of those commodities is strictly increasing in a unique unobservable taste variable, ε. In such a case, the analysis of nonparametric identification of the demand function and the distribution of ε can proceed using the methods developed in Matzkin (1999, 2003). The general situation considered in Matzkin (1999) is one where the value of an observable dependent variable, Y, is determined by an observable vector of explanatory variables, X, and an unobservable variable, ε, both arguments in a nonparametric function $m(X, \varepsilon)$. It is assumed that m is strictly increasing in ε, over the support of ε, and ε is distributed independently of X. Under these conditions, the unknown function m and the unknown distribution, F_ε, of ε satisfy for every x, ε, the equation

$$F_\varepsilon(\varepsilon) = F_{Y|X=x}(m(y, \varepsilon))$$

where $F_{Y|X=x}$ denotes the conditional distribution of Y given $X = x$. (see Matzkin, 1999). In our particular case, we can let Y denote the observable demand for one of the two commodities, $X = (p, I)$ denote the vector of observable explanatory variables, and ε denote the unobservable taste. Hence, if the demand is strictly increasing in ε, it follows by analogy that, for all (p, I) and ε,

$$F_\varepsilon(\varepsilon) = F_{Y|p,I}(d(p, I, \varepsilon))$$

where F_ε is the cumulative distribution of ε and $F_{Y|p,I}$ is the cumulative distribution of Y given (p, I). It is clear from this functional equation that without any further restrictions, it is not possible to identify both, F_ε and d, nonparametrically.

2.1.2.1 Normalizations. One approach that can be used to deal with the non-identification of the unknown functions is to specify a normalization for one of them. For this, it is convenient to first determine, for any pair, (d, F_ε), the set of pairs, $(\tilde{d}, F_{\tilde\varepsilon})$, which are observationally equivalent to (d, F_ε). We say that $(\tilde{d}, F_{\tilde\varepsilon})$ is *observationally equivalent* to (d, F_ε) if the distribution of Y given (p, I) generated by $(\tilde{d}, F_{\tilde\varepsilon})$ equals almost surely, in (p, I), the distribution of Y given (p, I) generated by (d, F_ε).

We assume, as above, that d and $\tilde{d}$ are strictly increasing in ε and $\tilde\varepsilon$, over their respective convex supports E and $\tilde{E}$, and that ε and $\tilde\varepsilon$ are distributed independently of X. Moreover, we will assume that F_ε and $F_{\tilde\varepsilon}$ are continuous. We can characterize d and $\tilde{d}$ by their inverse functions, v and $\tilde{v}$, defined by $y = d(p, I, v(y, p, I))$ and $y = \tilde{d}(p, I, \tilde{v}(y, p, I))$. Then, by the analysis in Matzkin (2003), it follows that, under our assumptions, $(\tilde{d}, F_{\tilde\varepsilon})$ is observationally equivalent to (d, F_ε) iff for some continuous and strictly increasing $g : E \to \tilde{E}$,

$$\tilde{v}(y, p, I) = g(v(y, p, I)) \quad \text{and} \quad F_{\tilde\varepsilon}(e) = F_\varepsilon\left(g^{-1}(e)\right).$$

This implies that the function d is identified up to a strictly increasing transformation of ε. Or, in other words, that the function d can be identified only up to the ordering of the values of ε. In particular, if on a given budget set, the demand for the commodity of one individual is different than the demand for the same commodity of another individual, then, one can identify which of the individuals has a larger value of ε, but one cannot identify the actual values of their corresponding tastes ε.

The implication of this analysis is that to select from each set of observationally equivalent pairs, a unique pair, one needs to impose restrictions on the set of functions v guaranteeing that no two functions can be expressed as strictly increasing transformations of each other. Alternatively, one may impose restrictions on the set of distributions guaranteeing that the random variables corresponding to any two distributions are not strictly increasing transformations of each other.

To normalize the set of inverse functions so that no two functions are strictly increasing transformations of each other, Matzkin (1999) proposed restricting all inverse functions v to satisfy that, at some value of the vector of explanatory variables, $(\overline{p}, \overline{I})$, and for all y,

$$v(y, \overline{p}, \overline{I}) = y.$$

This guarantees that if $\widetilde{v}$ is such that for some strictly increasing g and for all y, p, I

$$\widetilde{v}(y, p, I) = g(v(y, p, I)), \quad \text{and} \quad \widetilde{v}(y, \overline{p}, \overline{I}) = y$$

then $\widetilde{v} = v$. The demand functions corresponding to inverse functions satisfying the above restriction satisfy for all $\widetilde{\varepsilon}$,

$$\widetilde{d}(\overline{p}, \overline{I}, \widetilde{\varepsilon}) = \widetilde{\varepsilon}.$$

Hence, as long as one restricts the set of demand functions $\widetilde{d}$ to be such that at one budget $\left(\overline{p}, \overline{I}\right)$, for all values of $\widetilde{\varepsilon}$

$$\widetilde{d}(\overline{p}, \overline{I}, \widetilde{\varepsilon}) = \widetilde{\varepsilon}$$

it will not be possible to find two demand functions, d and $\widetilde{d}$ and two distributions F_ε and $F_{\widetilde{\varepsilon}}$, such that (d, F_ε) and $(\widetilde{d}, F_{\widetilde{\varepsilon}})$ are observationally equivalent. This normalization can be seen as a generalization of a linear demand with additive unobservables. In the latter, when the value of the explanatory variables equals zero, demand equals the value of the unobservable random term, after restricting the intercept of the linear function to be zero. (Note that we are not restricting the expectation of ε to be zero, as it is typically done in linear models. Hence assuming a zero intercept is not more restrictive than the standard assumption made in linear models.)

Under the above normalization, the distribution of ε can be read off from the distribution of the demand when $(p, I) = (\overline{p}, \overline{I})$. Specifically,

$$F_\varepsilon(e) = F_{Y|(p,I)=(\overline{p},\overline{I})}(e).$$

Then, for any $\widetilde{p}, \widetilde{I}, \widetilde{e}$

$$d\left(\widetilde{p}, \widetilde{I}, \widetilde{e}\right) = F_{Y|(p,I)=(\widetilde{p},\widetilde{I})}^{-1}\left(F_{Y|(p,I)=(\overline{p},\overline{I})}(\widetilde{e})\right).$$

Alternatively, one can specify the distribution of ε. In such case,

$$d\left(\widetilde{p}, \widetilde{I}, \widetilde{e}\right) = F_{Y|(p,I)=(\widetilde{p},\widetilde{I})}^{-1}\left(F_\varepsilon(\widetilde{e})\right).$$

In particular, when F_ε is the distribution of a $U(0, 1)$ random variable, the demand function is a conditional quantile function, whose estimation has been extensively studied. [See Imbens and Newey (2001) for the use of this normalization and Koenker (2005) for estimation methods for conditional quantiles.]

2.1.2.2 Restrictions. In some cases, economic theory might imply some properties on either the unknown function, d, or the unknown distribution, F_ε. These restrictions might allow us to identify these functions with fewer normalizations. Suppose, for example, that $V(y_1, y_2, \varepsilon) = \tilde{V}(y_1, y_2 + \varepsilon)$ for some function $\tilde{V}$. The demand function for $Y = y_1$ derived from such a utility function can be shown to have the form $d(p, I + \varepsilon)$, when p is the price of one unit of y_1 and the price of one unit of y_2 is normalized to 1. In this case, we can identify the demand function d and the distribution of ε by only normalizing the value of the demand function at one point, for example, $d(\bar{p}, \bar{\imath}) = \bar{y}$. In such a case, F_ε can be recovered from the distribution of demand at different values of income

$$F_\varepsilon(\varepsilon) = F_{Y|p=\bar{p}, I=\bar{\imath}-\varepsilon}(\bar{y})$$

and then, for any $(\tilde{p}, \tilde{I}, \varepsilon)$

$$d(\tilde{p}, \tilde{I} + \varepsilon) = F_{Y|(p,I)=(\tilde{p},\tilde{I})}^{-1}\left(F_{Y|\bar{p}, I=\bar{\imath}-\varepsilon}(\bar{y})\right).$$

2.1.2.3 Functionals of the Demand. Rather than considering different normalizations or restrictions, which would allow us to identify the unknown functions and distributions in the model, we might ask what can be identified without them. For example, given a consumer with unobservable taste ε, we might want to determine by how much his consumption would change if his budget set changed from $B(\tilde{p}, \tilde{I})$ to $B(p', I')$. This change in demand can be identified without normalizations or restrictions on the unknown functions, other than assuming that ε is distributed independently of (p, I), the demand function is strictly increasing in ε, and F_ε is strictly increasing at ε. Specifically,

$$d(p', I', \varepsilon) - d(\tilde{p}, \tilde{I}, \varepsilon)$$
$$= F_{Y|(p,I)=(p',I')}^{-1}\left(F_{Y|(p,I)=(\tilde{p},\tilde{I})}(y_1)\right) - y_1$$

where y_1 is the observed consumption of the individual when his budget is (p, I) (see Matzkin, 2006). When to the above assumptions one adds differentiability, one can obtain, using arguments as in Matzkin (1999) and Chesher (2003) that

$$\frac{\partial d(\tilde{p}, \tilde{I}, \varepsilon)}{\partial(p, I)}$$
$$= -\left[\frac{\partial F_{Y|(p,I)=(\tilde{p},\tilde{I})}(d(\tilde{p}, \tilde{I}, \varepsilon))}{\partial y}\right]^{-1} \frac{\partial F_{Y|(p,I)=(\tilde{p},\tilde{I})}(d(\tilde{p}, \tilde{I}, \varepsilon))}{\partial(p, I)}.$$

[See also Altonji and Matzkin (1997) and Athey and Imbens (2006) for related expressions.]

2.1.3   Identification When $K > 2$

When the number of unobservable taste variables, $\varepsilon_1, \ldots, \varepsilon_{K-1}$, is larger than one, the demand function for each commodity typically depends on all these unobservable variables. For example, in individual consumer demand, the chosen quantity of entertainment will depend on the taste of the individual for housing, since spending a large amount in housing will typically decrease the amount spent in entertainment. If one could impose some type of separability, so that the demand function depended on a one-dimensional function of the unobservables, then the methods for $K = 2$ might be used. When, however, this is not desirable, one needs to consider identification of functions whose arguments are unobservable. The analysis of identification in this case may be performed using results about identification of nonparametric simultaneous equations.

Roehrig (1988), following the approach in Brown (1983), established a rank condition for nonparametric simultaneous equations, which when satisfied, guarantees that the model is not identified. Benkard and Berry (2004) showed that when Roehrig's rank condition is not satisfied, the model might not be identified. Matzkin (2005) developed a different rank condition, which can be used to determine identification of simultaneous equation models, in general, and of system of demands, in particular. Other methods that have been recently developed to either identify or estimate equations in systems with simultaneity are Newey and Powell (1989, 2003), Brown and Matzkin (1998), Darolles, Florens, and Renault (2002), Hall and Horowitz (2003), Ai and Chen (2003), Matzkin (2004), Chernozhukov, Imbens, and Newey (2004), and Chernozhukov and Hansen (2005).

We follow Matzkin (2005). Assume that the first-order conditions for utility maximization subject to the budget constraint can be solved for ε, in terms of (y, p, I). Then, the model can be expressed as

$$\varepsilon = r(y, p, I).$$

We will assume that r is twice differentiable in (y, p, I), invertible in y, and the Jacobian determinant of r with respect to y, $|\partial r(y, p, I)/\partial y|$, is > 0. The later is the extension to multidimensional situations of the monotonicity requirement in the single equation, univariate unobservable demand function $d(p, I, \varepsilon)$ analyzed above for the case where $K = 2$. In the $K = 2$ case, it was only necessary to require that d be strictly increasing in ε.

To analyze identification in the $K > 2$ case, we can proceed as in the $K = 2$ case, by first characterizing the sets of pairs (r, f_ε), $(\tilde{r}, f_{\tilde{\varepsilon}})$ that are observationally equivalent among them. We assume that ε and $\tilde{\varepsilon}$ are distributed independently of (p, I) with differentiable densities f_ε and $f_{\tilde{\varepsilon}}$, that $\tilde{r}$ is twice differentiable in (y, p, I), invertible in y, and with Jacobian determinant with respect to y, $|\partial\tilde{r}(y, p, I)/\partial y| > 0$. We will also assume that (p, I) has a differentiable density and convex support. Under these conditions, we can say that the pairs (r, f_ε) and $(\tilde{r}, f_{\tilde{\varepsilon}})$ are *observationally equivalent* if for all y, p, I

$$f_\varepsilon(r(y, p, I)) \left| \frac{\partial r(y, p, I)}{\partial y} \right| = f_{\tilde{\varepsilon}}(\tilde{r}(y, p, I)) \left| \frac{\partial \tilde{r}(y, p, I)}{\partial y} \right|$$

This is clear because, when this condition is satisfied, both pairs (r, f_ε) and $(\tilde{r}, f_{\tilde{\varepsilon}})$ generate the same conditional densities, $f_{y|(p,I)}$, of y given (p, I). Under our assumptions, the distribution of y given p, I, which is generated by (r, f_ε) is

$$f_{y|p,I}(y) = f_\varepsilon(r(y, p, I)) \left| \frac{\partial r(y, p, I)}{\partial y} \right|$$

and this equals the conditional distribution of $f_{y|p,I}$ generated by $(\tilde{r}, f_{\tilde{\varepsilon}})$.

Example 2 *Suppose that for a twice differentiable, 1-1 function $g : E \to \tilde{E}$, with Jacobian determinant $|\partial g(\varepsilon)/\partial \varepsilon| > 0$*

$$\tilde{r}(y, p, I) = g(r(y, p, I)) \quad and \quad \tilde{\varepsilon} = g(\varepsilon)$$

where $E \subset R^{K-1}$ is the convex support of ε, and $E \subset R^{K-1}$, then, $(\tilde{r}, f_{\tilde{\varepsilon}})$ is observationally equivalent to (r, f_ε).

To see this, note that in this case

$$\tilde{\varepsilon} = g(\varepsilon) = g(r(y, p, I)) = \tilde{r}(y, p, I).$$

Using the relationship $\tilde{\varepsilon} = g(\varepsilon)$, to derive the distribution of ε from that of $\tilde{\varepsilon}$, and substituting $\tilde{r}(y, p, I)$ for $g(\varepsilon)$, we get that

$$f_\varepsilon(\varepsilon) = f_{\tilde{\varepsilon}}(g(\varepsilon)) \left| \frac{\partial g(\varepsilon)}{\partial \varepsilon} \right| = f_{\tilde{\varepsilon}}(\tilde{r}(y, p, I)) \left| \frac{\partial g(r(y, p, I))}{\partial \varepsilon} \right|.$$

Using the relationship $\tilde{r}(y, p, I) = g(r(y, p, I))$, we also get that

$$\left| \frac{\partial \tilde{r}(y, p, I)}{\partial y} \right| = \left| \frac{\partial g(r(y, p, I))}{\partial y} \right| = \left| \frac{\partial g(r(y, p, I))}{\partial \varepsilon} \right| \left| \frac{\partial r(y, p, I)}{\partial y} \right|.$$

Hence,

$$f_\varepsilon(r(y, p, I)) \left| \frac{\partial r(y, p, I)}{\partial y} \right| = f_{\tilde{\varepsilon}}(\tilde{r}(y, p, I)) \left| \frac{\partial \tilde{r}(y, p, I)}{\partial y} \right|. \qquad \blacksquare$$

Example 2 shows that invertible transformations, g, of $r(y, p, I)$, satisfying $|\partial g(\varepsilon)/\partial \varepsilon| > 0$, together with the associated vector of unobservables $\tilde{\varepsilon} = g(\varepsilon)$, generate pairs $(\tilde{r}, f_{\tilde{\varepsilon}})$ that are observationally equivalent to (r, f_ε). One may wonder, as Benkard and Berry (2004) did, whether invertible transformations that depend on the observable exogenous variables, (p, I), as well as on ε might also generate pairs, $(\tilde{r}, f_{\tilde{\varepsilon}})$, that are observationally equivalent to (r, f_ε). When $K = 2$, this is not possible, in general. Strictly increasing transformation of ε that also depends on $x = (p, I)$ will generate a random variable,

$\tilde{\varepsilon} = g(\varepsilon, x)$, which is not distributed independently of (p, I). [Example 3.3 in Matzkin (2005) provides a proof of this. See also Matzkin (2003).] Hence, when the number of commodities is 2, one can guarantee identification of the true pair (f_ε, r) in a set of pairs $(f_{\tilde{\varepsilon}}, \tilde{r})$ by eliminating from that set all pairs $(f_{\tilde{\varepsilon}}, \tilde{r})$ that are obtained by strictly increasing transformations, g, of ε. When, however, $K > 2$, invertible transformations of ε that depend on (p, I) might generate pairs that are also observationally equivalent to (r, f_ε). For general simultaneous equation models, this claim was recently shown by Benkard and Berry (2004, 2006).

Example 3 (Benkard and Berry, 2006). *Consider a simultaneous equation model with $\varepsilon \in R^2$ and*

$$\varepsilon = r(y, x)$$

where $y \in R^2$ is the vector of observable endogenous variables and $x \in R$ is a vector of observable exogenous variables. Suppose that ε is $N(0, I)$ and let

$$\tilde{\varepsilon} = g(\varepsilon, x) = \Gamma(x)'\varepsilon$$

where $\Gamma(x)$ is an orthonormal matrix that is a smooth function of x. Then, $\tilde{\varepsilon}$ is $N\left(0, \Gamma(x)'\Gamma(x)\right) = N(0, I)$. Let

$$\tilde{r}(y, x) = \Gamma(x)'r(y, x).$$

Then,

$$(r, f_\varepsilon) \text{ and } (\tilde{r}, f_{\tilde{\varepsilon}}) \text{ are observationally equivalent.}$$

To see this, note that for all y, x

$$
\begin{aligned}
f_{Y|X=x}(y) &= f_\varepsilon \left(r(y, x)\right) \left| \frac{\partial r(y, x)}{\partial y} \right| \\
&= (2\pi)^{-1} \exp\left(-\frac{\left(r(y, x)'r(y, x)\right)}{2} \right) \left| \frac{\partial r(y, x)}{\partial y} \right| \\
&= (2\pi)^{-1} \exp\left(-\frac{\left(r(y, x)'\Gamma(x)'\Gamma(x)r(y, x)\right)}{2} \right) |\Gamma(x)| \left| \frac{\partial r(y, x)}{\partial y} \right| \\
&= (2\pi)^{-1} \exp\left(-\frac{\left(\tilde{r}(y, x)'\tilde{r}(y, x)\right)}{2} \right) \left| \frac{\partial \tilde{r}(y, x)}{\partial y} \right| \\
&= f_{\tilde{\varepsilon}} \left(\tilde{r}(y, x)\right) \left| \frac{\partial \tilde{r}(y, x)}{\partial y} \right|.
\end{aligned}
$$

Hence, (f_ε, r) and $(f_{\tilde{\varepsilon}}, \tilde{r})$ are observationally equivalent. ∎

Conditions for identification in nonparametric simultaneous equations with nonadditive unobservables were provided by Matzkin (2005). To describe these results, let X denote the vector of observable exogenous variables. Let r^*, f_{ε^*} denote the true function and true distribution. Denote by P a set of functions to which r^* is assumed to belong, and denote by Γ the set of densities to which f_{ε^*} is assumed to belong. Assume that all functions $r \in P$ are such that (i) r is twice continuously differentiable, (ii) for all y, x, $|\partial r(y, x)/\partial y| > 0$, and (iii) for all $x, \widetilde{\varepsilon}$ there exists a unique $\widetilde{y}$ satisfying $\widetilde{\varepsilon} = \widetilde{r}(\widetilde{y}, x)$. Assume that the vector of observable exogenous variables, X, has a differentiable density, f_X, and convex support in R^K. Further, assume that for all $f_\varepsilon \in \Gamma$, f_ε is continuously differentiable and with convex support; and that for all $r \in P$ and all $f_\varepsilon \in \Gamma$, the distribution of Y given $X = x$, which is generated by r and f_ε, is continuously differentiable and has convex support in R^G. Then, by Matzkin (2005) it follows that.

Theorem   (Matzkin, 2005). *Under the above assumptions (r^*, f_{ε^*}) is identified within $(P \times \Gamma)$ if for all $r, \widetilde{r} \in P$, such that $r \neq \widetilde{r}$, and all $f_\varepsilon \in \Gamma$, there exists a value of (y, x) at which the density of (y, x) is strictly positive and the rank of the matrix*

$$
B(y, x; r, \widetilde{r}, f_\varepsilon)
$$
$$
= \left(\begin{array}{l} \left(\dfrac{\partial \widetilde{r}(y, x)}{\partial y} \right)' \Delta_y\left(y, x; \partial r, \partial^2 r, \partial \widetilde{r}, \partial^2 \widetilde{r}\right) - \dfrac{\partial \log(f_\varepsilon(r(y, x)))}{\partial \varepsilon} \dfrac{\partial r(y, x)}{\partial y} \\[3mm] \left(\dfrac{\partial \widetilde{r}(y, x)}{\partial x} \right)' \Delta_x\left(y, x; \partial r, \partial^2 r, \partial \widetilde{r}, \partial^2 \widetilde{r}\right) - \dfrac{\partial \log(f_\varepsilon(r(y, x)))}{\partial \varepsilon} \dfrac{\partial r(y, x)}{\partial x} \end{array} \right)
$$

is strictly larger than G, where

$$
\Delta_y\left(y, x; \partial r, \partial^2 r, \partial \widetilde{r}, \partial^2 \widetilde{r}\right) = \frac{\partial}{\partial y} \log \left| \frac{\partial r(y, x)}{\partial y} \right| - \frac{\partial}{\partial y} \log \left| \frac{\partial \widetilde{r}(y, x)}{\partial y} \right|
$$
$$
\Delta_x\left(y, x; \partial r, \partial^2 r, \partial \widetilde{r}, \partial^2 \widetilde{r}\right) = \frac{\partial}{\partial x} \log \left| \frac{\partial r(y, x)}{\partial y} \right| - \frac{\partial}{\partial x} \log \left| \frac{\partial \widetilde{r}(y, x)}{\partial y} \right|.
$$

∎

The following example applies this result to a random utility model where the utility function is of the type considered in Brown and Calsamiglia (2003).

Example 4   *Suppose that the utility for a consumer with tastes ε is*

$$
V(y_1, \ldots, y_K, \varepsilon_1, \ldots, \varepsilon_{K-1}) = U(y_1, \ldots, y_{K-1}) + \sum_{k=1}^{K-1} \varepsilon_k y_k + y_K.
$$

Denote the gradient of U by DU and the Hessian of U by $D^2 U$. Let $\overline{y}$ denote a value of y. For fixed $\alpha \in R^{K-1}$ and $\Lambda \in R$, let W denote the set of functions U such that $DU(\overline{y}) = \alpha$ and $|D^2 U(\overline{y})| = \Lambda$. Let ε^* denote a value of ε. Let Γ denote the set of densities, f_ε, such that (i) f_ε is differentiable, (ii) $f_\varepsilon(\varepsilon) > 0$ on a neighborhood of radius δ around ε^*, (iii) for all ε in the support of f_ε, $\partial \log(f_\varepsilon(\varepsilon))\partial \varepsilon = 0$ iff $\varepsilon = \varepsilon^*$, (iv) for all k, there exist two distinct values, ε' and ε'', in the δ-neighborhood of ε^* such that $f_\varepsilon(\varepsilon')$, $f_\varepsilon(\varepsilon'') > 0$, $\partial f_\varepsilon(\varepsilon')/\partial \varepsilon_k$, $\partial f_\varepsilon(\varepsilon'')/\partial \varepsilon_k \neq 0$, $\partial \log(f_\varepsilon(\varepsilon'))\partial \varepsilon_k \neq \partial \log(f_\varepsilon(\varepsilon'')/\partial \varepsilon_k$, and for $j \neq k$, $\partial \log(f_\varepsilon(\varepsilon'))\partial \varepsilon_j = \partial \log(f_\varepsilon(\varepsilon'')/\partial \varepsilon_j = 0$.

Let W and the support of p be such for all y, for all $U \in W$, there exist a set of prices, Q, such that the density of p is uniformly bounded away from zero on Q and the range of $DU(y) - p$, when considered as a function of p over Q, is the δ neighborhood of ε^*. Then, if U, $\tilde{U}$ belong to W and $D\tilde{U} \neq DU$, there exist, for all $f_\varepsilon \in \Gamma$, values y, p such that the rank of the matrix $B\left(y, p; DU, D\tilde{U}, f_\varepsilon\right)$ is larger than $K - 1$.

The proof of this result can be obtained by modifying an analogous theorem in Brown and Matzkin (1998).

2.1.4   Recovering the Distribution of Utility Functions When $K > 2$.

An implication of the last example is that, if the observable price vector p has an appropriate support and the utility function is given by

$$V(y_1, \ldots, y_K, \varepsilon_1, \ldots, \varepsilon_{K-1}) = U(y_1, \ldots, y_{K-1}) + \sum_{k=1}^{K-1} y_k \cdot \varepsilon_k + y_K \qquad (2.2)$$

then, the rank conditions for nonparametric identification of U and f_ε are satisfied. Under those conditions, we can constructively recover $DU(y)$ and f_ε from the distribution of demand, by applying the results in Section 6 of Matzkin (2005). [See Matzkin (2006).]

Example 4 (continued). Suppose that given any budget set (p, I), each consumer with unobservable tastes $(\varepsilon_1, \ldots, \varepsilon_{K-1})$ chooses his demand by maximizing $V(y_1, \ldots, y_K, \varepsilon_1, \ldots, \varepsilon_{K-1})$, as in (2.2), subject to $p \cdot y \leq I$. Let $f_{Y|p,I}$ denote the density of demand generated by the density of ε, over the budget set determined by (p, I). Suppose that U belongs to the set W, and f_ε belongs to the set of densities Γ. Then, the density of ε and the gradient, $DU(y)$, of U, can be recovered from $f_{Y|p,I}$, as long as this conditional density is strictly positive at the values from which DU and f_ε are recovered. In particular, for $(t_1, \ldots, t_{K-1})$,

$$f_\varepsilon(t_1, \ldots, t_{K-1}) = f_{Y|p_1=t_1+\alpha_1, \ldots, p_{K-1}=t_{K-1}+\alpha_{K-1}, I}(\overline{y}) \Lambda^{-1}$$

and for y,

$$DU(y) = p^* - \varepsilon^*$$

where p^* is the value of p that satisfies

$$\frac{\partial f_{Y|p=p^*,I}(y)}{\partial p} = 0.$$

2.2   Linear Choice Sets, Income Variation, No Price Variation

A critical requirement in the identification results in the previous section is that, given any bundle of commodities and any value for the marginal utility, one could always observe a price vector with the value necessary to identify that marginal utility. That requires a large support condition on these variables. In most situations, however, that large support condition is not satisfied. In fact, it is often the case that the available data corresponds to only a few values of prices. Blundell, Browning, and Crawford (2003) deal with this situation by ingeniously making use of observations on income. They note that, although the data corresponds to only a few price vectors, income across different individuals has a large support. They use this to estimate the income expansion paths of the average consumer. Assuming that the average consumer behaves as if maximizing a utility function, they use these choices to determine bounds on the demand of this average consumer on previously unobserved budget sets. These bounds are determined from reveled preference (see also Blundell, Browning, and Crawford, 2004, 2005; Blundell, Chen, and Kristensen, 2003).

2.2.1   Bounds on the Derivative of the Distribution of Demand with Respect to Price

The assumption that the average consumer behaves as if maximizing a utility function might be too restrictive in some circumstances. Blundell and Matzkin (2005) and Blundell, Kristensen, and Matzkin (2005) analyze what can be said when it is only assumed that each consumer acts as if maximizing a utility. No specific restrictions are imposed on the average consumer. In other words, they consider a population of consumers such that each consumer possesses a utility function

$$V(y, \varepsilon).$$

On each budget set, characterized by a price vector, p, and an income I, the distribution of ε generates a distribution of demand over the budget set determined by p and I. This gives rise, as in the previous sections, to a system of demand functions

$$y_1 = d_1(p, I, \varepsilon_1, \ldots, \varepsilon_{K-1})$$
$$y_2 = d_2(p, I, \varepsilon_1, \ldots, \varepsilon_{K-1})$$

$$\ldots$$

$$y_{K-1} = d_{K-1}(p, I, \varepsilon_1, \ldots, \varepsilon_{K-1}),$$

which, for each (p, I) and $(\varepsilon_1, \ldots, \varepsilon_{K-1})$, solve the maximization of $V(y, \varepsilon)$ subject to the budget constraint. Assuming that the system is invertible in $(\varepsilon_1, \ldots, \varepsilon_{K-1})$, we can express it as

$$\varepsilon_1 = r_1(p, I, y_1, \ldots, y_{K-1})$$
$$\varepsilon_2 = r_2(p, I, y_1, \ldots, y_{K-1})$$
$$\cdots$$
$$\varepsilon_{K-1} = r_{K-1}(p, I, y_1, \ldots, y_{K-1})$$

Making use of the variation in income, together with the implications of the Slutsky conditions for optimization, Blundell and Matzkin (2005) obtain bounds on the unobservable derivative of the density of demand with respect to price.

To provide an example of the type of restrictions that one can obtain, consider again the $K = 2$ case. Let $d(p, I, \varepsilon)$ denote the demand function for one of the commodities. If this demand function is generated from the maximization of a twice differentiable, strictly quasiconcave utility function, it satisfies the Slutsky condition

$$\frac{\partial d(p, I, \varepsilon)}{\partial p} + d(p, I, \varepsilon)\frac{\partial d(p, I, \varepsilon)}{\partial I} \leq 0.$$

Under the assumptions in Section 2.1.2.3, the derivative of the demand with respect to income, of a consumer that is observed demanding $y = d(p, I, \varepsilon)$ can be recovered from the distribution of demand over budget sets with a common price vector, p, and different income levels, I, by

$$\frac{\partial d(p, I, \varepsilon)}{\partial I} = \left(\frac{\partial F_{Y|(p,I)}(y)}{\partial y}\right)^{-1}\left(\frac{\partial F_{Y|(p,I)}(y)}{\partial I}\right).$$

Hence, an upper bound on the derivative of the demand with respect to price of a consumer that demands y at prices p and income I is given by

$$\frac{\partial d(p, I, \varepsilon)}{\partial p} \leq -y\left(\frac{\partial F_{Y|(p,I)}(y)}{\partial y}\right)^{-1}\left(\frac{\partial F_{Y|(p,I)}(y)}{\partial I}\right).$$

Note that ε need not be known to obtain such an expression.

2.2.2   Representation of Demand

In some cases, one may be able to analyze demand by using a representation of the system of demand. Blundell, Kristensen, and Matzkin (2005) consider one such representation. Suppose, as above, that the system of demand functions is given by

$$y_1 = d_1(p, I, \varepsilon_1, \ldots, \varepsilon_{K-1})$$
$$y_2 = d_2(p, I, \varepsilon_1, \ldots, \varepsilon_{K-1})$$
$$\cdots$$
$$y_{K-1} = d_{K-1}(p, I, \varepsilon_1, \ldots, \varepsilon_{K-1}),$$

A representation of this system, in terms of a different vector of unobservable variables, $(\eta_1, \ldots, \eta_{K-1})$, can be obtained by defining these unobservables sequentially as

$$\eta_1 = F_{Y_1|p,I}(y_1)$$

$$\eta_2 = F_{Y_2|\eta_1,p,I}(y_2)$$

$$\cdots$$

$$\eta_{K-1} = F_{Y_{K-1}|\eta_1,\eta_2,\ldots,\eta_{K-1},p,I}(y_{K-1})$$

where $F_{Y_1|p,I}$ is the conditional distribution of Y_1 given (p, I), $F_{Y_2|\eta_1,p,I}(y_2)$ is the conditional distribution of Y_2 given (η_1, p, I), and so on. [McFadden (1985) and Benkard and Berry (2004) previously considered also using this type of representations for simultaneous equation models.]

By construction, the system

$$y_1 = F^{-1}_{y_1|p,I}(\eta_1)$$

$$y_2 = F^{-1}_{y_1|p,I}(\eta_1, \eta_2)$$

$$\cdots$$

$$y_{K-1} = F^{-1}_{y_1|p,I}(\eta_1, \eta_2, \ldots, \eta_{K-1})$$

is observationally equivalent to

$$y_1 = d_1(p, I, \varepsilon_1, \ldots, \varepsilon_{K-1})$$

$$y_2 = d_2(p, I, \varepsilon_1, \ldots, \varepsilon_{K-1})$$

$$\cdots$$

$$y_{K-1} = d_{K-1}(p, I, \varepsilon_1, \ldots, \varepsilon_{K-1}).$$

Assuming that (p, I) has an appropriate large support, the connection between both systems can be analyzed using Theorem 3.1 in Matzkin (2005). Denote the mapping from (η, p, I) to y by

$$y = s(\eta, p, I)$$

and the mapping from (y, p, I) to ε by

$$\varepsilon = r(y, p, I).$$

Define the mapping by

$$\varepsilon = g(\eta, p, I)$$
$$= r(s(\eta, p, I), p, I).$$

Then, by Theorem 3.1 in Matzkin (2005),

$$
\left[-\frac{\partial \log(f_\eta(\eta))}{\partial \eta} + \frac{\partial}{\partial \eta} \log \left(\left| \frac{\partial g(\eta, p, I)}{\partial \eta} \right| \right) \right] \left[\left(\frac{\partial g(\eta, p, I)}{\partial \eta} \right)^{-1} \frac{\partial g(\eta, p, I)}{\partial (p, I)} \right]
$$

$$
= \frac{\partial}{\partial (p, I)} \log \left(\left| \frac{\partial g(\eta, p, I)}{\partial \eta} \right| \right).
$$

Making use of the relationships $g(\eta, p, I) = r(s(\eta, p, I), p, I)$ and $y = s(\eta, p, I)$, this expression can be written solely in terms of the unknown elements

$$
\frac{\partial r(y, p, I)}{\partial y}, \ \frac{\partial r(y, p, I)}{\partial (p, I)}, \ \frac{\partial}{\partial y} \log \left(\left| \frac{\partial r(y, p, I)}{\partial y} \right| \right), \ \text{and}
$$

$$
\frac{\partial}{\partial (p, I)} \log \left(\left| \frac{\partial r(y, p, I)}{\partial y} \right| \right)
$$

and the known elements

$$
\frac{\partial \log(f_\eta(\eta))}{\partial \eta}, \ \frac{\partial s(\eta, p, I)}{\partial \eta}, \ \frac{\partial s(\eta, p, I)}{\partial (p, I)},
$$

$$
\frac{\partial}{\partial \eta} \log \left(\left| \frac{\partial s(\eta, p, I)}{\partial \eta} \right| \right), \quad \text{and} \quad \frac{\partial}{\partial (p, I)} \log \left(\left| \frac{\partial s(\eta, p, I)}{\partial \eta} \right| \right).
$$

The latter group is known because s is constructed from the conditional distribution functions. One can then use the resulting expression, which contains the elements of both groups, to determine properties of the derivatives of the function r.

2.3   Linear Choice Sets, No Price Variation or Income Variation

In some cases, we may observe no variation in either prices or income. Only one budget set together with a distribution of choices over it is available for analysis. This is a similar problem to that considered in the hedonic models studied by Ekeland, Heckman, and Nesheim (2004) and Heckman, Matzkin, and Nesheim (2002), where observations correspond to only one price function, and consumers and firm locate along that function. Rather than using identification due to variation in prices, they achieve identification exploiting variation in observable characteristics. We next exemplify their method in the consumer demand model. Suppose that $z = (z_1, \ldots, z_{K-1})$ is a vector of observable characteristics. In analogy to the piecewise linear specification in the previous section, suppose that the random utility function is

$$
V(y_1, \ldots, y_K, \varepsilon_1, \ldots, \varepsilon_{K-1}, z_1, \ldots, z_{K-1})
$$

$$
= U(y_1, \ldots, y_{K-1}) + \sum_{k=1}^{K-1} y_k \cdot (\varepsilon_k + z_k) + y_K.
$$

Then, the first-order conditions for utility maximization are

$$\varepsilon_k = p_k - U_k(y_1, \dots, y_{K-1}) - z_k.$$

This is identical to the model in Section 2.1.1 where prices vary, after substituting p_k by $p_k - z_k$. Hence, the analysis of identification is analogous to that in Section 2.1. [See also the related literature on equivalence scales (e.g., Lewbel (1989).]

2.4 Nonlinear Choice Sets

In many situations, budget sets are nonlinear. These can be generated, for example, in the classical consumer demand models by prices that depend on quantities, in the labor supply model by regressive or progressive taxes, or in a characteristics model by feasible combinations of characteristics that can be obtained by existent products. Epstein (1981) provided integrability conditions in this case. Richter (1966), Matzkin (1991a, 1991b), and Yatchew (1985) provided revealed preference results. Hausman (1985) and Bloomquist and Newey (2002), among others, provided methods for estimation of some of these models.

Suppose that the choice problem of a consumer with unobserved ε is to maximize

$$V(y_1, \dots, y_{K-1}, \varepsilon_1, \dots, \varepsilon_{K-1}) + y_K$$
$$\text{subject to} \quad g(y_1, \dots, y_K, w) \leq 0$$

where w is an observable vector of variables (e.g., taxes, income) that affects choice sets and is distributed independently of ε, and for all $y_1, \dots, y_{K-1}, w$, g is strictly increasing in y_K. The first-order conditions for optimization are, for $k = 1, \dots, K-1$

$$V_k(y_1, \dots, y_{K-1}, \varepsilon_1, \dots, \varepsilon_{K-1}) = s_k(y_1, \dots, y_{K-1}, w)$$

where $s(y_1, \dots, y_{K-1}, w) = y_K$ such that $g(y_1, \dots, y_K, w) = 0$, and where s_k denotes the derivative of s with respect to its kth coordinate. (We assume that the solution to the FOC is unique and that second-order conditions are satisfied.)

This is a multidimensional case of the problem considered by Heckman, Matzkin, and Nesheim (2002), when the price function varies with z. Suppose that $DV(y_1, \dots, y_{K-1}, \varepsilon_1, \dots, \varepsilon_{K-1})$ is invertible in $\varepsilon = (\varepsilon_1, \dots, \varepsilon_{K-1})$. Let

$$\varepsilon = r(y_1, \dots, y_{K-1}, s_k(y_1, \dots, y_{K-1}, w)).$$

Consider an alternative gradient function $D\widetilde{V}(y_1, \dots, y_{K-1}, \varepsilon_1, \dots, \varepsilon_{K-1})$, which is also invertible in ε. Denote the inverse function of $D\widetilde{V}$ with respect to ε by $\widetilde{r}$, so that

$$\widetilde{\varepsilon} = \widetilde{r}(y_1, \dots, y_{K-1}, s_k(y_1, \dots, y_{K-1}, w)).$$

Then, again one can use the results in Matzkin (2005) to determine under what conditions $\widetilde{r}$ is not observationally equivalent to r. Constructive identification can be obtained by specifying the utility function as

$$U(y_1, \dots, y_{K-1}) + \sum_{k=1}^{K-1} \varepsilon_k y_k + y_K.$$

In this case, the first-order conditions become

$$\varepsilon = s_k(y_1, \dots, y_{K-1}, w) - U_k(y_1, \dots, y_{K-1}).$$

Specifying the value of the gradient $DU = (U_1, \dots, U_{K-1})$ of U at a point $\bar{y}$ and assuming that for each y and s_k, the value of $s_k(y_1, \dots, y_{K-1}, w)$ has an appropriate large support, as w varies, one can follow a method similar to that discussed in Sections 2.1.3 and 2.1.4 to directly recover f_ε and $DU(y) \equiv (U_1(y), \dots, U_{K-1}(y))$ from the distribution of the observable variables.

If w were not observed varying, this would become a situation like the single market observations in Ekeland, Heckman, and Nesheim (2004) and Heckman, Matzkin, and Nesheim (2002). Rather than exploiting exogenous variation in prices, one exploits exogenous variation in the observable characteristics of the consumers. Suppose, for example, that the choice problem of the consumer with unobserved ε is to maximize

$$U(y_1, \dots, y_{K-1}) + y_K + \sum_{k=1}^{K-1} (z_k + \varepsilon_k) y_k$$
$$\text{subject to} \quad g(y_1, \dots, y_K) \leq 0.$$

The first-order conditions for optimization are, for $k = 1, \dots, K-1$,

$$U_k(y_1, \dots, y_{K-1}) + z_k + \varepsilon_k = s_k(y_1, \dots, y_{K-1})$$

where $s(y_1, \dots, y_{K-1}, z) = y_K$ such that $g(y_1, \dots, y_K, z) = 0$. Hence, variation in the observable characteristics z can be used to recover the gradient of U and the density of ε.

2.5   Restrictions on the Distribution of Choices

Given a distribution of choices, over any type of choice sets, one may ask what restrictions optimization places on this distribution. This question was studied by McFadden and Richter (1970, 1990), Falmange (1978), Cohen (1980), and Barbera and Pattanaik (1986), among others, [see Fishburn (1998)]. Most recently, the issue has been studied by McFadden (2005). In particular, consider a discrete set of alternatives. Let $\tilde{R}$ denote the set of all possible orderings of those alternatives. The following is defined in McFadden and Richter (1990):

Axiom of Stochastic Revealed Preference: For every finite list $\{(B_1, C_1), \dots, (B_k, C_k)\}$ of subsets of alternatives, $C_1, \dots, C_k$, and choices from those alternatives, $B_1, \dots, B_k$,

$$\sum_{i=1}^{k} \pi_{B_i}(C_i) \leq \text{Max} \left\{ \sum_{i=1}^{k} \alpha(R, B_i, C_i) | R \in \tilde{R} \right\}$$

where $\pi_{B_i}(C_i)$ is the probability of choosing B_i from choice set C_i; $\alpha(R, B_i, C_i) = 1$ if ordering R selects B_i from C_i and $\alpha(R, B_i, C_i) = 0$ otherwise.

McFadden and Richter (1970) showed that this axiom is equivalent to the existence of a probability distribution over the space of orderings $\widetilde{R}$. They proved the following.

Theorem (McFadden and Richter, 1970): *The Axiom of Stochastic Revealed Preference is equivalent to the existence of a probability ξ on the space of ordering such that for all orderings $R \in \widetilde{R}$, all choice sets C, and all subsets B of C*

$$\pi_B(C) = \xi\left(\{R \in \widetilde{R} | R \text{ selects an element of } B \text{ from } C\}\right).$$

McFadden (2005) has generalized this result to nondiscrete budget sets. To provide an example of what this result means, consider two budget sets in R_+^2 that intersect. Restrict the set of random preferences to be such that each random preference admits a strictly monotone, strictly concave, and twice differentiable utility function, and the relationship between ε and the choice generated by ε is 1-1. Let A denote the set of points in the first budget line, C_1, that are included in the second budget set. Let B denote the set of points in the second budget line, C_2, that are included in the first budget set. The axiom implies that

$$\pi_A(C_1) + \pi_B(C_2) \le 1.$$

That is, the probability of the set of orderings that choose an element of C_1 plus the probability of the set of orderings that choose an element of C_2 has to be not larger than 1. If this sum were larger than 1, it would imply that the probability of the set of ordering that choose an element of C_1 in A and an element of C_2 in B is strictly positive.

3 DISCRETE CHOICE

In many situations in economics, a consumer's feasible set is only a finite set of alternatives. Discrete choice models (McFadden, 1974) provide the appropriate framework to analyze such situations. In these models, each alternative is characterized by a vector of characteristics. The consumer's utility of each alternative is given by a function, which may depend on observable characteristics of the consumer and the alternative, and on unobservable characteristics of either the consumer, the alternative, or both. It is assumed that the alternative chosen by the consumer is the one that provides the highest level of utility. In a standard textbook example, the available alternatives are to commute to work by either car or bus. The observable characteristics of each means of transportation are its time and its cost. Comfort might be one of the unobservable characteristics. The observable characteristics of the consumer are the number of cars owned by the commuter and his income.

Let J denote the set of feasible alternatives. Let $V_j(s, z_j, x_j, \omega)$ denote the utility for alternative j, where s denotes a vector of observable characteristics of the consumer, x_j denotes a vector of observable attributes of alternative j, z_j denotes an observable variable which denotes another attribute of the alternative, and ω is an unobservable random vector. Let $y = (y_1, \dots, y_J)$ be defined by

$$y_j = \begin{cases} 1 & \text{if} \quad V_j(s, z_j, x_j, \omega) > V_k(s, z_k, x_k, \omega) \quad \text{for all } k \neq j \\ 0 & \text{otherwise} \end{cases}.$$

Then, the conditional choice probability, for each $j = 1, \dots, J$, is

$$\Pr(\{y_j = 1 \mid s, x, z\})$$
$$= \Pr(\{\omega \mid V_j(s, z_j, x_j, \omega) > V_k(s, z_k, x_k, \omega) \text{ for all } k \neq j\}).$$

Since the choice probabilities of each alternative depend only on the differences between the utilities of the alternatives, only those differences can be identified. Hence, for simplicity, we will normalize $V_J(s, z_J, x_J, \omega)$ equal to 0 for all (s, z_J, x_J, ω). Then,

$$\Pr(\{y_J = 1 \mid s, x, z\}) = \Pr(\{\omega \mid 0 > V_k(s, z_k, x_k, \omega) \text{ for all } k \neq J\}).$$

(We assume that the probability of ties is zero.)

3.1   Subutilities Additive in the Unobservables

Assume that $\omega = (\omega_1, \dots, \omega_{J-1})$, each V_j depends only on one coordinate, ω_j of ω, and that each ω_j is additive. Then, under certain restrictions, one can identify the V_j functions and the distribution of ω nonparametrically. A result of this type, considered in Matzkin (1992, 1993, 1994), is where, for each j, V_j is specified as

$$V_j(s, x_j, z_j, \omega) = z_j + v_j(s, x_j) + \omega_j, \tag{3.1}$$

where v_j is a nonparametric function. Matzkin (1992, 1993, 1994) requires that $(z_1, \dots, z_{J-1})$ has an everywhere positive density, conditional on $(s, x_1, \dots, x_{J-1})$ and that $(\omega_1, \dots, \omega_{J-1})$ is distributed independently of $(s, z_1, \dots, z_{J-1}, x_1, \dots, x_{J-1})$. In addition, the vector of functions $(v_1, \dots, v_{J-1})$ is normalized by requiring that at a point, $(\bar{s}, \bar{x}_1, \dots, \bar{x}_{J-1})$, and for some values $(\alpha_1, \dots, \alpha_{J-1})$,

$$v_j(\bar{s}, \bar{x}_j) = \alpha_j. \tag{3.2}$$

Matzkin (1992, Example 3) shows that the functions v_j and the distribution of $(\omega_1, \dots, \omega_{J-1})$ are identified nonparametrically. Lewbel (2000) shows that to identify the distribution of $(v_1(s, x_1) + \omega_1, \dots, v_J(s, x_J) + \omega_J)$ given $(s, x_1, \dots, x_J)$, it suffices to require that $(\omega_1, \dots, \omega_{J-1})$ is distributed independently of $(z_1, \dots, z_{J-1})$, conditional on $(s, x_1, \dots, x_{J-1})$. To separately identify $(v_1(s, x_1), \dots, v_{J-1}(s, x_{J-1}))$ from the distribution of $(\omega_1, \dots, \omega_J)$, Lewbel imposes linearity of the functions v and a zero covariance between ω and $(s, x_1, \ldots, x_J)$. Alternatively, Lewbel uses instruments for $(s, x_1, \ldots, x_J)$.

In the past, the identification and estimation of these models, was analyzed using either parametric or semiparametric methods. McFadden (1974, 1981) specified each function V_j as linear in (s, z_j, x_j) and additive in ω_j. The distribution of ω was assumed to be known up to a finite-dimensional parameter. Manski (1975) developed an estimation method for the parameters of the linear function that did not require a parametric specification for the distribution of ω. Later, Cosslett (1983), Manski (1985), Powell, Stock, and Stoker (1989), Horowitz (1992), Ichimura (1993), and Klein and Spady (1993), among others, developed other methods that did not require a parametric specification for the distribution of ω. Matzkin (1991a, 1991b) developed methods in which the distribution of $(\omega_1, \ldots, \omega_{J-1})$ is parametric and the functions V_j are additive in ω_j but otherwise nonparametric. [See Briesch, Chintagunta, and Matzkin (2002) for an application of this latter method.]

To see how identification is achieved, consider the specification in (3.1) with the normalization in (3.2) and the assumption that $\omega = (\omega_1, \ldots, \omega_{J-1})$ is distributed independently of $(s, z, x) = (s, z_1, \ldots, z_J, x_1, \ldots, x_{J-1})$. Then,

$$\Pr(\{y_J = 1 \mid s, z_1, \ldots, z_{J-1}, x_1, \ldots, x_{J-1}\})$$
$$= \Pr(\{0 > z_j + v_j(s, x_j) + \omega_j \text{ for all } j \neq J \mid s, z_1, \ldots, z_{J-1}, x_1, \ldots, x_{J-1}\})$$
$$= \Pr(\{\omega_j < -z_j - v_j(s, x_j) \text{ for all } j \neq J \mid s, z_1, \ldots, z_{J-1}, x_1, \ldots, x_{J-1}\}).$$

Since independence between ω and (s, z, x) implies that ω is independent of z, conditional on (s, x), it follows from the last expression that fixing the values of (s, x) and varying the values of z, we can identify the distribution of ω. Specifically, by letting $(s, x) = (\overline{s}, \overline{x}_1, \ldots, \overline{x}_{J-1})$, it follows that

$$\Pr(\{y_J = 1 \mid \overline{s}, z_1, \ldots, z_{J-1}, \overline{x}_1, \ldots, \overline{x}_{J-1}\})$$
$$= \Pr(\{\omega_j < -z_j - \alpha_j \text{ for all } j \neq J \mid \overline{s}, z_1, \ldots, z_{J-1}, \overline{x}_1, \ldots, \overline{x}_{J-1}\}).$$

This shows that the distribution of $(\omega_1, \ldots, \omega_{J-1})$, conditional on $(s, x) = (\overline{s}, \overline{x}_1, \ldots, \overline{x}_{J-1})$ is identified. Since ω is distributed independently of (s, x), the marginal distribution of ω is the same as the conditional distribution of ω. Hence, for any $(t_1, \ldots, t_{J-1})$,

$$F_{\omega_1, \ldots, \omega_{J-1}}(t_1, \ldots, t_{J-1})$$
$$= \Pr(\{y_J = 1 \mid \overline{s}, z_1 = -\alpha_1 - t_1, \ldots, z_{J-1} = -\alpha_{J-1} - t_{J-1}, \overline{x}_1, \ldots, \overline{x}_{J-1}\}).$$

Once the distribution of the additive random terms is identified, one can identify the nonparametric functions V_j using, for example, the identification results in Matzkin (1991a 1991b), which assume that the distribution of ω is parametric.

3.2   Subutilities Nonadditive in the Unobservables

Matzkin (2005) considered a model where the vector of unobservables, $\omega = (\omega_1, \ldots, \omega_{J-1})$, entered in possibly nonadditive ways in each of the V_j

functions. The specification was, for each j,

$$V_j \left(s, x_j, z_j, \omega\right) = z_j + v_j \left(s, x_j, \omega\right), \tag{3.3}$$

where v_j is a nonparametric function, and ω is assumed to be distributed independently of $(s, z_1, \ldots, z_{J-1}, x_1, \ldots, x_{J-1})$. The analysis of identification makes use of the arguments in Matzkin (1992, 1993, 1994), Briesch, Chintagunta, and Matzkin (1997), and Lewbel (1998, 2000), together with the results about identification in nonparametric simultaneous equation models. Define U_j for each j by

$$U_j = v_j \left(s, x_j, \omega\right).$$

Since ω is distributed independently of (s, z, x), $(U_1, \ldots, U_{J-1})$ is distributed independently of z given (s, x). Hence, using the arguments in Lewbel (1998, 2000), from the probability of choosing alternative J, or any other alternative, conditional on (s, x), one can recover the distribution of $(U_1, \ldots, U_{J-1})$ given (s, x). Since the distribution of the observable variables (s, x) is observable, this is equivalent to observing the joint distribution of the dependent variables $(U_1, \ldots, U_{J-1})$ and the explanatory variables, $(s, x_1, \ldots, x_J)$, in the system of equations

$$U_1 = v_1 (s, x_1, \omega_1, \ldots, \omega_{J-1})$$
$$U_2 = v_2 (s, x_2, \omega_1, \ldots, \omega_{J-1})$$
$$\cdots$$

$$U_{J-1} = v_{J-1} (s, x_{J-1}, \omega_1, \ldots, \omega_{J-1}).$$

The identification and estimation of the functions $(v_1, \ldots, v_{J-1})$ in this system can be analyzed using the methods in Matzkin (2005).

For a simple example, that generalizes the model in 3.1 to functions that are nonadditive in one unobservable, suppose that each function V_j is of the form

$$V_j \left(s, x_j, z_j, \omega\right) = z_j + v_j \left(s, x_j, \omega_j\right), \tag{3.4}$$

where each nonparametric functions v_j is strictly increasing in ω_j. Then, assuming the ω is distributed independently of (s, z, x), one can identify the joint distribution of $(U_1, \ldots, U_{J-1}; s, x_1, \ldots, x_{J-1})$, where

$$U_1 = v_1(s, x_1, \omega_1)$$
$$U_2 = v_2(s, x_2, \omega_2)$$
$$\cdots$$

$$U_{J-1} = v_{J-1}(s, x_{J-1}, \omega_{J-1}).$$

Each of these v_j functions can be identified from the distribution of $\left(U_j, s, x_j\right)$ after either a normalization or a restriction. For example, one could require that each function v_j is separable into a known function of one coordinate of $\left(s, x_j\right)$ and ω_j, and the value of v_j is known at one point, or, one could specify a marginal distribution for ω_j.

One could also consider situations where the number of unobservables is larger than $J - 1$. Briesch, Chintagunta, and Matzkin (1997), for example, consider a situation where the utility function depends on an unobserved heterogeneity variable, θ. They specify, for each j

$$V\left(j, s, x_j, z_j, \theta, \omega_j\right) = z_j + v\left(j, s, x_j, \theta\right) + \omega_j$$

where θ is considered an unobservable heterogeneity parameter.

Ichimura and Thompson (1998) consider the model

$$V\left(j, s, x_j, z_j, \theta\right) = z_j + \theta x_j$$

where θ is an unobservable vector, distributed independently of (z, x), with an unknown distribution. Using Matzkin (2003, Appendix A), one can modify the model in Ichimura and Thompson (1998) to allow the random coefficients to enter in a nonparametric way. This can be done, for example, by specifying, for each j, that $V\left(j, s, x_j, z_j, \theta_j, \omega_j\right)$ is of the form

$$V(j, s, x_j, z_j, \theta_j, \omega_j) = z_j + \sum_{k=1}^{K} m_k(x_{j(k)}, \theta_{j(k)}) + \omega_j$$

where the nonparametric functions m_k are a.e. strictly increasing in θ_j, the θ_j are independently distributed among them and from (z, x), and for some $\overline{x}_j, \widetilde{x}_j$,

$$m_k\left(\widetilde{x}_{j(k)}, \theta_j\right) = 0 \quad \text{for all } \theta_j, \quad \text{and}$$
$$m_k\left(\overline{x}_{j(k)}, \theta_j\right) = \theta_j.$$

In the random coefficient model of Ichimura and Thompson (1998), these conditions are satisfied at $\widetilde{x}_{j(k)} = 0$ and $\overline{x}_{j(k)} = 1$.

4 CHOICES AS EXPLANATORY VARIABLES

In many models, choices appear as explanatory variables. When this choice depends on unobservables that affect the dependent variable of interest, we need to deal with an endogeneity problem, to be able to disentangle the effect of the observable choice variable from the effect of the unobservable variables. Suppose, for example, that the model of interest is

$$Y = m(X, \varepsilon)$$

where Y denotes output of a worker that possesses unobserved ability ε and X is the amount of hours of work. If the value of X is determined independently of ε, then one could analyze the identification of the function m and of the distribution of ε using Matzkin (1999), in a way similar to that used in the analysis of demand in Section 2.1. In particular, assuming that m is strictly increasing in ε, it follows by the independence between X and ε that for all x, e

$$F_\varepsilon(e) = F_{Y|X=x}(m(x, e)).$$

Suppose, in addition, that $f_\varepsilon(e) > 0$. Then, at $X = x$, the conditional distribution of Y given x when $Y = m(x, e)$ is strictly increasing. It follows that

$$m(x, e) = F_{Y|X=x}^{-1}(F_\varepsilon(e))$$

and that a change in the value of X from x to x' causes a change in the value of Y from $y_0 = m(x, e)$ to $y_1 = m(x, e)$ equal to:

$$y_1 - y_0 = F_{Y|X=x'}^{-1}\left(F_{Y|x=x}(y_0)\right) - y_0.$$

Suppose, however, that the amount of hours of work is chosen by the worker, as a function of his ability. In particular, suppose that, for some ξ,

$$X = v(\varepsilon, \xi)$$

where v is strictly increasing in ε. Then, there exists an inverse function r such that

$$\varepsilon = r(X, \xi).$$

The change in output, for a worker of ability ε, when the amount of X changes exogenously from x to x' is

$$y_1 - y_0 = m(x', r(x, \xi)) - m(x, r(x, \xi)).$$

Altonji and Matzkin (1997, 2005), Altonji and Ichimura (1997), Imbens and Newey (2001, 2003), Chesher (2002, 2003), and Matzkin (2003, 2004) consider local and global identification of m and of average derivatives of m, in nonseparable models, using conditional independence methods. Altonji and Matzkin (1997) also propose a method that uses shape restrictions on a conditional distribution of ε. All of these methods are based upon using additional data. Most are based on a control function approach, following the parametric methods in Heckman (1976, 1978, 1980), and later works by Heckman and Robb (1985), Blundell and Smith (1986, 1989), and Rivers and Vuong (1988). Control function approaches for nonparametric models that are additive on an unobservable have been studied by Newey, Powell, and Vella (1999), Ng and Pinske (1995), and Pinske (2000).

The shape-restricted method in Altonji and Matzkin (1997, 2005) assumes that there exists an external variable, Z, such that for each value x of X there exists a value z of Z such that for all e

$$f_{\varepsilon|X=x,Z=z}(e) = f_{\varepsilon|X=z,Z=x}(e).$$

In the above example, Z could be the amount of hours of that same worker at some other day. The assumption is that the distribution of ability, ε, given that the hours of work are x today and z at that other period is the same distribution as when the worker's hours today are z and the worker's hours at the other period are x. Assuming that m is strictly increasing in ε, this exchangeability restriction implies that

$$F_{Y|X=x,Z=z}(m(x,e)) = F_{Y|X=z,Z=x}(m(z,e)).$$

This is an equation in two unknowns, $m(x,e)$ and $m(z,e)$. Altonji and Matzkin (1997) use the normalization that at some $\bar{x}$, and for all e,

$$m(\bar{x}, e) = e.$$

This then allows one to identify $m(x, e)$ as

$$m(x, e) = F^{-1}_{Y|X=x,Z=\bar{x}} \left(F_{Y|X=\bar{x},Z=x}(e) \right).$$

The distribution $F_{\varepsilon|X=x}$ can next be identified by

$$F_{\varepsilon|X=x}(e) = F_{Y|X=x} \left(F^{-1}_{Y|X=x,Z=\bar{x}} \left(F_{Y|X=\bar{x},Z=x}(e) \right) \right).$$

Altonji and Matzkin (1997, 2005) also propose a method to estimate average derivatives of m using a control variable Z satisfying the conditional independence assumption that

$$F_{\varepsilon|X,Z}(e) = F_{\varepsilon|Z}(e). \tag{4.1}$$

Their object of interest is the average derivative of m with respect to x, when the distribution of ε given X remains unchanged:

$$\beta(x) = \int \frac{\partial m(x,e)}{\partial x} f_{\varepsilon|X=x}(e) \, de.$$

They show that under their conditional independence assumption, $\beta(x)$ can be recovered as a functional of the distribution of the observable variables (Y, X, Z). In particular,

$$\beta(x) = \int \frac{\partial E\,(Y|X=x, Z=z)}{\partial x} f(z|x) \, dz$$

where $E\,(Y|X=x, Z=z)$ denotes the conditional expectation of Y given $X = x, Z = z$, and $f(z|x)$ denotes the density of Z given $X = x$. Matzkin (2003) shows how condition (4.1) can also be used to identify m and the distribution of ε given X, using the normalization that at some $\bar{x}$, and for all ε

$$m\,(\bar{x}, \varepsilon) = \varepsilon.$$

Blundell and Powell (2000, 2003) and Imbens and Newey (2001, 2003) have considered situations where the control variable Z, satisfying (4.1) is estimated rather than observed. Blundell and Powell considered the average structural function

$$\int m(x, \varepsilon) \, f_\varepsilon(\varepsilon) \, d\varepsilon$$

as well as functionals of it and average derivatives. Imbens and Newey considered the quantile structural function, defined as

$$m(x, q_\varepsilon(\tau))$$

where $q_\varepsilon(\tau)$ is the τth quantile of ε, as well as the average structural function, functionals of both functions, and average derivatives (see Imbens, 2006).

Condition (4.1) together with strict monotonicity of m in ε implies that

$$F_{\varepsilon|Z}(\varepsilon) = F_{Y|X,Z}(m(x, \varepsilon)).$$

Multiplying both sides of the equation by $f(z)$ and integrating with respect to z, one gets

$$F_\varepsilon(\varepsilon) = \int F_{Y|X,Z}(m(x, \varepsilon)) \, f(z) \, dz$$

which can be solved for $m(x, \varepsilon)$ once one specifies the marginal distribution of ε.

The above approaches are based on conditional independence, given a variable, Z, which can be either observed or estimated. One may wonder, however, how to determine whether any given variable, Z, can be used to obtain conditional independence. Imbens and Newey (2001) provides one such example. They consider the model

$$Y = m(X, \varepsilon)$$
$$X = s(Z, \eta)$$

where s is strictly increasing in η, m is strictly increasing in ε, and Z is jointly independent of (ε, η). The latter assumption implies that ε is independent of X conditional on η, because conditional on η, X is a function of Z, which is independent of ε. Since the function s can be identified (Matzkin, 1999), one can estimate η, and use it to identify m. Chesher (2002, 2003) considered a model similar to the one in Imbens and Newey, and showed that to identify local derivatives of m, a local quantile insensitivity condition was sufficient (see also Ma and Koenker, 2004).

Matzkin (2004) shows that reversing the roles in the second equation in Imbens and Newey can, in some situations, considerably lessen the requirements for global identification. The model is

$$Y = m(X, \varepsilon)$$
$$X = s(Z, \eta)$$

where for one value, $\bar{z}$ of Z, ε is independent of η, conditional on $Z = \bar{z}$. It is assumed that m is strictly increasing in ε, $F_{\varepsilon|Z=\bar{z}}$ and $F_{X|Z=\bar{z}}$ are strictly increasing, and for each value x of X, $F_{\varepsilon|X=x,Z=\bar{z}}$ is strictly increasing. Under these assumptions, Matzkin (2004) shows that if η is independent of ε conditional on $Z = \bar{z}$, then for all x, e

$$m(x, e) = F_{Y|X=x,Z=\bar{z}}^{-1}\left(F_{\varepsilon|Z=\bar{z}}(e)\right) \quad \text{and}$$
$$F_{\varepsilon|X=x}(e) = F_{Y|X=x}\left(F_{Y|X=x,Z=\bar{z}}^{-1}\left(F_{\varepsilon|Z=\bar{z}}(e)\right)\right).$$

This result establishes the global identification of the function m and the distribution of (X, ε), up to a normalization on the conditional distribution $F_{\varepsilon|Z=\bar{z}}$. If, for example, we normalized the distribution of ε conditional on $Z = \bar{z}$ to be $U(0, 1)$, then, for all x and all $e \in (0, 1)$

$$m(x, e) = F_{Y|X=x, Z=\bar{z}}^{-1}(e) \quad \text{and} \quad F_{\varepsilon|X=x}(e) = F_{Y|X=x}\left(F_{Y|X=x, Z=\bar{z}}^{-1}(e)\right).$$

Endogeneity in discrete choice models can be handled similarly. In particular, Altonji and Matzkin's (1997, 2005) average derivative method can be applied to the case where Y is discrete as well as when Y is continuous. Blundell and Powell (2003) derive an estimator for a semiparametric binary response model with endogenous regressors, using a control function approach. Similarly to Blundell and Powell (2003), but with less structure, one can consider a nonparametric binary response model, as in Matzkin (2004). Consider the model

$$Y_1 = \begin{cases} 1 & \text{if } X_0 + v(X_1, Y_2, \xi) \geq \varepsilon \\ 0 & \text{otherwise} \end{cases}$$

where Y_1, Y_2, and X are observable and ξ and ε are unobservable. Suppose that ξ is not distributed independently of Y_2. Let

$$W = v(X_1, Y_2, \xi)$$

and assume that for some unknown function s, observable $\widetilde{Y}_2$, and unobservable η

$$Y_2 = s(\widetilde{Y}_2, \eta)$$

where η is independent of ξ conditional on $\widetilde{Y}_2$. Following arguments similar to those described in Section 3, one can identify the distribution of W given $(X_1, Y_2, \widetilde{Y}_2)$, from the distribution of Y_1 given $(X_0, X_1, Y_2, \widetilde{Y}_2)$, using X_0 as a special regressor (Lewbel, 2000). The system

$$W = v(X_1, Y_2, \xi)$$
$$Y_2 = s(\widetilde{Y}_2, \eta)$$

is a nonparametric triangular system whose identification can be analyzed using Chesher (2003), Imbens and Newey (2001, 2003), Matzkin (2004), or using methods for nonparametric simultaneous equation models, such as the ones mentioned in Section 3.

5 CONCLUSIONS

This paper has surveyed some of the current literature on nonparametric identification of models with unobserved heterogeneity. We considered models where choices are the dependent variables, such as the classical consumer demand model and discrete choice models, and models where choices are explanatory variables, such as the model where years of education is an explanatory variable in the determination of wages.

We concentrated on models where the unobservable random terms, representing unobserved heterogeneity, entered in the relationships in nonadditive ways. In some of the models, these unobservables could be considered as independently distributed from the observable explanatory variables. In others, they were conditionally independent of the explanatory variables. In some, such as in demand models generated from multivariate unobservables, we dealt with nonparametric models of simultaneous equations with nonadditive unobservables.

Several variations in the support of the data were considered. For the classical consumer demand model, in particular, we presented existent results that can be used when observed prices and income are continuously distributed, when only observed income is continuously distributed, and when neither prices nor income vary over observations. Linear and nonlinear budget constraints were considered.

References

AFRIAT, S. (1967): "The Construction of a Utility Function from Demand Data," *International Economic Review*, 8, 66–77.

AI, C. AND X. CHEN (2003): "Efficient Estimation of Models with Conditional Moments Restrictions Containing Unknown Functions," *Econometrica*, 71, 1795–1843.

ALTONJI, J. G. AND H. ICHIMURA (1997): "Estimating Derivatives in Nonseparable Models with Limited Dependent Variables," Mimeo.

ALTONJI, J. G. AND R. L. MATZKIN (1997, 2001): "Panel Data Estimators for Nonseparable Models with Endogenous Regressors," Mimeo, Northwestern University (1997), NBER Working Paper T0267 (2001).

——— (2005): "Cross Section and Panel Data Estimators for Nonseparable Models with Endogenous Regressors," *Econometrica*, 73(3), 1053–1102.

ATHEY, S. AND G. IMBENS (2006): "Identification and Inference in Nonlinear Difference-in-Difference Models," *Econometrica*, 74(2), 431–497.

BARBERA, S. AND P. K. PATTANAIK (1986): "Flamange and the Rationalizability of Stochastic Choices in Terms of Random Orderings," *Econometrica*, 54(3), 707–715.

BARTEN, A. P. (1968): "Estimating Demand Equations," *Econometrica*, 36(2), 213–251.

BECKERT, W. AND R. BLUNDELL (2005): "Heterogeneity and the Nonparametric Analysis of Consumer Choice: Conditions for Invertibility," CEMMAP Working Paper, CWP 09/05.

BENKARD, C. L. AND S. BERRY (2004, 2006): "On the Nonparametric Identification of Nonlinear Simultaneous Equations Models: Comment on B. Brown (1983) and Roehrig (1988)," Cowles Foundation Discussion Paper #1482 (2004), published in *Econometrica*, 74(5), 1429–1440 (2006).

BLOOMQUIST, S. AND W. NEWEY (2002): "Nonparametric Estimation with Nonlinear Budget Sets," *Econometrica*, 70(6), 2455–2480.

BLUNDELL, R., M. BROWNING, AND I. CRAWFORD (2003): "Nonparametric Engel Curves and Revealed Preference" *Econometrica*, 71(1), 205–240.

——— (2004): "Best Nonparametric Bounds on Demand Responses," Walras-Bowley lecture, IFS Working Paper, 05/03.

——— (2005): "Improving Revealed Preference Bounds on Demand Responses," Mimeo, IFS.

BLUNDELL, R., X. CHEN, AND D. KRISTENSEN (2003): "Semiparametric Engel Curves with Endogenous Expenditure," CEMMAP Working Paper, 15/03.

BLUNDELL, R., D. KRISTENSEN, AND R. L. MATZKIN (2005): "Stochastic Demand and Revealed Preference," Mimeo.

BLUNDELL, R. AND R. L. MATZKIN (2005): "Nonseparable Demand," Mimeo.

BLUNDELL, R. AND J. L. POWELL (2000): "Endogeneity in Nonparametric and Semiparametric Regression Models," Invited Lecture at the Eigth World Congress of the Econometric Society, Seattle, Washington, USA.

——— (2003): "Endogeneity in Nonparametric and Semiparametric Regression Models," in *Advances in Economics and Econometrics, Theory and Applications, Eighth World Congress*, Vol. II, edited by M. Dewatripont, L. P. Hansen, and S. J. Turnovsky, Cambridge, UK: Cambridge University Press.

——— (2004): "Endogeneity in Semiparametric Binary Response Models," *Review of Economics Studies*, 71(3), 655–679.

BLUNDELL, R. AND R. SMITH (1986): "An Exogeneity Test for a Simultaneous Equation Tobit Model with and Application to Labor Supply," *Econometrica*, 54, 3, 679–686.

——— (1989): "Estimation in a Class of Simultaneous Equation Limited Dependent Variable Models," *Review of Economic Studies*, 56, 37–58.

BRIESCH, R., P. CHINTAGUNTA, AND R. MATZKIN (1997): "Nonparametric Discrete Choice Models with Unobserved Heterogeneity," Mimeo, Northwestern University.

——— (2002): "Semiparametric Estimation of Choice Brand Behavior," *Journal of the American Statistical Association*, 97(460), Applications and Case Studies, pp. 973–982.

BROWN, B. W. (1983): "The Identification Problem in Systems Nonlinear in the Variables," *Econometrica*, 51, 175–196.

BROWN, D. J. AND C. CALSAMIGLIA (2003): "The Strong Law of Demand," CFDP #1399, Yale University.

BROWN, D. J. AND R. L. MATZKIN (1998): "Estimation of Nonparametric Functions in Simultaneous Equations Models, with an Application to Consumer Demand," Cowles Foundation Discussion Paper #1175.

BROWN, B. W. AND M. B. WALKER (1989): "The Random Utility Hypothesis and Inference in Demand Systems," *Econometrica*, 57, 815–829.

——— (1995): "Stochastic Specification in Random Production Models of Cost-Minimizing Firms," *Journal of Econometrics*, 66(1), 175–205.

CHERNOZHUKOV, V. AND C. HANSEN (2005): "An IV Model of Quantile Treatment Effects," *Econometrica*, 73, 245–261.

CHERNOZHUKOV, V., G. IMBENS, AND W. NEWEY (2004): "Instrumental Variable Identification and Estimation of Nonseparable Models via Quantile Conditions," Mimeo, Department of Economics, M.I.T., forthcoming in *Journal of Econometrics*.

CHESHER, A. (2002): "Local Identification in Nonseparable Models," CeMMAP Working Paper CWP 05/02.

——— (2003): "Identification in Nonseparable Models," *Econometrica*, 71(5), 1405–1441.

——— (2006): "Identification in Non-additive Structural Functions," presented at the Invited Symposium on Nonparametric Structural Models, 9th World Congress of the Econometric Society, London, 2005.

COHEN, M. (1980): "Random Utility Systems – the Infinite Case," *Journal of Mathematical Psychology*, 18, 52–72.

COSSLETT, S. R. (1983): "Distribution-free Maximum Likelihood Estimator of the Binary Choice Model," *Econometrica*, 51, 3, 765–782.

DAROLLES, S., J. P. FLORENS, AND E. RENAULT (2002): "Nonparametric Instrumental Regression," Mimeo, IDEI, Toulouse.

EKELAND, I., J. J. HECKMAN, AND L. NESHEIM (2004): "Identification and Estimation of Hedonic Models," *Journal of Political Economy*, 112(S1), S60–S109.

EPSTEIN, L. G. (1981): "Generalized Duality and Integrability," *Econometrica*, 49(3), 655–678.

FALMANGE, J. (1978): "A Representation Theorem for Finite Random Scale Systems," *Journal of Mathematical Psychology*, 18, 52–72.

FISHBURN, P. (1998): "Stochastic Utility," in *Handbook of Utility Theory*, edited by S. Barbera, P. Hammond, and C. Seidl, New York: Kluwer, pp. 273–320.

HALL, P. AND J. L. HOROWITZ (2003): "Nonparametric Methods for Inference in the Presence of Instrumental Variables," Mimeo, Northwestern University.

HAUSMAN, J. (1985): "The Econometrics of Nonlinear Choice Sets," *Econometrica*, 53(6), 1255–1282.

HECKMAN, J. J. (1974): "Effects of Day-Care Programs on Women's Work Effort," *Journal of Political Economy*, 82, 136–163.

——— (1976): "Simultaneous Equations Models with Continuous and Discrete Endogenous Variables and Structural Shifts," in *Studies in Nonlinear Estimation*, edited by S. Goldfeld and R. Quandt, Cambridge, MA: Ballinger.

——— (1978): "Dummy Endogenous Variables in a Simultaneous Equations System," *Econometrica*, 46, 931–961.

——— (1980): "Addendum to Sample Selection Bias as a Specification Error," in *Evaluation Studies*, Vol. 5, edited by E. Stromsdorfer and G. Farkas, San Francisco: Sage.

HECKMAN, J. J., R. L. MATZKIN, AND L. NESHEIM (2002): "Nonparametric Estimation of Nonadditive Hedonic Models," Mimeo, UCL.

HECKMAN, J. J. AND R. ROBB (1985): "Alternative Methods for Evaluating the Impacts of Interventions," in *Longitudinal Analysis of Labor Market Data*, Econometric Society Monograph 10, edited by J. J. Heckman and B. Singer, Cambridge: Cambridge University Press.

HECKMAN, J. J. AND B. SINGER (1984): "A Method of Minimizing the Impact of Distributional Assumptions in Econometric Models for Duration Data," *Econometrica*, 52, 271–320.

HECKMAN, J. J. AND R. WILLIS (1977): "A Beta-Logistic Model for the Analysis of Sequential Labor Force Participation by Married Women," *Journal of Political Economy*, 87(1), 197–201.

HOUTHAKKER, H. S. (1950): "Revealed Preference and the Utility Function," *Economica*, 17, 159–174.

HOROWITZ, J. L. (1992): "A Smoothed Maximum Score Estimator for the Binary Choice Model," *Econometrica*, 60, 505–531.

ICHIMURA, H. (1993): "Semiparametric Least Squares (SLS) ad Weighted SLS Estimation of Single Index Models," *Journal of Econometrics*, 58, 71–120.

ICHIMURA, H. AND T. S. THOMPSON (1998): "Maximum Likelihood Estimation of a Binary Choice Model with Random Coefficients of Unknown Distribution," *Journal of Econometrics*, 86(2), 269–295.

IMBENS, G. W. (2006): "Nonadditive Models with Endogenous Regressors," presented at the Invited Symposium on Nonparametric Structural Models, 9th World Congress of the Econometric Society, London, 2005.

IMBENS, G. W. AND W. K. NEWEY (2001, 2003): "Identification and Estimation of Triangular Simultaneous Equations Models Without Additivity," Mimeo, UCLA.

KLEIN R. AND R. H. SPADY (1993): "An Efficient Semiparametric Estimator for Discrete Choice Models," *Econometrica*, 61, 387–422.

KOENKER, R. (2005): *Quantile Regression*, Econometric Society Monograph Series, Cambridge: Cambridge University Press.

LANCASTER, T. (1979): "Econometric Methods for the Analysis of Unemployment" *Econometrica*, 47, 939–956.

LEWBEL, A. (1989): "Identification and Estimation of equivalence Scales under Weak Separability," *The Review of Economic Studies*, 56(2), 311–316.

——— (1998): "Semiparametric Latent Variables Model Estimation with Endogenous or Missmeasured Regressors," *Econometrica*, 66(1), 105–121.

——— (2000): "Semiparametric Qualitative Response Model Estimation with Unknown Heteroskedasticity and Instrumental Variables," *Journal of Econometrics*, 97, 145–177.

——— (2001): "Demand Systems With and Without Errors," *American Economic Review*, 91, 611–618.

MA, L. AND R. W. KOENKER (2004): "Quantile Regression Methods for Recursive Structural Equation Models," CeMMAP Working Paper WP 01/04, *Journal of Econometrics*, forthcoming.

MANSKI, C. F. (1975): "Maximum Score Estimation of the Stochastic Utility Model of Choice," *Journal of Econometrics*, 3, 205–228.

——— (1983): "Closest Empirical Distribution Estimation," *Econometrica*, 51(2), 305–320.

——— (1985): "Semiparametric Analysis of Discrete Response: Asymptotic Properties of the Maximum Score Estimator," *Journal of Econometrics*, 27(3), 313–333.

MAS-COLELL, A. (1977): "The Recoverability of Consumers' Preferences from Market Demand Behavior," *Econometrica*, 45(6), 1409–1430.

——— (1978): "On Revealed Preference Analysis," *Review of Economic Studies*, 45(1), 121–131.

MATZKIN, R. L. (1991a): "Semiparametric Estimation of Monotone and Concave Utility Functions for Polychotomous Choice Models," *Econometrica*, 59, 1315–1327.

——— (1991b): "Axioms of Revealed Preference for Nonlinear Choice Sets," *Econometrica*, 59(6), 1779–1786.

——— (1992): "Nonparametric and Distribution-Free Estimation of the Threshold Crossing and Binary Choice Models," *Econometrica*, 60, 239–270.

——— (1993): "Nonparametric Identification and Estimation of Polychotomous Choice Models," *Journal of Econometrics*, 58, 137–168.

——— (1994): "Restrictions of Economic Theory in Nonparametric Methods," in *Handbook of Econometrics*, Vol. IV, edited by R. F. Engel and D. L. McFadden, Amsterdam: Elsevier, Chapter 42.

——— (1999): "Nonparametric Estimation of Nonadditive Random Functions," Mimeo, Northwestern University, Invited Lecture at the Session on New Developments in the Estimation of Preferences and Production Functions, Cancun, Mexico, August 1999.

——— (2003): "Nonparametric Estimation of Nonadditive Random Functions," *Econometrica*, 71, 1339–1375.

——— (2004): "Unobservable Instruments," Mimeo, Northwestern University.

——— (2005): "Identification in Nonparametric Simultaneous Equations," Mimeo, Northwestern University.

———— (2006): "Nonparametric Identification," in *Handbook of Econometrics*, Vol. 6, edited by J. J. Heckman and E. E. Leamer, Amsterdam: Elsevier, forthcoming.

MATZKIN, R. L. AND M. K. RICHTER (1991): "Testing Strictly Concave Rationality," *Journal of Economic Theory*, 53, 287–303.

MCELROY, M. B. (1981): "Duality and the Error Structure in Demand Systems," Discussion Paper #81–82, Economics Research Center/NORC.

———— (1987): "Additive General Error Models for Production, Cost, and Derived Demand or Share Systems," *Journal of Political Economy*, 95, 737–757.

McFadden, D. L. (1974): "Conditional Logit Analysis of Qualitative Choice Behavior," in *Frontiers in Econometrics*, edited by P. Zarembka, New York: Academic Press.

———— (1978): "Cost, Revenue, and Profit Functions," in *Production Economics: A Dual Approach to Theory and Applications, Vol. I: The Theory of Production*, edited by M. Fuss and D. L. McFadden, Amsterdam: North-Holland.

———— (1981): "Econometric Models of Probabilstic Choice," in *Structural Analysis of Discrete Data with Econometric Applications*, edited by C . F. Manski and D. L. McFadden, Cambridge, MA: MIT Press, pp. 2–50.

———— (1985): Presidential Address, World Congress of the Econometric Society.

———— (2005): "Revealed Stochastic Preferences: A Synthesis," *Economic Theory*, 26(2), 245–264.

MCFADDEN, D. L. AND M. K. RICHTER (1970): "Revealed Stochastic Preference," Mimeo.

———— (1990): "Stochastic Rationality and Revealed Stochastic Preference," in *Preferences, Uncertainty, and Rationality*, edited by J. Chipman, D. McFadden, and M. K. Richter, Westview Press, pp. 187–202.

NEWEY, W. K. AND J. L. POWELL (1989): "Instrumental Variables Estimation for Nonparametric Models," Mimeo, Princeton University.

———— (2003): "Instrumental Variables Estimation for Nonparametric Models," *Econometrica*, 71, 1557–1569.

NEWEY, W. K., J. L. POWELL, AND F. VELLA (1999): "Nonparametric Estimation of Triangular Simultaneous Equations Models," *Econometrica* 67, 565–603.

NG, S. AND J. PINKSE (1995): "Nonparametric Two-Step Regression Estimation when Regressors and Errors and Dependent," Mimeo, University of Montreal.

PINKSE, J. (2000): "Nonparametric Two-Step Regression Estimation when Regressors and Errors are Dependent," *Canadian Journal of Statistics*, 28-2, 289–300.

POWELL, J. L., J. H. STOCK, AND T. M. STOKER (1989): "Semiparametric Estimation of Index Coefficients," *Econometrica*, 57, 1403–1430.

RICHTER, M. K. (1966): "Revealed Preference Theory," *Econometrica*, 34(3), 635–645.

RIVERS, D. AND Q. H. VUONG (1988): "Limited Information Estimators and Exogeneity Tests for Simultaneous Probit Models," *Journal of Econometrics*, 39, 347–366.

ROEHRIG, C. S. (1988): "Conditions for Identification in Nonparametric and Parametric Models," *Econometrica*, 56, 433–447.

SAMUELSON, P. A. (1938): "A Note on the Pure Theory of Consumer Behavior," *Economica*, 5, 61–71.

YATCHEW, A. (1985): "A Note on Nonparametric Tests of Consumer Behavior," *Economic Letters*, 18, 45–48.

CHAPTER 5

Modeling Heterogeneity
Arthur Lewbel[*]

1 INTRODUCTION

My goal here is to provide some synthesis of recent results regarding unobserved heterogeneity in nonlinear and semiparametric models, using as a context Matzkin (2005a) and Browning and Carro (2005), which were the papers
presented in the Modeling Heterogeneity session of the 2005 Econometric Society World Meetings in London. These papers themselves consist of enormously
heterogeneous content, ranging from high theory to Danish milk, which I will
attempt to homogenize.

The overall theme of this literature is that, in models of individual economic
agents, errors at least partly reflect unexplained heterogeneity in behavior, and
hence in tastes, technologies, etc. Economic theory can imply restrictions on the
structure of these errors, and in particular can generate nonadditive or nonseparable errors, which has profound implications for model specification, identification, estimation, and policy analysis.

2 STATISTICAL VERSUS STRUCTURAL MODELS OF HETEROGENEITY

Using one of Browning and Carro's models to fix ideas, suppose we have a sample of observations of a dependent variable Y such as a household's purchases of
organic whole milk, and a vector of covariates X, such as the prices of alternative
varieties of milk and demographic characteristics of the consuming household.
The heterogeneity we are concerned with here is unobserved heterogeneity,
specifically the behavioral variation in Y that is not explained by variation in
X. By behavioral, I mean variation that primarily reflects actual differences in
actions, tastes, technologies, etc., across the sampled economic agents, rather
than measurement or sampling errors. For simplicity, assume for this discussion that our data are independent, identically distributed observations of Y and

[*] Boston College.

X, without any complications associated with sample selection, censoring, or measurement errors.

One view of heterogeneity, which could be called the statistical model, is that unobserved heterogeneity is completely defined by $F(Y|X)$, that is, the conditional distribution of Y given X, since this gives the probability of any value of Y given any value of X. This can be easily estimated nonparametrically, and by this view the only purpose or reason to construct a model is dimension reduction or otherwise improving the efficiency of our estimate of F.

This may be contrasted with what I'll call the Micro Econometrician's view, which is that there is a behavioral or structural model $Y = g(X, \theta, U)$, which may include parameters θ and has unobservables (heterogeneity) U. We could also include endogeneity, by allowing U to correlate with X or by including Y into the function g, but ignore that complication for now.

We wish to understand and estimate this structural model because it is based on some economic model of behavior and its parameters may have implications for economic policy. The structural model g is more informative than F, because it tells us how F would change if some underlying parameters change. For example, θ could include production function parameters, which would then allow us to predict how the distribution of outputs across firms might change in response to an improvement in technology, or in the milk example θ provides information about the distribution of tastes across households, which we might use to predict the response to introduction of a new milk product, or the returns to a marketing campaign aimed at changing tastes.

To illustrate, the Micro Econometrician might assume a linear random coefficients model $Y = a + bX + \varepsilon = (a + e_1) + (b + e_2)X$, where the errors e_1 and e_2, representing unobserved variation in tastes, are distributed independently of each other and of X, and are normal so $e_j \backsim N(0, \sigma_j^2)$ and $\varepsilon = e_1 + e_2X$. This then implies the statistical model $F(Y|X) = N(a + bX, \sigma_1^2 + \sigma_2^2 X^2)$.

Given a scalar, continuously distributed Y, there is a trick Matzkin employs to construct a function that could be structural. Define an unobserved error term U by $U = F(Y|X)$, and a function G by $Y = G(X, U) = F^{-1}(U|X)$. The idea is then to assume that the true behavioral model $Y = g(X, \theta, U)$ is just $Y = G(X, U)$. By construction this error term U is independent of X, since it has a standard uniform distribution regardless of what value X takes on. We could further transform U by any known monotonic function, for example, converting U to a standard normal instead of a standard uniform. Matzkin then adds economically motivated assumptions regarding G and U for identification or to interpret G as structural, for example, if Y is output G might be interpreted as a production function with U being an unobserved input or factor of production, and with constant returns to scale implying that G is linearly homogeneous in X and U.

Taking $Y = G(X, U) = F^{-1}(U|X)$ to be a structural model is a very tempting construction. It says that, once we abandon the idea that errors must appear additively in models, we can assume that all unobserved heterogeneity takes the form of independent uniform errors! This would appear to conflict with

Browning's claim that the way we model errors is often too simplistic, that is, there is typically more (and more complicated) unobserved heterogeneity in the world than in our models.

The source of this conflict is that the clean error construction $Y = G(X, U)$ requires that G be the inverse of F, but a model $Y = g(X, \theta, U)$ that has some economically imposed structure is typically not the inverse of F. Equivalently, the construction of G assumes that the unobserved heterogeneity U equals conditional quantiles of Y, while a structural model g may assume errors of another form. For example, in the random coefficients model $Y = a + bX + (e_1 + e_2X)$ the error $\varepsilon = e_1 + e_2X$ appears additively, and imposing constant returns to scale in X, ε implies only $a = 0$. In contrast, with an independent uniform error U the model is $Y = G(X, U) = a + bX + (\sigma_1^2 + \sigma_2^2X^2)^{1/2}\Phi^{-1}(U)$ where Φ^{-1} is the inverse of the cumulative standard normal distribution function. I chose this example for its simplicity, but even in this model one can see that imposing structure like additivity in U or constant returns to scale in X, U would place very different restrictions on behavior than imposing additivity in ε or constant returns to scale in X, ε.

Browning and Carro consider structural models we could write generically as latent additive error models, $Y = g(h(x) + U)$. Knowing that we can always write $Y = G(X, U)$ with U independent of X, we might hope that after imposing a relatively mild restriction like latent additivity, the resulting errors U in $Y = g(h(x) + U)$ could still be close to independent. However, using panels that are long enough to permit separate estimation for each household, Browning and Carro find empirically that the distribution of U depends strongly on X in complicated ways.

3 MULTIPLE EQUATIONS, COHERENCE, AND INVERTIBILITY

Now consider multiple equation models, so Y is now a vector of endogenous variables. Once we allow for nonadditivity or nonlinearity of errors or endogenous regressors, the issue of coherency arises. An incoherent model is one in which, for some values of the errors or regressors, there is either no corresponding value for Y, or multiple values for Y (when the incoherence only takes the form of multiple solutions, the problem is sometimes called incompleteness). See Heckman (1978), Gourieroux, Laffont, and Monfort (1980), Blundell and Smith (1994), and Tamer (2003).

For example, consider the simple system of equations $Y_1 = I(Y_2 + U_1 \geq 0)$, $Y_2 = \alpha Y_1 + U_2$, where I is the indicator that equals one if its argument is true and zero otherwise. This system might arise as the reaction function of two players in a game, one of whom chooses a discrete strategy Y_1, and the other a continuous strategy Y_2. This innocuous looking model is incoherent. The system has multiple solutions, implying both $Y_1 = 0$ and $Y_1 = 1$, when $-a \leq U_1 + U_2 < 0$, and it has no solution, with neither $Y_1 = 0$ nor $Y_1 = 1$ satisfying the system, if $0 \leq U_1 + U_2 < -a$. This example is from Lewbel

(2005), who provides general conditions for coherency of models like these. Examples of incoherent or incomplete economic models similar to this example include Bresnahan and Reiss (1991) and Tamer (2003).

When we write down econometric models, coherence is usually taken for granted to such an extent that many researchers are unaware of the concept. This may be due to the fact that linear models, optimizing models, and triangular models are all generally coherent, or typically incomplete in only harmless ways, such as potential ties in optimizing solutions that occur with probability zero.

A coherent model is one that has a well-defined reduced form, that is, it's a model for which a function G exists such that $Y = G(X, U)$ for all values that X and U can take on. Closely related to coherence is invertibility. A model is invertible if a function H exists such that $U = H(Y, X)$, so a coherent model can be solved for Y and an invertible model can be solved for U. Invertibility is convenient for estimation, for example, it implies one can do maximum likelihood if the U distribution is parameterized, or one can construct moments for GMM estimation if U is uncorrelated with instruments. For structural models, if U represents unobserved taste or technology parameters, then invertibility generally means that we can estimate the distribution of these tastes or technologies.

Invertibility depends on how the structural model, and hence the corresponding errors, are defined. The probit model $Y = I(a + bX + e \geq 0)$ with standard normal e independent of X is, like most latent variable models, coherent but not invertible in the latent error e. However, this model can be rewritten as $Y = \Phi(a + bX) + \varepsilon$ which is invertible in the heteroskedastic error $\varepsilon = Y - E(Y|X)$.

With a continuously distributed vector Y, Matzkin uses an extension of the idea of inverting the distribution function to construct coherent, invertible models, with errors U that are independent of X. Let $Y = (Y_1, Y_2)$. Define errors $U = (U_1, U_2)$ by $U_1 = F_1(Y_1|X)$, and $U_2 = F_2(Y_2|X, U_1)$, where F_1 and F_2 are conditional distribution functions of Y_1 and Y_2. Then let $G_j = F_j^{-1}$ to obtain the coherent, invertible, triangular model $Y = G(X, U)$ defined by $Y_1 = G_1(X, U_1)$ and $Y_2 = G_2(X, U_1, U_2)$. The extension to Y_3 and up is immediate. As before, the question that arises is whether this construction of G is just a statistical trick or a model that represents underlying behavior, and whether economic modeling restrictions can be imposed on this G without reintroducing substantial dependence of U on X (and without introducing incoherence).

Consider the example where Y is a consumption bundle, that is, a K vector of quantities of goods that an individual consumes, determined by maximizing a utility function subject to a linear budget constraint. Then X is a vector consisting of the prices of the K goods, the consumer's income or total expenditures on goods, and observed characteristics of the consumer that affect or are otherwise correlated with the consumer's utility function. In this model, U is interpreted as a vector of unobserved utility function parameters. A necessary condition for coherence and invertibility of this model is that U have $K - 1$ elements. Roughly, this is because the demand functions for $K - 1$ of the goods each have an error term corresponding to an element of U, and then the budget constraint pins down the quantity of the K'th good.

Actually, achieving coherency and invertibility in this application is surprising difficult, because utility maximization imposes constraints on $Y = G(X, U)$, such as symmetry and negative semidefiniteness of the Slutsky matrix, that must be satisfied for every value that U can take on. See, for example, van Soest, Kapteyn, and Kooreman (1993). In particular, if consumers are price takers with fixed preferences, then the utility parameters U should be independent of prices, but semidefiniteness imposes inequality constraints on demand functions and hence upon U that, except for very special classes of preferences, will generally be functions of prices. Similarly, Lewbel (2001) shows that additive demand errors must generally be heteroskedastic. Another example that Browning mentions is that popular utility functions for empirical demand system estimation do not coherently encompass ordinary heterogeneity models such as random coefficients.

Brown and Matzkin (1998) provide one rather restrictive demand model that is coherent and invertible, which are demands derived from a random utility function of the form $V(Y) + \widetilde{Y}'U$, where $\widetilde{Y}$ denotes the K-vector Y with one element Y_K removed. Beckert and Blundell (2004) provide some generalizations of this model. See also the stochastic-revealed preference results summarized in McFadden (2005). Matzkin's paper combines these concepts, considering coherent, invertible demands with unobservables U independent of X, reparameterized using the above technique of sequentially inverting distribution functions, and gives conditions for their nonparametric identification.

4 NONPARAMETRIC IDENTIFICATION

There is a small but growing literature on identification with incomplete (and hence in that way incoherent) models, which is closely related to set identification concepts, but the vast bulk of the identification literature assumes coherent, complete models. I will focus on ordinary point identification assuming coherency, but note that the unknown objects we are identifying can be entire functions, not just finite parameter vectors.

The statistical model $F(Y|X)$ tells us everything we can know from the data about the response in Y to a change in X. We can therefore define identification as the ability to recover unknown structural parameters or functions from the statistical model. For example, in the normal random coefficients model $Y = (a + e_1) + (b + e_2)X$ identification means obtaining the parameter values, a, b, σ_1, and σ_2 from the distribution function F. With $F(Y|X) = N(a + bX, \sigma_1^2 + \sigma_2^2 X^2)$, the slope and intercept of the function $E(Y|X)$ are a and b, while the slope and intercept of the function $var(Y|X^2)$ are σ_1 and σ_2, so we have identification. More generally, in the random coefficients model the joint distribution of the two random variables $a + U_1$ and $b + U_2$ is nonparametrically identified assuming they are independent of X, a fact that Browning exploits in some of his work.

Brown (1983) and Roehrig (1988) provided general conditions for nonlinear and nonparametric identification of structural functions. Assume a coherent, invertible model with error vector U that is independent of X, and invert the structural model $Y = G(X, U)$ to obtain $U = H(Y, X)$. The model H or equivalently G is nonparametrically identified if there does not exist any other observationally equivalent model, that is, any alternative inverse model $\widetilde{H}(Y, X)$ such that $\widetilde{U}$ defined by $\widetilde{U} = \widetilde{H}(Y, X)$ is also independent of X, where $\widetilde{H}$ also possesses whatever properties were used to define or characterize H. These properties could be parameterizations or functional restrictions such as additivity, separability, homogeneity, monotonicity, or latent index constructions.

Such identification generally requires some normalizations of parameters or of functions, for example, we must rule out trivial cases where $\widetilde{H}$ is just a simple monotonic transformation of H. With some assumptions, Roehrig (1988) expressed this identification condition as a restriction on the rank of a matrix of derivatives of $\partial H(Y, X)/\partial Y$, $\partial H(Y, X)/\partial X$, $\partial \widetilde{H}(Y, X)/\partial Y$, and $\partial \widetilde{H}(Y, X)/\partial X$, and Brown (1983) earlier provided a similar expression based on parameterization.

Recently, Benkard and Berry (2004) found, by means of a counterexample, a flaw in this characterization of identification. The source of the problem is that one must consider both $H(Y, X)$ and the distribution function of U, $F_U(U) = F_U(H(Y, X))$. Matzkin (2005b) fixes the Brown and Roehrig results, showing that the matrix one actually needs to check the rank of depends on functions of derivatives of F_U and $F_{\widetilde{U}}$ as well as the above derivatives of H and $\widetilde{H}$.

Matzkin (2005a) applies this result to a range of coherent demand models. Some cleverness is required to find sufficient functional restrictions and normalizations to obtain nonparametric identification. This generally involves limiting the number and dimension of unknown functions by using additivity and separability restrictions. One example she considers is utility-derived demand systems with K goods and a linear budget constraint using the utility function $V(\widetilde{Y}) + \widetilde{Y}'U + Y_K$ with U independent of X. She shows nonparametric identification of V and the distribution of U in this model, essentially using this new nonparametric identification machinery to recast and extend results from Brown and Matzkin (1998).

Another example she considers is utility-derived demand systems with two goods and a linear budget constraint, which for coherence and invertibility requires that U equals a scalar U_1, and assuming U_1 is independent of X. A general utility function $V(Y_1, Y_2, U_1)$ is not identified from demand functions in this case, essentially because a general three-dimensional function cannot be recovered from two demand equations. Matzkin obtains nonparametric identification in this example by reducing the dimensionality of the problem, specifically by assuming the utility function has the additively separable form $V_1(Y_1, Y_2) + V_2(Y_1, U_1)$, where V_1, and V_2 are unknown functions that she shows can be nonparametrically identified from $F(Y|X)$ (essentially corresponding to non-parametric Marshallian demand functions), again assuming a suitably normalized U that is independent of X.

Matzkin also considers stronger restrictions on utility to obtain identification in cases where either total expenditures or prices are not observed. The former is closely related to nonlinear hedonic modeling (see, e.g., Ekeland, Heckman, and Nesheim, 2002) while the latter is concerned with Engel curve estimation. Regarding the latter, it would be useful to derive the connections between these new identification theorems and results in the older demand system literature on identification of Engel curve rank (Gorman, 1981; Lewbel, 1991), and identification of equivalence scales using Engel curve data and the related use of variation in characteristics to help identify price effects (Barten, 1964; Lewbel, 1989; Muellbauer, 1974).

5 DISCRETE CHOICE MODELS

In his presentation, Browning observed, "Conventional schemes have usually been devised by statisticians to introduce hetereogeneity in such a way as to allow us to immediately take it out again." This is particularly true in discrete choice models, where estimators, and associated assumptions about all types of errors (not just heterogeneity) are often chosen based on tractibility rather than behavioral realism. A particularly egregious example is the widespread use of the linear probability model to deal with measurement errors, endogeneity, or fixed effects.

Browning and Carro consider parametric dynamic discrete choice models allowing for substantial heterogeneity, including both fixed effects and coefficients that vary across individuals. They note that in short (fixed T) panels, the presence of individual-specific parameters implies that unbiased estimators for transition probabilities do not exist and they propose, as an alternative to maximum likelihood estimation, a bias adjusted maximum likelihood estimator and a minimum integrated mean squared error estimator. These results and estimators are essentially applications of recent theoretical advances in the larger literature on the incidental parameters problem. See, for example, Hahn and Newey (2004) and Woutersen (2004). However, it is informative to see just how much these adjustments matter in empirical work, and more importantly, how strong the evidence is for all kinds of unobserved heterogeneity

Turning to less parametric models, let Z be a scalar variable that is observed along with the vector X. Assume Y is conditionally independent of Z, conditioning on X. Assume now that we do *not* observe Y, but instead observe a discrete binary D given by the latent variable threshold crossing model $D = I(Y - Z > 0)$ where I is the indicator function that equals one when its argument is true and zero otherwise. For example, D could indicate the purchase of a good, where Z is a price faced by the consumer and Y is the consumer's unobserved reservation price. More generally, Y could be an unobserved benefit and Z the observed cost of some decision D, or Z could be any observed variable that monotonically affects the probability of choosing $D = 1$, and Y is all other observed and unobserved variables that determine D.

In this model $E(D|Z, X) = 1 - \Pr(Y \leq Z|X, Z) = 1 - F(Z|X)$, where as before F denotes the conditional distribution of the (now latent) Y conditioning on X. It follows that the distribution F is identified for all Y on the support of Z, and is therefore identified everywhere if the support of Z is large enough to contain the support of Y. Here Z is a special regressor as in Lewbel (2000), who uses this construction to estimate parameters in a model of Y.

Most of Matzkin's discrete choice identification results are variants of this construction. In particular, any set of assumptions that are used to identify a model $Y = g(X, U)$ where X and a continuous Y are observed can now alternatively be used to identify the latent variable discrete choice model $D = I(Z - g(X, U) \geq 0)$ where we instead observe D, Z, and X. Lewbel (2000) focused on linear $g(X, U)$ with errors U that are heteroskedastic or correlated with some elements of X (such as endogenous or mismeasured regressors). Lewbel, Linton, and McFadden (2004) use this model to estimate nonparametric conditional moments of Y. Matzkin considers cases such as nonparametric G assuming an independent U. Lewbel and Matzkin also both extend these ideas to multinomial choice, assuming we can observe a separate Z for each possible choice.

6   ENDOGENOUS REGRESSORS

Matzkin next considers identification of some general nonparametric models with endogenous regressors. In addition to the special regressor as above, another general technique for identifying such models is control function methods (See Lewbel, 2004 for a comparison of the two methods in the above discrete choice context when g is linear). The control function approach has a long history going back at least to Heckman (1978), but in its modern form assumes we observe vectors Y, X, and instruments Z where $Y = g(X, U)$ and $X = r(Z, e)$ and U and e are correlated. The key assumption here is that U and e are independent of Z, so the source of endogeneity is only through e, that is, X and U are correlated *only* because e and U are correlated. This then implies that X and U are conditionally independent, conditioning on e, so instead of identifying the g model based on $F(Y|X)$, we can instead use $F(Y|X, e)$. Essentially, the control function method consists of fixing the endogeneity problem by nonparametrically including e as an additional regressor in the model for Y. For example, If $Y = r(X'\beta + U)$, $X = Z'\alpha + e$, and $U = e\gamma + \varepsilon$, where ε is independent of e and Z, then $Y = r(X'\beta + e\gamma + \varepsilon)$ and ε must be independent of e and X, so including both X and e as regressors results in a model that no longer suffers from endogeneity.

We now have a whole range of tools that can be mixed and matched. Essentially, any of the earlier described techniques could be used in the first step to define and identify e in $X = r(Z, e)$, and again any might be used in the second step to define and identify U. For example, in the first stage if the endogenous

X is continuous then e could be defined by inverting the conditional distribution function of X given Z, or if the endogenous X is discrete then the distribution function of e could be obtained using a special regressor in the X model. Either method could also be used in the model for Y given X and e. Other variants can also be applied in either step, for example, semiparametric parameters of the Y model could be obtained when Y is discrete from a nonparametric regression of Y on X and e as in Blundell and Powell (2004). Matzkin (2004) suggests exchanging the roles of Z and e, letting e be an observed covariate and z be an unobserved instrument, which then removes the need to identify and estimate e. Other examples and variations include Altonji and Matzkin (2005), Chesher (2003), and Imbens and Newey (2003).

With such an assortment of models to choose from, there is little excuse for continued use of flawed specifications such as the linear probability model for dealing with problems like endogeneity and heterogeneity.

7 CONCLUSIONS

In classical econometrics, virtually all errors were treated (either essentially or literally) as measurement errors. Models such as McFadden (1973) that took errors seriously as heterogeneity parameters were the exception rather than the rule. However, it is clear that the errors in most microeconomic relationships are so large and systematic that they must to some extent represent true structural heterogeneity (though misspecification and mismeasurement may also loom large). Indeed, it is common in microeconomic models to see R^2 statistics far below a half, that is, often most of the variation in Y is unexplained individual variation. The errors matter more than the regressors! This is a humbling realization for the researcher, but it demonstrates the crucial importance of developing specification, identification, and estimation methods that incorporate realistic models of unobserved individual variation.

References

ALTONJI, J. AND R. L. MATZKIN (2005): "Cross Section and Panel Data Estimators for Nonseparable Models with Endogenous Regressors," *Econometrica*, 73, 1053–1102.

BARTEN, A. P. (1964): "Family Composition, Prices, and Expenditure Patterns," in *Econometric Analysis for National Economic Planning: 16th Symposium of the Colston Society*, edited by P. Hart, G. Mills, and J. K. Whitaker, pp. 277–292, London: Butterworth.

BECKERT, W. AND R. BLUNDELL (2004): "Invertibility of Nonparametric Stochastic Demand Functions," Birkbeck Working Papers in Economics and Finance No. 406.

BENKARD, C. L. AND S. BERRY (2004): "On the Nonparametric Identification of Nonlinear Simultaneous Equations Models": Comment on B. Brown (1983) and Roehrig (1988), Cowles Foundation Discussion Paper No. 1482.

BLUNDELL, R. AND J. L. POWELL (2004): "Endogeneity in Semiparametric Binary Response Models," *Review of Economic Studies*, 71, 581–913.

BLUNDELL, R. AND R. J. SMITH (1994): "Coherency and Estimation in Simultaneous Models with Censored or Qualitative Dependent Variables," *Journal of Econometrics*, 64, 355–373.

BRESNAHAN, T. F. AND P. C. REISS (1991): "Empirical Models of Discrete Games," *Journal of Econometrics*, 48, 57–81

BROWN, B. W. (1983): "The Identification Problem in Systems Nonlinear in the Variables," *Econometrica*, 51, 175–196.

BROWN, D. J. AND R. L. MATZKIN (1998): "Estimation of Nonparametric Functions in Simultaneous Equations Models, with an Application to Consumer Demand," Cowles Foundation Discussion Papers 1175, Cowles Foundation, Yale University.

BROWNING, M. AND J. CARRO (2005): "Heterogeneity in Dynamic Discrete Choice Models," 2005 Econometric Society World Meetings, London.

CHESHER, A. (2003): "Identification in Nonseparable Models," *Econometrica*, 71, 1405–1441.

EKELAND, I., J. HECKMAN, AND L. NESHEIM (2002): "Identifying Hedonic Models," *American Economic Review*, 92, 304–309.

GORMAN, W. M. (1981): "Some Engel Curves," in *Essays in the Theory and Measurement of Consumer Behaviour in Honor of Sir Richard Stone*, edited by Angus Deaton, Cambridge: Cambridge University Press.

GOURIEROUX, C., J. J. LAFFONT, AND A. MONFORT (1980): "Coherency Conditions in Simultaneous Linear Equations Models with Endogenous Switching Regimes," *Econometrica*, 48, 675–695.

HAHN, J. AND W. NEWEY (2004): "Jackknife and Analytical Bias Reduction for Nonlinear Panel Data Models," *Econometrica* 72, 1295–1319.

HECKMAN, J. J. (1978): "Dummy Endogenous Variables in Simultaneous Equation Systems," *Econometrica*, 46, 931–960.

IMBENS, G. AND W. NEWEY (2003): "Identification and Estimation of Triangular Simultaneous Equations Models without Additivity," Unpublished manuscript.

LEWBEL, A. (1989): "Identification and Estimation of Equivalence Scales Under Weak Separability," *Review of Economic Studies*, 56, 311–316.

———— (1991): "The Rank of Demand Systems: Theory and Nonparametric Estimation," *Econometrica*, 59, 711–730.

———— (2000): "Semiparametric Qualitative Response Model Estimation with Unknown Heteroscedasticity and Instrumental Variables," *Journal of Econometrics* 97, 145–177.

———— (2001): "Demand Systems with and without Errors," *American Economic Review*, 91, 611–618.

———— (2004): "Simple Estimators for Hard Problems," Unpublished manuscript.

———— (2005): "Coherence of Structural Models Containing a Dummy Endogenous Variable," Unpublished manuscript.

LEWBEL, A., O. LINTON, AND D. MCFADDEN (2004): "Estimating Features of a Distribution From Binomial Data," Unpublished manuscript.

MATZKIN, R. L. (2004): "Unobservable Instruments," Unpublished manuscript.

———— (2005a): "Heterogeneous Choice," 2005 Econometric Society World Meetings, London.

———— (2005b): "Identification in Simultaneous Nonparametric Equations," Unpublished manuscript.

MCFADDEN, D. L. (1973): "Conditional Logit Analysis of Qualitative Choice Behavior," in *Frontiers in Econometrics*, edited by P. Zarembka, New York: Academic Press.

McFADDEN, D. L. (2005): "Stochastic Revealed Preference: A Synthesis," *Economic Theory*, 26, 245–264.

MUELLBAUER, J. (1974): "Household Composition, Engel Curves and Welfare Comparisons Between Households," *European Economic Review*, 5, 103–22.

ROEHRIG, C. S. (1988): "Conditions for Identification in Nonparametric and Parametric Models," *Econometrica*, 56, 433–447.

TAMER, E. (2003): "Incomplete Simultaneous Discrete Response Model with Multiple Equilibria," *Review of Economics Studies*, 70, 147–165.

VAN SOEST, A., A. KAPTEYN, AND P. KOOREMAN (1993): "Coherency and Regularity of Demand Systems with Equality and Inequality Constraints," *Journal of Econometrics*. 57, 161–188.

WOUTERSEN, T. (2004): "Robustness Against Incidental Parameters," Unpublished manuscript.

CHAPTER 6

Inference with Weak Instruments[*]
Donald W. K. Andrews[†] and James H. Stock[‡]

Abstract: The standard approach to reporting empirical results in economics is to pro-vide point estimates and standard errors. With this information, confidence intervals (CIs) and tests are constructed using t tests and the normal critical values. In instrumen-tal variables (IVs) regression with weak IVs, this approach is problematic. The most widely used estimator, two-stage least squares (2SLS), has significant bias and is poorly approximated by a normal distribution when IVs are weak and the degree of endogene-ity is medium to strong. In fact, when the parameter space allows for arbitrarily weak IVs the exact finite-sample level of standard CIs of the form "estimate $\pm$ std error $\times$ constant" is zero and t tests have level one.

This paper reviews recent results in the literature on weak IVs that develop an al-ternative approach to inference with weak IVs. With this approach, one reports point estimates accompanied by CIs or tests that have levels that are robust to the strength of the IVs. In particular, CIs are formed by inverting tests that are robust to weak IVs. That is, a CI for a parameter β, say, is the set of points β_0 for which a weak IV robust test fails to reject the null hypothesis $H_0 : \beta = \beta_0$. This is the same method that is used to generate a CI of the form "estimate $\pm$ std error $\times$ constant" except that the test em-ployed is one whose level is robust to weak IVs, rather than a t test based on a normal approximation.

1 INTRODUCTION

This paper focuses on the linear IV model with a single right-hand side (rhs) endogenous variable and independent identically distributed (iid) homoskedas-tic normal errors. The majority of applications involve a single rhs endoge-nous variable. Interest usually is focused on the coefficient on this variable.

[*] This paper was prepared for an invited session at the 2005 Econometric Society World Congress in London. The authors thank Whitney Newey and Richard Smith for comments and the con-ference organizers for their organizational efforts. Andrews and Stock gratefully acknowledge the research support of the National Science Foundation via grant numbers SES-0001706, SES-0417911, and SBR-0214131, respectively.
[†] Cowles Foundation for Research in Economics, Yale University.
[‡] Department of Economics, Harvard University.

Although this basic model is relatively simple, it captures the essence of the problem. Tests whose levels are robust to weak IVs for this model can be extended to the case of non-normal errors, heteroskedastic and/or autocorrelated errors, multiple rhs endogenous variables, and nonlinear moment condition models. This paper discusses these extensions. Not all of them are completely satisfactory.

For a just-identified model, the Anderson-Rubin (AR) test, or a heteroskedasticity and/or autocorrelation robust version of it, is the preferred test because its level is robust to weak IVs and its power properties are quite good – optimal in certain respects. For over-identified models, the AR test still is robust to weak IVs, but its power properties are not as good because it effectively ignores parameter restrictions that arise naturally in the model. The literature has sought tests that are robust to weak IVs and are more powerful than the AR test in over-identified models.

Alternatives to the AR test that have been considered include an LM test and a conditional likelihood ratio (CLR) test. Both of these tests are robust to weak IVs. The power properties of the CLR test have been found to dominate those of the LM and AR tests (with iid homoskedastic normal errors). In fact, the CLR test is found to be essentially on a power envelope for two-sided invariant similar tests. Furthermore, there is no cost in terms of performance of the test when the IVs are strong – the test is asymptotically efficient under standard strong IV asymptotics.

"Conditioning" methods have been developed that can be used to convert t tests, such as the usual one based on the 2SLS estimator, into tests whose levels are robust to weak IVs. The power properties of such tests, however, are found to be distinctly inferior to those of the CLR test. Hence, the CLR test outperforms standard t tests both in terms of level and in terms of level-corrected power under weak IVs and is asymptotically efficient under strong IVs.

Although the CLR test is robust asymptotically to weak IVs and non-normality of the errors, it is not robust to heteroskedasticity and/or autocorrelation of the errors. Nevertheless, versions of the CLR test that are robust to these features have been developed. We recommend such tests and the CIs they generate for general use in IV regression with potentially weak IVs. Furthermore, generalizations of these CLR tests to moment condition models, which are typically estimated by generalized method of moments (GMM), also are available. For moment condition models, we recommend such tests because they are robust to weak IVs and can be expected to have relatively good power properties.

In addition to reviewing some of the recent literature on inference with weak IVs, this paper presents new results for testing under "many weak IV asymptotics." Such asymptotics are designed for the case in which the IVs are weak and the number of IVs, k, is relatively large compared to the sample size n. We find that in this setup the CLR test is still completely robust asymptotically to weak IVs and is essentially on the power envelope for two-sided invariant (similar or nonsimilar) tests. This holds no matter how one specifies the relative magnitude of the strength of the IVs to k in the asymptotics. Hence, the optimal power properties of the CLR test are quite robust to k. The AR and LM tests have power that lies off the power envelope – in some cases by a considerable extent. On the other hand, the level of the CLR test is not completely robust to the magnitude of k relative to n. One does not want to take k too large relative to n. With normal errors, we show that the CLR test has correct size asymptotically provided $k^{3/2}/n \to 0$ as $n \to \infty$. With non-normal errors, Andrews and Stock (2007) show that the same is true if $k^3/n \to 0$ as $n \to \infty$.

We conclude that the "many weak IV" results for the CLR test buttress the argument for employing this test (or heteroskedasticity or autocorrelation robust versions of it) in scenarios with potentially weak IVs.

This paper focuses on hypothesis tests and CIs that are robust to weak IVs, and pays less attention to two other aspects of the weak IV problem. The first neglected topic concerns pretesting for weak instruments: if the instruments are weak, one adopts a robust strategy, but if the instruments are strong, one uses 2SLS. This approach is now common empirical practice and is an improvement over the practice of a decade ago, in which 2SLS was always used without thought about the strength of the instruments. But this approach entails standard concerns about pretests, and as a result we find fully robust tests and CIs more appealing. The second neglected aspect is point estimation. Despite a great deal of work in the finite sample and Edgeworth expansion literatures, there are few sharp results concerning point estimates. Although it is generally found that 2SLS has particularly poor finite sample behavior, each alternative estimator seems to have its own pathologies when instruments are weak. We therefore have focused on testing and CIs that are robust to weak IVs, for which a solution is closer at hand than it is for estimation.

This paper does not discuss the recent literature on IV estimation of treatment effect models in which the treatment effects depend on unobserved individual-specific variables, for example, see Imbens and Angrist (1994) and Heckman and Vytlacil (2005).

The remainder of this paper is organized as follows. Section 2 introduces the model considered in much of the paper. Section 3 discusses what is meant by weak IVs and the problems with 2SLS estimators, tests, and CIs under weak IVs. Section 4 describes "weak IV asymptotics," "many IV asymptotics," and "many weak IV asymptotics." Section 5 covers formal methods for detecting weak IVs. Section 6 discusses the two approaches to tests and CIs mentioned above – t test-based CIs versus CIs obtained by inverting weak IV robust tests. Section 7 describes recent developments for tests whose levels are robust to weak IVs. This includes similar tests via conditioning, optimal power, robustness to heteroskedasticity and/or autocorrelation, power with non-normal errors, and extensions to multiple rhs endogenous variables, coefficients on exogenous variables, and moment condition models. Section 8 briefly outlines some recent developments for estimation with weak IVs. Section 9 does likewise for estimation with many weak IVs. Section 10 presents the new results for testing with many weak IVs.

We note that recent survey papers on weak IVs include Stock, Wright, and Yogo (2002), Dufour (2003), and Hahn and Hausman (2003b).

2 MODEL

We start by defining the model that we focus on for much of the paper. The model is an IV regression model with one endogenous rhs variable, multiple exogenous variables, multiple IVs, and independent identically distributed (iid) homoskedastic normal errors. The exogenous variables and IVs are treated as fixed (i.e., nonrandom).

The reasons for considering this special model are the following. First, the case of a single rhs endogenous variable is by far the most important in empirical applications. Second, asymptotic results for non-normal errors with random or fixed exogenous variables and IVs are analogous to the finite sample results for normal errors with fixed exogenous variables and IVs. Third, results for heteroskedastic and/or autocorrelated errors can be obtained by extending the results for iid homoskedastic errors. Below we discuss these extensions.

The model consists of a structural equation and a reduced-form equation:

$$y_1 = y_2\beta + X\gamma_1 + u,$$

$$y_2 = Z\pi + X\xi + v_2, \tag{2.1}$$

where $y_1, y_2 \in R^n$, $X \in R^{n \times p}$, and $Z \in R^{n \times k}$ are observed variables; $u, v_2 \in R^n$ are unobserved errors; and $\beta \in R$, $\pi \in R^k$, $\gamma_1 \in R^p$, and $\xi \in R^p$ are unknown parameters. We assume that Z is the matrix of residuals from the regression of some underlying IVs, say $\widetilde{Z} \in R^{n \times k}$, on X (i.e., $Z = M_X\widetilde{Z}$, where $M_X = I_n - P_X$ and $P_X = X(X'X)^{-1}X'$). Hence, $Z'X = 0$. The exogenous variable matrix X and the IV matrix Z are fixed (i.e., non-stochastic) and $[X : Z]$ has full column rank $p + k$. The $n \times 2$ matrix of errors $[u : v_2]$ is iid across rows with each row having a mean zero bivariate normal distribution.

The variable y_2 is endogenous in the equation for y_1 (i.e., y_2 and u may be correlated). Endogeneity may be due to simultaneity, left-out variables, or mismeasurement of an exogenous variable. Although we refer to the equation for y_1 as a structural equation, only in the case of simultaneity is the equation for y_1 really a structural equation.

The two reduced-form equations are

$$y_1 = Z\pi\beta + X\gamma + v_1$$
$$y_2 = Z\pi + X\xi + v_2, \quad \text{where}$$
$$\gamma = \gamma_1 + \xi\beta \text{ and } v_1 = u + v_2\beta. \tag{2.2}$$

The reduced-form errors $[v_1 : v_2]$ are iid across rows with each row having a mean zero bivariate normal distribution with 2×2 nonsingular covariance matrix Ω. The parameter space for $\theta = (\beta, \pi', \gamma', \xi')'$ is taken to be $R \times R^k \times R^p \times R^p$. Let $Y = [y_1 : y_2] \in R^{n \times 2}$ denote the matrix of endogenous variables.

In empirical applications, interest often is focused on the parameter β on the rhs endogenous variable y_2.

3   WEAK INSTRUMENTS

It is well known that there are two key properties for IVs: (i) exogeneity, that is, lack of correlation of the IVs with the structural equation error, and (ii) relevance, that is, the ability of the IVs to explain the rhs endogenous variables. For many years, considerable attention has been paid in applications to the issue of exogeneity. Only more recently has attention been paid to relevance. Weak IVs concern relevance.

IVs are weak if the mean component of y_2 that depends on the IVs, viz., $Z\pi$, is small relative to the variability of y_2, or equivalently, to the variability of the error v_2. This can be measured by the population partial R^2 of the equation (2.1) for y_2 (where the effect of the exogenous variables X is partialed out). In sample, it can be measured by the sample partial R^2 or, equivalently, by the F statistic for the null that $\pi = 0$ in (2.1), see Shea (1997), Godfrey (1999), and Section 5.

Note that IVs can be weak and the F statistic small, either because π is close to zero or because the variability of Z is low relative to the variability of v_2. Also, note that in practice the issue typically is how close to zero is π or $Z\pi$, not whether π or $Z\pi$ is exactly equal to zero.

There are numerous examples of weak IVs in the empirical literature. Here we mention three. The first is the classic example from labor economics of Angrist and Krueger's (1991) IV regression of wages on the endogenous variable years of education and additional covariates. Dummies for quarter of birth (with and without interactions with exogenous variables) are used as IVs for years of education. The argument is that quarter of birth is related to years of education via mandatory school laws for children aged sixteen and lower. At best, the relationship is weak, which leads to weak IVs.[1] A notable feature of this application is that weak instrument issues arise despite the fact that Angrist and Krueger use a 5% Census sample with hundreds of thousands of observations. Evidently, weak instruments should not be thought of as merely a small-sample problem, and the difficulties associated with weak instruments can arise even if the sample size is very large.

---

[1] Angrist and Krueger's (1991) results for models with covariates use 30 quarter of birth times year of birth IVs, see their Tables IV–VI, or these IVs plus 150 quarter of birth times state of birth IVs, see their Tables VII and VIII. In all of these cases, the IVs are found to be weak via the Stock and Yogo (2005a) tests for the null hypothesis of weak IVs described below – compare the first-stage F statistics reported in Staiger and Stock (1997, Tbl. II), which lie between 1.87 and 6.85, with level 0.05 critical values between 10.3 and 11.3 for the test based on 2SLS bias (discussed in Section 5). On the other hand, if one only uses three quarter of birth dummies as the IVs, then the IVs are not found to be weak via the Stock and Yogo (2005a, 2005b) tests for weak IVs – the first stage F statistics are 26.32 or 30.53 for the cases reported in Staiger and Stock (1997, Tbl. II).

The second example is from the macroeconomics/finance literature on the consumption CAPM. Interest concerns the elasticity of intertemporal substitution. In both linear and nonlinear versions of the model, IVs are weak, for example, see Neeley, Roy, and Whiteman (2001), Stock and Wright (2000), and Yogo (2004). In one specification of the linear model in Yogo (2004), the endogenous regressor is consumption growth and the IVs are twice lagged nominal interest rates, inflation, consumption growth, and log dividend–price ratio. Since log consumption is close to a random walk (see Hall, 1978), consumption growth is difficult to predict. This leads to the IVs being weak. For example, Yogo (2004) finds F statistics for the null hypothesis that $\pi = 0$ in the first stage regression that lie between 0.17 and 3.53 for different countries.

The third example is from the macroeconomics literature on the new Keynesian Phillips curve. Inference typically is carried out using IV methods, see Mavroeidis (2004), Nason and Smith (2005), and Dufour, Khalaf, and Kichian (2006). Twice-lagged real marginal cost (labor share in income) or change in inflation are used as IVs for current inflation growth. Given that changes in inflation are difficult to predict, the IVs are weak.

Much of the current interest in weak IVs started with two important papers by Nelson and Startz (1990a, 1990b) which showed the dramatically non-normal distributions of the 2SLS estimator and t statistic when instruments are weak. The effect of weak IVs on these 2SLS statistics depends considerably on the degree of endogeneity, which is measured by the correlation, ρ_{u,v_2}, between u and v_2. If $\rho_{u,v_2} = 0$ or ρ_{u,v_2} is close to zero, then standard procedures work well (in terms of low bias and test and CI levels being close to their nominal values). When the IVs are weak and the degree of endogeneity is fairly strong, however, the 2SLS estimator has appreciable bias and the normal approximation to its distribution is poor. See Nelson and Startz (1990a, 1990b), Maddala and Jeong (1992), and Woglom (2001).

There is also a considerable earlier literature that is relevant to this issue, see the references in Phillips (1984). But, most of the early finite sample literature tended not to focus on the properties of procedures when the IVs are weak, because the empirical relevance of this scenario was not recognized. On other hand, for the LIML estimator, Phillips (1984, 1989) and Choi and Phillips (1992) investigate the finite sample and asymptotic properties under the limiting case of completely irrelevant IVs (lack of identification) as well as the case of partial identification. Their results show quite different sampling properties under lack of identification or partial identification compared to strong identification. This suggests that problems arise when the model is identified, but the IVs are weak. [It is interesting to note that in models with stochastically and/or deterministically trending variables, such as cointegrated models, completely irrelevant IVs are not necessarily weak and the properties of IV procedures with completely irrelevant IVs can be quite different compared to models with non-trending variables, see Phillips (2005).]

An influential paper by Bound, Jaeger, and Baker (1995) analyzes the properties of 2SLS in the context of Angrist and Krueger's (1991) regression of wages on education and exogenous variables. It shows that even when the sample size is huge, the properties of 2SLS can be poor in the face of many weak IVs. The sample size is not the key parameter. What matters most is the concentration parameter, $\lambda_{\text{conc}} = \pi'Z'Z\pi/\sigma_{v_2}^2$ (where $\sigma_{v_2}^2$ is the variance of v_2) and the degree of endogeneity, ρ_{uv_2}. The earlier finite sample literature was aware of this, for example, see Rothenberg (1984).

Generic results for models with isolated unidentified points in the parameter space also have had an impact on the weak IV literature. Gleser and Hwang (1987) establish dramatic results concerning the levels of CIs and tests when the parameter space includes unidentified points. Dufour (1997) extends these results and applies them to the weak IV regression model. Consider any parametric model with parameters $(\beta, \pi) \in R^2$. Suppose the observations have common support. Suppose β is unidentified when $\pi = 0$. In this scenario, Gleser and Hwang's (1987) result states that a CI for β must have infinite length with positive probability – otherwise its (exact) level is zero. This result also holds (essentially by a continuity argument) if the parameter space is taken to be $\{(\beta, \pi) \in R^2 : \pi \neq 0\}$, which only includes identified points. The usual "estimator $\pm$ std error $\times$ constant" CI has finite length with probability one. Hence, the finite-sample confidence level of such a CI is zero under the specified conditions. Analogously, the finite sample significance levels of t tests and Wald tests are one. These conclusions do not apply to LR and LM tests and CIs based on them because these CIs are not necessarily finite with probability one.

The conclusion from the result of Gleser and Hwang (1987) and Dufour (1997) is that CIs and tests based on t tests and Wald tests cannot be fully robust to weak IVs. This concern is not just a theoretical nicety: numerical studies included in the papers cited in this section have demonstrated that coverage rates of conventional TSLS confidence intervals can be very poor when instruments are weak, even if the sample size is large, in designs calibrated to practical empirical applications such as the Angrist–Krueger data and the consumption CAPM.

4   ASYMPTOTICS

In this section we discuss some basic tools that are used in the weak IV literature, viz., different types of asymptotics. Asymptotic results are widely used in econometrics to provide approximations and to facilitate comparisons of estimators or tests. For the IV regression model, standard asymptotics let $n \to \infty$ and hold other features of the model fixed. We refer to these asymptotics as *strong IV asymptotics*. These asymptotics provide poor approximations in the IV regression model with weak IVs because (i) weak IVs correspond to a relatively small value of $\lambda = \pi'Z'Z\pi$, (ii) the finite sample properties of estimators and tests are sensitive to the magnitude of λ, and (iii) the asymptotic framework results in $\lambda \to \infty$.

In consequence, the literature on weak IVs has considered several alternative asymptotic frameworks. For linear models, Staiger and Stock (1997) consider asymptotics in which

$$\pi = C/\sqrt{n} \quad \text{for } n = 1, 2, \ldots \tag{4.1}$$

for some constant k-vector C. Combined with the standard assumption that $Z'Z/n \to D_Z$ as $n \to \infty$, for some $k \times k$ nonsingular matrix D_Z, this yields

$$\lambda = \pi'Z'Z\pi = C'(Z'Z/n)C \to C'D_ZC \quad \text{as } n \to \infty. \tag{4.2}$$

Thus, under this asymptotic setup, λ converges to a finite constant as $n \to \infty$. Depending on the magnitude of the constant, the IVs are weaker or stronger. We refer to these asymptotics as *weak IV asymptotics*. Weak IV asymptotics are analogous to local-to-unity asymptotics that are widely used in the unit root time series literature.

An attractive feature of weak IV asymptotics is that they provide better approximations than standard asymptotics for the case where λ is small, yet still allow for the usual simplifications regarding non-normality, heteroskedasticity, and/or autocorrelation of the errors as under standard asymptotics. Under weak IV asymptotics, estimation of the 2×2 reduced-form covariance matrix, Ω, is an order of magnitude easier than estimation of the structural parameters (β, γ_1). In consequence, one typically obtains the same weak IV asymptotic results whether Ω is known or estimated, which is another useful simplification.

Under weak IV asymptotics, the "limiting experiment" is essentially the same as the finite sample model with iid homoskedastic normal errors and known reduced-form covariance matrix Ω. This has the advantages listed in the previous paragraph, but the disadvantage that the finite-sample normal model is significantly more complicated than the usual Gaussian-shift limiting experiment.

A second type of asymptotics utilized in the literature lets $k \to \infty$ as $n \to \infty$ with π fixed for all n. We call this *many IV asymptotics*. These asymptotics are appropriate when k is relatively large. But, Bekker (1994) argues that these asymptotics provide better approximations than standard asymptotics even when k is small. Many IV asymptotics have been employed by Anderson (1976), Kunitomo (1980), Morimune (1983), Bekker (1994), Donald and Newey (2001), Hahn (2002), Hahn, Hausman, and Kuersteiner (2004), and Hansen, Hausman, and Newey (2005) among others.

A third type of asymptotics, introduced by Chao and Swanson (2005) and Han and Phillips (2006), are *many weak IV asymptotics* in which $k \to \infty$ and $\pi \to 0$ as $n \to \infty$. These asymptotics are designed for the case in which one has relatively many IVs that are weak. Many weak IV asymptotics are employed by Stock and Yogo (2005a), Anderson, Kunitomo, and Matsushita (2005), Hansen, Hausman, and Newey (2005), and Newey and Windmeijer (2005). Sections 9 and 10 consider estimation and testing under many weak IV asymptotics.

5   DETECTING WEAK IVs

A small first stage F statistic for $H_0 : \pi = 0$ (or, equivalently, a low partial R^2) provides evidence that IVs are weak. Stock and Yogo (2005b) develop formal tests based on the F statistic for the null hypothesis: (1) the bias of 2SLS is greater than 10% of the bias based on OLS. The null of weak IVs is rejected at the 5% level if the first stage F statistic exceeds a critical value that depends on the number of IVs and ranges between 9.1 and 11.5. They also consider the null hypothesis that (2) the null rejection rate of the nominal 5% 2SLS t test concerning β has a rejection rate of 10% or greater. The critical values for this test are larger than the critical values of the 10% bias test, so IVs that are weak according to the bias test also are weak according to the size test. Analogous tests when the null hypothesis is specified in terms of the LIML estimator or Fuller's (1977) modification of LIML are provided in Stock and Yogo (2005b). These tests have different (smaller) critical values.

The adverse effect of weak IVs on standard methods, such as 2SLS, depends on the degree of endogeneity present as measured by ρ_{uv_2}, the correlation between the structural and reduced-form errors u and v_2. But, ρ_{uv_2} is difficult to estimate precisely when the IVs are weak. In particular, ρ_{uv_2} cannot be consistently estimated under weak IVs asymptotics. (The reason is that the residuals used to estimate u depend on some estimator of β, and β cannot be consistently estimated under weak IV asymptotics.) In consequence, the F tests of Stock and Yogo (2005b) are designed to be valid for any value of ρ_{uv_2}.

An alternative test for the detection of weak IVs based on reverse regressions is given by Hahn and Hausman (2002). Unfortunately, this test has very low power and is not recommended, at least for the purpose of detecting weak instruments, see Hausman, Stock, and Yogo (2005).

If one uses an F test to detect weak IVs as a pre-test procedure, then the usual pre-testing issues arise for subsequent inference, for example, see Hall, Rudebusch, and Wilcox (1996). The approach of Chioda and Jansson (2004), which considers tests concerning β that are valid conditional on the value of the F statistic, can deal with such pre-testing issues. A drawback of this approach, however, is that it sacrifices power.

6   APPROACHES TO INFERENCE WITH WEAK IVs

In most areas of econometrics, the standard method is to report a parameter estimate along with its standard error. Then, one utilizes CIs of the form "estimator $\pm$ std error $\times$ constant," and one carries out t tests using critical values from the normal distribution. This approach is suitable if the estimator has a distribution that is centered approximately at the true value and is reasonably well approximated by the normal distribution. In the case of IV estimation, this approach does not work well if the IVs are weak, as discussed in Section 3.

One approach to dealing with weak IVs is to follow the "estimate/standard error" reporting method combined with a pre-test for weak IVs and/or a suitable choice of (bias-corrected) estimator, standard error estimator, and/or IVs in order to improve the normal approximation. For example, a sophisticated version of the latter is given in Donald and Newey (2001). See Hahn and Hausman (2003b), Hahn, Hausman, and Kuersteiner (2004), Hansen, Hausman, and Newey (2005), Newey and Windmeijer (2005), and Section 8 for results and references to the literature. This approach is justified if the parameter space is bounded away from the unidentified set of parameter values where $\pi = 0$. But, the approach is not fully robust to weak IVs.

An alternative approach is to report an estimate and CI, where the CI is fully robust to weak IVs asymptotically. By this we mean that the CI has asymptotically correct coverage probability under standard asymptotics for $\pi \neq 0$ and under weak IV asymptotics (which includes the standard asymptotic case with $\pi = 0$). For testing, this approach uses tests that are fully robust to weak IVs asymptotically. For the weak IV problem, this approach was advocated first by Anderson and Rubin (1949), and more recently by Dufour (1997) and Staiger and Stock (1997).

Fully-robust CIs can be obtained by inverting fully-robust tests. For example, a CI for β of (approximate) level $100(1 - \alpha)\%$ consists of all parameter values β_0 for which the null hypothesis $H_0 : \beta = \beta_0$ is not rejected at (approximate) level 5%. Note that standard CIs of the form "estimator $\pm$ std error $\times$ constant" are obtained by inverting t tests. Thus, the only difference between the CIs used in the first and second approaches is that the second approach employs tests that are fully robust to weak IVs rather than t tests. Papers that discuss the mechanics of the inversion of robust tests to form CIs include Zivot, Startz, and Nelson (1998), Dufour and Jasiak (2001), and Dufour and Taamouti (2005). Papers that report empirical results using CIs obtained by inverting fully-robust tests include Yogo (2004), Nason and Smith (2005), and Dufour, Khalaf, and Kichian (2006).

We advocate the second approach. In consequence, we view robust tests to be very important, and we focus more attention in this paper on testing than on estimation.

7 DEVELOPMENTS IN TESTING FOR THE LINEAR MODEL

In this section, we consider testing in the model specified in (2.1)–(2.2). In applications, interest often is focused on the parameter β on the rhs endogenous variable y_2. Hence, our interest is in the null and alternative hypotheses:

$$H_0 : \beta = \beta_0 \quad \text{and} \quad H_1 : \beta \neq \beta_0. \tag{7.1}$$

The parameter π, which determines the strength of the IVs, is a nuisance parameter that appears under the null and alternative hypotheses. The parameters γ, ξ, and Ω are also nuisance parameters, but are of lesser importance because tests concerning β typically are invariant to γ and ξ, and Ω is much more easily estimated than π.

We desire tests that are robust to weak IVs under normal or non-normal errors. In addition, we desire tests that exhibit robustness under weak and strong IV asymptotics to (i) left-out IVs, (ii) nonlinearity of the reduced-form equation for y_2, (iii) heteroskedasticity – in cross-section contexts, (iv) heteroskedasticity and/or autocorrelation – in some time series contexts, and (v) many IVs – in some contexts.

Some, for example, Dufour (1997), desire tests whose finite-sample null rejection rate is exactly the desired significance level under iid homoskedastic normal errors for any π. But, we view this as putting excessive weight on the iid homoskedastic normal assumptions, which are not likely to hold in practice.

Here we evaluate tests based on their significance levels and power functions. An alternative approach, based on decision theory, is studied by Chamberlain (2005) for the linear IV model. In the latter approach, nuisance parameters, such as π, are in general integrated out using a prior.

7.1   Anderson–Rubin and LM Tests

The first test employed specifically to deal with weak IVs is the Anderson and Rubin (1949) (AR) test, see Dufour (1997) and Staiger and Stock (1997). The AR test imposes the null $\beta = \beta_0$ and uses the F test for the artificial null hypothesis $H_0^* : \kappa = 0$ in the model

$$y_1 - y_2\beta_0 = Z\kappa + X\gamma + u. \tag{7.2}$$

The AR test statistic is

$$AR(\beta_0) = \frac{(y_1 - y_2\beta_0)' P_Z (y_1 - y_2\beta_0)/k}{\widehat{\sigma}_u^2(\beta_0)}, \quad \text{where}$$

$$\widehat{\sigma}_u^2(\beta_0) = \frac{(y_1 - y_2\beta_0)' M_{[Z:X]}(y_1 - y_2\beta_0)}{n - k - p}. \tag{7.3}$$

Under the null hypothesis $H_0 : \beta = \beta_0$, we have

$$AR(\beta_0) = \frac{u' P_Z u/k}{u' M_{[Z:X]} u/(n - k - p)}. \tag{7.4}$$

The null distribution of the AR statistic does not depend on π regardless of the distribution of the errors u and the AR test is fully robust to weak IVs. Under H_0, $AR(\beta_0) \rightarrow_d \chi_k^2/k$ under strong and weak IV asymptotics assuming iid homoskedastic errors u with two moments finite. Under the additional assumption of normal errors, $AR(\beta_0) \sim F_{k,n-k-p}$. Hence, an F critical value is typically employed with the AR test. As pointed out by Dufour (2003), the AR test does not rely on any assumptions concerning the reduced-form equation for y_2. But, the AR test is not robust to heteroskedasticity and/or autocorrelation of the structural equation error u.

Under the alternative hypothesis,

$$AR(\beta_0) = \frac{(u + Z\pi(\beta - \beta_0))' P_Z(u + Z\pi(\beta - \beta_0))}{u' M_{[Z:X]} u / (n - k - p)}. \tag{7.5}$$

In consequence, power depends on the magnitude of $\pi' Z' Z\pi(\beta - \beta_0)^2$. The power of the AR test is very good when $k = 1$. Moreira (2001) shows that it is UMP unbiased when the errors are iid homoskedastic normal, Ω is known, and $k = 1$. In the same scenario, AMS shows that it is UMP in terms of two-point average power in the class of invariant similar tests.

On the other hand, when $k > 1$, the power of the AR test is not so good. It is a k degrees of freedom test when only one parameter is under test. When the true parameter is β, the model can be written as

$$y_1 - y_2\beta_0 = Z\pi(\beta - \beta_0) + X\gamma + v_1. \tag{7.6}$$

The AR test tests whether Z enters this equation. The AR test sacrifices power because it ignores the restriction that $\kappa = \pi(\beta - \beta_0)$. Obviously, low power is an undesirable property for tests, and it leads to excessively long CIs based on such tests.

The literature has sought more powerful tests than the AR test that are robust to weak IVs. To start, one might consider the LR test of $H_0 : \beta = \beta_0$. The LR statistic combined with the conventional χ_1^2 critical value is not robust to weak IVs when $k > 1$. But, Wang and Zivot (1998) show that a larger critical value, obtained by bounding the asymptotic distribution of the LR statistic over π values, is robust to weak IVs. However, the resulting test is nonsimilar asymptotically under weak IV asymptotics (i.e., its asymptotic null rejection rate depends on π). In consequence, the test is biased and sacrifices power. For instance, the test is not asymptotically efficient under strong IV asymptotics.

Kleibergen (2002) and Moreira (2001) independently introduce an LM test whose null rejection rate is robust to weak IVs. They use different ideas to arrive at the LM test. Kleibergen's idea is as follows: The AR statistic projects $y_1 - y_2\beta_0$ onto the k-dimensional space spanned by Z. Instead, one can estimate π under the null hypothesis via the ML estimator, $\widehat{\pi}(\beta_0)$, and project onto the one-dimensional space spanned by $Z\widehat{\pi}(\beta_0)$. It turns out that $\widehat{\pi}(\beta_0)$ is asymptotically independent of $y_1 - y_2\beta_0$ under the null under strong and weak IV asymptotics. Hence, a suitably scaled version of the projection residuals is asymptotically χ_1^2 under the null hypothesis under both strong and weak IV asymptotics. The resulting test statistic is an LM statistic and it is fully robust to weak IVs. [For an alternative derivation of this LM statistic, see Poskitt and Skeels (2005).]

The power of the LM test often is better than that of the AR test when $k > 1$, but not always. A drawback of the LM test is that it exhibits quirky power properties including non-monotonicity in $|\beta - \beta_0|$, for example, see Andrews, Moreira, and Stock (2004, 2006b).

We note that when $k = 1$ the LM, LR, and AR tests are equivalent because the LM and LR statistics equal k times the AR statistic.

7.2   Similar Tests

Moreira (2001, 2003) gives a characterization of (exactly) similar tests of H_0 : $\beta = \beta_0$ for the model of (2.1)–(2.2) with normal errors and known Ω. Similar tests are necessarily fully robust to weak IVs because their null distribution does not depend on π. When Ω is unknown, a consistent estimator of Ω, say $\widehat{\Omega}$, can be plugged in for Ω and an exactly similar test becomes a test that is asymptotically similar under weak IV asymptotics (and typically under strong IV asymptotics as well).

By definition, a level α test $\phi(Y)$ (which equals one when the test rejects H_0 and zero otherwise) is similar if

$$E_\pi \phi(Y) = \alpha \text{ for all } \pi, \tag{7.7}$$

where $E_\pi(\cdot)$ denotes expectation under (β_0, π).

Moreira's argument leading to the characterization of similar tests is as follows. Under the null hypothesis, the unknown parameter is π. Using standard methods, for example, Lehmann (1986), the null-restricted ML estimator of π, $\widehat{\pi}(\beta_0)$, can be shown to be a complete sufficient statistic for π because the parametric model is in the exponential family of distributions. By definition, a sufficient statistic $\widehat{\pi}(\beta_0)$ is complete for π if, for any real function $h(\cdot)$, $E_\pi h(\widehat{\pi}(\beta_0)) = c$ for all π implies that $h(\cdot) = c$ a.s. for some constant c. Applying this definition of complete sufficiency with $h(\cdot) = E_\pi(\phi(Y)|\widehat{\pi}(\beta_0) = \cdot)$ and using the law of iterated expectations gives:

$$E_\pi h(\widehat{\pi}(\beta_0)) = E_\pi E_\pi(\phi(Y)|\widehat{\pi}(\beta_0)) = E_\pi \phi(Y) = \alpha \text{ for all } \pi \tag{7.8}$$

implies that $h(\cdot) = E_\pi(\phi(Y)|\widehat{\pi}(\beta_0) = \cdot) = \alpha$ a.s. That is, $\phi(Y)$ is similar with level α implies that

$$E_\pi(\phi(Y)|\widehat{\pi}(\beta_0) = x) = \alpha \text{ for all } x. \tag{7.9}$$

The converse is immediate by the law of iterated expectations.

Given this result, similar tests can be created from nonsimilar tests by employing a conditional critical value function $\kappa_{\phi,\alpha}(x)$ defined by

$$\kappa_{\phi,\alpha}(x) = E(\phi(Y)|\widehat{\pi}(\beta_0) = x) = \alpha \tag{7.10}$$

(where the expectation is taken under the null). Then, a similar test based on ϕ rejects H_0 if

$$\phi(Y) > \kappa_{\phi,\alpha}(\widehat{\pi}(\beta_0)). \tag{7.11}$$

This method generates "conditional tests" that are similar. For example, one can generate a conditional Wald test given an estimator such as 2SLS or LIML.

In addition, one can consider the CLR test. Moreira (2003) focuses on this test. It is a more sophisticated version of Wang and Zivot's (1998) LR test in which a critical value function replaces a constant to achieve the desired level α. The CLR test has higher power than the Wang–Zivot LR test.

The CLR test based on a plug-in value of Ω has asymptotic null rejection rate α under both weak and strong IV asymptotics and, hence, is fully robust to weak IVs.

Note that the critical value function $\kappa_{\phi,\alpha}(x)$ of (7.10) can be computed by numerical integration or simulation and then tabulated, see Andrews, Moreira, and Stock (2007) for an efficient algorithm and Andrews, Moreira, and Stock (2006b) for detailed tables.

Moreira, Porter, and Suarez (2004) introduce a residual-based bootstrap for the CLR test which is shown to be first-order correct under strong IV asymptotics whether $\pi = 0$ or $\pi \neq 0$. Its behavior under weak IV asymptotics is not discussed. This bootstrap does not deliver higher-order improvements.

7.3 Optimal Tests

The "conditioning" method leads to a surfeit of tests that are fully robust to weak IVs because any test can be made fully robust. Given this, Andrews, Moreira, and Stock (2006a) (AMS) address the question of optimal tests that are robust to weak IVs. They consider the class of similar tests for the model of (2.1)–(2.2) with iid homoskedastic normal errors and known Ω. If π is known, then it is plausible that an optimal two-sided test is just the t test of $H_0 : \beta = \beta_0$ in the model

$$y_1 - y_2\beta_0 = (Z\pi)(\beta - \beta_0) + X\gamma + u. \tag{7.12}$$

Indeed, Moreira (2001) shows that the two-sided t test for the case when π and Ω are known is UMP unbiased. But π is not known in practice, so no optimal two-sided test exists. The problem is that the class of tests considered is too large. In consequence, AMS restricts attention to similar tests that satisfy a rotational invariance property.

The data matrix Y has a multivariate normal distribution, which is a member of the exponential family of distributions. In consequence, low-dimensional sufficient statistics are available. For tests concerning β, there is no loss (in terms of attainable power functions) in considering tests that are based on the sufficient statistic $Z'Y$ for $(\beta, \pi')'$, see AMS. This eliminates the nuisance parameters (γ, ξ) from the problem. The nuisance parameter π remains. As in Moreira (2003), we consider a one-to-one transformation of $Z'Y$ given by $[S : T]$, where

$$S = (Z'Z)^{-1/2}Z'Yb_0 \cdot (b_0'\Omega b_0)^{-1/2},$$

$$T = (Z'Z)^{-1/2}Z'Y\Omega^{-1}a_0 \cdot (a_0'\Omega^{-1}a_0)^{-1/2},$$

$$b_0 = (1, -\beta_0)' \quad \text{and} \quad a_0 = (\beta_0, 1)'. \tag{7.13}$$

The invariant tests considered in AMS depend on S and T only through the maximal invariant statistic Q defined by

$$Q = [S{:}T]'[S{:}T] = \begin{bmatrix} S'S & S'T \\ T'S & T'T \end{bmatrix} = \begin{bmatrix} Q_S & Q_{ST} \\ Q_{ST} & Q_T \end{bmatrix}. \qquad (7.14)$$

(See AMS for the definition of the groups of transformations on the data matrix $[S{:}T]$ and the parameters (β, π) that yields the maximal invariant to be Q. Note that $Y'P_Z Y$ is an equivalent statistic to Q.)

For example, the AR, LM, and LR test statistics can be written as

$$AR = Q_S/k, \; LM = Q_{ST}^2/Q_T, \quad \text{and}$$

$$LR = \frac{1}{2}\left(Q_S - Q_T + \sqrt{(Q_S - Q_T)^2 + 4Q_{ST}^2}\right). \qquad (7.15)$$

The only tests that we are aware of that are not functions of Q are tests that involve leaving out some IVs and t tests based on Chamberlain and Imbens' (2004) many IV estimator.

The matrix Q has a noncentral Wishart distribution with means matrix of rank one and identity variance matrix. The distribution of Q (and hence of invariant similar tests) only depends on the unknown parameters β and

$$\lambda = \pi'Z'Z\pi \in R, \qquad (7.16)$$

where λ indicates the strength of the IVs (and is proportional to the concentration parameter λ_{conc}). The utilization of invariance has reduced the k-vector nuisance parameter π to a scalar nuisance parameter λ. The distribution of Q also depends on the number IVs, k, and the parameter of interest, β.

AMS derives a power envelope for two-sided invariant similar (IS) tests and compares new and existing tests to the power envelope. The power envelope is determined by the tests that are point optimal for each (β, λ) combination. There are several ways to impose two-sidedness. First, AMS considers average power against two points (β^*, λ^*) and (β_2^*, λ_2^*), where (β_2^*, λ_2^*) is selected given (β^*, λ^*) to be the unique point such that β_2^* is on the opposite side of the null value β_0 from β^* and such that the test that maximizes power against these two points is asymptotically efficient (AE) under strong IV asymptotics. The power envelope is then a function of (β^*, λ^*). Second, AMS considers tests that satisfy a sign-invariance condition that the test depends on Q_{ST} only through $|Q_{ST}|$. This is satisfied by most tests in the literature including the AR, LM, and CLR tests. Third, AMS considers locally unbiased tests. Andrews, Moreira, and Stock (2006b) show that the first and second approaches yield exactly the same power envelope. Furthermore, numerical calculations show that the third approach yields a power envelope that is hard to distinguish from the first and second.

Andrews, Moreira, and Stock (2004) develop a class of new tests based on maximizing weighted average power (WAP) given different weight functions on (β, λ). These tests and the AR, LM, and CLR tests are compared numerically to the two-sided power envelope for IS tests. The power envelope only depends on β, λ, k, $\rho = \text{corr}(v_1, v_2)$ and is smooth in these parameters. Hence, it is possible to make fairly exhaustive comparisons.

Figure 6.1 illustrates some of these comparisons for the case of $k = 5$ instruments. The figure plots the power of the AR, LM, and CLR tests as a function of β, along with the asymptotically efficient power envelope for two-sided invariant similar tests. The first three panels show the effect of varying $\rho = \text{corr}(v_1, v_2)$ (negative values of ρ correspond to reversing the sign of $\beta - \beta_0$) and for $\beta_0 = 0$ (taken without loss of generality). Panels (a)–(c) consider rather weak instruments, $\lambda = 10$, which corresponds to a first-stage F statistic having a mean of $\lambda/k + 1 = 3$ under the null. Panel (d) presents the power functions for a case of relatively strong instruments, $\lambda = 80$.

Figure 6.1 and other results in AMS and Andrews, Moreira, and Stock (2006b) show that the CLR test is essentially on the power envelope for all β, λ, k, and ρ. In contrast, the AR test typically is below the power envelope – the more so, the larger is k. In addition, the LM test has a quirky non-monotone power function that is sometimes on the power envelope and sometimes far from it. See AMS for an explanation of this behavior. Results in Andrews, Moreira, and Stock (2004) indicate that some point-optimal IS two-sided (POIS2) tests are very close to the power envelope, like the CLR test. This is also true of some WAP tests based on nondegenerate weight functions. But, these tests do not have as simple closed-form expressions as the LR test statistic.

One might ask the question of whether the restriction to similar tests is overly restrictive. Andrews, Moreira, and Stock (2006c) provide results for the power envelope for invariant nonsimilar tests using the least favorable distribution approach of Lehmann (1986). It is found to be very close to that for similar tests. Hence, the imposition of similarity does not appear to be overly restrictive.

The finite sample power envelope for known Ω that is determined in AMS is shown to be the same as the weak IV asymptotic power envelope for unknown Ω. Hence, the feasible CLR test is (essentially) on the weak IV asymptotic power envelope for two-sided IS tests under the assumption of normal errors. In addition, AMS shows that the CLR test (and the LM test) are asymptotically efficient under strong IV asymptotics.

Based on these results, we recommend the CLR test among tests that are designed for iid homoskedastic normal errors.

7.4 Conditional LR Test

There is a one-to-one transformation from the restricted ML estimator $\widehat{\pi}(\beta_0)$ to the statistic Q_T. Hence, the CLR test can be written such that it rejects the null hypothesis when

$$LR > \kappa_\alpha^{CLR}(Q_T), \tag{7.17}$$

where $\kappa_\alpha^{CLR}(Q_T)$ is defined to satisfy $P_{\beta_0}(LR > \kappa_\alpha^{CLR}(q_T)|Q_T = q_T) = \alpha$.

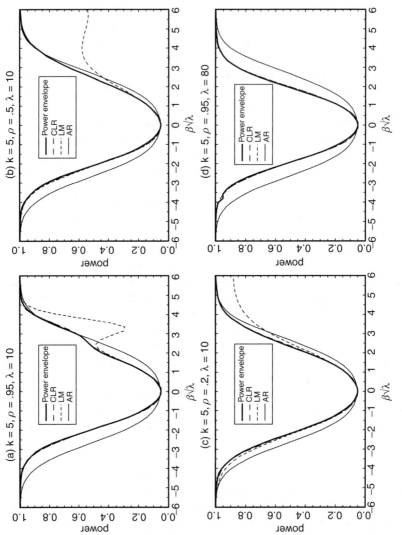

Figure 6.1. Asymptotically efficient two-sided power envelopes for invariant similar tests and power functions for the two-sided CLR, LM, and AR tests, $k = 5$, $\rho = 0.95, 0.5, 0.2$.

We note that the LR statistic combines the AR and LM statistics based on the magnitude of $Q_T - Q_S$. If Q_T is much larger than Q_S, then LR is essentially LM. If Q_T is much smaller than Q_S, then LR is essentially $k \cdot$AR. This can be seen more clearly by re-writing LR as follows:

$$LR = \frac{1}{2} \left(Q_S - Q_T + |Q_T - Q_S| \sqrt{1 + \frac{4Q_T}{(Q_T - Q_S)^2} LM} \right).$$

(7.18)

Now, as $Q_T \to \infty$ and $Q_S/Q_T \to 0$, we have (i) $Q_T - Q_S \to \infty$, (ii) $Q_T/(Q_T - Q_S)^2 \to 0$, (iii) the $\sqrt{\cdot}$ term is approximately $1 + 2[Q_T/(Q_T - Q_S)^2]LM$ by a mean-value expansion, (iv) $|Q_T - Q_S| = Q_T - Q_S$, (v) $|Q_T - Q_S|[Q_T/(Q_T - Q_S)^2]LM$ goes to LM, and (vi) LR goes to LM. On the other hand, as $Q_T \to 0$, (i) the $\sqrt{\cdot}$ term goes to 1, (ii) $Q_S - Q_T + |Q_T - Q_S|$ goes to $2Q_S$, and (iii) LR goes to $Q_S = k \cdot AR$.

Fast algorithms for computing confidence intervals by inverting the CLR test are now available, see Mikusheva and Poi (2006).

We briefly illustrate the use of the CLR test to construct CIs using some results from Yogo (2004). Yogo reports CIs for the elasticity of intertemporal substitution obtained from regressions of stock returns on consumption growth using quarterly data from 1970 to 1998 with four IVs: twice-lagged nominal interest rate, inflation, consumption growth, and log of the dividend/price ratio. CIs are obtained by inverting AR, LM, and CLR tests. Yogo (2004) reports results for several countries. For most countries, the CIs are $(-\infty, \infty)$ using all three methods because the IVs are very weak in this model specification. For Canada, the CIs are AR: [.02, 4.03], LM: [.05, .35], and CLR: [.04, .41]. In this case, the AR CI is much wider than LM and CLR CIs. For France, the CIs are AR: $[-.28, .20]$, LM: $(-\infty, \infty)$, and CLR: $[-.16, .11]$. In this case, the LM CI is uninformative and the CLR CI is noticeably shorter than the AR CI. These results illustrate that the power advantages of the CLR test translate into shorter more informative CIs (at least in these applications).

7.5   Conditional t Tests

The usual test employed in practice is a t test based on the 2SLS estimator. Analogously, the usual CI employed is a t test-generated CI of the form "estimator $\pm$ std error $\times$ constant." As noted above, a t test using the normal approximation is not robust to weak IVs. But, one can construct a conditional t test that is robust by using a conditional critical value function like that for the CLR test. In consequence, one can answer the question of how good is a t test in terms of power once it has been corrected to get its size correct.

Andrews, Moreira, and Stock (2007) compare the power properties of conditional t tests based on several estimators, including 2SLS, LIML, and Fuller's (1977) modification of LIML, to the CLR test and the power envelope for two-sided IS tests. In short, the results indicate that t tests have very poor power properties when the IVs are weak. Power is often very low on one side of the null hypothesis. The CLR test has much better power properties. We conclude that in the presence of weak IVs, t tests not only lack robustness to weak IVs in terms of size, but their power properties are also poor after size-correction by conditioning.

7.6   Robustness to Heteroskedasticity and/or Autocorrelation

Although the CLR test has good power properties, it is not robust to heteroskedasticity or autocorrelation. However, the LR test statistic can be replaced by a heteroskedasticity-robust version, HR-LR, or a heteroskedasticity and autocorrelation-robust version, HAR-LR, that is robust, see Andrews, Moreira, and Stock (2004).

Given the HR-LR or HAR-LR statistic, the same conditional critical value function as for the CLR test is used to yield HR-CLR and HAR-CLR tests. These tests are robust to heteroskedasticity and/or autocorrelation under weak and strong IV asymptotics. They are also robust to left-out IVs and nonlinear reduced form for y_2, which can be viewed to be causes of heteroskedasticity. Furthermore, the asymptotic properties of the HR-CLR and HAR-CLR tests under homoskedasticity are the same as those of the CLR test. So, HR-CLR and HAR-CLR tests are optimal IS two-sided tests under homoskedastic iid errors.

Kleibergen (2005, 2007) also gives heteroskedasticity and/or autocorrelation robust tests that reduce to the CLR test under homoskedasticity. Kleibergen's tests apply in the more general context of nonlinear moment conditions. Note that Kleibergen's tests are not the same as those in AMS under heteroskedasticity and/or autocorrelation even asymptotically under weak IV asymptotics. But, they are equivalent asymptotically under weak and strong IV asymptotics with homoskedastic iid errors.

Other tests that are robust to weak IVs as well as to heteroskedasticity and/or autocorrelation can be based on generalized empirical likelihood methods; these tests are discussed in Section 7.10.

7.7   Power with Non-Normal Errors

The power results of Section 7.3 are for normal errors. The question arises whether tests exist with good power for normal errors and higher power for non-normal errors. In certain contexts, the answer is yes. In particular, rank-based versions of the AR and CLR tests have this property, see Andrews and Marmer (2004) and Andrews and Soares (2007). With iid homoskedastic (possibly non-normal) errors and given certain conditions on the exogenous variables and IVs, the rank-based AR test based on normal scores has exact significance level α and has power that asymptotically dominates the power of the AR test. Specifically, its power is higher for thick-tailed error distributions. Hence, under the given conditions and $k = 1$ (in which case, the AR, LM, and CLR tests are the same), the rank-based AR test is quite attractive. It is robust to left-out

IVs and nonlinear reduced form for y_2. On the other hand, it is not robust to heteroskedasticity or autocorrelation of the structural errors u. It also relies on stronger assumptions concerning the exogenous variables and IVs than the AR test. Hence, there is a trade-off between the rank and non-rank tests.

When $k > 1$, the rank-based CLR test has power advantages over the CLR test for thick tailed errors. But, it is not robust to heteroskedasticity or autocorrelation. Hence, there is a trade-off between the rank-based CLR test and the HR-CLR and HAR-CLR tests in terms of power against non-normal errors and these robustness properties.

We conclude that in certain circumstances rank-based tests are preferable to the HR-CLR or HAR-CLR tests. But, in most circumstances, the latter are preferred.

7.8   Multiple Right-Hand Side Endogenous Variables

Next, suppose y_2 and β are vectors. The AR, LM, and CLR tests of $H_0 : \beta = \beta_0$ all generalize to this case, see Anderson and Rubin (1949), Kleibergen (2002), and Moreira (2003). All of these tests are robust to weak IVs. One would expect the relative power properties of these tests to be similar to those in the case of a scalar β. However, the optimal power properties of the CLR test established in AMS do not carry over in a straightforward manner because the Wishart distribution of the (data) matrix Q that appears in the vector β case has a means matrix of rank two or greater, rather than rank one. Nevertheless, based on the scalar β power comparisons, we recommend the CLR (HR-CLR, or HAR-CLR) test over the AR and LM tests. The CLR test does have the drawback that the conditional critical value function is higher-dimensional and, hence, more cumbersome in the vector β case.

To obtain a CI or test for an individual coefficient, say β_1, in the vector $\beta = (\beta_1, \beta_2')' \in R^m$, there are several approaches to inference when the IVs are weak – none is completely satisfactory. First, one can construct a CI via the projection method. The idea is to construct an approximate $100(1 - \alpha)\%$ confidence region in R^m for β using a test that is robust to weak IVs. Then, the approximate $100(1 - \alpha)\%$ CI for β_1 is the set of β_1 values for which $(\beta_1, \beta_2')'$ is in the confidence region for some β_2. In turn, an approximate level α test of $H_0 : \beta_1 = \beta_{10}$ rejects the null hypothesis if β_{10} is not in the CI for β_1. For the application of this method using the AR test, see Dufour and Jasiak (2001) and Dufour and Taamouti (2005). A drawback of this method is that it is conservative. Hence, it yields CIs that are longer than desirable.

An alternative method, discussed in Moreira (2005), relies on exclusion restrictions in the reduced-form equations for the endogenous variables whose coefficients are β_2 in the structural equation. Given suitable restrictions, tests are available that are asymptotically similar under weak and strong IV asymptotics. Such tests have the drawback of relying on exclusion restrictions and of sacrificing power – they are not asymptotically efficient under strong IV asymptotics.

A third approach is available that is partially robust to weak IVs. Suppose β_1 is asymptotically weakly identified and β_2 is asymptotically strongly identified. See Stock and Wright (2000), Kleibergen (2004), or Guggenberger and Smith (2005a) for precise definitions of what this means. Then, asymptotically non-conservative tests for β_1 are available by concentrating out β_2. Simulation results in Guggenberger and Smith (2005a) indicate that this method works fairly well in terms of size even if β_2 is not very strongly identified.

7.9   Inference on Other Coefficients

Suppose one is interested in a test or CI concerning a coefficient, say γ_a, on an exogenous variable, say X_a, in the structural equation for y_1, where $X\gamma_1 = X_a\gamma_a + X_b\gamma_b$. In this case, t tests based on the 2SLS or LIML estimator of γ_a do not necessarily perform poorly under weak IVs asymptotics. What is key for good performance asymptotically for 2SLS is that y_2 is explained asymptotically by more than just the part of X_a that is orthogonal to X_b. For example, one can show that consistency and asymptotic normality of the 2SLS estimator holds in the model of (2.1)–(2.2) with iid homoskedastic errors u with two moments finite if

$$\liminf_{n\to\infty}(\pi'Z'Z\pi + \xi_b^{*\prime}X_b'X_b\xi_b^*)/n > 0 \quad \text{and}$$

$$\lim_{n\to\infty} X_a^{*\prime}X_a^*/n = M > 0, \text{ where} \tag{7.19}$$

$$y_2 = Z\pi + X_a^*\xi_a + X_b\xi_b^*, \ X_a^* = M_{X_b}X_a, \quad \text{and}$$

$$\xi_b^* = \xi_b + (X_b'X_b)^{-1}X_b'X_a\xi_a.$$

Thus, consistency holds even if $\pi = C/\sqrt{n}$ provided $\liminf_{n\to\infty} \xi_b^{*\prime}X_b'X_b\xi_b^*/n > 0$ (and $\lim_{n\to\infty} X_a^{*\prime}X_a^*/n = M > 0$). This sort of result is closely related to results under partial identification of Phillips (1989).

There are several approaches to inference that are robust to weak IVs and small values of $\xi_b^{*\prime}X_b'X_b\xi_b^*$, but none is completely satisfactory. One can use projection as in Section 7.8, but this has the same potential drawback as described above. If X_a (or equivalently X_a^*) does not enter the reduced-form equation for y_2, then $\xi_a = 0$ and least squares estimation of y_1 on X_a^* yields a consistent estimator of γ_a and least squares t tests are invariant to π and ξ_b^*. But, such an exclusion restriction may not be plausible in a given application.

7.10   Tests in Nonlinear Moment Condition Models

Weak IVs appear not only in linear models, but also in nonlinear models specified by moment conditions. Such models typically are estimated by GMM, although generalized empirical likelihood (GEL) estimation also is possible. There have been significant contributions to the literature recently concerning inference in such models when the IVs are weak.

Stock and Wright (2000) extend weak IV asymptotics to nonlinear models by taking part of the population moment function to be local to zero for all values of the parameter as $n \to \infty$. This implies that part of the matrix of derivatives of the sample moments is local to zero as $n \to \infty$. These results allow one to assess both the null rejection probabilities of tests under weak IV asymptotics and their power properties. Stock and Wright (2000) consider extensions of the AR test and corresponding CIs to the nonlinear moment condition model.

Kleibergen (2002, 2005, 2007) extends the weak IV-robust LM test for the IV regression model to the moment condition model. This allows him to construct, by analogy, a CLR test for the nonlinear moment condition model, call it GMM-CLR. The GMM-CLR test is robust to weak IVs and allows for heteroskedasticity and/or autocorrelation. Its power properties have not been investigated, but one would think that in many cases they would reflect the power advantages of the CLR test in linear models.

Generalized empirical likelihood versions of the weak IV robust AR and LM tests have been constructed by Guggenberger and Smith (2005a, 2005b), Otsu (2006), and Caner (2003). These tests are robust to heteroskedasticity and/or autocorrelation. Their properties under the null and alternatives using the weak IV asymptotics of Stock and Wright (2000) are the same as those of the AR and LM moment condition tests. Hence, one would expect that these GEL tests are not as powerful as the GMM-CLR test, at least if the amount of heteroskedasticity and autocorrelation is not too large. We note that it should be possible to construct a GEL-based test that is an analogue of the CLR test. [In fact, Smith (2005) recently has done so.]

Given current knowledge, we recommend the GMM-CLR test of Kleibergen (2005, 2007) for dealing with weak IVs in moment condition models. However, knowledge in this area is not completely developed and it remains an open question whether a test that dominates GMM-CLR can be developed.

8   ESTIMATION WITH WEAK IVs

This section gives a brief discussion of estimation with weak IVs. Under weak IV asymptotics, what is relevant is estimation in the normal linear model with known Ω. There is a substantial older literature comparing estimators in this model. See Rothenberg (1984) and Phillips (1984) for references. But, the relevance of some of this literature is diminished for two reasons. First, many comparisons are based on higher-order expansions under standard SI asymptotics. For example, see Nagar (1959) and Rothenberg (1984) for further references. Hahn, Hausman, and Kuersteiner (2004) (HHK) and Chao and Swanson (2003) find such higher-order expansions are not accurate under weak IV parameter configurations. Second, Monte Carlo comparisons in the older literature tend to be for relatively strong IV parameter configurations, see HHK.

Chamberlain (2005) has provided a theoretical optimality result for the LIMLk estimator (i.e., LIML for the case of known Ω) in the model of (2.1)–(2.2). He shows that LIMLk is minimax for a particular bounded loss function.

He also shows that LIMLk minimizes average risk over certain ellipses in π-space independently of the radius of these ellipses. These are nice theoretical properties, but the lack of finite integer moments of LIML and LIMLk indicates that the loss function employed may not be desirable if one is concerned with large estimation errors.

Via simulation, HHK confirm that LIML displays high dispersion under weak IV parameter configurations relative to other estimators even when dispersion is measured by the interquartile range rather than by the variance (which is infinite for LIML and LIMLk). LIML does exhibit low median bias, which is consistent with LIMLk being exactly median unbiased.

Fuller's (1977) modification of LIML with $a = 1$ or 4 has finite moments and its median-bias is relatively small in HHK's simulations with weak IV parameter configurations. The jackknife 2SLS estimator also fares well in these simulations.

There has been recent research on Bayes estimators for the model of (2.1)–(2.2) that is relevant for weak IV contexts. Kleibergen and van Dijk (1998) consider a diffuse prior that is designed to handle lack of identification due to weak IVs. Kleibergen and Zivot (2003) consider priors that yield posteriors that are of the same form as the densities of 2SLS and LIML. Chao and Phillips (1998, 2002) construct the Jeffreys prior Bayes estimator for the limited information model. Zellner (1998) introduces a Bayesian method of moments estimator (BMOM), which is in the family of double k class estimators. Unlike the other Bayes estimators mentioned above, BMOM is not equivariant to shifts in β. Gao and Lahiri (1999) carry out Monte Carlo comparisons of several of these Bayes estimators under weak IV parameter configurations.

By standard results, Bayes estimators based on proper priors and their limits yield a complete class of estimators for the model with iid homoskedastic normal errors and known Ω. Hence, these estimators also form an asymptotically complete class under weak IV asymptotics when Ω is unknown and is replaced by a consistent estimator.

Other related papers include Forchini and Hillier (2003), who consider conditional estimation given the eigenvalues of the "first stage F" matrix, and Hahn and Hausman (2003a) and Kiviet and Niemczyk (2005), who consider the relative attributes of OLS and 2SLS.

We conclude this section by noting that there does not seem to be any dominant estimation method for the linear model with weak IVs. At this time, we recommend Fuller's (1977) modified LIML estimator with $a = 1$ or 4 as a good choice in terms of overall properties.

9 ESTIMATION WITH MANY WEAK IVs

To date the literature concerning models with many weak IVs has focused on estimation. Chao and Swanson (2005) consider asymptotics in which $k \to \infty$ and $\pi \to 0$ as $n \to \infty$. The idea of their paper is that a sufficient number of weak IVs may provide enough additional information regarding β to yield consistent estimation. Indeed, they establish that consistent estimation of β is possible even if $\pi = C/\sqrt{n}$ (as in weak IV asymptotics) provided $k \to \infty$. For consistency of LIML or the jackknife IV estimator (JIVE), one needs $\lambda/k^{1/2} \to \infty$ as $n \to \infty$, where $\lambda = \pi Z'Z\pi$ indexes the strength of the IVs. For consistency of 2SLS, on the other hand, one needs a faster growth rate of λ: $\lambda/k \to \infty$ as $n \to \infty$. This advantage of LIML over 2SLS is consistent with the higher-order bias properties of LIML and 2SLS under many (non-weak) IV asymptotics, see HHK.

Han and Phillips (2006) consider fixed weight-matrix GMM estimators for nonlinear moment condition models. Their results show that many different types of asymptotic behavior of such estimators is possible depending on the rates of growth of the strength of the IVs relative to k. They provide conditions for convergence in probability to a constant, which is not necessarily the true value. They provide results based on high-level conditions that indicate that the asymptotic distributions of fixed weight-matrix GMM estimators can be normal or non-normal.

Hansen, Hausman, and Newey (2005) and Newey and Windmeijer (2005) analyze LIML and Fuller's (1977) modified LIML estimators and GEL estimators, respectively, when $\lambda/k \to c$ as $n \to \infty$ for some constant $c > 0$. They show that these estimators are asymptotically normal, but with a variance matrix that has an additional term compared to the usual fixed k case. They provide a new asymptotic variance estimator that is asymptotically correct under many weak IV asymptotics when $\lambda/k \to c$. Although this variance estimator helps to robustify inference to many weak IVs, tests and CIs based on this asymptotic approximation are not fully robust to weak IVs or large k.

Anderson, Kunitomo, and Matsushita (2005) consider a (restricted) class of estimators in the linear IV model and show that the LIML estimator satisfies some asymptotic optimality properties within this class under many weak IV asymptotics when $\lambda/k \to c$ as $n \to \infty$ for some constant $c > 0$. [The same is true for Fuller's (1977) modified LIML estimator.]

Chamberlain and Imbens (2004) develop a random-effects quasi-ML estimator based on a random coefficients structure on the relation between the rhs endogenous variable and the IVs. This structure reduces the number of parameters to be estimated. (They do not consider the asymptotic distribution of the estimator under many weak IV asymptotics.)

Chao and Swanson (2003) introduce bias-corrected linear IV estimators based on sequential asymptotics in which $n \to \infty$ and then $\lambda_{conc}/k \to \infty$.

10 TESTING WITH MANY WEAK INSTRUMENTS

In this section, we present new results concerning tests in the asymptotic framework of many weak IVs. We are interested in the relative performance of the AR, LM, and CLR tests and in their performance relative to an asymptotic power envelope.

10.1   Asymptotic Distribution of Q for Large λ and k

We consider the model of (2.1)–(2.2) with iid homoskedastic normal errors. The hypotheses of interest are given in (7.1). The statistics S and T are defined in (7.13). As in AMS, we focus on invariant tests, which are functions of the maximal invariant Q defined in (7.14). Our goal is to obtain an asymptotic two-sided power envelope for invariant tests concerning β when $(\lambda, k) \to \infty$. To achieve this, we need to determine the asymptotic distribution of Q as $(\lambda, k) \to \infty$. For clarity, we sometimes denote Q by $Q_{\lambda,k}$.

The means of S and T depend on the following quantities:

$$\mu_\pi = (Z'Z)^{1/2}\pi \in R^k, \quad c_\beta = (\beta - \beta_0) \cdot (b_0'\Omega b_0)^{-1/2} \in R, \quad \text{and}$$

$$d_\beta = a'\Omega^{-1}a_0 \cdot (a_0'\Omega^{-1}a_0)^{-1/2} \in R, \quad \text{where } a = (\beta, 1)'. \quad (10.1)$$

The distributions of S and T are $S \sim N(c_\beta\mu_\pi, I_k)$, $T \sim N(d_\beta\mu_\pi, I_k)$, and S and T are independent, see Lemma 2 of AMS.

Under the model specification given above, the following assumption holds.

Assumption 1 $Q = Q_{\lambda,k} = [S{:}T]'[S{:}T]$, where $S \sim N(c_\beta\mu_\pi, I_k)$, $T \sim N(d_\beta\mu_\pi, I_k)$, S and T are independent, and $(\mu_\pi, c_\beta, d_\beta)$ are defined in (10.1).

By definition, under Assumption 1, Q has a noncentral Wishart distribution with mean matrix $M = \mu_\pi(c_\beta, d_\beta)'$ (of rank one) and identity covariance matrix. The distribution of Q only depends on μ_π through $\lambda = \mu_\pi'\mu_\pi$. The density of Q is given in Lemma 3 of AMS.

Next, we specify the rate at which λ and k diverge to infinity. Our results allow for a wide range of possibilities. All limits are as $(\lambda, k) \to \infty$. Let $\chi_1^2(\delta)$ denote a noncentral chi-square distribution with one degree of freedom and noncentrality parameter δ.

Assumption 2 $\lambda/k^\tau \to r_\tau$ for some constants $\tau \in (0, \infty)$ and $r_\tau \in [0, \infty)$.

The asymptotic distribution of Q depends on the following quantities:

$$V_{3,\tau} = \begin{cases} Diag\{2, 1, 2\} & \text{if } 0 < \tau \leq 1/2 \\ Diag\{2, 1, 0\} & \text{if } 1/2 < \tau < 1 \\ Diag\{2, 1 + d_{\beta_0}^2 r_1, 0\} & \text{if } \tau = 1 \\ Diag\{2, d_{\beta_0}^2 r_\tau, 0\} & \text{if } \tau > 1 \quad \text{and} \end{cases}$$

$$\gamma_B = (b_0'\Omega b_0)^{-1/2}d_{\beta_0}B \quad (10.2)$$

for a scalar constant B.

The asymptotic distribution of Q is given in the following theorem.

Theorem 1   *Suppose Assumptions 1 and 2 hold.*

(a) *If* $0 < \tau < 1/2$ *and* β *is fixed,*

$$\begin{pmatrix} (S'S - k)/k^{1/2} \\ S'T/k^{1/2} \\ (T'T - k)/k^{1/2} \end{pmatrix} \to_d \begin{pmatrix} \overline{Q}_{S,\infty} \\ \overline{Q}_{ST,\infty} \\ \overline{Q}_{T,\infty} \end{pmatrix} \sim N\left(\begin{pmatrix} 0 \\ 0 \\ 0 \end{pmatrix}, V_{3,\tau} \right),$$

$$(AR - 1)k^{1/2} \to_d \overline{Q}_{S,\infty} \sim N(0, 2), \quad LM \to_d \overline{Q}^2_{ST,\infty} \sim \chi^2_1(0), \quad and$$

$$LR/k^{1/2} \to_d \frac{1}{2}\left(\overline{Q}_{S,\infty} - \overline{Q}_{T,\infty} + \sqrt{(\overline{Q}_{T,\infty} - \overline{Q}_{S,\infty})^2 + 4\overline{Q}^2_{ST,\infty}} \right).$$

(b) *If* $\tau = 1/2$ *and* β *is fixed,*

$$\begin{pmatrix} (S'S - k)/k^{1/2} \\ S'T/k^{1/2} \\ (T'T - k)/k^{1/2} \end{pmatrix} \to_d \begin{pmatrix} \overline{Q}_{S,\infty} \\ \overline{Q}_{ST,\infty} \\ \overline{Q}_{T,\infty} \end{pmatrix} \sim N\left(\begin{pmatrix} c^2_\beta r_{1/2} \\ c_\beta d_\beta r_{1/2} \\ d^2_\beta r_{1/2} \end{pmatrix}, V_{3,1/2} \right),$$

$$(AR - 1)k^{1/2} \to_d \overline{Q}_{S,\infty} \sim N\left(c^2_\beta r_{1/2}, 2 \right),$$

$$LM \to_d \overline{Q}^2_{ST,\infty} \sim \chi^2_1\left(c^2_\beta d^2_\beta r^2_{1/2} \right), and$$

$$LR/k^{1/2} \to_d \frac{1}{2}\left(\overline{Q}_{S,\infty} - \overline{Q}_{T,\infty} + \sqrt{(\overline{Q}_{T,\infty} - \overline{Q}_{S,\infty})^2 + 4\overline{Q}^2_{ST,\infty}} \right).$$

(c) *If* $1/2 < \tau \leq 1$ *and* $\beta = \beta_0 + Bk^{1/2-\tau}$ *for a scalar constant* B,

$$\begin{pmatrix} (S'S - k)/k^{1/2} \\ S'T/k^{1/2} \\ (T'T - k)/k^{\tau} \end{pmatrix} \to_d \begin{pmatrix} \overline{Q}_{S,\infty} \\ \overline{Q}_{ST,\infty} \\ \overline{Q}_{T,\infty} \end{pmatrix} \sim N\left(\begin{pmatrix} 0 \\ \gamma_B r_\tau \\ d^2_{\beta_0} r_\tau \end{pmatrix}, V_{3,\tau} \right),$$

$$(AR - 1)k^{1/2} \to_d \overline{Q}_{S,\infty} \sim N(0, 2),$$

$$LM \to_d \overline{Q}^2_{ST,\infty} \sim \chi^2_1\left(\gamma^2_B r^2_\tau \right) \text{ when } 1/2 < \tau < 1,$$

$$LM \to_d \overline{Q}^2_{ST,\infty}/\left(1 + d^2_{\beta_0} r_1 \right) \sim \chi^2_1\left(\gamma^2_B r^2_\tau/\left(1 + d^2_{\beta_0} r_1 \right) \right) \text{ when } \tau=1,$$

$$LR = \left(1/\left(d^2_{\beta_0} r_\tau \right) \right) k^{1-\tau} LM(1 + o_p(1)) \text{ when } 1/2 < \tau < 1, \text{ and}$$

$$LR = \left(\left(1 + d^2_{\beta_0} r_1 \right)/\left(d^2_{\beta_0} r_1 \right) \right) LM + o_p(1) \text{ when } \tau = 1.$$

(d) *If* $\tau > 1$, $r_\tau > 0$, *and* $\beta = \beta_0 + Bk^{-\tau/2}$,

$$\begin{pmatrix} (S'S - k)/k^{1/2} \\ S'T/k^{\tau/2} \\ (T'T - k)/k^{\tau} \end{pmatrix} \to_d \begin{pmatrix} \overline{Q}_{S,\infty} \\ \overline{Q}_{ST,\infty} \\ \overline{Q}_{T,\infty} \end{pmatrix} \sim N\left(\begin{pmatrix} 0 \\ \gamma_B r_\tau \\ d^2_{\beta_0} r_\tau \end{pmatrix}, V_{3,\tau} \right),$$

$$(AR - 1)k^{1/2} \to_d \overline{Q}_{S,\infty} \sim N(0, 2),$$

$$LM \to_d \overline{Q}^2_{ST,\infty}/\left(d^2_{\beta_0} r_\tau \right) \sim \chi^2_1\left(\gamma^2_B r_\tau/d^2_{\beta_0} \right) \text{ provided } d_{\beta_0} \neq 0, \text{ and}$$

$$LR = LM + o_p(1).$$

Comments
1. An interesting feature of Theorem 1 is that the statistics $S'S$, $S'T$, and $T'T$ are asymptotically independent.
2. Part (a) of the Theorem shows that when the concentration parameter λ grows at a rate slower than $k^{1/2}$, the statistic Q has an asymptotic distribution that does not depend on the parameter β. Hence, in this case, no test has nontrivial asymptotic power.
3. The result of part (a) also holds when λ is fixed and $k \to \infty$.
4. Part (b) of the Theorem is the most interesting case. When the concentration parameter λ grows at the rate $k^{1/2}$, all three normalized statistics $S'S$, $S'T$, and $T'T$ have asymptotic distributions that depend on β. In this case, the growth in λ is not sufficiently fast that consistent estimation of β is possible (otherwise, tests with asymptotic power one against fixed alternatives would be available).
5. Parts (c) and (d) show that when λ grows at a rate faster than $k^{1/2}$, the AR statistic has trivial asymptotic power against local alternatives for which the LM and LR statistics have nontrivial power. Furthermore, in this case the LM and LR statistics are asymptotically equivalent.
6. The cases considered in Chao and Swanson (2005) and Han and Phillips (2006) correspond to $\tau > 1/2$. Those considered in Stock and Yogo (2005a), Anderson, Kunitomo, and Matsushita (2005), and Newey and Windmeijer (2005) correspond to the case where $\tau = 1$. Those considered in Hansen, Hausman, and Newey (2005) correspond to $\tau \geq 1$.

10.2 Two-Sided Asymptotic Power Envelopes

In the next several subsections, we determine asymptotic power envelopes for two-sided tests. We start with the most interesting case in which $\lambda/k^{1/2} \to r_{1/2}$, that is, the case $\tau = 1/2$. Subsequently, we consider the case $\tau > 1/2$. In contrast to the results in AMS, we do not restrict attention to tests that are asymptotically similar. Rather, we allow for both asymptotically similar and nonsimilar tests and show that the power envelope is determined by tests that are asymptotically similar.

There are several ways of constructing a two-sided power envelope depending on how one imposes the two-sidedness condition. The approach we take here is based on determining the highest possible average power against a point $(\beta, \lambda) = (\beta^*, \lambda^*)$ and another point, say (β_2^*, λ_2^*), for which β_2^* lies on the other side of the null value β_0 than β^*. [The power envelope then is a function of $(\beta, \lambda) = (\beta^*, \lambda^*)$.] Given (β^*, λ^*), we select (β_2^*, λ_2^*) in the same way as in AMS. In particular, the point (β_2^*, λ_2^*) has the property that the test that maximizes average power against these two points is *asymptotically efficient* under strong IV asymptotics when the number of IVs k is fixed as $\lambda \to \infty$. Furthermore, the power of the test that maximizes average power against these two points is the same for each of the two points. This choice also has the desirable properties that (a) the marginal distributions of Q_S, Q_{ST}, and Q_T under (β_2^*, λ_2^*) are the same as under (β^*, λ^*) and (b) the joint distribution of (Q_S, Q_{ST}, Q_T) under (β_2^*, λ_2^*) equals that of $(Q_S, -Q_{ST}, Q_T)$ under (β^*, λ^*), which corresponds to β_2^* being on the other side of the null from β^*.

Given (β^*, λ^*), the point (β_2^*, λ_2^*) that has these properties is shown in AMS to satisfy $(\lambda_2^*)^{1/2} c_{\beta_2^*} = -(\lambda^*)^{1/2} c_{\beta^*}$ $(\neq 0)$ and $(\lambda_2^*)^{1/2} d_{\beta_2^*} = (\lambda^*)^{1/2} d_{\beta^*}$ and is given by

$$\beta_2^* = \beta_0 - \frac{d_{\beta_0}(\beta^* - \beta_0)}{d_{\beta_0} + 2g(\beta^* - \beta_0)} \quad \text{and}$$

$$\lambda_2^* = \lambda^* \frac{(d_{\beta_0} + 2g(\beta^* - \beta_0))^2}{d_{\beta_0}^2}, \quad \text{where}$$

$$g = e_1' \Omega^{-1} a_0 \cdot (a_0' \Omega^{-1} a_0)^{-1/2} \quad \text{and} \quad e_1 = (1, 0)' \tag{10.3}$$

(provided $\beta^* \neq \beta_{AR}$, where β_{AR} denotes the point β at which $d_\beta = 0$, see AMS).

The average power of a test $\phi(Q)$ against the two points (β^*, λ^*) and (β_2^*, λ_2^*) is given by

$$K(\phi; \beta^*, \lambda^*) = \frac{1}{2} \left[E_{\beta^*, \lambda^*} \phi(Q) + E_{\beta_2^*, \lambda_2^*} \phi(Q) \right] = E_{\beta^*, \lambda^*}^* \phi(Q), \tag{10.4}$$

where $E_{\beta, \lambda}$ denotes expectation with respect to the density $f_{Q_1, Q_T}(q_1, q_T; \beta, \lambda)$, which is the joint density of (Q_1, Q_T) at (q_1, q_T) when (β, λ) are the true parameters, and E_{β^*, λ^*}^* denotes expectation with respect to the density

$$f_{Q_1, Q_T}^*(q_1, q_T; \beta^*, \lambda^*)$$
$$= \frac{1}{2} [f_{Q_1, Q_T}(q_1, q_T; \beta^*, \lambda^*) + f_{Q_1, Q_T}(q_1, q_T; \beta_2^*, \lambda_2^*)]. \tag{10.5}$$

Hence, the average power (AP) of $\phi(Q)$ against (β^*, λ^*) and (β_2^*, λ_2^*) can be written as the power against the single density $f_{Q_1, Q_T}^*(q_1, q_T; \beta^*, \lambda^*)$.

10.3 Asymptotic Power Envelope for $\tau = 1/2$

We now consider the case where $\tau = 1/2$. We restrict ourselves to invariant tests that depend on the data only through

$$\overline{Q}_{\lambda, k} = (Q_{\lambda, k} - kI_2)/k^{1/2}, \quad \text{where}$$
$$\text{vech}(\overline{Q}_{\lambda, k}) = (\overline{Q}_{S, k}, \overline{Q}_{ST, k}, \overline{Q}_{T, k})'. \tag{10.6}$$

A test $\phi_k(\overline{Q}_{\lambda, k})$ is $\{0, 1\}$-valued and rejects the null hypothesis when $\phi_k = 1$. We say that a sequence of tests $\{\phi_k : k \geq 1\}$ is a *convergent sequence of asymptotically level α tests* for $\tau = 1/2$ if there exists a $\{0, 1\}$-valued function ϕ such that under Assumption 1, under any sequence $\lambda/k^{1/2} \to r_{1/2}$ for any $r_{1/2}$

in some non-empty subset of $[0, \infty)$, and for any β in some set that includes $\{\beta_0, \beta^*, \beta_2^*\}$, we have

$$\phi_k(\overline{Q}_{\lambda,k}) \to_d \phi(\overline{Q}_\infty), \quad \text{where}$$

$$vech(\overline{Q}_\infty) = \begin{pmatrix} \overline{Q}_{S,\infty} \\ \overline{Q}_{ST,\infty} \\ \overline{Q}_{T,\infty} \end{pmatrix} \sim N\left(\begin{pmatrix} c_\beta^2 r_{1/2} \\ c_\beta d_\beta r_{1/2} \\ d_\beta^2 r_{1/2} \end{pmatrix}, V_{3,1/2} \right), \quad \text{and}$$

$$P_{\beta_0, r_{1/2}}(\phi(\overline{Q}_\infty) = 1) \leq \alpha, \tag{10.7}$$

where $P_{\beta, r_{1/2}}(\cdot)$ denotes probability when the true parameters are $(\beta, r_{1/2})$. By Theorem 1, examples of convergent sequences of asymptotically level α tests include sequences of CLR, LM, and AR tests. Standard Wald and LR tests are not asymptotically level α.

We now determine the average power envelope for the asymptotic testing problem. Let $\overline{Q}_\infty$ be distributed as in (10.7). The unknown parameters are β and $r_{1/2}$. We are interested in average power against two points $(\beta^*, r_{1/2}^*)$ and $(\beta_2^*, r_{2,1/2}^*)$, where β_2^* is as defined in (10.3) and $r_{2,1/2}^*$ is the asymptotic analogue of λ_2^* and is defined in (10.3) with λ^* replaced by $r_{1/2}^*$. As in (10.4), the average power of a test based on $\overline{Q}_\infty$ equals its power against the single alternative whose density is the average of the densities for the points $(\beta^*, r_{1/2}^*)$ and $(\beta_2^*, r_{2,1/2}^*)$.

The null hypothesis is composite and the alternative is simple, so we use the "least favorable" approach of Lehmann (1986, Sec. 3.8) to find a best test of level α. The idea is as follows. Given a distribution over the parameters in the null hypothesis, say $G(\cdot)$, one obtains a single distribution by integrating the null distribution with respect to $G(\cdot)$. For any $G(\cdot)$, one can construct the level α LR test for the simple null versus the simple alternative, and it is best according to the Neyman–Pearson Lemma. If one can find a distribution, $G_{LF}(\cdot)$, called a least favorable distribution, for which the simple versus simple LR test is of level α not just for the simple null but for the underlying composite null as well, then this LR test is the best level α test for the composite null versus the simple alternative. The reason is that this test is best against the simple alternative subject to the constraint that the average null rejection rate weighted by $G_{LF}(\cdot)$ is less than or equal to α, which is a weaker constraint than the constraint that the pointwise rejection rate is less than or equal to α for all points in the composite null.

The key step in the implementation of the least favorable approach is the determination of a least favorable distribution. In the present case, the parameter that appears under the null hypothesis is $r_{1/2}$, and it only affects the distribution of $\overline{Q}_{T,\infty}$ because $c_{\beta_0} = 0$ implies that $\overline{Q}_{S,\infty}$ and $\overline{Q}_{ST,\infty}$ have mean zero under H_0 (see (10.7)). The distribution of $\overline{Q}_{T,\infty}$ under $(\beta^*, r_{1/2}^*)$ and $(\beta_2^*, r_{2,1/2}^*)$ is the same because $d_{\beta^*}^2 r_{1/2}^* = d_{\beta_2^*}^2 r_{2,1/2}^*$, see (10.3), and $\overline{Q}_{T,\infty} \sim N(d_\beta^2 r_{1/2}, 2)$ under $(\beta, r_{1/2})$ by (10.7). Hence, the distribution of $\overline{Q}_{T,\infty}$ under the simple alternative whose density is the average of the densities for the points $(\beta^*, r_{1/2}^*)$ and $(\beta_2^*, r_{2,1/2}^*)$ is just $N(d_{\beta^*}^2 r_{1/2}^*, 2)$.

Under the null hypothesis, $\overline{Q}_{T,\infty} \sim N(d_{\beta_0}^2 r_{1/2}, 2)$. Hence, if we postulate that the least favorable distribution is a point mass at $r_{1/2}^{LF}$, where $d_{\beta_0}^2 r_{1/2}^{LF} = d_{\beta^*}^2 r_{1/2}^*$ or equivalently

$$r_{1/2}^{LF} = d_{\beta^*}^2 r_{1/2}^* / d_{\beta_0}^2, \tag{10.8}$$

then $\overline{Q}_{T,\infty}$ has the same distribution under the simple null hypothesis as under the simple alternative hypothesis. Given the independence of $(\overline{Q}_{S,\infty}, \overline{Q}_{ST,\infty})$ and $\overline{Q}_{T,\infty}$, the simple versus simple LR test statistic does not depend on $\overline{Q}_{T,\infty}$. This implies that the pointmass distribution at $r_{1/2}^{LF}$ is indeed least favorable because the simple versus simple LR statistic depends only on $(\overline{Q}_{S,\infty}, \overline{Q}_{ST,\infty})$, the null distribution of the latter does not depend on $r_{1/2}$, and hence, the pointwise null rejection rate of the simple versus simple level α LR test is α for each point in the null hypothesis.

The above discussion establishes that the best test for testing the composite null against the simple alternative based on the average density determined by $(\beta^*, r_{1/2}^*)$ and $(\beta_2^*, r_{2,1/2}^*)$ is given by the likelihood ratio for $(\overline{Q}_{S,\infty}, \overline{Q}_{ST,\infty})$. This likelihood ratio statistic is given by

$$LR^* \left(\overline{Q}_\infty; \beta^*, r_{1/2}^* \right) = LR^* \left(\overline{Q}_{S,\infty}, \overline{Q}_{ST,\infty}; \beta^*, r_{1/2}^* \right)$$

$$= \exp\left(-\frac{1}{4} \left(\overline{Q}_{S,\infty} - c_{\beta^*}^2 r_{1/2}^* \right)^2 \right)$$

$$\times \frac{\left(\exp\left(-\frac{1}{2} \left(\overline{Q}_{ST,\infty} - c_{\beta^*} d_{\beta^*} r_{1/2}^* \right)^2 \right) + \exp\left(-\frac{1}{2} \left(\overline{Q}_{ST,\infty} + c_{\beta^*} d_{\beta^*} r_{1/2}^* \right)^2 \right) \right)}{2 \exp\left(-\frac{1}{4} \overline{Q}_{S,\infty}^2 - \frac{1}{2} \overline{Q}_{ST,\infty}^2 \right)}$$

$$= \exp\left(-c_{\beta^*}^4 r_{1/2}^{*2}/4 - c_{\beta^*}^2 d_{\beta^*}^2 r_{1/2}^{*2}/2 \right) \exp\left(c_{\beta^*}^2 r_{1/2}^* \overline{Q}_{S,\infty}/2 \right) \tag{10.9}$$

$$\times \left(\exp\left(c_{\beta^*} d_{\beta^*} r_{1/2}^* \overline{Q}_{ST,\infty} \right) + \exp\left(-c_{\beta^*} d_{\beta^*} r_{1/2}^* \overline{Q}_{ST,\infty} \right) \right) /2$$

$$= \exp\left(-c_{\beta^*}^4 r_{1/2}^{*2}/4 - c_{\beta^*}^2 d_{\beta^*}^2 r_{1/2}^{*2}/2 \right) \exp\left(c_{\beta^*}^2 r_{1/2}^* \overline{Q}_{S,\infty}/2 \right)$$

$$\times \cosh\left(c_{\beta^*} d_{\beta^*} r_{1/2}^* \overline{Q}_{ST,\infty} \right).$$

The critical value, $\kappa_\alpha^*(\beta^*, r_{1/2}^*)$, for the LR^* test is defined by

$$P(LR^*(N_1, N_2; \beta^*, r_{1/2}^*) > \kappa_\alpha^*(\beta^*, r_{1/2}^*)) = \alpha, \text{ where}$$

$$(N_1, N_2)' \sim N(0, Diag\{2, 1\}). \tag{10.10}$$

By varying $(\beta^*, r_{1/2}^*)$, the power of the $LR^*(\overline{Q}_\infty; \beta^*, r_{1/2}^*)$ test traces out the average power envelope for level α similar tests for the asymptotic testing problem.

The results above lead to the following Theorem, which provides an upper bound on asymptotic average power.

Theorem 2 *The average power over (β^*, λ^*) and (β_2^*, λ_2^*) of any convergent sequence of invariant and asymptotically level α tests for $\tau = 1/2$, $\{\phi_k(\overline{Q}_{\lambda,k}) :$*

$k \geq 1\}$, *satisfies*

$$\lim_{k \to \infty} (1/2) \left[P_{\beta^*, \lambda^*}(\phi_k(\overline{Q}_{\lambda,k}) = 1) + P_{\beta_2^*, \lambda_2^*}(\phi_k(\overline{Q}_{\lambda,k}) = 1) \right]$$

$$= P_{\beta^*, r_{1/2}^*}^*(\phi(\overline{Q}_\infty) = 1)$$

$$\leq P_{\beta^*, r_{1/2}^*}^* \left(LR^*(\overline{Q}_\infty; \beta^*, r_{1/2}^*) > \kappa_\alpha(\beta^*, r_{1/2}^*) \right),$$

where $P_{\beta, \lambda}(\cdot)$ denotes probability when $Q_{\lambda,k}$ has the distribution specified in Assumption 1 with parameters (β, λ), $P_{\beta, r_{1/2}}(\cdot)$ denotes probability when $\overline{Q}_\infty$ has the distribution in (10.7), and $P_{\beta^*, r_{1/2}^*}^*(\cdot) = (1/2)[P_{\beta^*, r_{1/2}^*}(\cdot) + P_{\beta_2^*, r_{2,1/2}^*}(\cdot)]$.

The upper bound on average asymptotic power given in Theorem 2 is attained by a point optimal invariant two-sided (POI2) test that rejects H_0 if

$$LR^*(\overline{Q}_{S,k}, \overline{Q}_{ST,k}; \beta^*, r_{1/2}^*) > \kappa_\alpha^*(\beta^*, r_{1/2}^*). \qquad (10.11)$$

This test is asymptotically similar. Hence, the asymptotic power envelope for similar and nonsimilar invariant tests is the same. The asymptotic distribution of the test statistic in (10.11) is given in the following Corollary to Theorem 1(b) (which holds by the continuous mapping theorem).

Corollary 1 *Suppose Assumptions 1 and 2 hold with $\tau = 1/2$ and β is fixed. Then,*

$$LR^*(\overline{Q}_{\lambda,k}; \beta^*, r_{1/2}^*) \to_d LR^*(\overline{Q}_\infty; \beta^*, r_{1/2}^*),$$

where $\overline{Q}_\infty$ is distributed as in (10.7).

Comments
1. Corollary 1 implies that the POI2 test of (10.11) is a convergent sequence of invariant and asymptotically level α tests that attains the upper bound on asymptotic average power given in Theorem 2 at $(\beta^*, r_{1/2}^*)$.
2. Corollary 1 shows that the upper bound in Theorem 2 is attainable and, hence, that the upper bound is the asymptotic power envelope when $\tau = 1/2$.

10.4   Numerical Results for Many Weak Instruments

We now turn to a brief summary of the asymptotic properties of the many weak instrument power envelope and the AR, LM, and CLR tests under the $\tau = 1/2$ sequence obtained using numerical methods. The limiting power envelope and power functions for various values of $r_{1/2}$ are presented in Figure 6.2 for $\rho = 0.95$ and in Figure 6.3 for $\rho = 0.5$. These figures, and unreported additional numerical work, support three main conclusions. First, the power function of the CLR test is effectively on the limiting asymptotically efficient power envelope, so the CLR test is, in effect, UMP

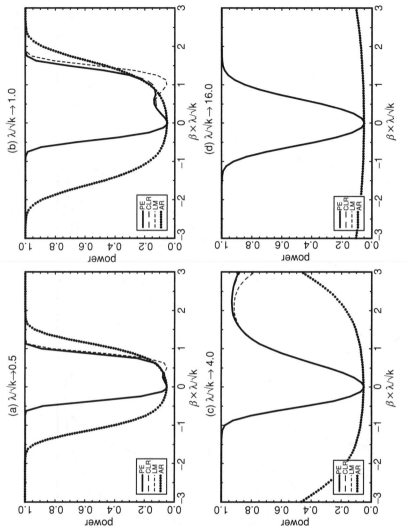

Figure 6.2. Many-instrument $\tau = \frac{1}{2}$ limiting power envelope and power functions of the CLR, LM, and AR tests, $\rho = 0.95$.

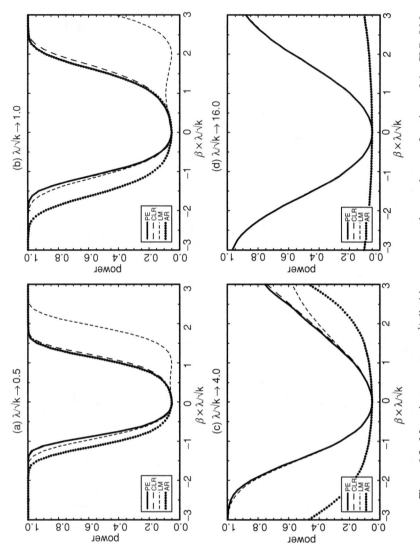

Figure 6.3. Many-instrument $\tau = \frac{1}{2}$ limiting power envelope and power functions of the CLR, LM, and AR tests, $\rho = 0.5$.

among asymptotically level invariant tests under the $\tau = 1/2$ sequence. Second, the power function of the LM test sometimes falls well below the power envelope and is not monotonic in the many-instrument limit. Third, the performance of the AR test, relative to the power envelope and the CLR and LM tests, depends heavily on the strength of the instruments. For very weak instruments, the AR power function is below the power envelope but the AR test still exhibits nontrivial power. As the strength of the instruments increases (i.e., as $r_{1/2}$ increases), the power of the AR test, relative to the other tests, is increasingly poor, and the power function is nearly flat in the case of panel (d) in both figures.

These results apply to the limit of the sequence (λ, k) as $\lambda/k^{1/2} \to r_{1/2}$. It is of interest to examine numerically the speed of convergence of the finite-k power envelopes and power functions to this limit. This is done in Figures 6.4 and 6.5, which present the power envelope and the CLR power function for various values of k and for the $k \to \infty$ limit. Evidently the speed of convergence, and the quality of the $k \to \infty$ approximation, depends on the strength of the instruments. For very weak instruments [panels (a) and (b)], the rate of convergence is fairly fast and the limiting functions are close to the finite-k approximations. For stronger instruments, the limiting approximation is less good and is achieved less quickly. An important point to note in Figures 6.4 and 6.5 is that for each parameter value and for each value of k, the CLR power function is effectively on the power envelope. Whether or not the $k \to \infty$ approximation is a good one for finite k, the CLR power function is in effect on the power envelope for asymptotically efficient two-sided invariant similar tests.

Figures 6.6 and 6.7 present a final set of numerical results, in which we consider performance of the CLR and AR tests along the sequence $\tau = 0$; this corresponds to the addition of irrelevant instruments as k increases. In the limit that $k \to \infty$, these tests have trivial power, but this result does not tell us directly how costly it is to err on the side of adding an irrelevant instrument. Perhaps surprisingly, for these and other cases not reported, adding a few irrelevant instruments is not very costly in terms of power for the CLR test; less surprisingly, adding a great number of irrelevant instruments drives the power to zero.

10.5 Asymptotic Power Envelope When $\tau > 1/2$

We now consider the asymptotic power envelope for the case where $\tau > 1/2$. In this case, the alternatives that we consider are local to the null hypothesis and significant simplifications occur. By Theorem 1(c) and (d), the asymptotic distribution of the normalized $Q_{\lambda,k}$ matrix only depends on the unknown localization parameter B through the distribution of $\overline{Q}_{ST,\infty}$ (because $\overline{Q}_{S,\infty} \sim N(0, 2)$ and $\overline{Q}_{T,\infty} = d_{\beta_0}^2 r_\tau$). The asymptotic testing problem concerns the hypotheses $H_0' : B = 0$ versus $H_1' : B \neq 0$ with no nuisance parameter

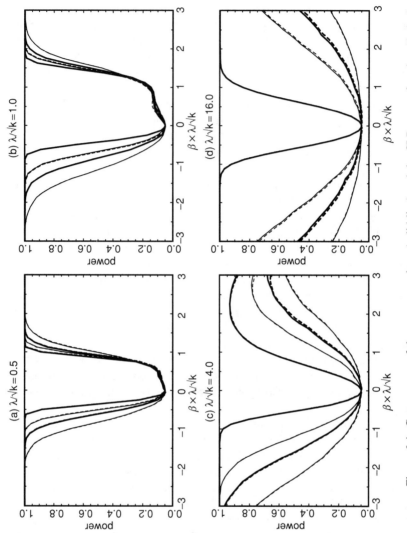

Figure 6.4. Convergence of the power envelope (solid line) and the CLR power function (dashed line) to the $\tau = \frac{1}{2}$, $K \to \infty$ limit, $K = 10$ (bottom pair), 40, 160, and ∞ (top pair), $\rho = 0.95$.

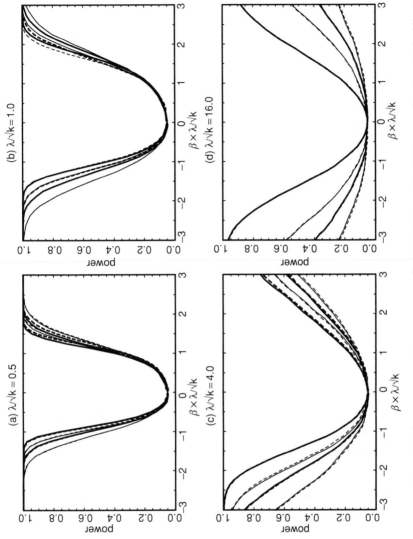

Figure 6.5. Convergence of the power envelope (solid line) and the CLR power function (dashed line) to the $\tau = \frac{1}{2}$, $K \to \infty$ limit, $K = 10$ (bottom pair), 40, 160, and ∞ (top pair), $\rho = 0.5$.

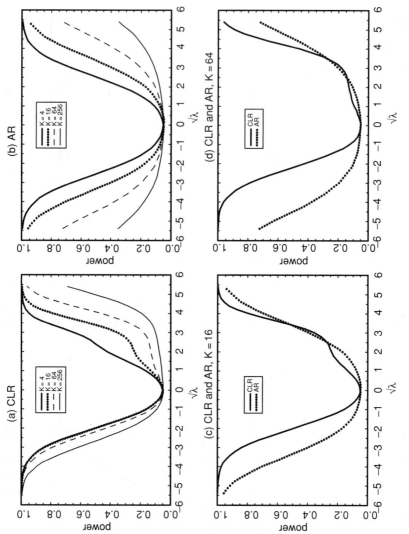

Figure 6.6. Effect of irrelevant instruments ($\tau = 0$) on the CLR and AR tests, $\lambda = 80$ and $\rho = 0.95$.

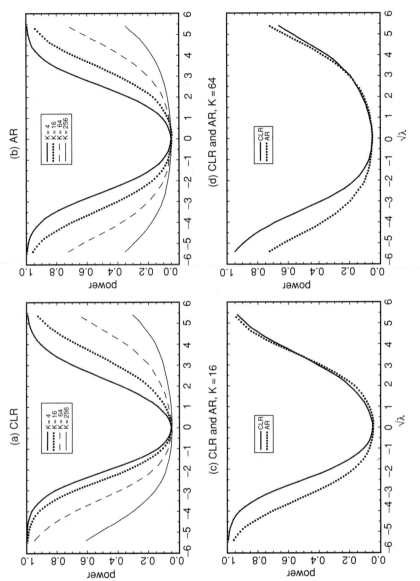

Figure 6.7. Effect of irrelevant instruments ($\tau = 0$) on the CLR and AR tests, $\lambda = 80$ and $\rho = 0.5$.

(because $\overline{Q}_{T,\infty} = d_{\beta_0}^2 r_\tau$ implies that r_τ is known asymptotically). An asymptotic sufficient statistic for B is $\overline{Q}_{ST,\infty}$, which has distribution

$$\overline{Q}_{ST,\infty} \sim \begin{cases} N(\gamma_B r_\tau, 1) & \text{when } 1/2 < \tau < 1 \\ N(\gamma_B r_1, 1 + d_{\beta_0}^2 r_1) & \text{when } \tau = 1 \\ N(\gamma_B r_\tau^{1/2}, d_{\beta_0}^2 r_\tau) & \text{when } \tau > 1. \end{cases} \tag{10.12}$$

Using the same sort of argument as in Section 10.3, by the Neyman–Pearson Lemma, the level α test based on $\overline{Q}_{ST,\infty}$ that maximizes average power against B^* and $-B^*$ is constructed using the following likelihood ratio statistic:

$$\begin{aligned} LR^{**} &= \frac{\exp\left(-\frac{1}{2}\left(\overline{Q}_{ST,\infty} - \gamma_{B^*} r_\tau\right)^2\right) + \exp\left(-\frac{1}{2}\left(\overline{Q}_{ST,\infty} + \gamma_{B^*} r_\tau\right)^2\right)}{2\exp\left(-\frac{1}{2}\overline{Q}_{ST,\infty}^2\right)} \\ &= \exp\left(-\gamma_{B^*}^2 r_\tau^2/2\right)\left(\exp\left(\gamma_{B^*} r_\tau \overline{Q}_{ST,\infty}\right) + \exp\left(-\gamma_{B^*} r_\tau \overline{Q}_{ST,\infty}\right)\right)/2 \\ &= \exp\left(-\gamma_{B^*}^2 r_\tau^2/2\right)\cosh\left(\gamma_{B^*} r_\tau \overline{Q}_{ST,\infty}\right) \end{aligned} \tag{10.13}$$

for the case $1/2 < \tau < 1$. The test that rejects when LR^{**} is large is equivalent to the test that rejects when $\overline{Q}_{ST,\infty}^2$ is large (because $\cosh(x)$ is increasing in $|x|$). Hence, the level α test that maximizes average power against B^* and $-B^*$ does not depend on B^*. The test rejects H_0' if

$$\overline{Q}_{ST,\infty}^2 > \chi_1^2(\alpha), \tag{10.14}$$

where $\chi_1^2(\alpha)$ denotes the $1 - \alpha$ quantile of a chi-squared distribution with one degree of freedom. Similar calculations for the cases $\tau = 1$ and $\tau > 1$ yield the same test as delivering maximal average power for any B^*.

Returning now to the finite sample testing problem, we restrict attention to invariant tests $\phi_k(\overline{Q}_{\lambda,k})$ that depend on the normalized data matrix

$$\overline{Q}_{\lambda,k} = \begin{pmatrix} (S'S - k)/k^{1/2} \\ S'T/k^{1/2} \\ (T'T - k)/k^\tau \end{pmatrix} \quad \text{or} \quad \overline{Q}_{\lambda,k} = \begin{pmatrix} (S'S - k)/k^{1/2} \\ S'T/k^{\tau/2} \\ (T'T - k)/k^\tau \end{pmatrix} \tag{10.15}$$

for $1/2 < \tau \le 1$ or $\tau > 1$, respectively. We say that a sequence of tests $\{\phi_k(\overline{Q}_{\lambda,k}) : k \ge 1\}$ is a *convergent sequence of asymptotically level α tests* for $\tau > 1/2$ if there exists a $\{0, 1\}$-valued function ϕ such that under Assumption 1, under any sequence $\lambda/k^\tau \to r_\tau$ for any r_τ in some non-empty subset of $[0, \infty)$, for $\beta = \beta_0 + Bk^{1/2-\tau}$ when $1/2 < \tau \le 1$ and $\beta = \beta_0 + Bk^{-\tau/2}$ when $\tau > 1$, and for any B in some set that includes $\{0, B^*, -B^*\}$, we have

$$\phi_k(\overline{Q}_{\lambda,k}) \to_d \phi(\overline{Q}_\infty), \quad \text{where}$$

$$vech(\overline{Q}_\infty) = \begin{pmatrix} \overline{Q}_{S,\infty} \\ \overline{Q}_{ST,\infty} \\ \overline{Q}_{T,\infty} \end{pmatrix} \sim N\left(\begin{pmatrix} 0 \\ \gamma_B \overline{r}_\tau \\ d_{\beta_0}^2 r_\tau \end{pmatrix}, V_{3,\tau} \right),$$

$$\overline{r}_\tau = \begin{cases} r_\tau & \text{when } 1/2 < \tau \leq 1 \\ r_\tau^{1/2} & \text{when } \tau > 1, \end{cases}$$

$$P_{\beta_0}(\phi(\overline{Q}_\infty) = 1) \leq \alpha, \tag{10.16}$$

and $P_{\beta_0}(\cdot)$ denotes probability when the true parameter is β_0. By Theorem 1, the CLR, LM, and AR tests are examples of convergent sequences of asymptotically level α tests for $\tau > 1/2$.

The next result provides an upper bound on average power for convergent sequences of invariant asymptotically level α tests.

Theorem 3 *The average power over B^* and $-B^*$ of any convergent sequence of invariant asymptotically level α tests for $\tau > 1/2$, $\{\phi_k(\overline{Q}_{\lambda,k}) : k \geq 1\}$, satisfies*

$$\lim_{k \to \infty} (1/2) \big[P_{\beta_k^*, \lambda}\big(\phi_k(\overline{Q}_{\lambda,k}) = 1\big) + P_{\beta_{2,k}^*, \lambda}\big(\phi_k(\overline{Q}_{\lambda,k}) = 1\big) \big]$$

$$= P_{B^*}^*(\phi(\overline{Q}_\infty) = 1) \leq P_{B^*}^*\big(\overline{Q}_{ST,\infty}^2 > \chi_1^2(\alpha)\big),$$

where $P_{\beta,\lambda}(\cdot)$ denotes probability when $Q_{\lambda,k}$ has the distribution specified in Assumption 1 with parameters (β, λ), $\lambda/k^\tau \to r_\tau$, $\beta_k^* = \beta_0 + B^* k^{1/2-\tau}$ and $\beta_{2,k}^* = \beta_0 - B^* k^{1/2-\tau}$ when $1/2 < \tau \leq 1$, $\beta_k^* = \beta_0 + B^* k^{-\tau/2}$ and $\beta_{2,k}^* = \beta_0 - B^* k^{-\tau/2}$ when $\tau > 1$, $P_B(\cdot)$ denotes probability when $\overline{Q}_{ST,\infty} \sim N(\gamma_B \overline{r}_\tau, 1)$, and $P_B^*(\cdot) = (1/2)[P_B(\cdot) + P_{-B}(\cdot)]$.

Comment

1. The upper bound on average asymptotic power given in Theorem 3 is attained for all B^* and $-B^*$ by the LM and CLR tests by Theorem 1(c) and (d) (because the LM and LR test statistics are scalar multiples of $\overline{Q}_{ST,\infty}^2$ asymptotically). In consequence, we say that these tests are *asymptotically efficient* when $\tau > 1/2$.

10.6 Asymptotic Power Envelope for Unknown Ω

The asymptotic power envelopes provided in the preceding sections presume that the covariance matrix Ω of the reduced-form errors in (2.2) is known. Tests based on $Q_{\lambda,k}$ have asymptotic level α only if the true Ω is used in their construction. In this section, we show that under fairly weak conditions on the growth rate of the number of IVs, k, these asymptotic power envelopes also apply when Ω is unknown. Obviously, an upper bound on asymptotic average power for known Ω is also an upper bound when Ω is unknown. Hence, to show that the upper bound is the power envelope, it suffices to show that it is attainable at each point by some sequence of tests.

We estimate Ω ($\in R^{2\times 2}$) via

$$\widehat{\Omega}_n = (n - k - p)^{-1} \widehat{V}' \widehat{V}, \quad \text{where } \widehat{V} = Y - P_Z Y - P_X Y. \quad (10.17)$$

We define analogues of S, T, and $Q_{\lambda,k}$ with Ω replaced by $\widehat{\Omega}_n$:

$$\widehat{S}_n = (Z'Z)^{-1/2} Z'Y b_0 \cdot (b_0' \widehat{\Omega}_n b_0)^{-1/2},$$

$$\widehat{T}_n = (Z'Z)^{-1/2} Z'Y \widehat{\Omega}_n^{-1} a_0 \cdot (a_0' \widehat{\Omega}_n^{-1} a_0)^{-1/2},$$

$$\widehat{Q}_{\lambda,k,n} = [\widehat{S}_n : \widehat{T}_n]'[\widehat{S}_n : \widehat{T}_n], \quad \text{and} \quad \overline{\widehat{Q}}_{\lambda,k,n} = (\widehat{Q}_{\lambda,k,n} - kI_2)/k^{1/2}. \quad (10.18)$$

The LR, LM, AR, and POIS2 test statistics for the case of unknown Ω are defined in the same way as when Ω is known, but with $\widehat{Q}_{\lambda,k,n}$ in place of $Q_{\lambda,k}$. Denote these test statistics by $\widehat{LR}_n$, $\widehat{LM}_n$, $\widehat{AR}_n$, and $\widehat{LR}_n^* = LR^*(\overline{\widehat{Q}}_{\lambda,k,n}; \beta^*, \lambda^*)$, respectively.

Consistency of $\widehat{\Omega}_n$ with rate $k^{1/2}$ is established in the following Lemma.

Lemma 1 *Suppose $\{V_i : i \geq 1\}$ are iid with mean zero, variance Ω, and finite fourth moment, and $k^{3/2}/n \to 0$. Then, $k^{1/2}(\widehat{\Omega}_n - \Omega) \to_p 0$ as $n \to \infty$.*

Lemma 1 can be used to show that $\widehat{Q}_{\lambda,k,n}$ and $Q_{\lambda,k}$ have the same asymptotic distributions.

Theorem 4 *Theorem 1 holds under the given assumptions with $(\widehat{S}_n, \widehat{T}_n)$ in place of (S, T) provided $(k, n) \to \infty$ such that $k^{3/2}/n \to 0$.*

Comments

1. Theorem 4 and the continuous mapping theorem combine to show that when $\tau = 1/2$ and β is fixed, then

$$\widehat{LR}_n^* = LR^*(\overline{\widehat{Q}}_{\lambda,k,n}; \beta^*, r_{1/2}^*) \to_d LR^*(\overline{Q}_\infty; \beta^*, r_{1/2}^*). \quad (10.19)$$

In consequence, the $\widehat{LR}_n^*$ and LR^* statistics are asymptotically equivalent under the null and fixed alternatives. Thus, the upper bound on asymptotic average power for $\tau = 1/2$ given in Theorem 2 is attained by the tests based on $\widehat{LR}_n^*$, which are asymptotically level α and similar, by varying $(\beta^*, r_{1/2}^*)$. In turn, this implies that the upper bound in Theorem 2 is the asymptotic power envelope whether or not Ω is known.

2. Similarly, Theorem 4 implies that when $\tau > 1/2$, $\widehat{LM}_n \to_d \overline{Q}_{ST,\infty}^2$ under the null hypothesis and local alternatives. Hence, the upper bound on average power given in Theorem 3 is attained for all B^* and $-B^*$ by the tests based on $\widehat{LM}_n$ and $\widehat{LR}_n$. The upper bound in Theorem 3 is the asymptotic power envelope whether or not Ω is known and the tests based on $\widehat{LM}_n$ and $\widehat{LR}_n$ are asymptotically efficient.

10.7   Asymptotics with Non-Normal Errors

Andrews and Stock (2007) investigate the asymptotic properties of the statistic $\widehat{Q}_{\lambda,k,n}$ and the test statistics $\widehat{LR}_n$, $\widehat{LM}_n$, and $\widehat{AR}_n$ when the errors are not necessarily normally distributed. For the case of $\tau \in [0, 2]$, they show that one obtains the same limit distributions (given in Theorem 1) when the errors are non-normal and Ω is estimated as when the errors are normal and Ω is known provided $k^3/n \to 0$ as $n \to \infty$.

To conclude, the many weak IV results given in this section show that the significance level of the CLR test is completely robust to weak IVs. The test, however, is not completely robust to many IVs. One cannot employ too many IVs relative to the sample size. For normal errors, the CLR test has correct asymptotic significance level provided $k^{3/2}/n \to 0$ as $n \to \infty$ regardless of the strength of the IVs. For non-normal errors, the restriction is greater: $k^3/n \to 0$ as $n \to \infty$. The power results show that the CLR test is essentially on the two-sided power envelope for invariant tests for any value of τ when the errors are iid homoskedastic normal.

These level and power results established for many IV asymptotics, combined with the properties of the CLR test under weak IV asymptotics, lead us to recommend the CLR test (or heteroskedasticity and/or autocorrelation robust versions of it) for general use in scenarios where the IVs may be weak.

APPENDIX OF PROOFS

In this Appendix, we prove the results stated in Section 10.1.

Proof of Theorem 1. First, we determine the means, variances, and covariances of the components of Q. Let $S = (S_1, \dots, S_k)'$, $\mu_S = ES = c_\beta \mu_\pi = (\mu_{S1}, \dots, \mu_{Sk})'$, $S^* = S - \mu_S = (S_1^*, \dots, S_k^*)' \sim N(0, I_k)$. Define T_j, μ_T, T^*, and T_j^* for $j = 1, \dots, k$ analogously. We have

$$ES'S = \sum_{j=1}^{k} E\left(S_j^* + \mu_{Sj}\right)^2 = \sum_{j=1}^{k}\left(1 + \mu_{Sj}^2\right) = k + c_\beta^2 \lambda,$$

$$E(S'S)^2 = E\left(\sum_{j=1}^{k} S_j^2\right)^2 = \sum_{j=1}^{k} E S_j^4 + \sum_{j=1}^{k}\sum_{j\neq\ell}^{k} E S_j^2 E S_\ell^2$$

$$= \sum_{j=1}^{k} E\left(S_j^* + \mu_{Sj}\right)^4 + \sum_{j=1}^{k}\sum_{\ell=1}^{k}\left(1 + \mu_{Sj}^2\right)\left(1 + \mu_{S\ell}^2\right) - \sum_{j=1}^{k}\left(1 + \mu_{Sj}^2\right)^2$$

$$= \sum_{j=1}^{k}\left(3 + 6\mu_{Sj}^2 + \mu_{Sj}^4\right) + \left(\sum_{j=1}^{k}\left(1 + \mu_{Sj}^2\right)\right)^2 - \sum_{j=1}^{k}\left(1 + \mu_{Sj}^2\right)^2$$

$$= 2k + 4c_\beta^2 \lambda + (ES'S)^2, \quad \text{and}$$

$$Var(S'S) = 2\left(k + 2c_\beta^2 \lambda\right). \tag{A.1}$$

Analogously,

$$ET'T = k + d_\beta^2 \lambda \quad \text{and} \quad Var(T'T) = 2\left(k + 2c_\beta^2 \lambda\right). \tag{A.2}$$

Next, we have

$$ES'T = ES'ET = c_\beta d_\beta \lambda,$$

$$E(S'T)^2 = E\left(\sum_{j=1}^k S_j T_j\right)^2 = \sum_{j=1}^k ES_j^2 ET_j^2 + \sum_{j \neq \ell}^k \sum^k ES_j ET_j ES_\ell ET_\ell$$

$$= \sum_{j=1}^k \left(1 + \mu_{Sj}^2\right)\left(1 + \mu_{Tj}^2\right) + \left(\sum_{j=1}^k ES_j ET_j\right)^2 - \sum_{j=1}^k (ES_j ET_j)^2$$

$$= \sum_{j=1}^k \left(1 + \mu_{Sj}^2 + \mu_{Tj}^2 + \mu_{Sj}^2 \mu_{Tj}^2\right) + (ES'T)^2 - \sum_{j=1}^k \mu_{Sj}^2 \mu_{Tj}^2$$

$$= k + \left(c_\beta^2 + d_\beta^2\right)\lambda + (ES'T)^2, \quad \text{and}$$

$$Var(S'T) = k + \left(c_\beta^2 + d_\beta^2\right)\lambda. \tag{A.3}$$

Finally, we have

$$E(S'SS'T) = \sum_{j=1}^k \sum_{\ell=1}^k ES_j^2 ES_\ell ET_\ell$$

$$= \sum_{j=1}^k ES_j^3 ET_j + \sum_{j=1}^k \sum_{\ell=1}^k ES_j^2 ES_\ell ET_\ell - \sum_{j=1}^k ES_j^2 ES_j ET_j$$

$$= \sum_{j=1}^k E\left(S_j^* + \mu_{Sj}\right)^3 \mu_{Tj} + ES'S \cdot ES'T - \sum_{j=1}^k ES_j^2 ES_j ET_j$$

$$= \sum_{j=1}^k \left(3\mu_{Sj}\mu_{Tj} + \mu_{Sj}^3 \mu_{Tj}\right) + ES'S \cdot ES'T$$

$$\quad - \sum_{j=1}^k \left(1 + \mu_{Sj}^2\right)\mu_{Sj}\mu_{Tj}, \quad \text{and}$$

$$Cov(S'S, S'T) = 2c_\beta d_\beta \lambda. \tag{A.4}$$

Using the Cramer–Wold device and the Liapounov CLT, we show that

$$\begin{pmatrix} \left(S'S - \left(k + c_\beta^2 \lambda\right)\right)/\left(2(k + 2c_\beta^2 \lambda)\right)^{1/2} \\ \left(S'T - c_\beta d_\beta \lambda\right)/\left(k + \left(c_\beta^2 + d_\beta^2\right)\lambda\right)^{1/2} \\ \left(T'T - \left(k + d_\beta^2 \lambda\right)\right)/\left(2(k + 2d_\beta^2 \lambda)\right)^{1/2} \end{pmatrix} \to_d N(0, I_3) \tag{A.5}$$

under the conditions of the theorem. The proof is as follows. Wlog, we can take $\mu_\pi = (\lambda/k)^{1/2} 1_k$, where $1_k = (1, 1, \ldots, 1)' \in R^k$ (because the distribution of Q only depends on μ_π through λ). Then, $\mu_{Sj} = c_\beta (\lambda/k)^{1/2}$ and $\mu_{Tj} = d_\beta (\lambda/k)^{1/2}$ for all j. We have

$$S'S - \left(k + c_\beta^2 \lambda\right) = \sum_{j=1}^{k} \left(\left(S_j^* + \mu_{Sj}\right)^2 - 1 - \mu_{Sj}^2 \right)$$

$$= \sum_{j=1}^{k} \left[\left(S_j^{*2} - 1\right) + 2\mu_{S1} S_j^* \right]. \tag{A.6}$$

By the Liapounov CLT, if $\{X_{kj} : j \le k, k \ge 1\}$ is a triangular array of mean zero row-wise iid random variables with $\sum_{j=1}^{k} Var(X_{kj}) = 1$ and $kE|X_{kj}|^{2+2\delta} = o(1)$ for some $\delta > 0$, then $\sum_{j=1}^{k} X_{kj} \to_d N(0, 1)$, for example, see Chow and Teicher (1978, Cor. 9.1.1, p. 293). If $X_{kj} = X_{kj1} + X_{kj2}$, where $\{X_{kjs} : j \le k, k \ge 1\}$ are iid across j for $s = 1, 2$, then by Minkowski's inequality it suffices to show that $kE|X_{kjs}|^{2+2\delta} = o(1)$ for $s = 1, 2$. We apply this CLT with

$$X_{kj1} = \left(S_j^{*2} - 1\right) / \left(2 \left(k + 2c_\beta^2 \lambda\right)\right)^{1/2} \quad \text{and}$$

$$X_{kj2} = 2\mu_{S1} S_j^* / \left(2 \left(k + 2c_\beta^2 \lambda\right)\right)^{1/2}. \tag{A.7}$$

We have

$$kE|X_{kj1}|^{2+2\delta} = \frac{kE|S_j^{*2} - 1|^{2+2\delta}}{\left(2\left(k + 2c_\beta^2 \lambda\right)\right)^{1+\delta}} = o(1) \text{ as } k \to \infty \quad \text{and}$$

$$kE|X_{kj2}|^{2+2\delta} = \frac{kE|2\mu_{S1} S_j^*|^{2+2\delta}}{\left(2\left(k + 2c_\beta^2 \lambda\right)\right)^{1+\delta}} = \frac{k(\lambda/k)^{1+\delta}|2c_\beta|^{2+2\delta} E|S_j^*|^{2+2\delta}}{\left(2\left(k + 2c_\beta^2 \lambda\right)\right)^{1+\delta}}$$

$$\tag{A.8}$$

using the fact that $S_j^* \sim N(0, 1)$ has all moments finite. The term $kE|X_{kj2}|^{2+2\delta}$ is $o(1)$ if $\tau < 1/2$ because then c_β is fixed. It is $o(1)$ when $1/2 < \tau \le 1$ because then $\lambda/k = O(1)$ and $c_\beta = O(1)$. It is $o(1)$ when $\tau > 1$ because then $c_\beta \propto k^{-\tau/2}$ and $(\lambda/k)^{1+\delta}|c_\beta|^{2+2\delta} = O((\lambda/k)^{1+\delta} k^{-\tau(1+\delta)}) = O((\lambda/k^\tau)^{1+\delta} k^{-(1+\delta)}) = o(1)$. Hence, the first element in (A.5) is asymptotically $N(0, 1)$. Analogous arguments apply to the second and third elements in (A.5).

To obtain the joint result in (A.5), we consider an arbitrary linear combination, say $\alpha = (\alpha_1, \alpha_2, \alpha_3)'$ with $\|\alpha\| = 1$, of the three terms in (A.5) and apply the above CLT. We have

$$\frac{Cov(S'S, S'T)}{Var^{1/2}(S'S) Var^{1/2}(S'T)} = \frac{2c_\beta d_\beta \lambda}{\left(2\left(k + 2c_\beta^2 \lambda\right)\right)^{1/2} \left(k + \left(c_\beta^2 + d_\beta^2\right)\lambda\right)^{1/2}}. \tag{A.9}$$

The rhs converges to zero because (i) $\lambda/k \to 0$ when $\tau < 1$ and (ii) $c_\beta = O(k^{-\tau/2}) = o(1)$ when $\tau \ge 1$. The same result holds with $S'S$ replaced by $T'T$.

Hence, the asymptotic covariances between the three terms in (A.5) are all zero. In consequence, although the variance of the inner product of α with the three terms in (A.5) is not one, it converges to one as $k \to \infty$ (which is sufficient for the CLT by rescaling). We establish the Liapounov condition $kE|X_{kj}|^{2+2\delta} = o(1)$ for the linear combination by the same method as above. This concludes the proof of (A.5).

Now, using (A.5), the first result in parts (a), (b), (c), and (d) of the theorem hold because (a) when $\tau < 1/2$, $\lambda/k^{1/2} \to 0$, (b) when $\tau = 1/2$, $\lambda/k \to 0$ and $\lambda/k^{1/2} \to r_{1/2}$, (c) when $1/2 < \tau \le 1$, (A.5) implies that $(T'T - k)/k^{\tau} \to_p d_{\beta_0}^2 r_{\tau}$, $c_{\beta}d_{\beta}\lambda/k^{1/2} = (b_0'\Omega b_0)^{-1/2}Bk^{1/2-\tau}d_{\beta}\lambda/k^{1/2} \to \gamma_B r_{\tau}$, and $c_{\beta}^2\lambda/k^{1/2} = \gamma_B^2 k^{1-2\tau}\lambda/k^{1/2} = o(1)$; when $1/2 < \tau < 1$, $(k + (c_{\beta}^2 + d_{\beta}^2)\lambda)/k \to 1$; when $\tau = 1$, $(k + (c_{\beta}^2 + d_{\beta}^2)\lambda)/k \to 1 + d_{\beta_0}^2 r_1$, and (d) when $\tau > 1$ and $r_{\tau} > 0$, (A.5) implies that $(T'T - k)/k^{\tau} \to_p d_{\beta_0}^2 r_{\tau}$, $(k + (c_{\beta}^2 + d_{\beta}^2)\lambda)/\lambda \to d_{\beta_0}^2$, $c_{\beta}d_{\beta}\lambda^{1/2} = (b_0'\Omega b_0)^{-1/2}Bk^{-\tau/2}d_{\beta}\lambda^{1/2} = (b_0'\Omega b_0)^{-1/2}Bd_{\beta}(\lambda/k^{\tau})^{1/2} \to \gamma_B r_{\tau}^{1/2}$, and $c_{\beta}^2\lambda^{1/2} \to 0$.

Next, we establish the results for the AR, LM, and LR statistics. The results of parts (a)–(d) for AR hold because $(AR - 1)k^{1/2} = (S'S - k)/k^{1/2}$. For parts (a)–(d) of the theorem, we have

(a) and (b) $LM = \dfrac{(S'T)^2}{T'T} = \dfrac{(S'T/k^{1/2})^2}{k^{-1/2}\left(\frac{T'T-k}{k^{1/2}}\right)+1} = (S'T/k^{1/2})^2(1 + o_p(1))$,

(c) $LM = \dfrac{(S'T/k^{1/2})^2}{k^{\tau-1}\left(\frac{T'T-k}{k^{\tau}}\right)+1} = \begin{cases} (S'T/k^{1/2})^2(1+o_p(1)) & \text{if } 1/2 < \tau < 1 \\ \dfrac{(S'T/k^{1/2})^2}{d_{\beta_0}^2 r_1 + 1 + o_p(1)} & \text{if } \tau = 1 \end{cases}$

(d) $LM = \dfrac{(S'T/k^{\tau/2})^2}{\left(\frac{T'T-k}{k^{\tau}}\right)+k^{1-\tau}} = \dfrac{(S'T/k^{\tau/2})^2}{d_{\beta_0}^2 r_{\tau} + o_p(1)} \to_d (Q_{ST,\infty}^2/(d_{\beta_0}r_{\tau}^{1/2}))^2.$

$$(A.10)$$

Combining these expressions with the asymptotic results for Q given in the theorem gives the stated asymptotic results for LM.

For the LR statistic, we use (7.18) and write

$$LR = \frac{1}{2}\left((Q_S - k) - (Q_T - k) + \sqrt{((Q_S - k) - (Q_T - k))^2 + 4Q_{ST}^2}\right).$$

$$(A.11)$$

The results of parts (a) and (b) follow from (A.11) by dividing through by $k^{1/2}$ and applying the results of parts (a) and (b) for the asymptotic distribution of Q.

Next, for the case where $\tau > 1/2$, by parts (c) and (d) for the asymptotic distribution of Q, we have

$$(T'T - k)k^{-\tau} \to_p d_{\beta_0}^2 r_\tau \quad \text{and} \quad (S'S - k)k^{-\tau} \to_p 0, \quad \text{and so}$$

(A.12)

$$\frac{Q_T}{(Q_T - Q_S)^2} = \frac{(Q_T - k)k^{-2\tau} + k^{1-2\tau}}{((Q_T - k)k^{-\tau} - (Q_S - k)k^{-\tau})^2}$$

$$= \frac{o_p(1)}{\left(d_{\beta_0}^2 r_\tau + o_p(1)\right)^2} = o_p(1).$$

By a mean-value expansion $\sqrt{1 + x} = 1 + (1/2)x(1 + o(1))$ as $x \to 0$. Hence,

$$LR = \frac{1}{2}\left(Q_S - Q_T + |Q_T - Q_S|\sqrt{1 + \frac{4Q_T}{(Q_T - Q_S)^2}LM}\right)$$

$$= \frac{1}{2}\left(Q_S - Q_T + |Q_T - Q_S|\left(1 + \frac{2Q_T(1 + o_p(1))}{(Q_T - Q_S)^2}LM\right)\right)$$

$$= \frac{Q_T(1 + o_p(1))}{Q_T - Q_S}LM,$$

(A.13)

where the third equality uses $|Q_T - Q_S| = Q_T - Q_S$ with probability that goes to one by the calculation in the denominator of (A.12). By results of parts (c) and (d) for Q, we have

$$\frac{Q_T}{Q_T - Q_S} = \frac{(Q_T - k)k^{-\tau} + k^{1-\tau}}{(Q_T - k)k^{-\tau} - (Q_S - k)k^{-\tau}} = \frac{d_{\beta_0}^2 r_\tau + o_p(1) + k^{1-\tau}}{d_{\beta_0}^2 r_\tau + o_p(1)}$$

$$= \begin{cases} 1 + o_p(1) & \text{if } \tau > 1 \\ \dfrac{1 + d_{\beta_0}^2 r_1}{d_{\beta_0}^2 r_1} + o_p(1) & \text{if } \tau = 1 \\ \dfrac{1 + o_p(1)}{d_{\beta_0}^2 r_\tau}k^{1-\tau} & \text{if } 1/2 < \tau < 1. \end{cases}$$

(A.14)

Equations (A.13) and (A.14) combine to give the results for LR stated in parts (c) and (d) of the Theorem. $\square$

Proof of Lemma 1. Let $\widehat{\Omega}_{n,rs}$ and Ω_{rs} denote the (r, s) elements of $\widehat{\Omega}_n$ and Ω, respectively, for $r, s = 1, 2$. Let $n_k = n - k - p$. We have

$$k^{1/2}(\widehat{\Omega}_{n,rs} - \Omega_{rs}) = \frac{k^{1/2}}{n_k}(v_r'v_s - n\Omega_{rs}) - \frac{k^{1/2}}{n_k}v_r'P_Z v_s - \frac{k^{1/2}}{n_k}v_r'P_X v_s$$

$$+ k^{1/2}\left(1 - \frac{n}{n_k}\right)\Omega_{rs}.$$

(10.15)

Next, we have

$$
0 \leq \frac{k^{1/2}}{n_k} E v_r' P_Z v_s = \frac{k^{1/2}}{n_k} tr(P_Z E v_r v_s')
$$
$$
= \frac{k^{1/2}}{n_k} tr(P_Z)\Omega_{rs} = \frac{k^{3/2}}{n_k}\Omega_{rs} \to 0 \tag{10.16}
$$

provided $k^{3/2}/n \to 0$. L^1-convergence implies convergence in probability. Hence, $(k^{1/2}/n_k)v_r' P_Z v_s \to_p 0$. Analogously, $(k^{1/2}/n_k)v_r' P_X v_s \to_p 0$. In addition, $k^{1/2}(1 - n/n_k) \to 0$.

Lastly, by Markov's inequality, for any $\varepsilon > 0$,

$$
P\left(\frac{k^{1/2}}{n_k}\left|v_r' v_s - n\Omega_{rs}\right| > \varepsilon\right) \leq \frac{kE\left(\sum_{i=1}^n (v_{i,r} v_{i,s} - \Omega_{rs})\right)^2}{n_k^2 \varepsilon^2}
$$
$$
= \frac{knE(v_{i,r} v_{i,s} - \Omega_{rs})^2}{n_k^2 \varepsilon^2} \to 0 \tag{10.17}
$$

provided $k/n \to 0$. The above results combine to prove the Lemma.   □

Proof of Theorem 4. It suffices to show that

$$
k^{-1/2}(\widehat{Q}_{\lambda,k,n} - kI_2) - k^{-1/2}(Q_{\lambda,k} - kI_2) \to_p 0 \quad \text{or}
$$
$$
k^{-1/2}(\widehat{Q}_{\lambda,k,n} - Q_{\lambda,k}) \to_p 0. \tag{10.18}
$$

Using (7.13), we have

$$
\widehat{S}_n'\widehat{S}_n - S'S = b_0'Y'Z(Z'Z)^{-1}Z'Yb_0 \cdot \left[\left(b_0'\widehat{\Omega}_n b_0\right)^{-1} - \left(b_0'\Omega b_0\right)^{-1}\right] \quad \text{and}
$$
$$
k^{-1/2}\left(\widehat{S}_n'\widehat{S}_n - S'S\right) = (S'S/k)\left(\frac{k^{1/2}(b_0'\Omega b_0 - b_0'\widehat{\Omega}_n b_0)}{b_0'\widehat{\Omega}_n b_0}\right) = o_p(1),
$$

$$
\tag{10.19}
$$

where the last equality uses Theorem 1 and Lemma 1. Similar arguments, but with more steps because Ω enters T in two places, yield $k^{-1/2}(\widehat{S}_n'\widehat{T}_n - S'T) = o_p(1)$ and $k^{-1/2}(\widehat{T}_n'\widehat{T}_n - T'T) = o_p(1)$. This completes the proof.   □

References

ANDERSON, T. W. (1976): "Estimation of Linear Functional Relationships: Approximate Distributions and Connections with Simultaneous Equations in Econometrics," *Journal of the Royal Statistical Society*, Ser. B, 38, 1–36.

ANDERSON, T. W., N. KUNITOMO, AND Y. MATSUSHITA (2005): "A New Light from Old Wisdoms: Alternative Estimation Methods of Simultaneous Equations and Microeconometric Models," Graduate School of Economics, University of Tokyo.

ANDERSON, T. W. AND H. RUBIN (1949): "Estimators of the Parameters of a Single Equation in a Complete Set of Stochastic Equations," *Annals of Mathematical Statistics*, 21, 570–582.

ANDREWS, D. W. K., AND V. MARMER (2004): "Exactly Distribution-Free Inference in Instrumental Variables Regression with Possibly Weak Instruments," Cowles Foundation Discussion Paper No. 1501, Yale University. Available at http://cowles.econ.yale.edu.

ANDREWS, D. W. K., M. J. MOREIRA, AND J. H. STOCK (2004): "Optimal Invariant Similar Tests for Instrumental Variables Regression with Weak Instruments," Cowles Foundation Discussion Paper No. 1476, Yale University. Available at http://cowles.econ.yale.edu.

——— (2006a): "Optimal Two-sided Invariant Similar Tests for Instrumental Variables Regression," *Econometrica*, 74, 715–752.

——— (2006b): "Supplement to 'Optimal Two-Sided Invariant Similar Tests for Instrumental Variables Regression,'" available on the *Econometric Society* website at www.econometricsociety.org under Supplemental Material and at http://ksghome.harvard.edu/~.JStock.Academic.Ksg/ams/websupp/index.htm.

——— (2006c): "Efficient Two-Sided Nonsimilar Invariant Tests in IV Regression with Weak Instruments," Unpublished Paper, Department of Economics, Harvard University.

——— (2007): "Performance of Conditional Wald Tests in IV Regression with Weak Instruments," *Journal of Econometrics*, forthcoming.

ANDREWS, D. W. K. AND G. SOARES (2007): "Rank Tests for Instrumental Variables Regression," *Econometric Theory*, 23, forthcoming.

ANDREWS, D. W. K. AND J. H. STOCK (2007): "Inference with Many Weak Instruments," *Journal of Econometrics*, forthcoming.

ANGRIST, J. D. AND A. B. KRUEGER (1991): "Does Compulsory School Attendance Affect Schooling and Earnings?" *Quarterly Journal of Economics*, 106, 979– 1014.

BEKKER, P. A. (1994): "Alternative Approximations to the Distributions of Instrumental Variable Estimators," *Econometrica*, 62, 657–681.

BOUND, J. D., A. JAEGER, AND R. M. BAKER (1995): "Problems with Instrumental Variables Estimation When the Correlation Between the Instruments and the Endogenous Explanatory Variable Is Weak," *Journal of the American Statistical Association,* 90, 443–450.

CANER, M. (2003): "Exponential Tilting with Weak Instruments: Estimation and Testing," Department of Economics, University of Pittsburgh.

CHAMBERLAIN, G. (2005): "Decision Theory Applied to an Instrumental Variables Model," Department of Economics, Harvard University.

CHAMBERLAIN, G. AND G. IMBENS (2004): "Random Effects Estimators with Many Instrumental Variables, *Econometrica*, 72, 295–306.

CHAO, J. C. AND P. C. B. PHILLIPS (1998): "Posterior Distributions in Limited Information Analysis of the Simultaneous Equations Model Using the Jeffreys Prior," *Journal of Econometrics*, 87, 49–86.

——— (2002): "Jeffreys Prior Analysis of the Simultaneous Equations Model in the Case with $n + 1$ Endogenous Variables," *Journal of Econometrics*, 111, 251–283.

CHAO, J. C. AND N. R. SWANSON (2003): "Alternative Approximations of the Bias and MSE of the IV Estimator under Weak Identification with an Application to Bias Correction," Cowles Foundation Discussion Paper No. 1418, Yale University.

——— (2005): "Consistent Estimation with a Large Number of Weak Instruments," *Econometrica*, 73, 1673–1692.

CHIODA, L. AND M. JANSSON (2004): "Optimal Inference for Instrumental Variables Regression," Department of Economics, University of California, Berkeley.

CHOI, I. AND P. C. B. PHILLIPS (1992): "Asymptotic and Finite Sample Distribution Theory for IV Estimators and Tests in Partially Identified Structural Equations," *Journal of Econometrics*, 51, 113–150.

CHOW Y.-C. AND H. TEICHER (1978): *Probability Theory*, New York: Springer.

DONALD, S. G. AND W. K. NEWEY (2001): "Choosing the Number of Instruments," *Econometrica*, 69, 1161–1191.

DUFOUR, J.-M. (1997): "Impossibility Theorems in Econometrics with Applications to Structural and Dynamic Models," *Econometrica*, 65, 1365–1387.

——— (2003): "Identification, Weak Instruments, and Statistical Inference in Econometrics," *Canadian Journal of Economics*, 36, 767–808.

DUFOUR, J.-M. AND J. JASIAK (2001): "Finite Sample Limited Information Inference Methods for Structural Equations and Models with Generated Regressors," *International Economic Review*, 42, 815–843.

DUFOUR, J.-M., L. KHALAF, AND M. KICHIAN (2006): "Inflation Dynamics and the New Keynesian Phillips Curve: An Identification Robust Econometric Analysis," *Journal of Economic Dynamics and Control*, 30, 1707–1727.

DUFOUR, J.-M. AND M. TAAMOUTI (2005): "Projection-Based Statistical Inference in Linear Structural Models with Possibly Weak Instruments," *Econometrica*, 73, 1351–1365.

FORCHINI, G. AND G. HILLIER (2003): "Conditional Inference for Possibly Unidentified Structural Equations," *Econometric Theory*, 19, 707–743.

FULLER, W. A. (1977): "Some Properties of a Modification of the Limited Information Estimator," *Econometrica*, 45, 939–954.

GAO, C. AND K. LAHIRI (1999): "A Comparison of Some Recent Bayesian and Classical Procedures for Simultaneous Equation Models with Weak Instruments," Department of Economics, SUNY, Albany.

GLESER, L. J. AND J. T. HWANG (1987): "The Nonexistence of $100(1-\alpha)\%$ Confidence Sets of Finite Expected Diameter in Errors-in-Variables and Related Models," *Annals of Statistics*, 15, 1351–1362.

GODFREY, L. (1999): "Instrument Relevance in Multivariate Linear Models," *Review of Economics and Statistics*, 81, 550–552.

GUGGENBERGER, P. AND R. J. SMITH (2005a): "Generalized Empirical Likelihood Estimators and Tests under Partial, Weak and Strong Identification," *Econometric Theory*, 21, 667–709.

——— (2005b): "Generalized Empirical Likelihood Tests in Time Series Models with Potential Identification Failure," Department of Economics, UCLA.

HAHN, J. (2002): "Optimal Inference with Many Instruments," *Econometric Theory*, 18, 140–168.

HAHN, J. AND J. HAUSMAN (2002): "A New Specification Test for the Validity of Instrumental Variables," *Econometrica*, 70, 163–189.

——— (2003a): "IV Estimation with Valid and Invalid Instruments," Department of Economics, M.I.T.

——— (2003b): "Weak Instruments: Diagnosis and Cures in Empirical Economics," *American Economic Review*, 93, 118–125.

HAHN, J., J. HAUSMAN, AND G. KUERSTEINER (2004): "Estimation with Weak Instruments: Accuracy of Higher-order Bias and MSE Approximations," *Econometrics Journal*, 7, 272–306.

HALL, A. R., G. D. RUDEBUSCH, AND D. W. WILCOX (1996): "Judging Instrument Relevance in Instrumental Variables Estimation," *International Economic Review*, 37, 283–298.

HALL, R. E. (1978): "Stochastic Implications of the Life Cycle-Permanent Income Hypothesis: Theory and Evidence," *Journal of Political Economy*, 86, 971–987.

HAN, C. AND P. C. B. PHILLIPS (2006): "GMM with Many Moment Conditions," *Econometrica*, 74, 147–192.

HANSEN, C., J. HAUSMAN, AND W. K. NEWEY (2005): "Estimation with Many Instrumental Variables," Department of Economics, M.I.T.

HAUSMAN, J., J. H. STOCK, AND M. YOGO (2005): "Asymptotic Properties of the Hahn-Hausman Test for Weak Instruments," *Economics Letters*, 89, 333–342.

HECKMAN, J. J. AND E. VYTLACIL (2005): "Structural Equations, Treatment Effects, and Econometric Policy Analysis," *Econometrica*, 73, 669–738.

IMBENS, G. W. AND J. D. ANGRIST (1994): "Identification and Estimation of Local Average Treatment Effects," *Econometrica*, 62, 467–476.

KIVIET, J. F. AND J. NIEMCZYK (2005): "The Asymptotic and Finite Sample Distributions of OLS and IV in Simultaneous Equations," Discussion Paper 2005/01, Department of Quantitative Economics, University of Amsterdam.

KLEIBERGEN, F. (2002): "Pivotal Statistics for Testing Structural Parameters in Instrumental Variables Regression," *Econometrica*, 70, 1781–1803.

——— (2004): "Testing Subsets of Structural Parameters in the Instrumental Variables Regression Model," *Review of Economics and Statistics*, 86, 418–423.

——— (2007): "Generalizing Weak Instrument Robust IV Statistics Towards Multiple Parameters, Unrestricted Covariance Matrices and Identification," *Journal of Econometrics*, forthcoming.

——— (2005b): "Testing Parameters in GMM without Assuming That They Are Identified," *Econometrica*, 73, 1103–1123.

KLEIBERGEN, F. AND H. K. VAN DIJK (1998): "Bayesian Simultaneous Equation Analysis Using Reduced Rank Structures," *Econometric Theory*, 14, 701–743.

KLEIBERGEN, F. AND E. ZIVOT (2003): "Bayesian and Classical Approaches to Instrumental Variable Regression," *Journal of Econometrics*, 114, 29–72.

KUNITOMO, N. (1980): "Asymptotic Expansions of the Distribution of Estimators in a Linear Functional Relationship and Simultaneous Equations," *Journal of the American Statistical Association*, 75, 693–700.

LEHMANN, E. L. (1986): *Testing Statistical Hypotheses*, New York: Wiley.

MADDALA, G. S. AND J. JEONG (1992): "On the Exact Small Sample Distribution of the Instrumental Variable Estimator," *Econometrica*, 60, 181–183.

MAVROEIDIS, S. (2004): "Weak Identification of Forward-looking Models in Monetary Models," *Oxford Bulletin of Economics and Statistics*, 66, Supplement, 609–635.

MIKUSHEVA, A. AND B. POI (2006): "Tests and Confidence Sets with Correct Size in the Simultaneous Equations Model with Potentially Weak Instruments," Department of Economics, Harvard University.

MOREIRA, M. J. (2001): "Tests with Correct Size When Instruments Can Be Arbitrarily Weak," Unpublished paper, Department of Economics, University of California, Berkeley.

——— (2003): "A Conditional Likelihood Ratio Test for Structural Models," *Econometrica*, 71, 1027–1048.

——— (2005): "Towards a General Theory of Hypothesis Testing for Structural Models," Department of Economics, Harvard University.

MOREIRA, M. J., J. R. PORTER, AND G. SUAREZ (2004): "Bootstrap and Higher-Order Expansion Validity When Instruments May Be Weak," Department of Economics, Harvard University.

MORIMUNE, K. (1983): "Approximate Distributions of the k-class Estimators when the Degree of Overidentifiability Is Large Compared with the Sample Size," *Econometrica*, 51, 821–841.

NAGAR, A. L. (1959): "The Bias and Moment Matrix of the General k-class Estimators of the Parameters in Simultaneous Equations," *Econometrica*, 27, 575–595.

NASON, J. M. AND G. W. SMITH (2005): "Identifying the New Keynesian Phillips Curve," Working Paper 2005-1, Federal Reserve Bank of Atlanta.

NEELEY, C. J., A. ROY, AND C. H. WHITEMAN (2001): "Risk Aversion Versus Intertemporal Substitution: A Case Study of Identification Failure in the Intertemporal Consumption Capital Asset Pricing Model," *Journal of Business and Economic Statistics*, 19, 395–403.

NELSON, C. R. AND R. STARTZ (1990a): "Some Further Results on the Exact Small Sample Properties of the Instrumental Variables Estimator," *Econometrica*, 58, 967–976.

——— (1990b): "The Distribution of the Instrumental Variables Estimator and Its t-Ratio When the Instrument Is a Poor One," *Journal of Business*, 63, S125–S140.

NEWEY, W. K. AND F. WINDMEIJER (2005): "Many Weak Moment Asymptotics for Generalized Empirical Likelihood Estimators," Department of Economics, M.I.T.

OTSU, T. (2006): "Generalized Empirical Likelihood Inference for Nonlinear and Time Series Models under Weak Identification," *Econometric Theory*, 22, 513–527.

PHILLIPS, P. C. B. (1984): "Exact Small Sample Theory in the Simultaneous Equations Model," in *Handbook of Econometrics*, Vol. 1, Amsterdam: North Holland.

——— (1989): "Partially Identified Econometric Models," *Econometric Theory*, 5, 181–240.

——— (2005): "Optimal Estimation of Cointegrated Systems with Irrelevant Instruments," unpublished paper, Cowles Foundation, Yale University.

POSKITT, D. S. AND C. L. SKEELS (2005): "Small Concentration Asymptotics and Instrumental Variables Inference," Department of Economics, University of Melbourne.

ROTHENBERG, T. J. (1984): "Approximating the Distributions of Econometric Estimators and Test Statistics," in *Handbook of Econometrics*, Vol. 2, Amsterdam: North Holland.

SHEA, J. (1997): "Instrument Relevance in Multivariate Linear Models: A Simple Measure," *Review of Economics and Statistics*, 79, 348–352.

SMITH, R. J. (2005): "Weak Instruments and Empirical Likelihood: A Discussion of the Papers by D. W. K. Andrews and J. H. Stock and Y. Kitamura," Unpublished paper, Faculty of Economics, University of Cambridge.

STAIGER, D. AND J. H. STOCK (1997): "Instrumental Variables Regression with Weak Instruments," *Econometrica*, 65, 557–586.

STOCK, J. H. AND J. H. WRIGHT (2000): "GMM with Weak Instruments," *Econometrica*, 68, 1055–1096.

STOCK, J. H., J. H. Wright, and M. Yogo (2002): "A Survey of Weak Instruments and Weak Identification in Generalized Method of Moments," *Journal of Business and Economic Statistics*, 20, 518–529.

STOCK, J. H. AND M. YOGO (2005a): "Asymptotic Distributions of Instrumental Variables Statistics with Many Instruments," in *Identification and Inference for Econometric Models: A Festschrift in Honor of Thomas J. Rothenberg*, edited by D. W. K. Andrews and J. H. Stock, Cambridge, UK: Cambridge University Press.

———— (2005b): "Testing for Weak Instruments in Linear IV Regression," in *Identification and Inference for Econometric Models: A Festschrift in Honor of Thomas J. Rothenberg*, edited by D. W. K. Andrews and J. H. Stock, Cambridge, UK: Cambridge University Press.

WANG, J. AND E. ZIVOT (1998): "Inference on Structural Parameters in Instrumental Variables Regression with Weak Instruments," *Econometrica*, 66, 1389–1404.

WOGLOM, G. (2001): "More Results on the Exact Small Sample Properties of the Instrumental Variable Estimator," *Econometrica*, 69, 1381–1389.

YOGO, M. (2004): "Estimating the Elasticity of Intertemporal Substitution When Instruments Are Weak," *Review of Economic Studies*, 86, 797–810.

ZELLNER, A. (1998): "The Finite Sample Properties of Simultaneous Equations' Estimates and Estimators: Bayesian and Non-Bayesian Approaches," *Journal of Econometrics*, 83, 185–212.

ZIVOT, E., R. STARTZ, AND C. R. NELSON (1998): "Valid Confidence Intervals and Inference in the Presence of Weak Instruments," *International Economic Review*, 39, 1119–1144.

CHAPTER 7

Empirical Likelihood Methods in Econometrics: Theory and Practice*
Yuichi Kitamura[†]

1 INTRODUCTION

Likelihood-based methods are of fundamental importance in econometrics. When the model is correctly specified, the maximum likelihood (ML) procedure automatically yields an estimator that is asymptotically efficient in several senses. For instance, the maximum likelihood estimator (MLE) is a best asymptotically normal (BAN) estimator under regularity conditions; see, for example, Chapter 4 of Serfling (1980). It is known that a bias corrected MLE is higher-order efficient (Ghosh, 1994). Other concepts of asymptotic efficiency also point to the superiority of MLE. For example, consider the following asymptotic efficiency criterion in terms of "large deviations" [see Chapter 10 of Serfling (1980) for discussions on large deviation theory]. Suppose a random sample $(z_1, \ldots, z_n)$ is generated according to a parametric probability model indexed by a finite-dimensional parameter vector θ, that is, $(z_1, \ldots, z_n) \sim P_\theta$. It is known that, in general, the probability of a consistent estimator $\theta_n = \theta_n(z_1, \ldots, z_n)$ missing its true value θ by a margin exceeding a fixed value c decays exponentially as n goes to infinity. The (negative of the) decay rate

$$\liminf_{n \to \infty} \frac{1}{n} \log P_\theta\{\|\theta_n - \theta\| > c\}, \quad c > 0 \tag{1.1}$$

has been used to measure the efficiency of θ_n. Obviously, an estimator that makes the "rate" (1.1) small is desirable. Kester and Kallenberg (1986) show that MLE achieves the lower bound of the above rate if the parametric model belongs to the convex exponential family. The last requirement is rather restrictive, but it is removable in the sense that MLE is generally optimal if the limit of the

* I acknowledge financial support from the National Science Foundation via grants SES-0241770 and SES-0551271. This paper is prepared for an invited symposium at the 9th World Congress of the Econometric Society in London. I thank Whitney Newey, Richard Smith, Kirill Evdokimov and participants of the World Congress for valuable comments.
† Department of Economics, Yale University, New Haven, CT.

rate (1.1) as $c \rightarrow 0$ is used as an efficiency criterion; see Bahadur (1960) and Bahadur, Zabell, and Gupta (1980).

Inference methods based on likelihood also possess a number of desirable properties. A leading example is the celebrated Neyman–Pearson Fundamental Lemma. Moreover, the large deviation principle (LDP) uncovers further optimality properties of the likelihood ratio test in broader contexts. Hoeffding (1963) considers a multinomial model and shows that the likelihood ratio test is optimal in terms of large deviation probabilities of type II errors. This optimality of the likelihood ratio test has been extended to more general hypothesis testing problems for parametric distributions (Zeitouni and Gutman, 1991).

As widely recognized, the validity of the likelihood approach generally depends on the assumption on the parametric form for the data distribution, and this fact has spurred the development of nonparametric and semiparametric methods. Perhaps one of the earliest ideas of treating the data distribution nonparametrically in statistical estimation and testing is to use the empirical distribution of the data by comparing it with the (family of) distribution(s) implied by a statistical model. This requires some measure of divergence between distributions. Standard testing methods such as the Kolmogorov–Smirnov test fall into this category, but the estimation theory based on the idea has been developed as well, as exemplified by the classic treatise by Wolfowitz (1957) on the minimum distance estimation. See Manski (1983) as well as Brown and Wegkamp (2002) for further developments of this line of research in econometrics. An estimation procedure that generalizes the minimum distance method by Wolfowitz is studied by Bickel et al. (1993), who call it the generalized minimum contrast (GMC) method; see Section 3 for more discussion on GMC. The minimum contrast approach yields procedures that are robust against distribution assumptions, though potentially at the cost of efficiency.

It has been recognized that the notion of likelihood can be introduced in the empirical minimum contrast framework just described above. This raises a conjecture: by using likelihood as a measure of distance, it may be possible to develop a method that is robust against distributional assumptions yet possesses good properties analogous to that of a parametric likelihood procedure. Remarkably, recent research shows that this conjecture holds, at least for certain classes of models that are important in econometrics. In particular, this idea yields a powerful and elegant procedure when applied to moment condition models. In his important paper, Owen (1988) has coined term "empirical likelihood" for this procedure. Its literature has been growing rapidly since then, as documented in Owen (2001). The current paper illustrates the method by connecting it with two important existing statistical frameworks, one being nonparametric MLE (NPMLE) and the other GMC. It also gives an updated review of the literature and provides some practical guidance for applied econometricians.

2   EL AS NPMLE

This section treats empirical likelihood as a nonparametric maximum likelihood estimation procedure (NPMLE). The basic idea of NPMLE is simple. Suppose the econometrician observes IID data $\{z_i\}_{i=1}^n$, where each z_i is distributed according to an unknown probability measure μ. The fundamental concept is the nonparametric (or empirical) log-likelihood function. Let Δ denote the simplex $\{(p_1, \ldots, p_n) : \sum_{i=1}^n p_i = 1, 0 \le p_i, i = 1, \ldots, n\}$. The nonparametric log likelihood at $(p_1, \ldots, p_n)$ is

$$\ell_{\mathrm{NP}}(p_1, \ldots, p_n) = \sum_{i=1}^n \log p_i, \quad (p_1, \ldots, p_n) \in \Delta. \tag{2.1}$$

This can be interpreted as the log likelihood for a multinomial model, where the support of the multinomial distribution is given by the empirical observations $\{z_i\}_{i=1}^n$, even though the distribution μ of z_i is not assumed to be multinomial. Rather, μ is left unspecified and therefore it is treated nonparametrically. It is obvious that the maximum of the above log-likelihood function is attained at $p_i = \frac{1}{n}$, therefore the empirical measure $\mu_n = \frac{1}{n} \sum_{i=1}^n \delta_{z_i}$ (δ_z denotes a unit mass at z) can be regarded as the NPMLE for the unknown probability measure μ. The maximum value of ℓ_{NP} is $-n \log n$. See Bickel et al. (1993) (Section 7.5 in particular) for a more rigorous derivation of the empirical measure μ_n as an NPMLE for μ.

The above example involves no model, but NPMLE works for well-specified econometric models as well. Owen (1990) made a crucial observation that the nonparametric maximum likelihood method shares many properties with conventional parametric likelihood when applied to moment condition models. Consider the model

$$E[g(z_i, \theta)] = \int g(z, \theta) d\mu = 0, \theta \in \Theta \mathbb{R}^k. \tag{2.2}$$

where g is a known $\mathbb{R}^q$-valued function. The parameter θ and the probability measure μ are unknown. The symbol θ_0 denotes the true value of θ.

Applying NPMLE, the moment condition model (2.2) is parameterized by $(\theta, p_1, \ldots, p_n)$ that resides in $\Theta \times \Delta$. The nonparametric log-likelihood function to be maximized is

$$\ell_{\mathrm{NP}} = \sum_{i=1}^n \log p_i, \quad \sum_{i=1}^n g(z_i, \theta) p_i = 0.$$

The value of $(\theta, p_1, \ldots, p_n) \in \Theta \times \Delta$ that maximizes ℓ_{NP} is called the (maximum) empirical likelihood estimator and denoted by $(\hat{\theta}_{\mathrm{EL}}, \hat{p}_{\mathrm{EL}1}, \ldots, \hat{p}_{\mathrm{EL}n})$. The NPMLE for θ and μ are $\hat{\theta}_{\mathrm{EL}}$ and $\hat{\mu}_{\mathrm{EL}} = \sum_{i=1}^n \hat{p}_{\mathrm{EL}i} \delta_{z_i}$. One might expect that the high dimensionality of the parameter space $\Theta \times \Delta$ makes the above maximization problem difficult to solve for any practical application. Fortunately, that is not the case. Instead of maximizing ℓ_{NP} with respect to the parameters $(\theta, p_1, \ldots, p_n)$ jointly, first fix θ at a given value of θ and consider the log likelihood with the parameters $(p_1, \ldots, p_n)$ "profiled out":

$$\ell(\theta) = \max \ell_{\mathrm{NP}}(p_1, \ldots, p_n) \text{ subject to } \sum_{i=1}^{n} p_i = 1, \sum_{i=1}^{n} p_i g(z_i, \theta) = 0.$$

(2.3)

Once this is done, maximize the profile likelihood $\ell(\theta)$ to obtain the empirical likelihood estimator. It turns out that (2.3) is easy to solve numerically, as illustrated below.

The Lagrangian associated with the constrained optimization problem (2.3) is

$$\mathcal{L} = \sum_{i=1}^{n} \log p_i + \lambda \left(1 - \sum_{i=1}^{n} p_i \right) - n \gamma' \sum_{i=1}^{n} p_i g(z_i, \theta),$$

where $\lambda \in \mathbb{R}$ and $\gamma \in \mathbb{R}^q$ are Lagrange multipliers. It is a straightforward exercise to show that the first-order conditions for $\mathcal{L}$ are solved by:

$$\hat{\lambda} = n, \quad \hat{\gamma}(\theta) = \operatorname*{argmin}_{\gamma \in \mathbb{R}^q} - \sum_{i=1}^{n} \log(1 + \gamma' g(z_i, \theta))), \quad \text{and}$$

$$\hat{p}_i(\theta) = \frac{1}{n(1 + \hat{\gamma}(\theta)' g(z_i, \theta))}, \tag{2.4}$$

yielding

$$\ell(\theta) = \min_{\gamma \in \mathbb{R}^q} - \sum_{i=1}^{n} \log(1 + \gamma' g(z_i, \theta))) - n \log n. \tag{2.5}$$

The empirical likelihood estimator for θ_0 is therefore

$$\hat{\theta}_{\mathrm{EL}} = \operatorname*{argmax}_{\theta \in \Theta} \ell(\theta) = \operatorname*{argmax}_{\theta \in \Theta} \min_{\gamma \in \mathbb{R}^q} - \sum_{i=1}^{n} \log(1 + \gamma' g(z_i, \theta)).$$

The numerical evaluation of the function $\ell(\cdot)$ is easy, because (2.5) is a low-dimensional convex maximization problem, for which a simple Newton algorithm works. The maximization of $\ell(\theta)$ with respect to θ is typically carried our using a nonlinear optimization algorithm. Once $\hat{\theta}_{\mathrm{EL}}$ is calculated, $\hat{p}_{\mathrm{EL}i}, i = 1, \ldots, n$ are obtained using the formula (2.4):

$$\hat{p}_{\mathrm{EL}i} = \frac{1}{n(1 + \hat{\gamma}(\hat{\theta}_{\mathrm{EL}})' g(z_i, \hat{\theta}_{\mathrm{EL}}))}. \tag{2.6}$$

More computational issues will be discussed in Section 8.

Qin and Lawless (1994) derived the asymptotic distribution of the empirical likelihood estimator. Let $D = E[\nabla_\theta g(z, \theta_0)]$ and $S = E[g(z, \theta_0) g(z, \theta_0)']$, then

$$\sqrt{n}(\hat{\theta}_{\mathrm{EL}} - \theta_0) \xrightarrow{d} \mathrm{N}(0, (D'SD)^{-1}). \tag{2.7}$$

The asymptotic variance coincides with the semiparametric efficiency bound derived by Chamberlain (1987). [Note that Chamberlain (1987) also uses a sequence of approximating multinomial models in his argument.] It is interesting to observe that maximizing the nonparametric likelihood function ℓ_{NP} for the moment condition model (2.2) automatically achieves efficiency. This is, a semiparametric analog of the standard result that maximizing the likelihood function of a parametric model yields an efficient estimator. The estimator $\hat{\mu}_{EL} = \sum_{i=1}^{n} \hat{p}_{ELi} \delta_{z_i}$ is also an efficient estimator for μ in the following sense. Suppose one wishes to estimate the expectation of a function $a(z, \theta_0)$ of z, that is, $E(a(z, \theta_0)) = \int a(z, \theta_0) d\mu$. Using $\hat{\mu}_{EL}$, let $E\widehat{(a(z, \theta_0))} = \int a(z, \hat{\theta}_{EL}) d\hat{\mu}_{EL} = \sum_{i=1}^{n} \hat{p}_{ELi} a(z_i, \hat{\theta}_{EL})$. This estimator is more efficient than a naive sample mean such as $\frac{1}{n} \sum_{i=1}^{n} a(z_i, \hat{\theta}_{EL})$, and can be shown to be semiparametrically efficient, using a result obtained by Brown and Newey (1998).

Empirical likelihood also applies to testing problems. Let R denote a known $\mathbb{R}^s$-valued function of θ. Suppose the econometrician poses a hypothesis that θ_0 is restricted as $R(\theta_0) = 0$ (and assume that the s restrictions are independent). This can be tested by forming a nonparametric analog of the parametric likelihood ratio statistic

$$
\begin{aligned}
r &= -2 \left(\sup_{\theta : R(\theta)=0} \ell(\theta) - \sup_{\theta \in \Theta} \ell \right) \\
&= -2 \left(\sup_{\theta : R(\theta)=0} \ell(\theta) - \ell(\hat{\theta}_{EL}) \right),
\end{aligned}
\tag{2.8}
$$

which obeys the chi-square distribution with s degrees of freedom asymptotically under the null that $R(\theta_0) = 0$. This is called the empirical likelihood ratio (ELR) statistic. Another interesting possibility is to define the empirical log-likelihood ratio *function*

$$
\text{elr}(\theta) = -2 \left[\ell(\theta) - (-n \log n) \right] = \max_{\gamma \in \mathbb{R}^q} 2 \sum_{i=1}^{n} \log(1 + \gamma' g(z_i, \theta))).
\tag{2.9}
$$

The first and the second terms in the square bracket are the maximized values of the log nonparametric likelihood with and without the restriction $\sum_{i=1}^{n} p_i g(z_i, \theta) = 0$, respectively. It can be shown that its value at θ_0, that is elr(θ_0), obeys the χ_q^2 distribution asymptotically under (2.2) and mild regularity conditions; see Owen (1991) and Section 3.5 of Owen (2001). Note that this procedure tests the overidentifying restrictions (2.2) and the parametric restriction $\theta = \theta_0$ jointly, since the restriction $\sum_{i=1}^{n} p_i g(z_i, \theta_0) = 0$ imposes the two restrictions simultaneously. Thus it is similar to the Anderson–Rubin test (Anderson and Rubin, 1949) in its scope. Finally, if one wants to test the overidentifying restrictions only, the restricted log likelihood in (2.9) is maximized under the constraint (2.2) but treating θ as a free parameter, therefore the corresponding restricted and the unrestricted empirical log likelihood are

$\ell(\hat{\theta}_{RL})$ and $-n \log n$, respectively. The empirical likelihood ratio statistic for the overidentification hypothesis (2.2), therefore, is $\mathrm{elr}(\hat{\theta}_{EL})$. This statistic obeys the chi-square distribution with $q - k$ degrees of freedom asymptotically.

Some may find having various versions of empirical likelihood ratio statistics rather confusing. The following elementary relationships among the statistics might help to clarify this. Suppose one wishes to test a parametric hypothesis of the form $\theta = \theta_0$. Then the appropriate statistic is $r = -2(\ell(\theta_0) - \ell(\hat{\theta}_{EL}))$, which is equal to

$$
\begin{aligned}
r &= -2\left(\ell(\theta_0) - \ell(\hat{\theta}_{EL})\right) \\
&= \left[-2\left(\ell(\theta_0) + n \log n\right)\right] - \left[-2\left(\ell(\hat{\theta}_{EL}) + n \log n\right)\right] \\
&= \mathrm{elr}(\theta_0) - \mathrm{elr}(\hat{\theta}_{EL}),
\end{aligned}
$$

or

$$
\mathrm{elr}(\theta_0) = r + \mathrm{elr}(\hat{\theta}_{EL}). \tag{2.10}
$$

This is similar to the decomposition noted in, for example, Stock and Wright (2000), p. 1066. The last equation shows that the test statistic $\mathrm{elr}(\theta_0)$, which tests the k parametric hypotheses and $q - k$ overidentifying restrictions simultaneously, splits into the empirical likelihood ratio test statistic for $\theta = \theta_0$ and the empirical likelihood-based test of the overidentifying restrictions.

A moment condition model is a prime example for which nonparametric maximum likelihood works very well. Note, however, that NPMLE has been applied to other models. For example, Cosslett (1983) considers a binary choice model

$$
y_i = 1\{x_i'\theta + \epsilon_i > 0\}, \theta \in \Theta \subset \mathbb{R}^k
$$

where ϵ_i is independent of x_i. Here the unknown parameters are the finite-dimensional parameter θ and the distribution of ϵ. To put Cosslett's estimator in our framework, consider a probability measure for ϵ that puts probability mass of p_i on each $\{-x_i'\theta\}$, $i = 1, \ldots, n$. Then the empirical log likelihood (or the nonparametric log likelihood) for $(\theta, p_1, \ldots, p_n)$ is given by

$$
\begin{aligned}
\ell_{NP} = \sum_{i=1}^{n} \Bigg[&y_i \left(\sum_{j=1}^{n} 1\{x_j'\theta \leq x_i'\theta\} p_i \right) \\
&+ (1 - y_i) \left(1 - \sum_{j=1}^{n} 1\{x_j'\theta \leq x_i'\theta\} p_i \right) \Bigg].
\end{aligned}
$$

Maximizing this empirical likelihood function for $(\theta, p_1, \ldots, p_n)$ over $\Theta \times \Delta$ yields Cosslett's estimator. Many other applications of NPMLE have been considered in the econometrics literature, for example, Heckman and Singer (1984); see also Cosslett (1997).

3   EL AS GMC

3.1   GMC and Duality

This section offers an interpretation of empirical likelihood alternative to the one as a nonparametric ML procedure given in the previous section. As noted by Bickel et al. (1993), it is useful to cast (parametric) MLE as a special case of the GMC estimation procedure. This principle can be applied here to construct a family of estimators to which EL belongs as a special case. Consider a function that measures the divergence between two probability measures P and Q:

$$D(P, Q) = \int \phi \left(\frac{dP}{dQ} \right) dQ, \tag{3.1}$$

where ϕ is chosen so that it is convex. If P is not absolutely continuous with respect to Q, define the divergence D to be ∞. $D(\cdot, P)$ is minimized at P.

The econometrician observes IID draws of an $\mathbb{R}^p$-valued random variable z that obeys the probability measure μ, and considers the model of the form (2.2). To interpret EL as a version of GMC, introduce the following notation. Let $\mathbf{M}$ denote the set of all probability measures on $\mathbb{R}^p$ and

$$\mathcal{P}(\theta) = \left\{ P \in \mathbf{M} : \int g(z, \theta) dP = 0 \right\}.$$

Define

$$\mathcal{P} = \cup_{\theta \in \Theta} \mathcal{P}(\theta), \tag{3.2}$$

which is the set of all probability measures that are compatible with the moment restriction (2.2). The set $\mathcal{P}$ is called a statistical model. It is correctly specified if and only if $\mathcal{P}$ includes the true measure μ as its member. At the population level, the GMC optimization problem is

$$\inf_{\theta \in \Theta} \rho(\theta, \mu), \quad \text{where} \quad \rho(\theta, \mu) = \inf_{P \in \mathcal{P}(\theta)} D(P, \mu). \tag{3.3}$$

If the model is correctly specified, the minimum of the contrast function $\rho(\cdot, \mu)$ is attained at $\theta = \theta_0$. Equation (3.3) is a variational problem as the minimization problem $\inf_{P \in \mathcal{P}(\theta)} D(P, \mu)$ involves optimization over functions. Using a variational problem as a basis of estimation may seem unpractical from a computational point of view. Fortunately, a duality theorem in the convex analysis comes to rescue. Define $p = \frac{dP}{d\mu}$, then $D(P, \mu) = \int \phi(p) d\mu$. For a value θ in Θ, consider the infinite-dimensional constrained optimization problem

$$v(\theta) = \inf_p \int \phi(p) d\mu \quad \text{subject to} \int g(z, \theta) p d\mu = 0, \int p d\mu = 1,$$

$$\tag{P}$$

where $v(\theta)$ is the value function corresponding a particular choice of θ. The nonnegativity of p is maintained if ϕ is modified so that $\phi(p) = \infty$ for $p < 0$; see Borwein and Lewis (1991). The primal problem (**P**) has a dual problem

$$v^*(\theta) = \max_{\lambda \in \mathbb{R}, \gamma \in \mathbb{R}^q} \left[\lambda - \int \phi^*(\lambda + \gamma' g(z, \theta)) d\mu \right], \tag{DP}$$

where ϕ^* is the convex conjugate (or the Legendre transformation) of ϕ;[1] see Borwein and Lewis (1991). Note (**DP**) is a finite-dimensional unconstrained convex maximization problem.

The Fenchel duality theorem (see Borwein and Lewis, 1991) implies that

$$v(\theta) = v^*(\theta). \tag{3.4}$$

Let $(\phi')^{-1}$ denote the inverse of the derivative of ϕ, and suppose $(\bar{\lambda}, \bar{\gamma}')' \in \mathbb{R}^{q+1}$ solves (**DP**), then the minimum of (**P**) is attained by

$$\bar{p}(\theta) = (\phi')^{-1}(\bar{\lambda} + \bar{\gamma}' g(z, \theta)). \tag{3.5}$$

See Borwein and Lewis (1991) for details. Equations (3.3), (**P**), (**DP**), and (3.4) show that θ_0 solves the minimization problem

$$\inf_{\theta \in \Theta} v^*(\theta) = \inf_{\theta \in \Theta} \max_{\lambda \in \mathbb{R}, \gamma \in \mathbb{R}^q} \left[\lambda - \int \phi^*(\lambda + \gamma' g(z, \theta)) d\mu \right]. \tag{3.6}$$

The preceding discussion focused on the population. Statistical procedures can be obtained by replacing the unknown μ with the empirical measure μ_n. By the definition (3.1), an appropriate sample version of the GMC problem (3.3) is

$$\text{minimize } \frac{1}{n} \sum_{i=1}^{n} \phi(n p_i), \quad \text{s.t. } \sum_{i=1}^{n} p_i g(z_i, \theta) = 0, \sum_{i=1}^{n} p_i = 1, \theta \in \Theta. \tag{3.7}$$

This leads to the following definition of the GMC estimator for θ:

$$\hat{\theta} = \underset{\theta \in \Theta}{\operatorname{argmin}} \, \hat{v}(\theta), \quad \hat{v}(\theta) = \inf_{\substack{\sum_{i=1}^{n} p_i g(z_i, \theta) = 0 \\ \sum_{i=1}^{n} p_i = 1}} \frac{1}{n} \sum_{i=1}^{n} \phi(n p_i). \tag{3.8}$$

The formulation (3.8) based on the sample version of the GMC problem corresponds to the use of "empirical discrepancy statistics" by Corcoran (1998). See also Kitamura (1996b), where it is noted that the discrepancy measure $D(P, \mu) = \int \phi\left(\frac{dP}{d\mu}\right) d\mu$ is essentially the f-divergence by Csiszàr (1967). Newey and Smith (2004) refer to the sample GMC-based estimator as the minimum distance estimator.

---

[1] For a convex function $f(x)$, its convex conjugate f^* is given by

$$f^*(y) = \sup_x [xy - f(x)].$$

The duality theorem shows that (3.8) is equivalent to a computationally convenient form

$$\hat{\theta} = \operatorname*{argmin}_{\theta \in \Theta} \hat{v}^{\star}(\theta), \quad \hat{v}^{\star}(\theta) = \max_{\lambda \in \mathbb{R}, \gamma \in \mathbb{R}^q} \left[\lambda - \frac{1}{n} \sum_{i=1}^{n} \phi^*(\lambda + \gamma' g(z_i, \theta)) \right],$$

(3.9)

obtained by replacing μ with μ_n in (3.6). This also suggests a natural estimator for μ. Let $(\hat{\lambda}, \hat{\gamma}')' \in \mathbb{R}^{q+1}$ solve the $(q + 1)$-dimensional maximization problem that is necessary for calculating the sample dual value function $\hat{v}^*(\theta)$ in (3.9). The density formula (3.5) yields

$$\widehat{\mu(A)} = \int_A (\phi')^{-1}(\hat{\lambda} + \hat{\gamma}' g(z, \hat{\theta})) d\mu_n$$

$$= \frac{1}{n} \sum_{z_i \in A} (\phi')^{-1}(\hat{\lambda} + \hat{\gamma}' g(z_i, \hat{\theta}))$$

(3.10)

as an estimator for $\mu(A)$ for every Borel set A defined on the sample space of z_i.

Choosing $\phi(x)$ to be $-\log(x)$ corresponds to empirical likelihood, because letting $\phi(x) = -\log(x)$ in (3.8) yields a GMC estimator of the form:

$$\hat{\theta} = \operatorname*{argmin}_{\theta \in \Theta} \inf_{\substack{\sum_{i=1}^{n} p_i g(z_i, \theta)=0 \\ \sum_{i=1}^{n} p_i=1}} \frac{1}{n} \sum_{i=1}^{n} -\log(np_i),$$

(3.11)

which is exactly the definition of the empirical likelihood estimator given in Section 2. Note that the convex conjugate of $\phi(x) = -\log(x)$ is $\phi^*(y) = -1 - \log(-y)$. Using this expression in (3.9) and concentrating λ out, obtain

$$\hat{\theta} = \operatorname*{argmin}_{\theta \in \Theta} \max_{\lambda \in \mathbb{R}, \gamma \in \mathbb{R}^q} \left[\lambda + 1 + \frac{1}{n} \sum_{i=1}^{n} \log(-\lambda - \gamma' g(z_i, \theta)) \right]$$

$$= \operatorname*{argmin}_{\theta \in \Theta} \max_{\gamma \in \mathbb{R}^q} \left[\frac{1}{n} \sum_{i=1}^{n} \log(1 + \gamma' g(z_i, \theta)) \right].$$

(3.12)

The last expression again matches the characterization of the EL estimator provided in Section 2, showing that the somewhat mysterious "saddle point" formulation of the EL estimator provided there is a natural consequence of the Fenchel duality. According to the original definition, the EL estimator solves the twofold minimization problem (3.11); it is an estimator that minimizes a contrast function. But its dual form (3.12) replaces the second minimization in (3.11) with a (computationally more tractable) low-dimensional maximization problem, thereby yielding the saddle point formula (3.12).

Note also that the form of the contrast function corresponding to the choice $\phi(x) = -\log(x)$ is

$$\rho(\theta, \mu) = \inf_{P \in \mathcal{P}(\theta)} \int \log \frac{d\mu}{dP} d\mu = \inf_{P \in \mathcal{P}(\theta)} K(\mu, P),$$

where $K(P, Q) = \int \log \frac{dP}{dQ} dP$ denotes the Kullback–Leibler (KL) divergence between probability measures P and Q. That is, the EL estimator solves the minimization problem

$$\inf_{\theta \in \Theta} \inf_{P \in \mathcal{P}(\theta)} K(\mu_n, P) = \inf_{P \in \mathcal{P}} K(\mu_n, P). \tag{3.13}$$

The fact that empirical likelihood minimizes the KL divergence between the empirical measure μ_n and the moment condition model $\mathcal{P}$ plays an important role in the analysis of empirical likelihood with the large deviations theory presented in Section 4.

Choices of ϕ other than $-\log$ have been considered in the literature. Let $\phi(x) = x \log(x)$, then the divergence function evaluated at P is $D(P, \mu) = \int \log \frac{dP}{d\mu} dP = K(P, \mu)$. This is similar to empirical likelihood in that the divergence function is given by the KL divergence measure, but note that the roles of P and μ are reversed. The Legendre transform of $\phi(x)$ is $\phi^*(y) = e^{y-1}$. Using this in (3.9) and concentrating λ out, one obtains $\hat{\theta}$ as a solution to

$$\inf_{\theta \in \Theta} \max_{\gamma \in \mathbb{R}^q} \left[-\frac{1}{n} \sum_{i=1}^{n} e^{\gamma' g(z_i, \theta)} \right]. \tag{3.14}$$

This is the saddle-point estimator proposed by Kitamura and Stutzer (1997). It is sometimes called the exponential tilting estimator for θ. Note that $\phi^{-1}(y) = e^{y-1}$ for this case, so the definition (3.10) yields

$$\widehat{\mu(A)} = \int_A e^{\hat{\gamma}' g(z, \hat{\theta})} d\mu_n = \frac{1}{n} \sum_{z_i \in A} e^{\hat{\gamma}' g(z_i, \hat{\theta})} \tag{3.15}$$

where $\hat{\gamma}$ is the value of γ at the saddle-point of (3.14) corresponding to $\hat{\theta}$.

Yet another popular choice of ϕ is $\phi(x) = \frac{1}{2}(x^2 - 1)$, which yields $\frac{1}{2n} \sum_{i=1}^{n} (np_i - 1)^2$ as the minimand of the GMC minimization problem (3.7). This is called the "Euclidean likelihood" by Owen (1991). Its Legendre transformation is $\phi^*(y) = \frac{1}{2}(y^2 + 1)$. In this case the numerical optimization to evaluate the function $\widehat{v}^*(\theta)$, $\theta \in \Theta$ is unnecessary. Let $\bar{g}(\theta) = \frac{1}{n} \sum_{i=1}^{n} g(z_i, \theta)$ and $\hat{S} = \frac{1}{n} \sum_{i=1}^{n} [g(z_i, \theta) - \bar{g}(\theta)][g(z_i, \theta) - \bar{g}(\theta)]'$. It is easy to see that for the quadratic ϕ^* the maximization problem that defines $\widehat{v}^*(\theta)$ [see (3.9)] has an explicit solution and the resulting GMC estimator solves

$$\inf_{\theta \in \Theta} \bar{g}(\theta)' \hat{S}^{-1}(\theta) \bar{g}(\theta).$$

Therefore, the choice $\phi(x) = \frac{1}{2}(x^2 - 1)$ leads to the continuous updating GMM estimator by Hansen, Heaton, and Yaron (1996); this connection between (continuous updating) GMM and Euclidean likelihood is noted in Kitamura (1996b).

Finally, Baggerly (1998), Kitamura (1996b), and Newey and Smith (2004) suggest using the Cressie–Read divergence family, which corresponds to the choice $\phi(x) = \frac{2}{\alpha(\alpha+1)}(x^{-\alpha} - 1)$ indexed by the parameter α. The conjugate ϕ^* of ϕ in this case is given by $\phi^*(y) = -\frac{2}{\alpha}[-\frac{\alpha+1}{2} y]^{\frac{\alpha}{\alpha+1}} + \frac{2}{\alpha(\alpha+1)}$. Using this ϕ^* in (3.9) yields the estimation procedure in Theorem 2.2 of Newey and

Smith (2004). Parameter values $\alpha = -2, -1, 0$, and 1 yield Euclidean likelihood, exponential tilt, empirical likelihood and Pearson's χ^2, respectively.

3.2   GMC and GEL

It is unnecessary to use a specific function or a specific parametric family of functions for ϕ or ϕ^* to define a GMC estimator $\hat{\theta}$. Kitamura (1996b) suggests a general family of estimator by considering ϕ's that are convex functions on $(0, +\infty)$. Alternatively, one may use the dual representation instead to define a class of estimators

$$\left\{ \hat{\theta} = \underset{\theta \in \Theta}{\text{argmin}} \max_{\lambda \in \mathbb{R}, \gamma \in \mathbb{R}^q} \left[\lambda - \frac{1}{n} \sum_{i=1}^{n} \phi^*(\lambda + \gamma' g(z_i, \theta)) \right] : \phi^* \text{ is convex} \right\}.$$

If ϕ takes the form of the Cressie–Read family, then ϕ^* is convex and homogeneous (plus an additive constant). Consequently, concentrating λ out and re-defining γ as γ/λ yields $\hat{\theta}$ as

$$\hat{\theta} = \underset{\theta \in \Theta}{\text{argmin}} \max_{\gamma \in \mathbb{R}^q} \left[-\frac{1}{n} \sum_{i=1}^{n} \phi^*(1 + \gamma' g(z_i, \theta)) \right]. \tag{3.16}$$

Define $\kappa(y) = -\phi^*(y + 1)$, then

$$\hat{\theta} = \underset{\theta \in \Theta}{\text{argmin}} \max_{\gamma \in \mathbb{R}^q} \left[\frac{1}{n} \sum_{i=1}^{n} \kappa(\gamma' g(z_i, \theta)) \right]. \tag{3.17}$$

This is essentially equivalent to the Generalized Empirical Likelihood (GEL) estimator by Smith (1997), though his original derivation of GEL is based on an interesting application of the method of Chesher and Smith (1997). It is therefore quite different from the GMC-based derivation outlined above. Also, Smith's formulation of GEL demands only concavity on κ in (3.17). The GEL family and the GMC family therefore do not completely coincide, though the difference between the two does not seem to matter much for practitioners as they both include commonly used estimators such as EL, exponential tilt and continuous updating as special cases. Smith (2004) provides a detailed account for GEL.

3.3   Some Properties

The procedures based on GMC or GEL share some common properties. First, both family yield estimators that have the same asymptotic distribution as in (2.7) under reasonable conditions; see Kitamura and Stutzer (1997), Smith (1997), Imbens, Spady, and Johnson (1998), and Newey and Smith (2004). It is well known that the two-step (optimal) GMM (Hansen, 1982), also yields the same first-order asymptotics. Second, the value of the objective function can be used for inference. It has already been observed in Section 2 that one can construct a nonparametric analogue of the likelihood ratio statistic which has an appropriate χ^2-distribution asymptotically. This carries over to the procedures discussed in Section 3. For example, suppose one is interested in testing the null hypothesis that $\theta_0 \in \Theta_0 \subset \Theta$, $\dim(\Theta_0) = k - s$ in (2.2),[2] which puts s restrictions on the parameter space for θ. Under the hypothesis, the difference in the constrained and unconstrained objective function values obeys the following asymptotic distribution:

$$-2\left(\inf_{\theta \in \Theta} \widehat{v}(\theta) - \inf_{\theta \in \Theta_0} \widehat{v}(\theta) \right) \xrightarrow{d} \chi_s^2. \tag{3.18}$$

Third, a similar argument applies to overidentifying restrictions testing. One can use the maximum value of the GMC objective function to test the null hypothesis that $\mu \in \mathcal{P}$ (i.e., the model is correctly specified, or the overidentifying restrictions hold). Under this null,

$$\inf_{\theta \in \Theta} 2\widehat{v}(\theta) \xrightarrow{d} \chi_{q-k}^2.$$

Smith (2000) discusses various EL-based specification tests for (2.2). See also Ramalho and Smith (2002).

Asymptotic properties similar to those presented above also hold for the conventional two-step GMM (Hansen, 1982), but there are distinctive features of GMC/GEL that are not shared by the two-step GMM. Subsequent sections investigate those properties theoretically, though some informal arguments that have been often made in favor of GMC/GEL-type estimators are worth noting here.

The two-step GMM requires a preliminary estimator of the weighting matrix, which often causes problems in finite samples, whereas GMC or GEL avoids explicit estimation of it. Some theoretical advantages associated with this fact are discussed in Section 5, though one interesting consequence is the normalization invariance property of GMC/GEL. Suppose one obtains a moment condition of the form (2.2) as an implication of the economic model. It is obvious that one can replace g by $\tilde{g} = Ag$, where $A(\theta)$ is a nonsingular matrix that can depend on θ, and obtain an equivalent condition $E[\tilde{g}(z, \theta_0)] = 0$, $\theta_0 \in \Theta$. There should be no economic reason to prefer one representation over the other. The two-step GMM, however, yields different results in finite samples, depending on the choice of A. See Gali and Gertler (1999) for an example of this phenomenon in an actual empirical setting. All the estimators discussed in the previous section are invariant with respect to the choice of A.

The properties described above are interesting and desirable, though more theoretical developments are required to uncover decisive advantages of

---

[2] This requirement refers to the local dimension of Θ_0 at θ_0. Here and henceforth the symbol dim is often used to denote such local dimensions.

GMC/GEL estimators, and, in particular, those of empirical likelihood. This will be the main theme of the next two sections.

4 LARGE DEVIATIONS

One can pick an arbitrary convex function ϕ in GMC (or a concave function κ in GEL) to define an estimator. This introduces a great deal of arbitrariness in estimating (2.2), and raises a natural and important question: which member of GMC (or GEL) should be used? Theoretical, practical, and computational considerations are necessary to answer this question. This section and the next attempt to provide theoretical accounts, followed by more practical discussions in Section 8. Note that the results in this section provide a theoretical answer to the above question, but they have further implications. The optimality result here holds for a class of very general statistical procedures, including those which do not belong to GMC or GEL.

The conventional *first-order, local* asymptotic theory discussed in Sections 2 and 3 predicts identical asymptotic behavior for members of GMC/GEL estimators as far as the moment condition model (2.2) is correctly specified. Likewise, all comparable tests that belong to these families share identical properties under appropriate null and local alternative hypotheses. This is a consequence of the fundamental nature of the conventional asymptotic distribution theory, which relies on first-order linear approximations. In reality, however, these estimators and tests can behave wildly differently in finite samples [see, e.g., simulation results in Kitamura (2001) and Kitamura and Otsu (2005)]. While the conventional asymptotic method is a useful device, it is important to explore approaches that go beyond local first-order approximations to resolve these problems. At least two alternative approaches exist. One approach, taken by some researchers, is to explore local higher-order asymptotic theory. This often yields useful and insightful results as will be discussed in Section 5, though it generally involves rather intricate calculations and delicate regularity conditions. Alternatively, first-order, global efficiency properties of GMC can be explored. Taking this approach enables us to evaluate the statistical implications of *global* and *nonlinear* structures of various GMC estimators not captured by local linear theory. This is a powerful tool for studying differences in the behavior of GMM, empirical likelihood, and other estimators. Such an investigation belongs to the domain of the so-called large deviation theory, which is the theme of the current section.

The rest of this section covers two topics. The first is the large deviation theory of estimation in the moment condition model (2.2). The second is the large deviations analysis of various hypothesis testing problems, including inference concerning θ as well as testing the overidentifying restrictions of the model. Interestingly, in both cases empirical likelihood (i.e., GMC with $\phi(x) = -\log(x)$) yields optimality results, implying that empirical likelihood has a special status among competing procedures. Note, however, that obtaining an optimal estimator in terms of large deviations requires some modifications to the maximum empirical likelihood estimator discussed in Sections 2 and 3.

4.1   Large Deviations and Minimax Estimation

Consider again the moment condition model (2.2). θ_0, or its subvector, is the parameter of interest. The conventional asymptotic efficiency theory focuses on the behavior of estimators in a shrinking neighborhood of the true parameter value. In contrast, efficiency theory with LDP deals with a fixed neighborhood of the true value. For an estimator θ_n, consider the probability that it misses the true value θ_0 by a margin exceeding $c > 0$

$$\Pr\{\|\theta_n - \theta_0\| > c\}, \tag{4.1}$$

where $\| \cdot \|$ is the (Euclidean) norm.

The expression (4.1) can be interpreted as the expected risk $E[L(\hat{\theta})]$ of the estimator θ_n under the loss function $L(\theta) = 1\{\|\theta_n - \theta_0\| > c\}$. It should be emphasized that other loss functions can be employed. It is generally possible to derive a large deviation optimal estimator under an alternative loss function, at least at the theoretical level. The treatment here focuses on the indicator loss function, however. It is a natural loss function, and commonly used in the literature (e.g., Bahadur, 1964). A nice feature of the indicator loss is that it leads to a practical and computationally convenient procedure, as discussed later in this section.

The parameter c in (4.1) is a loss function parameter that is chosen by the decision maker (i.e., the econometrician). In a typical empirical application, the econometrician would tolerate estimation errors within a certain margin. If one subscribes to the view that a model is an approximation of reality, it would be natural to allow a certain margin of error. Also, a number of authors argued the importance the concept of "economic significance" in econometrics; with that view, c can be chosen by considering a range within which errors are economically insignificant. In sum, c should be determined based on economic considerations. As an example, suppose the risk aversion parameter in a dynamic optimization model of consumers is being estimated. The econometrician then would have a range within which differences in the degree of risk aversion are economically not significant. The parameter c is a part of the econometrician's loss function and therefore should be decided based on the economic meaning of the parameter.

Once the parameter c is chosen, the next step is to make the probability (4.1) "small." The precise meaning of "small" will be defined shortly.

Evaluating (4.1) in finite samples is unrealistic unless the model is completely specified and extremely simple. On the other hand, simply letting n go to infinity is not informative, as the limit would be either 1 or 0 depending on whether θ_n is consistent or not. The theory of large deviations focuses on the asymptotic behavior of

$$(\Pr\{\|\theta_n - \theta_0\| > c\})^{1/n}. \tag{4.2}$$

or its logarithmic version

$$\frac{1}{n} \log \left(\Pr\{ \|\theta_n - \theta_0\| > c \} \right). \tag{4.3}$$

Letting n go to infinity in the latter gives the negative of the asymptotic decreasing rate of the probability that the estimator misses the true value by a margin that exceeds c. The goal would be then to make this limit as small as possible. The problem of minimizing the rate as in (4.3) has been considered in the context of parametric estimation, for example, Bahadur (1960) and Fu (1973). These studies, however, usually require that the model belongs to the exponential family and do not extend to other models.

The moment condition model (2.2) is not a member of the exponential family, but there is a way to proceed. Kitamura and Otsu (2005) note that an asymptotic minimax criterion leads to an estimator for θ that possesses optimal properties in terms of large deviations, by using an approach proposed by Puhalskii and Spokoiny (1998). Consider, instead of (4.3), its maximum over all possible combinations of (θ, P):

$$\sup_{\theta \in \Theta} \sup_{P \in \mathcal{P}(\theta)} \frac{1}{n} \log \left(P^{\otimes n} \{ \|\theta_n - \theta\| > c \} \right), \tag{4.4}$$

where $P^{\otimes n} = P \otimes P \otimes \cdots \otimes P$ denotes the n-fold product measure of P. (Since $z_i \sim_{iid} P$, the sample obeys the law $(z_1, \ldots, z_n) \sim P^{\otimes n}$.)

Let $B \leq 0$ denote an asymptotic lower bound for (4.4), that is,

$$\liminf_{n \to \infty} \inf_{\theta_n \in \mathcal{F}_n} \sup_{\theta \in \Theta} \sup_{P \in \mathcal{P}(\theta)} \frac{1}{n} \log \left(P^{\otimes n} \{ \|\theta_n - \theta\| > c \} \right) \geq B, \tag{4.5}$$

where $\mathcal{F}_n$ denotes the set of all Θ-valued measurable functions of data $(z_1, \ldots, z_n)$, that is, the set of all estimators. The following constant B^* satisfies (4.5):

$$B^* = \sup_{Q \in \mathbf{M}} \inf_{\theta^* \in \Theta} \sup_{\theta \in \Theta : \|\theta^* - \theta\| > c} \sup_{P \in \mathcal{P}(\theta)} -K(Q, P). \tag{4.6}$$

(Recall $\mathbf{M}$ denotes the set of all probability measures on $\mathbb{R}^p$.) Moreover, this bound B^* turns out to be tight, therefore called the asymptotic minimax bound. The qualification "asymptotic" refers to $\liminf_{n \to \infty}$, whereas the term "minimax" corresponds to the operation $\inf_{\theta_n \in \mathcal{F}_n} \sup_{\theta \in \Theta} \sup_{P \in \mathcal{P}(\theta)}$.

The minimax bound (4.6) can be achieved by an estimator based on empirical likelihood function (Kitamura and Otsu, 2005). Let $\hat{\theta}_{ld}$ denote the minimizer of the objective function

$$Q_n(\theta) = \sup_{\theta^* \in \Theta : \|\theta^* - \theta\| > c} \ell(\theta^*),$$

where $\ell(\cdot)$ is the log empirical likelihood function defined in (2.5). The estimator $\hat{\theta}_{ld}$ is a minimax estimator in the large deviation sense, as it reaches the bound B^* asymptotically:

$$\limsup_{n \to \infty} \sup_{\theta \in \Theta} \sup_{P \in \mathcal{P}(\theta)} \frac{1}{n} \log \left(P^{\otimes n} \{ \|\hat{\theta}_{ld} - \theta\| > c \} \right) = B^*.$$

See Kitamura and Otsu (2005) for a proof. Note that $\hat{\theta}_{\mathrm{ld}}^1$ generally differs from the empirical likelihood estimator $\hat{\theta}_{\mathrm{EL}}$, unless, say, the sample empirical likelihood function $\ell(\cdot)$ is symmetric around $\hat{\theta}_{\mathrm{EL}}$. Practical implementation of $\hat{\theta}_{\mathrm{ld}}$ is straightforward, at least when $k = \dim(\Theta)$ is low, since the objective function Q_n is a rather simple function of the log empirical likelihood $\ell(\cdot)$, whose numerical evaluation is easy (see Sections 2, 3, and 8).

If the dimension of θ is high, it is also possible to focus on a low-dimensional subvector of θ and obtain a large deviation minimax estimator for it, treating the rest as nuisance parameters. This is potentially useful in practice, since it is often the case that a small number of "key parameters" in a model are economically interesting. Even in a case where every element of θ is important, one may want to apply the following procedure to each component of θ to lessen computational burden. Wlog, let $\theta = (\theta^{1\prime}, \theta^{2\prime})'$, where $\theta^1 \in \Theta^1$. Suppose the researcher chooses the loss function $1\{\|\theta^1 - \theta_n^1\| > c\}$ to evaluate the performance of an estimator θ_n^1 for θ^1. The corresponding maximum (log) risk function is given by

$$\sup_{\theta \in \Theta} \sup_{P \in \mathcal{P}(\theta)} \frac{1}{n} \log \left(P^{\otimes n} \{ \|\theta_n^1 - \theta^1\| > c \} \right). \tag{4.7}$$

The limit inferior of the above display is bounded below by

$$B_1^* = \sup_{Q \in \mathbf{M}} \inf_{\theta^{1*} \in \Theta^1} \sup_{\theta \in \Theta: \|\theta^{1*} - \theta^1\| > c} \sup_{P \in \mathcal{P}(\theta)} -K(Q, P).$$

Let $\hat{\theta}_{\mathrm{ld}}^1$ minimize the function

$$Q_n^1(\theta^1) = \sup_{\theta^* \in \Theta: \|\theta^{1*} - \theta_1\| > c} \ell(\theta^*).$$

This is a minimax estimator, in the sense that it achieves the lower bound of the maximum risk (4.7) asymptotically:

$$\lim_{n \to \infty} \sup_{\theta \in \Theta} \sup_{P \in \mathcal{P}(\theta)} \frac{1}{n} \log \left(P^{\otimes n} \{ \|\hat{\theta}_{\mathrm{ld}}^1 - \theta^1\| > c \} \right) = B_1^*.$$

If the parameter of interest θ_1 is scalar, it is possible to provide an interesting and practically useful characterization of the minimax estimator $\hat{\theta}_{\mathrm{ld}}^1$. Assume, for the sake of argument, that the minimum of Q_n^1 is attained uniquely by $\hat{\theta}_{\mathrm{ld}}^1$. Then

$$\begin{aligned}
\hat{\theta}_{\mathrm{ld}}^1 &= \operatorname*{argmin}_{\theta^1 \in \Theta^1} \sup_{\theta^* \in \Theta: |\theta^{1*} - \theta^1| > c} \ell(\theta) \\
&= \operatorname*{argmin}_{\theta^1 \in \Theta^1} \sup_{\theta_1^* \in \Theta^1: |\theta^{1*} - \theta^1| > c} \sup_{\theta^{2*}} \ell(\theta^{1*}, \theta^{2*}) \\
&= \operatorname*{argmin}_{\theta^1 \in \Theta^1} \sup_{\theta_1^* \in \Theta^1: |\theta^{1*} - \theta^1| > c} \ell_1(\theta^{1*}), \tag{4.8}
\end{aligned}$$

where $\ell^1(\theta^1) = \sup_{\theta^2} \ell(\theta^1, \theta^2)$ is the log empirical likelihood function with the nuisance parameter θ^2 profiled out. Imagine the function $\ell^1(\cdot)$ plotted against the parameter space Θ^1 of θ^1, which is (a subset of) $\mathbb{R}$. Choose a level set of $\ell^1(\cdot)$ so that its length is $2c$, then the estimator $\hat{\theta}^1_{\text{ld}}$ is the midpoint of the level set. To see this, notice that the last expression in (4.8) indicates that the value of $\hat{\theta}^1_{\text{ld}}$ is chosen so that the maximum of ℓ^1 outside of the c-ball with center $\hat{\theta}^1_{\text{ld}}$ becomes as small as possible. If an alternative value $\check{\theta}^1$ in place of $\hat{\theta}^1_{\text{ld}}$ is used, the c-ball around it will exclude some points where the values of $\ell^1(\cdot)$ are higher than $Q^1_n(\hat{\theta}^1_{\text{ld}})$, making $Q^1_n(\check{\theta}^1)$ larger than $Q^1_n(\hat{\theta}^1_{\text{ld}})$. This is true for any $\check{\theta}_1 \neq \hat{\theta}^1_{\text{ld}}$, therefore $\hat{\theta}^1_{\text{ld}}$ minimizes Q^1_n.

The above characterization of $\hat{\theta}^1_{\text{ld}}$ implies that the estimator can be interpreted as a "robustified" version of the original empirical likelihood estimator. Again, imagine the profiled empirical likelihood function ℓ^1 plotted against the space of θ^1. Suppose the function has a "plateau" of length $2c$. This should include the maximizer of ℓ^1, but the maximum can occur at a point that is close to one of the end points of the plateau. The empirical likelihood estimator follows small fluctuations over the plateau, since it has to correspond to the exact maximum. In contrast, the minimax estimator always chooses the center of the plateau and therefore is robust against these small fluctuations. This is reminiscent of arguments that favor a posterior mean Bayes estimator over MLE, on the ground that the former takes a weighted average of the likelihood function and is more robust against sample fluctuations of the likelihood function than the latter. This interpretation of $\hat{\theta}^1_{\text{ld}}$ as a robustified estimator applies to the case where θ^1 is multidimensional as well.

The preceding discussion described the new procedure as a point estimator, though it may be better understood as a fixed-length interval estimation method. The concept of fixed-length interval estimators can be found, for example, in Wald (1950). As before, let θ^1 denote the parameter of interest in the vector θ and suppose it is a scalar. Consider the set $\mathcal{I}_n$ of interval estimators I_n of length $2c$ for θ^1. From the above discussion, the large deviation probability of such an interval not containing the true value is asymptotically bounded from below by B_1^*, which is attained by the interval estimator $\hat{I}_{\text{ld}} = [\hat{\theta}^1_{\text{ld}} - c, \hat{\theta}^1_{\text{ld}} + c]$. That is,

$$\liminf_{n \to \infty} \inf_{I_n \in \mathcal{I}_n} \sup_{\theta \in \Theta} \sup_{P \in \mathcal{P}(\theta)} \frac{1}{n} \log \left(P^{\otimes n} \{ \theta^1 \notin I_n \} \right) = B_1^*$$

$$= \lim_{n \to \infty} \sup_{\theta \in \Theta} \sup_{P \in \mathcal{P}(\theta)} \frac{1}{n} \log \left(P^{\otimes n} \{ \theta^1 \notin \hat{I}_{\text{ld}} \} \right).$$

The interval estimator $\hat{I}_{\text{ld}}$ is therefore optimal. $\hat{\theta}^1_{\text{ld}}$ is not necessarily consistent when viewed as a point estimator, but the corresponding $\hat{I}_{\text{ld}}$ is consistent in the sense that it contains the true parameter value with probability approaching 1.

The choice of the parameter c should be determined by the goal of the economic analysis as discussed at the beginning of this section, though some further remarks on this issue are in order.

First, experimental results from Kitamura and Otsu (2005) suggest that a wide range of values of c work for realistic sample sizes. See Section 8 for more information on finite sample properties of the minimax estimator and other estimators.

Second, it is reasonable to assume that the researcher would choose a smaller value of c, when a larger data set is available and therefore more accurate estimation would be possible. If one calculates $\hat{\theta}_{1d}^1$ for a sequence of constants $\{c_n\}_{n=1}^{\infty}$ that converges to 0 slowly, the estimator is consistent as a point estimator, while it may be still possible to show that it has an asymptotic optimality property. Such an investigation would involve the theory of moderate deviations, which has been applied to estimation problems; see, for example, Kallenberg (1983).

4.2   Minimax Testing

Section 4.1 applied an asymptotic minimax approach to parameter estimation. Kitamura and Otsu (2005) show that the similar approach (cf. Puhalskii and Spokoiny, 1998) leads to a testing procedure that has a large deviation minimax optimality property in the model (2.2). Let Θ_0 be a subset of the parameter space Θ of θ. Consider testing

$$H_0 : \theta \in \Theta_0$$

against

$$H_1 : \theta \in \Theta_0^c$$

(Θ_0^c denotes the complement of Θ_0 in Θ). To derive a minimax test, a few decision theoretic concepts are useful. The econometrician observes the data $\{z_1, \dots, z_n\}$ to reach a decision to accept H_0 or reject it in favor of H_1. So it can be represented by a binary-valued function $d_n = d_n(z_1, \dots, z_n)$, taking the value of 0 if H_0 is accepted and the value of 1 otherwise. An appropriate loss function for decision d_n is

$$L(d_n) = w 1\{d_n = 1, H_0 \text{ holds}\} + (1 - w) 1\{d_n = 0, H_1 \text{ holds}\}$$

where the weighting factor w belongs to $[0, 1]$. The econometrician chooses w; as seen below, this parameter determines the critical value of the minimax test. Applying the same argument as in Section 4.1 yields a decision function that is large deviation minimax optimal. Let $\mathcal{P}_0 = \cup_{\theta \in \Theta_0} \mathcal{P}(\theta)$ and $\mathcal{P}_1 = \cup_{\theta \in \Theta_1} \mathcal{P}(\theta)$. The maximum log expected risk, normalized by $\frac{1}{n}$ is

$$\frac{1}{n} \max \left\{ \log \left(w^n \sup_{P \in \mathcal{P}_0} P^{\otimes n} \{d_n = 1\} \right), \log \left((1 - w)^n \sup_{P \in \mathcal{P}_1} P^{\otimes n} \{d_n = 0\} \right) \right\}.$$

This corresponds to (4.4) in the estimation problem. The limit inferior of the above display (as n tends to infinity) is bounded below by

$$C^* = \sup_{Q \in M} \min \left\{ \log w + \sup_{P \in \mathcal{P}_0} -K(Q, P), \log(1 - w) + \sup_{P \in \mathcal{P}_1} -K(Q, P) \right\}.$$

It can be shown that this large deviation bound is attained by the following decision function

$$\hat{d}_{\mathrm{ld}} = 1 \left\{ \log \frac{w}{1 - w} < \sup_{\theta \in \Theta} l(\theta) - \sup_{\theta \in \Theta_0} l(\theta) \right\}, \tag{4.9}$$

that is,

$$\lim_{n \to \infty} \frac{1}{n} \max \left\{ \log \left(w^n \sup_{P \in \mathcal{P}_0} P^{\otimes n} \{\hat{d}_{\mathrm{ld}} = 1\} \right), \right.$$
$$\left. \log \left((1 - w)^n \sup_{P \in \mathcal{P}_1} P^{\otimes n} \{\hat{d}_{\mathrm{ld}} = 0\} \right) \right\} = C^*$$

if $\frac{1}{2} \le w \le 1$. (If the econometrician chooses w that is less than $\frac{1}{2}$, $\hat{d}_{\mathrm{ld}}$ needs to be modified so that the first supremum in the above definition of $\hat{d}_{\mathrm{ld}}$ is taken over Θ_1.) The testing procedure (4.9) is the empirical likelihood ratio (ELR) test for H_0 with critical value $2 \log \frac{w}{1-w}$ as described in Section 2; see also Equation (3.18). That is, ELR is minimax, large deviation optimal for testing H_0 against H_1.

4.3   GNP-Optimality of Empirical Likelihood

Specification analysis of moment condition models is often carried out using the GMM-based overidentifying restrictions test by Hansen (1982). The null hypothesis of Hansen's test takes the form (2.2), that is, the moment condition holds for *some* θ in Θ. It can be expressed using the notation in Section 3.1 as

$$\mu \in \mathcal{P}. \tag{H}$$

Previous sections introduced alternative tests for (**H**), including the ELR overidentification test based on $\mathrm{elr}(\hat{\theta}_{\mathrm{EL}})$; see Equation (2.9) and discussions thereafter.

Again, the existence of alternative procedures raises the question of which test should be used. Various asymptotic efficiency criteria can be applied for comparing competing tests for (**H**). See Serfling (1980) for a comprehensive catalog of asymptotic efficiency criteria. Among them, the well-known Pitman efficiency criterion uses local first-order approximations and is not informative here, for the same reason discussed at the beginning of this section. The asymptotic efficiency criterion by Hoeffding (1963), however, reveals that the ELR test is optimal in a asymptotic large deviations sense. This conclusion, obtained by Kitamura (2001), is in a sense stronger than the results in the previous section on parametric hypothesis testing. It claims that the ELR is *uniformly* most powerful, whereas the previous result is about minimax optimality. This kind of property is sometimes called a generalized Neyman–Pearson (GNP)-type lemma.

As before, a test is represented by a sequence of binary functions $d_n = d_n(z_1, \ldots, z_n), n = 1, 2, \ldots$ which takes the value of 0 if the test accept (**H**) and 1 otherwise. The conventional asymptotic power comparison is based on the type II error probabilities of tests that have comparable type I error probabilities. Hoeffding (1963) takes this approach as well, but he evaluates type I and type II errors using LDP. In the present context, size properties of competing tests are made comparable by requiring that, for a parameter $\eta > 0$, each test d_n satisfies

$$\sup_{P \in \mathcal{P}} \limsup_{n \to \infty} \frac{1}{n} \log P^{\otimes n}\{d_n = 1\} \leq -\eta \qquad \text{(L)}$$

Therefore η determines the level of a test via large deviations.

Now, use the η in (**L**) to define the ELR test as follows:

$$d_{\text{ELR},n} = \begin{cases} 0 & \text{if } \frac{1}{2n}\text{elr}(\hat{\theta}_{\text{EL}}) \leq -\eta \\ 1 & \text{otherwise.} \end{cases}$$

Kitamura (2001) shows the following two facts under weak regularity conditions.

(I) $d_{\text{ELR},n}$ satisfies the condition (**L**).
(II) For every test d_n that satisfies (**L**),

$$\limsup_{n \to \infty} \frac{1}{n} \log P^{\otimes n}\{d_n = 0\} \geq \limsup_{n \to \infty} \frac{1}{n} \log P^{\otimes n}\{d_{ELR,n} = 0\} \qquad (4.12)$$

for every $P \notin \mathcal{P}$.

Fact (I) shows that the large deviation rate of the type I error probability of the ELR test defined as above satisfies the size requirement (**L**). The left-hand side and the right-hand side of the inequality in Fact (II) correspond to the LDP of the type II errors of the arbitrary test d_n and that of the ELR test $d_{\text{ELR},n}$, respectively. The two facts therefore mean that, among all the tests that satisfies the LDP level condition (**L**) [and the regularity conditions discussed in Kitamura (2001)], there exists no test that outperforms the ELR test in terms of the large deviation power property. Note that Fact (II) holds for every $P \notin \mathcal{P}$, therefore ELR is uniformly most powerful in terms of LDP. That is, ELR is a GNP test.

To illustrate this result, take the simplest example: suppose $z_i \sim_{iid} \mu, i = 1, \ldots, n$ and $E[z_i] = m \in \mathbb{R}$. The null hypothesis $m = m_0$ is tested against $m \neq m_0$. In absence of further distributional assumptions, a standard procedure described in textbooks is to carry out a large sample test based on the statistic $n(\bar{z} - m_0)^2/\hat{s}_z$, where $\bar{z} = \frac{1}{n}\sum_{i=1}^{n} z_i$ and $\hat{s}_z$ is a consistent estimator for the variance of z. The above result shows that the standard procedure as above is suboptimal, since the ELR is the uniformly most powerful in Hoeffding's criterion. The simulation experiments reported in Section 8.2.2 considers this setting and provides strong support for the theoretical implications described above.

4.4   EL, Large Deviations, and Sanov's Theorem

The analysis in the previous two sections shows various efficiency properties of empirical likelihood in terms of large deviations. This phenomenon is by no means a coincidence. The fundamental reason why empirical likelihood emerges as an optimal procedure comes from an LDP for empirical measures, called Sanov's theorem [Sanov (1961); see also Deuschel and Stroock (1989), Theorem 3.1.17]. Suppose $z_i \sim_{iid} \mu$, $i = 1, \ldots, n$, and equip the space of all probability measures $\mathbf{M}$ with the topology of weak convergence. For an arbitrary set $\mathcal{G} \in \mathbf{M}$, let $\mathcal{G}^o$ and $\bar{\mathcal{G}}$ denote the interior and the closure of $\mathcal{G}$, respectively. Sanov's Theorem shows that the empirical measure μ_n satisfies

$$\liminf_{n \to \infty} \frac{1}{n} \log \Pr(\mu_n \in \mathcal{G}^o) \geq - \inf_{\nu \in \mathcal{G}^o} K(\nu, \mu)$$

$$\limsup_{n \to \infty} \frac{1}{n} \log \Pr(\mu_n \in \bar{\mathcal{G}}) \leq - \inf_{\nu \in \bar{\mathcal{G}}} K(\nu, \mu).$$

Put loosely, the probability that the empirical measure falls into the set $\mathcal{G}$ is governed by the minimum value of the Kullback–Leibler divergence number between the probability measure and $\mathcal{G}$. The moment condition model is represented by the set $\mathcal{P}$, so it is reasonable to expect that using the minimum KL divergence $\inf_{P \in \mathcal{P}} K(\mu, P)$, or more precisely, its empirical version $\inf_{P \in \mathcal{P}} K(\mu_n, P)$, as a statistical criterion leads to optimal procedures. As seen in (3.13), however, empirical likelihood solves the empirical KL minimization problem and therefore often achieves optimality in a large deviations sense. The choice of $\phi(x) = -\log(x)$ emerges naturally from the LDP, not as a consequence of an arbitrary and artificial choice of an econometric objective function.

5   HIGHER-ORDER THEORY

The LDP-based approach, presented in the previous section, utilized global first-order approximations of empirical likelihood and other related methods. This section presents some results from an alternative approach based on local higher-order approximations. Interestingly, the two quite different approaches tend to yield similar conclusions; empirical likelihood often exhibits desirable properties in terms of higher-order comparisons as well, though there are some differences in the conclusions obtained from the two approaches.

5.1   Estimation

Newey and Smith (2004) investigate higher-order properties of the GEL family of estimators. They find that GEL estimators have good properties in terms of the second-order bias. Moreover, empirical likelihood has a special bias reducing property among the GEL estimators. To illustrate their findings, it is instructive to consider the conventional two-step GMM estimator for (2.2) and compare it with GEL estimators. Write $\bar{D}(\theta) = \frac{1}{n}\sum_{i=1}^{n}\nabla_\theta g(z_i, \theta)$, $\bar{S}(\theta) = \frac{1}{n}\sum_{i=1}^{n}g(z_i, \theta)g(z_i, \theta)'$ and $\bar{g}(\theta) = \frac{1}{n}\sum_{i=1}^{n}g(z_i, \theta)$. The two-step GMM, denoted by $\hat{\theta}_{\text{GMM}}$, based on a preliminary estimator $\check{\theta}$ is a root of the following first-order condition:

$$\bar{D}(\hat{\theta}_{\text{GMM}})'\bar{S}(\check{\theta})^{-1}\bar{g}(\hat{\theta}_{\text{GMM}}) = 0. \tag{5.1}$$

This can be regarded as a feasible version of the infeasible optimally weighted sample moment condition with $D = E[\nabla_{\theta_0}g(z, \theta)]$, $S = E[g(z_i, \theta_0)g(z_i, \theta_0)']$, which would yield an "ideal" estimator $\hat{\theta}_{\text{ideal}}$ as its root:

$$D'S^{-1}\bar{g}(\hat{\theta}_{\text{ideal}}) = 0. \tag{5.2}$$

The effect of replacing D and S with $\bar{D}(\hat{\theta}_{\text{GMM}})$ and $\bar{S}(\check{\theta})$ is negligible in the conventional first-order asymptotics by Slutsky's theorem. These terms, however, do affect the bias of $\hat{\theta}_{\text{GMM}}$ of order $O(\frac{1}{n})$ for two reasons. First, even evaluated at the true value θ_0, these two sample moments are correlated with the sample mean of g, and these correlations show up in the second-order bias term of $\hat{\theta}_{\text{GMM}}$. Second, the effect of the preliminary estimator $\check{\theta}$ also appears in the second-order bias term. In particular, the first effect from the correlations tend to grow with the number of moment conditions q. See Newey and Smith (2004), Donald, Imbens, and Newey (2003), and Imbens and Spady (2006).

The situation changes for the EL estimator $\hat{\theta}_{\text{EL}}$. Appendix shows that the first-order condition for $\hat{\theta}_{\text{EL}}$, using the notation $\hat{D}(\theta) = \sum_{i=1}^{n}\hat{p}_{\text{EL}i}\nabla_\theta g(z_i, \theta)$ and $\hat{S}(\theta) = \sum_{i=1}^{n}\hat{p}_{\text{EL}i}g(z_i, \theta)g(z_i, \theta)'$, can be written as

$$\hat{D}(\hat{\theta}_{\text{EL}})'\hat{S}^{-1}(\hat{\theta}_{\text{EL}})\bar{g}(\hat{\theta}_{\text{EL}}) = 0; \tag{5.3}$$

see Theorem 2.3 of Newey and Smith (2004) as well as Donald and Newey (2000). This is similar to the first-order condition (5.1) for GMM, though there are important differences. Notice that D and S that appear in the "ideal" first-order condition (5.2) are estimated by $\hat{D}(\hat{\theta}_{\text{EL}})$ and $\hat{S}(\hat{\theta}_{\text{EL}})$ in (5.3). These are semiparametrically efficient estimators of D and S under the moment restriction (2.2), as discussions in Section 2 imply. This means that they are asymptotically uncorrelated with $\bar{g}(\theta_0)$, removing the important source of the second-order bias of GMM. Moreover, the EL estimator does not involve a preliminary estimator, thereby eliminating the other source of the second-order bias in GMM mentioned above. Newey and Smith (2004) formalize this intuition and obtain an important conclusion that the second-order bias of the EL estimator is equal to that of the infeasible "ideal" estimator $\hat{\theta}_{\text{ideal}}$. Schennach (2004) and Ragusa (2005) present interesting higher-order asymptotic results that are closely related to those of Newey and Smith (2004).

Some, if not all, of the nice second bias properties of EL are shared by other members of the GEL (or GMC) family. Newey and Smith (2004) observe that the Jacobian term D in the first-order condition of GEL estimators is efficiently estimated, therefore the second-order bias term due to the correlation between $\bar{g}$ and the estimator for D is absent. Also, they are free from second-order bias from preliminary estimation, because they are one-step estimators. Therefore, they possess merits over GMM in terms of higher-order bias due to these factors.

In general, however, members of GEL other than EL have first-order conditions where S is not efficiently estimated, and this can potentially cause bias through its correlation with $\bar{g}$. To see this point, take the continuous updating GMM estimator (CUE), which is a member of GMC as discussed in Section 3. Let $\tilde{D}(\theta) = \nabla_\theta \bar{g}(\theta) - \left(\frac{1}{n} \sum_{i=1}^n \nabla_\theta g(z_i, \theta) g(z_i, \theta)\right) \bar{S}^{-1}(\theta) \bar{g}(\theta)$, then the first-order condition for CUE is

$$\tilde{D}(\hat{\theta}_{\text{cue}})' \bar{S}^{-1}(\hat{\theta}_{\text{cue}}) \bar{g}(\hat{\theta}_{\text{cue}}) = 0 \tag{5.4}$$

(see Appendix). The term subtracted from $\nabla_\theta \bar{g}(\hat{\theta}_{\text{cue}})$ in $\tilde{D}(\hat{\theta}_{\text{cue}})$ makes it a semiparametrically efficient estimator for D. $\bar{S}(\hat{\theta}_{\text{cue}})$, however, is just a sample average and therefore not an efficient estimator for S; see Brown and Newey (2002). This, in turn, contributes to the second-order bias of the continuous updating GMM. It has been recognized that the effect of the *estimated* weighting matrix of GMM is an important source of bias; see Altonji and Segal (1996) for an experimental study on this problem. Altonji and Segal (1996), based on their finding, recommend using the q-dimensional identify matrix for weighting $\bar{g}$ to avoid this problem, though this solution has the cost of not being efficient asymptotically. The higher-order theory reviewed in this section suggests that empirical likelihood successfully addresses this problem, whereas other GEL or GMC estimators in general do not. Newey and Smith (2004) also analyze higher-order MSE of bias-corrected GMM and GEL and note that the bias-corrected empirical likelihood estimator is third-order efficient. A recent paper by Kunitomo and Matsushita (2003) provides a detailed numerical study of EL and GMM, emphasizing on cases where the number of moments q is large. They find that the distribution of the EL estimator tends to be more centered and concentrated around the true parameter value compared with that of GMM. They also report that the asymptotic normal approximation appears to be more appropriate for EL than for GMM.

In a related recent study, Newey and Windmeijer (2006) consider asymptotics of GEL and GMM under "many weak moment conditions." An interesting aspect of this asymptotic scheme is that it captures an additional variance term in the asymptotic distribution of GEL due to the randomness in the (implicitly) estimated Jacobian term D. They find that the two-step GMM is asymptotically biased under this scheme, whereas GEL is not. They further propose an appropriate variance estimator for GEL in this case.

5.2   Testing

One of the significant findings in the early literature of empirical likelihood is the Bartlett correctability of the empirical likelihood ratio test, discovered by DiCiccio, Hall, and Romano (1991). A well-known result for parametric likelihood shows that one can improve the accuracy of the parametric likelihood ratio (LR) test by adjusting it by a constant called the Bartlett factor. DiCiccio, Hall, and Romano (1991) prove that this result holds for empirical likelihood.

They consider testing a hypothesis of the form $\theta = \theta_0$ in (2.2) when the model is just-identified, that is, $q = k$. The relationship (2.10) implies that the empirical likelihood ratio statistic r for the constraint and elr(θ_0) are identical for this case. Recall that the asymptotic distribution of elr(θ_0) (see (2.9)) is chi-square with q degrees of freedom, that is, $\Pr\{\text{elr}(\theta_0) \leq x\} \to \Pr\{\chi_q^2 \leq x\}$ for $x \geq 0$ as $n \to \infty$. It can be shown that the accuracy of this approximation is of order n^{-1}:

$$\Pr\{\text{elr}(\theta_0) \leq x\} = \Pr\left\{\chi_q^2 \leq x\right\} + O(n^{-1}).$$

The error rate n^{-1} is good but not surprising since it can be achieved by other conventional tests, such as the Wald test. What is surprising about the Bartlett correctability result discovered by DiCiccio, Hall, and Romano (1991) is that the ELR test, which is nonparametric, permits Bartlett correction and it yields the same accuracy rate as in the parametric case. Let a denote the Bartlett factor, then

$$\Pr\{\text{elr}(\theta_0)(1 + n^{-1}a) \leq x\} = \Pr\left\{\chi_q^2 \leq x\right\} + O(n^{-2}).$$

See DiCiccio, Hall, and Romano (1991) for an analytical expression of a. The Bartlett factor can be replaced by an appropriate estimator without affecting the error rate n^{-2}. Notice that no element of the parameter vector θ is estimated in the testing problem considered by DiCiccio, Hall, and Romano (1991). Showing Bartlett correctability of ELR for more complex testing problems is harder, though some progress has been made. For example, Chen and Cui (2005) consider Bartlett correctability in the case where the model is just identified ($q = k$), and one is interested in testing an s-dimensional subvector of the parameter θ with $s < k$. See also Chen and Cui (2004). Though their result is stated in terms of just identified models, the Chen–Cui theorem immediately implies the Bartlett correctability of the empirical likelihood-based overidentifying restrictions test statistic elr($\hat{\theta}_{\text{EL}}$), which is important in econometric applications. Whang (2006) reports strongly supportive experimental evidence for the Bartlett correction for quantile regression models. See also Chen, Leung, and Qin (2003) for simulation results on Bartlett correction in an interesting application of EL. On the other hand, it should be added that Corcoran, Davison, and Spady (1995) raise a question concerning the empirical relevance of Bartlett correction. These issues deserve further investigation.

6   SOME VARIATIONS OF EL

6.1   Estimation Under Conditional Moment Restrictions

The moment condition model (2.2) is standard, though it is sometimes useful to consider a model stated in terms of a conditional moment restriction. Suppose, instead of (2.2), random variables x and z satisfy the condition

$$E[g(z, \theta)|x] = 0, \theta \in \Theta. \tag{6.1}$$

This is trivially satisfied for the standard mean regression model $E[y|x] = m(x, \theta)$ by setting $g(z, \theta) = y - m(x, \theta)$ and $z = (x, y)$. It also holds for many models of dynamic optimization, where (6.1) is interpreted as a stochastic Euler equation. The condition (6.1) implies (2.2), thus the former is stronger than the latter. This feature often leads to a common practice where a researcher picks an arbitrary matrix-valued function $a(x)$ of x as a matrix of instruments, then applies GMM, EL or other methods to an implication of (2.2):

$$E[a(x)g(z, \theta)] = 0.$$

Such a procedure is used under the presumption that the chosen instrument $a(x)$ identifies θ, which is not necessarily true even if θ is identified in the original model (6.1); see Dominguez and Lobato (2004) on this issue and other identification problems in the standard treatment of conditional moment restriction models. Moreover, it fails to fully utilize the information contained in the conditional moment restriction, and the resulting estimator does not achieve the semiparametric efficiency bound in general. A more satisfactory approach is to directly impose (6.1) in estimating θ.

Let $D(x) = E[\nabla_\theta g(z, \theta)|x]$ and $V(x) = E[g(z, \theta)g(z, \theta)'|x]$. Chamberlain (1987) shows that the semiparametric efficiency bound for the model (6.1) is given by

$$\mathcal{I}^{-1} = \left[E[D(x)'V^{-1}(x)D(x)] \right]^{-1}, \tag{6.2}$$

which can be attained by setting $a^*(x) = D'(x)V^{-1}(x)$ as instruments. One way to achieve this bound in practice is to apply a two-step procedure. In the first step, one obtains an inefficient preliminary estimator $\tilde{\theta}$ for θ, and the unknown functions $D(x)$ and $V(x)$ are estimated by running nonparametric regressions of $\nabla_\theta g(z, \tilde{\theta})$ and $g(z, \tilde{\theta})g'(z, \tilde{\theta})$ on x. The nonparametric estimates $\tilde{D}(x)$ and $\tilde{V}(x)$ evaluated at x_i, $i = 1, \ldots, n$ are used to construct estimated optimal instruments $\tilde{a}^*(x_i)$, $i = 1, \ldots, n$. In the second step, the optimal GMM is implemented using $\tilde{a}^*(x_i)$, $i = 1, \ldots, n$ as instruments. See Robinson (1987) and Newey (1990) for details of this approach.

The two-step approach is asymptotically valid under relatively mild conditions, but it is important to explore alternative approaches based on empirical likelihood for the following reasons. First, the validity of the two-step approach relies on the availability of a preliminary consistent estimator for θ. This can be in principle achieved by choosing an appropriate function $a(x)$ that identifies θ, but this is by no means guaranteed, as noted in the study by Dominguez and Lobato (2004) mentioned above. Second, Dominguez and Lobato (2004) also find that even if the form of the optimal IV a^* were known, the resulting moment condition $E[a^*(x)g(z, \theta)] = 0$ may fail to identify θ while the original model (6.1) identifies it. Third, the theoretical analysis in previous sections on unconditional moment condition models shows that GMC/GEL-type methods – empirical likelihood in particular – have various advantages over two-step procedures.

The rest of this subsection discusses two distinct empirical likelihood-based approaches to conditional moment restriction models, one proposed by Kitamura, Tripathi, and Ahn (2004) and the other by Donald, Imbens, and Newey (2003). The first uses kernel smoothing or a similar nonparametric regression technique to incorporate local restrictions implied by (6.1). The second employs an expanding set of unconditional moment restrictions so that the conditional moment restriction is "spanned" asymptotically. Both EL-based approaches address the two issues for the two-step approach regarding identification due to the choice of instruments; see more discussions below.

The approach taken by Kitamura, Tripathi, and Ahn (2004) utilizes kernel regression to calculate localized empirical log likelihood, though other nonparametric regression techniques work for the purpose as well. Let K and h be an appropriate kernel function and bandwidth, and define a version of nonparametric log likelihood localized at x_i,

$$\ell_{\text{LNP}i}(p_{i1}, \ldots, p_{in}) = \sum_{j=1}^{n} w_{ij} \log p_{ij},$$

$$w_{ij} = \frac{K\left(\frac{x_i - x_j}{h}\right)}{\sum_{j=1}^{n} K\left(\frac{x_i - x_j}{h}\right)}, \quad (p_{i1}, \ldots, p_{in}) \in \Delta, \qquad (6.3)$$

which is to be maximized subject to the conditional mean zero constraint for a given value of θ:

$$\sum_{j=1}^{n} p_{ij} g(z_j, \theta) = 0.$$

The idea of applying a nonparametric regression technique to likelihood is reminiscent of the expected log-likelihood criterion that justifies the local likelihood methodology (Hastie and Tibshirani, 1986). The maximum value of the above optimization problem is used as the empirical log-likelihood contribution of the ith observation, and in what follows denoted by $\ell_i(\theta)$. The duality result in Section 3 shows that

$$\ell_i(\theta) = w_{ij} \log w_{ij} - \max_{\gamma_i \in \mathbb{R}^q} \sum_{j=1}^{n} w_{ij} \log(1 + \lambda_i' g(z_j, \theta)). \qquad (6.4)$$

The dual form formulation (6.4) is obviously preferred over the primal form formulation (6.3) from the computational point of view. Define the log-likelihood function for $\theta \in \Theta$ conditional on $X = \{x_i\}_{i=1}^{n}$ as

$$\ell_{\text{CEL}}(\theta) = \sum_{i=1}^{n} \ell_i(\theta). \qquad (6.5)$$

The maximizer of $\ell_{\text{CEL}}(\theta)$ may be termed the conditional empirical likelihood estimator (or the smoothed empirical likelihood estimator) for θ for obvious reasons,[3] and will be denoted by $\hat{\theta}_{CEL}$. See also LeBlanc and Crowley (1995) and Zhang and Gijbels (2003) for similar estimators.

Kitamura, Tripathi, and Ahn (2004) show that the limiting distribution of the conditional empirical likelihood estimator $\hat{\theta}_{CEL}$ is given by

$$\sqrt{n}(\hat{\theta}_{CEL} - \theta) \xrightarrow{d} N(0, \mathcal{I}^{-1}),$$

that is, it achieves the semiparametric efficiency bound defined by (6.2). Unlike a two-stage procedure where the choice of instruments in the first stage can affect identifiability, this estimator directly exploits the identification power of (6.1). Even in the examples presented by Dominguez and Lobato (2004) where the optimal IV a^* fails to deliver identification, the conditional empirical likelihood estimator is consistent as far as the original model (6.1) identifies θ. One may find this fact rather paradoxical, though this is due to the global properties of the objective functions. The likelihood nature of ℓ_{CEL} guarantees that its value is globally maximized at the true value asymptotically. In contrast, the form of optimal IV is based on local efficiency considerations, therefore the objective function of the corresponding GMM with optimal IV may fail to deliver identification. Also, the estimator $\hat{\theta}_{CEL}$ avoids explicit estimation of the functions $D(x)$ and $V(x)$. This feature also applies to inference, that is, testing and confidence interval calculation. To test a hypothesis of the form $\theta \in \Theta_0$, $\dim(\Theta_0) = k - s$, form a likelihood ratio statistic based on ℓ_{CEL}:

$$r_{CEL} = -2 \left(\sup_{\theta \in \Theta_0} \ell_{CEL}(\theta) - \sup_{\theta \in \Theta} \ell_{CEL}(\theta) \right).$$

This converges to a χ_s^2 random variable in distribution under the null hypothesis. The same result, of course, can be used for constructing confidence intervals by inverting the likelihood ratio statistic.

Kitamura, Tripathi, and Ahn (2004) report some Monte Carlo results of this estimator and existing two-step estimators. The conditional EL estimator $\hat{\theta}_{CEL}$ performs remarkably well, and often works substantially better than the two-step estimators in their simulations. For example, the precision of the conditional EL estimator, in terms of various dispersion measures, is close to that of the infeasible ideal estimator based on the unknown optimal IV even for a moderate sample size. They also report that the likelihood-ratio test based on r_{CEL} works well, in terms of its size. Other asymptotically valid tests based on efficient and inefficient estimators tend to over-reject when the null is correct, whereas rejection probabilities of the r_{CEL}-based test are close to the nominal level in their experiments. Kitamura, Tripathi, and Ahn (2004) note that the performance

---

[3] Kitamura, Tripathi, and Ahn (2004) allow the support of x to be unbounded, and they use trimming to deal with technical problems associated with it. The treatment in this section ignores this issue to simplify presentation. Kitamura, Tripathi, and Ahn (2004) report that the use of trimming factors did not affect the result of their simulation experiments qualitatively.

of their procedure is insensitive to the choice of bandwidth, and the standard cross-validation seems appropriate for selecting it automatically.

Smith (2003) extends the analysis of Kitamura, Tripathi, and Ahn (2004) by replacing the log-likelihood criterion with a Cressie–Read-type divergence (see Section 3 for discussion on the Cressie–Read family of divergence). That is, he replaces (6.3) with

$$\sum_{j=1}^{n} w_{ij} \frac{2}{\alpha(\alpha+1)} \left[\left(\frac{p_{ij}}{w_{ij}} \right)^{-\alpha} - 1 \right]. \tag{6.6}$$

His estimator therefore includes the conditional empirical likelihood estimator as a special case where α is 0. This is analogous to the treatment of EL as a GMC presented in Section 3. Smith (2003) shows that his estimator for θ is first-order equivalent to $\hat{\theta}_{\text{CEL}}$. A related paper by Smith (2005) uses the GEL formulation to analyze the problem. It replaces $\log(1 + y)$ in the dual form of log-likelihood contributions (6.4) with a general concave function. The resulting estimator corresponds to the dual formulation (3.16) of GMC, modified by kernel regression. It, therefore, further generalizes the Cressie–Read-type estimator in Smith (2003) mentioned above. This line of research has been also pursued by Antoine, Bonnal, and Renault (2006). They replace the likelihood criterion in (6.3) with a chi-square distance. This corresponds to the criterion in (6.6) with $\alpha = -1$, and can be interpreted as a localized version of Euclidean likelihood discussed in Section 3. As noted there, this choice of criterion for GMC yields an explicit solution, which also applies to the localized version as well. This might lead to a modest saving of computational costs. Gagliardini, Gourieroux, and Renault (2004) develop a creative use of the Euclidean likelihood version of the conditional empirical likelihood procedure in option pricing.

An alternative empirical likelihood-based approach to estimate (6.1) has been suggested by Donald, Imbens, and Newey (2003). They use a series of functions of x to form a vector of instruments, and let the dimension of the vector increase as the sample size goes to infinity. Let $q^K(x)$ be such a vector, then the conditional moment restriction implies the unconditional moment restriction $E[g(z, \theta) \otimes q^K(x)] = 0$. Donald, Imbens, and Newey (2003) apply unconditional versions of empirical likelihood and GEL (hence GMC) to the implied unconditional moment condition model. Since the optimal GMM with instruments $\{a^*(x_i)\}_{i=1}^{n}$ is asymptotically efficient, if the vector q^K approximates a^* as $K \to \infty$, the optimal GMM applied to $g(z, \theta) \otimes q^K$ would be asymptotically efficient as well. A leading choice for q^K is spline: the sth-order spline with knots $t_1, \ldots, t_{K-s-1}$ is given by $q^K(x) = (1, x, \ldots, x^s, [(x - t_1 \vee 0)]^s, \ldots, [(x - t_{K-s-1}) \vee 0]^s)$. This means, however, that the dimension of the estimating function is high even for a moderate sample size. In view of the result by Newey and Smith (2004) described in Section 5.1, the two-step GMM for θ is likely to suffer from severe bias due to this high-dimensionality, whereas it is natural to expect empirical likelihood to perform well in a situation where the dimension of moments grows with the sample size. Donald, Imbens, and Newey (2003) develop asymptotic theory for the (generalized) empirical likelihood estimator for (6.1) under this environment. They show that this procedure also achieves the semiparametric efficiency bound $\mathcal{I}^{-1}$.

It is important to note that neither of the two EL-based procedures does not assume that the econometrician has *a priori* knowledge about a finite-dimensional instrument vector a that identifies θ. Such knowledge is crucial for a two-step procedure discussed above. The treatment of the EL estimator in Donald, Imbens, and Newey (2003) imposes restrictions on the distribution of x, such as its density being bounded away from zero, and these are somewhat stronger that those assumed in Kitamura, Tripathi, and Ahn (2004). The two are quite different algorithmically. Maximization of the former is in some sense simpler than the latter, which requires calculation of local likelihood (6.4) at each x_i; on the other hand, the former involves construction of q^K, including choosing the basis functions and selection of the dimension of instruments K.

6.2   Nonparametric Specification Testing

A large literature exists for nonparametric goodness-of-fit testing for regression function. Let $y \in \mathbb{R}$ and $x \in \mathbb{R}^s$ be a pair of random elements, and consider the regression function $E[y|x] = m(x)$. Suppose one wishes to test a parametric specification $m(x) = m(x, \theta)$, such as a linear specification $m(x, \theta) = x'\theta$, against nonparametric alternatives. Many authors, including Eubank and Spiegelman (1990) and Härdle and Mammen (1993), consider this problem. See Hart (1997) for a review. A conventional approach to this problem is to compare predicted values from the parametric regression model and a nonparametric regression method in terms of an L_2-distance. The rest of this subsection discusses application of empirical likelihood to this problem. As the standard empirical likelihood ratio test possesses many desirable properties (see Sections 4 and 5), it is of interest to consider empirical likelihood-based nonparametric specification testing. It turns out that certain EL-based tests have asymptotic optimality properties.

The regression specification testing problem described above is a special case of the following. Consider a parametric function $g(z, \theta), \theta \in \Theta \in \mathbb{R}^k$, of random variable z as in previous sections. Let x be a random variable such that under the null hypothesis

$$E[g(z, \theta)|x] = 0 \quad a.s. \text{ for some } \theta \in \Theta. \tag{6.7}$$

Letting $z = (y, x)$ and $g(z, \theta) = y - m(x, \theta)$, one obtains the regression specification hypothesis. The null hypothesis (6.7) is the identification restriction used in the previous section. Testing it, therefore, is equivalent to test the overidentifying restrictions in the model (6.1). This motivates the following test proposed by Tripathi and Kitamura (2003). It can be regarded as a nonparametric version of the likelihood ratio test.

Tripathi and Kitamura (2003) consider testing the conditional mean zero restriction over a compact set S, that is, $E[g(z, \theta)|x] = 0, \theta \in \Theta$ for $x \in S$. This is a common formulation used in the literature of nonparametric specification testing: see Aït-Sahalia, Bickel, and Stoker (2001), for example. With this in mind, define the conditional nonparametric log-likelihood function as a sum of localized nonparametric log-likelihood functions in (6.3) weighted by $t(x) = 1\{x \in S\}$:

$$\ell_{\text{CNP}}(p_{11}, p_{12}, \dots, p_{nn}) = \sum_{i=1}^{n} t(x_i)\ell_{\text{LNP}i}(p_{i1}, \dots, p_{in}).$$

Let ℓ_{CEL}^r signify the restricted maximum value of ℓ_{CNP} under the conditional moment constraints

$$\sum_{j=1}^{n} p_{ij}g(z_j, \theta) = 0, i = 1, \dots, n, \theta \in \Theta. \tag{6.8}$$

Calculations similar to ones presented in the previous section show that.[4]

$$\ell_{\text{CEL}}^r = \sum_{i=1}^{n} t(x_i)w_{ij} \log w_{ij} + \sup_{\theta \in \Theta} \sum_{i=1}^{n} t(x_i) \min_{\gamma_i \in \mathbb{R}^q}$$
$$- \sum_{j=1}^{n} w_{ij} \log(1 + \lambda_i' g(z_j, \hat{\theta}_{\text{CEL}})).$$

It is straightforward to see that the maximum of ℓ_{CNP} without the restrictions (6.8) is attained at $p_{ij} = w_{ij}$, giving

$$\ell_{\text{CEL}}^u = \sum_{i=1}^{n} t(x_i) \sum_{j=1}^{n} w_{ij} \log w_{ij}.$$

The log-likelihood ratio statistic is therefore

$$r_C = -2 \left(\ell_{\text{CEL}}^r - \ell_{\text{CEL}}^u \right) \tag{6.9}$$
$$= 2 \inf_{\theta \in \Theta} \sum_{i=1}^{n} t(x_i) \max_{\gamma_i \in \mathbb{R}^q} \sum_{j=1}^{n} w_{ij} \log(1 + \lambda_i' g(z_j, \theta)).$$

It is not essential that the second line in the definition of r_C is evaluated at θ that minimizes the expression. Other $\sqrt{n}$-consistent estimators for θ work without affecting the asymptotics.

Tripathi and Kitamura (2003) derive the limiting distribution of r_C under the null (6.7). Let S be $[0, 1]^{\times s}$. This assumption is innocuous since it can be achieved by an appropriate transformation of x. Let $c_1(K) = \int K(u)^2 du$ be the roughness of the kernel function K used in (6.3). Define also

---

[4] Note that Tripathi and Kitamura (2003) use a different normalization for p_{ij}'s, though this difference does not matter in implementing the test.

$c_2(K) = \int [\int K(v)K(u - v)dv]^2 du$. Tripathi and Kitamura (2003) show the following: under the null hypothesis (6.7),

$$\frac{r_C - h^{-s}qc_1(K)}{\sqrt{2h^{-s}qc_2(K)}} \xrightarrow{d} N(0, 1) \tag{6.10}$$

given that $s \leq 3$. Studentization of r_C for cases with $s > 3$ is possible, though more involved; see Tripathi and Kitamura (2003) for a formula that is valid for a general s. In practice, it seems that it is best to bootstrap r_C to obtain a reliable critical value for the empirical likelihood-based test [see simulation results in Tripathi and Kitamura (2003)], as critical values based on the first-order approximation tend to lead to under-rejection. This is a phenomenon commonly observed throughout the literature of nonparametric specification testing; see, for example, Härdle and Mammen (1993).

The empirical likelihood test statistic r_C has features that distinguish it from other known procedures. To discuss these features of r_C, consider a large class of nonparametric testing procedures that includes standard tests such as Härdle and Mammen (1993) as a special case. For simplicity, suppose both x and g are scalar-valued. Consider a weighted L_2-distance statistic based on kernel regression:

$$J_n(a) = h \sum_{i=1}^{n} a(x_i) \sum_{j=1}^{n} [w_{ij}g(z_j, \theta_n)]^2, a : [0, 1] \to \mathbb{R}_+, \int a(x)^2 dx = 1.$$

Note that the choice of the weighting function a is arbitrary. The statistic J_n can be standardized using the conditional variance function $\sigma^2(x) = \text{var}(g(z_j, \theta_0)|x)$:

$$j_n(a) = \frac{h^{-1/2}[J_n(a) - c_1(K) \int \sigma a dx]}{\sqrt{2c_2(K) \int \sigma^2 a^2 dx}}.$$

The standardized weighted L_2-statistic $j_n(a)$ converges to a standard normal random variable in distribution under the null hypothesis. Note that the use of the kernel method above is inconsequential; other nonparametric methods yield results that are essentially the same.

The above asymptotic approximation result is valid under weak regularity conditions and can be used for testing the null hypothesis (6.7). The statistic $j_n(a)$, however, lacks an invariance property that r_C possesses. Let $b(x)$ be an arbitrary measurable function of x, and define $g^*(z, \theta) = b(x)g^*(z, \theta)$. Note that the null hypothesis (6.7) can be expressed in an alternative form $E[g^*(z, \theta)|x] = 0, \theta \in \Theta$ for every b. There is no mathematical or economic reason to prefer one parameterization over the other, since they are mathematically equivalent. Nevertheless, this reformulation affects the test since it essentially changes its weighting factor a. This dependence of empirical outcomes of the test on the formulation of the null hypothesis seems undesirable. In contrast, the empirical likelihood ratio statistic r_C is invariant with respect to the choice of b, since any change in b is absorbed into the variables λ_i, $i = 1, \ldots, n$ in the definition of r_C in (6.9).

The empirical likelihood test based on r_C has an additional advantage in terms of its asymptotic power. Note that the tests based on r_C or $j_n(a)$ have nontrivial power against alternatives in an $n^{-1/2}h^{-s/4}$-neighborhood of the null. To fix ideas, consider an alternative given by a function δ:

$$E[g(z, \theta_0)|x] = n^{-1/2}h^{-s/4}\delta(x), \quad \theta \in \Theta.$$

Let f_x be the density function of x, and define

$$\mu(a, \delta) = \frac{\int_0^1 \delta^2 a f_x dx}{\sqrt{2c_2(K) \int_0^1 \sigma^2 a^2 dx}}.$$

The statistic $j_n(a)$ converges to $N(\mu(a, \delta), 1)$ asymptotically under the sequence of alternatives. Let Φ denote the standard normal CDF, then if one chooses a critical value c for $j_n(a)$, the power function is given by

$$\pi(a, \delta) = 1 - \Phi(c - \mu(a, \delta)).$$

Tripathi and Kitamura (2003) show that the above results for $j_n(a)$ hold for the empirical likelihood ratio with a particular form of a:

$$a_{\text{EL}}(x) = \frac{1}{\sigma(x) \int_0^1 \sigma^{-2} dx}.$$

Though the power function $\pi(a, \delta)$ can be maximized at $a^* = \text{const.} \times \delta^2(x) f_x(x)/\sigma^2(x)$ for a given δ, it depends on δ. Therefore such a procedure is infeasible in practice. One way to proceed is to integrate δ out from the power function $\pi(a, \delta)$ using a measure over the space of δ and to attempt maximizing the average power criterion. Wald (1943), facing a similar situation in a parametric multiparameter testing problem, suggested the following. Suppose a hypothesis on a finite-dimensional parameter takes the form $\theta = \theta_0 \in \mathbb{R}^p$. Let $\pi(\delta)$ denote the power function corresponding to a local alternative of the form $\theta_a = \theta_0 + n^{-1/2}\delta$. The average power function with weight P_δ is $\pi = \int \pi(\delta)dP_\delta$. Wald suggests using P_δ that is essentially the probability measure implied by the asymptotic distribution of the MLE for θ_0. Tripathi and Kitamura (2003) extend this principle to nonparametric specification testing. They suggest using the distribution of a continuous random function $\tilde{\delta}(x)$ on $s = [0, 1]$ that mimics the distribution of the nonparametric conditional moment estimator

$$\hat{\delta}(x) = \frac{\sum_{i=1}^n K(\frac{x_i - x}{h})g(x_i, \theta)}{\sum_{j=1}^n K(\frac{x_j - x}{h})}$$

to weight $\pi(a, \delta)$. Let $C([0, 1])$ denote the set of continuous functions over $S = [0, 1]$, then the random function $\tilde{\delta}(x)$ is a $C([0, 1])$-valued random element.

Let P_δ be the probability measure for the random function $\tilde{\delta}(x)$. The average power function is

$$\pi(a) = \int_{C[0,1]} \pi(a, \tilde{\delta}) d P_\delta(\tilde{\delta}).$$

Calculus of variation shows that $\pi(a)$ is maximized at $a = a_{\text{EL}}$ (Tripathi and Kitamura, 2003). That is, the empirical likelihood test is asymptotically optimal according to the average power criterion.

The methodology by Tripathi and Kitamura (2003) has been extended in various directions. Chen, Härdle, and Li (2003) investigate a method that is similar to the empirical likelihood test above. Their construction of empirical likelihood applies kernel regression to the function g, not likelihood. This also provides an asymptotically valid procedure. However, since it uses nonparametric regression of g on x, its finite sample behavior is not invariant with respect to multiplicative renormalization of g with a function of x. This is in contrast to the methodology by Tripathi and Kitamura (2003), which has the invariance property since it smoothes the likelihood function rather than the moment function. On the other hand, Chen, Härdle, and Li (2003) develop asymptotic theory of their test for dependent processes. This extension is important, as they apply their method to test a defusion model for asset returns. Smith (2003) extends the test statistic r_C by replacing the log-likelihood criterion with a Cressie–Read-type divergence measure. Smith's test, therefore, is also invariant against renormalization. It is natural to expect that his test possesses the average power optimality property of the r_C-based test.

There is a different empirical likelihood-approach for testing the conditional moment restriction (6.7). The insight that multiplying $g(z, \theta)$ by a growing number of appropriate instruments asymptotically imposes the conditional moment restrictions, used by Donald, Imbens, and Newey (2003) for obtaining an asymptotically efficient EL estimator, is valid here as well. Recall that the ELR function (2.9) evaluated at $\hat{\theta}_{\text{EL}}$ serves as an appropriate test statistic for testing the overidentifying restrictions for the unconditional moment restriction model (2.2) with a fixed number of moment conditions. Testing (6.7) is asymptotically equivalent to testing a growing number of unconditional overidentifying restrictions of the form $E[g(z, \theta) \otimes q^K] = 0$ in the notation used in Section 6.1. It is, therefore, natural to use the maximum value of the ELR function calculated for the moment function $g \otimes q^K$ as a test statistic. Donald, Imbens, and Newey (2003) show that the test statistic

$$\frac{\sup_{\theta \in \Theta} \text{elr}(\theta) - (qK - k)}{\sqrt{2(qK - k)}}$$

is distributed according to the standard normal distribution asymptotically under the null hypothesis (6.7), which corresponds to the limiting distribution for r_C obtained in (6.10).

6.3   Dependent Data

6.3.1   The Problem

The foregoing sections explored empirical likelihood methods with independent observations. This section points out various impacts of dependence on the results discussed so far in the current paper, and presents empirical likelihood-based approaches that are suitable for time series data. The introduction of dependence typically necessitates modification of the definition of empirical likelihood. This should be clear from the form of the nonparametric log likelihood (2.1), which is interpreted as the log likelihood of independent multinomial data. Some of the standard asymptotic properties of empirical likelihood no longer hold under dependence without appropriate modifications. To see this point, suppose stationary and weakly-dependent time series observations $\{z_t\}_{t=1}^T$ are given. [See Kitamura (1997) for some discussions on the notion of weak dependence.] Consider an unconditional moment condition model as in Section 2:

$$E[g(z_t, \theta_0)] = 0, \quad \theta_0 \in \Theta. \tag{6.11}$$

The only difference from (2.2) is that z_t is a dependent process in (6.11). Recall that the standard EL estimator solves the FOC of the form (5.3). As $\hat{D}(\hat{\theta}_{\mathrm{EL}})$ and $\hat{S}(\hat{\theta}_{\mathrm{EL}})$ are weighted averages, they converge to their population counterparts $D = E[\nabla_\theta g(z_t, \theta_0)]$ and $S = E[g(z_t, \theta_0)g(z_t, \theta_0)']$ in probability. Expanding (5.3) with respect to $\hat{\theta}_{\mathrm{EL}}$ in $\bar{g}$ around θ_0 and solving for $\hat{\theta}_{\mathrm{EL}} - \theta_0$,

$$\sqrt{T}(\hat{\theta}_{\mathrm{EL}} - \theta_0) = (D'S^{-1}D)^{-1}D'S^{-1}\sqrt{T}\,\bar{g}(\theta_0) + o_p(1),$$

$$\bar{g}(\theta_0) = T^{-1}\sum_{t=1}^T g(z_t, \theta_0). \tag{6.12}$$

Under a mild mixing condition, such as the one used in Kitamura (1997), the term $\sqrt{T}\,\bar{g}(\theta_0)$ follows the central limit theorem:

$$\sqrt{T}\,\bar{g}(\theta_0) \overset{d}{\to} \mathrm{N}(0, \Omega), \quad \Omega = \sum_{j=-\infty}^{\infty} E[g(z_t, \theta_0)g(z_{t+j}, \theta_0)'],$$

yielding

$$\sqrt{T}(\hat{\theta}_{\mathrm{EL}} - \theta_0) \overset{d}{\to} \mathrm{N}(0, (D'S^{-1}D)^{-1}D'S^{-1}\Omega D S^{-1}(D'S^{-1}D)^{-1}).$$

What this means is that the EL estimator $\hat{\theta}_{\mathrm{EL}}$ is asymptotically first-order equivalent to the GMM estimator with a sub-optimal weighting matrix ($= S^{-1}$), whereas Ω^{-1} should be used for optimal weighting. The standard empirical likelihood therefore yields an estimator that is $T^{1/2}$-consistent and obeys a normal law asymptotically, but it is less efficient than the optimally weighted GMM estimator. This fact also affects EL-based inference. Suppose one is interested in testing the hypothesis $\theta_0 \in \Theta_0 \subset \Theta$. Arguments as above show that the ELR statistic defined in (2.8) is asymptotically equivalent to the difference between the minimum values of the quadratic form $T\bar{g}(\theta)S^{-1}\bar{g}(\theta)$ with and without the constraint $\theta \in \Theta_0$. Since the quadratic form is not weighted by the appropriate matrix Ω^{-1}, the ELR statistic fails to converge to the desired chi-square random variable with the degrees of freedom $\dim(\Theta) - \dim(\Theta_0)$.

There are some possible approaches to solve the above problems. The first uses a parametric model, and the second avoids such parametric modeling. The third strikes a middle ground between the two approaches. The fourth uses a spectral method, which has a limited range of applications relative to the other methods.

6.3.2   Parametric Approach

A rather obvious method to deal with dependence is to introduce a parametric model to remove dependence in the data. For example, one may use a pth-order (vector) autoregressive model for the purpose. Let L denote the backshift operator, that is, $Lx_t = x_{t-1}$. Consider a pth-order polynomial $B(L; \xi)$ parameterized by a finite-dimensional vector $\xi \in \Xi \subset \mathbb{R}^J$. Suppose operating $B(L, \xi_0)$ to $g(x_t, \theta_0)$ yields $\epsilon_t = B(L, \xi_0)g(x_t, \theta_0)$ which is a martingale difference sequence (mds). Define $z_t^* = (z_t, z_{t-1}, \dots, z_{t-p})$, $t = p + 1, \dots, T$ and $\theta^* = (\theta', \xi')' \in \Theta^* = \Theta \times \Xi$. Then the function $g^*(z_t^*, \theta^*) = [B(L, \xi)g(z_t, \theta)] \otimes [1, g(z_{t-1}, \theta)', \dots, g(z_{t-p}, \theta)']'$ satisfies moment restrictions, that is, $E[g^*(z_t^*, \theta^*)] = 0$ at $\theta^* = \theta_0^* = (\theta_0', \xi_0')'$. If such θ^* is unique, application of EL to g^* is justified. Moreover, the sequence $\{g^*(z_t^*, \theta_0^*)\}_{t=1}^T$ is also an mds by construction. An application of the martingale difference CLT to $\bar{g}^*(\theta_0^*) = T^{-1}\sum_{t=p+1}^T g(z_t^*, \theta_0^*)$ yields

$$\sqrt{T}\bar{g}^*(\theta_0, \xi_0) \xrightarrow{d} \mathrm{N}(0, S^*), \quad S^* = E[g^*(z_t^*, \theta_0^*)g^*(z_t^*, \theta_0^*)'].$$

The standard empirical likelihood estimator in Section 2 applied to g^* yields an appropriate estimator $\hat{\theta}_{\mathrm{EL}}^*$, in the sense that

$$\sqrt{T}(\hat{\theta}_{\mathrm{EL}}^* - \theta_0^*) \xrightarrow{d} \mathrm{N}(0, (D^{*\prime}S^{*-1}D^*)^{-1}), \quad D^* = E[\nabla_{\theta^*}g^*(z_t^*, \theta_0^*)].$$
$$(6.13)$$

This gives the joint limiting distribution for the empirical likelihood estimator for the parameter of interest θ_0 and the nuisance parameter ξ_0. Suppose the $B(L, \xi)$ is parameterized as an unrestricted pth-order VAR, that is,

$$B(L, \xi) = I_q - \sum_{j=1}^p \Xi_j L^j, \xi = (vec\,\Xi_1', \dots, vec\,\Xi_p')'$$

Write $\hat{\theta}_{\mathrm{EL}}^* = (\hat{\theta}_{\mathrm{EL}}', \hat{\xi}_{\mathrm{EL}}')'$, then a calculation shows that the marginal limiting distribution for $\hat{\theta}_{\mathrm{EL}}$ in the joint distribution given in (6.13) is

$$\sqrt{T}(\hat{\theta}_{\mathrm{EL}}^* - \theta_0) \xrightarrow{d} \mathrm{N}(0, (D'\Omega^{-1}D)^{-1}).$$

Therefore, $\hat{\theta}_{\mathrm{EL}}^*$ achieves the same asymptotic efficiency as the optimally weighted GMM for (6.11). It appears that the method described above to

estimate the model (6.11) is new, though some researchers considered procedures related to the above methodology. They focus on time series models such
as an AR model rather than a structural model (6.11), therefore $g(z_t, \theta) = z_t$.
They are concerned with inference for the parameter ξ_0 in $B(L, \xi_0)$. One can
use a sieve method where the order p of the polynomial $B(L, \xi)$ goes to infinity
as the sample size T grows (e.g., Bravo, 2005b).

6.3.3   Nonparametric Approach

The above approach has some aspects that are not entirely satisfactory, as it
relies on the parametric filter $B(L, \xi)$. This reduces the appeal of empirical
likelihood as a nonparametric procedure. It also involves joint estimation of
the parameter of interest θ_0 and the nuisance parameters ξ_0, which can be
high-dimensional for a moderate or large p. Fortunately, it is possible to treat
dependence fully nonparametrically in empirical likelihood analysis without
relying on a time series model as used above. The idea is to use blocks of
consecutive observations to retrieve information about dependence in data nonparametrically, therefore termed blockwise empirical likelihood (BEL). This
is the approach first proposed by Kitamura (1997) and Kitamura and Stutzer
(1997). There is interesting parallelism between the bootstrap and empirical
likelihood as pointed out, among others, by Hall and LaScala (1990), and this
is no exception: BEL is closely related to the blockwise bootstrap proposed by
Hall (1985), Carlstein (1986), and Künsch (1989).

Implementation of blockwise empirical likelihood proceeds as follows.
Again, consider (6.11) where $\{z_t\}_{t=1}^{T}$ are weakly dependent.

The first step is to form blocks of observations. The following description
specializes to the "fully overlapped blocking" scheme in the terminology of
Kitamura (1997), for the sake of simplicity. This is essentially equivalent to
the "time-smoothing" method proposed by Kitamura and Stutzer (1997). A
general blocking scheme that includes overlapping blocking and nonoverlapping blocking as two extreme special cases is discussed in Kitamura (1997).
The first step is to form data blocks: the tth block of observations is given by
$B_t = (z_t, z_{t+1}, \dots, z_{t+M-1}), t = 1, \dots, T - M + 1$ for an integer M. Suppose
$M \to \infty$ and $M = o(T^{1/2})$ as $T \to \infty$. The purpose of blocking is to retain the
dependence pattern of z_t's in each block B_t of length M. Since M grows slowly
as the sample size grows, it captures information about weak dependence in
the data asymptotically in a fully nonparametric way. The second step is to
calculate what Kitamura and Stutzer (1997) call the tth "smoothed moment
function":

$$\psi(B_t, \theta) = M^{-1} \sum_{s=0}^{M-1} g(z_{t+s}, \theta).$$

The third step is to apply the empirical likelihood procedure discussed in
Section 2 with $g(z_i, \theta), i = 1, \dots, n$ with $\psi(B_t, \theta), t = 1, \dots, T - M + 1$.

Proceeding as before yields the blockwise empirical likelihood function profiled at θ:

$$\ell_{\text{block}}(\theta) = \min_{\gamma \in \mathbb{R}^q} - \sum_{t=1}^{T-M+1} \log(1 + \gamma'\psi(B_t, \theta)))$$
$$- (T - M + 1)\log(T - M + 1). \tag{6.14}$$

This corresponds to (2.5). Let $\hat{\theta}_{\text{block}}$ denote the maximizer of ℓ_{block} over Θ; this is the blockwise empirical likelihood estimator of Kitamura (1997). Kitamura (1997) shows that the BEL estimator has the following limiting distribution

$$\sqrt{T}(\hat{\theta}_{\text{block}} - \theta_0) \xrightarrow{d} N(0, (D'\Omega^{-1}D)^{-1}). \tag{6.15}$$

The blockwise empirical likelihood incorporates information about dependence in the estimator. It achieves the same asymptotic efficiency as an optimally weighted GMM in a fully nonparametric way, but it avoids preliminary estimation of the optimal weighting matrix Ω^{-1}. The latter fact means that the BEL estimator shares some advantages with the standard EL estimator, such as its invariance property with respect to renormalization of the moment condition vector g.

It is easy to see how the "right" asymptotic distribution in (6.15) is achieved by BEL. BEL replaces the original moment function g with ψ. An approximation similar to (6.12) holds after this replacement, but the relationships $E[\nabla_\theta \psi(z_t, \theta_0)] = D$ and $\lim_{M \to \infty} E[M\psi(B_t, \theta_0)\psi(B_t, \theta_0)'] = \Omega$ imply that

$$\sqrt{T}(\hat{\theta}_{\text{block}} - \theta_0) = (D'\Omega^{-1}D)^{-1}D\Omega^{-1}\sqrt{T}\bar{\psi}(\theta_0) + o_p(1), \tag{6.16}$$
$$\bar{\psi}(\theta_0) = (T - M + 1)^{-1} \sum_{t=1}^{T-M+1} \psi(B_t, \theta_0).$$

Noting that $T^{1/2}\bar{\psi}(\theta_0) \xrightarrow{d} N(0, \Omega)$, (6.15) follows. This argument shows that BEL implicitly "estimates" $\Omega = \lim_{M \to \infty} E[M\psi(B_t, \theta_0)\psi(B_t, \theta_0)']$ by its sample counterpart. The "correct" weighting matrix $\Omega = \sum_{-\infty}^{\infty} E[g(z_t, \theta_0) g(z_t, \theta_0)']$ emerges in the approximation (6.16) from the probability limit of a weighted average of $M\psi(B_t, \theta_0)\psi(B_t, \theta_0)'$, $t = 1, \ldots, T - M + 1$. Note that the normalized sample variance of the form

$$\hat{\Omega} = (T - M + 1)^{-1} \sum_{t=1}^{T-M+1} M\psi(B_t, \theta_0)\psi(B_t, \theta_0)'$$

corresponds to the Bartlett kernel estimator of the "long-run covariance matrix" as proposed by Newey and West (1987) with lag length $M - 1$. This suggests that one may select M in BEL by using a lag-selection rule developed in the literature of long-run covariance estimation [see, for example, Andrews (1991) and Priestley (1981)]. The above observation also implies that it is possible to use weights other than the flat weighting by M^{-1} in calculating ψ above. Such alternative weights correspond to other kernel estimators of long-run covariances, as pointed out by Kitamura and Stutzer (1997) and Kitamura (1997). See Smith (2004) for a comprehensive account of this correspondence in the context of GEL.

The blockwise empirical likelihood function ℓ_{block} also yields a likelihood ratio test statistic to which standard asymptotic results apply. Suppose one is interested in testing a hypothesis $\theta_0 \in \Theta_0$ with $\dim(\Theta_0) = k - s$. Let

$$r_{\text{block}} = -2c_T^{-1}\left(\sup_{\theta \in \Theta_0} \ell_{\text{block}}(\theta) - \sup_{\theta \in \Theta} \ell_{\text{block}}(\theta)\right), \quad c_T = \frac{(T - M + 1)M}{T}.$$

The factor c_T is necessary to account for the fact that blocks are overlapping, in the following sense. There are $T - M + 1$ blocks of observations and each data block B_t consists of M observations $z_t, \ldots, z_{t-M+1}$, therefore seemingly $(T - M + 1)M$ observations enter the likelihood function ℓ_{block}. But the actual number of observation is T, thus c_T measures how many times each observation gets double-counted. The above likelihood ratio statistic with the correction term c_T^{-1} converges to a chi-squared random variable with s degrees of freedom in distribution under the null hypothesis. Similarly, modify the definition of the ELR function in (2.9) to define

$$\text{elr}_{\text{block}}(\theta) = -2c_T^{-1}[\ell_{\text{block}}(\theta) + (T - M + 1)\log(T - M + 1)].$$

It can be shown that $\text{elr}_{\text{block}}(\theta_0) \xrightarrow{d} \chi_s^2$, which can be used for a test that is analogous to the Anderson–Rubin test. Likewise, the value of $\text{elr}_{\text{block}}$ at the BEL estimator asymptotically obeys the χ_{q-k}^2 law; therefore, it offers a test for the overidentifying restrictions of the moment condition model (6.11) for time series data. Kitamura (1997) also extends the Bartlett correctability result by DiCiccio, Hall, and Romano (1991) of $\text{elr}(\theta_0)$ for iid data to $\text{elr}_{\text{block}}(\theta_0)$ with weakly-dependent data. Let a denote the Bartlett factor [see Kitamura (1997) for its expression]. The result obtained in the paper shows that adjusting $\text{elr}_{\text{block}}(\theta_0)$ by a improves the accuracy of the chi-square approximation for the distribution of the test statistic from

$$\Pr\{\text{elr}_{\text{block}}(\theta_0) \le x\} = \Pr\left\{\chi_q^2 \le x\right\} + O(T^{-2/3})$$

to

$$\Pr\{\text{elr}_{\text{block}}(\theta_0)(1 + T^{-1}a) \le x\} = \Pr\left\{\chi_q^2 \le x\right\} + O(T^{-5/6}).$$

Kitamura (1997) also shows that the idea of using blocks of data to construct empirical likelihood can be extended to inference for infinite-dimensional parameters, such as the spectral density of z_t.

The blockwise empirical likelihood method has been extended in various directions. Nordman, Sibbertsen, and Lahiri (2006) make an interesting discovery by considering inference for the mean $E[z_t]$ when the process z_t exhibits the so-called long-range dependence behavior. It is known in the literature that blocking methods used in the bootstrap and subsampling tend to break down under long-range dependence. A long-range dependent process can be characterized by how slow its autocovariance function decays, or, alternatively by the behavior of its spectral density at the origin. Using the latter formulation, suppose the spectral density $f_z(\omega)$ of the process $\{z_t\}_{t=-\infty}^{\infty}$ at frequency ω is of the same order as $|\omega|^{-2d}$, $d \in (-\frac{1}{2}, \frac{1}{2})$. A non-zero value of d corresponds to long-range dependence. The essence of the discovery of the Nordman, Sibbertsen, and Lahiri (2006) is that the blockwise empirical likelihood procedure by Kitamura (1997) remains valid for long-range dependent processes if the adjustment factor c_T in the definition of r_{block} is modified suitably. In particular, they propose to replace the original factor $c_T = \frac{(T-M+1)M}{T}$ with its generalization:

$$c_{T,n} = (T - M + 1)\left(\frac{M}{T}\right)^{1-2d}.$$

The value of d is zero if z_t is weakly dependent. In that case $c_{0,T} = c_T$ and the factor reduces to the one proposed by Kitamura (1997).

Kitamura and Stutzer (1997) apply a variant of the blocking scheme as above to develop an exponential tilting estimator for weakly-dependent processes. Indeed, a number of subsequent papers that study various aspects of BEL have appeared. Smith (1997) notes that Kitamura and Stutzer's blocking method remains valid for the entire GEL family; hence the same is expected to hold for the GMC family in Section 3 as well. Higher-order properties of BEL and other blockwise versions of GEL estimators, in the spirit of Newey and Smith (2004), are investigated by Anatolyev (2005). Bravo (2005a) studies the application of the blocking-based method by Kitamura (1997) as well as the blocking-after-prewhitening method by Kitamura (1996a) described in the next section to the saddle-point exponential tilting estimator by Kitamura and Stutzer (1997). Likewise, Lin and Zhang (2001) and Bravo (2002) replace empirical likelihood in (6.14) with Euclidean likelihood and the Cressie–Read divergence, respectively, and confirm that the first-order asymptotic results for estimation and testing derived for BEL in Kitamura (1997) still hold.

You, Chen, and Zhou (2006) find a different application of BEL to what essentially is a random effects model for longitudinal data. In their application a block is formed per individual, so the length of each block is equal to the number of observations available for each individual. Therefore, it does not go to infinity in their asymptotics. This method is robust against heteroskedasticity and within-group correlation. You, Chen, and Zhou (2006) report experimental results that indicate that BEL tends to produce much shorter confidence intervals than others with comparable coverage probabilities, such as those obtained based on normal approximations with robust standard errors. This fact is consistent with the optimal power properties of the empirical likelihood ratio test as outlined in Sections 4.2 and 4.3. Zhang (2006) applies BEL to NA (negatively associated) time series [see Joag-Dev and Proschan (1983) for a definition of an NA process] and proves its asymptotic validity. Allen, Gregory, and Shimotsu (2005) propose a bootstrapping procedure based on BEL. Their idea is to extend the EL-based bootstrap method by Brown and Newey (2002), which will be described in Section 8, to dependence data using BEL.

6.3.4   A Middle Ground

The blocking approach avoids arbitrary specification of dynamics. Therefore, the empirical likelihood function is obtained without imposing restrictions other than the model restriction (6.11). When observations are highly persistent, however, in the sense that the autocorrelation function decays slowly as the number of lags increases, it might take long blocks to capture dependence in the data. This requires the data size to be large. If the data process under consideration appears highly persistent and the size of the available data set is small, the blocking approach might need a modification. One possibility is to merge the parametric and blocking approaches, borrowing the idea of prewhitening from the literature of spectral density estimation. See Section 7.4.1 of Priestley (1981) for the prewhitening method and Andrews and Monahan (1992) for an application in econometrics. The idea of prewhitening in the spectral analysis of highly persistent processes is as follows. First, fit a lower-order (vector) autoregressive model to the original series and use it as a filter to reduce its dependence, so that the process is closer to white noise after filtering. This is the prewhitening step. Second, apply a standard spectral method to estimate the spectrum of the prewhitened process. Third, use the coefficients of the (V)AR model used in prewhitening to obtain an estimate of the spectrum of the original process. This last step is called recoloring.

Applications of prewhitening in empirical likelihood have been investigated by Kitamura (1996a). Consider the model (6.11) once again, where z_t is highly persistent. As before, apply a parametric VAR model $B(L, \xi)$ to filter the process $\{g(z_t, \theta)\}_{t=1}^{T}$, though $B(L, \xi)$ is not meant to be the true model that generates the process $g(z_t, \theta_0)$. Therefore, the filtered process $B(L, \xi)g(z_t, \theta)$ would exhibit a certain degree of dependence for every value of $\theta^* = (\theta', \xi')'$; in particular, it is not supposed to be an mds. The purpose of the filter $B(L, \xi)$ is to reduce the dependence in the process, not eliminating it. A low-order filter, even a first-order model, may suffice for the purpose. Such a choice avoids the problem of overparameterization, which can be a serious issue in the purely parametric approach of Section 6.3.2. Now let $z_t^* = (z_t, \ldots, z_{t-p})$ and apply the blocking technique described above to the process $g^*(z_t^*, \theta, \xi) = [B(L, \xi)g(z_t, \theta)] \otimes (1, g(z_{t-1}, \theta)', \ldots, g(z_{t-p}, \theta)')'$ to deal with the dependence not captured by the filter:

$$\psi^*(B_t^*, \theta, \xi) = M^{-1} \sum_{s=1}^{M-1} g^*(z_{t+s}^*, \theta, \xi), \quad B_t^* = (z_t^*, \ldots, z_{t+M-1}^*),$$

$$t = p + 1, \ldots, T - M + 1.$$

The blockwise empirical log likelihood with prewhitening is

$$\ell_{\text{pwblock}}(\theta) = \sup_{\xi \in \Xi} \min_{\gamma \in \mathbb{R}^{q+\dim \Xi}} - \sum_{t=p+1}^{T-M+1} \log(1 + \gamma' \psi^*(B_t^*, \theta, \xi)))$$

$$- (T - M - p + 1) \log(T - M - p + 1). \quad (6.17)$$

Let $\hat{\theta}_{\text{pwblock}}$ denote the maximizer of $\ell_{\text{pwblock}}(\theta)$. The block length parameter M needs to go to infinity such that $M = o(T^{1/2})$, as assumed for BEL. Since the filter $B(L, \xi)$ is not a model, $\hat{\xi}_{\text{pwblock}}$ would converge to some "pseudo-true" value and therefore its asymptotic behavior is not of main interest. Regarding the parameter of interest θ_0, the following holds

$$\sqrt{T}(\hat{\theta}_{\text{pwblock}} - \theta_0) \xrightarrow{d} N(0, (D'\Omega^{-1}D)^{-1}).$$

To carry out inference, replace $\ell_{\text{block}}(\theta)$ with $\ell_{\text{pwblock}}(\theta)$ in the definitions of r_{block} and $\text{elr}_{\text{block}}(\theta), \theta \in \Theta$. The resulting prewhitened versions r_{pwblock} and $\text{elr}_{\text{pwblock}}(\theta), \theta \in \Theta$ have the same asymptotic properties as their BEL counterparts without prewhitening. An interesting feature of this procedure is that there is no need to apply recoloring explicitly, since it is done implicitly in the empirical likelihood algorithm.

6.3.5   *Frequency Domain Approach*

Yet another approach to deal with dependence in the empirical likelihood analysis is to apply frequency domain methods, as proposed by Monti (1997). This work follows the Whittle likelihood methodology, therefore a parametric model for the spectral density (e.g., the spectral density function implied by a parametric ARMA model) is considered. The method is suitable for parametric time series models and differs from the block-based methodologies discussed in Sections 6.3.3 and 6.3.4, where the goal is to treat dependence nonparametrically. Nordman and Lahiri (2004) shows that the frequency domain empirical likelihood applies to a class of statistics termed ratio statistics (see Dahlhaus and Janas 1996), allowing possible long-range dependence.

6.4   **Further Applications of EL**

An interesting aspect of empirical likelihood is that it allows the researcher to combine information from two data sets in a natural manner. Chen, Leung, and Qin (2003) discuss an application of empirical likelihood when a complete data set (validation set) and a data set that includes covariates and surrogates (nonvalidation set) are available. They find that their empirical likelihood-based method yields highly accurate confidence intervals. Hellerstein and Imbens (1999) discuss the use of empirical likelihood to estimate a regression model when information on some moments is available from auxiliary data.

Wang and Rao (2002) develop a valid empirical likelihood ratio test in a missing data problem, where nonparametric imputation is used under the missing at random (MAR) assumption. They also derive an empirical likelihood estimator that incorporates information in additional moment conditions. Tripathi (2005) considers EL-based estimation of moment condition models with stratified data. See Cosslett (1993) for a detailed review of applications of NPMLE (thus EL) to models with endogenously stratified data. This line of research aims at dealing with the distribution of exogenous covariates nonparametrically, as in the estimator by Cosslett (1981a, 1981b) for choice-based samples.

Empirical likelihood has been applied to the problem of weak instruments; see Caner (2003), Guggenberger and Smith (2005), and Otsu (2006). These papers use empirical likelihood or GEL mainly in an LM-test setting (which, if appropriately defined, is known to work for the weak IV problem; see Kleibergen, 2002). This is a rather tricky problem for EL, because many distinctive properties of empirical likelihood-based inference crucially depend on the structure of the empirical likelihood ratio test statistic, and they do not generally carry over to LM-type tests.

7   MISSPECIFICATION

It is well-known that OLS and parametric MLE yield results that can be regarded as best approximations, where the criteria are mean square error (White, 1980) and the Kullback–Leibler divergence [see Akaike (1973) and White (1982)], respectively. Such a best approximation result does not carry over to the two-step GMM, since the probability limit of the two-step GMM depends on the weighting matrices used in both steps in an uninterpretable manner. A one-step estimation with a weighting matrix that does not depend on the model specification may avoid this issue, but such an estimator loses efficiency when the model is correctly specified.

Interestingly, the GMC estimator possesses an approximation property analogous to that of MLE. To illustrate this point, it is useful to summarize basic results from the theory of parametric ML. Suppose $\{z_i\}_{i=1}^n \sim_{iid} \mu$. The econometrician uses a finite-dimensional vector $\upsilon \in \Upsilon$ for parameterization, so the model is given by $\mathcal{P}_{\mathrm{par}} = \{P_\upsilon | \upsilon \in \Upsilon\}$. The model $\mathcal{P}_{\mathrm{par}}$ is misspecified if it does not contain μ. MLE then converges to υ^* such that $P_{\upsilon^*} = \mathrm{argmin}_{P \in \mathcal{P}_{\mathrm{par}}} K(P, \mu)$. That is, MLE finds the probability measure that is closest to the true distribution μ in terms of the KL divergence.

Now, consider the moment condition model (2.2). This means that the statistical model is given by $\mathcal{P}$ defined in (3.2), instead of $\mathcal{P}_{\mathrm{par}}$ above. Suppose $\mathcal{P}$ is misspecified. A useful fact is that a GMC estimator finds the best approximation for the true measure μ, where the approximation criterion is given by the contrast function (3.1). For example, Kitamura (1998) studies the asymptotic behavior of the exponential tilt saddle-point estimator (3.14). The main results are as follows. Let θ^* denote the value of $\theta \in \Theta$ that minimizes $\rho(\theta, \mu) = \inf_{P \in \mathcal{P}_\theta} K(P, \mu)$. Obviously, $\rho(\theta^*, \mu) = \inf_{P \in \mathcal{P}} K(P, \mu)$, that is, θ^* corresponds to the solution of the approximation problem $\inf_{P \in \mathcal{P}} K(P, \mu)$. Also, suppose P^* minimizes $K(P, \mu), P \in \mathcal{P}$. Kitamura (1998) shows that the exponential tilt estimator $\hat{\theta}$ and the corresponding probability measure estimator $\widehat{\mu(\cdot)}$ in (3.15) converge to θ^* and P^* asymptotically. Imbens (1997) makes a related observation that the empirical likelihood estimator minimizes the Kullback–Leibler divergence between the empirical distribution and the probability distribution under the moment constraint; see also Chen, Hong, and Shum (2001). These results are expected to extend to other members of GMC.

Recall that some GEL estimators can be interpreted as dual GMC estimators when κ in (3.17) is obtained from the convex conjugate of a Cressie–Read divergence measure. It is therefore obvious that the best approximation result holds for the corresponding subset of the GEL family. In general, however, GEL estimators may not be represented as GMC. For this reason some GEL's do not seem to provide best approximation interpretations presented here.

Kitamura (1998) also derives the asymptotic distribution of the exponential tilting estimator under misspecification and extends Vuong's model comparison test (Vuong, 1989). Vuong's original test is concerned with likelihood-ratio testing between two non-nested parametric models. His model comparison measure for two parametric models $\mathcal{P}_{\text{par}}$ and $\mathcal{Q}_{\text{par}}$ is

$$\delta = \inf_{P \in \mathcal{P}_{\text{par}}} K(\mu, P) - \inf_{Q \in \mathcal{Q}_{\text{par}}} K(\mu, Q). \tag{7.1}$$

Vuong (1989) shows that a normalized likelihood ratio statistic ($= LR$) converges to δ in probability. This can be used to test the null hypothesis $\delta = 0$, since $\sqrt{n}LR/s$, where s is an appropriate studentization factor, converges to the standard normal distribution.

Kitamura (1998) shows that this idea works for moment condition models. The motivation of the paper originates from the notion that many economic models are best viewed as approximations. Even though moment condition models are considered to be more robust than parametric models, they still often come from highly stylized economic models. The researcher needs to confront the issue of misspecification in such a situation. For example, take empirical asset pricing models as considered in the classic study by Hansen and Singleton (1982). If one subjects such a model to specification tests, oftentimes negative results emerge, implying potential misspecification of the model. Moreover, there are many other non-nested moment conditions implied by different asset pricing models, such as cash-in-advance models. It is then of interest to compare two potentially misspecified competing moment condition models. This is the goal of the following procedure, which permits a wide range of statistical measures for model evaluation.

Consider two moment conditions that are non-nested, and possibly misspecified:

$$E[g_1(z, \theta_1)] = 0, \theta_1 \in \Theta_1 \quad \text{and} \quad E[g_2(z, \theta_2)] = 0, \theta_2 \in \Theta_2.$$

From these conditions define two sets of probability measures as in (3.2). Call them $\mathcal{P}_1$ and $\mathcal{P}_2$. Suppose the researcher decides to use a contrast function of the form (3.1) to measure the divergence between the true probability measure and the probability measures implied by the model. Discussions in Section 3.1 imply that different choices of ϕ generate a wide variety of goodness-of-fit criteria. Once a criterion is chosen, define

$$\delta = \inf_{\theta_1 \in \Theta_1} v_1(\theta_1) - \inf_{\theta_2 \in \Theta_2} v_2(\theta_2)$$

where $\theta_1 \in \Theta_1$ and $\theta_2 \in \Theta_2$ are the unknown parameters in the two moment condition models, and v_1 and v_2 are the corresponding value functions (see Equation (P) in Section 3). $\delta = 0$ means that Models $\mathcal{P}_1$ and $\mathcal{P}_2$ are equally good approximations of the true probability measure μ in terms of the researcher's criterion function. Likewise, a positive (negative) δ implies that $\mathcal{P}_2$ ($\mathcal{P}_1$) fits to the true data distribution better than P_1 (P_2) does. Using the sample dual form (3.9), define:

$$\hat{\delta} = \inf_{\theta_1 \in \Theta_1} \max_{\lambda_1 \in \mathbb{R}, \gamma_1 \in \mathbb{R}^q} \left[\lambda_1 - \frac{1}{n} \sum_{i=1}^{n} \phi^*(\lambda_1 + \gamma_1' g_1(z_i, \theta_1)) \right]$$
$$- \inf_{\theta_2 \in \Theta_2} \max_{\lambda_2 \in \mathbb{R}, \gamma_2 \in \mathbb{R}^q} \left[\lambda_2 - \frac{1}{n} \sum_{i=1}^{n} \phi^*(\lambda_2 + \gamma_2' g_2(z_i, \theta_2)) \right]. \quad (7.2)$$

Kitamura (1998) considers the asymptotic distribution of $\hat{\delta}$ for the case where the divergence function is given by the Kullback–Leibler divergence measure $K(\cdot, \mu)$, therefore the resulting estimators are the exponential tilt estimators (3.14). As in Vuong's test, with an appropriate scaling factor $s > 0$, the asymptotic distribution of the statistic under the null hypothesis $\delta = 0$ is standard normal:

$$\frac{n^{1/2} \hat{\delta}}{s} \xrightarrow{d} N(0, 1).$$

Kitamura (1998) also discusses how to estimate s. See Christoffersen, Hahn, and Inoue (2001) for an application of this model comparison test to value-at-risk modeling.

Chen, Hong, and Shum (2001) note that such an idea can be also used to carry out model comparison between a parametric specification and a semiparametric one. In their case, $\mathcal{P}_1$ comes from a parametric model: the researcher parameterizes the distribution of data z as P_v, $v \in \Upsilon$, so $\mathcal{P}_1 = \{P_v | v \in \Upsilon\}$. This model is compared against a moment condition model, which generates $\mathcal{P}_2$. Chen, Hong, and Shum (2001) use $D(P, \mu) = \int \log \frac{d\mu}{dP} d\mu$ as the divergence function.

Kitamura (2002) explores the issue of model comparison tests, focusing on the case where there exist covariates. This study considers estimation of conditional moment restriction models of the form $E[g(z, \theta)|x] = 0$. For example, suppose one considers modeling the conditional mean of a variable y given x using a parametric function, for example, $E[y|x] = \beta'x$. Alternatively, a median regression $\text{med}(y|x) = \beta'x$ can be used. These models are non-nested, therefore conventional testing methods do not work for testing one against the other.

Note also that the presence of covariates is crucial in these models. A typical choice of instrumental variables for these models is x, but moment conditions such as $E[x(y - \beta'x)] = 0$ impose a just-identifying restriction so that the corresponding set of measures $\mathcal{P}$ always include μ. GMC-based testing methods discussed above therefore do not work, since $\inf_{P \in \mathcal{P}} D(P, \mu) = 0$ no matter how badly the regression function is specified. It is of course possible to add more instruments to obtain overidentifying restrictions, but such a method involves an *ad hoc* choice of instruments. A solution to this problem by Kitamura (2002) is to impose the conditional moment restriction directly and apply GMC by following the methodology in Kitamura, Tripathi, and Ahn (2004) described in Section 6. Kitamura (2002) also develops asymptotic theory for misspecified quantile regression models. This is a topic that has attracted attention in the recent literature [see Kim and White (2002) and Angrist, Chernozhukov, and Fernandez (2005)]. For example, Angrist, Chernozhukov, and Fernandez (2005) investigate the asymptotic behavior of the linear quantile regression estimator of Koenker and Bassett (1978). In contrast, Kitamura (2002) considers the asymptotics of the CEL estimator by Kitamura, Tripathi, and Ahn (2004) and provides its best approximation characterization. The method in Kitamura (2002) is also useful in evaluating and comparing a parametric model with covariates with mean/quantile regression models. Otsu and Whang (2005) also consider an application of the CEL method to non-nested models. While the above test in Kitamura (2002) is a Vuong-test analog for conditional moment restriction models, Otsu and Whang (2005) investigate a Cox-test analog.

The consideration on misspecification also raises an interesting issue about robustness. If one accepts the view that the econometric model under consideration (e.g., the moment condition model (2.2)) is a reasonable yet misspecified approximation of the unknown true structure, it may be desirable to use an estimator that is robust to misspecification. Roughly speaking, there are two issues involved in assessing the robustness of an estimator. One is about the bias of the estimator due to the misspecification, that is, how the limit θ^* of a GMC $\hat{\theta}$ behaves as the model $\mathcal{P}$ moves away from the true probability measure μ. The other is the dispersion behavior of the estimator, such as its asymptotic variance. [Some claims on the latter issue can be found in Schennach (2004).] As far as one considers a global misspecification (as opposed to a local misspecification, in which the model approaches the true probability measure at a certain rate), the former is typically dominant of the two, which makes the latter a second-order issue. An alternative approach to the robustness issue is to consider the effect of local misspecification within a shrinking topological neighborhood of the true probability distribution, so that both bias and variance matter asymptotically. Such analysis, put loosely, enables the researcher to compare robustness in terms of MSE. This approach appears to be useful if one is interested in analyzing the robustness of empirical likelihood and other methods. Note that this line of research has been carried out in the robustness literature on parametric models. Some researchers in this literature argue for the use of minimum Hellinger distance methods. This is interesting because the GEL/GMC families include the Hellinger distance as a special case, since it is the Cressie–Read divergence with $\alpha = -\frac{1}{2}$. Detailed investigation toward a robustness theory of empirical likelihood is left for a separate paper.

8 COMPUTATIONAL ISSUES AND NUMERICAL EXAMPLES

Empirical likelihood or its generalizations have desirable theoretical properties, as described in the foregoing sections. This section turns to practical matters. First, issues associated with actual implementation are explored. Some numerical algorithms are discussed. Second, numerical examples of some of the methods discussed in the preceding sections are presented.

8.1   Implementing Empirical Likelihood

Computational issues for empirical likelihood are best described by considering the unconditional moment restrictions model (2.2). It appears that the most stable way to compute the EL estimator $\hat{\theta}_{EL}$ is to utilize the profile likelihood at θ as given by (2.5) and write a nested optimization routine. See Chapter 12 in Owen (2001) for this and other types of algorithms. The nested optimization method requires a routine for the *inner loop minimization*, which takes θ as an argument and return the value

$$\min_{\gamma \in \mathbb{R}^q} Q_n(\theta, \gamma), \quad Q_n(\theta, \gamma) = -\sum_{i=1}^{n} \log(1 + \gamma' g(z_i, \theta)). \tag{8.1}$$

This is equal to the profile likelihood function $\ell(\theta)$ in (2.5), up to a constant which is irrelevant in estimating θ. Once this routine is defined, it is maximized with respect to θ. This part can be called the *outer loop maximization*. To compute $\hat{\theta}_{EL}$, one uses a nested optimization algorithm where the outer maximization loop encloses the inner minimization loop. Some comments on the inner loop and the outer loop are in order. In particular, the problem associated with the situation where the convex hull spanned by $g(z_i, \theta), i = 1, \ldots, n$ does not include the origin deserves a special attention.

The objective function Q_n in the inner loop is convex in γ. Moreover, the analytical expressions for its Jacobian and Hessian are readily available:

$$\nabla_\gamma Q_n(\theta, \gamma) = -\sum_{i=1}^{n} \frac{g(z_i, \theta)}{1 + \gamma' g(z_i, \theta)}, \quad \nabla_{\gamma\gamma} Q_n(\theta, \gamma)$$

$$= \sum_{i=1}^{n} \frac{g(z_i, \theta)g(z_i, \theta)'}{(1 + \gamma' g(z_i, \theta))^2}.$$

It is therefore reasonable to carry out Newton iterations using these expressions. Hansen (2006) suggests a rule for the choice of Newton step lengths. Even though the Hessian is positive definite by its definition, sometimes inverting it numerically is difficult when the model is not well-behaved, in particular for a value of θ that is distant from the optimal point $\hat{\theta}_{EL}$. In such a situation one may consider replacing it according to a quasi-Newton method or further modifying it along the line suggested by Shanno (1970). Alternatively, one can use a nonlinear numerical optimization routine based on numerical derivatives to minimize Q_n with respect to γ.

Sometimes it may be advantageous to transform the parameter space of γ using (an approximation for) the Hessian matrix, as often done in a nonlinear numerical optimization algorithm. For the inner loop problem above, this can be achieved by premultiplying $g(z_i, \theta)$ with an appropriate matrix, such as the inverse of the Cholesky decomposition of $\sum_{i=1}^{n} g(z_i, \theta)g(z_i, \theta)'$, which is suggested by Bruce Hansen in his GAUSS code for EL. This does not alter the value function $\min_{\gamma \in \mathbb{R}^q} Q_n(\theta, \gamma)$; only the definition of γ changes to $\gamma^* = [\sum_{i=1}^{n} g(z_i, \theta)g(z_i, \theta)']^{1/2'}\gamma$. The coordinate change is likely to make the Hessian $\nabla_{\gamma^*\gamma^*} Q$ close to the q-dimensional identity matrix, and it may help the convergence of the optimization process when the dimension q is high.

The inner loop optimization is generally a well-behaved convex programming problem, when there is a solution. In some situations, however, it does not have a solution. This should be clear from the primal problem (2.3). If for a given θ the condition

$$0 \in \text{co}\{g(z_1, \theta), \ldots, g(z_n, \theta)\} \tag{C}$$

fails to hold, that is, the convex hull of the n vectors of the moment function evaluated at the observations $\{z_i\}_{i=1}^n$ does not include the origin of $\mathbb{R}^q$, the problem (2.3) does not have a feasible solution. Note that this is more of a practical problem than a theoretical one. If (C) fails, it is theoretically appropriate to set the value of the empirical likelihood $\ell(\theta)$ at $-\infty$ as a convention. After all, a failure of (C) at a value of θ should be regarded as strong evidence against the possibility that it is the true value. As far as $E[g(z, \theta_0)] = 0$, which holds if the model is correctly specified, the condition (C) holds with probability approaching one at $\theta = \theta_0$.

In practice, however, (C) can fail in finite samples even if the model is correctly specified, partly because a numerical search in the outer maximization loop can take θ to areas that are far from the true value θ_0. Also, the vectors $\{g(z_i, \theta)\}_{i=1}^n$ are more likely to fail to span the origin, if the dimension of the space becomes higher or the number of the vectors becomes smaller. In other words, the condition (C) may occasionally fail for a large q and/or a small n. Finally, when the model is misspecified as discussed in Section 7, this becomes an important issue. One needs to proceed with caution when it happens.

Consider again the inner loop minimization problem (8.1), and suppose one starts a Newton algorithm from an initial value (e.g., $\gamma = 0$). If (C) fails, a Newton iteration would make γ grow (in absolute value). Theoretically, γ that "solves" the inner loop minimization (8.1) should be at infinity in a direction where $\gamma'g(z_i, \theta)$ is positive for all i.[5] This makes the value of Q_n negative infinity, which is consistent with the convention introduced above. It may, however, cause a problem when implementing a numerical algorithm such as Newton's method. For example, the first-order gradient can still be large at the end of the algorithm if the maximum number of iterations is set too low. More importantly, when the elements of γ are large in absolute value, it is likely that some of the logs in Q_n would have negative arguments at a γ value the (Newton) algorithm "tries." This causes a naive algorithm to stop. It is the author's impression that a common mistake is to use a rather arbitrary value such as zero to impute the value of $\min_{\gamma \in \mathbb{R}^q} Q_n(\theta, \gamma)$ when an algorithm halts for this situation. Recall that theoretically the value of empirical log likelihood should be negative infinity in the event of the failure of (**C**), so using inappropriate values for this situation leads to quite misleading results. This might explain some puzzling results of Monte Carlo experiments reported in the literature. This is especially relevant when the power of ELR or the behavior of the EL estimator under misspecification are being evaluated by simulations, since obviously the failure of (**C**) is an issue in these situations. It can be in principle prevented by assigning an appropriate value when this happens, but this should be done with caution as well, so that the numerical search in the outer maximization loop over θ would not remain trapped in the region where the violation of (**C**) occurs.

A practical approach to deal with the above problem is to modify the algorithm to prevent the problem associated with potential negative values in log terms of Q_n. One possibility is to use a constrained optimization routine to optimize Q_n while keeping the arguments of the log terms positive. That is, the objective function $Q_n(\theta, \gamma)$ for a given value of θ is minimized over the region $\{\gamma \in \mathbb{R}^q : 1 + \gamma'g(z_i, \theta) \geq \delta$ for all $i\}$ in the inner loop, where δ is a small number chosen by the econometrician. The resulting minimum values of Q_n is then maximized over θ in the outer loop. This method appears to work reasonably well in practice, even in a situation where the problem associated with the violation of (**C**) is rather severe. Another potential solution, suggested by Owen (2001), is to replace log in Q_n by a function that allows negative arguments. He suggests choosing a small number $\delta > 0$ and use

$$\log_\star(y) = \begin{cases} \log(y) & \text{if } y > \delta \\ \log(\delta) - 1.5 + 2\frac{y}{\delta} - \frac{y^2}{2\delta^2} & \text{if } y \leq \delta, \end{cases}$$

which is twice continuously differentiable and concave. This makes the objective function

$$Q_{\star n}(\theta, \gamma) = -\sum_{i=1}^{n} \log_\star(1 + \gamma'g(z_i, \theta))$$

well-defined for all $\gamma \in \mathbb{R}^q$.

---

[5] The separating hyperplane theorem shows that such a direction exists if the condition (**C**) is violated.

Once the empirical likelihood function is calculated, it can be used for inference as seen in the preceding sections. Standard empirical likelihood ratio statistics possess χ^2 limiting distributions and therefore provide methods for asymptotically valid inference. Moreover, under regularity conditions, the second-order derivative of the empirical log-likelihood function $\ell(\theta)$ normalized by $-\frac{1}{n}$ and evaluated at $\hat{\theta}_{EL}$ converges to the appropriate asymptotic variance matrix of $\hat{\theta}_{EL}$, that is,

$$-\frac{1}{n}\nabla_{\theta\theta}\ell(\hat{\theta}_{EL}) \xrightarrow{p} (D'SD)^{-1}.$$

This provides asymptotic standard error estimates, though the optimal power results (e.g., the generalized Neyman–Pearson property described in Section 4) strongly indicate that the empirical likelihood ratio test has theoretical advantages over other methods, including a Wald-type test or an LM-type test based on the asymptotic covariance matrix estimate $-\frac{1}{n}\nabla_{\theta\theta}\ell(\hat{\theta}_{EL})$. The same optimality results also imply that it is best to invert the likelihood ratio test statistic to obtain a confidence interval if it is computationally feasible. Many simulation studies report that empirical likelihood ratio-based confidence intervals tend to be substantially shorter than other asymptotically valid intervals with comparable coverage probabilities.

In terms of size, however, the asymptotic chi-square approximation of the empirical likelihood ratio statistic may not be accurate enough when the sample size is small. One potential way to correct this is to use Bartlett adjustment discussed in Section 5.2. Analytical expressions for Bartlett factors tend to be complicated even for a relatively simple model, and are probably hard to derive for a complex structural model often used in econometrics. An alternative way to improve the size properties of empirical likelihood ratio tests is to apply the bootstrap, sometimes called the bootstrap calibration in the literature. Consider again the problem of testing the hypothesis $R(\theta_0) = 0$ discussed in Section 2, where the empirical likelihood ratio statistic r has been introduced. The nonparametric bootstrap can be implemented as follows. Resample $\{z_i\}_{i=1}^n$ according to the empirical measure μ_n with replacements in the usual manner to obtain bootstrapped data $\{z_i^{*(b)}\}_{i=1}^n, b = 1, \ldots, B$, where B is the number of bootstrap replications. Define

$$\tilde{g}(z_i^{*(b)}, \theta) = g(z_i^{*(b)}, \theta) - \frac{1}{n}\sum_{i=1}^n g(z_i, \hat{\theta}_{EL}), \quad i = 1, \ldots, n, b = 1, \ldots, B.$$

This recentering resolves the issue associated with bootstrapping under overidentifying restrictions [see, for example, Hall and Horowitz (1996)]. Use this to obtain

$$\ell^{*(b)}(\theta) = \min_{\gamma \in \mathbb{R}^q} -\sum_{i=1}^n \log\left(1 + \gamma'\tilde{g}\left(z_i^{*(b)}, \theta\right)\right) - n\log n, \quad b = 1, \ldots, B.$$

The bth bootstrap version of the empirical likelihood ratio statistic is

$$r^{*(b)} = -2 \left(\sup_{\theta \in \Theta : R(\theta) = R(\hat{\theta}_{\mathrm{EL}})} \ell^{*(b)}(\theta) - \sup_{\theta \in \Theta} \ell^{*(b)}(\theta) \right), \quad b = 1, \ldots, B.$$

Alternatively, one may resample according to an EL-based estimate of the probability measure μ, borrowing the idea of "efficient bootstrapping" by Brown and Newey (2002). For example, use the constrained EL estimator $\hat{\theta}_{\mathrm{EL}}^c = arg max_{\theta \in \Theta : R(\theta) = 0} \ell(\theta)$ to calculate the NPMLE weights as in (2.6) under the constraint $R(\theta) = 0$:

$$\hat{p}_{\mathrm{EL}i}^c = \frac{1}{n(1 + \hat{\gamma}(\hat{\theta}_{\mathrm{EL}}^c)' g(z_i, \hat{\theta}_{\mathrm{EL}}^c)}, \quad i = 1, \ldots, n.$$

One would then resample $\{z_i\}_{i=1}^n$ according to the probability measure $\hat{\mu}^c = \sum_{i=1}^n \hat{p}_{\mathrm{EL}i}^c \delta_{z_i}$ to generate $\{z_i^{*(b)}\}_{i=1}^n$, $b = 1, \ldots, B$, from which bootstrap empirical likelihood ratio statistics are obtained:

$$r^{*(b)} = -2 \left(\sup_{\theta \in \Theta : R(\theta) = 0} \ell^{*(b)}(\theta) - \sup_{\theta \in \Theta} \ell^{*(b)}(\theta) \right), \quad b = 1, \ldots, B.$$

Note that the latter fully exploits the imposed restrictions in constructing the resampling distribution. The $(1 - \alpha)$-quantile of the distribution of $\{r^{*(b)}\}_{b=1}^B$ obtained in either way can be then used as a bootstrap $100(1 - \alpha)\%$ critical value for r.

It is also possible to bootstrap the empirical likelihood ratio test statistic $\mathrm{elr}(\hat{\theta}_{\mathrm{EL}})$ for overidentifying restrictions in similar ways. One way is to use the empirical distribution μ_n for resampling to generate $\{z_i^{*(b)}\}_{i=1}^n$, $b = 1, \ldots, B$, then define $\{\tilde{g}(z_i^{*(b)}, \theta)\}_{i=1}^n\}_{b=1}^B$ as above to obtain

$$\mathrm{elr}^{*(b)}(\theta) = \max_{\gamma \in \mathbb{R}^q} 2 \sum_{i=1}^n \log(1 + \gamma' \tilde{g}(z_i^{*(b)}, \theta)), \quad b = 1, \ldots, B.$$

Evaluate each $\mathrm{elr}^{*(b)}(\theta)$ at its maximizer $\hat{\theta}^{*(b)}$ to obtain $\mathrm{elr}^{*(b)}(\hat{\theta}_{\mathrm{EL}}^{*(b)})$. The bootstrap empirical distribution of these values yields critical values for $\mathrm{elr}(\hat{\theta}_{\mathrm{EL}})$. If, however, one uses $\hat{\mu}_{\mathrm{EL}} = \sum_{i=1}^n \hat{p}_{\mathrm{EL}} \delta_{z_i}$ derived in Section 2 for resampling as in Brown and Newey (2002), the recentering step is unnecessary.

The above discussions focused on the bootstrap calibration in which the researcher uses the distribution of bootstrap versions of empirical likelihood ratio statistics in place of the appropriate chi-square distribution. There is another potentially interesting way to use bootstrap test statistic values to improve accuracy of inference. Recall that empirical likelihood ratio statistics are generally Bartlett-correctable (Section 5.2). The essence of Bartlett correction is to adjust a likelihood ratio statistic (parametric or empirical) by its expected value. Suppose, for example, one wishes to compare $\mathrm{elr}(\hat{\theta}_{\mathrm{EL}})$ with its limiting distribution χ_{q-k}^2. Then $E[\mathrm{elr}(\hat{\theta}_{\mathrm{EL}})] = (q - k)(1 + n^{-1}a) + O(n^{-2})$ for the Bartlett factor a, and the Bartlett-corrected statistic is $\mathrm{elr}(\hat{\theta}_{\mathrm{EL}})/(1 + n^{-1}a)$. The factor a needs to be estimated, but its expression can be overwhelmingly complex. One can, however, estimate the factor in the denominator by taking the average of bootstrapped statistics generated by either of the two algorithms described above. This yields a Bartlett-corrected empirical likelihood ratio statistic via bootstrapping:

$$\frac{(q - k)\mathrm{elr}(\hat{\theta}_{\mathrm{EL}})}{\frac{1}{B}\sum_{b=1}^{B} \mathrm{elr}^{*(b)}(\hat{\theta}_{\mathrm{EL}}^{*(b)})}$$

The distribution of the above statistic can be approximated by the χ^2_{q-k} distribution up to errors of order $O(n^{-2})$.

Bootstrap Bartlett correction has been used in parametric likelihood ratio testing. In particular, Rocke (1989) considers the parametric LR test in a seemingly unrelated regression model and finds that bootstrap Bartlett correction achieves accuracy comparable to conventional bootstrap methods with a substantially smaller number of bootstrap replications. See also Zaman (1996) for a discussion on the topic. It is therefore worthwhile to consider the use of bootstrap Bartlett correction for empirical likelihood in complex models where bootstrapping is costly. Chen, Leung, and Qin (2003) report a striking performance of the bootstrap Bartlett correction for their empirical likelihood ratio test with validation data.

8.2   Simulation Results

The theoretical analysis in Sections 4 and 5 indicates that empirical likelihood-based methods possess theoretical advantages over other competing methods. The following numerical examples provide some insights on finite sample properties of these estimators.

8.2.1   Experiment 1

The first simulation design is taken from Blundell and Bond (1998) and Bond, Bowsher, and Windmeijer (2001). The focus of this experiment is the relative finite sample performance of EL-based estimators and the conventional GMM.[6] It is concerned with a dynamic panel data model: $y_{it} = \theta_0 y_{t-1} + \eta_i + u_{it}, i = 1, \ldots, n, t = 1, \ldots, T$ where $\eta_i \sim_{iid} N(0, 1)$, $u_{it} \sim_{iid} N(0, 1)$, and $e_i \sim_{iid} N(0, \frac{1}{1-\theta_0^2})$, and these shocks are independent. The initial value is drawn according to $y_{i1} = \frac{\eta_i}{1-\theta_0} + e_i$. The two equations, together with the independence assumptions, imply that

$$E[y_{i,s}(\Delta y_{it} - \theta_0 \Delta y_{it-1})] = 0, t = 1, \ldots, T, s = 1, \ldots, t - 2 \quad (8.2)$$

---

[6] Further details of this experiment are to be found in Kitamura and Otsu (2005).

and

$$E[\Delta y_{it-1}(y_{it} - \theta_0 y_{it-1})] = 0, t = 3, \ldots, T. \tag{8.3}$$

The task is to estimate the parameter θ_0 using the moment conditions (8.2) and (8.3). The following estimators are considered: (i) the two-step GMM with its weighting matrix obtained by the usual robust estimator as described in Blundell and Bond (1998) ($\hat{\theta}_{GMM}$), (ii) the continuous updating GMM by Hansen, Heaton, and Yaron (1996) ($\hat{\theta}_{CUE}$), (iii) the maximum empirical likelihood estimator ($\hat{\theta}_{EL}$), and (iv) and the minimax estimator by Kitamura and Otsu (2005) ($\hat{\theta}_{ld}$) with $c = 0.1$ and 0.2. The second design is based on Bond, Bowsher, and Windmeijer (2001), where u_{it} is replaced by a conditionally heteroskedastic process of the form $u_{it}|y_{it-1} \sim N(0, 0.4 + 0.3y_{it-1}^2)$. The initial condition is generated using fifty pre-sample draws as in Bond, Bowsher, and Windmeijer (2001). The third design is the same as the second, except that u_{it} is the (standardized) chi-square distribution with one degree of freedom: $u_{ii} \sim_{iid} (\chi_1^2 - 1)/\sqrt{(0.4 + 0.3y_{it-1}^2)/2}$. Experimenting with asymmetric errors such as this specification is important, since one of the main advantages of GMM, EL or other moment-based estimators is its robustness against distributional assumptions. Also, asymmetric shocks appear to be an important characteristic of empirical models of income dynamics [see Geweke and Keane (2000) and Hirano (2002)], which is one of the main applications of dynamic panel data models. For these three designs, the true value for the autoregressive parameter θ is set at 0.8. The fourth is the same as the first, except that the AR parameter θ is set at 0.4. The panel dimensions are $n = 100$ and $T = 6$, and the number of Monte Carlo replications is 1000 for each design. The first and second panels of Table 7.1 (Table 7.2) display results from the first and second (the third and the fourth) designs, respectively. The five columns of each panel correspond to bias, root mean square errors (RMSE), mean absolute errors (MAE) and the probabilities of the estimators deviating from the true value by more than $d = 0.1$ and 0.2, respectively.

The results of the experiment are intriguing, and in accordance with the theoretical results presented in Sections 4 and 5. Some caution needs to be exercised in interpreting figures such as RMSE, as the existence of moments of these estimators can be an issue; see, for example, Kunitomo and Matsushita (2003).

In the first design with homoskedastic and normal idiosyncratic shocks, all of the estimators work reasonably well, though the minimax estimation method by Kitamura and Otsu (2005) leads to substantial efficiency gain in terms of MAE. Also, the deviation probabilities for $d = 0.1$ are much lower for the minimax estimators than for CUE and EL. While the performance of (two-step) GMM is only slightly worse than that of the minimax estimators in this design, that changes dramatically in the second design, where conditional heteroskedasticity is introduced. Even though the bias of the minimax estimators is slightly inflated relative to that of EL, it is offset by their variance reduction. This is consistent with our interpretation that the minimax method "robustifies" the original EL

Table 7.1. *Estimation of dynamic panel data model (1)*

| | Homoskedastic u_{it} | | | | | Heteroskedastic u_{it} | | | | |
| | | | | $\Pr\{|\theta_n - \theta_0| > d\}$ | | | | | $\Pr\{|\theta_n - \theta_0| > d\}$ | |
	Bias	RMSE	MAE	$d = 0.1$	$d = 0.2$	Bias	RMSE	MAE	$d = 0.1$	$d = 0.2$
$\hat{\theta}_{\text{GMM}}$	0.014	0.096	0.071	0.296	0.029	−0.253	0.364	0.261	0.815	0.614
$\hat{\theta}_{\text{CUE}}$	0.001	0.113	0.084	0.390	0.054	−0.080	0.264	0.148	0.643	0.368
$\hat{\theta}_{\text{EL}}$	−0.005	0.113	0.080	0.370	0.056	−0.059	0.189	0.119	0.570	0.275
$\hat{\theta}_{\text{ld}}$ $\quad c = 0.1$	−0.016	0.100	0.061	0.274	0.047	−0.064	0.182	0.110	0.542	0.258
$\phantom{\hat{\theta}_{\text{ld}}}\quad c = 0.2$	−0.027	0.090	0.056	0.233	0.037	−0.076	0.166	0.100	0.503	0.215

Table 7.2. *Estimation of dynamic panel data model (2)*

| | Heteroskedastic & asymmetric u_{it} | | | | | $\theta = 0.4$, Heteroskedastic u_{it} | | | | |
| | | | | $\Pr\{|\theta_n - \theta_0| > d\}$ | | | | | $\Pr\{|\theta_n - \theta_0| > d\}$ | |
	Bias	RMSE	MAE	$d = 0.1$	$d = 0.2$	Bias	RMSE	MAE	$d = 0.1$	$d = 0.2$
$\hat{\theta}_{\mathrm{GMM}}$	−0.209	0.292	0.220	0.770	0.538	−0.005	0.134	0.091	0.457	0.124
$\hat{\theta}_{\mathrm{CUE}}$	−0.031	0.235	0.165	0.710	0.393	−0.025	0.141	0.095	0.477	0.131
$\hat{\theta}_{\mathrm{EL}}$	−0.038	0.178	0.135	0.613	0.289	−0.0018	0.119	0.079	0.388	0.075
$\hat{\theta}_{\mathrm{ld}}$ $c = 0.1$	−0.037	0.174	0.130	0.600	0.273	−0.0016	0.115	0.076	0.373	0.067
$c = 0.2$	−0.037	0.165	0.120	0.573	0.226	−0.0010	0.104	0.070	0.340	0.053

Table 7.3. *Standard normal, size* $= 0.01$

	Size uncorrected		Size corrected	
c	ℓ_{EL}	W	ℓ_{EL}	W
0.0	0.012	0.013	0.010	0.010
0.3	0.322	0.348	0.300	0.303
0.5	0.809	0.832	0.789	0.794

estimator. Deviation probabilities for this design exhibit an interesting pattern. Take the case with $d = 0.2$. GMM falls outside of the interval 0.8 ± 0.2 with 61 percent probability. CUE is much better than GMM (37 percent), though still it is high. EL has a good performance (28 percent), and by using the minimax method with $c = 0.2$, the probability is reduced to 21 percent, nearly one third of that of GMM. The last result seems to support the theoretical results by Kitamura and Otsu (2005) discussed in Section 4.1. Similar patterns emerge for the third design with asymmetric errors; again, note the drastic reduction of the deviation probability with $d = 0.2$ by the minimax estimator with $c = 0.2$ (the probability is 23 percent, compared with the 54 deviation probability of GMM, for example). In the fourth design, EL and its minimax versions continue to outperform GMM and CUE.

8.2.2   Experiment 2

This experiment is concerned with testing, in particular the power properties of the empirical likelihood ratio test. Pseudo-samples $\{z_i\}_{i=1}^n$ are independently drawn from a distribution F, and by adding a location shift term c, $x_i = z_i + c, i = 1, \ldots, n$, are calculated. Three specifications of F are considered: (1) standard normal $\Phi(z)$, (2) normal mixture $0.1\Phi(z - 9) + 0.9\Phi(z + 1)$, and (3) lognormal $\Phi(\log(z))$, $z > 0$. The null hypothesis is: $E[x] = 0$. This is the simplest possible example of overidentifying restrictions: the number of moment conditions is one and no parameters are estimated, so the degree of overidentification is one. Two statistics are used to test this null; one is the empirical likelihood ratio ℓ_{EL} and the other is $W = n(\bar{x}^2)/n^{-1}\sum_{i=1}^n(x_i - \bar{x})^2$, where $\bar{x} = n^{-1}\sum_{i=1}^n x_i$ ("W" stands for "Wald"). The "Wald" statistic is a feasible J-statistic in this simple setting. The sample size n is set to be 50. Tables 7.3–7.6 report rejection frequencies of the two tests.

The standard normal distribution belongs to the family of distributions discussed by Kariya (1981), for which W is uniformly most powerful invariant (UMPI). In this sense, the experimental design with normal z's (Table 7.3) is favorable to W, since no other invariant test should outperform W after size correction, for any finite sample size. Nevertheless, Table 7.3 shows that the power of the empirical likelihood ratio keeps up with that of W reasonably well. (The power curves for the standard normal are symmetric, so only the results for nonnegative c's are reported in Table 7.3.)

Table 7.4. *Normal mixture, size* = 0.01

c	Size uncorrected		Size corrected	
	ℓ_{EL}	W	ℓ_{EL}	W
−1.2	0.887	0.574	0.868	0.028
−0.6	0.174	0.043	0.148	0.001
0.0	0.011	0.041	0.010	0.010
0.6	0.082	0.206	0.073	0.075
−1.2	0.344	0.553	0.320	0.263

Table 7.5. *Normal mixture, size* = 0.05

c	Size uncorrected		Size corrected	
	ℓ_{EL}	W	ℓ_{EL}	W
−1.2	0.961	0.876	0.960	0.729
−0.6	0.361	0.199	0.353	0.093
0.0	0.055	0.085	0.050	0.050
0.6	0.225	0.348	0.207	0.224
−1.2	0.614	0.727	0.594	0.605

Table 7.6. *Lognormal, size* = 0.01

c	Size uncorrected		Size corrected	
	ℓ_{EL}	W	ℓ_{EL}	W
−1.0	0.582	0.752	0.404	0.468
−0.6	0.325	0.480	0.176	0.201
0.0	0.034	0.056	0.010	0.010
0.6	0.640	0.248	0.421	0.003
1.0	1.000	0.947	0.998	0.338

In the normal mixture and lognormal cases, the size distortion of W makes power comparison difficult and misleading, and size corrected power might give a better picture. Table 7.4 shows the excellent power properties of the empirical likelihood ratio test. When the deviation from the null is $c = -1.2$, the power of ℓ_{EL} is nearly 90 percent, whereas the power of W is extremely poor (2.8 percent). Qualitatively similar results are obtained for larger nominal sizes (see Table 7.5), and for other distributions such as the lognormal (see Table 7.6). In summary, the simulation results seem to be consistent with the large deviation optimality results of the empirical likelihood ratio test in Section 4.

9 CONCLUSION

This paper has discussed several aspects of empirical likelihood. Two different but interconnected interpretations for empirical likelihood have been offered.

One can view empirical likelihood as NPMLE, which has a long history in statistics. The literature on empirical likelihood initiated by Owen (1988) demonstrates that NPMLE applied to a moment restriction model yields an attractive procedure, both practically and theoretically. Moreover, applications of empirical likelihood extend to other problems that are important in applied economics, as discussed in the present paper. Alternatively, one can view empirical likelihood as GMC with a particular choice of the "contrast function." This line of argument yields a variety of empirical likelihood-type estimators and tests, depending on the choice of the contrast function. The theory of convex duality shows a clear connection between GMC and other related estimators, including Smith's GEL. Theoretical considerations seem to indicate that the contrast function used for empirical likelihood is often the most preferred choice.

A natural conjecture sometimes made in the literature is that empirical likelihood may bring efficiency properties analogous to those of parametric likelihood to semiparametric analysis, while retaining the distribution-free character of certain nonparametric procedures. The results described in this paper present affirmative answers to this conjecture. In particular, the large deviation principle (LDP) provides compelling theoretical foundations for the use of empirical likelihood through Sanov's theorem.

Another attractive aspect of empirical likelihood is that it directly uses the empirical distribution of the data, which has intuitive and practical appeal. It avoids, or at least lessens, the problem of choosing tuning parameters that often introduce a fair amount of arbitrariness to nonparametric and semiparametric procedures. A related and important point is the practicality of empirical likelihood. The use of convex duality transforms seemingly complex optimization problems into their simple dual forms, thereby making empirical likelihood a highly usable method. This paper has provided discussions on the implementation of empirical likelihood as well as numerical examples, so that they offer practical guidance to applied economists who wish to use empirical likelihood in their research.

APPENDIX

Derivation of Equations (5.3) and (5.4)   The objective function to be maximized is

$$-\sum_{i=1}^{n} \log(1 + \hat{\gamma}(\theta)'g(z_i, \theta)).$$

Consider the first-order condition. Since the $\hat{\gamma}(\theta)$ is an optimizer (for a given θ), the derivative of $\hat{\gamma}$ with respect to θ drops out by the envelop theorem. Therefore:

$$\sum_{i=1}^{n} \frac{\nabla_\theta g(z_i, \hat{\theta}_{EL})'\hat{\gamma}}{1 + \hat{\gamma}'g(z_i, \hat{\theta}_{EL})} = 0, \quad \hat{\gamma} = \hat{\gamma}(\hat{\theta}_{EL}). \tag{A.1}$$

Now, the first-order condition for $\hat{\gamma}$ is

$$\sum_{i=1}^{n} \frac{g(z_i, \theta)}{1 + \hat{\gamma}' g(z_i, \theta)} = 0.$$

Manipulating this yields

$$\hat{\gamma} = \left[\sum_{i=1}^{n} \frac{g(z_i, \hat{\theta}_{\mathrm{EL}}) g(z_i, \hat{\theta}_{\mathrm{EL}})'}{n(1 + \hat{\gamma}' g(z_i, \hat{\theta}_{\mathrm{EL}}))} \right]^{-1} \bar{g}(\hat{\theta}_{\mathrm{EL}}). \tag{A.2}$$

By (A.1) and (A.2),

$$\left[\sum_{i=1}^{n} \frac{\nabla_\theta g(z_i, \hat{\theta}_{\mathrm{EL}})}{1 + \hat{\gamma}' g(z_i, \hat{\theta}_{\mathrm{EL}})} \right]' \left[\sum_{i=1}^{n} \frac{g(z_i, \hat{\theta}_{\mathrm{EL}}) g(z_i, \hat{\theta}_{\mathrm{EL}})'}{n(1 + \hat{\gamma}' g(z_i, \hat{\theta}_{\mathrm{EL}}))} \right]^{-1} \bar{g}(\hat{\theta}_{\mathrm{EL}}) = 0.$$

Use the definition of $\hat{p}_{\mathrm{EL}i}$ given by (2.6) to obtain (5.3).
To obtain (5.4), differentiate $\bar{g}(\theta)' \bar{S}(\theta)^{-1} \bar{g}(\theta)$ by θ (assume that θ is a scalar for the ease of presentation) to obtain

$$\nabla_\theta \bar{g}(\hat{\theta}_{\mathrm{cue}})' \bar{S}^{-1}(\hat{\theta}_{\mathrm{cue}}) \bar{g}(\hat{\theta}_{\mathrm{cue}})$$

$$- \bar{g}(\hat{\theta}_{\mathrm{cue}}) \bar{S}^{-1}(\hat{\theta}_{\mathrm{cue}}) \frac{1}{n} \sum_{i=1}^{n} g(z_i, \hat{\theta}_{\mathrm{cue}}) \nabla_\theta g(z_i, \hat{\theta}_{\mathrm{cue}})' \bar{S}^{-1}(\hat{\theta}_{\mathrm{cue}}) \bar{g}(\hat{\theta}_{\mathrm{cue}})$$

$$= \left[\nabla_\theta \bar{g}(\hat{\theta}_{\mathrm{cue}}) - \left(\frac{1}{n} \sum_{i=1}^{n} \nabla_\theta g(z_i, \hat{\theta}_{\mathrm{cue}}) g(z_i, \hat{\theta}_{\mathrm{cue}}) \right) \bar{S}^{-1}(\hat{\theta}_{\mathrm{cue}}) \bar{g}(\hat{\theta}_{\mathrm{cue}}) \right]'$$

$$\times \bar{S}^{-1}(\hat{\theta}_{\mathrm{cue}}) \bar{g}(\hat{\theta}_{\mathrm{cue}})$$

$$= \tilde{D}(\hat{\theta}_{\mathrm{cue}})' \bar{S}^{-1}(\hat{\theta}_{\mathrm{cue}}) \bar{g}(\hat{\theta}_{\mathrm{cue}})$$

$$= 0.$$

References

AÏT-SAHALIA, Y., P. BICKEL, AND T. STOKER (2001): "Goodness-of-fit Tests for Kernel Regression with an Application to Option Implied Volatilities," *Journal of Econometrics*, 105, 363–412.

AKAIKE, H. (1973): "Information Theory and an Extension of the Likelihood Ratio Principle," in *Proceedings of the Second International Symposium of Information Theory*, Budapest: Akademiai Kiado, pp. 257–281.

ALLEN, J., A. GREGORY, AND K. SHIMOTSU (2005): "Empirical Likelihood Block Bootstrap," Manuscript, Department of Economics, Queen's University.

ALTONJI, J. AND L. M. SEGAL (1996): "Small Sample Bias in GMM Estimation of Covariance Structures," *Journal Business and Economic Statistics*, 14, 353–366.

ANATOLYEV, S. (2005): "GMM, GEL, Serial Correlation, and Asymptotic Bias," *Econometrica*, 73, 983–1002.

ANDERSON, T. W. AND H. RUBIN (1949): "Estimators of the Parameters of a Single Equation in a Complete Set of Stochastic Equations," *Annals of Mathematical Statistics*, 21, 570–582.

ANDREWS, D. W. (1991): "Heteroskedasticity and Autocorrelation Consistent Covariance Matrix Estimation," *Econometrica*, 59, 817–858.

ANDREWS, D. W. AND C. MONAHAN (1992): "An Improved Heteroskedasticity and Autocorrelation Consistent Covariance Matrix Estimator," *Econometrica*, 60, 953–966.

ANGRIST, J., V. CHERNOZHUKOV, AND I. FERNANDEZ (2005): "Quantile Regression Under Misspecification, with an Application to the U.S. Wage Structures," *Econometrica*, 74, 539–563.

ANTOINE, B., H. BONNAL, AND E. RENAULT (2006): "On the Efficient Use of the Informational Content of Estimating Equations: Implied Probabilities and Euclidean Likelihood," *Journal of Econometrics*, forthcoming.

BAGGERLY, K. (1998): "Empirical Likelihood as a Goodness-of-fit Measure," *Biometrika*, 85, 535–547.

BAHADUR, R. (1960): "On the Asymptotic Efficiency of Tests and Estimators," *Sankhyā*, 22, 229–252.

———— (1964): "On Fisher's Bound for Asymptotic Variances," *Annals of Mathematical Statistics*, 35, 1545–1552.

BAHADUR, R., S. ZABELL, AND J. GUPTA (1980): "Large Deviations, Tests, and Estimates," in *Asymptotic Theory of Statistical Tests and Estimation*, edited by I. M. Chaterabarli, New York: Academic Press, pp. 33–64.

BICKEL, P., C. KLASSEN, Y. RITOV, AND J. WELLNER (1993): *Efficient and Adaptive Estimation for Semiparametric Models*, Baltimore: Johns Hopkins Press.

BLUNDELL, R. AND S. BOND (1998): "Initial Conditions and Moment Restrictions in Dynamic Panel Data Models," *Journal of Econometrics*, 87, 115–143.

BOND, S., C. BOWSHER, AND F. WINDMEIJER (2001): "Criterion-Based Inference for GMM in Autoregressive Panel Data Models," *Economics Letters*, 73, 379–388.

BORWEIN, J. M. AND A. S. LEWIS (1991): "Duality Relationships for Entropy-type Minimization Problems," *SIAM Journal of Control and Optimization*, 29, 325–338.

BRAVO, F. (2002): "Blockwise Empirical Cressie–Read Test statistics for α-mixing Processes," *Statistics and Probability Letters*, 58, 319–325.

———— (2005a): "Blockwise Empirical Entropy Tests for Time Series Regressions," *Journal of Time Series Analysis*, 26, 157–321.

———— (2005b): "Sieve Empirical Likelihood for Unit Root Tests," Manuscript, University of York.

BROWN, B. W. AND W. K. NEWEY (1998): "Efficient Semiparametric Estimation of Expectations," *Econometrica*, 66, 453–464.

———— (2002): "Generalized Method of Moments, Efficient Bootstrapping, and Improved Inference," *Journal of Business and Economic Statistics*, 20, 507–517.

BROWN, D. J. AND M. H. WEGKAMP (2002): "Weighted Minimum Mean-Square Distance from Independence Estimation," *Econometrica*, 70, 2035–2051.

CANER, M. (2003): "Exponential Tilting with Weak Instruments: Estimation and Testing," Manuscript, University of Pittsburgh.

CARLSTEIN, E. (1986): "The Use of Subseries Values for Estimating the Variance of a General Statistic from Stationary Processes," *Annals of Statistics*, 14, 1171–1179.

CHAMBERLAIN, G. (1987): "Asymptotic Efficiency in Estimation with Conditional Moment Restrictions," *Journal of Econometrics*, 34, 305–334.

CHEN, S. X. AND H. CUI (2004): "On the Second Order Properties of Empirical Likelihood with Moment Conditions," Manuscript.

———— (2005): "On Bartlett Correction of Empirical Likelihood in the Presence of Nuisance Parameters," *Biometrika*, forthcoming.

CHEN, S. X., W. HÄRDLE, AND M. LI (2003): "An Empirical Likelihood Goodness-of-fit Test for Time Series," *Journal of The Royal Statistical Society, Series B*, 65, 663–678.

CHEN, S. X., D. H. Y. LEUNG, AND J. QIN (2003): "Information Recovery in a Study with Surrogate Endpoints," *Journal of the American Statistical Association*, 98, 1052–1062.

CHEN, X., H. HONG, AND M. SHUM (2001): "Nonparametric Likelihood Selection Tests for Parametric versus Moment Condition Models," *Journal of Econometrics*, forthcoming.

CHESHER, A. AND R. SMITH (1997): "Likelihood Ratio Specification Tests," *Econometrica*, 65, 627–646.

CHRISTOFFERSEN, P., J. HAHN, AND A. INOUE (2001): "Testing and Comparing Value at Risk Measures," *Journal of Empirical Finance*, 8, 325–342.

CORCORAN, S. A. (1998): "Bartlett Adjustment of Empirical Discrepancy Statistics," *Biometrika*, 85, 967–972.

CORCORAN, S. A., A. C. DAVISON, AND R. H. SPADY (1995): "Reliable Inference from Empirical Likelihood," Working Paper, Nuffield College, Oxford University.

COSSLETT, S. (1981a): "Efficient Estimation of Discrete Choice Models," in *Structural Analysis of Discrete Data with Econometric Applications*, edited by C. F. Manski and D. L. McFadden, Cambridge, MA: MIT Press, pp. 51–111.

———— (1981b): "Maximum Likelihood Estimation for Choice-based Samples," *Econometrica*, 49, 1289–1316.

———— (1983): "Distribution-free Maximum Likelihood Estimator of the Binary Choice Model," *Econometrica*, 51, 765–782.

———— (1993): "Estimation from Endogenously Stratified Samples," in *Handbook of Statistics*, edited by G. Maddala, C. Rao, and H. Vinod, Amsterdam: Elsevier Science, pp. 1–43.

———— (1997): "Nonparametric Maximum Likelihood Methods," in *Handbook of Statistics*, edited by G. Maddala, C. Rao, and H. Vinod, Amsterdam: Elsevier Science, pp. 385–404.

CSISZÀR (1967): "On Topological Properties of f-Divergences," *Studia Scientriarum Mathematicarum Hungaria*, 2, 329–339.

DAHLHAUS, R. AND D. JANAS (1996): "A Frequency Domain Bootstrap for Ratio Statistics in Time Series Analysis," *The Annals of Statistics*, 24(5), 1934–1963.

DEUSCHEL, J. D. AND D. W. STROOCK (1989): *Large Deviations*, New York: Academic Press.

DICICCIO, T., P. HALL, AND J. ROMANO (1991): "Empirical Likelihood is Bartlett-Correctable," *Annals of Statisics*, 19, 1053–1061.

DOMINGUEZ, M. AND I. LOBATO (2004): "Consistent Estimation of Models Defined by Conditional Moment Restrictions," *Econometrica*, 72, 1601–1615.

DONALD, S. G., G. W. IMBENS, AND W. K. NEWEY (2003): "Empirical Likelihood Estimation and Consistent Tests with Conditional Moment Restrictions," *Journal of Econometrics*, 117, 55–93.

DONALD, S. G. AND W. K. NEWEY (2000): "A Jackknife Interpretation of the Continuous Updating Estimator," *Economics Letters*, 67, 239–244.

EUBANK, R. AND C. SPIEGELMAN (1990): "Testing the Goodness of Fit of a Linear Model via Nonparametric Regression Techniques," *Journal of the American Statistical Association*, 85, 387–392.

FU, J. C. (1973): "On a Theorem of Bahadur on the Rate of Convergence of Point Estimators," *Annals of Statistics*, 1, 745–749.

GAGLIARDINI, P., C. GOURIEROUX, AND E. RENAULT (2004): "Efficient Derivative Pricing by Extended Method of Moments," Working Paper.

GALI, J. AND M. GERTLER (1999): "Inflation Dynamics: A Structural Econometric Analysis," *Journal of Monetary Economics*, 44, 195–222.

GEWEKE, J. AND M. KEANE (2000): "An Empirical Analysis of Earnings Dynamics Among Men in the PSID: 1968–1989," *Journal of Econometrics*, 96, 293–356.

GHOSH, J. K. (1994): *Higher Order Asymptotics*, Hayward, CA: Institute of Mathematical Statistics.

GUGGENBERGER, P. AND R. H. SMITH (2005): "Generalized Empirical Likelihood Estimators and Tests Under Partial, Weak and Strong Identification," *Econometric Theory*, 21, 667–709.

HALL, P. (1985): "Resampling a Coverage Process," *Stochastic Processes and Their Applications*, 19, 259–269.

HALL, P. AND J. L. HOROWITZ (1996): "Bootstrap Critical Values for Tests Based on Generalized Method of Moments Estimators," *Econometrica*, 64, 891–916.

HALL, P. AND B. LASCALA (1990): "Methodology and Algorithms for Empirical Likelihood," *International Statistical Review*, 58, 109–127.

HANSEN, B. E. (2006): "Econometrics," Manuscript, Department of Economics, University of Wisconsin.

HANSEN, L. P. (1982): "Large Sample Properties of Generalized Methods of Moments Estimators," *Econometrica*, 50, 1029–1054.

HANSEN, L. P., J. HEATON, AND A. YARON (1996): "Finite-Sample Properties of Some Alternative GMM Estimators," *Journal of Business and Economic Statistics*, 14, 262–280.

HANSEN, L. P. AND K. SINGLETON (1982): "Generalized Instrumental Variable Estimation of Nonlinear Rational Expectations Models," *Econometrica*, 50, 1269–1286.

HÄRDLE, W. AND E. MAMMEN (1993): "Comparing Nonparametric versus Parametric Regression Fits," *Annals of Statistics*, 21, 1926–1947.

HART, J. D. (1997): *Nonparametric Smoothing and Lack-of-fit Tests*, New York: Springer-Verlag.

HASTIE, T. AND R. TIBSHIRANI (1986): "Generalized Additive Models," *Statistical Science*, 1, 297–318.

HECKMAN, J. J. AND B. SINGER (1984): "A Method of Minimizing the Impact of Distributional Assumptions in Econometric Models for Duration Data," *Econometrica*, 52, 271–320.

HELLERSTEIN, J. K. AND G. W. IMBENS (1999): "Imposing Moment Restrictions from Auxiliary Data by Weighting," *Review of Economics and Statistics*, 81, 1–14.

HIRANO, K. (2002): "Semiparametric Bayesian Inference in Autoregressive Panel Data Models," *Econometrica*, 70, 781–799.

HOEFFDING, W. (1963): "Asymptotically Optimal Tests for Multinomial Distributions," *Annals of Mathematical Statistics*, 36, 369–408.

IMBENS, G. W. (1997): "One-Step Estimators for Over-Identified Generalized Method of Moments Models," *Review of Economic Studies*, 64, 359–383.

IMBENS, G. W. AND R. H. SPADY (2006): "The Performance of Empirical Likelihood and Its Generalizations," in *Identification and Inference for Economic Models: Essays in Honor of Thomas Rothenberg*, edited by D. W. K. Andrews and J. H. Stock, Cambridge, UK: Cambridge University Press, pp. 216–244.

IMBENS, G. W., R. H. SPADY, AND P. JOHNSON (1998): "Information Theoretic Approaches to Inference in Moment Condition Models," *Econometrica*, 66, 333–357.

JOAG-DEV, K. AND F. PROSCHAN (1983): "Negative Association of Random Variables with Applications," *Annals of Statistics*, 11, 286–295.

KALLENBERG, W. (1983): "On Moderate Deviation Theory in Estimation," *Annals of Statistics*, 11, 498–504.

KARIYA, T. (1981): "A Robustness Property of Hotelling's Test," *Annals of Statistics*, 9, 211–214.

KESTER, A. AND W. KALLENBERG (1986): "Large Deviations of Estimators," *Annals of Statistics*, 14, 648–664.

KIM, T.-H. AND H. WHITE (2003): "Estimation, Inference, and Specification Testing for Possibly Misspecified Quantile Regression," in *Maximum Likelihood Estimation of Misspecified Models: Twenty Years Later*, edited by T. Fomby and R. C. Hill, New York: Elsevier, pp. 107–132.

KITAMURA, Y. (1996a): "Empirical Likelihood and the Bootstrap for Time Series Regressions," Working Paper, Department of Economics, University of Minnesota.

——— (1996b): "GNP-Optimal Tests for Moment Restrictions," Working Paper, Department of Economics, University of Minnesota.

——— (1997): "Empirical Likelihood Methods with Weakly Dependent Processes," *Annals of Statistics*, 25, 2084–2102.

——— (1998): "Comparing Misspecified Dynamic Econometric Models Using Nonparametric Likelihood," Working Paper, Department of Economics, University of Wisconsin.

——— (2001): "Asymptotic Optimality of Empirical Likelihood for Testing Moment Restrictions," *Econometrica*, 69, 1661–1672.

——— (2002): "A Likelihood-based Approach to the Analysis of a Class of Nested and Non-nested Models," Working Paper, Department of Economics, University of Pennsylvania.

KITAMURA, Y. AND T. OTSU (2005): "Minimax Estimation and Testing for Moment Condition Models via Large Deviations," Manuscript, Department of Economics, Yale University.

KITAMURA, Y. AND M. STUTZER (1997): "An Information Theoretic Alternative to Generalized Method of Moments Estimation," *Econometrica*, 65(4), 861–874.

KITAMURA, Y., G. TRIPATHI, AND H. AHN (2004): "Empirical Likelihood Based Inference in Conditional Moment Restriction Models," *Econometrica*, 72, 1667–1714.

KLEIBERGEN, F. (2002): "Pivotal Statistics for Testing Structural Parameters in Instrumental Variables Regression," *Econometrica*, 70, 1781–1803.

KOENKER, R. AND G. BASSETT (1978): "Regression Quantiles," *Econometrica*, 46, 33–50.

KUNITOMO, N. AND Y. MATSUSHITA (2003): "On Finite Sample Distributions of the Empirical Likelihood Estimator and the GMM Estimator," Manuscript.

KÜNSCH, H. R. (1989): "The Jacknife and the Bootstrap for General Stationary Observations," *Annals of Statistics*, 17, 1217–1241.

LEBLANC, M. AND J. CROWLEY (1995): "Semiparametric Regression Functionals," *Journal of the American Statistical Association*, 90(429), 95–105.

LIN, L. AND R. ZHANG (2001): "Blockwise Empirical Euclidean Likelihood for Weakly Dependent Processes," *Statistics and Probability Letters*, 53, 143–152.

MANSKI, C. F. (1983): "Closest Empirical Distribution Estimation," *Econometrica*, 51, 305–319.

MONTI, A. C. (1997): "Empirical Likelihood Confidence Regions in Time Series Analysis," *Biometrika*, 84, 395–405.

NEWEY, W. K. (1990): "Efficient Instrumental Variables Estimation of Nonlinear Models," *Econometrica*, 58, 809–837.

NEWEY, W. K. AND R. J. SMITH (2004): "Higher Order Properties of GMM and Generalized Empirical Likelihood Estimators," *Econometrica*, 72, 219–255.

NEWEY, W. K. AND K. D. WEST (1987): "A Simple, Positive Semi-Definite, Heteroskedasticity and Autocorrelation Consistent Covariance Matrix," *Econometrica*, 55(3), 703–708.

NEWEY, W. K. AND F. WINDMEIJER (2006): "GMM with Many Weak Moment Conditions," Working Paper, Department of Economics, MIT.

NORDMAN, D. AND S. N. LAHIRI (2004): "A Frequency Domain Empirical Likelihood for Short- and Long-Range Dependence," Manuscript, Department of Economics, University of Iowa.

NORDMAN, D., P. SIBBERTSEN, AND S. N. LAHIRI (2006): "Empirical Likelihood Confidence Intervals for the Mean of a Long-Range Dependent Process," *Annals of Statistics*, forthcoming.

OTSU, T. (2006): "Generalized Empirical Likelihood Under Weak Identification," *Econometric Theory*, 22, 513–527.

OTSU, T. AND Y.-J. WHANG (2005): "Testing for Non-Nested Conditional Moment Restrictions via Conditional Empirical Likelihood," Manuscript, Yale University and Seoul National University.

OWEN, A. (1988): "Empirical Likelihood Ratio Confidence Intervals for a Single Functional," *Biometrika*, 75(2), 237–249.

——— (1990): "Empirical Likelihood Ratio Confidence Regions," *The Annals of Statistics*, 18(1), 90–120.

——— (1991): "Empirical Likelihood for Linear Models," *The Annals of Statistics*, 19(4), 1725–1747.

——— (2001): *Empirical Likelihood*, London: Chapman and Hall/CRC.

PRIESTLEY, M. B. (1981): *Spectral Analysis and Time Series*, New York: Academic Press.

PUHALSKII, A. AND V. SPOKOINY (1998): "On Large-Deviation Efficiency in Statistical Inference," *Bernoulli*, 4, 203–272.

QIN, J. AND J. LAWLESS (1994): "Empirical Likelihood and General Estimating Equations," *Annals of Statistics*, 22, 300–325.

RAGUSA, G. (2005): "Properties of Minimum Divergence Estimators," Manuscript.

RAMALHO, J. J. S. AND R. J. SMITH (2002): "Generalized Empirical Likelihood Non-Nested Tests," *Journal of Econometrics*, 107, 99–125.

ROBINSON, P. M. (1987): "Asymptotically Efficient Estimation in the Presence of Heteroskedasticity of Unknown Form," *Econometrica*, 55, 875–891.

ROCKE, D. M. (1989): "Bootstrap Bartlett Adjustment in Seemingly Unrelated Regression," *Journal of the American Statistical Association*, 84(406), 598–601.

SANOV, I. N. (1961): "On the Probability of Large Deviations of Random Variables," *Selected Translations in Mathematical Statistics and Probability*, I, 213–244.

SCHENNACH, S. M. (2004): "Exponentially Tilted Empirical Likelihood," Discussion Paper, University of Chicago.

SERFLING, R. J. (1980): *Approximation Theorems of Mathematical Statistics*, New York: John Wiley.

SHANNO, D. F. (1970): "Parameter Selection for Modified Newton Methods for Function Minimization," *SIAM Journal on Numerical Analysis*, 7(3), 366–372.

SMITH, R. J. (1997): "Alternative Semi-Parametric Likelihood Approaches to Generalized Method of Moments Estimation," *Economic Journal*, 107, 503–519.

—— (2000): "Empirical Likelihood Estimation and Inference," in *Applications of Differential Geometry to Econometrics*, edited by M. Salmon and P. Marriott, Cambridge: Cambridge University Press, pp. 119–150.

—— (2003): "Efficient Information Theoretic Inference for Conditional Moment Restrictions," Working Paper, University of Cambridge.

—— (2004): "GEL Criteria for Moment Condition Models," Working Paper, University of Warwick.

—— (2005): "Local GEL Methods for Conditional Moment Restrictions," Working Paper, University of Cambridge.

STOCK, J. H. AND J. H. WRIGHT (2000): "GMM with Weak Identification," *Econometrica*, 68(5), 1055–1096.

TRIPATHI, G. (2005): "Moment Based Inference with Stratified Data," Working Paper, Department of Economics, University of Connecticut.

TRIPATHI, G. AND Y. KITAMURA (2003): "Testing Conditional Moment Restrictions," *Annals of Statisics*, 31, 2059–2095.

VUONG, Q. (1989): "Likelihood Ratio Tests for Model Selection and Non-Nested Hypotheses," *Econometrica*, 57, 307–333.

WALD, A. (1943): "Tests of Statistical Hypotheses Concerning Several Parameters When the Number of Observations is Large," *Transactions of the American Mathematical Society*, 54, 426–482.

—— (1950): *Statistical Decision Functions*, New York: Wiley.

WANG, Q. AND J. N. K. RAO (2002): "Empirical Likelihood-based Inference Under Imputation for Missing Response Data," *Annals of Statistics*, 30, 896–924.

WHANG, Y.-J. (2006): "Smoothed Empirical Likelihood Methods for Quantile Regression Models," *Econometric Theory*, 22, 173–205.

WHITE, H. (1980): "Using Least Squares to Approximate Unknown Regression Functions," *International Economic Review*, 21, 149–170.

—— (1982): "Maximum Likelihood Estimation of Misspecified Models," *Econometrica*, 50, 1–25.

WOLFOWITZ, J. (1957): "The Minimum Distance Method," *Annals of Methematical Statistics*, 28, 75–88.

YOU, J., G. CHEN, AND Y. ZHOU (2006): "Block Empirical Likelihood for Longitudinal Partially Linear Regression Models," *Canadian Journal of Statistics*, 34(1), 79–96.

ZAMAN, A. (1996): *Statistical Foundations for Econometric Techniques*, New York: Academic Press.

ZEITOUNI, O. AND M. GUTMAN (1991): "On Universal Hypothesis Testing via Large Deviations," *IEE Transactions on Information Theory*, 37, 285–290.

ZHANG, J. (2006): "Empirical Likelihood for NA Series," *Statistics and Probability Letters*, 76, 153–160.

ZHANG, J. AND I. GIJBELS (2003): "Sieve Empirical Likelihood and Extensions of the Generalized Least Squares," *Scandinavian Journal of Statistics*, 30, 1–24.

CHAPTER 8

Weak Instruments and Empirical Likelihood: A Discussion of the Papers by D. W. K. Andrews and J. H. Stock and Y. Kitamura[*]

Richard J. Smith[†]

1 INTRODUCTION

These two papers represent the fruition of important and thorough investigations undertaken by the authors of their respective fields of enquiry. I feel that they will add considerably to our understanding of these topics. Before describing the contents of my discussion I initially and briefly outline the contributions of both sets of authors.

Andrews and Stock (2005), henceforth referred to as AS, continues the program of research initiated with the papers by Moreira (2001, 2003) through Andrews, Moriera, and Stock (2004), henceforth AMS. Like those contributions, this paper is primarily concerned with the weak instrument problem for the classical two variable linear simultaneous equations model with normally distributed reduced form errors and known error variance matrix. The particular advantage of using a well-understood classical framework for analysis is that results here as elsewhere should have important implications and conclusions for estimators and statistics in more general settings enabling specific recommendations for practice. Apart from reviewing and detailing existing results, this paper provides a comprehensive treatment of the many weak instrumental variables problem for this model. Generally speaking with weak instruments standard point estimators such as 2SLS and LIML are no longer consistent and have nonstandard limiting distributions which cannot be consistently estimated. Therefore recourse is typically made to tests based on unconditionally or conditionally pivotal statistics. Acceptance regions associated with these tests may then be inverted to provide valid confidence interval estimators for the parameters of interest. I now briefly summarize their findings and conclusions.

[*] This paper reports the Invited Discussion of the Symposium on Weak Instruments and Empirical Likelihood held at the Econometric Society World Congress, U.C.L., London (2005). I am grateful for insightful discussions with G. H. Hillier which helped me formulate the weak identification section of my discussion. Neither he nor anyone else bears responsibility for any misconceptions that remain. The research for this Invited Discussion benefitted from the financial support of a 2002 Leverhulme Major Research Fellowship.
[†] cemmap, U.C.L and I.F.S., and Faculty of Economics, University of Cambridge.

AMS obtains the power envelope for two-sided similar tests of the structural parameter *via* consideration of point optimal tests. The power envelope changes little between similar and nonsimilar tests. A new test class is obtained which maximizes weighted average power. However, the conditional likelihood ratio (CLR) test due to Moreira (2003), also a similar test, comes close to reaching the power envelope as does the CLR test with estimated reduced form error variance matrix. Apart from surveying extant results in the literature, AS again mostly confines attention to invariant similar tests and extends the analysis of AMS for many weak instruments. Let λ_π denote the concentration parameter, k the number of instruments and n the sample size. AS characterize the various situations under consideration by the limit of the ratio $\lambda_\pi / k^\tau \to r_\tau, r_\tau \in [0, \infty)$, $\tau \in (0, \infty)$, where $k \to \infty, n \to \infty$. Briefly, (a) $\tau \in (0, 1/2)$, there is no test with nontrivial power, (b) $\tau = 1/2$, the Anderson–Rubin (AR), Lagrange multiplier (LM), and likelihood ratio (LR) statistics all have nontrivial power, (c) $\tau > 1/2$, the AR statistic has trivial power whereas the LM and LR statistics are asymptotically equivalent and have nontrivial power. AS also obtain the asymptotic power envelopes using a least favorable distribution approach to circumvent the difficulty of the composite null hypothesis, thus, enabling the application of classical Neyman–Pearson theory. They find that for $\tau = 1/2$ the CLR test is close to the asymptotically efficient power envelope and that for $\tau > 1/2$ the LM and CLR tests are asymptotically equivalent. As a consequence, tests based on the CLR statistic are to be recommended as a useful and powerful tool in weakly identified models.

Kitamura (2005), henceforth K, provides an extensive overview of empirical likelihood (EL), see Owen (2001). K demonstrates the well-known result that EL is a nonparametric maximum likelihood estimator but, of particular note, also reinterprets EL as a generalized minimum contrast (GMC) estimator using an information-theoretic treatment based on Fenchel duality, see Borwein and Lewis (1991). This GMC interpretation of EL is particularly useful when considering issues of estimation and inference in the presence of misspecification, allowing a generalization of the analysis of likelihood ratio test statistics of Vuong (1989) to the nested and non-nested moment restrictions environment. Both unconditional and conditional moment settings are treated.

A broader question concerns why the more computationally complex EL should be entertained instead of GMM [Hansen (1982)]. It is now commonly appreciated that EL possesses some desirable higher-order properties. The asymptotic bias of EL is that of an infeasible GMM estimator when Jacobian and moment indicator variance matrices are known. Furthermore, bias-corrected EL is higher-order efficient. See Newey and Smith (2004), henceforth NS. A particularly innovative approach taken by K is the application of the theory of large deviations. Recent work co-authored with Otsu shows that a minimax EL estimator achieves the asymptotic minimax lower bound. The EL criterion function statistic also provides an asymptotically optimal test, see Kitamura (2001). This statistic has the added advantage of Bartlett correctability. K provides some simulation evidence on the efficacy of these procedures, minimax

EL generally appearing superior and good coverage probabilities for the EL criterion function statistics. It is worth noting that when heteroskedastic models are considered EL is generally competitive, being internally self-studentized, as compared with homoskedastic environments. A number of other applications of EL are also briefly surveyed by K including time series moment condition models, conditional moment restrictions, and weak instruments among many others.

Because the breadth of the topics covered by AS and K is so vast, I must necessarily confine my discussion to a limited number of topics. To provide some focus, I use generalized empirical likelihood (GEL) as an organizational tool. Section 2 briefly summarizes the first-order theory concerning GEL and defines some objects needed later.

Weak identification is the subject of Section 3. By considering a model specified by nonlinear moment conditions, an appropriate GEL estimation problem allows consideration of objects which mirror in an asymptotic sense those which form the basis of the exact theory in AMS and AS. As a consequence, we define asymptotically pivotal statistics, the acceptance regions of which may then be inverted to provide asymptotically valid confidence interval estimators for the parameters of interests. The resultant statistics are compared and contrasted with those already extant in the literature and some new statistics are also defined which may warrant further investigation.

Paralleling the information theoretic development of EL in K, Section 4 briefly discusses the contribution of Corcoran (1998) which provides a general minimum distance (MD) approach to estimation and is the empirical counterpart to the analysis given by K. By comparing first-order conditions as in Newey and Smith (2001), similarly to K, it is immediately apparent that although the MD class has many members in common with GEL they do not coincide.

Schennach (2004) casts some doubt on the efficacy of EL in misspecified situations and proves that an alternative estimator which embeds exponential tilting (ET) empirical probabilities in the EL criterion not only has desirable asymptotic properties under misspecification but when bias-corrected is also higher-order efficient, sharing the higher-order bias and variance properties of EL when the moment restrictions are correct. Section 5 suggests an equivalent approach based on GEL rather than ET empirical probabilities. We show that the resultant estimator has the same asymptotic bias as EL and hazard that its higher-order variance also coincides with that of EL. Furthermore, this estimator should also have useful properties for misspecified moment conditions as discussed in Section 6.

2   GEL

We consider a model defined by a finite number of nonlinear moment restrictions. That is, the model has a true parameter β_0 satisfying the moment condition

$$E[g(z, \beta_0)] = 0,$$

where $g(z, \beta)$ is an m-vector of functions of the data observation z and β, a p-vector of parameters, $m \geq p$ and $E[.]$ denotes expectation taken with respect to the distribution of z. We assume throughout this discussion that z_i, $(i = 1, \dots, n)$, are i.i.d. observations on the data vector z.

Let $g_i(\beta) \equiv g(z_i, \beta)$, $\hat{g}(\beta) \equiv n^{-1} \sum_{i=1}^{n} g_i(\beta)$ and $\hat{\Omega}(\beta) \equiv n^{-1} \sum_{i=1}^{n} g_i(\beta) g_i(\beta)'$.

The class of GEL estimators, [NS, Smith (1997, 2001)], is based on $\rho(v)$, a function of a scalar v that is concave on its domain, an open interval $\mathcal{V}$ containing zero, and, without loss of generality, normalized with $\rho_1 = \rho_2 = -1$ where $\rho_j(v) = \partial^j \rho(v)/\partial v^j$ and $\rho_j = \rho_j(0)$, $(j = 0, 1, 2, \dots)$. Let $\hat{\Lambda}_n(\beta) = \{\lambda : \lambda' g_i(\beta) \in \mathcal{V}, i = 1, \dots, n\}$. The GEL estimator is the solution to a saddle point problem

$$\hat{\beta} = \arg \min_{\beta \in \mathcal{B}} \sup_{\lambda \in \hat{\Lambda}_n(\beta)} \sum_{i=1}^{n} \rho(\lambda' g_i(\beta)), \tag{2.1}$$

where $\mathcal{B}$ denotes the parameter space. Both EL and exponential tilting (ET) estimators are special cases of GEL with $\rho(v) = \log(1 - v)$ and $\mathcal{V} = (-\infty, 1)$, [Qin and Lawless (1994), Imbens (1997), and Smith (1997)] and $\rho(v) = -\exp(v)$, [Kitamura and Stutzer (1997), Imbens, Spady, and Johnson (1998), and Smith (1997)], respectively, as is the continuous updating estimator (CUE), [Hansen, Heaton, and Yaron (1996)], if $\rho(v)$ is quadratic as shown by NS (2004, Theorem 2.1, p. 223).[1]

We adopt the following assumptions from NS. Let $G \equiv E[\partial g(z, \beta_0)/\partial \beta']$, $\Omega \equiv E[g(z, \beta_0) g(z, \beta_0)']$, and $\mathcal{N}$ denote a neighborhood of β_0.

Assumption 2.1   (a) $\beta_0 \in \mathcal{B}$ is the unique solution to $E[g(z, \beta)] = 0$; (b) $\mathcal{B}$ is compact; (c) $g(z, \beta)$ is continuous at each $\beta \in \mathcal{B}$ with probability one; (d) $E\left[\sup_{\beta \in \mathcal{B}} \|g(z, \beta)\|^\alpha\right] < \infty$ for some $\alpha > 2$; (e) Ω is nonsingular; (f) $\rho(v)$ is twice continuously differentiable in a neighborhood of zero.

Assumption 2.2   (a) $\beta_0 \in int(\mathcal{B})$; (b) $g(z, \beta)$ is continuously differentiable in $\mathcal{N}$ and $E[\sup_{\beta \in \mathcal{N}} \|\partial g(z, \beta)/\partial \beta'\|] < \infty$; (c) $rank(G) = p$.

Assumption 2.1 is sufficient for the consistency of $\hat{\beta}$ for β_0 whereas taken together with Assumption 2.2 the large sample normality of $\hat{\beta}$ and $\hat{\lambda}$ may be shown. See NS, Theorems 3.1 and 3.2.

Let $\hat{\lambda} \equiv \hat{\lambda}(\hat{\beta})$ where $\hat{\lambda}(\beta) \equiv \arg \sup_{\lambda \in \hat{\Lambda}_n(\beta)} \sum_{i=1}^{n} \rho(\lambda' g_i(\beta))/n$.

---

[1] The CUE is analogous to GMM and is given by $\hat{\beta}_{CUE} = \arg \min_{\beta \in \mathcal{B}} \hat{g}(\beta)' \hat{\Omega}(\beta)^- \hat{g}(\beta)$, where A^- denotes any generalized inverse of a matrix A satisfying $AA^-A = A$. The two-step GMM estimator is $\hat{\beta}_{GMM} = \arg \min_{\beta \in \mathcal{B}} \hat{g}(\beta)' \hat{\Omega}(\tilde{\beta})^{-1} \hat{g}(\beta)$, where $\tilde{\beta}$ is some preliminary consistent estimator for β_0.

Theorem 2.1 *If Assumptions 2.1 and 2.2 are satisfied then*

$$n^{1/2} \begin{pmatrix} \hat{\beta} - \beta_0 \\ \hat{\lambda} \end{pmatrix} \xrightarrow{d} N(0, \text{diag}(\Sigma, P)),$$

$$2n \left[\sum_{i=1}^{n} \rho(\hat{\lambda}' g_i(\hat{\beta}))/n - \rho_0 \right] \xrightarrow{d} \chi^2(m - p),$$

where $\Sigma \equiv (G' \Omega^{-1} G)^{-1}$ *and* $P \equiv \Omega^{-1} - \Omega^{-1} G \Sigma G' \Omega^{-1}$.

Given $\rho(v)$, empirical probabilities for the observations may also be described

$$\pi_i(\beta) \equiv \frac{\rho_1(\hat{\lambda}(\beta)' g_i(\beta))}{\sum_{j=1}^{n} \rho_1(\hat{\lambda}(\beta)' g_j(\beta))}, \quad (i = 1, \dots, n); \tag{2.2}$$

cf. Back and Brown (1993). The GEL empirical probabilities $\pi_i(\beta)$, $(i = 1, \dots, n)$, sum to one by construction, satisfy the sample moment condition $\sum_{i=1}^{n} \pi_i(\beta) g_i(\beta) = 0$ when the first-order conditions for $\hat{\lambda}(\beta)$ hold, and are positive when $\hat{\lambda}(\hat{\beta})' \hat{g}_i(\hat{\beta})$ is small uniformly in i. From Brown and Newey (1998), $\sum_{i=1}^{n} \pi_i(\hat{\beta}) a(z_i, \hat{\beta})$ is a semiparametrically efficient estimator of $E[a(z, \beta_0)]$.

3 WEAK IDENTIFICATION

This section addresses weak identification when the moment indicators are nonlinear in β. The setup used here is based on Guggenberger and Smith (2005a), henceforth GS.

Assumption 2.1 (a) implies that β_0 is strongly identified, a conclusion that Assumption 2.2 (c) makes explicit. Therefore, we will need to revise these assumptions appropriately to address weak identification of β_0. As is now well documented, standard GMM and GEL estimators in the weakly identified context are inconsistent and have limiting representations which depend on parameters which cannot be consistently estimated rendering their use for estimation and inference purposes currently infeasible. See Stock and Wright (2000) for results on GMM and GS for GEL. In particular, the limit normal distributions of Theorem 2.1 will no longer hold. As a consequence, and similarly to AS, recent research for the nonlinear case has sought acceptance regions of tests for $\beta = \beta_0$ based on asymptotically pivotal statistics which may then be inverted to provide well-defined interval estimates for β_0.

We will require some additional notation. Let $G(z, \beta) \equiv \partial g(z, \beta)/\partial \beta'$ and $G_i(\beta) \equiv G(z_i, \beta)$.

Our interest will concern tests for the hypothesis $H_0 : \beta = \beta_0$. To make transparent the relation between the analysis in AS and that for GEL-based procedures, we treat the Jacobian matrix G as mp additional parameters to be estimated with associated moment conditions

$$E[G(z, \beta_0) - G] = 0. \tag{3.1}$$

The resultant GEL criterion which incorporates the hypothesis $H_0 : \beta = \beta_0$ is then $\sum_{i=1}^{n} \rho(\lambda' g_i(\beta_0) + \mu' vec(G_i(\beta_0) - G)))/n$ with the mp-vector μ of auxiliary parameters associated with the additional moment constraints (3.1). It is straightforward to see that the auxiliary parameter μ is estimated as identically zero. Thus, the auxiliary parameter estimator $\tilde{\lambda} = \hat{\lambda}(\beta_0)$. Moreover, the corresponding GEL estimator for G is given by

$$\tilde{G} = \sum_{i=1}^{n} \pi_i(\beta_0) G_i(\beta_0), \tag{3.2}$$

where the empirical probabilities $\pi_i(\beta_0)$, $(i = 1, \ldots, n)$, are defined in (2.2).[2]

To describe the weakly identified setup and to detail the limiting properties of the estimators, we adapt Assumptions Θ, ID, ρ, and M_θ of GS.

Assumption 3.1   (a) $\beta_0 \in int(\mathcal{B})$; (b) $\mathcal{B}$ is compact.

Assumption 3.2 $E[\hat{g}(\beta)] = n^{-1/2} m(\beta)$, where $m(\beta)$ is a continuous function of $\beta \in \mathcal{B}$ and $m(\beta_0) = 0$.

Assumption 3.3 $\rho(v)$ is twice continuously differentiable in a neighborhood of zero.

Assumption 3.2 encapsulates weak identification of β_0 in the nonlinear moment restrictions setting. Next we detail the necessary moment assumptions.

Assumption 3.4   (a) $E\left[\sup_{\beta \in \mathcal{B}} \|g(z, \beta)\|^\alpha\right] < \infty$ for some $\alpha > 2$; (b) $\Omega(\beta)$ is nonsingular; (c) $g(z, \beta)$ is continuously differentiable in $\mathcal{N}$ and $E[\sup_{\beta \in \mathcal{N}} \|\partial g_i(\beta)/\partial \beta'\|^\alpha] < \infty$ for some $\alpha > 2$; (d) $V(\beta) \equiv var[(g(z, \beta)', (vecG(z, \beta))')'] $ is positive definite.

Partition $V(\beta)$ conformably with $g(z, \beta)$ and $vecG(z, \beta)$ as

$$V(\beta) \equiv \begin{pmatrix} \Omega(\beta) & \Delta_G(\beta)' \\ \Delta_G(\beta) & \Delta_{GG}(\beta) \end{pmatrix}.$$

The hypotheses of GS Assumption M_θ are therefore satisfied. For example, from Assumptions 3.4 (a) and (c), by an i.i.d. WLLN, $\hat{\Omega}(\beta) \xrightarrow{P} \Omega(\beta)$ and $n^{-1} \sum_{i=1}^{n} g_i(\beta)(vecG_i(\beta))' \xrightarrow{P} \Delta_G(\beta)$. Furthermore, by an i.i.d. CLT, on $\mathcal{N}$, $n^{-1/2} \sum_{i=1}^{n} ((g_i(\beta) - E[g_i(\beta)])', (vec(G_i(\beta) - E[G_i(\beta)]))')' \xrightarrow{d} N(0, V(\beta))$.

---

[2] When G is strongly identified, the Jacobian estimator $\tilde{G}$ is an efficient estimator for G under $H_0 : \beta = \beta_0$; see Brown and Newey (1998).

Assumption 3.4 (c) ensures that $\partial E[\hat{g}(\beta)]/\partial \beta' = E[\partial \hat{g}(\beta)/\partial \beta']$ on $\mathcal{N}$ and, thus, from Assumption 3.2, $E[\hat{G}(\beta)] = n^{-1/2}M(\beta)$ where $M(\beta) \equiv \partial m(\beta)/\partial \beta'$.

The following theorem is the counterpart to Theorem 2.1 above for the weakly identified context.[3]

Theorem 3.1   *Under Assumptions 3.1–3.4,*

$$n^{1/2}\begin{pmatrix} \tilde{\lambda} \\ vec(\tilde{G}) \end{pmatrix} \overset{d}{\to} N((0', (vecM)')', \mathrm{diag}(\Omega^{-1}, \Delta_{GG} - \Delta_G'\Omega^{-1}\Delta_G)),$$

where $M \equiv M(\beta_0)$, $\Delta_{GG} \equiv \Delta_{GG}(\beta_0)$ *and* $\Delta_G \equiv \Delta_G(\beta_0)$.

To aid comparison with AMS and AS, we will assume that $p = 1$ in the remainder of this section unless otherwise indicated. AS concentrated their search for optimal tests of the hypothesis $H_0 : \beta = \beta_0$ on invariant and similar tests. Invariance restricts attention to statistics based on the random matrix Q whereas similarity requires consideration of tests defined in terms of Q conditional on Q_T. See AS, sections 7.2 and 7.3.

First, note that $n^{1/2}\tilde{\lambda} = -\Omega^{-1}n^{1/2}\hat{g} + o_p(1)$. As a consequence, in large samples, it follows immediately from Theorem 3.1 that the normalized vectors

$$\tilde{S} \equiv \Omega^{-1/2}n^{1/2}\hat{g} \overset{d}{\to} Z_S \sim N(0, I_m),$$
$$\tilde{T} \equiv (\Delta_{GG} - \Delta_G'\Omega^{-1}\Delta_G)^{-1/2}n^{1/2}\tilde{G} \overset{d}{\to} Z_T \sim N(M, I_m),$$

and are mutually asymptotically independent.[4] Because they are constructed from analogous objects apposite for the nonlinear setting, the random vectors $\tilde{S}$ and $\tilde{T}$ parallel S and T respectively in AS in the construction of asymptotically pivotal statistics for tests of $H_0 : \beta = \beta_0$; cf. AS, eq. (7.13). Therefore, to make the analogy with AS explicit, define the random matrix $\tilde{Q}$ as

$$\tilde{Q} \equiv (\tilde{S}, \tilde{T})'(\tilde{S}, \tilde{T}) = \begin{pmatrix} \tilde{S}'\tilde{S} & \tilde{S}'\tilde{T} \\ \tilde{T}'\tilde{S} & \tilde{T}'\tilde{T} \end{pmatrix} = \begin{pmatrix} \tilde{Q}_S & \tilde{Q}_{ST} \\ \tilde{Q}_{TS} & \tilde{Q}_T \end{pmatrix}.$$

The matrices $\tilde{Q}$ and $\tilde{Q}_T$ thus mirror the maximal invariant Q and Q_T in AS, eq. (7.14). It follows from Theorem 3.1 that

$$\tilde{Q} \overset{d}{\to} (Z_S, Z_T)'(Z_S, Z_T)$$

---

[3] If Assumption 3.2 were modified as $E[\hat{g}(\beta)] = n^{-\tau}m(\beta)$, $\tau \in (0, 1]$, Theorem 3.1 would need to be altered appropriately, cf. AS, Theorem 1. Thus, (a) $\tau \in (0, 1/2)$, $n^{1/2}vec(\tilde{G}) \overset{d}{\to} N(0, \Delta_{GG} - \Delta_G'\Omega^{-1}\Delta_G)$ and all of the tests discussed below have trivial asymptotic power, (b) $\tau = 1/2$, the results are as stated in Theorems 3.1 and 3.2, (c) $\tau > 1/2$, $n^{1-\tau}\tilde{G} \overset{p}{\to} M(\beta_0)$ and the first-order large sample properties of the tests are as in the strongly identified case when $\tau = 1$.

[4] For expositional purposes only we will assume that the variance matrices Ω and $\Delta_{GG} - \Delta_G'\Omega^{-1}\Delta_G$ are known. As noted above, their components may be consistently estimated using the outer product form.

which is noncentral Wishart distributed with variance matrix I_2 and noncentrality parameter $(0, M)'(0, M)$. The asymptotic counterparts to Q and Q_T are thus $(Z_S, Z_T)'(Z_S, Z_T)$ and $Z_T'Z_T$.[5]

Therefore, statistics corresponding to the Anderson–Rubin (AR), Lagrange multiplier (LM) and likelihood ratio (LR) statistics in AS, eq. (7.15), also see AMS, eq. (3.4), may likewise be defined as

$$\widetilde{AR} = \tilde{Q}_S, \quad \widetilde{LM} = \tilde{Q}_{ST}^2/\tilde{Q}_T,$$

$$\widetilde{LR} = \frac{1}{2}\left(\tilde{Q}_S - \tilde{Q}_T + \sqrt{(\tilde{Q}_S - \tilde{Q}_T)^2 + 4\tilde{Q}_{ST}^2}\right).$$

That is, letting $\Delta \equiv \Delta_{GG} - \Delta_G'\Omega^{-1}\Delta_G$,

$$\widetilde{AR} \equiv n\hat{g}'\Omega^{-1}\hat{g},$$

$$\widetilde{LM} \equiv (n\tilde{G}'\Delta^{-1/2}\Omega^{-1/2}\hat{g})^2/(n\tilde{G}'\Delta^{-1}\tilde{G}),$$

$$\widetilde{LR} = \frac{1}{2}\left(\widetilde{AR} - n\tilde{G}'\Delta^{-1}\tilde{G}\right.$$

$$\left. + \sqrt{(\widetilde{AR} - n\tilde{G}'\Delta^{-1}\tilde{G})^2 + 4\widetilde{LM}(n\tilde{G}'\Delta^{-1}\tilde{G})}\right).$$

Theorem 3.2 *Let Assumptions 3.1–3.4 hold. Then, under $H_0 : \beta = \beta_0$, conditional on Z_T, $\widetilde{AR}$ and $\widetilde{LM}$ converge in distribution to chi-square random variables with m and one degrees of freedom respectively and $\widetilde{LR}$ converges in distribution to a random variable whose distribution is characterized by*

$$\frac{1}{2}\left(\chi^2(1) + \chi^2(m-1) - Z_T'Z_T\right.$$

$$\left. + \sqrt{(\chi^2(1) + \chi^2(m-1) - Z_T'Z_T)^2 + 4\chi^2(1)(Z_T'Z_T)}\right),$$

where $\chi^2(1)$ and $\chi^2(m-1)$ denote independent chi-square random variables with one and $m - 1$ degrees of freedom respectively.

The various statistics suggested in the literature may be related to $\widetilde{AR}$, $\widetilde{LM}$, and $\widetilde{LR}$. Asymptotic equivalence, denoted by $=^a$, is under $H_0 : \beta = \beta_0$.

First, analogues of $\widetilde{AR}$ may be constructed using the GEL criterion function statistic and the auxiliary parameter estimator $\tilde{\lambda}$, viz.

$$\mathcal{GELR}(\beta_0) \equiv 2\sum_{i=1}^{n}(\rho(\tilde{\lambda}'g_i(\beta_0)) - \rho_0)$$

$$=^a n\tilde{\lambda}'\Omega\tilde{\lambda}$$

$$=^a n\hat{g}'\Omega^{-1}\hat{g}.$$

[5] It is interesting to note that when G is strongly identified $\tilde{G}'\Omega^{-1}\tilde{G}$ is an estimator for the semiparametric counterpart of the information matrix in fully parametric models. Conditioning on such objects or their asymptotic representations, i.e., $\tilde{G}$ or Z_T here, follows a long tradition in statistics. See, for example, Reid (1995).

Stock and Wright (2000) suggested the CUE version of $\widetilde{AR}$. The quadratic form statistics in $\tilde{\lambda}$ and $\hat{g}$ for CUE are given in Kleibergen (2005) for CUE, in which case they coincide, and for GEL by GS. GS also suggest the GEL criterion function statistic $\mathcal{GELR}(\beta_0)$. Caner (2003) also describes similar statistics based on ET.

Secondly, LM and score statistics that have appeared in the literature are adaptations of statistics suggested in Newey and West (1987). These statistics use a slightly different normalization to that for $\widetilde{LM}$ given above although their limiting distribution remains that of a chi-square random variable with one degree of freedom, *viz.*

$$\mathcal{LM}(\beta_0) \equiv (n\tilde{G}'\Omega^{-1}\hat{g})^2/(n\tilde{G}'\Omega^{-1}\tilde{G})$$
$$= {}^a(n\tilde{G}'\tilde{\lambda})^2/(n\tilde{G}'\Omega^{-1}\tilde{G})$$
$$\equiv \mathcal{S}(\beta_0).$$

Kleibergen (2005) details the Lagrange multiplier $\mathcal{LM}(\beta_0)$ statistic for CUE, which again coincides with the score statistic $\mathcal{S}(\beta_0)$.[6] GS describe $\mathcal{LM}(\beta_0)$ and $\mathcal{S}(\beta_0)$ for GEL whereas Caner (2003) gives their ET counterparts. Otsu (2006) suggests an alternative statistic based on the GEL criterion which is related and asymptotically equivalent to $\mathcal{LM}(\beta_0)$ and $\mathcal{S}(\beta_0)$. Let $\tilde{G}_i(\beta_0) \equiv \pi_i(\beta_0)G_i(\beta_0)$ and define $\tilde{\xi} \equiv \arg\max_{\xi \in \hat{\Xi}_n(\beta_0)} \sum_{i=1}^n \rho(\xi'\tilde{G}_i(\beta_0)'\Omega^{-1}g_i(\beta_0))/n$ where $\hat{\Xi}_n(\beta) \equiv \{\xi : \xi'\tilde{G}_i(\beta)'\Omega^{-1}g_i(\beta) \in \mathcal{V}, i = 1, \ldots, n\}$. The statistic is then given by $2\sum_{i=1}^n (\rho(\tilde{\xi}'\tilde{G}_i(\beta_0)'\Omega^{-1}g_i(\beta_0)) - \rho_0)$ but requires two maximizations, one for $\tilde{\lambda}$ in $\tilde{G}_i(\beta_0)$ and the other for $\tilde{\xi}$. As noted in Guggenberger and Smith (2005b), the latter maximization may be simply avoided by the substitution of either $-(\tilde{G}'\Omega^{-1}\tilde{G})^{-1}\tilde{G}'\Omega^{-1}\hat{g}(\beta_0)$ or $(\tilde{G}'\Omega^{-1}\tilde{G})^{-1}\tilde{G}'\tilde{\lambda}$ for $\tilde{\xi}$. The function $\rho(v)$ used to obtain $\tilde{\lambda}$ in $\tilde{G}$ may be different from that defining the statistic as long as both satisfy Assumption 3.3.

Finally, numerous analogues of $\widetilde{LR}$ may also be described. For example,

$$\mathcal{LR}(\beta_0) \equiv \frac{1}{2}\left(\mathcal{GELR}(\beta_0) - n\tilde{G}'\Delta^{-1}\tilde{G} \right.$$
$$\left. + \sqrt{(\mathcal{GELR}(\beta_0) - n\tilde{G}'\Delta^{-1}\tilde{G})^2 + 4\widetilde{LM}(n\tilde{G}'\Delta^{-1}\tilde{G})} \right),$$

in which $\widetilde{AR}$ has been replaced by the GEL criterion function statistic $\mathcal{GELR}(\beta_0)$ (or $n\tilde{\lambda}'\Omega\tilde{\lambda}$). Similarly, $\widetilde{LM}$ might be replaced by $\mathcal{LM}(\beta_0)$ or $\mathcal{S}(\beta_0)$ with Δ substituted by Ω. A CUE version of $\mathcal{LR}(\beta_0)$ was proposed in Kleibergen (2005, eq. (31), p. 1113) in which $\mathcal{LM}(\beta_0)$ and Ω replace $\widetilde{LM}$ and Δ. The limiting distribution of $\mathcal{LR}(\beta_0)$ with $\mathcal{GELR}(\beta_0)$ or $n\tilde{\lambda}'\Omega\tilde{\lambda}$ substituted for $\widetilde{AR}$ remains that for $\widetilde{LR}$ given in Theorem 3.2 above. If $\widetilde{LM}$ is replaced by $\mathcal{LM}(\beta_0)$

---

[6] It is interesting to note that Kleibergen's (2002) statistic for the single linear simultaneous equations model may be viewed as an adaptation of the CUE version of $\mathcal{LM}(\beta_0)$ which incorporates a homoskedastic error assumption. The resultant formulation for $\tilde{G}$ is thus that which arises in LIML estimation.

or $\mathcal{S}(\beta_0)$ and Δ by Ω, then the limiting representation must be altered by sub-stituting likewise $Z_T' \Delta^{1/2} \Omega^{-1} \Delta^{1/2} Z_T$ for $Z_T' Z_T$. Note that if $n\tilde{G}'\Delta^{-1}\tilde{G} \xrightarrow{p} \infty$, corresponding to the strong identification of G, then $\mathcal{LR}(\beta_0) - \mathcal{LM}(\beta_0) \xrightarrow{p} 0$, confirming the asymptotic equivalence of these statistics in this circumstance, cf. AS, section 7.4.

The large sample representation for $\widetilde{LR}$, $\mathcal{LR}(\beta_0)$ or any of its analogues may easily be consistently estimated by simulation, thus enabling an asymp-totically valid interval estimator for β_0 to be obtained by inversion of the ac-ceptance region of the LR-type test for $H_0 : \beta = \beta_0$. Given $\tilde{G}$, realizations of $\mathcal{LR}(\beta_0)$ based on its limiting representation are given from simulation of independent chi-square random variables with one and $m - 1$ degrees of free-dom respectively. An estimator of the asymptotic conditional distribution func-tion of $\mathcal{LR}(\beta_0)$ given Z_T may then be simply obtained [cf. Kleibergen (2005, p. 1114)].

When $p > 1$, Kleibergen (2005, section 5.1, pp. 1113–5) suggests replacing $n\tilde{G}'\Omega^{-1}\tilde{G}$ in the CUE version of $\mathcal{LR}(\beta_0)$, after substitution of Ω and $\mathcal{LM}(\beta_0)$ for Δ and $\widetilde{LM}$ respectively, by a statistic which incorporates $H_0 : \beta = \beta_0$ ap-propriate for testing $rk[G] = p - 1$ against $rk[G] = p$ based on $\tilde{G}$. Examples of such statistics are given in Cragg and Donald (1996, 1997), Kleibergen and Paap (2006), and Robin and Smith (2000).

4 GMC AND GEL

K provides an information-theoretic characterization of GMC estimators which includes EL as a special case. Corcoran (1998) formulated a general class of MD estimators which are the empirical counterparts of those GMC estimators detailed in K. NS, see also Newey and Smith (2001), compared GEL with the MD type of estimator discussed by Corcoran (1998) which helps explain the form of the probabilities in (2.2) and connects their results with the existing literature.

Let $h(\pi)$ be a convex function that can depend on n of a scalar π that measures the discrepancy between π and the empirical probability $1/n$ of a single observation. Consider the optimization problem

$$\min_{\pi_1,\dots,\pi_n,\beta} \sum_{i=1}^{n} h(\pi_i), \ s.t. \ \sum_{i=1}^{n} \pi_i g_i(\beta) = 0, \ \sum_{i=1}^{n} \pi_i = 1. \tag{4.3}$$

The resultant MD estimator is defined by

$$\hat{\beta}_{MD} = \arg \min_{\beta \in \mathcal{B}, \pi_1,\dots,\pi_n} \sum_{i=1}^{n} h(\pi_i), \ s.t. \ \sum_{i=1}^{n} \pi_i g_i(\beta) = 0, \ \sum_{i=1}^{n} \pi_i = 1.$$

Like GEL, this class also includes as special cases EL, ET, and CUE, where $h(\pi)$ is $-\log(\pi)$, $\pi \log(\pi)$, and $[(n\pi)^2 - 1]/2n$ respectively together with members of the Cressie–Read (1984) family of power divergence criteria discussed below. When the solutions $\hat{\pi}_1, \dots, \hat{\pi}_n$ of this problem are nonnegative, they can be interpreted as empirical probabilities that minimize the discrepancy with the empirical measure subject to the moment conditions.

To relate MD and GEL estimators we compare their first-order conditions. For an m-vector of Lagrange multipliers $\hat{\alpha}_{MD}$ associated with the first constraint and a scalar $\hat{\mu}_{MD}$ for the second in (4.3), the MD first-order conditions for $\hat{\pi}_i$ are $h_\pi(\hat{\pi}_i) = -\hat{\alpha}'_{MD}g_i(\hat{\beta}_{MD}) + \hat{\mu}_{MD}$ which, if $h_\pi(.)$ is one-to-one, may be solved for $\hat{\pi}_i$, $(i = 1, \ldots, n)$. Substituting into the first-order conditions for $\hat{\beta}_{MD}$, $\hat{\alpha}_{MD}$ and $\hat{\mu}_{MD}$ gives

$$\sum_{i=1}^{n} h_\pi^{-1}(-\hat{\alpha}'_{MD}g_i(\hat{\beta}_{MD}) + \hat{\mu}_{MD})G_i(\hat{\beta}_{MD})'\hat{\alpha}_{MD} = 0, \qquad (4.4)$$

$$\sum_{i=1}^{n} h_\pi^{-1}(-\hat{\alpha}'_{MD}g_i(\hat{\beta}_{MD}) + \hat{\mu}_{MD})g_i(\hat{\beta}_{MD}) = 0,$$

and $\sum_{i=1}^{n} h_\pi^{-1}(-\hat{\alpha}'_{MD}g_i(\hat{\beta}_{MD}) + \hat{\mu}_{MD}) = 1$. For comparison, the GEL first-order conditions are

$$\sum_{i=1}^{n} \rho_1(\hat{\lambda}'g_i(\hat{\beta}))G_i(\hat{\beta})'\hat{\lambda} = 0, \qquad (4.5)$$

$$\sum_{i=1}^{n} \rho_1(\hat{\lambda}'g_i(\hat{\beta}))g_i(\hat{\beta}) = 0.$$

In general, the first-order conditions for GEL and MD are different, and hence so are the estimators of β. However, if $h_\pi^{-1}(\cdot)$ is homogenous, the Lagrange multiplier $\hat{\mu}_{MD}$ can be factored out of (4.4). Then the first-order conditions (4.4) and (4.5) coincide for

$$\hat{\lambda} = \hat{\alpha}_{MD}/\hat{\mu}_{MD}. \qquad (4.6)$$

In this case the GEL saddle point problem is a dual of the MD one, in the sense that $\hat{\lambda}$ is a ratio of Lagrange multipliers (4.6) from MD. If $h_\pi^{-1}(\cdot)$ is not homogenous, MD and GEL estimators are different. In general, though, for large n, the GEL class is obtained from a much smaller-dimensional optimization problem than MD and is consequently computationally less complex. Duality also justifies the GEL empirical probabilities $\pi_i(\beta)$ (2.2) as MD estimates which may thus be used to efficiently estimate the distribution of the data by $\widehat{\mathcal{P}}\{z \leq c\} = \sum_{i=1}^{n} \pi_i(\hat{\beta})\mathbb{I}(z_i \leq c)$.

A particular example of the relationship between MD and GEL occurs when $h(\cdot)$ is a member of the Cressie–Read (1984) power divergence criteria in which $h(\pi) = [\gamma(\gamma + 1)]^{-1}[(n\pi)^{\gamma+1} - 1]/n$. We interpret expressions as limits for $\gamma = 0$ or $\gamma = -1$. In this case $h_\pi^{-1}(\cdot)$ is homogenous and, hence, for each MD estimator there is a dual GEL estimator in this case. The following is Theorem 2.2, p. 224, in NS.[7]

---

[7] Duality between MD and GEL estimators occurs for EL when $\gamma = -1$, for ET when $\gamma = 0$ and for CUE when $\gamma = 1$ as well as for all the other members of the Cressie–Read (1984) family.

Theorem 4.1 *If $g(z, \beta)$ is continuously differentiable in β, for some scalar γ*

$$\rho(v) = -(1 + \gamma v)^{(\gamma+1)/\gamma}/(\gamma + 1), \tag{4.7}$$

the solutions to (2.1) and (4.3) occur in the interior of $\mathcal{B}$, $\hat{\lambda}$ exists, and $\sum_{i=1}^{n} \rho_2(\hat{\lambda}' \hat{g}_i) \hat{g}_i \hat{g}_i'$ is nonsingular, then the first-order conditions for GEL and MD coincide for $\hat{\beta} = \hat{\beta}_{MD}$, $\pi_i(\hat{\beta}) = \hat{\pi}_i^{MD}$, $(i = 1, \dots, n)$, and $\hat{\lambda} = \hat{\alpha}_{MD}/(\gamma \hat{\mu}_{MD})$ for $\gamma \neq 0$ and $\hat{\lambda} = \hat{\alpha}_{MD}$ for $\gamma = 0$.

5 ASYMPTOTIC BIAS

Schennach (2004) recently reconsidered EL and examined an alternative estimator, exponentially tilted empirical likelihood EL(ET), which embeds the ET implied probabilities in the EL criterion function. EL(ET) has been considered elsewhere by Jing and Wood (1996) and Corcoran (1998, section 4, pp. 971–972). Although the EL(ET) criterion is not Bartlett correctable, see Jing and Wood (1996), Schennach (2004) proves that EL(ET) possesses the same higher-order bias and variance properties as EL and, hence, like EL, is higher-order efficient among bias-corrected estimators.

Rather than, as Schennach (2004) suggests, embedding the ET implied probabilities in the EL criterion, we substitute the GEL implied probabilities. Given a suitable choice for $\rho(v)$, even with unbounded $g_i(\beta)$, the implied probabilities $\pi_i(\beta)$ (2.2) will always be positive, for example, members of the Cressie–Read family for which $\gamma \leq 0$.[8] As a consequence, the EL(GEL) criterion is defined as

$$\log \mathcal{L}_{EL(GEL)}(\beta) = \sum_{i=1}^{n} \log \pi_i(\beta)/n$$

$$= \sum_{i=1}^{n} \log \rho_1(\hat{\lambda}(\beta)' g_i(\beta))/n - \log \sum_{j=1}^{n} \rho_1(\hat{\lambda}(\beta)' g_j(\beta))/n,$$

where $\hat{\lambda}(\beta)$ is defined in Section 2 and satisfies $\sum_{i=1}^{n} \rho_1(\hat{\lambda}(\beta)' g_i(\beta)) g_i(\beta) = 0$. We show that EL(GEL) shares the same bias properties as EL.

The following assumption mirrors the hypotheses of Schennach (2004, Theorem 5).

Assumption 5.1 (a) $E[\sup_{\beta \in \mathcal{N}} \|g_i(\beta)\|^4] < \infty$ and $E[\sup_{\beta \in \mathcal{N}} \|G_i(\beta)\|^2] < \infty$; (b) for each $\beta \in \mathcal{N}$, $\|\partial g(z, \beta)/\partial \beta' - \partial g(z, \beta_0)/\partial \beta'\| \leq b(z)\|\beta - \beta_0\|$ such that $E[b(z)] < \infty$; (d) $\rho(v)$ is four times continuously differentiable with Lipschitz fourth derivative in a neighborhood of zero.

---

[8] Negative $\pi_i(\beta)$ may be avoided by incorporating a shrinkage factor; *viz.*

$$\pi_i^*(\beta) = \frac{1}{1 - \varepsilon_n} \pi_i(\beta) - \frac{\varepsilon_n}{1 - \varepsilon_n} \frac{1}{n},$$

where $\varepsilon_n = n \min[\min_{1 \leq i \leq n} \pi_i(\beta), 0]$. Cf. Bonnal and Renault (2003).

The next theorem follows as a consequence.

Theorem 5.5   *Let Assumptions 2.1, 2.2, and 5.1 hold. Then*

$$\hat{\beta}_{EL(GEL)} - \hat{\beta}_{EL} = O_p(n^{-3/2}).$$

An immediate consequence of Theorem 5.1 is that the EL(GEL) and EL estimators share the same asymptotic bias. Hence, we adopt Assumption 3 in NS; *viz.*

Assumption 5.2   *There is $b(z)$ with $E[b(z_i)^6] < \infty$ such that for $0 \le j \le 4$ and all z, $\nabla^j g(z, \beta)$ exists on a neighborhood $\mathcal{N}$ of β_0, $\sup_{\beta \in \mathcal{N}} \|\nabla^j g(z, \beta)\| \le b(z)$, and for each $\beta \in \mathcal{N}$, $\|\nabla^4 g(z, \beta) - \nabla^4 g(z, \beta_0)\| \le b(z)\|\beta - \beta_0\|$, $\rho(v)$ is four times continuously differentiable with Lipschitz fourth derivative in a neighborhood of zero.*

Let $H \equiv \Sigma G' \Omega^{-1}$ and $a(\beta_0)$ be an m-vector such that

$$a_j(\beta_0) \equiv tr(\Sigma E[\partial^2 g_{ij}(\beta_0)/\partial \beta \partial \beta'])/2, (j = 1, \dots, m), \qquad (5.8)$$

where $g_{ij}(\beta)$ denotes the jth element of $g_i(\beta)$, and e_j the jth unit vector. Therefore,

Theorem 5.2   *If Assumptions 2.1, 2.2, and 5.2 are satisfied, then to $O(n^{-2})$*

$$Bias\,(\hat{\beta}_{EL(GEL)}) = H(-a(\beta_0) + E[G_i(\beta_0) H g_i(\beta_0)])/n.$$

Cf. NS, Theorem 4.1, p. 228, and Corollary 4.3, p. 229.

Given the $O_p(n^{-3/2})$ equivalence between EL and EL(GEL) estimators, an open question remains concerning whether EL(GEL) is also higher-order efficient, sharing the same higher-order variance as EL and EL(ET).

6   MISSPECIFICATION

Schennach (2004, Theorem 1) also proves that, when the moment condition model is misspecified, EL is no longer root-n consistent for its pseudo true value (PTV) if $g(z, \beta)$ has unbounded support. The difficulty for EL under misspecification arises because its influence function is unbounded, a property shared by other members of the Cressie–Read family for which $\gamma < 0$, whereas that for ET is, see Imbens, Spady and Johnson (1998, p. 337). Schennach (2004, Theorem 10) shows that EL(ET) is, however, root-n consistent for its PTV which may be advantageous for the properties of ET *vis-à-vis* EL. We provide a similar result below for EL(GEL) estimators defined for GEL criteria with bounded influence functions under misspecification, that is, if there exists no $\beta \in \mathcal{B}$ such that $E[g(z, \beta)] = 0$.

Following Schennach (2004), we reformulate the estimation problem as a just-identified GMM system to facilitate the derivation of the large sample properties of EL(GEL) by the introduction of the additional auxiliary scalar and m-vector parameters ρ_1 and μ. Computationally, of course, this reparameterization is unnecessary to obtain the EL(GEL) estimators.

For brevity, we write $g_i \equiv g_i(\beta)$, $G_i \equiv G_i(\beta)$, $\rho_{1i} \equiv \rho_1(\lambda' g_i)$ and $\rho_{2i} \equiv \rho_2(\lambda' g_i), (i = 1, \ldots, n)$. The EL(GEL) and auxiliary parameter estimators may then be obtained *via* the following lemma; cf. Schennach (2004, Lemma 9).

Lemma 6.1 *The EL(GEL) and auxiliary parameter estimators $\hat{\beta}_{EL(GEL)}$ and $\hat{\lambda}_{EL(GEL)}$ are given as appropriate subvectors of $\hat{\theta} = (\hat{\rho}_1, \hat{\mu}', \hat{\lambda}, \hat{\beta})'$ which is the solution to*

$$\sum_{i=1}^{n} \psi(z_i, \hat{\theta})/n = 0,$$

where

$$\psi(z_i, \theta) \equiv \begin{pmatrix} \rho_{1i} - \rho_1 \\ \rho_{1i} g_i \\ (\rho_{2i} g_i g_i')\mu + ((\rho_1 \rho_{2i}/\rho_{1i}) - \rho_{2i})g_i \\ \rho_{1i} G_i' \mu + \rho_{2i} G_i' \lambda g_i' \mu + ((\rho_1 \rho_{2i}/\rho_{1i}) - \rho_{2i})G_i' \lambda \end{pmatrix}.$$

Likewise, see Schennach (2004, eq. (30)), the structure of the moment indicator vector $\psi(z_i, \theta)$ becomes more transparent when re-expressed as

$$\psi(z_i, \theta) = \begin{pmatrix} \rho_{1i} - \rho_1 \\ \partial(\rho_{1i} g_i' \mu + \rho_1 \log(\rho_{1i} \exp(-\rho_{1i}/\rho_1)))/\partial\mu \\ \partial(\rho_{1i} g_i' \mu + \rho_1 \log(\rho_{1i} \exp(-\rho_{1i}/\rho_1)))/\partial\lambda \\ \partial(\rho_{1i} g_i' \mu + \rho_1 \log(\rho_{1i} \exp(-\rho_{1i}/\rho_1)))/\partial\beta \end{pmatrix}.$$

Let $\lambda(\beta)$ be the unique solution of $E[\rho_1(\lambda' g(z, \beta))g(z, \beta)] = 0$ which exists by the concavity of $\rho(\cdot)$. We also define $\mathcal{N}$ as a neighborhood of the PTV β_*, see Assumption 6.1 (b) below, and $P(\beta) \equiv E[\rho(\lambda(\beta)'(g(z, \beta) - E[g(z, \beta)]))]$. The following assumption adapts Schennach (2004, Assumption 3) for EL(GEL). Let $g^j(z, \beta)$ be the jth element of $g(z, \beta), (j = 1, \ldots, m)$.

Assumption 6.1 (a) $\mathcal{B}$ *is compact;* (b) $P(\beta)$ *is minimized at the unique PTV $\beta_* \in int(\mathcal{B})$;* (c) $g(z, \beta)$ *is continuous at each $\beta \in \mathcal{B}$ with probability one;* (d) $\Lambda(\beta)$ *is a compact set such that $\lambda(\beta) \in \Lambda(\beta)$ and $E[\sup_{\beta \in \mathcal{B}} \sup_{\lambda \in \Lambda(\beta)} |\rho(\lambda' g(z, \beta))|] < \infty$;* (e) $g(z, \beta)$ *is twice continuously differentiable on $\mathcal{N}$;* (f) *there is $b(z)$ with $E[\sup_{\beta \in \mathcal{N}} \sup_{\lambda \in \Lambda(\beta)} \prod_{j=1}^{3} |\rho_j(\lambda' g(z, \beta))|^{k_j} b(z)^k] < \infty$ for $0 \le k \le 4$ such that $\|g(z, \beta)\|$, $\|\partial g(z, \beta)/\partial\beta'\|$, $\|\partial^2 g^j(z, \beta)/\partial\beta\partial\beta'\| < b(z)$, $(j = 1, \ldots, m)$, and $k_3 = 0$ unless $-1 \le k_1 \le 0$, when $k_2 = 0$, $k_3 = 1$, if $-2 \le k_1 \le -1$, $k_2 = 2$ and if $0 \le k_1, k_2 \le 2, 1 \le k_1 + k_2 \le 2$.*

The just-identified GMM system based on the moment indicator vector $\psi(z, \theta)$ allows the use of standard results on the large sample behavior of GMM estimators to be employed, for example, Newey and McFadden (1994, Theorem 3.4, p. 2148).

Theorem 6.1 *Let $G_\theta^* = E[\partial \psi(z, \theta_*)/\partial \theta']$ and $\Omega_\theta^* = E[\psi(z, \theta_*)\psi(z, \theta_*)']$. If Assumption 6.1 satisfied and G_θ^* is nonsingular, then $n^{1/2}(\hat\theta - \theta_*) \overset{d}{\to} N(0, (G_\theta^*)^{-1}\Omega_\theta^*(G_\theta^*)'^{-1})$.*

APPENDIX: PROOFS

Proof of Theorem 3.2: Given Theorem 3.1, it is straightforward to see that, under $H_0 : \beta = \beta_0$, $\widetilde{AR}$ converges in distribution to $Z_S'Z_S$ and, thus, has a limiting $\chi^2(m)$ distribution. Similarly, $n\tilde{G}'\Delta^{-1/2}\Omega^{-1/2}\hat{g}$ converges in distribution to $Z_T'Z_S$. Given Z_T, $Z_T'Z_S \sim N(0, Z_T'Z_T)$ and, thus, $Z_T'Z_S/(Z_T'Z_T)^{1/2}$ is standard normally distributed and independent of $Z_T'Z_T$. Therefore, as $n\tilde{G}'\Delta^{-1}\tilde{G} \overset{d}{\to} Z_T'Z_T$, $\widetilde{LM}$ has a limiting $\chi^2(1)$ distribution under $H_0 : \beta = \beta_0$. Finally, $\widetilde{LR}$ converges in distribution to $(Z_S'Z_S - Z_T'Z_T + \sqrt{(Z_S'Z_S - Z_T'Z_T)^2 + 4(Z_T'Z_S)^2})/2$. Write $Z_S'Z_S = (Z_T'Z_S)^2/Z_T'Z_T + (Z_S'Z_S - (Z_T'Z_S)^2/Z_T'Z_T)$ which are independent $\chi^2(1)$ and $\chi^2(m - 1)$ random variates respectively independent of $Z_T'Z_T$. Therefore, conditionally on Z_T, $\widetilde{LR}$ has a limiting distribution described by

$$\frac{1}{2}\left(\chi^2(1) + \chi^2(m - 1) - Z_T'Z_T \right.$$

$$\left. + \sqrt{(\chi^2(1) + \chi^2(m - 1) - Z_T'Z_T)^2 + 4\chi^2(1)(Z_T'Z_T)}\right). \qquad \square$$

Proof of Theorem 5.1: Let $\hat{g}_i = g_i(\hat\beta)$, $\hat{G}_i = G_i(\hat\beta)$, $\hat\rho_{1i} = \rho_1(\hat\lambda'\hat{g}_i)$ and $\hat\rho_{2i} = \rho_2(\hat\lambda'\hat{g}_i)$, $(i = 1, \ldots, n)$. The first-order conditions defining the EL(GEL) estimator are

$$0 = \frac{\partial \hat\lambda(\hat\beta)'}{\partial \beta} \sum_{i=1}^n \left(\frac{1}{n\hat\rho_{1i}} - \frac{1}{\sum_{j=1}^n \hat\rho_{1j}}\right) \hat\rho_{2i}\hat{g}_i \qquad (A.1)$$

$$+ \sum_{i=1}^n \left(\frac{1}{n\hat\rho_{1i}} - \frac{1}{\sum_{j=1}^n \hat\rho_{1j}}\right) \hat\rho_{2i}\hat{G}_i'\hat\lambda,$$

cf. Schennach (2004, eq. (52)). As $\rho(v)$ is continuously differentiable to the fourth order, a similar argument to Schennach (2004, eq. (55)) yields

$$\hat\rho_{ji} = -1 + \rho_{j+1}\hat\lambda'\hat{g}_i + \frac{1}{2}\rho_{j+2}(\hat\lambda'\hat{g}_i)^2 + O_p(n^{-3/2})\|\hat{g}_i\|^3,$$

$$\sum_{k=1}^n \hat\rho_{jk}/n = -1 + O_p(n^{-1}), (j = 1, 2).$$

The remainders here and below are uniform in i, $(i = 1, \ldots, n)$. Hence, noting $\hat{g} = n^{-1} \sum_{i=1}^{n} \hat{g}_i = O_p(n^{-1/2})$ and $\hat{\lambda} = O_p(n^{-1/2})$,

$$\hat{\rho}_{2i} - \hat{\rho}_{1i} = (\rho_3 + 1)\hat{\lambda}'\hat{g}_i + \frac{1}{2}(\rho_4 - \rho_3)(\hat{\lambda}'\hat{g}_i)^2 + O_p(n^{-3/2})\|\hat{g}_i\|^3,$$

$$\frac{\hat{\rho}_{2i} - \hat{\rho}_{1i}}{\hat{\rho}_{1i}} = -(\rho_3 + 1)\hat{\lambda}'\hat{g}_i - \frac{1}{2}(\rho_4 - \rho_3)(\hat{\lambda}'\hat{g}_i)^2 + (\rho_3 + 1)(\hat{\lambda}'\hat{g}_i)^2$$

$$+ O_p(n^{-3/2})\|\hat{g}_i\|^3,$$

$$\frac{n(\hat{\rho}_{2i} - \hat{\rho}_{1i})}{\sum_{k=1}^{n} \hat{\rho}_{1k}} = -(\rho_3 + 1)\hat{\lambda}'\hat{g}_i - \frac{1}{2}(\rho_4 - \rho_3)(\hat{\lambda}'\hat{g}_i)^2$$

$$+ O_p(n^{-3/2})(\|\hat{g}_i\| + \|\hat{g}_i\|^2 + \|\hat{g}_i\|^3).$$

Therefore, after cancellation, substitution of these expressions in (A.1) yields

$$\sum_{i=1}^{n} \left(\frac{1}{n\hat{\rho}_{1i}} - \frac{1}{\sum_{j=1}^{n} \hat{\rho}_{1j}} \right) \hat{\rho}_{2i}\hat{g}_i = \frac{1}{n}\sum_{i=1}^{n}(1 - n\hat{\pi}_i)\hat{g}_i \qquad (A.2)$$

$$+ (\rho_3 + 1)\frac{1}{n}\sum_{i=1}^{n}(\hat{\lambda}'\hat{g}_i)^2\hat{g}_i + O_p(n^{-3/2})\frac{1}{n}\sum_{i=1}^{n}\|\hat{g}_i\|^3\,\hat{g}_i$$

$$= \hat{g} + (\rho_3 + 1)\frac{1}{n}\sum_{i=1}^{n}(\hat{\lambda}'\hat{g}_i)^2\hat{g}_i + O_p(n^{-3/2}),$$

as $\sum_{i=1}^{n} \hat{\pi}_i\hat{g}_i = 0$, where $\hat{\pi}_i = \pi_i(\hat{\beta})$, $(i = 1, \ldots, n)$. Furthermore,

$$\sum_{i=1}^{n} \left(\frac{1}{n\hat{\rho}_{1i}} - \frac{1}{\sum_{j=1}^{n} \hat{\rho}_{1j}} \right) \hat{\rho}_{2i}\hat{G}_i'\hat{\lambda} \qquad (A.3)$$

$$= \frac{1}{n}\sum_{i=1}^{n}(1 - n\hat{\pi}_i + O_p(n^{-1})\|\hat{g}_i\|^2)\hat{G}_i'\hat{\lambda}$$

$$= \frac{1}{n}\sum_{i=1}^{n}(1 - n\hat{\pi}_i)\hat{G}_i'\hat{\lambda} + O_p(n^{-3/2})$$

$$= -\frac{1}{n}\sum_{i=1}^{n}(\hat{\lambda}'\hat{g}_i)\hat{G}_i'\hat{\lambda} + O_p(n^{-3/2}),$$

as $n\hat{\pi}_i = 1 + \hat{\lambda}'\hat{g}_i + O_p(n^{-1})\|\hat{g}_i\|^2$, $(i = 1, \ldots, n)$; cf. Schennach (2004, eq. (57)).

Now, similarly to Schennach (2004, eq. (56)), from the first-order conditions determining $\hat{\lambda}(\beta)$, substituting for $n\hat{\pi}_i$, $(i = 1, \ldots, n)$,

$$\sum_{i=1}^{n} \hat{\pi}_i \hat{g}_i = \hat{g} + \frac{1}{n}\sum_{i=1}^{n} \hat{g}_i \hat{g}_i' \hat{\lambda} + O_p(n^{-1})\frac{1}{n}\sum_{i=1}^{n} \|\hat{g}_i\|^2 \hat{g}_i$$

$$= \hat{g} + \sum_{i=1}^{n} \hat{\pi}_i \hat{g}_i \hat{g}_i' \hat{\lambda} + \frac{1}{n}\sum_{i=1}^{n}(1 - n\hat{\pi}_i)\hat{g}_i \hat{g}_i' \hat{\lambda} + O_p(n^{-1})$$

$$= \hat{g} + \tilde{\Omega}\hat{\lambda} + O_p(n^{-1}),$$

where $\tilde{\Omega} = \sum_{i=1}^{n} \hat{\pi}_i \hat{g}_i \hat{g}_i'$. Hence, as $\tilde{\Omega} = O_p(1)$ and is p.d. w.p.a.1,

$$\hat{\lambda} = -\tilde{\Omega}^{-1}\hat{g} + O_p(n^{-1}). \tag{A.4}$$

Therefore, from (A.3),

$$\sum_{i=1}^{n}\left(\frac{1}{n\hat{\rho}_{1i}} - \frac{1}{\sum_{j=1}^{n} \hat{\rho}_{1j}}\right)\hat{\rho}_{2i}\hat{G}_i'\hat{\lambda} = \hat{g}'\tilde{\Omega}^{-1}\frac{1}{n}\sum_{i=1}^{n} \hat{g}_i \hat{G}_i'\hat{\lambda} + O_p(n^{-3/2}), \tag{A.5}$$

as $n^{-1}\sum_{i=1}^{n} \hat{g}_i \hat{G}_i'\hat{\lambda} = O_p(n^{-1/2})$.

The total differential of the first-order conditions determining $\hat{\lambda}(\beta)$ at $\hat{\beta}$ is

$$\sum_{i=1}^{n} \hat{\rho}_{2i}\hat{g}_i \hat{g}_i' d\hat{\lambda} + \sum_{i=1}^{n}[\hat{\rho}_{1i}I_m + \hat{\rho}_{2i}\hat{g}_i \hat{\lambda}']\hat{G}_i d\beta = 0.$$

Now,

$$\sum_{i=1}^{n}\left[\frac{\hat{\rho}_{1i}}{\sum_{j=1}^{n} \hat{\rho}_{1j}}I_m + \frac{\hat{\rho}_{2i}}{\sum_{j=1}^{n} \hat{\rho}_{1j}}\hat{g}_i \hat{\lambda}'\right]\hat{G}_i$$

$$= \sum_{i=1}^{n} \hat{\pi}_i \hat{G}_i + \sum_{i=1}^{n} \hat{\pi}_i \hat{g}_i \hat{\lambda}'\hat{G}_i$$

$$- \frac{1}{n}\sum_{i=1}^{n}\left[(\rho_3 + 1)\hat{\lambda}'\hat{g}_i + O_p(n^{-1})\|\hat{g}_i\|^2\right]\hat{g}_i \hat{\lambda}'\hat{G}_i$$

$$= \tilde{G} + \sum_{i=1}^{n} \hat{\pi}_i \hat{g}_i \hat{\lambda}'\hat{G}_i - (\rho_3 + 1)\frac{1}{n}\sum_{i=1}^{n} \hat{g}_i \hat{g}_i' \hat{\lambda}\hat{\lambda}'\hat{G}_i + O_p(n^{-3/2})$$

$$= \tilde{G} + \sum_{i=1}^{n} \hat{\pi}_i \hat{g}_i \hat{\lambda}'\hat{G}_i + O_p(n^{-1}),$$

where $\tilde{G} = \sum_{i=1}^{n} \hat{\pi}_i \hat{G}_i$. Therefore,

$$
\frac{\partial \hat{\lambda}(\hat{\beta})}{\partial \beta'} = -\tilde{\Omega}^{-1} \sum_{i=1}^{n} \left[\frac{\hat{\rho}_{1i}}{\sum_{j=1}^{n} \hat{\rho}_{1j}} I_m + \frac{\hat{\rho}_{2i}}{\sum_{j=1}^{n} \hat{\rho}_{1j}} \hat{g}_i \hat{\lambda}' \right] \hat{G}_i \qquad (A.6)
$$

$$
- \tilde{\Omega}^{-1} \sum_{i=1}^{n} \frac{\hat{\rho}_{2i} - \hat{\rho}_{1i}}{\sum_{k=1}^{n} \hat{\rho}_{1k}} \hat{g}_i \hat{g}_i' \frac{\partial \hat{\lambda}(\hat{\beta})}{\partial \beta'}
$$

$$
= -\tilde{\Omega}^{-1} \tilde{G} - \tilde{\Omega}^{-1} \sum_{i=1}^{n} \hat{\pi}_i \hat{g}_i \hat{\lambda}' \hat{G}_i + O_p(n^{-1})
$$

$$
+ (\rho_3 + 1)\tilde{\Omega}^{-1} \frac{1}{n} \sum_{i=1}^{n} (\hat{\lambda}' \hat{g}_i + O_p(n^{-1}) \|\hat{g}_i\|^2) \hat{g}_i \hat{g}_i' \frac{\partial \hat{\lambda}(\hat{\beta})}{\partial \beta'}
$$

$$
= -\tilde{\Omega}^{-1} \tilde{G} - \tilde{\Omega}^{-1} \sum_{i=1}^{n} \hat{\pi}_i \hat{g}_i \hat{\lambda}' \hat{G}_i + O_p(n^{-1})
$$

$$
- (\rho_3 + 1)\tilde{\Omega}^{-1} \frac{1}{n} \sum_{i=1}^{n} [(\hat{\lambda}' \hat{g}_i) \hat{g}_i \hat{g}_i' + O_p(n^{-1}) \|\hat{g}_i\|^4] \tilde{\Omega}^{-1} [\tilde{G} + O_p(n^{-1/2})]
$$

$$
= -\tilde{\Omega}^{-1} \tilde{G} - \tilde{\Omega}^{-1} \sum_{i=1}^{n} \hat{\pi}_i \hat{g}_i \hat{\lambda}' \hat{G}_i
$$

$$
- (\rho_3 + 1)\tilde{\Omega}^{-1} \frac{1}{n} \sum_{i=1}^{n} (\hat{\lambda}' \hat{g}_i) \hat{g}_i \hat{g}_i' \tilde{\Omega}^{-1} \tilde{G} + O_p(n^{-1});
$$

cf. Schennach (2004, eq. (54)).

Therefore, after substitution of (A.2) and (A.6) into the first term of the first-order conditions (A.1) defining the EL(GEL) estimator,

$$
\frac{\partial \hat{\lambda}(\hat{\beta})'}{\partial \beta} \sum_{i=1}^{n} \left(\frac{1}{n\hat{\rho}_{1i}} - \frac{1}{\sum_{j=1}^{n} \hat{\rho}_{1j}} \right) \hat{\rho}_{2i} \hat{g}_i \qquad (A.7)
$$

$$
= -\tilde{G}' \tilde{\Omega}^{-1} \hat{g} - (\rho_3 + 1)\tilde{G}' \tilde{\Omega}^{-1} \frac{1}{n} \sum_{i=1}^{n} \hat{g}_i (\hat{\lambda}' \hat{g}_i)^2
$$

$$
- \sum_{i=1}^{n} \hat{\pi}_i \hat{G}_i' \hat{\lambda} \hat{g}_i' \tilde{\Omega}^{-1} \hat{g}
$$

$$
- (\rho_3 + 1)\tilde{G}' \tilde{\Omega}^{-1} \frac{1}{n} \sum_{i=1}^{n} \hat{g}_i (\hat{\lambda}' \hat{g}_i) \hat{g}_i' \tilde{\Omega}^{-1} \hat{g} + O_p(n^{-3/2})
$$

$$
= -\tilde{G}' \tilde{\Omega}^{-1} \hat{g} - \sum_{i=1}^{n} \hat{\pi}_i \hat{G}_i' \hat{\lambda} \hat{g}_i' \tilde{\Omega}^{-1} \hat{g} + O_p(n^{-3/2}),
$$

where the second equality follows from (A.4). Combining (A.5) and (A.7) in (A.1) yields

$$
0 = -\tilde{G}' \tilde{\Omega}^{-1} \hat{g} + O_p(n^{-3/2}).
$$

As $n(\hat{\pi}_i - \hat{\pi}_i^{EL}) = O_p(n^{-1}) \|\hat{g}_i\|^2$, $(i = 1, \ldots, n)$, $\tilde{G} = \tilde{G}_{EL} + O_p(n^{-1})$ and $\tilde{\Omega} = \tilde{\Omega}_{EL} + O_p(n^{-1})$, where $\tilde{G}_{EL} = \sum_{i=1}^{n} \hat{\pi}_i^{EL} \hat{G}_i$, $\tilde{\Omega}_{EL} = \sum_{i=1}^{n} \hat{\pi}_i^{EL} \hat{g}_i \hat{g}_i'$ and $\hat{\pi}_i^{EL}$, $(i = 1, \ldots, n)$, denote the EL probabilities evaluated at the EL(GEL) estimator $\hat{\beta}$. Therefore, as $\hat{g} = O_p(n^{-1/2})$, the EL(GEL) estimator $\hat{\beta}$ satisfies the same first-order conditions as the EL estimator (to $O_p(n^{-3/2})$), $\tilde{G}_{EL}' \tilde{\Omega}_{EL}^{-1} \hat{g} = O_p(n^{-3/2})$, and so

$$\hat{\beta} - \hat{\beta}_{EL} = O_p(n^{-3/2}). \qquad \square$$

Proof of Lemma 6.1. Let $\hat{\rho}_{1i}(\beta) = \rho_1(\hat{\lambda}(\beta)g_i(\beta))$ and $\hat{\rho}_{2i}(\beta) = \rho_2(\hat{\lambda}(\beta)g_i(\beta))$, $(i = 1, \ldots, n)$. The total differential of the first-order conditions determining $\hat{\lambda}(\beta)$ at $\hat{\beta}$ is given by

$$\sum_{i=1}^{n} \hat{\rho}_{2i}(\beta)g_i(\beta)g_i(\beta)'d\hat{\lambda}(\beta) + \sum_{i=1}^{n} [\hat{\rho}_{1i}(\beta)I_m + \hat{\rho}_{2i}(\beta)g_i(\beta)\hat{\lambda}(\beta)']G_i(\beta)d\beta = 0,$$

from which the derivative matrix $\partial\hat{\lambda}(\beta)/\partial\beta'$ may be derived. Therefore, the first-order conditions defining the EL(GEL) and auxiliary parameter estimators are

$$0 = -\sum_{i=1}^{n} G_i' [\rho_{1i}I_m + \rho_{2i}\lambda g_i'] \left(\sum_{i=1}^{n} \rho_{2i}g_i g_i'\right)^{-1} \sum_{i=1}^{n} \left(\frac{1}{n\rho_{1i}} - \frac{1}{\sum_{j=1}^{n} \rho_{1j}}\right)\rho_{2i}g_i$$
$$+ \sum_{i=1}^{n} \left(\frac{1}{n\rho_{1i}} - \frac{1}{\sum_{j=1}^{n} \rho_{1j}}\right)\rho_{2i}G_i'\lambda$$
$$0 = \sum_{i=1}^{n} \rho_{1i}g_i.$$

Write the additional scalar and m-vector parameter estimators ρ_1 and μ as

$$\rho_1 \equiv \sum_{i=1}^{n} \rho_{1i}/n, \mu \equiv -\left(\sum_{i=1}^{n} \rho_{2i}g_i g_i'/n\right)^{-1} \sum_{i=1}^{n} ((\rho_1\rho_{2i}/\rho_{1i}) - \rho_{2i})g_i/n.$$

The first-order conditions determining ρ_1, μ, λ, and β then become

$$0 = \sum_{i=1}^{n} \begin{pmatrix} \rho_{1i} - \rho_1 \\ \rho_{1i}g_i \\ (\rho_{2i}g_i g_i')\mu + ((\rho_1\rho_{2i}/\rho_{1i}) - \rho_{2i})g_i \\ \rho_{1i}G_i'\mu + \rho_{2i}G_i'\lambda g_i'\mu + ((\rho_1\rho_{2i}/\rho_{1i}) - \rho_{2i})G_i'\lambda \end{pmatrix}$$
$$= \sum_{i=1}^{n} \begin{pmatrix} \rho_{1i} - \rho_1 \\ \partial(\rho_{1i}g_i'\mu - \rho_1\log(\rho_{1i}\exp(-\rho_{1i}/\rho_1)))/\partial\mu \\ \partial(\rho_{1i}g_i'\mu - \rho_1\log(\rho_{1i}\exp(-\rho_{1i}/\rho_1)))/\partial\lambda \\ \partial(\rho_{1i}g_i'\mu - \rho_1\log(\rho_{1i}\exp(-\rho_{1i}/\rho_1)))/\partial\beta \end{pmatrix}. \qquad \square$$

Proof of Theorem 6.1. The proof is an adaptation for EL(GEL) of that of Schennach (2004, Theorem 10). We first demonstrate consistency of $\hat{\beta}$ for β_* and $\hat{\lambda}(\hat{\beta})$ for $\lambda_* \equiv \lambda(\beta_*)$.

Now, from Assumptions 6.1 (a) and (b), by Newey and McFadden (1994, Lemma 2.4, p. 2129), $\hat{P}(\beta, \lambda) \equiv \sum_{i=1}^{n} \rho(\lambda'(g_i(\beta) - E[g(z, \beta)])) \xrightarrow{p} P(\beta, \lambda) \equiv E[\rho(\lambda'(g(z, \beta) - E[g(z, \beta)]))]$ uniformly $(\beta, \lambda) \in \mathcal{B} \times \Lambda(\beta)$. By a similar argument to that in Schennach (2004, Proof of Theorem 10), $\sup_{\beta \in \mathcal{B}} \|\bar{\lambda}(\beta) - \lambda(\beta)\| \to 0$ where $\bar{\lambda}(\beta) \equiv \arg\max_{\lambda \in \Lambda(\beta)} \sum_{i=1}^{n} \rho(\lambda' g_i(\beta))/n$. Likewise $\sup_{\beta \in \mathcal{B}} \|\hat{\lambda}(\beta) - \lambda(\beta)\| \xrightarrow{p} 0$.

Next, $\sup_{\beta \in \mathcal{B}} |\hat{P}(\beta, \hat{\lambda}(\beta)) - P(\beta, \lambda(\beta))| \xrightarrow{p} 0$ by Assumptions 6.1 (c) and (d) and the concavity of $\rho(\cdot)$. As $P(\beta, \lambda(\beta))$ is uniquely minimized at β_* from Assumption 6.1 (b), $\hat{\beta} \xrightarrow{p} \beta_*$ and, thus, $\hat{\lambda}(\hat{\beta}) \xrightarrow{p} \lambda(\beta_*)$.

Finally, $\hat{\rho}_1$ and $\hat{\mu}$ are explicit continuous functions of $\hat{\lambda}$ and $\hat{\beta}$. Let $g_* \equiv g(z, \beta_*)$. Hence,

$$\hat{\rho}_1 \xrightarrow{p} \rho_{1*} \equiv E\left[\rho_1(\lambda'_* g_*)\right],$$

$$\hat{\mu} \xrightarrow{p} \mu_* \equiv -(E\left[\rho_2(\lambda'_* g_*) g_* g'_*\right])^{-1}$$
$$\times E\left[((\rho_{1*}\rho_2(\lambda'_* g_*)/\rho_1(\lambda'_* g_*)) - \rho_2(\lambda'_* g_*))g_*\right],$$

noting that $E[\rho_2(\lambda'_* g_*) g_* g'_*]$ is nonsingular follows as G_θ^* is n.s.

To show the asymptotic normality of the EL(GEL) and auxiliary parameter estimators, from Newey and McFadden (1994, Theorem 3.4, p. 2148), we need to establish (a) $E[\sup_{\theta \in \Theta} \|\partial \psi(z, \theta)/\partial \theta'\|] < \infty$ and (b) $E[\psi(z, \theta_*)\psi(z, \theta_*)']$ exists. First, for (a), the normed derivative matrix $\|\partial \psi(z, \theta)/\partial \theta'\|$ (apart from multiplicative factors that are bounded) consists of terms like

$$\prod_{j=1}^{3} |\rho_j(\lambda' g(z, \beta))|^{k_j} \|g(z, \beta)\|^{k_{g0}} \|\partial g(z, \beta)/\partial \beta'\|^{k_{g1}} \|\partial^2 g^l(z, \beta)/\partial \beta \partial \beta'\|^{k_{g2}},$$

$$(l = 1, \ldots, m),$$

where $1 \leq k_{g0} + k_{g1} + k_{g1} \leq 3$, which is bounded by $\prod_{j=1}^{3} |\rho_j(\lambda' g(z, \beta))|^{k_j} b(z)^k$, $1 \leq k \leq 3$. The indices k_j, $(j = 1, 2, 3)$, obey (a) $k_3 = 0$ unless $-1 \leq k_1 \leq 0$ when $k_2 = 0$, $k_3 = 1$, (b) if $-2 \leq k_1 \leq -1$, $k_1 + k_2 = 0$, (c) if $0 \leq k_1 \leq 1$, $k_1 + k_2 = 1$ where $k_1, k_2 \geq 0$. Therefore, for some positive constant C,

$$E[\sup_{\theta \in \Theta} \|\partial \psi(z, \theta)/\partial \theta'\|] \leq CE\left[\sup_{\theta \in \Theta} \prod_{j=1}^{3} |\rho_j(\lambda' g(z, \beta))|^{k_j} b(z)^k\right]$$

$$= CE\left[\sup_{\beta \in \mathcal{B}} \sup_{\lambda \in \Lambda(\beta)} \prod_{j=1}^{3} |\rho_j(\lambda' g(z, \beta))|^{k_j} b(z)^k\right] < \infty.$$

Likewise, the normed matrix $\|\psi(z, \theta)\psi(z, \theta)'\|$ has terms of the form

$$\prod_{j=1}^{2} |\rho_j(\lambda'g(z, \beta))|^{k_j} \|g(z, \beta)\|^{k_{g0}} \|\partial g(z, \beta)/\partial \beta'\|^{k_{g1}} \|\partial^2 g^l(z, \beta)/\partial \beta \partial \beta'\|^{k_{g2}},$$

$$(l = 1, \ldots, m),$$

where $0 \le k_{g0} + k_{g1} + k_{g1} \le 4$, which is bounded by $\prod_{j=1}^{2} |\rho_j(\lambda'g(z, \beta))|^{k_j} b(z)^k$, $0 \le k \le 4$. The indices k_j, $(j = 1, 2)$, obey (a) if $-2 \le k_1 \le -1$, $k_2 = 2$, (b) if $k_1 = 0$, $1 \le k_2 \le 2$, (c) if $1 \le k_1 \le 2$, $k_1 + k_2 = 2$ where $k_2 \ge 0$. That $E[\psi(z, \theta_*)\psi(z, \theta_*)']$ exists then follows as above. $\square$

References

ANDREWS, D. W. K., M. J. MOREIRA, AND J. H. STOCK (2004): "Optimal Invariant Similar Tests for Instrumental Variables Regression," Cowles Foundation Discussion Paper No. 1476.

ANDREWS, D. W. K. AND J. H. STOCK (2005): "Inference with Weak Instruments," Invited paper presented at the Econometric Society World Congress, U.C.L., London.

BACK, K. AND D. BROWN (1993): "Implied Probabilities in GMM Estimators," *Econometrica*, 61, 971–976.

BONNAL, H. AND E. RENAULT (2003): "On the Efficient Use of the Informational Content of Estimating Equations: Implied Probabilities and Maximum Euclidean Likelihood," Working Paper, Département de Sciences Économiques, Université de Montréal.

BORWEIN, J. M. AND A. S. LEWIS (1991): "Duality Relations for Entropy-Like Minimisation Problems," *SIAM Journal of Control and Optimisation*, 29, 325–338.

BROWN, B. W. AND W. K. NEWEY (1998): "Efficient Semiparametric Estimation of Expectations," *Econometrica*, 66, 453–464.

CANER, M. (2003): "Exponential Tilting with Weak Instruments: Estimation and Testing," Working Paper, University of Pittsburg.

CORCORAN, S. A. (1998): "Bartlett Adjustment of Empirical Discrepancy Statistics," *Biometrika*, 85, 967–972.

CRAGG, J. G. AND S. G. DONALD (1996): "On the Asymptotic Properties of LDU-Based Tests of the Rank of a Matrix," *Journal of the American Statistical Association*, 91, 1301–1309.

——— (1997): "Inferring the Rank of a Matrix," *Journal of Econometrics*, 76, 223–250.

CRESSIE, N. AND T. READ (1984): "Multinomial Goodness-of-Fit Tests," *Journal of the Royal Statistical Society Series B*, 46, 440–464.

GUGGENBERGER, P. AND R. J. SMITH (2005a): "Generalized Empirical Likelihood Estimators and Tests under Partial, Weak and Strong Identification," *Econometric Theory*, 21, 667–709.

——— (2005b): "Generalized Empirical Likelihood Tests in Time Series Models With Potential Identification Failure," Working Paper, U.C.L.A..

HANSEN, L. P. (1982): "Large Sample Properties of Generalized Method of Moments Estimators," *Econometrica*, 50, 1029–1054.

HANSEN, L. P., J. HEATON, AND A. YARON (1996): "Finite-Sample Properties of Some Alternative GMM Estimators," *Journal of Business and Economic Statistics*, 14, 262–280.

IMBENS, G. W. (1997): "One-Step Estimators for Over-Identified Generalized Method of Moments Models," *Review of Economic Studies*, 64, 359–383.

IMBENS, G. W., R. H. SPADY, AND P. JOHNSON (1998): "Information Theoretic Approaches to Inference in Moment Condition Models," *Econometrica*, 66, 333–357.

JING, B.-Y. AND A. T. A. WOOD (1996): "Exponential Empirical Likelihood Is Not Bartlett Correctable," *Annals of Statistics*, 24, 365–369.

KITAMURA, Y. (2001): "Asymptotic Optimality of Empirical Likelihood for Testing Moment Restriction," *Econometrica*, 69, 1661–1672.

——— (2005): "Empirical Likelihood Methods in Econometrics: Theory and Practice," Invited paper presented at the Econometric Society World Congress, U.C.L., London.

KITAMURA, Y. AND M. STUTZER (1997): "An Information-Theoretic Alternative to Generalized Method of Moments Estimation," *Econometrica*, 65, 861–874.

KLEIBERGEN, F. (2002): "Pivotal Statistics for Testing Structural Parameters in Instrumental Variables Regression," *Econometrica*, 70, 1781–1803.

——— (2005): "Testing Parameters in GMM Without Assuming that They Are Identified," *Econometrica*, 73, 1103–1123.

KLEIBERGEN, F. AND R. PAAP (2006): "Generalized Reduced Rank Tests Using the Singular Value Decomposition," *Journal of Econometrics*, 133, 97–126.

MOREIRA, M. J. (2001): "Tests with Correct Size When Instruments Can Be Arbitrarily Weak," Working Paper, University of California, Berkeley.

——— (2003): "A Conditional Likelihood Ratio Test for Structural Models," *Econometrica*, 71, 1027–1048.

NEWEY, W. K. AND D. L. MCFADDEN (1994): "Large Sample Estimation and Hypothesis Testing," in *Handbook of Econometrics*, Vol. 4, edited by R. Engle and D. L. McFadden, New York: North Holland.

NEWEY, W. K. AND R. J. SMITH (2001): "Asymptotic Bias and Equivalence of GMM and GEL Estimators," Working Paper No. 01/517, University of Bristol.

——— (2004): "Higher-Order Properties of GMM and Generalized Empirical Likelihood," *Econometrica*, 72, 219–255.

NEWEY, W. K. AND K. D. WEST (1987): "Hypothesis Testing with Efficient Method of Moments Estimation," *International Economic Review*, 28, 777–787.

OTSU, T. (2006): "Generalized Empirical Likelihood Inference for Nonlinear and Time Series Models Under Weak Identification," *Econometric Theory*, 22, 513–527.

OWEN, A. (2001): *Empirical Likelihood*, New York: Chapman and Hall.

QIN, J. AND J. LAWLESS (1994): "Empirical Likelihood and General Estimating Equations," *Annals of Statistics*, 22, 300–325.

REID, N. (1995): "The Roles of Conditioning in Inference," *Statistical Science*, 10, 138–157.

ROBIN, J.-M. AND R. J. SMITH (2000): "Tests of Rank," *Econometric Theory*, 16, 151–175.

SCHENNACH, S. M. (2004): "Exponentially Tilted Empirical Likelihood," Working Paper, University of Chicago.

SMITH, R. J. (1997): "Alternative Semi-Parametric Likelihood Approaches to Generalized Method of Moments Estimation," *Economic Journal*, 107, 503–519.

SMITH, R. J. (2001): "GEL Methods for Moment Condition Models," Working Paper, University of Bristol. Revised version CWP 19/04, cemmap, I.F.S. and U.C.L. http://cemmap.ifs.org.uk/wps/cwp0419.pdf.

STOCK, J. H. AND J. H. WRIGHT (2000): "GMM with Weak Identification," *Econometrica*, 68, 1055–1096.

VUONG, Q. (1989): "Likelihood Ratio Tests for Model Selection and Non-Nested Hypotheses," *Econometrica*, 57, 307–333.

CHAPTER 9

Estimating Continuous-Time Models
with Discretely Sampled Data[*]
Yacine Aït-Sahalia[†]

1 INTRODUCTION

Since Merton's seminal work in the 1970s, the continuous-time paradigm has
proved to be an immensely useful tool in finance and more generally economics.
Continuous time models are widely used to study issues that include the decision
to optimally consume, save, and invest; portfolio choice under a variety of
constraints; contingent claim pricing; capital accumulation; resource extraction;
game theory and more recently contract theory. The objective of this lecture is
to review some of the developments in the econometric literature devoted to the
estimation and testing of these models.

The unifying theme of the class of the problems I will discuss is that the data
generating process is assumed to be a continuous-time process describing the
evolution of state variable(s), but the process is sampled, or observed, at discrete
time intervals. The issues that arise, and the problems that are of interest, at
the interface between the continuous-time model and the discrete-time data are
quite different from those that we typically encounter in standard time series
analysis. As a result, there has been a large amount of research activity in this
area.

I will start with the simplest possible model, under many assumptions that
restrict its generality, and describe how different inference strategies can be
developed to work under progressively richer settings, where I relax either some
aspect of the model's specification and/or the manner in which the process
is sampled. I will attempt to systematize the treatment of different methods,
present them in a unified framework and, when relevant, compare them. If
nothing else, the reader should find these seemingly disparate methods presented
using a common notation!

Let me apologize from the onset for the necessarily selective coverage that
I will be able to achieve in this limited amount of space. Without any doubt,

[*] Invited Lecture, 2005 World Congress of the Econometric Society. I am grateful to Oliver Lin-
ton, the discussant, for many useful comments. Financial support from the NSF under grant
SBR-0350772 is also gratefully acknowledged.
[†] Princeton University and NBER.

I will not be able to do justice to important strands of the literature and will instead put the emphasis on a selected set of methods – not surprisingly, those primarily associated with my own work!

2 THE SIMPLEST MODEL

The basic dynamic model for the state variable(s) of interest X_t is a stochastic differential equation

$$dX_t = \mu dt + \sigma dW_t \tag{2.1}$$

where W_t a standard Brownian motion. The process X_t is observed at the discrete times $\tau_0 = 0, \tau_1, \tau_2, \dots, \tau_N$, in the interval $[0, T]$, and I write the sampling intervals as $\Delta_n = \tau_n - \tau_{n-1}$. In a typical example, X_t will represent the log-price of an asset.

I define the simplest model as one where the following assumptions are satisfied:

Assumption 1 *X is a Markov process.*

Assumption 2 *X is a diffusion.*

Assumption 3 *X is a univariate process.*

Assumption 4 *X has constant drift μ and diffusion σ.*

Assumption 5 *X is sampled at a fixed time interval $\Delta = T/N$.*

Assumption 6 *X is observed without error.*

For this model, any reasonable estimation strategy (MLE, OLS, GMM using the variance as a moment condition) ends up with the same estimator for the diffusion parameter σ^2. Let's write it to be even simpler for $\mu = 0$; otherwise one can simply subtract the natural estimator of μ from the (discrete) log-returns $X_{\tau_{n+1}} - X_{\tau_n}$. Indeed, the log-returns in this case are i.i.d. $N(0, \sigma^2\Delta)$, and so the MLE for σ^2 is

$$\hat{\sigma}^2 \equiv T^{-1}[X, X]_T = T^{-1} \sum_{n=1}^{N} (X_{\tau_{n+1}} - X_{\tau_n})^2, \tag{2.2}$$

and has the asymptotic distribution

$$N^{1/2} \left(\hat{\sigma}^2 - \sigma^2 \right) \underset{N \to \infty}{\longrightarrow} N(0, 2\sigma^4). \tag{2.3}$$

3 MORE REALISTIC ASSUMPTIONS

In each of the sections below, one or more of these assumptions will be relaxed; as a general rule, the above assumptions that are not explicitly stated as being relaxed are maintained.

The rest of the lecture is devoted to exploring what can be done when the assumptions of the simplest model are relaxed. I will relax Assumption 1 to test whether the process is Markovian; relax Assumption 2 to include jumps and test for their presence; relax Assumption 3 to cover multivariate models; relax Assumption 4 to cover general parametric models as well as nonparametric models; relax Assumption 5 to allow for random sampling; and relax Assumption 6 to allow for market microstructure noise.

Each generalization falls into one of the following three classes: different data generating processes; different observation schemes; different sampling schemes.

3.1   Different Data Generating Processes

More general processes will be considered:

Assumption 7 X is a multivariate process of dimension m.

Assumption 8 X has drift $\mu(x; \theta)$ and diffusion $\sigma(x; \theta)$ which are known functions except for an unknown parameter vector θ.

Assumption 9   The drift and diffusion functions of X are unknown time-homogenous smooth functions $\mu(x)$ and $\sigma(x)$.

I will allow for departure from the continuity of the sample paths according to either:

Assumption 10 X is a jump-diffusion process with drift $\mu(x; \theta)$, diffusion $\sigma(x; \theta)$ and (possibly random) jump amplitude J_t. The arrival intensity of the Poisson jumps is $\lambda(x; \theta)$. The Brownian motion, Poisson process, and jump amplitude are all independent.

Assumption 11 X is a Lévy process with characteristics (b, c, v) where b is the drift, σ the volatility from the continuous part and v the Lévy measure from the pure jump part.

In many but not all instances, it will be necessary to assume that:

Assumption 12   The drift and diffusion functions of X, and its initial distribution (of X_0).are such that X is a stationary process.

3.2   Different Observation Schemes

Different assumptions can be made regarding the way(s) in which the process X is observed:

Assumption 13   All components of the vector X are observed.

Assumption 14 $X_t = [S_t; V_t]'$, where the $(m - q)$-dimensional vector S_t is observed but the q-dimensional V_t is not.

And, especially when dealing with high frequency financial data, it will be important to allow for the fact that X may be observed with a fair amount of noise, as this is an essential feature of the observed data:

Assumption 15 X is observed with additive error, $Y_{\tau_n} = X_{\tau_n} + \varepsilon_{\tau_n}$.

The next two assumptions represent the baseline case for modeling additive noise:

Assumption 16 ε is independent of X.

Assumption 17 ε_{τ_n} in Assumption 15 is i.i.d.

They can be relaxed by allowing ε to be correlated with the X process, and by allowing ε to be autocorrelated:

Assumption 18 ε_{τ_n} in Assumption 15 is (when viewed as a process in index n) stationary and strong mixing with the mixing coefficients decaying exponentially; and, there exists $\kappa > 0$ such that $E\varepsilon^{4+\kappa} < \infty$.

An alternative model for the noise is the following:

Assumption 19 X is observed with rounding error at some level $\alpha > 0$: $Y_t = \alpha[X_t/\alpha]$ where $[.]$ denotes the integer part of a real number.

Finally, an additional source of error, beyond market microstructure noise captured by the above assumptions, is the fact that, under Assumption 7 and the components of the vector X represent different asset prices, these assets may not be observed at the same instants because the assets do not trade, or see their quotes being revised, synchronously. This gives rise to:

Assumption 20 The ith component of X, $X^{(i)}$, is observed at instants $\tau_0 = 0$, $\tau_1^{(i)}, \tau_2^{(i)}, \ldots, \tau_{n^{(i)}}^{(i)}$ which may not coincide for all $i = 1, \ldots, m$.

3.3   Different Sampling Schemes

Instead of Assumption 5, the sampling intervals at which the observations are recorded can be of different types:

Assumption 21 X is sampled at an increasingly finer time interval, $\Delta \to 0$.

Assumption 22 *The sampling intervals $\Delta_n = \tau_n - \tau_{n-1}$ are drawn at time τ_{n-1} so as to be conditionally independent of the future of the process X given the past data $(Y_{n-1}, \Delta_{n-1}, Y_{n-2}, \Delta_{n-2}, \ldots, Y_1, \Delta_1)$ where $Y_n = X_{\tau_n}$.*

4 RELAXING THE MODEL SPECIFICATION: ALLOWING FOR MULTIVARIATE PARAMETRIC DYNAMICS

Of course, many models of interest require that we relax Assumption 4. To save space, I will describe how to conduct likelihood inference for arbitrary multivariate diffusion models, that is, relax Assumption, 3 at the same time. That is, suppose now that we are under Assumptions 7 and 8. For now, also assume that the vector X is fully observed so that Assumption 13 holds.

The SDE driving the X process takes the multivariate parametric form

$$dX_t = \mu(X_t; \theta)dt + \sigma(X_t; \theta)dW_t \qquad (4.1)$$

where W_t is an m-dimensional standard Brownian motion. I will first discuss the maximum likelihood estimation of θ before turning to alternative, non-likelihood, approaches. When conducting likelihood inference, Assumption 12 is not necessary. Stationarity will however be a key requirement for some of the other methods.

4.1 Likelihood Inference

One major impediment to both theoretical modeling and empirical work with continuous-time models of this type is the fact that in most cases little can be said about the implications of the instantaneous dynamics for X_t under these assumptions for longer time intervals. That is, unlike the simple situation where (2.1) implied that log-returns are i.i.d. and normally distributed, one cannot in general characterize in closed form an object as simple (and fundamental for everything from prediction to estimation and derivative pricing) as the conditional density of $X_{t+\Delta}$ given the current value X_t. For a list of the rare exceptions, see Wong (1964). In finance, the well-known models of Black and Scholes (1973), Vasicek (1977), and Cox, Ingersoll, and Ross (1985) rely on these existing closed-form expressions.

In Aït-Sahalia (1999) (examples and application to interest rate data), Aït-Sahalia, (2002b) (univariate theory), and Aït-Sahalia (2001) (multivariate theory), I developed a method which produces very accurate approximations *in closed form* to the unknown transition function $p_X(x|x_0, \Delta; \theta)$, that is, the conditional density of $X_{n\Delta} = x$ given $X_{(n-1)\Delta} = x_0$ implied by the model in equation (4.1). (When there is no risk of ambiguity, I will write simply p instead of p_X; but, as will become clear below, the construction of p_X requires a change of variable from X to some Y so it is best to indicate explicitly which variable's transition density we are talking about.)

Bayes' rule combined with the Markovian nature of the process, which the discrete data inherit, imply that the log-likelihood function has the simple form

$$\ell_N(\theta, \Delta) \equiv \sum_{n=1}^{N} l_X\left(X_{n\Delta} | X_{(n-1)\Delta}, \Delta; \theta\right) \tag{4.2}$$

where $l_X \equiv \ln p_X$, and the asymptotically irrelevant density of the initial observation, X_0, has been left out. As is clear from (4.2), the availability of tractable formulae for l_X is what makes likelihood inference feasible under these conditions.

In the past, a computational challenge for such estimation was the tractable construction of a likelihood function since existing methods required solving numerically the Fokker–Planck–Kolmogorov partial differential equation [see e.g., Lo (1988)], or simulating a large number of sample paths along which the process is sampled very finely (Pedersen, 1995). Both classes of methods result in a large computational effort since the likelihood must be recomputed for each observed realization of the state vector, and each value of the parameter vector θ along the maximization. By contrast, the closed form likelihood expressions that I will summarize below make MLE a feasible choice for estimating θ.

Jensen and Poulsen (2002), Stramer and Yan (2005), and Hurn, Jeisman, and Lindsay (2005) conducted extensive comparisons of different techniques for approximating transition function and demonstrated that the method is both the most accurate and the fastest to implement for the types of problems and sampling frequencies one encounters in finance. The method has been extended to time inhomogeneous processes by Egorov, Li, and Xu (2003) and to jump-diffusions by Schaumburg (2001) and Yu (2003) (described in Section 8). DiPietro (2001) has extended the methodology to make it applicable in a Bayesian setting. Bakshi and Yu (2005) proposed a refinement to the method in the univariate case.

Identification of the parameter vector must be ensured. In fact, identifying a multivariate continuous-time Markov process from discrete-time data can be problematic when the process is not reversible, as an aliasing problem can be present [see Philips (1973) and Hansen and Sargent (1983)]. As for the distributional properties of the resulting estimator, a fixed interval sample of a time-homogenous continuous-time Markov process is a Markov process in discrete time. Given that the Markov state vector is observed and the unknown parameters are identified, properties of the ML estimator follow from what is known about ML estimation of discrete-time Markov processes (see Billingsley, 1961). In the stationary case of Assumption 12, the MLE will under standard regularity conditions converge at speed $n^{1/2}$ to a normal distribution whose variance is given by the inverse of Fisher's information matrix. The nonstationary case is discussed in Section 7.

4.1.1   Reducibilty

Whenever possible, it is advisable to start with a change of variable. As defined in Aït-Sahalia (2001), a diffusion X is *reducible* if and only if there exists a one-to-one transformation of the diffusion X into a diffusion Y whose diffusion matrix σ_Y is the identity matrix. That is, there exists an invertible function $\gamma(x; \theta)$ such that $Y_t \equiv \gamma(X_t; \theta)$ satisfies the stochastic differential equation

$$dY_t = \mu_Y(Y_t; \theta)dt + dW_t. \tag{4.3}$$

Every univariate diffusion is reducible, through the simple transformation $Y_t = \int^{X_t} du/\sigma(u; \theta)$. The basic construction in Aït-Sahalia, (2002b) in the univariate case proceeds by first changing X into Y, and showing that the density of Y can be approximated around an $N(0, 1)$ distribution in the form of an expansion in Hermite polynomials. The unit diffusion in (4.3) is what yields the $N(0, 1)$ distribution in the limit where Δ becomes small. The choice of Hermite (as opposed to other) polynomials is dictated by the fact that they are the orthonormal family in L^2 for the normal density. The key aspect is then that the coefficients of the expansion can be computed in closed form in the form of a Taylor expansion in Δ.

However, not every multivariate diffusion is reducible. As a result, the passage from the univariate to the multivariate cases does not just reduce to a simple matter of scalars becoming matrices. Whether or not a given multivariate diffusion is reducible depends on the specification of its σ matrix. Proposition 1 of Aït-Sahalia (2001) provides a necessary and sufficient condition for reducibility: the diffusion X is reducible if and only if the inverse diffusion matrix $\sigma^{-1} = [\sigma_{i,j}^{-1}]_{i,j=1,\dots,m}$ satisfies the condition that

$$\frac{\partial \sigma_{ij}^{-1}(x; \theta)}{\partial x_k} = \frac{\partial \sigma_{ik}^{-1}(x; \theta)}{\partial x_j} \tag{4.4}$$

for each triplet $(i, j, k) = 1, \dots, m$ such that $k > j$, or equivalently

$$\sum_{l=1}^{m} \frac{\partial \sigma_{ik}(x; \theta)}{\partial x_l} \sigma_{lj}(x; \theta) = \sum_{l=1}^{m} \frac{\partial \sigma_{ij}(x; \theta)}{\partial x_l} \sigma_{lk}(x; \theta). \tag{4.5}$$

Whenever a diffusion is reducible, an expansion can be computed for the transition density p_X of X by first computing it for the density p_Y of Y and then transforming Y back into X. When a diffusion is not reducible, the situation is more involved (see Section 4.1.2). The expansion for l_Y is of the form

$$l_Y^{(K)}(y|y_0, \Delta; \theta) = -\frac{m}{2} \ln(2\pi\Delta) + \frac{C_Y^{(-1)}(y|y_0; \theta)}{\Delta}$$
$$+ \sum_{k=0}^{K} C_Y^{(k)}(y|y_0; \theta) \frac{\Delta^k}{k!}. \tag{4.6}$$

As shown in Theorem 1 of Aït-Sahalia (2001), the coefficients of the expansion are given explicitly by

$$C_Y^{(-1)}(y|y_0; \theta) = -\frac{1}{2} \sum_{i=1}^{m} (y_i - y_{0i})^2 \tag{4.7}$$

$$C_Y^{(0)}(y|y_0; \theta) = \sum_{i=1}^{m} (y_i - y_{0i}) \int_0^1 \mu_{Y_i}(y_0 + u(y - y_0); \theta) \, du \tag{4.8}$$

and, for $k \geq 1$,

$$C_Y^{(k)}(y|y_0; \theta) = k \int_0^1 G_Y^{(k)}(y_0 + u(y - y_0)|y_0; \theta) u^{k-1} du \tag{4.9}$$

where $G_Y^{(k)}(y|y_0; \theta)$ is given explicitly as a function of μ_{Y_i} and $C_Y^{(j-1)}$, $j = 1, \ldots, k$.

Given an expansion for the density p_Y of Y, an expansion for the density p_X of X can be obtained by a direct application of the Jacobian formula:

$$l_X^{(K)}(x|x_0, \Delta; \theta) = -\frac{m}{2} \ln(2\pi\Delta) - D_v(x; \theta) + \frac{C_Y^{(-1)}(\gamma(x; \theta)|\gamma(x_0; \theta); \theta)}{\Delta}$$

$$+ \sum_{k=0}^{K} C_Y^{(k)}(\gamma(x; \theta)|\gamma(x_0; \theta); \theta) \frac{\Delta^k}{k!} \tag{4.10}$$

from $l_Y^{(K)}$ given in (4.6), using the coefficients $C_Y^{(k)}$, $k = -1, 0, \ldots, K$ given above, and where

$$D_v(x; \theta) \equiv \frac{1}{2} \ln(Det[v(x; \theta)]) \tag{4.11}$$

with $v(x; \theta) \equiv \sigma(x; \theta) \sigma^T(x; \theta)$.

4.1.2 The Irreducible Case

In the irreducible case, no such Y exists and the expansion of the log-likelihood l_X has the form

$$l_X^{(K)}(x|x_0, \Delta; \theta) = -\frac{m}{2} \ln(2\pi\Delta) - D_v(x; \theta)$$

$$+ \frac{C_X^{(-1)}(x|x_0; \theta)}{\Delta} + \sum_{k=0}^{K} C_X^{(k)}(x|x_0; \theta) \frac{\Delta^k}{k!}. \tag{4.12}$$

The approach is to calculate a Taylor series in $(x - x_0)$ of each coefficient $C_X^{(k)}$, at order j_k in $(x - x_0)$. Such an expansion will be denoted by $C_X^{(j_k, k)}$ at order $j_k = 2(K - k)$, for $k = -1, 0, \ldots, K$.

The resulting expansion will then be

$$\bar{l}_X^{(K)}(x|x_0, \Delta; \theta) = -\frac{m}{2}\ln(2\pi\Delta) - D_v(x;\theta) + \frac{C_X^{(j_{-1},-1)}(x|x_0;\theta)}{\Delta}$$

$$+ \sum_{k=0}^{K} C_X^{(j_k,k)}(x|x_0;\theta)\frac{\Delta^k}{k!} \qquad (4.13)$$

Such a Taylor expansion was unnecessary in the reducible case: the expressions given above provide the explicit expressions of the coefficients $C_Y^{(k)}$ and then in (4.10) we have the corresponding ones for $C_X^{(k)}$. However, even for an irreducible diffusion, it is still possible to compute the coefficients $C_X^{(j_k,k)}$ explicitly.

As in the reducible case, the system of equations determining the coefficients is obtained by forcing the expansion (4.12) to satisfy, to order Δ^J, the forward and backward Fokker–Planck–Kolmogorov equations, either in their familiar form for the transition density p_X, or in their equivalent form for $\ln p_X$. For instance, the forward equation for $\ln p_X$ is of the form:

$$\frac{\partial l_X}{\partial\Delta} = -\sum_{i=1}^{m}\frac{\partial\mu_i^P(x)}{\partial x_i} + \frac{1}{2}\sum_{i=1}^{m}\sum_{j=1}^{m}\frac{\partial^2 v_{ij}(x)}{\partial x_i\partial x_j}$$

$$+ \sum_{i=1}^{m}\mu_i^P(x)\frac{\partial l_X}{\partial x_i} + \sum_{i=1}^{m}\sum_{j=1}^{m}\frac{\partial v_{ij}(x)}{\partial x_i}\frac{\partial l_X}{\partial x_j}$$

$$+ \frac{1}{2}\sum_{i=1}^{m}\sum_{j=1}^{m}v_{ij}(x)\frac{\partial^2 l_X}{\partial x_i\partial x_j} + \frac{1}{2}\sum_{i=1}^{m}\sum_{j=1}^{m}\frac{\partial l_X}{\partial x_i}v_{ij}(x)\frac{\partial l_X}{\partial x_j}.$$

$$(4.14)$$

For each $k = -1, 0, \ldots, K$, the coefficient $C_X^{(k)}(x|x_0;\theta)$ in (4.12) solves the equation

$$f_X^{(k-1)}(x|x_0;\theta) = C_X^{(k)}(x|x_0;\theta) - \sum_{i=1}^{m}\sum_{j=1}^{m}$$

$$v_{ij}(x;\theta)\frac{\partial C_X^{(-1)}(x|x_0;\theta)}{\partial x_i}\frac{\partial C_X^{(k)}(x|x_0;\theta)}{\partial x_j} - G_X^{(k)}(x|x_0;\theta) = 0$$

Each function $G_X^{(k)}$, $k = 0, 1, \ldots, K$ involves only the coefficients $C_X^{(h)}$ for $h = -1, \ldots, k-1$, so this system of equation can be utilized to solve recursively for each coefficient at a time. Specifically, the equation $f_X^{(-2)} = 0$ determines $C_X^{(-1)}$; given $C_X^{(-1)}$, $G_X^{(0)}$ becomes known and the equation $f_X^{(-1)} = 0$ determines $C_X^{(0)}$; given $C_X^{(-1)}$ and $C_X^{(0)}$, $G_X^{(1)}$ becomes known and the equation $f_X^{(0)} = 0$ then determines $C_X^{(1)}$, etc. It turns out that this results in a system of linear equations in the coefficients of the polynomials $C_X^{(j_k,k)}$, so each one of these equations can be solved explicitly in the form of the Taylor expansion $C_X^{(j_k,k)}$ of the coefficient $C_X^{(k)}$, at order j_k in $(x - x_0)$.

Aït-Sahalia and Yu (2006) developed an alternative strategy for constructing closed form approximations to the transition density of a continuous time Markov process. Instead of expanding the transition function in orthogonal polynomials around a leading term, we rely on the saddle-point method, which originates in the work of Daniels (1954). We showed that, in the case of diffusions, it is possible by expanding the cumulant generating function of the process to obtain an alternative closed form expansion of its transition density. We also showed that this approach provides an alternative gathering of the correction terms beyond the leading term that is equivalent at order Δ to the irreducible expansion of the transition density given in Aït-Sahalia (2001).

4.2   Alternative Non-Likelihood Methods

Because of the Cramer–Rao lower bound, maximum likelihood estimation will, at least asymptotically, be efficient and should consequently be the method of choice especially given the availability of closed-form, numerically tractable, likelihood expansions. There are, however, a number of alternative methods available to estimate θ.

4.2.1   Moment Conditions, Contrast Functions, and Estimating Equations

Consider a class of estimators for the parameter vector θ under Assumption 8 obtained by minimizing a quadratic criterion function, or equivalent setting to zero its θ-gradient. To estimate the d-dimensional parameter vector θ, we can select a vector of r moment conditions $h(y_1, y_0, \delta, \theta)$, $r \geq d$, which is continuously differentiable in θ. Here y_1 plays the role of the forward state variable, y_0 the role of the backward state variable, δ the sampling interval.

At this level of generality, of course, everything is possible. The question is to find actual functions h which are tractable. In particular to avoid any bias in the resulting estimator, h must be such that

$$E\left[h(Y_1, Y_0, \Delta, \theta_0)\right] = 0. \tag{4.15}$$

Whenever h depends on both Y_1 and Y_0, in a nontrivial manner, this requires that we be able to compute the expected value of a candidate h under the law of $Y_1|Y_0$ (by first conditioning on Y_0 and applying the law of iterated expectations), that is, under the transition density $p(Y_1|Y_0, \Delta; \theta)$. This is a tough requirement to fulfill in closed form, and one which severely limits the types of moment conditions which can be implemented.

Hansen and Scheinkman (1995) provide the only example of h functions which can be computed under a general specification of Assumption 8 (as opposed to just for special cases of μ and σ, such as the Ornstein–Uhlenbeck process), and in fact apply under more general Markov processes (i.e., allow us to relax Assumption 2). These moment conditions are in the form of expectations of the infinitesimal generator, one unconditional (C1) and one conditional (C2), that are applied to test functions. Stationarity, that is, Assumption 12, is a crucial requirement of the method.

The C1 moment condition takes a sufficiently differentiable function $\psi(y_0, \theta)$ in the domain of the infinitesimal generator A_θ and forms the moment condition

$$h_{C1}(y_1, y_0, \delta, \theta) \equiv A_\theta \cdot \psi(y_0, \theta) \equiv \mu(y_0, \theta)\frac{\partial \psi}{\partial y_0} + \frac{1}{2}\sigma^2(y_0; \theta)\frac{\partial^2 \psi}{\partial y_0^2},$$

(4.16)

with the last equality written for convenience under Assumption 3.

The C1 estimating equation relies on the fact that we have the unbiasedness condition

$$E\left[A_{\theta_0} \cdot \psi(Y_0, \theta)\right] = 0.$$

(4.17)

Once A_θ is evaluated at θ_0, this is true for any value of θ in ψ, including θ_0. A consequence of this is that the resulting estimator is unbiased for any function ψ (recall (4.15)).

The C2 method takes two functions ψ_0 and ψ_1, again satisfying smoothness and regularity conditions, and forms the "back to the future" estimating function

$$h_{C2}(y_1, y_0, \delta, \theta) \equiv \{A_\theta \cdot \psi_1(y_1, \theta)\} \times \psi_0(y_0, \theta)$$

$$- \{A_\theta \cdot \psi_0(y_0, \theta)\} \times \psi_1(y_1, \theta).$$

(4.18)

In general, the second of the two A_θ should be replaced by the infinitesimal generator associated with the reverse time process, A_θ^*. But under regularity conditions, univariate stationary diffusions are time reversible (see Kent, 1978) and so the infinitesimal generator of the process is self-adjoint .

The C2 estimating equation relies on the fact that

$$E\left[\{A_{\theta_0} \cdot \psi_1(Y_1, \theta)\} \times \psi_0(Y_0, \theta) - \{A_{\theta_0} \cdot \psi_0(Y_0, \theta)\} \times \psi_1(Y_1, \theta)\right] = 0.$$

(4.19)

Once A_θ is evaluated at θ_0, this is true for any value of θ in ψ, including θ_0.

Equation (4.19) is again a consequence of the stationarity of the process X. Namely, the expectation of any function of $(X_t, X_{t+\delta})$, such as $E_{X_t, X_{t+\delta}}\left[\psi_0(X_t, \theta)\psi_1(X_{t+\delta}, \theta)\right]$, does not depend upon the date t (it can of course depend upon the time lag δ between the two observations): hence

$$\frac{\partial}{\partial t}E_{X_t, X_{t+\delta}}\left[\psi_0(X_t, \theta)\psi_1(X_{t+\delta}, \theta)\right] = 0$$

from which (4.19) follows.

Unlike the typical use of the method of moments, one cannot in general select as moment conditions the "natural" conditional moments of the process since explicit expressions for the conditional mean, variance, skewness, etc. are not available in closed-form. Rather, the moment conditions in this case, that is, the h functions, are in the form of the infinitesimal generator of the process applied to arbitrary test functions. One additional aspect of the method is that it does not permit full identification of all the parameters of the model since multiplying the drift and diffusion functions by the same constant results in identical moment conditions. So parameters are only identified up to scale.

Bibby and Sørensen (1995) proposed moment conditions in the form

$$h(y_1, y_0, \delta, \theta) = \frac{\partial \mu(y_0; \theta) / \partial \theta \partial \theta'}{\sigma^2(y_0; \theta)} (y_1 - E[Y_1 | Y_0 = y_0]). \qquad (4.20)$$

By construction, (4.15), but except in special cases, $E[Y_1 | Y_0 = y_0]$ does not have an explicit form, and any approximation of misspecification of it will induce bias.

Kessler and Sørensen (1999) proposed to use a more general version of (4.20), namely

$$h(y_1, y_0, \delta, \theta) = a(y_0, \delta, \theta)(\phi(y_1, \theta) - E[\phi(Y_1, \theta) | Y_0 = y_0])$$
$$(4.21)$$

where a is a weighting function, and to select the function ϕ in such a way as to make the computation of $E[\phi(Y_1, \theta) | Y_0 = y_0]$ tractable. This can be achieved by considering the eigenfunctions of the infinitesimal operator: let λ_j and ϕ_j, $j = 0, 1, \ldots$, denote respectively the eigenvalues and eigenfunctions of the operator A_θ defined by

$$A_\theta \cdot \phi_j(y_0, \theta) = -\lambda_j(\theta)\phi_j(y_0, \theta).$$

This will imply that

$$E[\phi(Y_1, \theta) | Y_0 = y_0] = \exp(-\lambda_j(\theta)\Delta)\phi_j(y_0, \theta)$$

[for regularity conditions and related material on the infinitesimal generator, see e.g., Aït-Sahalia, Hansen, and Scheinkman (2002)]. But, unfortunately, for the general parametric model of Assumption 8, these moment functions are not explicit either, because the (λ_j, ϕ_j)'s cannot be computed in closed form except in special cases. Bibby, Jacobsen, and Sørensen (2002) provides a detailed review of these and other types of estimating equations.

4.2.2   Simulation-Based Methods of Moments

A different type of moment functions is obtained by simulation. The moment function is the expected value under the model whose parameters one wishes to estimate of the score function from an auxiliary model. The idea is that the auxiliary model should be easier to estimate; in particular, the parameters of the auxiliary model appearing in the moment function are replaced by their quasi-maximum likelihood estimates. The parameters of the model of interest are then estimated by minimizing a GMM-like criterion. This method has the advantage of being applicable to a wide class of models. On the other hand, the estimates are obtained by simulations which are computationally intensive and they require the selection of an arbitrary auxiliary model, so the parameter estimates for the model of interest will vary based on both the set of simulations and the choice of auxiliary model.

Related implementations of this idea are due to Smith (1993), Gouriéroux, Monfort, and Renault (1993), and Gallant and Tauchen (1996); see Gallant and Tauchen (2002) for a survey of this literature.

4.2.3   Two-Step Estimation Based on the Continuous Record Likelihood

Phillips and Yu (2005) proposed the following method. Suppose that the parameter vector is split according to $\theta = (\theta_1, \theta_2)'$ where μ depends on θ through θ_1 only and σ through θ_2 only. If the full continuous time path were observable, and θ_2 were known, then the log-likelihood for θ_1 is given by Girsanov's Theorem:

$$\ell_n(\theta_1) = \int_0^T \frac{\mu(X_t, \theta_1)}{\sigma^2(X_t, \theta_2)} dX_t - \frac{1}{2} \int_0^T \frac{\mu^2(X_t, \theta_1)}{\sigma^2(X_t, \theta_2)} dt. \qquad (4.22)$$

Suppose now that we also have $\sigma(X_t, \theta_2) = \theta_2$ constant. Then the quadratic variation of the process is $\langle X, X \rangle_T = \int_0^T \sigma^2(X_t, \theta_2) dt = \theta_2^2 T$. And the realized volatility $[X, X]_T$, defined as in (2.2), makes it possible to estimate θ_2 as $\hat{\theta}_2 = T^{-1/2}[X, X]_T^{1/2}$. Plug that into the continuous-record likelihood

$$\ell_n(\theta_1) = \int_0^T \frac{\mu(X_t, \theta_1)}{\sigma^2(X_t, \hat{\theta}_2)} dX_t - \frac{1}{2} \int_0^T \frac{\mu^2(X_t, \theta_1)}{\sigma^2(X_t, \hat{\theta}_2)} dt,$$

approximate the integral with a sum

$$\sum_{i=2}^n \frac{\mu(X_{(i-1)\Delta}, \theta_1)}{\sigma^2(X_{(i-1)\Delta}, \hat{\theta}_2)} (X_{i\Delta} - X_{(i-1)\Delta}) - \frac{1}{2} \sum_{i=2}^n \frac{\mu^2(X_{(i-1)\Delta}, \theta_1)}{\sigma^2(X_{(i-1)\Delta}, \hat{\theta}_2)} \Delta$$

and maximize over θ_1. Approximations to the continuous-record likelihood are discussed in Sørensen (2001).

When $\sigma(X_t, \theta_2) = \theta_2 f(X_t)$ and f is a known function, the same method applies: $\langle X, X \rangle_T = \int_0^T \sigma^2(X_t, \theta_2) dt = \theta_2^2 \int_0^T f(X_t) dt$, estimate $\int_0^T f(X_t) dt$ using $\sum_{i=2}^n f(X_{(i-1)\Delta}) \Delta$, and using $[X, X]_T$ to estimate $\langle X, X \rangle_T$, we have an estimator of θ_2 again. For more general σ functions, one can estimate θ_2 by minimizing a scaled distance (for instance quadratic) between $\langle X, X \rangle_T = \int_0^T \sigma^2(X_t, \theta_2) dt$ (or rather a sum that approximates the integral) and $[X, X]_T$ inside each subinterval; then proceed as before by plugging that into the continuous record likelihood and maximize over θ_1.

5   RELAXING THE MODEL SPECIFICATION: ALLOWING FOR A PARTIALLY OBSERVED STATE VECTOR

Under Assumption 13, the vector X_t is fully observed. This assumption can be violated in many practical situations when some components of the state vector are latent. I now examine likelihood inference for models where Assumption 13 is replaced by Assumption 14. Unlike likelihood-based inference, however, relatively little changes for the simulation-based methods described in Section 4.2.2; they remain applicable in this context (although without asymptotic efficiency). Estimating equations that are applicable to partially observed state vectors are discussed in Genon-Catalot, Jeantheau, and Larédo (1999).

Two typical examples in finance consist of stochastic volatility models, where V_t is the volatility state variable(s), and term structure models, where V_t is a vector of factors or yields. I will discuss how to conduct likelihood inference in this setting, without resorting to the statistically sound but computationally infeasible integration of the latent variables from the likelihood function. The idea is simple: write down in closed form an expansion for the log-likelihood of the state vector X, including its unobservable components. Then enlarge the observation state by adding variables that are observed and functions of X. For example, in the stochastic volatility case, an option price or an option-implied volatility; in term structure models, as many bonds as there are factors. Then, using the Jacobian formula, write down the likelihood function of the pair consisting of the observed components of X and the additional observed variables, and maximize it.

5.1   Likelihood Inference for Stochastic Volatility Models

In a stochastic volatility model, the asset price process S_t follows

$$dS_t = (r - \delta) S_t dt + \sigma_1(X_t; \theta) dW_t^Q \tag{5.1}$$

where r is the risk-free rate, δ is the dividend yield paid by the asset (both taken to be constant for simplicity only), σ_1 denotes the first row of the matrix σ and Q denotes the equivalent martingale measure (see e.g., Harrison and Kreps, 1979). The volatility state variables V_t then follow an SDE on their own. For example, in the Heston (1993) model, $m = 2$ and $q = 1$:

$$dX_t = d \begin{bmatrix} S_t \\ V_t \end{bmatrix} = \begin{bmatrix} (r - \delta) S_t \\ \kappa(\gamma - V_t) \end{bmatrix} dt$$

$$+ \begin{bmatrix} \sqrt{(1 - \rho^2) V_t} S_t & \rho \sqrt{V_t} S_t \\ 0 & \sigma \sqrt{V_t} \end{bmatrix} d \begin{bmatrix} W_1^Q(t) \\ W_2^Q(t) \end{bmatrix}. \tag{5.2}$$

The model is completed by the specification of a vector of market prices of risk for the different sources of risk (W_1 and W_2 here), such as

$$\Lambda(X_t; \theta) = \begin{bmatrix} \lambda_1 \sqrt{(1 - \rho^2) V_t}, & \lambda_2 \sqrt{V_t} \end{bmatrix}', \tag{5.3}$$

which characterizes the change of measure from Q back to the physical probability measure P.

Likelihood inference for this and other stochastic volatility models is discussed in Aït-Sahalia and Kimmel (2004). Given a time series of observations of both the asset price, S_t, and a vector of option prices (which, for simplicity, we take to be call options) C_t, the time series of V_t can then be inferred from the observed C_t. If V_t is multidimensional, sufficiently many options are required with varying strike prices and maturities to allow extraction of the current value of V_t from the observed stock and call prices. Otherwise, only a single option is needed. For reasons of statistical efficiency, we seek to determine the joint likelihood function of the observed data, as opposed to, for example, conditional or unconditional moments. We employ the closed-form approximation technique described above, which yields in closed form the joint likelihood function of $[S_t; V_t]'$. From there, the joint likelihood function of the observations on $G_t = [S_t; C_t]' = f(X_t; \theta)$ is obtained simply by multiplying the likelihood of $X_t = [S_t; V_t]'$ by the Jacobian term J_t:

$$\ln p_G(g|g_0, \Delta; \theta) = -\ln J_t(g|g_0, \Delta; \theta)$$
$$+ l_X(f^{-1}(g; \theta)|f^{-1}(g_0; \theta); \Delta, \theta) \qquad (5.4)$$

with l_X obtained in Section 4.

If a proxy for V_t is used directly, this last step is not necessary. Indeed, we can avoid the computation of the function f by first transforming C_t into a proxy for V_t. The simplest one consists in using the Black–Scholes implied volatility of a short-maturity at-the-money option in place of the true instantaneous volatility state variable. The use of this proxy is justified in theory by the fact that the implied volatility of such an option converges to the instantaneous volatility of the logarithmic stock price as the maturity of the option goes to zero. An alternate proxy (which we call the integrated volatility proxy) corrects for the effect of mean reversion in volatility during the life of an option. If V_t is the instantaneous variance of the logarithmic stock price, we can express the integral of variance from time t to T as

$$V(t, T) = \int_t^T V_u du. \qquad (5.5)$$

If the volatility process is instantaneously uncorrelated with the logarithmic stock price process, then we can calculate option prices by taking the expected value of the Black–Scholes option price (with $V(t, T)$ as implied variance) over the probability distribution of $V(t, T)$ (see Hull and White (1987)). If the two processes are correlated, then the price of the option is a weighted average of Black–Scholes prices evaluated at different stock prices and volatilities (see Romano and Touzi, 1997).

The proxy we examine is determined by calculating the expected value of $V(t, T)$ first, and substituting this value into the Black–Scholes formula as implied variance. This proxy is model-free, in that it can be calculated whether or not an exact volatility can be computed and results in a straightforward estimation procedure. On the other hand, this procedure is in general approximate, first because the volatility process is unlikely to be instantaneously uncorrelated with the logarithmic stock price process, and second, because the expectation is taken before substituting $V(t, T)$ into the Black–Scholes formula rather than after and we examine in Monte Carlo simulations the respective impact of these approximations, with the objective of determining whether the trade-off involved between simplicity and exactitude is worthwhile.

The idea is to adjust the Black–Scholes implied volatility for the effect of mean reversion in volatility, essentially undoing the averaging that takes place in equation (5.5). Specifically, if the Q-measure drift of Y_t is of the form $a + bY_t$ (as it is in many of the stochastic volatility models in use), then the expected value of $V(t, T)$ is given by

$$E_t[V(t, T)] = \left(\frac{e^{b(T-t)} - 1}{b} \right) \left(V_t + \frac{a}{b} \right) - \frac{a}{b}(T - t).$$ (5.6)

A similar expression can be derived in the special case where $b = 0$. By taking the expected value on the left-hand side to be the observed implied variance $V_{imp}(t, T)$ of a short maturity T at-the-money option, our adjusted proxy is then given by

$$V_t \approx \frac{bV_{imp}(t, T) + a(T - t)}{e^{b(T-t)} - 1} - \frac{a}{b}.$$ (5.7)

Then we can simply take $[S_t; V_{imp}(t, T)]'$ as the state vector, write its likelihood from that of $[S_t; V_t]'$ using a Jacobian term for the change of variable (5.7).

It is possible to refine the implied volatility proxy by expressing it in the form of a Taylor series in the "volatility of volatility" parameter σ in the case of the CEV model, where the Q-measure drift of Y_t is of the form $a + bY_t$, and the Q-measure diffusion of Y_t is of the form σY_t^β (Lewis, 2000). However, unlike (5.7), the relationship between the observed $V_{imp}(t, T)$ and the latent Y_t is not invertible without numerical computation of the parameter-dependent integral.

5.2   Likelihood Inference for Term Structure Models

Another example of model for which inference must be conducted under Assumption 14 consist of term structure models. A multivariate term structure model specifies that the instantaneous riskless rate r_t is a deterministic function of an m-dimensional vector of state variables, X_t:

$$r_t = r(X_t; \theta).$$ (5.8)

Under the equivalent martingale measure Q, the state vector follows the dynamics given in (4.1). To avoid arbitrage opportunities, the price at t of a zero-coupon bond maturing at T is given by the Feynman–Kac representation:

$$P(x, t, T; \theta) = E^Q \left[\exp\left(- \int_t^T r_u du \right) \middle| X_t = x \right].$$ (5.9)

An affine yield model is any model where the short rate (5.8) is an affine function of the state vector and the risk-neutral dynamics (4.1) are affine:

$$dX_t = \left(\tilde{A} + \tilde{B}X_t\right)dt + \Sigma\sqrt{S(X_t; \alpha, \beta)}dW_t^Q \tag{5.10}$$

where $\tilde{A}$ is an m-element column vector, $\tilde{B}$ and Σ are $m \times m$ matrices, and $S(X_t; \alpha, \beta)$ is the diagonal matrix with elements $S_{ii} = \alpha_i + X_t'\beta_i$, with each α_i a scalar and each β_i an $m \times 1$ vector, $1 \leq i \leq m$ (see Dai and Singleton, 2000).

It can then be shown that, in affine models, bond prices have the exponential affine form

$$P(x, t, T; \theta) = \exp\left(-\gamma_0(\tau; \theta) - \gamma(\tau; \theta)' x\right) \tag{5.11}$$

where $\tau = T - t$ is the bond's time to maturity. That is, bond yields (non-annualized, and denoted by $g(x, t, T; \theta) = -\ln(P(x, t, T; \theta))$) are affine functions of the state vector:

$$g(x, t, T; \theta) = \gamma_0(\tau; \theta) + \gamma(\tau; \theta)' x. \tag{5.12}$$

Alternatively, one can start with the requirement that the yields be affine, and show that the dynamics of the state vector must be affine (see Duffie and Kan, 1996).

The final condition for the bond price implies that $\gamma_0(0; \theta) = \gamma(0; \theta) = 0$, while

$$r_t = \delta_0 + \delta'x. \tag{5.13}$$

Affine yield models owe much of their popularity to the fact that bond prices can be calculated quickly as solutions to a system of ordinary differential equations. Under nonlinear term structure models, bond prices will normally be solutions to a partial differential equation that is far more difficult to solve.

Aït-Sahalia and Kimmel (2002) consider likelihood inference for affine term structure models. This requires evaluation of the likelihood of an observed panel of yield data for each parameter vector considered during a search procedure. The procedure for evaluating the likelihood of the observed yields at a particular value of the parameter vector consists of four steps. First, we extract the value of the state vector X_t (which is not directly observed) from those yields that are treated as observed without error. Second, we evaluate the joint likelihood of the series of implied observations of the state vector X_t, using the closed-form approximations to the likelihood function described in Section 4. Third, we multiply this joint likelihood by a Jacobian term, to find the likelihood of the panel of observations of the yields observed without error. Finally, we calculate the likelihood of the observation errors for those yields observed with error, and multiply this likelihood by the likelihood found in the previous step, to find the joint likelihood of the panel of all yields.

The first task is therefore to infer the state vector X_t at date t from the cross-section of bond yields at date t with different maturities. Affine yield models, as their name implies, make yields of zero coupon bonds affine functions of the state vector. Given this simple relationship between yields and the state vector, the likelihood function of bond yields is a simple transformation of the likelihood function of the state vector.

If the number of observed yields at that point in time is smaller than the number N of state variables in the model, then the state is not completely observed, and the vector of observed yields does not follow a Markov process, even if the (unobserved) state vector does, enormously complicating maximum likelihood estimation. On the other hand, if the number of observed yields is larger than the number of state variables, then some of the yields can be expressed as deterministic functions of other observed yields, without error. Even tiny deviations from the predicted values have a likelihood of zero. This problem can be avoided by using a number of yields exactly equal to the number of state variables in the underlying model, but, in general, the market price of risk parameters will not all be identified. Specifically, there are affine yield models that generate identical dynamics for yields with a given set of maturities, but different dynamics for yields with other maturities. A common practice (see, e.g., Duffee, 2002) is to use more yields than state variables, and to assume that certain benchmark yields are observed precisely, whereas the other yields are observed with measurement error. The measurement errors are generally held to be i.i.d., and also independent of the state variable processes.

We take this latter approach, and use $N + H$ observed yields, $H \geq 0$, in the postulated model, and include observation errors for H of those yields. At each date t, the state vector X_t is then exactly identified by the yields observed without error, and these N yields jointly follow a Markov process. Denoting the times to maturity of the yields observed without error as $\tau_1, \ldots, \tau_N$, the observed values of these yields, on the left-hand side, are equated with the predicted values (from (5.12)) given the model parameters and the current values of the state variables, X_t:

$$g_t = \Gamma_0(\theta) + \Gamma(\theta)' X_t. \tag{5.14}$$

The current value of the state vector X_t is obtained by inverting this equation:

$$X_t = \left[\Gamma(\theta)'\right]^{-1} \left[g_t - \Gamma_0(\theta)\right]. \tag{5.15}$$

While the only parameters entering the transformation from observed yields to the state variables are the parameters of the risk-neutral (or Q-measure) dynamics of the state variables, once we have constructed our time series of values of X_t sampled at dates $\tau_0, \tau_1, \ldots, \tau_n$, the dynamics of the state variable that we will be able to infer from this time series are the dynamics under the physical measure (denoted by P). The first step in the estimation procedure is the only place where we rely on the tractability of the affine bond pricing model. In particular, we can now specify freely (that is, without regard for considerations of analytical tractability) the market prices of risk of the different Brownian motions

$$dX_t = \mu^P(X_t; \theta) \, dt + \sigma(X_t; \theta) \, dW_t^P$$
$$= \left\{ \mu^Q(X_t; \theta) + \sigma(X_t; \theta) \, \Lambda(X_t; \theta) \right\} dt + \sigma(X_t; \theta) \, dW_t^P. \qquad (5.16)$$

We adopt the simple specification for the market price of risk

$$\Lambda(X_t; \theta) = \sigma(X_t; \theta)' \lambda \qquad (5.17)$$

with λ an $m \times 1$ vector of constant parameters, so that under P, the instantaneous drift of each state variables is its drift under the risk-neutral measure, plus a constant times its volatility squared. Under this specification, the drift of the state vector is then affine under both the physical and risk-neutral measures, since

$$\mu^P(X_t; \theta) = \left(\tilde{A} + \tilde{B} X_t \right) + \Sigma S(X_t; \beta)' \Sigma' \lambda \equiv A + B X_t. \qquad (5.18)$$

An affine μ^P is not required for our likelihood expansions. Since we can derive likelihood expansions for arbitrary diffusions, μ^P may contain terms that are non-affine, such as the square root of linear functions of the state vector, as in Duarte (2004) for instance. Duffee (2002) and Cheridito, Filipović, and Kimmel (2007) also allow for a more general market price of risk specifications than Dai and Singleton (2000), but retain the affinity of μ^Q and μ^P (and also of the diffusion matrix). However, we do rely on the affine character of the dynamics under Q because those allow us to go from state to yields in the tractable manner given by (5.15).

6 RELAXING THE MODEL SPECIFICATION: ALLOWING FOR NONPARAMETRIC DYNAMICS

I now relax Assumption 4 to Assumption 9. I first describe specification tests that are designed to test any particular model, given by Assumption 8, against the nonparametric alternative Assumption 9. Then I discuss the non- and semi-parametric estimation of the functions $\mu(x)$ and $\sigma(x)$. Throughout this section, Assumption 12 holds. Conditions on the function μ and σ can be given to ensure that Assumption 12 is satisfied (see e.g., Aït-Sahalia, 1996c).

6.1   Specification Testing Against Nonparametric Alternatives

Consider a given parameterization for a diffusion given by Assumption 8, that is, a joint parametric family:

$$\mathcal{P} \equiv \left\{ \left(\mu(\cdot, \theta), \sigma^2(\cdot, \theta) \right) \mid \theta \in \Theta \right\} \qquad (6.1)$$

where Θ is a compact subset of R^K. If we believe that the true process is a diffusion with drift and diffusion functions $(\mu_0(\cdot), \sigma_0^2(\cdot))$, a specification test asks whether there are values of the parameters in Θ for which the parametric model $\mathcal{P}$ is an acceptable representation of the true process, that is, do the functions $(\mu_0(\cdot), \sigma_0^2(\cdot))$ belong to the parametric family $\mathcal{P}$? Formally, the null and alternative hypotheses are

$$H_0 : \exists \theta_0 \in \Theta \text{ such that } \mu(\cdot, \theta_0) = \mu_0(\cdot) \text{ and } \sigma^2(\cdot, \theta_0) = \sigma_0^2(\cdot)$$
$$H_1 : \left(\mu_0(\cdot), \sigma_0^2(\cdot)\right) \notin \mathcal{P}. \tag{6.2}$$

Because $(\mu_0(\cdot), \sigma_0^2(\cdot))$ cannot easily be estimated directly from discretely sampled data, Aït-Sahalia, (1996c) proposed to test the parametric specification using an indirect approach. Let $\pi(\cdot, \theta)$ denote the marginal density implied by the parametric model in Assumption 8, and $p(\Delta, \cdot | \cdot, \theta)$ the transition density. Under regularity assumptions, $(\mu(\cdot, \theta), \sigma^2(\cdot, \theta))$ will uniquely characterize the marginal and transition densities over discrete time intervals. For example, the Ornstein–Uhlenbeck process $dX_t = \beta(\alpha - X_t) dt + \gamma dW_t$ specified by Vasicek (1977) generates Gaussian marginal and transitional densities. The square-root process $dX_t = \beta(\alpha - X_t) dt + \gamma X_t^{1/2} dW_t$ used by Cox, Ingersoll, and Ross (1985) yields a Gamma marginal and noncentral chi-squared transitional densities.

More generally, any parameterization $\mathcal{P}$ of μ and σ^2 corresponds to a parametrization of the marginal and transitional densities:

$$\left\{(\pi(\cdot, \theta), p(\Delta, \cdot, | \cdot, \theta)) \mid \left(\mu(\cdot, \theta), \sigma^2(\cdot, \theta)\right) \in \mathcal{P}, \ \theta \in \Theta\right\}. \tag{6.3}$$

While the direct estimation of μ and σ^2 with discrete data is problematic, the estimation of the densities explicitly take into account the discreteness of the data. The basic idea in Aït-Sahalia (1996c) is to use the mapping between the drift and diffusion on the one hand, and the marginal and transitional densities on the other, to test the model's specification using densities at the observed discrete frequency (π, p) instead of the infinitesimal characteristics of the process (μ, σ^2):

$$\text{Drift and Diffusion} \quad \Longleftrightarrow \quad \text{Marginal and Transitional Densities}$$
$$\tag{6.4}$$

Aït-Sahalia (1996c) proposed two tests, one based on the marginal density π, the other on the transition density p and derived their asymptotic distributions under the Assumption 12.

6.1.1   Testing the Marginal Specification

I start with the first specification test proposed for discretely sampled diffusions, the marginal density-based specification test in Aït-Sahalia (1996c). Let $\{\pi(\cdot, \theta) \mid (\mu(\cdot, \theta), \sigma^2(\cdot, \theta)) \in \mathcal{P}, \ \theta \in \Theta\}$ denote the parametric family of marginal densities implied by the specification of the parametric model in Assumption 8. This family is characterized by the fact that the density $\pi(\cdot, \theta)$ corresponding to the pair $(\mu(\cdot, \theta), \sigma^2(\cdot, \theta))$ is

$$\pi(x, \theta) = \frac{\xi(\theta)}{\sigma^2(x, \theta)} \exp\left\{\int^x \frac{2\mu(u, \theta)}{\sigma^2(u, \theta)} du\right\} \tag{6.5}$$

where the choice of the lower bound of integration in the interior of the domain of the diffusion is irrelevant, and is absorbed in the normalization constant $\xi(\theta)$ determined to insure that the density integrates to one. If we let the true marginal density of the process be

$$\pi_0(x) = \frac{\xi_0}{\sigma_0^2(x)} \exp\left\{ \int^x \frac{2\mu_0(u)}{\sigma_0^2(u)} du \right\} \tag{6.6}$$

we can then test

$$H_{M0} : \quad \exists\, \theta_0 \in \Theta \text{ such that } \pi\,(\cdot, \theta_0) = \pi_0(\cdot)$$
$$H_{M1} : \quad \pi_0\,(\cdot) \notin \Pi_M. \tag{6.7}$$

It is necessary that H_{M0} be true for H_0 to be true. If the true density $\pi_0\,(\cdot)$ were known, we could simply check to see if it belonged to the proposed parametric class. Since it is unknown, we must estimate it, and do so with an estimator that does not already assume that the null hypothesis is correct (otherwise there is obviously no way of testing it). We use for that purpose a nonparametric estimator – that is, free of all parametric assumptions regarding μ and σ^2 – which will converge to the true density whether or not the parametric model in Assumption 8 is correctly specified. Now consider a parametric estimator of the implied density $\pi(\cdot, \theta_0)$. It will converge to the true density only if the model is correctly specified. Therefore the parametric and nonparametric density estimators should be close together if the parametric model is correct, and far from each other otherwise. A measure of distance M between the two density estimates provides a natural statistic to test the null hypothesis of correct parametric specification. Aït-Sahalia (1996c) suggested to test H_{M0} using the distance measure between the densities:

$$M \equiv \min_{\theta \in \Theta} \int_{\underline{x}}^{\bar{x}} (\pi(x, \theta) - \pi_0(x))^2\, \pi_0(x)\, w(x) dx \tag{6.8}$$

where w is a weight (or trimming) function, for instance $w(x) = 1\{|x| \le c\}$ for some constant c or $w(x) = 1$. The former is used to analyze the fixed-point trimming, and the second no trimming or the fixed-percentage trimming. When the state space has finite boundaries, trimming can be advisable.

The test statistic is based on

$$\hat{M} = nh \min_{\theta \in \Theta} \int_D (\pi(x, \theta) - \hat{\pi}(x))^2\, \hat{\pi}(x) w(x) dx, \tag{6.9}$$

where $\hat{\pi}$ is the nonparametric density estimate of π_0, computed with bandwidth h. The null hypothesis is therefore rejected when the test statistic $\hat{M}$ is large enough. The test evaluates the distance between the densities at the "best possible" parametric estimator:

$$\hat{\theta}_M \equiv \arg\min_{\theta \in \Theta} \int_D (\pi(x, \theta) - \hat{\pi}(x))^2\, \hat{\pi}(x) w(x) dx. \tag{6.10}$$

The test rejects the parametric specification $\pi(\cdot, \theta)$ if $\hat{M}$ takes a large value. The intuition for the test is straightforward. If $\pi(\cdot, \theta)$ is the correct specification, $\hat{M}$ should be small.

Under stationarity, $\hat{M}$ is shown in Aït-Sahalia (1996c) to be asymptotically Normally distributed and the critical value $c(\alpha)$ of the size α test is given by

$$\hat{c}(\alpha) = \hat{E}_M + z_{1-\alpha} h^{1/2} \hat{V}_M^{-1/2},$$

where $z_{1-\alpha}$ is the one-sided Normal cutoff for α, and

$$\hat{E}_M = c_1 \int_{-\infty}^{\infty} \hat{\pi}^2(x) w(x)\, dx \quad \text{and} \quad \hat{V}_M = c_2 \int_{-\infty}^{\infty} \hat{\pi}^4(x) w(x) dx$$

for constants c_1 and c_2 dependent upon the kernel function only, and given by

$$c_1 = \int_{-\infty}^{+\infty} K^2(x)\, dx$$

$$c_2 = 2 \int_{-\infty}^{+\infty} \left\{ \int_{-\infty}^{+\infty} K(u) K(u+x)\, du \right\}^2 dx.$$

Following that work, Pritzker (1998) noted that, in small samples, the near-nonstationarity of empirical interest rate data can lead to over rejection of the null hypothesis when critical values are computed based on the asymptotic distribution derived under stationarity [see also Chapman and Pearson (2000), and Chen and Gao (2004b) for a critique of the critique]. I will revisit this issue in Section 7.

6.1.2   Testing the Specification of Transitions: An Indirect Approach

The stationary marginal density of the process, as just discussed, does not summarize all the information available in the data. Aït-Sahalia (1996c) shows how to exploit stationarity (in fact, just time-homogeneity) by combining the Kolmogorov forward and backward equations characterizing the transition function $p(y, t|x, s)$ in a way that eliminates the time derivatives of p – which are unobservable with discrete data. Consider the forward Kolmogorov equation, with the natural initial condition (x and s are fixed):

$$\frac{\partial p(y, t|x, s)}{\partial t} = -\frac{\partial}{\partial y}(\mu(y) p(y, t|x, s)) + \frac{1}{2} \frac{\partial^2}{\partial y^2}(\sigma^2(y) p(y, t|x, s))$$

$$(6.11)$$

for all y in the interior of the domain S of the diffusion and t such that $t > s$. The backward equation (y and t are fixed) is

$$-\frac{\partial p(y, t | x, s)}{\partial s} = \mu(x) \frac{\partial}{\partial x}(p(y, t | x, s)) + \frac{1}{2}\sigma^2(x) \frac{\partial^2}{\partial x^2}(p(y, t | x, s))$$

(6.12)

for all x in S and s such that $0 \leq s < t$.

Unfortunately, these two equations cannot be used as such to estimate the parameters because their left-hand side contains the derivative of the transition density with respect to time. Time derivatives cannot be estimated without observations on how the process changes over small intervals of time. But we can work around this problem by getting rid of the time derivatives as follows. Under time-homogeneity, $p(y, t | x, s) = p(y, t - s | x, 0) \equiv p(y | x, t - s)$ and therefore: $\partial p / \partial t = -\partial p / \partial s$. Combining the two equations (6.11)–(6.12) then yields the transition discrepancy:

$$K(y | x, \Delta) \equiv \left\{ \frac{1}{2} \frac{\partial^2}{\partial y^2}(\sigma^2(y) \, p(y | x, \Delta)) - \frac{\partial}{\partial y}(\mu(y) \, p(y | x, \Delta)) \right\}$$

(6.13)

$$- \left\{ \mu(x) \frac{\partial}{\partial x}(p(y | x, \Delta)) + \frac{1}{2}\sigma^2(x, \theta) \frac{\partial^2}{\partial x^2}(p(y | x, \Delta)) \right\}$$

where $\Delta = t - s$. For every (x, y) in S^2 and $\Delta > 0$, $K(y | x, \Delta)$ must be zero. Note that this must hold for every time interval Δ, not just small ones.

If we now parameterize the diffusion process, then K (with μ and σ^2 replaced by their assumed parametric form $\mu(\cdot, \theta)$ and $\sigma^2(\cdot, \theta)$ respectively) must be zero at the true parameter value under the null of correct parametric specification. Given nonparametric estimates of the transition function, $K = 0$ provides a testable implication. While the above discussion focuses on diffusions, the Kolmogorov equations have natural extensions for more general Markov processes (such as processes with jumps) and the corresponding transition discrepancy can be defined.

6.1.3   Testing the Specification of Transitions: A Direct Approach

In what follows, I discuss different approaches to understanding the behavior of transition functions. I consider specification tests for any given parameterization; tests for the Markov hypothesis; tests for the continuity of sample paths; all are based on nonparametric estimation of the transition functions.

Aït-Sahalia, Fan, and Peng (2005a) propose to develop an alternative specification test for the transition density of the process, based on a direct comparison of the nonparametric estimate of the transition function to the assumed parametric transition function instead of the indirect transition discrepancy criterion, that is in the form

$$H_0 : p(y|x, \Delta) = p(y|x, \Delta, \theta) \quad \text{vs.} \quad H_1 : p(y|x, \Delta) \neq p(y|x, \Delta, \theta)$$
(6.14)

instead of the indirect approach

$$H_0 : K(y|x, \Delta, \theta) = 0 \quad \text{vs.} \quad H_1 : K(y|x, \Delta, \theta) \neq 0.$$
(6.15)

What makes this new direct testing approach possible is the subsequent development described in Section 4 of closed form expansions for $p(y|x, \Delta, \theta)$, which, as noted above, is rarely known in closed form; this is required for (6.14), whereas (6.15) does not require knowledge of $p(y|x, \Delta, \theta)$. A complementary approach to this is the one proposed by Hong and Li (2005), who use the fact that under the null hypothesis, the random variables $\{P(X_{i\Delta}|X_{(i-1)\Delta}, \Delta, \theta)\}$ are a sequence of i.i.d. uniform random variables; see also Thompson (2004), Chen and Gao (2004a), and Corradi and Swanson (2005). Using for P the closed form approximations of Aït-Sahalia (2002b), they proposed to detect the departure from the null hypothesis by comparing the kernel-estimated bivariate density of $\{(Z_i, Z_{i+\Delta})\}$ with that of the uniform distribution on the unit square, where $Z_i = P(X_{i\Delta}|X_{(i-1)\Delta}, \Delta, \theta)$. They need to deal with the boundary issues for the kernel density estimates on a finite region.

As in the parametric situation of (4.2), note that the logarithm of the likelihood function of the observed data $\{X_1, \cdots, X_{n+\Delta}\}$ is

$$\ell(p) = \sum_{i=1}^{n} \ln p\big(X_{(i+1)\Delta}|X_{i\Delta}, \Delta\big),$$

after ignoring the stationary density $\pi(X_1)$. A natural test statistic is to compare the likelihood ratio under the null hypothesis and the alternative hypothesis. This leads to the test statistic

$$T_0 = \sum_{i=1}^{n} \ln\big(\hat{p}(X_{(i+1)\Delta}|X_{i\Delta}, \Delta)/p(X_{(i+1)\Delta}|X_i, \Delta, \hat{\theta})\big) w\big(X_{i\Delta}, X_{(i+1)\Delta}\big),$$
(6.16)

where w is a weight function. Note that this is not the maximum likelihood ratio test, since the estimate under the alternative model is not derived from the maximum likelihood estimate.

Under the null hypothesis (6.14), the parametric and nonparametric estimators are approximately the same. Using for p the locally linear estimator described below, the null distribution of T_0 is usually obtained by Taylor's expansion:

$$T_0 \approx \sum_{i=1}^{n} \frac{\hat{p}(X_{(i+1)\Delta}|X_{i\Delta}, \Delta) - p(X_{i+\Delta}|X_{i\Delta}, \Delta, \hat{\theta})}{p(X_{(i+1)\Delta}|X_i, \Delta, \hat{\theta})} w\left(X_{i\Delta}, X_{(i+1)\Delta}\right)$$

$$+ \frac{1}{2} \sum_{i=1}^{n} \left\{ \frac{\hat{p}(X_{(i+1)\Delta}|X_{i\Delta}) - p(X_{(i+1)\Delta}|X_{i\Delta}, \Delta, \hat{\theta})}{p(X_{(i+1)\Delta}|X_{i\Delta}, \Delta, \hat{\theta})} \right\}^2 w\left(X_{i\Delta}, X_{(i+1)\Delta}\right).$$

As the local linear estimator $\hat{p}$ is not an MLE, it is not clear whether the first term is asymptotically negligible. To avoid unnecessary technicality, we will consider the following χ^2-test statistic

$$T_1 = \sum_{i=1}^{n} \left\{ \frac{\hat{p}(X_{(i+1)\Delta}|X_{i\Delta}, \Delta) - p(X_{(i+1)\Delta}|X_{i\Delta}, \Delta, \hat{\theta})}{p(X_{(i+1)\Delta}|X_{i\Delta}, \Delta, \hat{\theta})} \right\}^2 w\left(X_{i\Delta}, X_{(i+1)\Delta}\right).$$

$$(6.17)$$

A natural alternative method to T_2 is

$$T_2 = \sum_{i=1}^{n} \left\{ \hat{p}\left(X_{(i+1)\Delta}|X_{i\Delta}, \Delta\right) - p\left(X_{(i+1)\Delta}|X_{i\Delta}, \Delta, \hat{\theta}\right) \right\}^2 w\left(X_{i\Delta}, X_{(i+1)\Delta}\right).$$

$$(6.18)$$

The transition-density-based test depends on two smoothing parameters h_1 and h_2. It is somewhat hard to implement. Like the Cramer–von Mises test, a viable alternative method is to compare the discrepancies between transition distributions. This leads to the test statistic

$$T_3 = \sum_{i=1}^{n} \left\{ \hat{P}\left(X_{(i+1)\Delta}|X_{i\Delta}, \Delta\right) - P\left(X_{(i+1)\Delta}|X_{i\Delta}, \Delta, \hat{\theta}\right) \right\}^2 w\left(X_{i\Delta}, X_{(i+1)\Delta}\right).$$

$$(6.19)$$

As we describe in the paper, the tests T_1 and T_2 are more powerful for detecting local departures from the null model, while T_3 is more powerful for detecting the global departures. The former involves an additional choice of bandwidth h_2. We derive the distribution of these statistics and investigate their power properties in departure directions that are relevant for empirical work in finance. The null distribution of T_3 can be better approximated by its asymptotic counterpart, as T_3 only localizes in the x-direction and hence uses many more local data points. This also makes its implementation more stable.

6.2   Nonparametric Estimation

6.2.1   *Nonparametric Global Estimation*

In the case where sampling occurs at a fixed $\Delta > 0$, that is, under Assumption 5, nonparametric estimation options are limited. Under Assumption 12,

Aït-Sahalia (1996b) shows that

$$\sigma^2(x) = \frac{2}{\pi(x)} \int^x \mu(u) \, \pi(u) \, du, \tag{6.20}$$

where π is the stationary (marginal) density of the process. Suppose we parameterize μ to be affine in the state variable, $\mu(x) = \beta(\sigma - x)$. In that case,

$$E[X_\Delta | X_0] = \alpha + e^{-\beta \Delta}(X_0 - \alpha). \tag{6.21}$$

This conditional moment condition applies for any $\Delta > 0$. As a consequence, (α, β) can be recovered by estimating a first-order scalar autoregression via least squares from data sampled at any interval Δ. The implied drift estimator may be plugged into formula (6.20) to produce a semiparametric estimator of $\sigma^2(x)$. Since neither (6.21) nor (6.20) requires that the time interval be small, this estimator of $\sigma^2(x)$ can be computed from data sampled at any time interval Δ, not just small ones.

6.2.2   Nonparametric Local Estimation

Under Assumption 21, the infinitesimal drift and diffusion functions can be defined as the limits of the conditional mean and variance of the process:

$$\mu(x) = \lim_{\Delta \to 0} \frac{1}{\Delta} \int_{|y-x^*|<\varepsilon} (y - x) \, p(y|x, \Delta) dy \tag{6.22}$$

$$\sigma^2(x) = \lim_{\Delta \to 0} \frac{1}{\Delta} \int_{|y-x^*|<\varepsilon} (y - x)^2 p(y|x, \Delta) dy. \tag{6.23}$$

These local characterizations suggest a regression-based estimation of μ and σ, since they can be rewritten as

$$E\left[\Delta^{-1/2}\xi_{i\Delta} | X_{(i-1)\Delta} = x\right] = \mu(x) + o(\Delta)$$
$$E\left[\xi_{i\Delta}^2 | X_{(i-1)\Delta} = x\right] = \sigma^2(x) + o(\Delta)$$

where $\xi_{i\Delta} = \Delta^{-1/2}(X_{i\Delta} - X_{(i-1)\Delta})$ denotes the scaled increments of the process.

Kernel estimators of the type

$$\hat{\mu}(x) = \frac{\sum_{i=1}^{n} \Delta^{-1/2}\xi_{i\Delta} K_h\left(X_{(i-1)\Delta} - x\right)}{\sum_{i=1}^{n} K_h\left(X_{(i-1)\Delta} - x\right)} \quad \text{and}$$

$$\hat{\sigma}^2(x) = \frac{\sum_{i=1}^{n} \xi_{i\Delta}^2 K_h\left(X_{(i-1)\Delta} - x\right)}{\sum_{i=1}^{n} K_h\left(X_{(i-1)\Delta} - x\right)}$$

where K is the kernel function, h the bandwidth, and $K_h(z) = h^{-1}K(z/h)$, have been considered by Florens-Zmirou (1989), Stanton (1997), Jiang and Knight (1997), Bandi and Phillips (2003), and Kristensen (2004). Instead of a kernel estimator (which is a locally constant estimator), Fan and Yao (1998) apply locally linear regression to this problem. This results in an estimator which has better boundary behavior than the kernel estimator.

These estimators are based on a form of state-domain smoothing, that is, they rely on using information on observations that are locally close together in space. But it is possible to use instead information on observations that are locally close together in time. And to combine both sources of information for potential efficiency gains.

6.2.3   Nonparametric Estimation of Transition Densities

To estimate the transition density $p(y|x, \Delta)$ nonparametrically using discretely sampled data on X at time intervals Δ, we can use a Nadaraya–Watson kernel estimator for the conditional density, or use a locally linear estimator (see Fan, Yao, and Tong 1996). A kernel estimator is simply based on the fact that $p(y|x, \Delta)$ is the ratio of the join density of (X_Δ, X_0) to the marginal density of X_0, that is

$$\hat{p}(y|x, \Delta) = \frac{\sum_{i=1}^{n} K_h(X_{i\Delta} - y) K_h\left(X_{(i-1)\Delta} - x\right)}{\sum_{i=1}^{n} K_h\left(X_{(i-1)\Delta} - x\right)}. \tag{6.24}$$

Consider now two bandwidths h_1 and h_2 and two kernel functions K and W. The locally linear estimator of p is based on observing that as $h_2 \to 0$

$$E\left\{K_{h_2}\left(X_{(i+1)\Delta} - y\right)|X_{i\Delta} = x\right\} \approx p(y|x), \tag{6.25}$$

where $K_h(z) = K(z/h)/h$. The left-hand side of (6.25) is the regression function of the random variable $K_{h_2}(X_{(i+1)\Delta} - y)$ given $X_{i\Delta} = x$. Hence, the local linear fit can be used to estimate this regression function. For each given x, one minimizes

$$\sum_{i=1}^{n} \left\{K_{h_2}\left(X_{(i+1)\Delta} - y\right) - \alpha - \beta(X_{i\Delta} - x)\right\}^2 W_{h_1}(X_{i\Delta} - x) \tag{6.26}$$

with respect to the local parameters α and β. The resulting estimate of the conditional density is simply $\hat{\alpha}$. The estimator can be explicitly expressed as

$$\hat{p}(y|x, \Delta) = \frac{1}{nh_1h_2} \sum_{i=1}^{n} W_n\left(\frac{X_{i\Delta} - x}{h_1}; x\right) K\left(\frac{X_{(i+1)\Delta} - y}{h_2}\right), \tag{6.27}$$

where W_n is the effective kernel induced by the local linear fit. Explicitly, it is given by

$$W_n(z; x) = W(z)\frac{s_{n,2}(x) - zs_{n,1}(x)}{s_{n,0}(x)s_{n,2}(x) - s_{n,1}(x)^2},$$

where

$$s_{n,j}(x) = \frac{1}{nh_1} \sum_{i=1}^{n} \left(\frac{X_{i\Delta} - x}{h_1}\right)^j W\left(\frac{X_{i\Delta} - x}{h_1}\right).$$

Note that the effective kernel W_n depends on the sampling data points and the location x.

From (6.27), a possible estimate of the transition distribution $P(y|x, \Delta) = P(X_{i+\Delta} < y | X_i = x, \Delta)$ is given by

$$\hat{P}(y|x, \Delta) = \int_{-\infty}^{y} \hat{p}(z|x)dz$$

$$= \frac{1}{nh_1} \sum_{i=1}^{n} W_n\left(\frac{X_{i\Delta} - x}{h_1}; x\right) \bar{K}\left(\frac{X_{(i+1)\Delta} - y}{h_2}\right),$$

where $\bar{K}(u) = \int_{u}^{\infty} K(z)dz$.

6.2.4   Nonparametric Option-Based Estimation of Transition Densities

A different approach is to estimate the transition density using discretely sampled observations on option prices instead of the prices of the underlying asset. A method to achieve this either nonparametrically or semiparametrically was proposed by Aït-Sahalia and Lo (1998).

Under standard assumptions the price of a derivative, written on the underlying asset with price process X, and with European payoff function $g(.)$ to be received Δ units of time from now is simply

$$H(x, \Delta) = e^{-r\Delta} \int_{0}^{+\infty} g(y) \, p^*(y|x, \Delta)dy \tag{6.28}$$

where r is the riskless rate and $p^*(y|x, \Delta)$ denotes the transition density corresponding to the risk-neutral dynamics of X. If the observed dynamics of X are given by Assumption 9, then the risk-neutral ones correspond to replacing $\mu(x)$ by $(r - q)x$ where q denotes the dividend rate paid by the asset (r and q are assumed constant for simplicity.)

If we specialize (6.28) to the payoff of a call option with strike price K, then $g_K(y) = \max(0, y - K)$ and it follows that

$$p^*(y|x, \Delta) = e^{r\Delta} \left[\frac{\partial^2 H_K(x, \Delta)}{\partial K^2}\right]_{K=y} \tag{6.29}$$

where H_K is the price of a call option with strike K (see Breeden and Litzenberger, 1978). One can then estimate by nonparametric regression the call pricing function H_K and differentiate twice with respect to K. Aït-Sahalia and Lo (1998) discuss the twin curses of dimensionality and differentiation as they relate to this problem and suggest various solutions, including a semiparametric regression at the level of implied volatilities.

Note that the theory imposes the restriction that the price of a call option must be a decreasing and convex function of the option's strike price. Aït-Sahalia and Duarte (2003) show how to impose these types of shape restrictions on p^* as a simple modification of nonparametric locally polynomial estimators. Their estimators satisfy in all samples these shapes restrictions.

Aït-Sahalia and Lo (2000) show how these types of transition density estimators can be used to infer the representative agent's preferences that are implicit in the market prices of options. If we let $p(y|x, \Delta)$ denote the transition density of X under its observed dynamics, then in an exchange economy where X is the only consumption good the representative agent maximizes the utility of consumption at date t, $U_t(X)$, then

$$p^*(y|x, \Delta) = c \, \zeta_\Delta(y|x) \, p(y|x, \Delta),$$

where $\zeta_\Delta(y|x) = U'_\Delta(y) / U'_0(x)$ is the agent's marginal rate of substitution and c is a constant so that the left-hand side integrates to one. The coefficient of local risk aversion of the agent is then

$$\gamma(y|x, \Delta) \equiv -\frac{U''_\Delta(y)}{U'_0(x)} = -\frac{\partial \zeta_\Delta(y|x)/\partial y}{\zeta_\Delta(y|x)}$$

$$= \frac{\partial p(y|x, \Delta)/\partial y}{p(y|x, \Delta)} - \frac{\partial p^*(y|x, \Delta)/\partial y}{p^*(y|x, \Delta)}$$

which can be estimated directly from estimates of the two transition densities p and p^*.

7   RELAXING THE MODEL SPECIFICATION: ALLOWING FOR NONSTATIONARY DYNAMICS

In this section, I discuss inference and testing when Assumption 12 is not satisfied.

7.1   Likelihood Estimation Under Nonstationarity

There is an extensive literature applicable to discrete-time stationary Markov processes starting with the work of Billingsley, (1961). The asymptotic co-variance matrix for the ML estimator is the inverse of the score covariance or information matrix where the score at date t is $\partial \ln p(X_{t+\Delta}|X_t, \Delta, \theta)/\partial\theta$ where $\ln p(\cdot|x, \Delta, \theta)$ is the logarithm of the conditional density over an interval of time Δ and a parameter value θ.

When the underlying Markov process is nonstationary, the score process inherits this nonstationarity. The rate of convergence and the limiting distribution of the maximum likelihood estimator depends upon growth properties of the score process [e.g., see Hall and Heyde (1980) Chapter 6.2]. A nondegenerate limiting distribution can be obtained when the score process behaves in a sufficiently regular fashion. The limiting distribution can be deduced by showing that general results pertaining to time series asymptotics (see e.g., Jeganathan, 1995) can be applied to the present context. One first establishes that the likelihood ratio has the locally asymptotically quadratic (LAQ) structure, then within that class separates between the locally asymptotically mixed Normal (LAMN), locally asymptotically Normal (LAN), and locally asymptotically

Brownian functional (LABF) structures. As we have seen, when the data generating process is stationary and ergodic, the estimation is typically in the LAN class. The LAMN class can be used to justify many of the standard inference methods given the ability to estimate the covariance matrix pertinent for the conditional normal approximating distribution. Rules for inference are special for the LABF case. These structures are familiar from the linear time series literature on unit roots and cointegration. Details for the case of a nonlinear Markov process can be found in Aït-Sahalia (2002b).

7.2   Nonparametric Local Estimation Under Nonstationarity

The properties of the estimators described in Section 6.2.2 have been studied by Bandi and Phillips (2003); see Bandi and Phillips (2002) for a survey of these results. Asymptotic results for these local estimators can be obtained, in the absence of a stationary distribution for the process, under conditions such as recurrence of the process.

7.3   Specification Testing When the Underlying
Process is Nonstationary

Recall now the specification test I described in Section 6 above for stationary processes, based on the marginal density. Aït-Sahalia and Park (2005) study the behavior of the marginal-based test in the local-to-unity framework. The idea is to draw a parallel with what happens in the unit root literature in time series: when studying an AR(1) model with autoregressive parameter ρ, in the nearly-integrated situation where ρ is close to one, it is often the case that the small sample distribution of the parameter estimate of ρ is better approximated by assuming that the process has a unit root (the discrete equivalent to our Brownian motion) than by assuming that the process has ρ close to but strictly smaller than one (in which case the process is stationary). We investigate the ability of that limiting distribution to better approximate the small behavior of the test when in fact the data generating process is stationary but exhibits very low speeds of mean reversion – as is the case for US interest rates, for instance. This will involve extensive use of the local time of the process.

In other words, if one fits an AR(1) process (i.e., Ornstein–Uhlenbeck) process to US short-term rates, $\rho = 0.99$ at the daily frequency, 0.95 at the monthly frequency. The process is still formally stationary (because of strong mean reversion at the extremes), but the asymptotics based on assuming stationarity are slow to converge. And it may well be that the asymptotic behavior of the test derived under nonstationarity is a better approximation to the small sample behavior of the test, just like the Dickey–Fuller distribution is a better approximation to the properties of $\hat{\rho}$ when the true value of ρ is 0.95, say.

As before, X is observed at intervals of length Δ over time $[0, T]$. We let $T \to \infty$ and possibly $\Delta \to 0$. Suppose we apply the marginal density-based test above, which is designed for stationary processes. Nonstationarity can be viewed as a different form of misspecification (compared to misspecifying the form of μ and σ). For nonstationary diffusions, there is no stationary density. Therefore, any parametric family of densities π cannot correctly specify the underlying density. And the test must be able to reject the null of correct specification.

What does the kernel density estimator $\hat{\pi}$ now estimate? It turns out that

$$\hat{\pi}(x) = \frac{L(T, x)}{T} + o_p(1)$$

where L is the local time of the process (see Akonom 1993). This also plays a crucial role in the estimation of nonstationary processes (see Bandi and Phillips, 2003). The local time L of X at x is

$$L(T, x) = \lim_{\varepsilon \to 0} \frac{1}{2\varepsilon} \int_0^T 1\{|X_t - x| < \varepsilon\} \, dt.$$

Intuitively, $L(T, x)$ denote the time spent by X in the neighborhood of point x between time 0 and time T. The occupation times formula states that

$$\int_0^T f(X_t) dt = \int_{-\infty}^\infty f(x) L(T, x) \, dx$$

for any nonnegative function f on $\mathbb{R}$, allows one to switch between time and space integrals.

Of critical importance here will be the behavior of the local time of the process asymptotically in T. We asume that, for the processes of interest, there exists $\kappa \in [0, 1]$ such that for each x, $L(T, x) = O_p(T^\kappa)$ as $T \to \infty$. A stationary process should be expected to spend more time near any given value x than an explosive process, which barely visits each point. Indeed, $\kappa = 1$ for stationary (or positive recurrent) diffusions: as $T \to \infty$,

$$\frac{L(T, x)}{T} \to \pi(x) \quad \text{a.s.}$$

By contrast, $\kappa = 0$ for transient processes. We also give examples illustrating the intermediary range $0 < \kappa < 1$, including Brownian motion for which $\kappa = 1/2$ and

$$L(T, x) =_d T^{1/2} L(1, T^{-1/2} x)$$

where for fixed x, as $T \to \infty$, we have

$$L(1, T^{-1/2} x) \to L(1, 0)$$

due to the continuity of $L(1, \cdot)$. The distribution of $L(1, 0)$ or more generally $L(T, 0)$ is given by

$$\Pr(L(T, 0) \geq u) = \sqrt{\frac{2}{\pi T}} \int_u^{+\infty} \exp\left(-\frac{y^2}{2T}\right) dy. \tag{7.1}$$

A heuristic argument that gives the result goes as follows. Since the test is an integral of a power of $\hat{\pi}$, and $\hat{\pi} = \frac{L}{T} + o_p(1)$ we will have to study integrals of powers of the local time L. We have $L(T, x) = T^\kappa \ell_T(x)$. But we must also have $\int_{-\infty}^{\infty} L(T, x)dx \equiv T$ since the total time spent between 0 and T in the neighborhood of *all* points is T. Therefore $\int_{-\infty}^{\infty} \ell_T(x)dx = T^{1-\kappa}$ where ℓ_T is neither exploding nor vanishing on its support. For these two things to happen together, we expect the support of ℓ_T to expand at rate $T^{1-\kappa}$ as $T \to \infty$. On its support, $\ell_T^q(x) \sim 1$ and we may therefore expect to have

$$\int_{-\infty}^{\infty} x^p L^q(T, x)dx \sim T^{q\kappa} \int_{-T^{1-\kappa}}^{T^{1-\kappa}} x^p \ell_T^q(x)dx \sim T^{(p+1)(1-\kappa)+q\kappa}$$

and for a bounded function b:

$$\int_{-\infty}^{\infty} b(x)L^q(T, x)dx \sim T^{q\kappa} \int_{-T^{1-\kappa}}^{T^{1-\kappa}} b(x)\ell_T^q(x)dx \sim T^{q\kappa}.$$

The first set of results concern the consistency of the test. So let us assume that the model is misspecified even if the diffusion is stationary. Aït-Sahalia and Park (2005) show that the test is consistent if $\Delta = o(T^{(9\kappa-5)/4-\delta})$ for some $\delta > 0$. So the test is consistent if Δ is sufficiently small relative to T. Intuitively, as Δ decreases we collect more information and as T increases the underlying diffusions exhibit more nonstationary characteristics. For stationary diffusions, the result implies that the misspecified models are rejected asymptotically with probability one, under no conditions other than $T \to \infty$. Indeed, in this case we have $\kappa = 1$, and the condition requires that $\Delta = o(T^{1-\delta})$ for some $\delta > 0$. But as κ decreases down from 1, we need more stringent conditions for the test to be consistent. For Brownian motion, we have $\kappa = 1/2$. The required condition for the test consistency becomes $\Delta = o(T^{-1/8-\delta})$. Now, in most practical applications, Δ is much smaller than the reciprocal of any fractional power of the time span T. If we use daily observations, then $\Delta \approx 1/252 = 0.004$. Even for $T = 100$ years, we have $T^{-1/8} \approx 0.5623$, which is much bigger. So for the usual values of T and Δ, the test is likely to reject.

We can use this finding to predict the performance of the test for stationary diffusions which are nearly nonstationary. For instance, consider a highly persistent Ornstein–Uhlenbeck process (i.e., with mean-reversion parameter positive but close to 0). In that situation, the test is expected to over-reject the null in small samples against any parametric specification, and this is what is found empirically by Pritzker (1998).

Next, we derive the asymptotic distribution of the test statistic $\hat{M}$ when the data generating process is nearly Brownian motion, and later investigate the ability of that limiting distribution to approximate the small behavior of the test when in fact the data generating process is stationary but exhibits very low speeds of mean reversion – as is the case for US interest rates, for instance. We let X be generated as

$$dX_t = -\frac{\delta}{T} X_t dt + \sigma dW_t, \tag{7.2}$$

that is, an Ornstein–Uhlenbeck process with the mean reversion parameter $\beta = \delta/T$ for some $\delta \geq 0$ and $X_0 = 0$. Clearly, X reduces to a Brownian motion, if $\delta = 0$. We have that

$$X_t = \sigma \int_0^t \exp\left[-(\delta/T)(t-s)\right] dW_s$$

$$=_d \sigma\sqrt{T} \int_0^{t/T} \exp\left[-\delta(t/T-s)\right] dW_s$$

$$= \sigma\sqrt{T} V_{t/T}^\delta, \tag{7.3}$$

where V^δ is the Ornstein–Uhlenbeck process with the mean reversion parameter $\delta > 0$, unit variance and $V_0^\delta = 0$ a.s. The result in (7.3) follows in particular from the scale invariant property of the Brownian motion W, that is, $W_{Ts} =_d \sqrt{T} W_s$.

For the nearly Brownian motion in (7.2), we may obtain the limit distribution of the test statistic $\hat{M}$ more explicitly. We let $h \to 0$, $T \to \infty$ and $\Delta/h^2 \to 0$. Aït-Sahalia and Park (2005) show that for the near Brownian motion in (7.2), we have

$$\frac{\Delta}{h\sqrt{T}} \hat{M} \to_d \frac{L_\delta(1,0)}{\sigma} \min_{\theta\in\Theta} \int_{-\infty}^{\infty} \pi^2(x,\theta)w(x)\,dx, \tag{7.4}$$

where L_δ is the local time of the Ornstein–Uhlenbeck process V^δ. The distribution of $L_0(1,0)$ is given in (7.1). Of course, the constant term in the limiting distribution of $\hat{M}$ can be computed once the parametric family $\pi(\cdot,\theta)$ is specified. For Brownian motion, the variance of the marginal distribution increases and explodes without a bound as $T \to \infty$. Therefore, the density that most closely approximates the (nonexisting) limiting marginal density of Brownian motion is naturally given by the most diffuse distribution in the family, that is, the distribution with the largest variance in case of the normal family. The mean becomes unimportant in this case. Given this observation, it is intuitive that the distribution of $\hat{M}$ involves the maximal variance and no mean parameter.

8   RELAXING THE MODEL SPECIFICATION: ALLOWING FOR DISCONTINUOUS DYNAMICS

The fact that jumps play an important role in many variables in economics and finance, such as asset returns, interest rates or currencies, as well as a sense of diminishing marginal returns in studies of the "simple" diffusive case, has led to a flurry of recent activity dealing with jump processes. I now examine some of these questions, thereby relaxing Assumption 2 to allow for jumps. Assumptions 1 and 3 are maintained.

8.1   Testing for Jumps Using the Transition Density

In Aït-Sahalia (1996a, 2002c) I investigated whether discretely sampled financial data can help us decide which continuous-time models are sensible.

Diffusion processes are characterized by the continuity of their sample paths. This cannot be verified from the discrete sample path: even if the underlying path were continuous, data sampled at discrete times will always appear as a succession of jumps. Instead, I relied on a necessary and sufficient characterization of the transition density to determine whether the discontinuities observed are the result of the discreteness of sampling, or rather evidence of genuine jump dynamics for the underlying continuous-time process.

So, what can be said if the process is only observed at a finite observation interval Δ? Consider a family of probability distributions for the Markov process X with state space $\mathbb{R}$, and indexed by the time interval Δ: $P(\cdot|x, \Delta)$. Could this family of densities have come from a scalar diffusion process, that is, a process with continuous sample paths, or must jumps be included? As discussed in these two papers, this question can be addressed in light of the total positivity characterization of Karlin and McGregor (1959b). The relevant result here is the fact that P_θ represents the family of transition densities for a (univariate) diffusion if and only if the transition function of any diffusion process must obey the *total positivity* inequality. While total positivity has a more general representation and probabilistic interpretation, it implies

$$P(B|x, \Delta)\, P\left(\tilde{B}|\tilde{x}, \Delta\right) - P(B|\tilde{x}, \Delta)\, P\left(\tilde{B}|x, \Delta\right) > 0 \qquad (8.1)$$

whenever, $x < \tilde{x}$ and $B < \tilde{B}$ (where $B < \tilde{B}$ is interpreted to mean that every element of B is less than every element of $\tilde{B}$). Since this must hold for any choice of $\tilde{x}$ and $\tilde{B}$, there is a local (in the state) counterpart that we express using the logarithm of the density:

$$\frac{\partial^2}{\partial x \partial y} \ln p(y|x, \Delta) > 0 \qquad (8.2)$$

for all x and y and interval Δ. This cross-derivative restriction for each choice of x, y, and Δ is a necessary condition for transition distributions to be those implied by a scalar diffusion. A partial converse is also available. Suppose that the family of distribution functions of a Markov process on $\mathbb{R}$ satisfies (8.1) for any positive Δ. Then under a side condition, there exists a realization of the process such that almost all sample paths are continuous. Aït-Sahalia (2002c) shows how to build and justify formally a statistical test, in the parametric case, of this cross-derivative restriction for data sampled at a given sampling interval Δ.

The following example shows how criterion (8.2) can be used to eliminate some transition densities as coming from a model of a scalar diffusion. Suppose that $p(y|x, \Delta)$ depends on the state (y, x) only through $y - x$. Using the criterion (8.2), it can be shown that the only admissible solutions is

$$p(y|x, \Delta) = (2\pi \beta^2 \Delta)^{-1/2} \exp\left\{ -\frac{(y - x - \alpha\Delta)^2}{2\beta^2 \Delta} \right\} \qquad (8.3)$$

where $\theta = (\alpha, \beta)$, that is the transition density of an arithmetic Brownian motion. Consider the generalized Cauchy density

$$\ln p(y|x, \Delta) = -\ln \pi + \ln a(\Delta) - \ln[a(\Delta)^2 + (y - x)^2]$$

where $a(\Delta)$ is positive. The criterion (8.2) will fail for large $y - x$. Aït-Sahalia (2002c) contains other examples.

More generally, total positivity implies restrictions on processes defined on state spaces other than $\mathbb{R}$. Consider a continuous-time, stationary, Markov chain that can only take countable discrete values, say, $\{\ldots, -1, 0, 1, \ldots\}$. When does such a process have continuous sample paths? Obviously, the notion of continuity of a sample path depends on the state space: in $\mathbb{R}$, this is the usual definition of a continuous function. More generally, by continuity one means continuity with respect to the order topology of the state space of the process. In a discrete-state space, the appropriate notion of continuity of the chain's sample paths is the following intuitive one: it constrains the chain to never jump by more than one state at a time, either up or down. It turns out that the restriction on the chain's transition probabilities analogous to (8.1) characterizes precisely this form of continuity: total positivity across all intervals restricts the process to be a so-called birth-and-death process (see Karlin and McGregor, 1959a). In this sense, a birth-and-death process is the discrete-state analog to a scalar diffusion. See Aït-Sahalia (2002c) for further discussion and implications for derivative pricing methods, such as binomial trees.

For a fixed Δ, total positivity is a necessary restriction on the transition distribution but not a sufficient one. Given a candidate transition distribution over an interval Δ, we did not construct a diffusion with that transition density. Frydman and Singer (1979) study the analogous question for a finite state birth and death process. In their study they show that to embed a single transition matrix (over an interval Δ) satisfying total positivity in a continuous-time Markov process it is sometimes necessary that the continuous-time process be time-inhomogeneous. They show that the total positivity function is a weaker restriction than embeddability for a continuous-time process that is restricted to be time-homogeneous.

But what if we are not willing to take a stand on a parametric specification for the transition density p? Aït-Sahalia and Fan (2005a) propose to design and implement a test for restriction (8.2) based on nonparametric estimators of p. There are several methods to testing the constraints (8.2). They can be classified as local and global approaches. The local test is to examine whether constraints (8.2) are violated at various places, while global approaches consist in testing whether the minimum of (8.2) for (x, y) over a compact set, which contains for instance 80% of data, is positive. In both cases, we face the challenge of the estimation of the second partial derivatives. With such estimates, the nonparametric test statistics can easily be formulated.

There are three possible approaches to estimating $\partial^2 \ln p(y|x, \Delta)/\partial x \partial y$. The naive one is the substitution estimator, using one of the estimators discussed in Section 6.2.3. The second approach is to extend the local likelihood estimation of the density function [see Hjort and Jones (1996) and Loader (1996)] to the estimation of the conditional density. Combining this with the local linear modeling of Fan (1992), a direct estimator of $\partial^2 \ln p(y|x, \Delta)/\partial x \partial y$ can be obtained. The third approach is to extend the "parametric-start" idea of Hjort and Glad (1995), Efron and Tibshirani (1996), and Glad (1998) to estimating nonparametrically the transition density. Take a parametric family of transition density such as those in Aït-Sahalia (2002c) as a starting point, correct the possible biases in the parametric estimation by using a nonparametric estimation to the difference. This kind of idea originates from the prewhitening technique of Press and Turkey (1956) on the estimation of spectral density. The advantage is that it allows us to incorporate the prior knowledge on the shape of the transition density. When the bandwidths of the nonparametric estimates are very large, the nonparametric estimates reduce to parametric estimates. This provides a smooth family of estimates indexed by the bandwidths, starting from parametric estimates of the transition density to full nonparametric estimate of transition density as bandwidths vary. This is particularly useful for our problem, as we need to estimate the difficult quantity $\partial^2 \ln p(y|x, \Delta)/\partial x \partial y$. On one hand, nonparametric estimates give a very slow rate of convergence while on the other the parametric estimates enjoy the usual root-n consistency. Our approach bridges the gaps between these two important approaches, allowing us to incorporate prior knowledge and making practical implementation feasible.

Other approaches to testing for jumps are based on the behavior of short dated options (Carr and Wu, 2003) or the different limiting behavior of the quadratic variation and related quantities, in the presence of jumps [see Barndorff-Nielsen and Shephard (2003), Andersen, Bollerslev, and Diebold (2003), and Huang and Tauchen (2006).]

8.2   Estimating the Volatility Parameter in the Presence of Jumps

A different issue related to the presence of jumps is whether they have an impact on our ability to estimate the other parameters of the process. In Aït-Sahalia (2004), I asked whether the presence of jumps impact our ability to estimate the diffusion parameter σ^2. Despite intuition that seems to suggest that the identification of σ^2 is hampered by the presence of the jumps, I showed that maximum likelihood can actually *perfectly* disentangle Brownian noise from jumps provided one samples frequently enough. For instance, suppose that, instead of Assumption 4 we are under Assumption 10. For simplicity, let us start by further assuming that (μ, σ, λ) are constant and that J_t is normally distributed in

$$dX_t = \mu dt + \sigma dW_t + J_t dN_t. \tag{8.4}$$

I first show this result in the context of a compound Poisson process, that is, the jump-diffusion model in (8.4).

The first result there showed that it is still possible, using maximum likelihood, to identify σ^2 with the same degree of precision as if there were no jumps, namely that when the Brownian motion is contaminated by compound Poisson jumps, it remains the case that

$$\text{AVAR}_{\text{MLE}}(\sigma^2) = 2\sigma^4\Delta + o(\Delta) \tag{8.5}$$

so that in the limit where sampling occurs infinitely often ($\Delta \to 0$), the MLE estimator of σ^2 has the same asymptotic distribution as if no jumps were present. These arguments are asymptotic in small Δ, that is, take the form of a Taylor expansion in Δ around $\Delta = 0$.

Note also that this result states that the presence of the jumps imposes no cost on our ability to estimate σ^2 : the variance which is squared in the leading term is only the diffusive variance σ^2, not the total variance $\sigma^2 + (\beta^2 + \eta)\lambda$. This can be contrasted with what would happen if, say, we contaminated the Brownian motion with another independent Brownian motion with known variance v. In that case, we could also estimate σ^2, but the asymptotic variance of the MLE would be $2(\sigma^2 + v)^2\Delta$.

What is happening here is that, as Δ gets smaller, our ability to identify price discontinuities improves. This is because these Poisson discontinuities are, by construction, discrete, and there are few of them relative to the diffusive moves. Then if we can see them, we can exclude them, and do as if they did not happen in the first place. More challenging therefore will be the case where the jumps are both infinitely frequent and infinitely small.

One may indeed wonder whether this result is driven by the fact that Poisson jumps share the dual characteristic of being large and infrequent. Is it possible to perturb the Brownian noise by a Lévy pure jump process other than Poisson, and still recover the parameter σ^2 as if no jumps were present? The reason one might expect this not to be possible is the fact that, among Lévy pure jump processes, the Poisson process is the only one with a finite number of jumps in a finite time interval. All other pure jump processes exhibit an *infinite number of small jumps* in any finite time interval. Intuitively, these tiny jumps ought to be harder to distinguish from Brownian noise, which is itself made up of many small moves. Perhaps more surprisingly then, I will show that maximum likelihood can still perfectly discriminate between Brownian noise and a Cauchy process, a canonical example of such processes.

I then examine whether the perfect distinction afforded by MLE is specific to the fact that the jump process considered so far was a compound Poisson process, or whether it extends to other types of jump processes. Among the class of continuous-time Markov processes, it is natural to look at Lévy processes. Poisson jumps are a unique case in the Lévy universe. Yet, it is possible to find examples of other pure jump processes for which the same result continues to hold, which cannot be explained away as easily as in the Poisson case.

A Lévy process can be decomposed as the sum of three independent components: a linear drift, a Brownian motion, and a pure jump process. Correspondingly, the log-characteristic function of a sum of independent random variables being the sum of their individual characteristic functions, the characteristic function of a Lévy process given in Assumption 11 is given by the Lévy–Khintchine formula, which states that there exist constants $b \in \mathbb{R}$, $c \geq 0$ and a positive sigma-finite measure $v(\cdot)$ on $\mathbb{R}\backslash\{0\}$ (extended to $\mathbb{R}$ by setting $v(\{0\}) = 0$) satisfying $\int_{-\infty}^{+\infty} \min(1, z^2)\, v(dz) < \infty$ such that the log-characteristic function $\psi(u)$ has the form for $u \in \mathbb{R}$:

$$\psi(u) = ibu - \frac{c^2}{2}u^2 + \int_{-\infty}^{+\infty} \left(e^{iuz} - 1 - iuzh(z)\right) v(dz). \qquad (8.6)$$

The three quantities $(\gamma_c, \sigma, v(\cdot))$, called the characteristics of the Lévy process, completely describe the probabilistic behavior of the process. γ_c is the drift rate of the process, σ its volatility from the Brownian component and the measure $v(\cdot)$ describes the pure jump component. It is known as the Lévy measure and has the interpretation that $v(E)$ for any subset $E \subset \mathbb{R}$ is the rate at which the process takes jumps of size $x \in E$, that is, the number of jumps of size falling in E per unit of time. Sample paths of the process are continuous if and only if $v \equiv 0$. Note that $v(\cdot)$ is not necessarily a probability measure, in that $v(\mathbb{R})$ may be finite or infinite. The function $h(z)$ is a weighting function whose role is to make the integrand in (8.6) integrable.

Examples of Lévy processes include the Brownian motion ($h = 0$, $b = 0$, $c = 1$, $v = 0$), the Poisson process ($h = 0$, $b = 0$, $c = 0$, $v(dx) = \lambda\delta_1(dx)$ where δ_1 is a Dirac point mass at $x = 1$) and the Poisson jump-diffusion I considered above in (8.4), corresponding to $h = 0$, $b = \mu$, $c > 0$, $v(dx) = \lambda n(x; \beta, \eta)dx$ where $n(x; \beta, \eta)$ is the Normal density with mean β and variance η.

The question I will address is whether it is possible to perturb the Brownian noise by a Lévy pure jump process other than Poisson, and still recover the parameter σ^2 as if no jumps were present. The reason one might expect this not to be possible is the fact that, among Lévy pure jump processes, the Poisson process is the only one with a finite $v(\mathbb{R})$, that is, a finite number of jumps in a finite time interval (and the sample paths are piecewise constant). In that case, define $\lambda = v(\mathbb{R})$ and the distribution of the jumps has measure $n(dx) = v(dx)/\lambda$. All other pure jump processes are such that $v([-\varepsilon, +\varepsilon]) = \infty$ for any $\varepsilon > 0$, so that the process exhibits an infinite number of small jumps in any finite time interval. Intuitively, these tiny jumps ought to be harder to distinguish from Brownian noise, which is itself made up of many small moves. Can the likelihood still tell them perfectly apart from Brownian noise?

I considered in Aït-Sahalia (2004) as an example of the Cauchy process, which is the pure jump process ($c = 0$) with Lévy measure $v(dx) = \alpha dx/x^2$ and, with weight function $h(z) = 1/(1 + z^2)$, $\gamma_c = 0$. This is an example of a symmetric stable distribution of index $0 < \xi < 2$ and rate $\alpha > 0$, with log characteristic function proportional to $\psi(u) = -(\alpha |u|)^\xi$, and Lévy measure $v(dx) = \alpha^\xi \xi dx/|x|^{1+\xi}$. The Cauchy process corresponds to $\xi = 1$, while the limit $\xi \to 2$ (from below) produces a Gaussian distribution.

So I next look at the situation where $dX_t = \mu dt + \sigma dW_t + dC_t$, where C_t is a Cauchy process independent of the Brownian motion W_t. The answer is, surprisingly, yes: when the Brownian motion is contaminated by Cauchy jumps, it still remains the case that

$$\text{AVAR}_{\text{MLE}}(\sigma^2) = 2\sigma^4 \Delta + o(\Delta). \tag{8.7}$$

Intuitively, while there is an infinite number of small jumps in a Cauchy process, this "infinity" remains relatively small (just like the cardinal of the set of integers is smaller than the cardinal of the set of reals) and while the jumps are infinitesimally small, they remain relatively bigger than the increments of a Brownian motion during the same time interval Δ. In other words, they are harder to pick up from inspection of the sample path than Poisson jumps are, but with a fine enough microscope, still possible. And the likelihood is the best microscope there is, in light of the Cramer–Rao lower bound.

8.3   Jumps versus Volatility: Questions of Uniformity

Whether these results continue to hold for general Lévy jump processes is investigated in Aït-Sahalia and Jacod (2004, 2006). The idea is to characterize precisely the class of jump processes which can still perfectly be distinguished from Brownian volatility. Let the Fisher information at stage n for σ^2 be $nI(\sigma^2, \Delta, G)$, where G denotes the law of the pure jump process.

If we are interested in σ^2 only, it is natural to consider the law of the jump process, that is G, as a nuisance parameter. Hence the idea of proving a convergence like (8.5) and (8.7) – for AVAR_{MLE} which is Δ times the inverse of I, or equivalently for I itself – which is uniform in G. Here, G is arbitrary in the set $\mathcal{G}$ of all infinitely divisible law with vanishing Gaussian part. The closure of $\mathcal{G}$ (for the weak convergence) contains all Gaussian laws: so if the convergence were uniform in $G \in \mathcal{G}$ it would hold as well when the Lévy process is also a Wiener process with variance, say, v: then the best one can do is to estimate $\sigma^2 + v$, and as noted above one cannot have even consistent estimators for σ^2 when v is altogether unknown.

So the idea is to restrict the set $\mathcal{G}$ to a subset which lies at a positive distance of all Gaussian laws. For this, we recall that $G \in \mathcal{G}$ is characterized by its drift $b \in I\!R$ and its Lévy measure F, through the Lévy–Khintchine representation of infinitely divisible distributions, given in (8.6). For any constant K and index $\alpha \in [0, 2]$ we denote by $\mathcal{G}(K, \alpha)$ the family of all infinitely divisible laws of the form (8.6) with

$$|b| \leq K, \quad F([-x, x]^c) \leq K\left(1 \vee \frac{1}{x^\alpha}\right) \quad \forall\, x > 0. \tag{8.8}$$

A stable law of index $\alpha < 2$, which has $F(dx)$ is proportional to $|x|^{-\alpha-1}\, dx$, belongs to $\mathcal{G}(K, \alpha)$ for some K. Any infinitely divisible law without Gaussian part belongs to $\mathcal{G}(K, 2)$ for some K. If $G \in \mathcal{G}(K, 0)$ then Y is a compound Poisson process plus a drift. The closure of $\mathcal{G}(K, 2)$ contains Gaussian laws, but if $\alpha < 2$ the set $\mathcal{G}(K, \alpha)$ is closed and does not contain any nontrivial Gaussian law.

We then prove results of the following type, giving both the uniformity of the convergence on the set $\mathcal{G}(K, \alpha)$, and the lack of uniformity otherwise: For all $K > 0$ and $\alpha \in [0, 2)$ and $\sigma^2 > 0$ we have

$$\sup_{G \in \mathcal{G}(K,\alpha)} \left(\frac{1}{2\sigma^4} - I(\sigma^2, \Delta, G) \right) \to 0 \quad \text{as } \Delta \to 0. \tag{8.9}$$

For each n let G^n be the symmetric stable law with index $\alpha_n \in (0, 2)$ and scale parameter $v/2$ (i.e., its characteristic function id $u \mapsto \exp(-\frac{v}{2}|u|^{\alpha_n})$. Then if $\alpha_n \to 2$, for all sequences $\Delta_n \to 0$ satisfying $(2 - \alpha_n) \log \Delta_n \to 0$ we have

$$I(\sigma^2, \Delta_n, G^n) \to \frac{1}{2(\sigma^2 + v)^2}. \tag{8.10}$$

8.4   GMM Estimation in the Presence of Jumps

Can the identification of σ^2 achieved by the likelihood, despite the presence of jumps, be reproduced by conditional moments of the process of integer or noninteger type, and which moments or combinations of moments come closest to achieving maximum likelihood efficiency. While it is clear that MLE is the preferred method, and as discussed above has been used extensively in that context, it is nevertheless instructive to determine which specific choices of moment functions do best in terms of approximating its efficiency.

In Aït-Sahalia (2004), I studied GMM moment conditions to estimate the parameters in the presence of jumps, with the objective of studying their ability to reproduce the efficiency of MLE. I consider in particular absolute moments of order r (i.e., the plims of the power variations). To form unbiased moment conditions, I need an exact expression for these moments, $M_a(\delta, \theta, r)$, which I derive in closed form. I form moment functions of the type $h(y, \delta, \theta) = y^r - M(\delta, \theta, r)$ and/or $h(y, \delta, \theta) = |y|^r - M_a(\delta, \theta, r)$ for various values of r. By construction, these moment functions are unbiased and all the GMM estimators considered will be consistent. The question becomes one of comparing their asymptotic variances among themselves, and to that of MLE. I refer to different GMM estimators of θ by listing the moments $M(\Delta, \theta, r)$ and/or $M_a(\Delta, \theta, r)$ that are used for that particular estimator. For example, the estimator of σ^2 obtained by using the single moment $M(\Delta, \theta, 2)$ corresponds to the discrete approximation to the quadratic variation of the process. Estimators based on the single moment $M_a(\delta, \theta, r)$ correspond to the power variation, etc. By using Taylor expansions in Δ, I characterize in closed form the properties of these different GMM estimators. The end result is a direct comparison of the different types of moment conditions, and the selection of optimal combinations of moment conditions for the purpose of estimating the parameters of a jump-diffusion.

Aït-Sahalia and Jacod (2006) consider GMM-type estimators for the model

$$dX_t = \sigma \, dW_t + dY_t,$$

where W is a standard Brownian motion or, more generally, a symmetric stable process of index β and the process Y is another Lévy process without Brownian (or continuous) part and with jumps dominated by those of W. The aim is to construct estimators for σ which behave under the model $X_t = \sigma W_t + Y_t$ as well as under the model $X_t = \sigma W_t$ asymptotically as $\Delta_n \to 0$ and $n \to \infty$. In some applications, the jump perturbation Y may represent frictions that are due to the mechanics of the trading process. Or in the case of compound Poisson jumps it may represent the infrequent arrival of relevant information related to the asset, in which case the law of Y may be difficult to pin down due to the peso problem.

Let us distinguish between a parametric case, where the law of Y is known, and a semiparametric case, where it is not. In the parametric case, we construct estimators which are asymptotically efficient. In the semiparametric case, obtaining asymptotically efficient estimators requires Δ_n to go fast enough to 0. We can then construct estimators that are efficient uniformly when the law of Y stays in a set sufficiently separated from the law of W. The estimators are based on a variety of moment conditions, such as the empirical characteristic function or power and truncated power functions.

8.5   Option-Based Transition Densities in the Presence of Jumps

Recall the discussion of option-based transition densities in Section 6.2.4. Aït-Sahalia, Wang, and Yared (2001) infer information from different estimates of p^*. The estimator of p^* constructed from (6.29) is a cross-sectional estimator because it uses information on a set of option prices with different strikes at one point in time. But recalling that under Assumption 9, p^* corresponds to the dynamics of X with drift set to $(r - q)x$ and local volatility function $\sigma(x)$ unchanged, it is possible to construct a different estimate of p^* that uses time series observations on X. Since $\sigma(x)$ is the same under both the risk-neutral and actual probability measures, the function $\sigma(x)$ can be estimated from the observed dynamics of X. Then, since $r - q$ is observable from the price of a forward contract written on X, an estimate of p^* can be computed to be the transition function corresponding to the SDE with (now known) drift $(r - q)x$ and volatility $\sigma(x)$: one could use the method described in Section 4.1 to construct this estimator in closed form. One can then test the overidentifying restriction that the cross-sectional and time series p^* are identical.

Empirical results based on S&P 500 options suggest that a peso problem is at play: the cross-sectional p^* prices options as if X were susceptible to large (downward) jumps, even though those jumps are generally absent from the time series data. Consequently, the time series p^* will not show any evidence of jumps whereas the cross-sectional one will. When the actual dynamics of

X are given by a nonparametric version of Assumption 10, the risk-neutral dynamics of X become

$$dX_t = (r - q - \lambda^* \kappa^*) X_t dt + \sigma(X_t) dW_t + J_t X_t dN_t$$

where κ^* is the risk-neutral-expected value of the jump size J_t and λ^* is the risk-neutral intensity of the Poisson process N_t. Under a peso problem situation, the occurrence of jumps in the time series of actual observations on X is infrequent, so we can use the same estimator of $\sigma(\cdot)$ as if no jumps had been observed during the period of interest. However, when we simulate the risk-neutral dynamics, we can draw from a process that incorporates the jump term. Now, λ^* and κ^* are determined by investors' preferences, so without assumptions on preferences, the equality between the cross-sectional and time series p^* is no longer an overidentifying restriction. Instead, it allows us to restore the exact identification of the system and we can infer the arrival rate of jumps required to make the two p^* equal.

8.6   Likelihood Estimation for Jump-Diffusions

It is possible to extend the basic closed form likelihood expansion described in Section 4 for diffusions to cover the situation where Assumptions 4 and 8 are generalized to processes driven by a Brownian motion and a compound Poisson process, that is, Assumption 10.

The expression, due to Yu (2003), is of the form:

$$p_X^{(K)}(\Delta, x | x_0; \theta) = \exp\left(-\frac{m}{2} \ln(2\pi\Delta) - D_v(x; \theta) + \frac{c_X^{(-1)}(x|x_0; \theta)}{\Delta} \right)$$

$$\times \sum_{k=0}^{K} c_X^{(k)}(x|x_0; \theta) \frac{\Delta^k}{k!} + \sum_{k=1}^{K} d_X^{(k)}(x|x_0; \theta) \frac{\Delta^k}{k!}.$$

$$(8.11)$$

Again, the series can be calculated up to arbitrary order K and the unknowns are the coefficients $c_X^{(k)}$ and $d_X^{(k)}$. The difference between the coefficients $c_X^{(k)}$ in (8.11) and $C_X^{(k)}$ in (4.12) is due to the fact that the former is written for $\ln p_X$ while the latter is for p_X itself; the two coefficients families match once the terms of the Taylor series of $\ln(p_X^{(K)})$ in Δ are matched to the coefficients $C_X^{(k)}$ of the direct Taylor series $\ln p_X^{(K)}$. The coefficients $d_X^{(k)}$ are the new terms needed to capture the presence of the jumps in the transition function. The latter terms are needed to capture the different behavior of the tails of the transition density when jumps are present. (These tails are not exponential in x, hence the absence of a factor $\exp(c_X^{(-1)} \Delta^{-1})$ in front of the sum of $d_X^{(k)}$ coefficients.) The coefficients can be computed analogously to the pure diffusive case.

An alternative extension of Aït-Sahalia (2002b) which applies to processes driven by more general Lévy jump processes than compound Poisson is due to Schaumburg (2001). There are cases where that expansion is not fully computable in closed form, as it requires computation of the orthonormal polynomials associated with the Lévy jump measure (just like the Hermite polynomials which form the basis for the method in the basic diffusive case are the natural family to use when the driving process is Brownian motion, i.e., Gaussian.)

9 RELAXING THE MODEL SPECIFICATION: ALLOWING FOR NON-MARKOV DYNAMICS

Doing inference without Assumption 1 is asking for too much at this point. However, it is possible to test that hypothesis. The specification analysis described in Section 6 assumes that the process is Markovian. In Aït-Sahalia (1996a, 2002a) , I describe a set of observable implications which follow from the Markov property. A necessary condition for the process X to be Markovian is that its transition function satisfy the Chapman–Kolmogorov equation in the form

$$p(y, t_3|x, t_1) = \int_{z \in S} p(y, t_3|z, t_2)\, p(z, t_2|x, t_1)\, dz \tag{9.1}$$

for every $t_3 > t_2 > t_1 \geq 0$, x and y in S.

Under time-homogeneity, the Markov hypothesis can then be tested in the form H_0 against H_1, where

$$\begin{cases} H_0 : & p(y|x, 2\Delta) - r(y|x, 2\Delta) = 0 \quad \text{for all } (x, y) \in S^2 \\ H_1 : & p(y|x, 2\Delta) - r(y|x, 2\Delta) \neq 0 \quad \text{for some } (x, y) \in S^2 \end{cases} \tag{9.2}$$

with

$$r(y|x, 2\Delta) \equiv \int_{z \in S} p(y|z, \Delta)\, p(z|x, \Delta)\, dz. \tag{9.3}$$

Both $p(y|x, \Delta)$ and $p(y|x, 2\Delta)$ can be estimated from data sampled at interval Δ, thanks to time homogeneity. The successive pairs of observed data (x_0, x_Δ), $(x_\Delta, x_{2\Delta})$, $(x_{2\Delta}, x_{3\Delta})$, etc., form a sample from the distribution with density $p(y|x, \Delta)$, from which the estimator $\hat{p}(y|x, \Delta)$ can be constructed and then $\hat{r}(y|x, 2\Delta)$ as indicated in equation (9.3). Meanwhile, the successive pairs $(x_0, x_{2\Delta})$, $(x_\Delta, x_{3\Delta})$, ..., form a sample from the distribution with density $p(y|x, 2\Delta)$ which can be used to form the direct estimator $\hat{p}(y|x, 2\Delta)$.

In other words, the test compares a direct estimator of the 2Δ-interval conditional density, $\hat{p}(y|x, 2\Delta)$, to an indirect estimator of the 2Δ-interval conditional density, $\hat{r}(y|x, 2\Delta)$, obtained by iterating a direct Δ interval estimator of $\hat{p}(y|x, \Delta)$ according to (9.3). If the process is actually Markovian, then the two estimates should be close (for some distance measure) in a sense made precise by the use of the statistical distribution of these estimators.

If instead of 2Δ transitions we test the replicability of $j\Delta$ transitions, where j is an integer greater or equal to 2, there is no need to explore all the possible combinations of these $j\Delta$ transitions in terms of shorter ones $(1, j - 1)$, $(2, j - 2), \dots$: verifying equation (9.1) for one combination is sufficient as can be seen by a recursion argument. In the event of a rejection of H_0 in (9.2), there is no need to consider transitions of order j. In general, a vector of "transition equalities" can be tested in a single pass in a GMM framework with as many moment conditions as transition intervals.

In Aït-Sahalia and Fan (2005b), we propose two classes of tests for restriction (9.2) based on nonparametric estimation of the transition densities and distributions. To be more specific, observe that

$$r(y|x, 2\Delta) = E\{p(y|X_\Delta, \Delta)|X_0 = x\}. \tag{9.4}$$

Hence, the function $r(y|x, 2\Delta)$ can be estimated by regressing nonparametrically $\hat{p}(y|X_{j\Delta}, \Delta)$ on $X_{(j-1)\Delta}$. This avoids integration in (9.3) and makes implementations and theoretical studies easier. Local linear estimator will be applied, resulting in an estimator $\hat{r}(y|x, 2\Delta)$. A nonparametric test statistic for problem (9.2) is naturally

$$T_4 = \sum_{i=1}^{n} \{\hat{p}(X_{(i+1)\Delta}|X_{i\Delta}, 2\Delta)$$
$$- \hat{r}(X_{(i+1)\Delta}|X_{i\Delta}, 2\Delta)\}^2 w(X_{i\Delta}, X_{(i+1)\Delta}). \tag{9.5}$$

The transition distribution-based tests can be formulated too. Let $\hat{P}(y|x, 2\Delta)$ be the direct estimator for the 2Δ-conditional distribution. Let $R(y|x, 2\Delta)$ be the cumulated version of $r(y|x, 2\Delta)$, which can be estimated by regression transition distribution $\hat{P}(y|X_{j\Delta}, \Delta)$ on $X_{(j-1)\Delta}$, yielding $\hat{R}(y|x, 2\Delta)$. The transition distribution-based test will naturally be

$$T_5 = \sum_{i=1}^{n} \{\hat{P}(X_{(i+1)\Delta}|X_{i\Delta}, 2\Delta)$$
$$- \hat{R}(X_{(i+1)\Delta}|X_{i\Delta}, 2\Delta)\}^2 w(X_{i\Delta}, X_{(i+1)\Delta}). \tag{9.6}$$

Note that this test statistic involves only one-dimensional smoothing. Hence, it is expected to be more stable than T_4. In addition, the null distribution can be better approximated by the asymptotic null distribution.

10   RELAXING THE SAMPLING ASSUMPTIONS: ALLOWING FOR RANDOMLY SPACED SAMPLING INTERVALS

Transaction-level data are not only discretely sampled in time, they are also sampled at random time intervals. In discrete time, models allowing for random times have been studied by Engle and Russell (1998) and Engle (2000).

In the context of continuous-time, this calls for relaxing Assumption 5, at least to Assumption 22. For example, if the Δ_i's are random and i.i.d., then $E[\Delta]$ has the usual meaning, but even if this is not the case, by $E[\Delta]$ we mean the limit (in probability, or just the limit if the Δ_i's are nonrandom) of $\sum_{i=1}^{n} \Delta_i/n$ as n tends to infinity. This permits the inclusion of the random non-i.i.d. and the nonrandom (but possibly irregularly spaced) cases for the Δ_i's.

At the cost of further complications, the theory allows for dependence in the sampling intervals, whereby Δ_n is drawn conditionally on (Y_{n-1}, Δ_{n-1}), which is the assumption under which Aït-Sahalia and Mykland (2003) work. Renault and Werker (2003) argue for more general specification of the randomness driving the sampling intervals than allowed under Assumption 22, which would give rise to more general version of the likelihood function than just discussed [see the related discussion on causality pp. 491–494 in Aït-Sahalia and Mykland (2003)].

To concentrate on the main ideas, I will focus here on Assumption 22 only.

10.1   Likelihood Inference with Random Sampling Intervals

In Aït-Sahalia and Mykland (2003), we describe the additional effect that the randomness of the sampling intervals might have when estimating a continuous-time model with discrete data, as would be the case with transaction-level returns data. We disentangle the effect of the sampling randomness from the effect of the sampling discreteness, and compare their relative magnitudes. We also examine the effect of simply ignoring the sampling randomness. We achieve this by comparing the properties of three likelihood-based estimators, which make different use of the observations on the state process and the times at which these observations have been recorded. We design these estimators in such a way that each one of them is subject to a specific subset of the effects we wish to measure. As a result, the differences in their properties allow us to zero in and isolate these different effects.

I will now describe the effect that the very existence of such a distribution (as opposed to having nonrandom times between trades) would have on the behavior of estimators of continuous-time models for the price process, as well as with the interesting issues arising at the interface of the continuous and discrete time domains. We assume that the discrete data we observe have been generated by a time-homogeneous stationary diffusion on the real line $dX_t = \mu(X_t; \kappa)dt + \sigma dW_t$. We will show that the properties of estimators vary widely depending upon whether only the drift or the diffusion parameters, or both together, are estimated. Hence, we consider the three cases of estimating $\theta = (\kappa, \sigma^2)$ jointly, estimating $\theta = \kappa$ with $\sigma^2 = \sigma_0^2$ known or estimating $\theta = \sigma^2$ with $\kappa = \kappa_0$ known. The parameter vector θ is to be estimated at time T on the basis of $N_T + 1$ discrete observations, the Y_n's given by $Y_n = X_{\tau_n}$. We let the sampling intervals $\Delta_n = \tau_n - \tau_{n-1}$ be random variables.

The first estimator of θ we consider is the full information maximum likelihood (FIML) estimator, using the bivariate observations (Y_n, Δ_n); the second is the partial information maximum likelihood estimator using only the state observations Y_n, with the sampling intervals integrated out (IOML for integrated out maximum likelihood); the third is the pseudo maximum likelihood estimator pretending that the observations times are fixed (PFML for pretend fixed maximum likelihood). Not surprisingly, the first estimator, FIML, is asymptotically efficient, making the best possible use of the joint data (Y_n, Δ_n).

The second estimator, IOML, corresponds to the asymptotically optimal choice if one recognizes that the sampling intervals Δ_n's are random but does not observe them. The third estimator, PFML, corresponds to the "head-in-the-sand" policy consisting of acting as if the sampling intervals were all identical (pretending that $\Delta_n = \bar{\Delta}$ for all n) when in fact they are random.

Both FIML and IOML confront the randomness issue head-on. FIML uses the recorded sampling times, IOML does not, but still recognizes their relevance by integrating them out in the absence of observations on them. Because the data are always discretely sampled, each estimator is subject to the "cost of discreteness," which we define to be the additional variance relative to the variance of an asymptotically efficient estimator based on the full continuous-time sample path. It also represents the error that one would make if one were to use continuous-time asymptotics when the data are in fact discretely sampled. However, FIML is only subject to the cost of discreteness, while IOML is penalized by both the fact that the data are discrete (the continuous-time sample path is not observed) and randomly spaced in time (the sampling intervals are not observed). The additional variance of IOML over that of FIML will therefore be identified as the "cost of randomness," or the cost of not observing the randomly-spaced sampling intervals. But if in fact one had recorded the observations times but chosen not to use them in the empirical estimation phase, then what we call the cost of randomness can be interpreted as the cost of throwing away, or not using, these data.

By contrast, PFML does as if the sampling times were simply not randomly spaced. Comparing it to FIML gives rise to the cost imputable to *ignoring* the randomness of the sampling intervals, as opposed to the what we call the cost of randomness, which is the cost due to *not observing* the randomly-spaced sampling intervals. In the former case, one (mistakenly) uses PFML, while in the latter case one realizes that the intervals are informative but, in their absence, IOML is the best one can do. Different types of estimation strategies in empirical market microstructure that do not use the sampling intervals can be viewed as versions of either IOML or PFML, depending upon their treatment of the sampling intervals: throw them away, or ignore their randomness. They will often be suboptimal versions of these estimators because they are subject to an additional efficiency loss if they do not use maximum likelihood.

All three estimators rely on maximizing a version of the likelihood function of the observations. Let $p(y_1|y_0, \delta, \theta)$ denote the transition function of the process X. Because of the time homogeneity of the model, the transition function p depends only on δ and not on $(t, t + \delta)$ separately. All three estimators make use of some functional of the density p: namely, $p(Y_n|Y_{n-1}, \Delta_n, \theta)$ for FIML; the expectation $\tilde{p}(Y_n|Y_{n-1}, \theta)$ of $p(Y_n|Y_{n-1}, \Delta_n, \theta)$ over the law of $\Delta_n|Y_{n-1}$ for IOML; and $p(Y_n|Y_{n-1}, \bar{\Delta}, \theta)$ for PFML (i.e., like FIML except that $\bar{\Delta}$ is used in place of the actual Δ_n). In practice, even though most diffusion models do not admit closed-form transition densities, all three estimators can be calculated for any diffusion X using arbitrarily accurate closed-form approximations of the transition function p (see Aït-Sahalia, 2002b, described above). We also show that $\tilde{p}$ can be obtained in closed form in an important special case.

Under Assumption 12, we have that

$$T^{1/2}(\hat{\theta} - \bar{\theta}) \to N(0, \Omega_\theta)$$

with

$$\Omega_\theta = \begin{pmatrix} \omega_\kappa & \omega_{\kappa\sigma^2} \\ \omega_{\kappa\sigma^2} & \omega_{\sigma^2} \end{pmatrix}. \tag{10.1}$$

For FIML and IOML, $\bar{\theta} = \theta_0$, but PFML is going to be asymptotically biased.

We then derive Taylor expansions of the asymptotic variance and bias of these estimators. We denote a random variable from the common distribution of the sampling intervals as

$$\Delta = \varepsilon \Delta_0, \tag{10.2}$$

where ε is deterministic and Δ_0 has a given finite distribution conditional on Y_0, whose density we write as $d(\Delta|Y_0)$. We compute Taylor expansions in ε of the expectations of interest, around $\varepsilon = 0$ (the limiting case were the full continuous-time sample path is observable), leading to results of the type:

$$\Omega_\theta = \Omega_\theta^{(0)} + \varepsilon\,\Omega_\theta^{(1)} + \varepsilon^2\,\Omega_\theta^{(2)} + O(\varepsilon^3)$$
$$\bar{\theta} - \theta_0 = \varepsilon\,b_\theta^{(1)} + \varepsilon^2\,b_\theta^{(2)} + O(\varepsilon^3)$$

where the higher-order terms in ε correct the leading term for the discreteness of the sampling. Differences between estimation methods and data use show up in the functions $\Omega_\theta^{(i)}$ and $b_\theta^{(i)}$, $i = 0, 1, \ldots$.

These calculations are based on a new operator, the *generalized infinitesimal generator* Γ of the diffusion X. We show that

$$E\left[f(X, X_0, \Delta, \theta, \varepsilon)|X_0, \Delta\right] = \sum_{j=0}^{J} \frac{\Delta^j}{j!}\Gamma^j \cdot f + O\left(\Delta^{J+1}\right)$$

where Γ is the operator that returns

$$\Gamma \cdot f = \Delta_0\,\mathcal{A} \cdot f + \frac{\partial f}{\partial \varepsilon} + \frac{\partial f}{\partial \theta}\frac{\partial \theta}{\partial \varepsilon} \tag{10.3}$$

with $\mathcal{A}$ denoting the standard infinitesimal generator, which for a diffusion yields:

$$\mathcal{A} \cdot f = \frac{\partial f}{\partial \delta} + \mu\frac{\partial f}{\partial y_1} + \frac{1}{2}\sigma_0^2\frac{\partial^2 f}{\partial y_1^2}$$

The operator Γ is random in that it depends on Δ_0.

Specifically, the log-likelihood function using all information is

$$\sum_{n=1}^{N-1} \ln p(X_{\tau_n}|X_{\tau_{n-1}}, \Delta_n, \theta) + \sum_{n=1}^{N-1} \ln d(\Delta_n|X_{\tau_{n-1}})$$

where d is the density of the sampling interval given the most recent price observation (recall Assumption 22). Since we only care about θ (not the parameters, if any, entering the density d) we maximize

$$l_T(\theta) = \sum_{n=1}^{N-1} \ln p(X_{\tau_n}|X_{\tau_{n-1}}, \Delta_n, \theta).$$

Suppose now that the observation times are either not observable or discarded prior to conducting inference on θ. They can be integrated out to obtain a proper likelihood. We would then base inference on the density

$$\tilde{p}(x|x_0, \theta) = E_\Delta \left[p(x|X_0, \Delta, \theta)|X_0 = x_0 \right].$$

The part of the log-likelihood function dependent on θ is then

$$\lambda_T(\theta) = \sum_{n=1}^{N-1} \ln \tilde{p}\left(X_{\tau_n}|X_{\tau_{n-1}}, \theta\right).$$

Using the Hermite-based closed-form expansion of the transition function $p(x|x_0, \Delta, \theta)$ described above, the corresponding expansion for the density $\tilde{p}$ can also be obtained explicitly in the important special case where the density d of Δ given X_0 is exponential with mean $E[\Delta|X_0]$:

$$\tilde{p}^{(J)}(x|x_0, \theta) = \exp\left(\int_{x_0}^x \frac{\mu(w, \kappa)}{\sigma^2} dw \right)$$
$$\times \sum_{j=0}^J \left\{ c_j\left(\frac{x}{\sigma} \bigg| \frac{x_0}{\sigma}, \theta\right) \frac{2^{(1-2j)/4} E[\Delta|X_0]^{(2j-3)/4}}{j! \pi^{1/2} \sigma^{j+(3/2)}} \right.$$
$$\left. \times B_{j+(1/2)}\left(\frac{2^{1/2} |x - x_0|}{E[\Delta|X_0]^{1/2}\sigma} \right) |x - x_0|^{(2j+1)/2} \right\},$$

where $B_{j+(1/2)}(z)$ is the Bessel K function of half-integer order $j + (1/2)$, which is in closed-form for any j.

The cost of discreteness is the cost attributable to not observing the full continuous-time sample path. It is the coefficient at the first-order i in ε for which the FIML variance differs from its continuous-time limit $\Omega_\theta^{(0)}$. It is also the error that one would make if one were to use continuous-time asymptotics ($\Omega_\theta^{(0)}$) instead of the full Ω_θ when the data are in fact discretely sampled. The cost of randomness is the extra variance due to not using the sampling intervals: it is the first-order i in ε at which the coefficient $\Omega_\theta^{(i)}$ for IOML differs from the corresponding coefficient $\Omega_\theta^{(i)}$ for FIML, and how much bigger the IOML coefficient at that order is compared to the FIML coefficient. It turns out that the cost of randomness is at least as great, and often substantially greater than the cost of discreteness.

Specifically, we have that

$$\Omega_\kappa^{\text{FIML}} = \Omega_\kappa^{(\text{FIML},0)} + O(\varepsilon^2) \tag{10.4}$$

$$\Omega_\kappa^{\text{IOML}} = \Omega_\kappa^{(\text{IOML},0)} + \varepsilon \, \Omega_\kappa^{(\text{IOML},1)} + O(\varepsilon^2), \tag{10.5}$$

where

$$\Omega_\kappa^{(\text{FIML},0)} = \Omega_\kappa^{(\text{IOML},0)} = \left(E_{Y_0} \big[\sigma^{-2}(Y_0, \gamma_0)(\partial \mu(Y_0, \kappa_0)/\partial \kappa)^2 \big] \right)^{-1} \tag{10.6}$$

which is the leading term in Ω_κ corresponding to efficient estimation of κ with a continuous record of observations.

And the price of ignoring the sampling times $\tau_0, \tau_1, \ldots$ when estimating κ is, to first-order, represented by

$$\Omega_\kappa^{(\text{IOML},1)} = \frac{E[Var[\Delta_0 | \chi_1^2 \Delta_0]]}{E[\Delta_0]} V,$$

and "χ_1^2" is a χ_1^2 distributed random variable independent of Δ_0, and

$$V = \frac{\left(E_{Y_0}\left[\sigma_0^4 \left(\frac{\partial^2 \mu(Y_0, \beta_0)}{\partial y \partial \kappa} \right)^2 \right] - 2 E_{Y_0}\left[\sigma_0^2 \frac{\partial \mu(Y_0, \kappa_0)}{\partial y} \left(\frac{\partial \mu(Y_0, \kappa_0)}{\partial \kappa} \right)^2 \right] \right)}{4 \, E_{Y_0}\left[\left(\frac{\partial \mu(Y_0, \kappa_0)}{\partial \kappa} \right)^2 \right]^2}. \tag{10.7}$$

Note that $V \geq 0$ by the asymptotic efficiency of FIML.

And the leading term in Ω_γ corresponding to efficient estimation of γ is

$$\Omega_\gamma^{\text{FIML}} = \varepsilon \, \Omega_\gamma^{(\text{FIML},1)} + O(\varepsilon^2)$$

$$\Omega_\gamma^{\text{IOML}} = \varepsilon \, \Omega_\gamma^{(\text{IOML},1)} + O(\varepsilon^2),$$

where

$$\Omega_\gamma^{(\text{FIML},1)} = \Omega_\gamma^{(\text{IOML},1)}$$

$$= E\left[\Delta_0\right] \left(2 E_{Y_0}\big[(\partial \sigma(Y_0, \gamma_0)/\partial \gamma)^2 \sigma(Y_0, \gamma_0)^{-2} \big] \right)^{-1}.$$

In the special case where σ^2 is constant ($\gamma = \sigma^2$), this becomes the standard AVAR of MLE from i.i.d. Gaussian observations, that is, $\Omega_\gamma^{(1)} = 2\sigma_0^4 E\left[\Delta_0\right]$.

These leading terms are achieved in particular when h is the likelihood score for κ and γ respectively, as analyzed in Aït-Sahalia and Mykland (2003), but also by other estimating functions that are able to mimic the behavior of the likelihood score at the leading order.

In other words, when estimating γ, the costs incurred due to the discreteness and the randomness of time both appear at the same order ε^1, while the limiting variance (the term of order ε^0) is zero if the full continuous time sample path is observed. The loss due to not using sampling times can be an arbitrarily large *multiple* of the loss due to the discreteness of the data. When estimating

κ, the cost of randomness is of order ε^1: it is therefore an order of magnitude in ε bigger than the loss from observing the process discretely rather than continuously (which is of order ε^2). However, both are small relative to the sampling variable that is present even if the full continuous time sample path is observed (order ε^0).

The cost of ignoring the randomness is the cost imputable to *ignoring* the randomness of the sampling intervals, by doing *as if* the Δ_n's were not random, as opposed to the cost of randomness, which is the cost due to *not observing* the randomly-spaced sampling intervals but still accounting for their randomness. In terms of RMSE, any biased estimator such as PFML will always do worse than an unbiased estimator since its variance is $O(T^{-1})$ whereas the squared bias is $O(1)$.

10.2   GMM Under Random Sampling Intervals

Aït-Sahalia and Mykland (2004) study the asymptotic properties of estimators based on general moment conditions, of the type described in Section 4.2.1, when the data are sampled not only discretely but also randomly (Assumption 22). Of course, the results also apply to the situation of Assumption 5 as a special case (where $\Delta_n = \bar{\Delta}$ for all n, corresponding to the distribution of Δ_n being a Dirac mass at $\bar{\Delta}$) so this section covers the asymptotics for all the estimators described in Section 4.2.1 under Assumption 5.

The moment conditions are $h(y_1, y_0, \delta, \theta, \varepsilon)$. Compared to the situation discussed in Section 4.2.1, where Assumption 5 held, the moment conditions under Assumption 22 could conceivably depend on ε in addition or instead of δ (ε is defined in (10.2)). As before, y_1 plays the role of the forward state variable, y_0 the role of the backward state variable and δ the sampling interval.

Then let

$$m_T(\theta) \equiv N_T^{-1} \sum_{n=1}^{N_T-1} h(Y_n, Y_{n-1}, \Delta_n, \theta, \varepsilon) \tag{10.8}$$

where $Y_n = X_{\tau_n}$ and obtain $\hat{\theta}$ by minimizing the quadratic form

$$Q_T(\theta) \equiv m_T(\theta)' W_T m_T(\theta) \tag{10.9}$$

where W_T is an $r \times r$ positive definite weight matrix assumed to converge in probability to a positive definite limit W_θ. If the system is exactly identified, $r = d$, the choice of W_T is irrelevant and minimizing (10.9) amounts to setting $m_T(\theta)$ to 0. The function h is known in the econometric literature as a "moment function" (see Hansen, 1982) and in the statistical literature as an "estimating equation" [see e.g., Godambe (1960) and Heyde (1997)].

Consistency of $\hat{\theta}$ is guaranteed as long as h is such that

$$E_{\Delta, Y_1, Y_0}[h(Y_1, Y_0, \Delta, \theta_0, \varepsilon)] = 0, \tag{10.10}$$

where E_{Δ, Y_1, Y_0} denotes expectations taken with respect to the joint law of (Δ, Y_1, Y_0) at the true parameter θ_0, and write E_{Δ, Y_1}, etc., for expectations taken from the appropriate marginal laws of (Δ, Y_1), etc.

Some otherwise fairly natural estimating strategies lead to inconsistent estimators. To allow for this, we do not assume that (10.10) is necessarily satisfied. Rather, we simply assume that the equation

$$E_{\Delta, Y_1, Y_0} [h(Y_1, Y_0, \Delta, \theta, \varepsilon)] = 0 \tag{10.11}$$

admits a unique root in θ, which we define as $\bar{\theta} = \bar{\theta}(\theta_0, \varepsilon)$.

For the estimator to be consistent, it must be that $\bar{\theta} \equiv \theta_0$ but, again, this will not be the case for every estimation method. However, in all the cases we consider, and one may argue for *any* reasonable estimation method, the bias will disappear in the limit where $\varepsilon \to 0$, that is, $\bar{\theta}(\theta_0, 0) = \theta_0$ (so that there is no bias in the limiting case of continuous sampling) and we have an expansion of the form

$$\bar{\theta} = \bar{\theta}(\theta_0, \varepsilon) = \theta_0 + b^{(1)}\varepsilon + b^{(2)}\varepsilon^2 + O(\varepsilon^3). \tag{10.12}$$

With N_T / T converging in probability to $(E[\Delta])^{-1}$, it follows from standard arguments (see e.g., Hansen, 1982) that $\sqrt{T}(\hat{\theta} - \bar{\theta})$ converges in law to $N(0, \Omega_\theta)$, with

$$\Omega_\theta^{-1} = (E[\Delta])^{-1} D_\theta' S_\theta^{-1} D_\theta, \tag{10.13}$$

where

$$D_\theta \equiv E_{\Delta, Y_1, Y_0} \left[\dot{h}(Y_1, Y_0, \Delta, \bar{\theta}, \varepsilon) \right],$$
$$S_{\theta, j} \equiv E_{\Delta, Y_1, Y_0} \left[h(Y_{1+j}, Y_j, \Delta, \bar{\theta}, \varepsilon) h(Y_1, Y_0, \Delta, \bar{\theta}, \varepsilon)' \right]$$

and $S_\theta \equiv \sum_{j=-\infty}^{+\infty} S_{\theta, j}$. If $r > d$, the weight matrix W_T is assumed to be any consistent estimator of S_θ^{-1}; otherwise its choice is irrelevant. A consistent first-step estimator of θ, needed to compute the optimal weight matrix, can be obtained by minimizing (10.9) with $W_T = Id$.

The simplest case arises when the moment function is a martingale, that is,

$$E_{\Delta, Y_1} [h(Y_1, Y_0, \Delta, \theta_0, \varepsilon)|Y_0] = 0 \tag{10.14}$$

since then $S_{\theta, j} = 0$ for all $j \neq 0$. However, this property will not be satisfied by many otherwise relevant examples, and so Aït-Sahalia and Mykland (2004) also allow for near-martingale moment conditions. To define the distance from a moment function to a martingale, denote by h_i the ith component of h, and define q_i and α_i by

$$E_{\Delta, Y_1} \left[h_i(Y_1, Y_0, \Delta, \bar{\theta}, \varepsilon)|Y_0 \right] = \varepsilon^{\alpha_i} q_i(Y_0, \beta_0, 0) + O(\varepsilon^{\alpha_i + 1}), \tag{10.15}$$

where α_i is an integer greater than or equal to zero for each moment function h_i. α_i is an index of the order at which the moment component h_i deviates from a martingale. A martingale moment function corresponds to the limiting case where $\alpha_i = +\infty$. When the moment functions are not martingales, the difference $T_\theta \equiv S_\theta - S_{\theta,0}$ is a matrix whose element (i, j) has a leading term of order $O\left(\varepsilon^{\min(\alpha_i, \alpha_j)}\right)$. Intuitively, the closer h will be to a martingale, the smaller T_θ.

This is all nice and well, but, for given h function(s), how does one compute the matrices D_θ and S_θ in (10.13), and the coefficients of the bias expansion (10.12)? Using the same tools as in the special case of the likelihood, that is, the generalized infinitesimal general defined in (10.3), Aït-Sahalia and Mykland (2004) derive expressions of the form

$$\Omega_\theta = \Omega_\theta^{(0)} + \varepsilon\,\Omega_\theta^{(1)} + \varepsilon^2\,\Omega_\theta^{(2)} + O(\varepsilon^3) \tag{10.16}$$

and detail the effects of the choice of inference strategy and/or distribution of the sampling intervals, as they show up in the functions $\Omega_\theta^{(i)}$, $i = 0, 1, \dots$ and in the bias coefficients $b^{(i)}$, $i = 0, 1, \dots$ of (10.12), since these coefficients are derived in closed form for arbitrary h moment conditions.

These general results can be applied to exact likelihood inference as in Aït-Sahalia and Mykland (2003), but also to study the properties of estimators of the drift and diffusion coefficients obtained by replacing the true likelihood function $l(y_1|y_0, \delta, \theta)$ with its discrete Euler approximation

$$l^E(y_1|y_0, \delta, \theta) = -\frac{1}{2}\ln(2\pi\sigma^2(y_0; \gamma)\delta) - \frac{(y_1 - y_0 - \mu(y_0; \kappa)\delta)^2}{2\sigma^2(y_0; \gamma)\delta}. \tag{10.17}$$

This estimator is commonly used in empirical work in finance, where researchers often write a theoretical model set in continuous-time but then switch gear in their empirical work, in effect estimating the parameters of the discrete time series model

$$X_{t+\Delta} - X_t = \mu(X_t; \kappa)\Delta + \sigma(X_t; \gamma)\sqrt{\Delta}\,\eta_{t+\Delta} \tag{10.18}$$

where the disturbance η is $N(0, 1)$. The properties of this estimator have been studied in the case where Δ is not random by Florens-Zmirou (1989). Our results apply to this particular situation as a special case.

In the terminology of the general case, our vector of moment functions is the Euler score

$$h(y_1, y_0, \delta, \theta, \varepsilon) = \begin{bmatrix} \dot{l}^E_\theta(y_1|y_0, \delta, \theta) \\ \dot{l}^E_{\sigma^2}(y_1|y_0, \delta, \theta) \end{bmatrix}. \tag{10.19}$$

We find that the asymptotic variance is, to first-order in ε, the same as for MLE inference. The impact of using the approximation is second-order in variances (and of course is responsible for bias in the estimator). When estimating one of the two parameters with the other known, the impact of the discretization approximation on the variance (which MLE avoids) is one order of magnitude higher than the effect of the discreteness of the data (which MLE is also subject to).

In Aït-Sahalia and Mykland (2005), we apply this general theory to determine the asymptotic properties of estimators using the C1 and C2 moment conditions of Hansen and Scheinkman (1995) discussed in Section 4.2.1; as a special case, our results give these properties in the form (10.16) – these estimators are unbiased, so all the coefficients in (10.12) are identically zero – when the sampling intervals are fixed and deterministic, but also when they are random. Since we have closed form expressions for the coefficients $\Omega_\theta^{(i)}$, we then derive the optimal choice of test functions by minimizing the asymptotic variance of the estimator and compare the results to the efficient choice represented by likelihood inference (where h is given by the log-likelihood score function).

11   RELAXING THE SAMPLING ASSUMPTIONS: ALLOWING FOR MARKET MICROSTRUCTURE NOISE

Over the past few years, price data sampled at very high frequency have become increasingly available, in the form of the Olsen data set of currency exchange rates or the TAQ database of NYSE stocks. In earlier work, I informally warned about the potential dangers of using high-frequency financial data without accounting for their inherent noise [see page 529 of Aït-Sahalia (1996b)], and I now discuss a formal modelization of that phenomenon.

So, inference will now be conducted when Assumption 6 is relaxed and instead explicitly allow for the presence of observation errors. Under Assumption 15, the observed transaction or quoted log-price will be Y_t, and take the form of the unobservable efficient log-price X_t plus some noise component due to the imperfections of the trading process, ε_t, collectively known as market microstructure noise.

So consider now the implications of Assumption 15 for the estimation of the volatility of the efficient log-price process, X_t, assumed to follow an SDE of the type studied in the previous sections:

$$dX_t = \mu_t dt + \sigma_t dW_t,$$

using discretely sampled data on the transaction price process at times 0, Δ, $\ldots, N\Delta = T$.

With either quote or transaction data, we are in a situation where Δ will be measured in seconds rather than minutes or hours. Under these circumstances, the drift is of course irrelevant, both economically and statistically, and so we shall focus on functionals of the σ_t process and set $\mu_t = 0$. It is also the case that transactions and quotes data series in finance are often observed at random time intervals (see Section 10 for inference under these circumstances). We make essentially no assumptions on the σ_t process: its driving process can of course be correlated with the Brownian motion W_t driving the asset price process, and it need not even have continuous sample paths.

The noise term ε summarizes a diverse array of market microstructure effects, which can be roughly divided into three groups. First, ε represents the frictions inherent in the trading process: bid-ask bounces, discreteness of price changes and rounding, trades occurring on different markets or networks, etc. Second, ε captures informational effects: differences in trade sizes or informational content of price changes, gradual response of prices to a block trade, the strategic component of the order flow, inventory control effects, etc. Third, ε encompasses measurement or data recording errors such as prices entered as zero, misplaced decimal points, etc., which are surprisingly prevalent in these types of data. As is clear from the laundry list of potential sources of noise, the data generating process for ε is likely to be quite involved. Therefore, robustness to departures from any assumptions on ε is desirable.

Different solutions have been proposed for this problem. In the constant σ case, Zhou (1996) who proposes a bias correcting approach based on autocovariances. The behavior of this estimator has been studied by Zumbach et al. (2002). In the constant σ case, efficient likelihood estimation of σ is studied by Aït-Sahalia, Mykland, and Zhang (2005b), showing that incorporating ε explicitly in the likelihood function of the observed log-returns Y provides consistent, asymptotically normal and efficient estimators of the parameters.

Hansen and Lunde (2006) study the Zhou estimator and extensions in the case where volatility is time varying but conditionally nonrandom. Related contributions have been made by Oomen (2006) and Bandi and Russell (2003). The Zhou estimator and its extensions, however, are inconsistent despite being unbiased. This means in this particular case that, as the frequency of observation increases, the estimator diverges instead of converging to the object of interest.

In the parametric case, Aït-Sahalia, Mykland, and Zhang (2005b) show that modeling ε explicitly through the likelihood restores the first-order statistical effect that sampling as often as possible is optimal. But, more surprisingly, this is true even if one misspecifies the distribution of ε. This robustness result argues for incorporating ε when estimating continuous time models with high-frequency financial data, even if one is unsure about the true distribution of the noise term. We also study the same questions when the observations are sampled at random time intervals Δ, which are an essential empirical feature of transaction-level data.

In the nonparametric or stochastic volatility case, the first consistent estimator is due to Zhang, Mykland, and Aït-Sahalia (2005). Ignoring the noise is worse than in the parametric case, in that the quadratic variation no longer estimates a mixture of the price volatility and the noise, but now estimates exclusively the variance of the noise. What makes this situation nonstandard among the class of measurement error problems is the fact that the contribution of the measurement error to the quantity being measured is the dominating one (typically, the effect of the measurement error is of the same magnitude, or smaller, than that of the signal). We propose a solution based on subsampling and averaging, which again makes use of the full data; for reasons that will become clear below, we call this estimator two scales realized volatility (TSRV).

11.1   Parametric Modeling: Likelihood Corrections and Robustness

Suppose for now that market microstructure noise is present, under Assumptions 15 and 17, but that the presence of the $\varepsilon's$ (i.i.d., mean 0, variance a^2) is ignored when estimating σ^2. Assume also that we are under Assumption 4 (with $\mu = 0$ since the drift is essentially impossible to measure accurately at these frequencies) and Assumption 5.

In other words, we use the same $N(0, \sigma^2\Delta)$ likelihood as under Section 2 even though the true structure of the observed log-returns Y is given by an MA(1) process since

$$Y_i = \sigma\left(W_{\tau_i} - W_{\tau_{i-1}}\right) + \varepsilon_{\tau_i} - \varepsilon_{\tau_{i-1}}. \tag{11.1}$$

The variance and first-order correlation coefficient of the log-returns are (γ^2, η) where $\gamma^2(1 + \eta^2) = Var[Y_i] = \sigma^2\Delta + 2a^2$ and $\gamma^2\eta = cov(Y_i, Y_{i-1}) = -a^2$.

Theorem 1 of Aït-Sahalia, Mykland, and Zhang (2005b) gives an exact small sample (finite T) result for the bias and variance of the estimator $\hat{\sigma}^2$. Its RMSE has a unique minimum in Δ which is reached at the optimal sampling interval:

$$\Delta^* = \left(\frac{2a^4T}{\sigma^4}\right)^{1/3}\left(\left(1 - \left(1 - \frac{2\left(3a^4 + \text{Cum}_4\,[\varepsilon]\right)^3}{27\sigma^4a^8T^2}\right)^{1/2}\right)^{1/3}\right.$$

$$\left. + \left(1 + \left(1 - \frac{2\left(3a^4 + \text{Cum}_4\,[\varepsilon]\right)^3}{27\sigma^4a^8T^2}\right)^{1/2}\right)^{1/3}\right) \tag{11.2}$$

where $\text{Cum}_4\,[\varepsilon]$ denotes the fourth cumulant of the random variable ε.

But this solution provides at best a partial answer to the problem. Indeed, the presence of the noise is acknowledged by reducing the sampling frequency, but this cannot be the optimal answer. Such an answer must proceed by fully specifying the likelihood function of the observations, including the noise. This immediately raises the question of what distribution to assume for the noise. To start, let us suppose that $\varepsilon \sim N(0, a^2)$. Then the likelihood function for the $Y's$ is then given by

$$l(\sigma^2, a^2) = -\ln\det(V)/2 - N\ln(2\pi\gamma^2)/2 - (2\gamma^2)^{-1}Y'V^{-1}Y$$

$$V = [v_{ij}] = \begin{pmatrix} 1+\eta^2 & \eta & \cdots & 0 \\ \eta & 1+\eta^2 & \ddots & \vdots \\ \vdots & \ddots & \ddots & \eta \\ 0 & \cdots & \eta & 1+\eta^2 \end{pmatrix}. \tag{11.3}$$

We can see that the MLE $(\hat{\sigma}^2, \hat{a}^2)$ is consistent and its asymptotic variance is given by

$$
\text{AVAR}_{\text{normal}}(\hat{\sigma}^2, \hat{a}^2)
$$
$$
= \begin{pmatrix} 4(\sigma^6\Delta(4a^2 + \sigma^2\Delta))^{1/2} + 2\sigma^4\Delta & -\sigma^2\Delta h \\ \bullet & \frac{\Delta}{2}(2a^2 + \sigma^2\Delta)h \end{pmatrix} \tag{11.4}
$$

with $h \equiv 2a^2 + (\sigma^2\Delta(4a^2 + \sigma^2\Delta))^{1/2} + \sigma^2\Delta$. Since $\text{AVAR}_{\text{normal}}(\hat{\sigma}^2)$ is increasing in Δ, it is optimal to sample as often as possible. Further, since

$$
\text{AVAR}_{\text{normal}}(\hat{\sigma}^2) = 8\sigma^3 a\Delta^{1/2} + 2\sigma^4\Delta + o(\Delta), \tag{11.5}
$$

the loss of efficiency relative to the case where no market microstructure noise is present (and $\text{AVAR}(\hat{\sigma}^2) = 2\sigma^4\Delta$ as given in (11.5) if $a^2 = 0$ is not estimated, or $\text{AVAR}(\hat{\sigma}^2) = 6\sigma^4\Delta$ if $a^2 = 0$ is estimated) is at order $\Delta^{1/2}$.

Of course, we can only compute this MLE if we assume a model for the noise distribution, in this case $\varepsilon \sim N(0, a^2)$. Given the complexity and diversity of the mechanisms giving rise to market microstructure noise, it is somewhat likely that any parametric assumption on the noise distribution would be misspecified. What, then, is the effect of misspecifying the distribution of the microstructure noise? Specifically, we consider the case where the $\varepsilon's$ are assumed by the econometrician to be normally distributed when they are not. We still suppose that the $\varepsilon's$ are i.i.d. with mean zero and variance a^2. Since the econometrician assumes $\varepsilon \sim N$, inference is still done with the Gaussian log-likelihood $l(\sigma^2, a^2)$, using the scores $\dot{l}_{\sigma^2}$ and $\dot{l}_{a^2}$ as moment functions. But since the expected values of $\dot{l}_{\sigma^2}$ and $\dot{l}_{a^2}$ only depend on the second-order moment structure of the log-returns Y, which is unchanged by the absence of normality, the moment functions are unbiased $E_{\text{true}}[\dot{l}_{\sigma^2}] = E_{\text{true}}[\dot{l}_{a^2}] = 0$ where "true" denotes the true distribution of the $Y's$. Hence, the estimator $(\hat{\sigma}^2, \hat{a}^2)$ based on these moment functions remains consistent and the effect of misspecification therefore lies in the AVAR. By using the cumulants of the distribution of ε, we express the AVAR in terms of deviations from normality.

Theorem 2 shows that the estimator $(\hat{\sigma}^2, \hat{a}^2)$ is consistent and its asymptotic variance is given by

$$
\text{AVAR}_{\text{true}}(\hat{\sigma}^2, \hat{a}^2) = \text{AVAR}_{\text{normal}}(\hat{\sigma}^2, \hat{a}^2) + \text{Cum}_4[\varepsilon]\begin{pmatrix} 0 & 0 \\ 0 & \Delta \end{pmatrix} \tag{11.6}
$$

where $\text{AVAR}_{\text{normal}}(\hat{\sigma}^2, \hat{a}^2)$ is the asymptotic variance in the case where the distribution of ε is Normal. We have therefore shown that $\text{AVAR}_{\text{normal}}(\hat{\sigma}^2, \hat{a}^2)$ coincides with $\text{AVAR}_{\text{true}}(\hat{\sigma}^2, \hat{a}^2)$ for all but the (a^2, a^2) term.

We show in the paper how to interpret this in terms of the profile likelihood and the second Bartlett identity. Next, we relax Assumption 5 by considering the case where the $\Delta_i's$ are random (for simplicity i.i.d., independent of the W process), which is a special case of Assumption 22. We Taylor-expand around

$\bar{\Delta} = E[\Delta] : \Delta_i = \bar{\Delta}(1 + \epsilon\xi_i)$, where ϵ and $\bar{\Delta}$ are nonrandom and the $\xi_i's$ are i.i.d. random variables with mean zero. we show that in that situation the MLE $(\hat{\sigma}^2, \hat{a}^2)$ is again consistent, this time with asymptotic variance obtained in closed form as

$$\text{AVAR}(\hat{\sigma}^2, \hat{a}^2) = A^{(0)} + \epsilon^2 A^{(2)} + O(\epsilon^3) \tag{11.7}$$

where $A^{(0)}$ is the asymptotic variance matrix already present in the deterministic sampling case except that it is evaluated at $\bar{\Delta}$, and the second-order correction term $A^{(2)}$ is proportional to $Var[\xi]$ and is therefore zero in the absence of sampling randomness.

Further extensions considered in the paper include: the presence of a drift coefficient, which, because of the block-diagonality of the asymptotic variance matrix, does not affect our earlier conclusions; serially correlated noise which, instead of being i.i.d. (Assumption 17) follows a mean reverting process (a special case of Assumption 18). This type of noise could capture the gradual adjustment of prices in response to a shock such as a large trade. Now, the variance contributed by the noise is of order $O(\Delta)$, that is of the same order as the variance of the efficient price process $\sigma^2\Delta$, instead of being of order $O(1)$ under Assumption 17. We show that this type of noise is not nearly as bad as i.i.d. noise for the purpose of inferring σ^2. The final extension covers the case where the noise is correlated with the price process, thereby relaxing Assumption 16: microstructure noise attributable to informational effects could be correlated with the efficient price process, since it is generated by the response of market participants to information signals. We show how the form of the variance matrix of the observed log-returns Y must be altered in that case.

11.2 The Nonparametric Stochastic Volatility Case: The TSRV Estimator

I now examine the situation where we relax Assumption 4, and allow for stochastic volatility. We also replace Assumption 5 with Assumption 21, since there is no other way in the presence of unobserved stochastic volatility. With $dX_t = \sigma_t dW_t$, the object of interest is now the quadratic variation

$$\langle X, X \rangle_T = \int_0^T \sigma_t^2 dt \tag{11.8}$$

over a fixed time period $[0, T]$, typically one day in empirical applications. This quantity can then be used to hedge a derivatives' portfolio, forecast the next day's integrated volatility, etc. Without noise, $Y = X$ and the realized volatility (RV) estimator $[Y, Y]_T^{(\text{all})} = \sum_{i=1}^n (Y_{t_{i+1}} - Y_{t_i})^2$ provides an estimate of the quantity $\langle X, X \rangle_T$, and asymptotic theory would lead one to sample as often as possible, or use all the data available, hence the "all" superscript. The sum $[Y, Y]_T^{(\text{all})}$ converges to the integral $\langle X, X \rangle_T$, with a known distribution, a result which dates back to Jacod (1994) and Jacod and Protter (1998) in great generality (i.e., for continuous semi-martingales):

$$[Y, Y]_T^{(all)} \overset{\mathcal{L}}{\approx} \langle X, X \rangle_T + \left[\frac{2T}{n} \int_0^T \sigma_t^4 dt \right]^{1/2} Z \tag{11.9}$$

conditionally on the X process, where Z denotes a standard normal variable; Barndorff-Nielsen and Shephard (2002) looked at the special case of Brownian motion. Mykland and Zhang (2006) studied general sampling schemes. This expression naturally reduces to the simple (2.3) when volatility is not stochastic, $\sigma_t = \sigma$.

In the context where volatility is stochastic and sampling is increasingly frequent, Zhang, Mykland, and Aït-Sahalia (2005)showed that ignoring market microstructure noise (of the type described in Assumptions 15, 16, and 17) leads to an even more dangerous situation than the one described above, where σ is constant and $T \to \infty$. After suitable scaling, the realized volatility is a consistent and asymptotically normal estimator – but of the quantity $2nE[\varepsilon^2]$. In general, this quantity has nothing to do with the object of interest, the quadratic variation $\langle X, X \rangle_T$. Said differently, market microstructure noise totally swamps the variance of the price signal at the level of the realized volatility.

Indeed, if one uses all the data (say sampled every second), we showed that

$$[Y, Y]_T^{(all)} \overset{\mathcal{L}}{\approx} \underbrace{\langle X, X \rangle_T}_{\text{object of interest}} + \underbrace{2nE[\varepsilon^2]}_{\text{bias due to noise}} \tag{11.10}$$

$$+ \underbrace{\left[\underbrace{4nE[\varepsilon^4]}_{\text{due to noise}} + \underbrace{\frac{2T}{n} \int_0^T \sigma_t^4 dt}_{\text{due to discretization}} \right]^{1/2} Z_{\text{total}}.}_{\text{total variance}}$$

conditionally on the X process. Therefore, the realized volatility $[Y, Y]_T^{(all)}$ has a positive bias whose magnitude increases linearly with the sample size n, as in the parametric case.

Of course, completely ignoring the noise and sampling as prescribed by $[Y, Y]_T^{(all)}$ is not what the empirical literature does in practice (see e.g., Andersen et al., 2001). There, one uses the estimator $[Y, Y]_T^{(sparse)}$, constructed as above but using sparse sampling once every, say, 5 minutes. For example, if $T = 1$ NYSE day and we start with stock returns data sampled every $\delta = 1$ second, then for the full data set the sample size is $n = T/\delta = 23{,}400$. But sampling sparsely once every 5 minutes means throwing out 299 out of every 300 observations, and the sample size is now only $n_{\text{sparse}} = 78$. There is a large literature devoted to this estimator: see the survey Andersen, Bollerslev, and Diebold (2002). As in the parametric case, if one insists upon sampling sparsely, we showed in Zhang, Mykland, and Aït-Sahalia (2005) how to determine optimally the sparse sampling frequency:

$$n_{\text{sparse}}^* = \left(\frac{T}{4E[\varepsilon^2]^2} \int_0^T \sigma_t^4 dt \right)^{1/3}. \tag{11.11}$$

So, one could benefit from using infrequently sampled data. And yet, one of the most basic lessons of statistics is that one should not do this. Zhang, Mykland, and Aït-Sahalia (2005) present a method to tackle the problem. We partition the original grid of observation times, $G = \{t_0, \ldots, t_n\}$ into subsamples, $G^{(k)}$, $k = 1, \ldots, K$ where $n/K \to \infty$ as $n \to \infty$. For example, for $G^{(1)}$ start at the first observation and take an observation every 5 minutes; for $G^{(2)}$, start at the second observation and take an observation every 5 minutes, etc. Then we average the estimators obtained on the subsamples. To the extent that there is a benefit to subsampling, this benefit can now be retained, while the variation of the estimator can be lessened by the averaging. Subsampling and averaging together gives rise to the estimator

$$[Y, Y]_T^{(\text{avg})} = \frac{1}{K} \sum_{k=1}^{K} [Y, Y]_T^{(\text{sparse},k)} \tag{11.12}$$

constructed by averaging the estimators $[Y, Y]_T^{(\text{sparse},k)}$ obtained by sampling sparsely on each of the K grids of average size $\bar{n}$. We show that:

$$[Y, Y]_T^{(\text{avg})} \overset{\mathcal{L}}{\approx} \underbrace{\langle X, X \rangle_T}_{\text{object of interest}} + \underbrace{2\bar{n} E[\varepsilon^2]}_{\text{bias due to noise}} \tag{11.13}$$

$$+ \underbrace{\left[\underbrace{4\frac{\bar{n}}{K} E[\varepsilon^4]}_{\text{due to noise}} + \underbrace{\frac{4T}{3\bar{n}} \int_0^T \sigma_t^4 dt}_{\text{due to discretization}} \right]^{1/2}}_{\text{total variance}} Z_{\text{total}}.$$

So, $[Y, Y]_T^{(\text{avg})}$ remains a biased estimator of the quadratic variation $\langle X, X \rangle_T$ of the true return process. But the bias $2\bar{n} E[\varepsilon^2]$ now increases with the average size of the subsamples, and $\bar{n} \leq n$. Thus, $[Y, Y]_T^{(\text{avg})}$ is a better estimator than $[Y, Y]_T^{(\text{all})}$, but is still biased.

But the lower bias can now be removed. Recall indeed that $E[\varepsilon^2]$ can be consistently approximated by

$$\widehat{E[\varepsilon^2]} = \frac{1}{2n} [Y, Y]_T^{(\text{all})}. \tag{11.14}$$

Hence a bias-adjusted estimator for $\langle X, X \rangle$ can thus be constructed as

$$\widehat{\langle X, X \rangle}_T^{(\text{tsrv})} = \underbrace{[Y, Y]_T^{(\text{avg})}}_{\text{slow time scale}} - \underbrace{\frac{\bar{n}}{n} [Y, Y]_T^{(\text{all})}}_{\text{fast time scale}} \tag{11.15}$$

and we call this, now for obvious reasons, the two scales realized volatility estimator.

If the number of subsamples is optimally selected as $K^* = cn^{2/3}$, then TSRV has the following distribution:

$$\widehat{\langle X, X \rangle}_T^{(tsrv)} \overset{\mathcal{L}}{\approx} \underbrace{\langle X, X \rangle_T}_{\text{object of interest}} + \frac{1}{n^{1/6}} \left[\underbrace{\frac{8}{c^2} E[\epsilon^2]^2}_{\text{due to noise}} + \underbrace{c \frac{4T}{3} \int_0^T \sigma_t^4 dt}_{\text{due to discretization}} \right]^{1/2} Z_{\text{total}}$$

$$\underbrace{\hphantom{\frac{8}{c^2} E[\epsilon^2]^2 + c \frac{4T}{3} \int_0^T \sigma_t^4 dt}}_{\text{total variance}}$$

(11.16)

and the constant c can be set to minimize the total asymptotic variance above.

Unlike all the previously considered ones, this estimator is now correctly centered, and to the best of our knowledge is the first consistent estimator for $\langle X, X \rangle_T$ in the presence of market microstructure noise. Unbiased, but inconsistent, estimators have been studied by Zhou (1996), who, in the parametric case of constant σ, proposed a bias correcting approach based on autocovariances. The behavior of this estimator has been studied by Zumbach, Corsi, and Trapletti (2002). Related studies are Hansen and Lunde (2006) and Bandi and Russell (2003); both papers consider time varying σ in the conditionally nonrandom case, and by Oomen (2006). These estimators are unfortunately also inconsistent. Under different assumptions (a pure jump process), the corresponding estimation problem is studied by Large (2005).

A small sample refinement to $\widehat{\langle X, X \rangle}_T^{(tsrv)}$ can be constructed as follows

$$\widehat{\langle X, X \rangle}_T^{(tsrv, adj)} = \left(1 - \frac{\bar{n}}{n} \right)^{-1} \widehat{\langle X, X \rangle}_T^{(tsrv)}.$$

(11.17)

The difference from the estimator in (11.15) is of order $O_p(\bar{n}/n) = O_p(K^{-1})$, and thus the two estimators behave identically to the asymptotic order that we consider. The estimator (11.17), however, has the appeal of being unbiased to higher order.

Just like the marginal distribution of the noise is likely to be unknown, its degree of dependence is also likely to be unknown. This calls for relaxing Assumption 17, and we developed in Aït-Sahalia, Mykland, and Zhang (2005c) a serial-dependence-robust TSRV estimator under Assumption 18. In a nutshell, we continue combining two different time scales, but rather than starting with the fastest possible time scale as our starting point, one now needs to be adjust how fast the fast time scale is. We also analyze there the impact of serial dependence in the noise on the distribution of the RV estimators, $[Y, Y]_T^{(all)}$ and $[Y, Y]_T^{(sparse)}$, and on a further refinement to this approach, called multiple scales realized volatility (MSRV), which achieves further asymptotic efficiency gains over TSRV (see Zhang, 2004).

Following our work, Barndorff-Nielsen et al. (2006) have shown that our TSRV estimator can be viewed as a form of kernel-based estimator. However, all kernel-based estimators are inconsistent estimators of $\langle X, X \rangle_T$ under the presence of market microstructure noise. When viewed as a kernel-based estimator, TSRV owes its consistency to its automatic selection of end effects which must be added "manually" to a kernel estimator to make it match TSRV. Optimizing over the kernel weights leads to an estimator with the same properties as MSRV, although the optimal kernel weights will have to be found numerically, whereas the optimal weights for MSRV will be explicit (see Zhang, 2004). With optimal weights, the rate of convergence can be improved from $n^{-1/6}$ for TSRV to $n^{-1/4}$ for MSRV as the cost of the higher complexity involved in combining $O(n^{1/2})$ time scales instead of just two as in (11.15). In the fully parametric case we studied in Aït-Sahalia, Mykland, and Zhang (2005b), we showed that when $\sigma_t = \sigma$ is constant, the MLE for σ^2 converges for T fixed and $\Delta \to 0$ at rate $\Delta^{1/4}/T^{1/4} = n^{-1/4}$ [see equation (31) p. 369 in Aït-Sahalia, Mykland, and Zhang (2005b)]. This establishes $n^{-1/4}$ as the best possible asymptotic rate improvement over (11.16).

To conclude, in the parametric case of constant volatility, we showed that in the presence of market microstructure noise that is unaccounted for, it is optimal to sample less often than would otherwise be the case: we derive the optimal sampling frequency. A better solution, however, is to model the noise term explicitly, for example by likelihood methods, which restores the first-order statistical effect that sampling as often as possible is optimal. But, more surprisingly, we also demonstrate that the likelihood correction is robust to misspecification of the assumed distribution of the noise term. In the nonparametric case of stochastic volatility, it is possible to correct for the noise by subsampling and averaging and obtain well-behaved estimators that make use of all the data. These results collectively suggest that attempts to incorporate market microstructure noise when estimating continuous-time models based on high-frequency data should have beneficial effects. And one final important message of these two papers: any time one has an impulse to sample sparsely, one can always do better: for example, using likelihood corrections in the parametric case or subsampling and averaging in the nonparametric case.

An alternative to the additive noise model of Assumption 15 is that described by Assumption 19, which captures the rounding that takes place in many financial markets, where prices are often quoted as a multiple of a given tick size. This form of measurement error has been studied by Jacod (1996), Delattre and Jacod (1997), and Gloter and Jacod (2000).

In the multivariate case of Assumption 7, an additional source of error is represented by the nonsynchronous trading of the different assets making up the X vector. Hayashi and Yoshida (2005) study the estimation of the quadratic covariation $\langle X^{(i)}, X^{(j)} \rangle_T$, defined analogously to (11.8) under Assumption 20, without market microstructure noise, that is, under Assumption 6. Zhang (2005) generalizes this to the situation where both Assumptions 15 and 20 hold.

References

AÏT-SAHALIA, Y. (1996a): "Do Interest Rates Really Follow Continuous-Time Markov Diffusions?" Technical Report, University of Chicago Working Paper.

——— (1996b): "Nonparametric Pricing of Interest Rate Derivative Securities," *Econometrica*, 64, 527–560.

—————— (1996c): "Testing Continuous-Time Models of the Spot Interest Rate," *Review of Financial Studies*, 9, 385–426.

—————— (1999): "Transition Densities for Interest Rate and Other Nonlinear Diffusions," *Journal of Finance*, 54, 1361–1395.

—————— (2001): "Closed-Form Likelihood Expansions for Multivariate Diffusions," Technical Report, Princeton University.

—————— (2002a): "Empirical Option Pricing and the Markov Property," Technical Report, Princeton University.

—————— (2002b): "Maximum-Likelihood Estimation of Discretely-Sampled Diffusions: A Closed-Form Approximation Approach," *Econometrica*, 70, 223–262.

—————— (2002c): "Telling from Discrete Data Whether the Underlying Continuous-Time Model is a Diffusion," *Journal of Finance*, 57, 2075–2112.

—————— (2004): "Disentangling Diffusion from Jumps," *Journal of Financial Economics*, 74, 487–528.

AÏT-SAHALIA, Y. AND J. DUARTE (2003): "Nonparametric Option Pricing under Shape Restrictions," *Journal of Econometrics*, 116, 9–47.

AÏT-SAHALIA, Y. AND J. FAN (2005a): "Nonparametric Transition Density-Based Tests for Jumps," Technical Report, Princeton University.

—————— (2005b): "Nonparametric Transition Density-Based Tests of the Markov Hypothesis," Technical Report, Princeton University.

AÏT-SAHALIA, Y., J. FAN, AND H. PENG (2005a): "Nonparametric Transition-Based Tests for Diffusions," Technical Report, Princeton University.

AÏT-SAHALIA, Y., L. P. HANSEN, AND J. A. SCHEINKMAN (2002): "Operator Methods for Continuous-Time Markov Processes," in *Handbook of Financial Econometrics*, edited by Y. Aït-Sahalia and L. P. Hansen, Amsterdam, The Netherlands: North Holland.

AÏT-SAHALIA, Y. AND J. JACOD (2004): "Fisher's Information for Discretely Sampled Lévy Processes," Technical Report, Princeton University and Université de Paris 6.

—————— (2006): "Volatility Estimators for Discretely Sampled Lévy Processes," *Annals of Statistics*, forthcoming.

AÏT-SAHALIA, Y. AND R. KIMMEL (2002): "Estimating Affine Multifactor Term Structure Models using Closed-Form Likelihood Expansions," Technical Report, Princeton University.

—————— (2004): "Maximum Likelihood Estimation of Stochastic Volatility Models," *Journal of Financial Economics,* forthcoming.

AÏT-SAHALIA, Y. AND A. LO (1998): "Nonparametric Estimation of State-Price-Densities Implicit in Financial Asset Prices," *Journal of Finance*, 53, 499–547.

—————— (2000): "Nonparametric Risk Management and Implied Risk Aversion," *Journal of Econometrics*, 94, 9–51.

AÏT-SAHALIA, Y. AND P. A. MYKLAND (2003): "The Effects of Random and Discrete Sampling when Estimating Continuous-Time Diffusions," *Econometrica*, 71, 483–549.

—————— (2004): "Estimators of Diffusions with Randomly Spaced Discrete Observations: A General Theory," *The Annals of Statistics*, 32, 2186–2222.

—————— (2005): "An Analysis of Hansen–Scheinkman Moment Estimators for Discretely and Randomly Sampled Diffusions," Technical Report, Princeton University.

AÏT-SAHALIA, Y., P. A. MYKLAND, AND L. ZHANG (2005b): "How Often to Sample a Continuous-Time Process in the Presence of Market Microstructure Noise," *Review of Financial Studies*, 18, 351–416.

——— (2005c): "Ultra High Frequency Volatility Estimation with Dependent Microstructure Noise," Technical Report, Princeton University.

AÏT-SAHALIA, Y. AND J. PARK (2005): "Specification Testing for Nonstationary Diffusions," Technical Report, Princeton University and Rice University.

AÏT-SAHALIA, Y., Y. WANG, AND F. YARED (2001): "Do Option Markets Correctly Price the Probabilities of Movement of the Underlying Asset?" *Journal of Econometrics*, 102, 67–110.

AÏT-SAHALIA, Y. AND J. YU (2006): "Saddlepoint Approximations for Continuous-Time Markov Processes," *Journal of Econometrics*, 134, 507–551.

AKONOM, J. (1993): "Comportement Asymptotique du Temps d'Occupation du Processus des Sommes Partielles," *Annales de l'Institut Henri Poincaré*, 29, 57–81.

ANDERSEN, T. G., T. BOLLERSLEV, AND F. X. DIEBOLD (2002): "Parametric and Nonparametric Measurements of Volatility," in *Handbook of Financial Econometrics*, edited by Y. Aït-Sahalia and L. P. Hansen, Amsterdam, The Netherlands: North Holland.

ANDERSEN, T. G., T. BOLLERSLEV, AND F. X. DIEBOLD (2003): "Some Like It Smooth, and Some Like It Rough," Technical Report, Northwestern University.

ANDERSEN, T. G., T. BOLLERSLEV, F. X. DIEBOLD, AND P. LABYS (2001): "The Distribution of Exchange Rate Realized Volatility," *Journal of the American Statistical Association*, 96, 42–55.

BAKSHI, G. S. AND N. YU (2005): "A Refinement to Aït-Sahalia's (2002) 'Maximum Likelihood Estimation of Discretely Sampled Diffusions: A Closed-form Approximation Approach'," *Journal of Business*, 78, 2037–2052.

BANDI, F. M. AND P. C. B. PHILLIPS (2002): "Nonstationary Continuous-Time Processes," in *Handbook of Financial Econometrics*, edited by Y. Aït-Sahalia and L. P. Hansen, Amsterdam, The Netherlands: North Holland.

——— (2003): "Fully Nonparametric Estimation of Scalar Diffusion Models," *Econometrica*, 71, 241–283.

BANDI, F. M. AND J. R. RUSSELL (2003): "Microstructure Noise, Realized Volatility and Optimal Sampling," Technical Report, University of Chicago Graduate School of Business.

BARNDORFF-NIELSEN, O. E., P. R. HANSEN, A. LUNDE, AND N. SHEPHARD (2006): "Regular and Modified Kernel-Based Estimators of Integrated Variance: The Case with Independent Noise," Technical Report, Department of Mathematical Sciences, University of Aarhus.

BARNDORFF-NIELSEN, O. E. AND N. SHEPHARD (2002): "Econometric Analysis of Realized Volatility and Its Use in Estimating Stochastic Volatility Models," *Journal of the Royal Statistical Society, B*, 64, 253–280.

——— (2003): "Power Variation with Stochastic Volatility and Jumps," Technical Report, University of Aarhus.

BIBBY, B. M., M. JACOBSEN, AND M. SØRENSEN (2002): "Estimating Functions for Discretely Sampled Diffusion-Type Models," in *Handbook of Financial Econometrics*, edited by Y. Aït-Sahalia and L. P. Hansen, Amsterdam, The Netherlands: North Holland.

BIBBY, B. M. AND M. S. SØRENSEN (1995): "Estimation Functions for Discretely Observed Diffusion Processes," *Bernoulli*, 1, 17–39.

BILLINGSLEY, P. (1961): *Statistical Inference for Markov Processes*, Chicago: The University of Chicago Press.

BLACK, F. AND M. SCHOLES (1973): "The Pricing of Options and Corporate Liabilities," *Journal of Political Economy*, 81, 637–654.

BREEDEN, D. AND R. H. LITZENBERGER (1978): "Prices of State-Contingent Claims Implicit in Option Prices," *Journal of Business*, 51, 621–651.

CARR, P. AND L. WU (2003): "What Type of Process Underlies Options? A Simple Robust Test," *Journal of Finance*, 58, 2581–2610.

CHAPMAN, D. A. AND N. PEARSON (2000): "Is the Short Rate Drift Actually Nonlinear?" *Journal of Finance*, 55, 355–388.

CHEN, S. X. AND J. GAO (2004a): "An Adaptive Empirical Likelihood Test for Time Series Models," Technical Report, Iowa State University.

——— (2004b): "On the Use of the Kernel Method for Specification Tests of Diffusion Models," Technical Report, Iowa State University.

CHERIDITO, P., D. FILIPOVIĆ, AND R. L. KIMMEL (2007): "Market Price of Risk Specifications for Affine Models: Theory and Evidence," *Journal of Financial Economics*, 83, 123–170.

CORRADI, V. AND N. R. SWANSON (2005): "A Bootstrap Specification Test for Diffusion Processes," *Journal of Econometrics*, 124, 117–148.

COX, J. C., J. E. INGERSOLL, AND S. A. ROSS (1985): "A Theory of the Term Structure of Interest Rates," *Econometrica*, 53, 385–408.

DAI, Q. AND K. J. SINGLETON (2000): "Specification Analysis of Affine Term Structure Models," *Journal of Finance*, 55, 1943–1978.

DANIELS, H. (1954): "Saddlepoint Approximations in Statistics," *Annals of Mathematical Statistics*, 25, 631–650.

DELATTRE, S. AND J. JACOD (1997): "A Central Limit Theorem for Normalized Functions of the Increments of a Diffusion Process, in the Presence of Round-Off Errors," *Bernoulli*, 3, 1–28.

DIPIETRO, M. (2001): "Bayesian Inference for Discretely Sampled Diffusion Processes with Financial Applications," Ph.D. thesis, Department of Statistics, Carnegie-Mellon University.

DUARTE, J. (2004): "Evaluating an Alternative Risk Preference in Affine Term Structure Models," *Review of Financial Studies*, 17, 379–404.

DUFFEE, G. R. (2002): "Term Premia and Interest Rate Forecasts in Affine Models," *Journal of Finance*, 57, 405–443.

DUFFIE, D. AND R. KAN (1996): "A Yield-Factor Model of Interest Rates," *Mathematical Finance*, 6, 379–406.

EFRON, B. AND R. TIBSHIRANI (1996): "Using Specially Designed Exponential Families for Density Estimation," *The Annals of Statistics*, 24, 2431–2461.

EGOROV, A. V., H. LI, AND Y. XU (2003): "Maximum Likelihood Estimation of Time Inhomogeneous Diffusions", *Journal of Econometrics*, 114, 107–139.

ENGLE, R. F. (2000): "The Econometrics of Ultra-High Frequency Data," *Econometrica*, 68, 1–22.

ENGLE, R. F. AND J. R. RUSSELL (1998): "Autoregressive Conditional Duration: A New Model for Irregularly Spaced Transaction Data," *Econometrica*, 66, 1127–1162.

FAN, J. (1992): "Design-Adaptive Nonparametric Regression," *Journal of the American Statistical Association*, 87, 998–1004.

FAN, J. AND Q. YAO (1998): "Efficient Estimation of Conditional Variance Functions in Stochastic Regression," *Biometrika*, 85, 645–660.

FAN, J., Q. YAO, AND H. TONG (1996): "Estimation of Conditional Densities and Sensitivity Measures in Nonlinear Dynamical Systems," *Biometrika*, 83, 189–206.

FLORENS-ZMIROU, D. (1989): "Approximate Discrete-Time Schemes for Statistics of Diffusion Processes," *Statistics*, 20, 547–557.

FRYDMAN, H. AND B. SINGER (1979): "Total Positivity and the Embedding Problem for Markov Chains," *Mathematical Proceedings of the Cambridge Philosophical Society*, 86, 339–344.

GALLANT, A. R. AND G. T. TAUCHEN (1996): "Which Moments to Match?" *Econometric Theory*, 12, 657–681.

——— (2002): "Simulated Score Methods and Indirect Inference for Continuous-time Models," in *Handbook of Financial Econometrics*, edited by Y. Aït-Sahalia and L. P. Hansen, Amsterdam, The Netherlands: North Holland.

GENON-CATALOT, V., T. JEANTHEAU, AND C. LARÉDO (1999): "Parameter Estimation for Discretely Observed Stochastic Volatility Models," *Bernoulli*, 5, 855–872.

GLAD, I. K. (1998): "Parametrically Guided Non-Parametric Regression," *Scandinavian Journal of Statistics*, 25, 649–668.

GLOTER, A. AND J. JACOD (2000): "Diffusions with Measurement Errors: I – Local Asymptotic Normality and II – Optimal Estimators," Technical Report, Université de Paris VI.

GODAMBE, V. P. (1960): "An Optimum Property of Regular Maximum Likelihood Estimation," *Annals of Mathematical Statistics*, 31, 1208–1211.

GOURIÉROUX, C., A. MONFORT, AND E. RENAULT (1993): "Indirect Inference," *Journal of Applied Econometrics*, 8, S85–S118.

HALL, P. AND C. C. HEYDE (1980): *Martingale Limit Theory and Its Application*, Boston: Academic Press.

HANSEN, L. P. (1982): "Large Sample Properties of Generalized Method of Moments Estimators," *Econometrica*, 50, 1029–1054.

HANSEN, L. P. AND T. J. SARGENT (1983): "The Dimensionality of the Aliasing Problem in Models with Rational Spectral Densities," *Econometrica*, 51, 377–387.

HANSEN, L. P. AND J. A. SCHEINKMAN (1995): "Back to the Future: Generating Moment Implications for Continuous-Time Markov Processes," *Econometrica*, 63, 767–804.

HANSEN, P. R. AND A. LUNDE (2006): Realized "Variance and Market Microstructure Noise," *Journal of Business and Economic Statistics*, 24, 127–161.

HARRISON, M. AND D. KREPS (1979): "Martingales and Arbitrage in Multiperiod Securities Markets," *Journal of Economic Theory*, 20, 381–408.

HAYASHI, T. AND N. YOSHIDA (2005): "On Covariance Estimation of Nonsynchronously Observed Diffusion Processes," Technical Report, Columbia University.

HESTON, S. (1993): "A Closed-Form Solution for Options with Stochastic Volatility with Applications to Bonds and Currency Options," *Review of Financial Studies*, 6, 327–343.

HEYDE, C. C. (1997): *Quasi-Likelihood and Its Application*, New York: Springer-Verlag.

HJORT, N. L. AND I. K. GLAD (1995): "Nonparametric Density Estimation with a Parametric Start," *The Annals of Statistics*, 23, 882–904.

HJORT, N. L. AND M. JONES (1996): "Locally Parametric Nonparametric Density Estimation," *The Annals of Statistics*, 24, 1619–1647.

HONG, Y. AND H. LI (2005): "Nonparametric Specification Testing for Continuous-Time Models with Applications to Term Structure of Interest Rates," *Review of Financial Studies*, 18, 37–84.

HUANG, X. AND G. TAUCHEN (2006): "The Relative Contribution of Jumps to Total Price Variance," *Journal of Financial Econometrics*, 4, 456–499.

HULL, J. AND A. WHITE (1987): "The Pricing of Options on Assets with Stochastic Volatilities," *Journal of Finance*, 42, 281–300.

HURN, A. S., J. JEISMAN, AND K. LINDSAY (2005): "Seeing the Wood for the Trees: A Critical Evaluation of Methods to Estimate the Parameters of Stochastic Differential Equations," Technical Report, School of Economics and Finance, Queensland University of Technology.

JACOD, J. (1994): "Limit of Random Measures Associated with the Increments of a Brownian Semimartingale," Technical Report, Université de Paris VI.

——— (1996): "La Variation Quadratique du Brownien en Présence d'Erreurs d'Arrondi," *Astérisque*, 236, 155–162.

JACOD, J. AND P. PROTTER (1998): "Asymptotic Error Distributions for the Euler Method for Stochastic Differential Equations," *Annals of Probability*, 26, 267–307.

JEGANATHAN, P. (1995): "Some Aspects of Asymptotic Theory with Applications to Time Series Models," *Econometric Theory*, 11, 818–887.

JENSEN, B. AND R. POULSEN (2002): "Transition Densities of Diffusion Processes: Numerical Comparison of Approximation Techniques," *Journal of Derivatives*, 9, 1–15.

JIANG, G. J. AND J. KNIGHT (1997): "A Nonparametric Approach to the Estimation of Diffusion Processes – with an Application to a Short-Term Interest Rate Model," *Econometric Theory*, 13, 615–645.

KARLIN, S. AND J. McGREGOR (1959a): "Coincidence Probabilities," *Pacific Journal of Mathematics*, 9, 1141–1164.

——— (1959b): "Coincidence Properties of Birth-and-Death Processes," *Pacific Journal of Mathematics*, 9, 1109–1140.

KENT, J. (1978): "Time Reversible Diffusions," *Advanced Applied Probability*, 10, 819–835.

KESSLER, M. AND M. SØRENSEN (1999): "Estimating Equations Based on Eigenfunctions for a Discretely Observed Diffusion," *Bernoulli*, 5, 299–314.

KRISTENSEN, D. (2004): "Estimation in Two Classes of Semiparametric Diffusion Models,"Technical Report, University of Wisconsin-Madison.

LARGE, J. (2005): "Quadratic Variation when Quotes Change One Tick at a Time," Technical Report, Oxford University.

LEWIS, A. L. (2000): *Option Valuation under Stochastic Volatility*, Newport Beach, CA: Finance Press.

LO, A. W. (1988): "Maximum Likelihood Estimation of Generalized Itô Processes with Discretely Sampled Data," *Econometric Theory*, 4, 231–247.

LOADER, C. R. (1996): "Local Likelihood Density Estimation," *The Annals of Statistics*, 24, 1602–1618.

MYKLAND, P. A. AND L. ZHANG (2006): "ANOVA for Diffusions," *The Annals of Statistics*, 34, 1931–1963.

OOMEN, R. C. (2006): "Properties of Realized Variance under Alternative Sampling Schemes," *Journal of Business and Economic Statistics*, 24, 219–237.

PEDERSEN, A. R. (1995): "A New Approach to Maximum-Likelihood Estimation for Stochastic Differential Equations Based on Discrete Observations," *Scandinavian Journal of Statistics*, 22, 55–71.

PHILIPS, P. C. B. (1973): "The Problem of Identification in Finite Parameter Continuous Time Models," *Journal of Econometrics*, 1, 351–362.

PHILLIPS, P. C. AND J. YU (2005): "A Two-Stage Realized Volatility Approach to the Estimation of Diffusion Processes from Discrete Observations," Technical Report, Singapore Management University.

PRESS, H. AND J. W. TURKEY (1956): *Power Spectral Methods of Analysis and Their Application to Problems in Airplane Dynamics*, Bell Telephone System Monograph 2606.

PRITZKER, M. (1998): "Nonparametric Density Estimation and Tests of Continuous Time Interest Rate Models," *Review of Financial Studies*, 11, 449–487.

RENAULT, E. AND B. J. WERKER (2003): "Stochastic Volatility Models with Transaction Time Risk," Technical Report, Tilburg University.

ROMANO, M. AND N. TOUZI (1997): "Contingent Claims and Market Completeness in a Stochastic Volatility Model," *Mathematical Finance*, 7, 399–412.

SCHAUMBURG, E. (2001): "Maximum Likelihood Estimation of Jump Processes with Applications to Finance," Ph.D. thesis, Princeton University.

SMITH, A. A. (1993): "Estimating Nonlinear Time Series Models using Simulated Vector Autoregressions," *Journal of Applied Econometrics*, 8, S63–S84.

SØRENSEN, H. (2001): "Discretely Observed Diffusions: Approximation of the Continuous-Time Score Function," *Scandinavian Journal of Statistics*, 28, 113–121.

STANTON, R. (1997): "A Nonparametric Model of Term Structure Dynamics and the Market Price of Interest Rate Risk," *Journal of Finance*, 52, 1973–2002.

STRAMER, O. AND J. YAN (2005): "On Simulated Likelihood of Discretely Observed Diffusion Processes and Comparison to Closed-Form Approximation," Technical Report, University of Iowa.

THOMPSON, S. (2004): "Identifying Term Structure Volatility from the LIBOR-Swap Curve," Technical Report, Harvard University.

VASICEK, O. (1977): "An Equilibrium Characterization of the Term Structure," *Journal of Financial Economics*, 5, 177–188.

WONG, E. (1964): "The Construction of a Class of Stationary Markoff Processes," in *Sixteenth Symposium in Applied Mathematics – Stochastic Processes in Mathematical Physics and Engineering*, edited by R. Bellman, Providence, RI: American Mathematical Society, pp. 264–276.

YU, J. (2003): "Closed-Form Likelihood Estimation of Jump-Diffusions with an Application to the Realignment Risk Premium of the Chinese Yuan," Ph.D. thesis, Princeton University.

ZHANG, L. (2004): "Efficient Estimation of Stochastic Volatility using Noisy Observations: A Multi-Scale Approach," Technical Report, Carnegie-Mellon University.

——— (2005): "Estimating Covariation: Epps Effect and Microstructure Noise," Technical Report, Carnegie-Mellon University.

ZHANG, L., P. A. MYKLAND, AND Y. AÏT-SAHALIA (2005): "A Tale of Two Time Scales: Determining Integrated Volatility with Noisy High-Frequency Data," *Journal of the American Statistical Association*, 100, 1394–1411.

ZHOU, B. (1996): "High-Frequency Data and Volatility in Foreign-Exchange Rates," *Journal of Business and Economic Statistics*, 14, 45–52.

ZUMBACH, G., F. CORSI, AND A. TRAPLETTI (2002): "Efficient Estimation of Volatility using High Frequency Data," Technical Report, Olsen & Associates.

CHAPTER 10

Variation, Jumps and High-Frequency Data in Financial Econometrics

Ole E. Barndorff-Nielsen[*] and Neil Shephard[†]

1 INTRODUCTION

We will review the econometrics of nonparametric estimation of the components of the variation of asset prices. This very active literature has been stimulated by the recent advent of complete records of transaction prices, quote data, and order books. In our view the interaction of the new data sources with new econometric methodology is leading to a paradigm shift in one of the most important areas in econometrics: volatility measurement, modeling, and forecasting.

We will describe this new paradigm which draws together econometrics with arbitrage-free financial economics theory. Perhaps the two most influential papers in this area have been Andersen, Bollerslev, Diebold, and Labys (2001) and Barndorff-Nielsen and Shephard (2002), but many other papers have made important contributions. This work is likely to have deep impacts on the econometrics of asset allocation and risk management. One of the most challenging problems in this context is dealing with various forms of market frictions, which obscure the efficient price from the econometrician. Here we briefly discuss how econometricians have been attempting to overcome them.

In Section 2, we will set out the basis of the econometrics of arbitrage-free price processes, focusing on the centrality of quadratic variation. In Section 3, we will discuss central limit theorems for estimators of the QV process, while in Section 4, the role of jumps in QV will be highlighted, with bipower and multipower variation being used to identify them and to test the hypothesis that there are no jumps in the price process. In Section 5, we write about the econometrics of market frictions, while in Section 6, we conclude.

[*] The T.N. Thiele Centre for Mathematics in Natural Science, Department of Mathematical Sciences, University of Aarhus, Ny Munkegade, DK-8000 Aarhus C, Denmark. E-mail: oebn@imf.au.dk.

[†] Nuffield College, Oxford OX1 1NF, UK. E-mail: neil.shephard@nuf.ox.ac.uk.

2   ARBITRAGE-FREE, FRICTIONLESS PRICE PROCESSES

2.1   Semimartingales and Quadratic Variation

Given a complete record of transaction or quote prices it is natural to model prices in continuous time (e.g., Engle, 2000). This matches with the vast continuous time financial economic arbitrage-free theory based on a frictionless market. In this section and the next, we will discuss how to make inferences on the degree of variation in such frictionless worlds. Section 5 will extend this by characterizing the types of frictions seen in practice and discuss strategies econometricians have been using to overcome these difficulties.

In its most general case the fundamental theory of asset prices says that a vector of log-prices at time t,

$$Y_t = \left(Y_t^1, \ldots, Y_t^p\right)',$$

must obey a *semimartingale* process (written $Y \in \mathcal{SM}$) on some filtered probability space $\left(\Omega, \mathcal{F}, (\mathcal{F}_t)_{t \geq 0}, P\right)$ in a frictionless market. The semimartingale is defined as being a process which can be written as

$$Y = A + M, \tag{1}$$

where A is a local finite variation process ($A \in \mathcal{FV}_{loc}$) and M is a local martingale ($M \in \mathcal{M}_{loc}$). Compact introductions to the economics and mathematics of semimartingales are given in Back (1991) and Protter (2004), respectively. Informally, we can think of A as being the financial reward for being exposed to the pure risk M. The use of localization[1] in the definition of a semimartingale is a technical condition which extends the scope of these processes beyond martingales[2] plus finite variation processes. However, localization is not the essential econometric feature here and so readers who are not familiar with localization are not advised to immediately focus on that aspect of semimartingales.

The Y process can exhibit jumps. It is tempting to decompose $Y = Y^{ct} + Y^d$, where Y^{ct} and Y^d are the purely continuous and discontinuous sample path components of Y. However, technically this definition is not clear as the jumps

---

[1] Recall a stochastic process Y is said to possess a given property *locally* if there exists an increasing sequence of stopping times T_n, with $\lim_{n \to \infty} T_n = \infty$ a.s., such that, for every n, the property holds for the stopped process $Y_t^{T_n}$. In turn a nonnegative random variable T is said to be a stopping time if $\{T \leq t\} \in \mathcal{F}_t$ for every $t \geq 0$.

[2] An example of this is a stochastic volatility process $M_t = \int_0^t \sigma_u dW_u$, where W is Brownian motion. For this to be a local martingale we need that $\int_0^t \sigma_u^2 du < \infty$, while for it to be a martingale we need the additional condition that

$$\mathrm{E}\left(\sqrt{\int_0^t \sigma_u^2 du}\right) < \infty,$$

in order that $\mathrm{E}|M_t| < \infty$.

of the Y process can be so active that they cannot be summed up. Thus we will define

$$Y^{ct} = A^c + M^c,$$

where M^c is the continuous part of the local martingale component of Y and A^c is A minus the sum of the jumps of A.[3] Likewise, the continuous sample path subsets of SM and M_{loc} will be denoted by SM^c and M_{loc}^c.

Crucial to semimartingales, and to the economics of financial risk, is the *quadratic variation* (QV) process of $(Y', X')' \in SM$. This can be defined as

$$[Y, X]_t = \text{p--}\lim_{n \to \infty} \sum_{j=1}^{t_j \le t} (Y_{t_j} - Y_{t_{j-1}})(X_{t_j} - X_{t_{j-1}})', \tag{2}$$

[e.g., Protter (2004, pp. 66–77)] for any deterministic sequence[4] of partitions $0 = t_0 < t_1 < \cdots < t_n = T$ with $\sup_j \{t_{j+1} - t_j\} \to 0$ for $n \to \infty$. The convergence is also locally uniform in time. It can be shown that this probability limit exists for all semimartingales.

Throughout we employ the notation that

$$[Y]_t = [Y, Y]_t,$$

while we will sometimes refer to $\sqrt{[Y^l]_t}$ as the quadratic volatility (QVol) process for Y^l where $l = 1, 2, \ldots, p$. It is well known that[5]

$$[Y] = [Y^{ct}] + [Y^d], \quad \text{where} \quad [Y^d]_t = \sum_{0 \le u \le t} \Delta Y_u \Delta Y_u' \tag{3}$$

where $\Delta Y_t = Y_t - Y_{t-}$ are the jumps in Y and noting that $[A^{ct}] = 0$. In the probability literature QV is usually defined in a different, but equivalent, manner [see, e.g., Protter (2004, p. 66)]

$$[Y]_t = Y_t Y_t' - 2 \int_0^t Y_{u-} \mathrm{d}Y_u'. \tag{4}$$

2.2 Brownian Semimartingales

In economics the most familiar semimartingale is the *Brownian semimartingale* $(Y \in BSM)$

$$Y_t = \int_0^t a_u \mathrm{d}u + \int_0^t \sigma_u \mathrm{d}W_u, \tag{5}$$

---

[3] It is tempting to use the notation Y^c for Y^{ct}, but in the probability literature if $Y \in SM$ then $Y^c = M^c$, so Y^c ignores A^c.

[4] The assumption that the times are deterministic can be relaxed to allow them to be any Riemann sequence of adapted subdivisions. This is discussed in, for example, Jacod and Shiryaev (2003, p. 51). Economically, this is important for it means that we can also think of the limiting argument as the result of a joint process of Y and a counting process N whose arrival times are the t_j. So long as Y and N are adapted to at least their bivariate natural filtration the limiting argument holds as the intensity of N increases off to infinity with n.

[5] Although the sum of jumps of Y does not exist in general when $Y \in SM$, the sum of outer products of the jumps always does exist. Hence $[Y^d]$ can be properly defined.

where a is a vector of predictable drifts, σ is a matrix volatility process whose elements are càdlàg and W is a vector Brownian motion. The stochastic integral $(\sigma \bullet W)_t$, where $(f \bullet g)_t$ is generic notation for the process $\int_0^t f_u \mathrm{d}g_u$, is said to be a stochastic volatility process $(\sigma \bullet W \in \mathcal{SV})$ – for example, the reviews in Ghysels, Harvey, and Renault (1996) and Shephard (2005). This vector process has elements which are $\mathcal{M}^c_{loc}$. Doob (1953) showed that all continuous local martingales with absolutely continuous quadratic variation can be written in the form of an SV process (see Karatzas and Shreve, 1991, pp. 170–172).[6] The drift $\int_0^t a_u \mathrm{d}u$ has elements which are absolutely continuous – an assumption which looks ad hoc, however arbitrage freeness plus the SV model implies this property must hold [Karatzas and Shreve (1998, p. 3) and Andersen, Bollerslev, Diebold, and Labys (2003, p. 583)]. Hence $Y \in \mathcal{BSM}$ is a rather canonical model in the finance theory of continuous sample path processes. Its use is bolstered by the facts that Ito calculus for continuous sample path processes is relatively simple.

If $Y \in \mathcal{BSM}$ then

$$[Y]_t = \int_0^t \Sigma_u \mathrm{d}u$$

the integrated covariance process, while

$$\mathrm{d}Y_t | \mathcal{F}_t \sim N\left(a_t \mathrm{d}t, \Sigma_t \mathrm{d}t\right), \quad \text{where} \quad \Sigma_t = \sigma_t \sigma_t', \tag{6}$$

where $\mathcal{F}_t$ is the natural filtration – that is the information from the entire sample path of Y up to time t. Thus $a_t \mathrm{d}t$ and $\Sigma_t \mathrm{d}t$ have clear interpretations as the infinitesimal predictive mean and covariance of asset returns. This implies that $A_t = \int_0^t \mathrm{E}\left(\mathrm{d}Y_u | \mathcal{F}_u\right) \mathrm{d}u$ while, centrally to our interests,

$$\mathrm{d}[Y]_t = \mathrm{Cov}\left(\mathrm{d}Y_t | \mathcal{F}_t\right) \quad \text{and} \quad [Y]_t = \int_0^t \mathrm{Cov}\left(\mathrm{d}Y_u | \mathcal{F}_u\right) \mathrm{d}u.$$

Thus A and $[Y]$ are the integrated infinitesimal predictive mean and covariance of the asset prices, respectively.

2.3   Adding Jump Processes

There is no plausible economic theory which says that prices must follow continuous sample path processes. Indeed we will see later that statistically it is rather easy to reject this hypothesis even for price processes drawn from very thickly traded markets. In this paper we will add a finite activity jump process (this means there are a finite number of jumps in a fixed time interval)

---

[6] An example of a continuous local martingale which has no SV representation is a time-change Brownian motion where the time-change takes the form of the so-called "devil's staircase," which is continuous and nondecreasing but not absolutely continuous [see, e.g., Munroe (1953, Section 27)]. This relates to the work of, for example, Calvet and Fisher (2002) on multifractals.

$J_t = \sum_{j=1}^{N_t} C_j$, adapted to the filtration generated by Y, to the Brownian semi-martingale model. This yields

$$Y_t = \int_0^t a_u du + \int_0^t \sigma_u dW_u + \sum_{j=1}^{N_t} C_j. \tag{7}$$

Here N is a simple counting process and the C are the associated nonzero jumps (which we assume have a covariance) which happen at times $0 = \tau_0 < \tau_1 < \tau_2 < \dots$. It is helpful to decompose J into $J = J^A + J^M$, where, assuming J has an absolutely continuous intensity, $J_t^A = \int_0^t c_u du$, and $c_t = \mathrm{E}(dJ_t|\mathcal{F}_t)$. Then J^M is the compensated jump process, so $J^M \in \mathcal{M}$, while $J^A \in \mathcal{FV}_{loc}^{ct}$. Thus Y has the decomposition as in (1), with $A_t = \int_0^t (a_u + c_u) du$ and

$$M_t = \int_0^t \sigma_u dW_u + \sum_{j=1}^{N_t} C_j - \int_0^t c_u du.$$

It is easy to see that $[Y^d]_t = \sum_{j=1}^{N_t} C_j C_j'$ and so

$$[Y]_t = \int_0^t \Sigma_u du + \sum_{j=1}^{N_t} C_j C_j'.$$

Again we note that $\mathrm{E}(dY_t|\mathcal{F}_t) = (a_t + c_t) dt$, but now,

$$\mathrm{Cov}(\sigma_t dW_t, dJ_t|\mathcal{F}_t) = 0, \tag{8}$$

so

$$\mathrm{Cov}(dY_t|\mathcal{F}_t) = \Sigma_t dt + \mathrm{Cov}(dJ_t|\mathcal{F}_t) \neq d[Y]_t.$$

This means that the QV process aggregates the components of the variation of prices and so is not sufficient to learn the integrated covariance process $\int_0^t \Sigma_u du$.

To identify the components of the QV process we can use the bipower variation (BPV) process introduced by Barndorff-Nielsen and Shephard (2006a). So long as it exists, the $p \times p$ matrix BPV process $\{Y\}$ has l, kth element

$$\{Y^l, Y^k\} = \frac{1}{4} \left(\{Y^l + Y^k\} - \{Y^l - Y^k\} \right), \quad l, k, = 1, 2, \dots, p, \tag{9}$$

where, so long as the limit exists and the convergence is locally uniform in t,[7]

$$\{Y^l\}_t = \mathrm{p-}\lim_{\delta \downarrow 0} \sum_{j=1}^{\lfloor t/\delta \rfloor} \left| Y_{\delta(j-1)}^l - Y_{\delta(j-2)}^l \right| \left| Y_{\delta j}^l - Y_{\delta(j-1)}^l \right|. \tag{10}$$

---

[7] To simplify some of the later results we consistently ignore end effects in variation statistics. This can be justified in two ways, either by (a) setting $Y_t = 0$ for $t < 0$, (b) letting Y start being a semi-martingale at zero at time before $t = 0$. The latter seems realistic when dealing with markets open 24 hours a day, borrowing returns from small periods of the previous day. It means that there is a modest degree of wash over from one day's variation statistics into the next day. There seems little econometric reasons why this should be a worry. Assumption (b) can also be used in equity markets when combined with some form of stochastic imputation, adding in artifical simulated returns for the missing period – see the related comments in Barndorff-Nielsen and Shephard (2002).

Here $\lfloor x \rfloor$ is the floor function, which is the largest integer less than or equal to x. Combining the results in Barndorff-Nielsen and Shephard (2006a) and Barndorff-Nielsen, Graversen, Jacod, Podolskij, and Shephard (2006) if Y is the form of (7) then, without any additional assumptions,

$$\mu_1^{-2} \{Y\}_t = \int_0^t \Sigma_u du,$$

where $\mu_r = \mathrm{E} |U|^r$, $U \sim N(0, 1)$ and $r > 0$, which means that

$$[Y]_t - \mu_1^{-2} \{Y\}_t = \sum_{j=1}^{N_t} C_j C_j'.$$

At first sight the robustness of BPV looks rather magical, but it is a consequence of the fact that only a finite number of terms in the sum (10) are affected by jumps, while each return which does not have a jump goes to zero in probability. Therefore, since the probability of jumps in contiguous time intervals goes to zero as $\delta \downarrow 0$, those terms which do include jumps do not impact the probability limit. The extension of this result to the case where J is an infinite activity jump process is discussed in Section 4.4.

2.4 Forecasting

Suppose Y obeys (7) and introduce the generic notation

$$y_{t+s,t} = Y_{t+s} - Y_t$$
$$= a_{t+s,t} + m_{t+s,t}, \quad t, s > 0.$$

So long as the covariance exists,

$$\mathrm{Cov}\left(y_{t+s,t}|\mathcal{F}_t\right) = \mathrm{Cov}\left(a_{t+s,t}|\mathcal{F}_t\right) + \mathrm{Cov}\left(m_{t+s,t}|\mathcal{F}_t\right)$$
$$+ \mathrm{Cov}\left(a_{t+s,t}, m_{t+s,t}|\mathcal{F}_t\right) + \mathrm{Cov}\left(m_{t+s,t}, a_{t+s,t}, |\mathcal{F}_t\right).$$

Notice how complicated this expression is compared to the covariance in (6), which is due to the fact that s is not necessarily dt and so $a_{t+s,t}$ is no longer known given $\mathcal{F}_t$ – while $\int_t^{t+dt} a_u du$ was. However, in all likelihood for small s, a makes a rather modest contribution to the predictive covariance of Y.

This suggests using the approximation that

$$\mathrm{Cov}\left(y_{t+s,t}|\mathcal{F}_t\right) \simeq \mathrm{Cov}\left(m_{t+s,t}|\mathcal{F}_t\right).$$

Now using (8) so

$$\mathrm{Cov}\left(m_{t+s,t}|\mathcal{F}_t\right)$$
$$= \mathrm{E}\left([Y]_{t+s} - [Y]_t|\mathcal{F}_t\right) - \mathrm{E}\left\{\left(\int_t^{t+s} c_u du\right)\left(\int_t^{t+s} c_u du\right)' |\mathcal{F}_t\right\}.$$

Hence if c or s is small then we might approximate

$$\text{Cov}\,(Y_{t+s} - Y_t | \mathcal{F}_t) \simeq \text{E}\,([Y]_{t+s} - [Y]_t | \mathcal{F}_t)$$
$$= \text{E}\,([\sigma \bullet W]_{t+s} - [\sigma \bullet W]_t | \mathcal{F}_t) + \text{E}\,([J]_{t+s} - [J]_t | \mathcal{F}_t)\,.$$

Thus an interesting forecasting strategy for covariances is to forecast the increments of the QV process or its components. As the QV process and its components are themselves estimable, though with substantial possible error, this is feasible. This approach to forecasting has been advocated in a series of influential papers by Andersen, Bollerslev, Diebold, and Labys (2001, 2003) and Andersen, Bollerslev, Diebold, and Ebens (2001), while the important earlier paper by Andersen and Bollerslev (1998a) was stimulating in the context of measuring the forecast performance of GARCH models. The use of forecasting using estimates of the increments of the components of QV was introduced by Andersen, Bollerslev, and Diebold (2003). We will return to it in Section 3.9 when we have developed an asymptotic theory for estimating the QV process and its components.

2.5   Realized QV and BPV

The QV process can be estimated in many different ways. The most immediate is the realized QV estimator

$$[Y_\delta]_t = \sum_{j=1}^{\lfloor t/\delta \rfloor} \left(Y_{j\delta} - Y_{(j-1)\delta}\right) \left(Y_{j\delta} - Y_{(j-1)\delta}\right)',$$

where $\delta > 0$. This is the outer product of returns computed over a fixed interval of time of length δ. By construction, as $\delta \downarrow 0$, $[Y_\delta]_t \overset{p}{\to} [Y]_t$. Likewise

$$\{Y_\delta^l\}_t = \sum_{j=1}^{\lfloor t/\delta \rfloor} \left|Y_{\delta(j-1)}^l - Y_{\delta(j-2)}^l\right| \left|Y_{\delta j}^l - Y_{\delta(j-1)}^l\right|, \quad l = 1, 2, \dots, p,$$

$$(11)$$

$\{Y_\delta^l, Y_\delta^k\} = \frac{1}{4}(\{Y_\delta^l + Y_\delta^k\} - \{Y_\delta^l - Y_\delta^k\})$ and $\{Y_\delta\} \overset{p}{\to} \{Y\}$. In practice, the presence of market frictions can potentially mean that this limiting argument is not really available as an accurate guide to the behavior of these statistics for small δ. Such difficulties with limiting arguments, which are present in almost all areas of econometrics and statistics, do not invalidate the use of asymptotics, for it is used to provide predictions about finite sample behavior. Probability limits are, of course, coarse and we will respond to this by refining our understanding by developing central limit theorems and hope they will make good predictions when δ is moderately small. For very small δ these asymptotic predictions become poor guides as frictions bite hard and this will be discussed in Section 5.

In financial econometrics the focus is often on the increments of the QV and realized QV over set time intervals, like one day. Let us define the daily QV

$$V_i = [Y]_{hi} - [Y]_{h(i-1)}, \quad i = 1, 2, \dots$$

while it is estimated by the realized daily QV

$$\widehat{V}_i = [Y_\delta]_{hi} - [Y_\delta]_{h(i-1)}, \quad i = 1, 2, \dots.$$

Clearly $\widehat{V}_i \xrightarrow{p} V_i$ as $\delta \downarrow 0$. The lth diagonal element of $\widehat{V}_i$, written $\widehat{V}_i^{l,l}$ is called the realized variance[8] of asset l, while its square root is its realized volatility. The latter estimates $\sqrt{V_i^{l,l}}$, the daily QVol process of asset l. The l, kth element of $\widehat{V}_i$, $\widehat{V}_i^{l,k}$, is called the realized covariance between assets l and k. Of these objects we can define standard dependence measures, like realized regression

$$\widehat{\beta}_i^{l,k} = \frac{\widehat{V}_i^{l,k}}{\widehat{V}_i^{k,k}} \xrightarrow{p} \beta_i^{l,k} = \frac{V_i^{l,k}}{V_i^{k,k}},$$

which estimates the QV regression and the realized correlation

$$\widehat{\rho}_i^{l,k} = \frac{\widehat{V}_i^{l,k}}{\sqrt{\widehat{V}_i^{l,l}\widehat{V}_i^{k,k}}} \xrightarrow{p} \rho_i^{l,k} = \frac{V_i^{l,k}}{\sqrt{V_i^{l,l}V_i^{k,k}}},$$

which estimates the QV correlation. Similar daily objects can be calculated of the realized BPV process

$$\widehat{B}_i = \mu_1^{-2} \left\{ \{Y_\delta\}_{hi} - \{Y_\delta\}_{h(i-1)} \right\}, \quad i = 1, 2, \dots$$

which estimates

$$B_i = \left[Y^{ct}\right]_{hi} - \left[Y^{ct}\right]_{h(i-1)} = \int_{h(i-1)}^{hi} \sigma_u^2 \mathrm{d}u, \quad i = 1, 2, \dots.$$

Realized volatility has a very long history in financial economics. It appears in, for example, Rosenberg (1972), Officer (1973), Merton (1980), French, Schwert, and Stambaugh (1987), Schwert (1989) and Schwert (1998), with Merton (1980) making the implicit connection with the case where $\delta \downarrow 0$ in the pure scaled Brownian motion plus drift case. Of course, in probability theory QV was discussed as early as Wiener (1924) and Lévy (1937) and appears as a crucial object in the development of the stochastic analysis of semimartingales which occurred in the second half of the last century. For more general financial processes a closer connection between realized QV and QV, and its use for econometric purposes, was made in a series of independent and concurrent papers by Comte and Renault (1998), Barndorff-Nielsen and Shephard (2001), and Andersen, Bollerslev, Diebold, and Labys (2001). The realized regressions and correlations were defined and studied in detail by Andersen, Bollerslev, Diebold, and Labys (2003) and Barndorff-Nielsen and Shephard (2004).

A major motivation for Barndorff-Nielsen and Shephard (2002) and Andersen, Bollerslev, Diebold, and Labys (2001) was the fact that volatility in financial markets is highly and unstably diurnal within a day, responding to regularly

---

[8] Some authors call $\widehat{V}_i^{l,l}$ the realized volatility, but throughout this paper we follow the tradition in finance of using volatility to mean standard deviation-type objects.

timed macroeconomic news announcements, social norms such as lunch times and sleeping or the opening of other markets. This makes estimating

$$\lim_{\varepsilon \downarrow 0} \left([Y]_{t+\varepsilon} - [Y]_t \right) / \varepsilon$$

extremely difficult. The very stimulating work of Genon-Catalot, Larédo, and Picard (1992), Foster and Nelson (1996), Mykland and Zhang (2002, 2006), Fan, Fan, and Lv (2005) tries to tackle this problem using a double asymptotics, as $\delta \downarrow 0$ and $\varepsilon \downarrow 0$. However, in the last 5 years many econometrics researchers have mostly focused on naturally diurnally robust quantities like the daily or weekly QV.

2.6   Derivatives Based on Realized QV and QVol

In the last 10 years an over the counter market in realized QV and QVol has been rapidly developing. This has been stimulated by interests in hedging volatility risk – see Neuberger (1990), Carr and Madan (1998), Demeterfi et al. (1999), and Carr and Lewis (2004). Examples of such options are where the payoffs are

$$\max \left([Y_\delta]_t - K_1, 0 \right), \quad \max \left(\sqrt{[Y_\delta]_t} - K_2, 0 \right). \tag{12}$$

Interesting δ is typically taken as a day. Such options approximate, potentially poorly,

$$\max \left([Y]_t - K_1, 0 \right), \quad \max \left(\sqrt{[Y]_t} - K_2, 0 \right). \tag{13}$$

The fair value of options of the type (13) has been studied by a number of authors, for various volatility models. For example, Brockhaus and Long (1999) employs the Heston (1993) SV model, Javaheri, Wilmott, and Haug (2002) GARCH diffusion, while Howison, Rafailidis, and Rasmussen (2004) study log-Gaussian OU processes. Carr et al. (2005) look at the same problem based upon pure jump processes. Carr and Lee (2003a) have studied how one might value such options based on replication without being specific about the volatility model. See also the overview of Branger and Schlag (2005).

The common feature of these papers is that the calculations are based on replacing (12) by (13). These authors do not take into account, to our knowledge, the potentially large difference between using $[Y_\delta]_t$ and $[Y]_t$.

2.7   Empirical Illustrations: Measurement

To illustrate some of the empirical features of realized daily QV, and particularly their precision as estimators of daily QV, we have used a series which records the log of the number of German Deutsche Mark a single US Dollar buys (written Y^1) and the log of the Japanese Yen/Dollar rate (written Y^2). It covers 1st December 1986 until 30th November 1996 and was kindly supplied to us

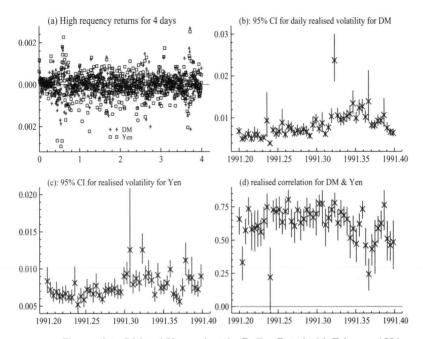

Figure 10.1. DM and Yen against the Dollar. Data is 4th February 1991 onwards for 50 active trading days. (a) 10 minute returns on the two exchange
rates for the first 4 days of the data set. (b) Realized volatility for the DM
series. This is marked with a cross, while the bars denote 95% confidence
intervals. (c) Realized covariance. (d) Realized correlation.

by Olsen and Associates in Zurich (see Dacorogna et al. 2001), although we
have made slightly different adjustments to deal with some missing data [de-
scribed in detail in Barndorff-Nielsen and Shephard (2002)]. Capturing time-
stamped indicative bid and ask quotes from a Reuters screen, they computed
prices at each 5-minute period by linear interpolation by averaging the log bid
and log ask for the two closest ticks.

Figure 10.1 provides some descriptive statistics for the exchange rates
starting on 4th February 1991. Figure 10.1(a) shows the first four active days of
the data set, displaying the bivariate 10 minute returns.[9] Figure 10.1(b) details
the daily realized volatilities for the DM $\sqrt{\widehat{V}_i^1}$, together with 95% confidence
intervals. These confidence intervals are based on the log-version of the limit
theory for the realized variance we will develop in the next subsection. When
the volatility is high, the confidence intervals tend to be very large as well. In
Figure 10.1(c) we have drawn the realized covariance $\widehat{V}_i^{1,2}$ against i, together
with the associated confidence intervals. These terms move rather violently
through this period. The corresponding realized correlations $\widehat{\rho}_i^{1,2}$ are given in
Figure 10.1(d). These are quite stable through time with only a single realized

---

[9] This time resolution was selected so that the results are not very sensitive to market frictions.

Table 10.1. *Daily statistics for 100 times DM/Dollar return series: estimated QV, BPV, conditional variance for GARCH and squared daily returns. Reported is the mean, standard deviation and correlations*

Daily	Mean	Standard Dev/Cor			
QV : $\widehat{V}_i^1$	0.509	0.50			
BPV : $\widehat{B}_i^1$	0.441	0.95	0.40		
GARCH: h_i	0.512	0.55	0.57	0.22	
$(Y_i^1 - Y_{i-1}^1)^2$	0.504	0.54	0.48	0.39	1.05

correlation standing out from the others in the sample. The correlations are not particularly precisely estimated, with the confidence intervals typically being around 0.2 wide.

Table 10.1 provides some additional daily summary statistics for 100 times the daily data (the scaling is introduced to make the tables easier to read). It shows the means of the squared daily returns $(Y_i^1 - Y_{i-1}^1)^2$ and the estimated daily QVs $\widehat{V}_i^1$ are in line, but that the realized BPV $\widehat{B}_i^1$ is below them. The RV and BPV quantities are highly correlated, but the BPV has a smaller standard deviation. A GARCH(1,1) model is also fitted to the daily return data and its conditional, one-step ahead predicted variances h_i, computed. These have similar means and lower standard deviations, but h_i is less strongly correlated with squared returns than the realized measures.

2.8   Empirical Illustration: Time Series Behavior

Figure 10.2 shows summaries of the time series behavior of daily raw and realized DM quantities. They are computed using the whole run of 10 years of 10 minute return data. Figure 10.2(a) shows the raw daily returns and 10.2(b) gives the corresponding correlogram of daily squared and absolute returns. As usual absolute returns are moderately more autocorrelated than squared returns, with the degree of autocorrelation in these plots being modest, while the memory lasts a large number of lags.

Figure 10.2(c) shows a time series plot of the daily realized volatilities $\sqrt{\widehat{V}_i^1}$ for the DM series, indicating bursts of high volatility and periods of rather tranquil activity. The correlogram for this series is given in Figure 10.2(d). This shows lagged one correlations of around one half and is around 0.25 at 10 lags. The correlogram then declines irregularly at larger lags. Figure 10.2(e) shows $\sqrt{\widehat{B}_i^1}$ using the lagged two bipower variation measure. This series does not display the peaks and troughs of the realized QVol statistics and its correlogram in Figure 10.2(d) is modestly higher with its first lag being around 0.56 compared to 0.47. The corresponding estimated jump QVol measure $\sqrt{\max\left(0, \widehat{V}_i^1 - \widehat{B}_i^1\right)}$ is displayed in Figure 10.2(f), while its correlogram is given in Figure 10.2(d), which shows a very small degree of autocorrelation.

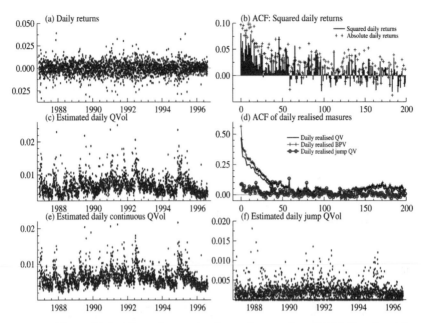

Figure 10.2. All graphs use 5 minute changes data DM/Dollar. Top left: daily returns. Middle left: estimated daily QVol $\sqrt{\widehat{V}_i}$, bottom left: estimated daily continuous QVol $\sqrt{\widehat{B}_i}$. Bottom right: estimated continuous QVol $\sqrt{\max\left(0, \widehat{V}_i - \widehat{B}_i\right)}$. Top right: ACF of squared and absolute returns. X-axis is marked off in days. Middle right: ACF of various realized estimators.

2.9   Empirical Illustration: A More Subtle Example

2.9.1   *Interpolation, Last Price, Quotes and Trades*

So far we have not focused on the details of how we compute the prices used in these calculations. This is important if we wish to try to exploit information buried in returns recorded for very small values of δ, such as a handful of seconds. Our discussion will be based on data taken from the London Stock Exchange's electronic order book, called SETS, in January 2004. The market is open from 8 a.m. to 4.30 p.m., but we remove the first 15 minutes of each day following Engle and Russell (1998). Times are accurate up to 1 second. We will use three pieces of the database: transactions, best bid, and best ask. Note the bid, and ask are firm quotes, not indicative like the exchange rate data previous studied. We average the bid and ask to produce a mid-quote, which is taken to proxy the efficient price. We also give some results based on transaction prices. We will focus on four high value stocks: Vodafone (telecoms), BP (hydrocarbons), AstraZeneca (pharmaceuticals), and HSBC (banking).

The top row of Figure 10.3 shows the log of the mid-quotes, recorded every 6 seconds on the 2nd working day in January. The graphs indicate the striking

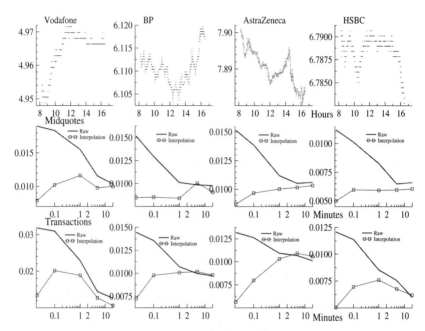

Figure 10.3. LSE's electronic order book on the 2nd working day in January 2004. Top graphs: mid-quote log-price every 6 seconds, from 8.15 a.m. to 4.30 p.m. X-axis is in hours. Middle graphs: realized daily QVol computed using 0.015, 0.1, 1, 5, and 20 minute midpoint returns. X-axis is in minutes. Lower graphs: realized daily QVol computed using 0.1, 1, 5, and 20 minute transaction returns. Middle and lower graphs are computed using interpolation and the last tick method.

discreteness of the price processes, which is particularly important for the Vodafone series. Table 10.2 gives the tick size, the number of mid-point updates and transactions for each asset. It shows the usual result that as the tick size, as a percentage of the price increases, then the number of mid-quote price updates will tend to fall as larger tick sizes mean that there is a larger cost to impatience, that is jumping the queue in the order book by offering a better price than the best current and so updating the best quotes.

The middle row of Figure 10.3 shows the corresponding daily realized QVol, computed using 0.015, 0.1, 1, 5, and 20 minute intervals based on mid-quotes. These are related to the signature plots of Andersen et al. (2000). As the times of the mid-quotes fall irregularly in time, there is the question of how to approximate the price at these time points. The Olsen method uses linear interpolation between the prices at the nearest observations before and after the correct time point. Another method is to use the last datapoint before the relevant time – the last tick or raw method (e.g., Wasserfallen and Zimmermann, 1985). Typically, the former leads to falls in realized QVol as δ falls, indeed in theory it converges to zero as $\delta \downarrow 0$ as its interpolated price process is of continuous bounded variation (Hansen and Lunde, 2006b), while the latter increases modestly.

Table 10.2. *Top part of table: Average daily volatility. Open is the mid-price at 8.15 a.m., close is the mid-price at 4.30 p.m. Open–open looks at daily returns. Reported are the sample standard deviations of the returns over 20 days and sample correlation between the open–close and open–open daily returns. Bottom part of table: descriptive statistics about the size of the data set*

	Vodafone	BP	AstraZeneca	HSBC
	Daily volatility			
Open–close	0.00968	0.00941	0.0143	0.00730
Open–open	0.0159	0.0140	0.0140	0.00720
Correlation	0.861	0.851	0.912	0.731
Tick size	0.25	0.25	1.0	0.5
# of Mid-quotes per day	333	1,434	1,666	598
# of Transactions per day	3,018	2,995	2,233	2,264

The sensitivity to δ tends to be larger in cases where the tick size is large as a percentage of price and this is the case here. Overall we have the conclusion that the realized QVol does not change much when δ is 5 minutes or above and that it is more stable for interpolation than for last price. When we use smaller time intervals there are large dangers lurking. We will formally discuss the effect of market frictions in Section 5.

The bottom row in Figure 10.3 shows the corresponding results for realized QVols computed using the transactions database. This ignores some very large over the counter trades. Realized QVol increases more strongly as δ falls when we use the last tick rather than mid-quote data. This is particularly the case for Vodafone, where bid/ask bounce has a large impact. Even the interpolation method has difficulties with transaction data. Overall, one gets the impression from this study that basing the analysis on mid-quote data is sound for the LSE data.[10]

A fundamental difficulty with equity data is that the equity markets are only open for a fraction of the whole day and so it is quite possible that a large degree of their variation is at times when there is little data. This is certainly true for the U.K. equity markets which are closed during a high percentage of the time when U.S. markets are open. Table 10.2 gives daily volatility for open to close and open to open returns, as well as the correlation between the two return measures. It shows the open to close measures account for a high degree of the volatility in the prices, with high correlations between the two returns. The weakest relationship is for the Vodafone series, with the strongest for AstraZeneca. Hansen and Lunde (2005b) have studied how one can use high-frequency information to estimate the QV throughout the day, taking into account closed periods.

---

[10] A good alternative would be to carry out the entire analysis on either all the best bids or all the best asks. This approach is used by Hansen and Lunde (2005b) and Large (2005).

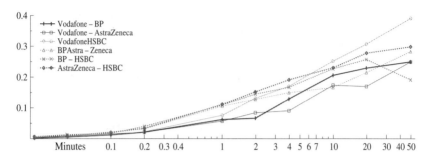

Figure 10.4. LSE data during January 2004. Realized correlation computed daily, averaged over the month. Realized quantities are computed using data at the frequency on the X-axis.

2.9.2   *Epps Effects*

Market frictions affect the estimation of QVol, but if the asset is highly active, the tick size is small as a percentage of the price, δ is well above a minute and the midquote/interpolation method is used, then the effects are modest. The situation is much less rosy when we look at estimating quadratic covariations due to the so-called Epps (1979) effect. This has been documented in very great detail by Sheppard (2005), who provides various theoretical explanations. We will come back to them in Sections 3.8.3 and 5. For the moment it suffices to look at Figure 10.4 which shows the average daily realized correlation computed in January 2004 for the four stocks looked at above. Throughout prices are computed using mid-quotes and interpolation. The graph shows how this average varies with respect to δ. It trends downwards to zero as $\delta \downarrow 0$, with extremely low dependence measures for low values of δ. This is probably caused by the fact that asset prices tend not to simultaneously move due to nonsynchronous trading and the differential rate at which information of different types is absorbed into individual stock prices.

3   MEASUREMENT ERROR WHEN $Y \in \mathcal{BSM}$

3.1   Infeasible Asymptotics

Market frictions mean that it is not wise to use realized variation objects based on very small δ. This suggests refining our convergence in probability arguments to give a central limit theorem which may provide reasonable predictions about the behavior of RV statistics for moderate values of δ, such as 5 or 10 minutes, where frictions are less likely to bite hard. Such CLTs will be the focus of attention in this section. At the end of the section, in addition, we will briefly discuss various alternative measures of variation, such as realized range, subsampling and kernel, which have recently been introduced to the literature. Finally, we will also discuss how realized objects can contribute to the practical forecasting of volatility.

We will derive the central limit theorem for $[Y_\delta]_t$ which can then be discretized to produce the CLT for $\widehat{V}_i$. Univariate results will be presented, since this has less notational clutter. The results were developed in a series of papers by Jacod (1994), Jacod and Protter (1998), Barndorff-Nielsen and Shephard (2002, 2004).

Theorem 1 *Suppose that $Y \in \mathcal{BSM}$ is one-dimensional and that (for all $t < \infty$) $\int_0^t a_u^2 du < \infty$, then as $\delta \downarrow 0$ so*

$$\delta^{-1/2} \left([Y_\delta]_t - [Y]_t\right) \to \sqrt{2} \int_0^t \sigma_u^2 dB_u, \tag{14}$$

where B is a Brownian motion which is independent from Y and the convergence is in law stable as a process.

Proof. By Ito's lemma for continuous semimartingales

$$Y^2 = [Y] + 2Y \bullet Y,$$

then

$$\left(Y_{j\delta} - Y_{(j-1)\delta}\right)^2 = [Y]_{\delta j} - [Y]_{\delta(j-1)} + 2 \int_{\delta(j-1)}^{\delta j} (Y_u - Y_{(j-1)\delta}) dY_u.$$

This implies that

$$\delta^{-1/2} \left([Y_\delta]_t - [Y]_t\right) = 2\delta^{-1/2} \sum_{j=1}^{\lfloor t/\delta \rfloor} \int_{\delta(j-1)}^{\delta j} (Y_u - Y_{(j-1)\delta}) dY_u$$

$$= 2\delta^{-1/2} \int_0^{\delta \lfloor t/\delta \rfloor} (Y_u - Y_{\delta \lfloor u/\delta \rfloor}) dY_u.$$

Jacod and Protter (1998, Theorem 5.5) show that for Y satisfying the conditions in Theorem 1 then[11]

$$\delta^{-1/2} \int_0^t (Y_u - Y_{\delta \lfloor u/\delta \rfloor}) dY_u \to \frac{1}{\sqrt{2}} \int_0^t \sigma_u^2 dB_u,$$

where $B \perp\!\!\!\perp Y$ and the convergence is in law stable as a process. This implies

$$\delta^{-1/2} \left([Y_\delta] - [Y]\right) \to \sqrt{2} \left(\sigma^2 \bullet B\right). \qquad \square$$

---

[11] At an intuitive level, if we ignore the drift then

$$\int_{\delta(j-1)}^{\delta j} (Y_u - Y_{(j-1)\delta}) dY_u \simeq \sigma_{\delta(j-1)}^2 \int_{\delta(j-1)}^{\delta j} (W_u - W_{(j-1)\delta}) dW_u,$$

which is a martingale difference sequence in j with zero mean and conditional variance of $\frac{1}{2}\sigma_{\delta(j-1)}^2$. Applying a triangular martingale CLT one would expect this result, although formalizing it requires a considerable number of additional steps.

Remark 1 *The concept and role of stable convergence may be unfamiliar to some readers and we therefore add some words of explanation. In the simplest case of stable convergence of sequences of random variables, rather than processes, the concise mathematical definition is as follows. Let X_n denote a sequence of random variables defined on a probability space $(\Omega, \mathcal{F}, P)$. Then we say that X_n converges stably in law if there exists a probability measure μ on $(\Omega \times \mathbb{R}, \mathcal{F} \times \mathcal{B})$ (where $\mathcal{B}$ denotes the Borel σ-algebra on $\mathbb{R}$) such that for every bounded random variable Z on $(\Omega, \mathcal{F}, P)$ and every bounded and continuous function g on $\mathbb{R}$ we have that, for $n \to \infty$,*

$$\mathrm{E}\,(Zg\,(X_n)) \to \int Z\,(\omega)\,g\,(x)\,\mu\,(\mathrm{d}\omega, \mathrm{d}x)\,.$$

If X_n converges stably in law then, in particular, it converges in distribution (or in law or weak convergence), the limiting law being $\mu\,(\Omega, \cdot)$. Accordingly, one says that X_n converges stably to some random variable X if there exists a probability measure μ as above such that X has law $\mu\,(\Omega, \cdot)$. This concept and its extension to stable convergence of processes is discussed in Jacod and Shiryaev (2003, pp. 512–518). For earlier expositions, see Hall and Heyde (1980, pp. 56–58), and Jacod (1997). An early use of this concept in econometrics was Phillips and Ouliaris (1990) in their work on the limit distribution of cointegration tests.

However, this formalization does not reveal the key nature of stable convergence which is that $X_n \to X$ stably implies that for any random variable Z, the pair (Z, X_n) converges in law to (Z, X). In the context the present paper considers the following simple example of the above result. Let $n = \lfloor t/\delta \rfloor$,

$$X_n = \sqrt{n}\,([Y_\delta]_t - [Y]_t)$$

and

$$Z = \sqrt{\int_0^t \sigma_u^4 \mathrm{d}u}\,.$$

Our focus is on $X_n/\sqrt{Z}$ and our convergence in law stably implies that

$$\sqrt{n}\,([Y_\delta]_t - [Y]_t)/\sqrt{\int_0^t \sigma_u^4 \mathrm{d}u} \overset{law}{\to} N(0, 2). \tag{15}$$

Without the convergence in law stably, (15) could not be deduced.

The key point of this theorem is that $B \perp\!\!\!\perp Y$. The appearance of the additional Brownian motion B is striking. This means that Theorem 1 implies, for a single t,

$$\delta^{-1/2}\,([Y_\delta]_t - [Y]_t) \overset{L}{\to} MN\left(0, 2\int_0^t \sigma_u^4 \mathrm{d}u\right), \tag{16}$$

where MN denotes a mixed Gaussian distribution. This result implies in particular that, for $i \neq j$,

$$\delta^{-1/2} \begin{pmatrix} \widehat{V}_i - V_i \\ \widehat{V}_j - V_j \end{pmatrix} \xrightarrow{L} MN \left(\begin{pmatrix} 0 \\ 0 \end{pmatrix}, 2 \begin{pmatrix} \int_{h(i-1)}^{hi} \sigma_u^4 du & 0 \\ 0 & \int_{h(j-1)}^{hj} \sigma_u^4 du \end{pmatrix} \right),$$

so $\widehat{V}_i - V_i$ are asymptotically uncorrelated, so long as Var $(\widehat{V}_i - V_i) < \infty$, through time.

Barndorff-Nielsen and Shephard (2002) showed that Theorem 1 can be used in practice as the *integrated quarticity* $\int_0^t \sigma_u^4 du$ can be consistently estimated using $(1/3) \{Y_\delta\}_t^{[4]}$ where

$$\{Y_\delta\}_t^{[4]} = \delta^{-1} \sum_{j=1}^{\lfloor t/\delta \rfloor} \left(Y_{j\delta} - Y_{(j-1)\delta} \right)^4. \tag{17}$$

In particular then

$$\frac{\delta^{-1/2} ([Y_\delta]_t - [Y]_t)}{\sqrt{\frac{2}{3} \{Y_\delta\}_t^{[4]}}} \xrightarrow{L} N(0, 1). \tag{18}$$

This is a nonparametric result as it does not require us to specify the form of a or σ.

The multivariate version of (14) has that as $\delta \downarrow 0$ so

$$\delta^{-1/2} \left([Y_\delta]_{(kl)} - [Y]_{(kl)} \right)$$

$$\rightarrow \frac{1}{\sqrt{2}} \sum_{b=1}^{q} \sum_{c=1}^{q} \left\{ \left(\sigma_{(kb)} \sigma_{(cl)} + \sigma_{(lb)} \sigma_{(ck)} \right) \bullet B_{(bc)} \right\}, \quad k, l = 1, \ldots, q, \tag{19}$$

where B is a $q \times q$ matrix of independent Brownian motions, independent of Y and the convergence is in law stable as a process. In the mixed normal version of this result, the asymptotic covariance is a $q \times q \times q \times q$ array with elements

$$\left\{ \int_0^t \{ \Sigma_{(kk')u} \Sigma_{(ll')u} + \Sigma_{(kl')u} \Sigma_{(lk')u} + \Sigma_{(kl)u} \Sigma_{(k'l')u} \} du \right\}_{k,k',l,l'=1,\ldots,q}. \tag{20}$$

Barndorff-Nielsen and Shephard (2004) showed how to use high-frequency data to estimate this array of processes. We refer the reader to that paper, and also Mykland and Zhang (2006), for details.

3.2   Finite Sample Performance and the Bootstrap

Our analysis of $[Y_\delta]_t - [Y]_t$ has been asymptotic as $\delta \downarrow 0$. Of course it is crucial to know if this analysis is informative for the kind of moderate values of δ we see in practice. A number of authors have studied the finite sample behavior of the feasible limit theory given in (18) and a log-version, derived using the delta-rule

$$\frac{\delta^{-1/2} \left(\log[Y_\delta]_t - \log[Y]_t\right)}{\sqrt{\frac{2}{3} \frac{\{Y_\delta\}_t^{[4]}}{([Y_\delta]_t)^2}}} \xrightarrow{L} N(0, 1). \tag{21}$$

We refer readers to Barndorff-Nielsen and Shephard (2005), Meddahi (2002), Goncalves and Meddahi (2004), and Nielsen and Frederiksen (2005). The overall conclusion is that (18) is quite poorly sized, but that (21) performs pretty well. The asymptotic theory is challenged in cases where there are components in volatility which are very quickly mean reverting. In the multivariate case, Barndorff-Nielsen and Shephard (2004) studied the finite sample behavior of realized regression and correlation statistics. They suggest various transformations which improve the finite sample behavior of these statistics, including the use of the Fisher transformation for the realized correlation.

Goncalves and Meddahi (2004) have studied how one might try to bootstrap the realized daily QV estimator. Their overall conclusions are that the usual Edgeworth expansions, which justify the order improvement associated with the bootstrap, are not reliable guides to the finite sample behavior of the statistics. However, it is possible to design bootstraps which provide very significant improvements over the limiting theory in (18). This seems an interesting avenue to follow up, particularly in the multivariate case.

3.3   Irregularly Spaced Data

Mykland and Zhang (2006) have recently generalized (14) to cover the case where prices are recorded at irregular time intervals. See also the related work of Barndorff-Nielsen and Shephard (2006b) and Barndorff-Nielsen et al. (2004). Mykland and Zhang (2006) define a random sequence of times, independent of Y,[12] over the interval $t \in [0, T]$,

$$\mathcal{G}_n = \{0 = t_0 < t_1 < \ldots < t_n = T\},$$

then continue to have $\delta = T/n$, and define the estimated QV process

$$[Y_{\mathcal{G}_n}]_t = \sum_{j=1}^{t_j \le t} \left(Y_{t_j} - Y_{t_{j-1}}\right)^2 \xrightarrow{p} [Y]_t.$$

---

[12] It is tempting to think of the t_j as the time of the jth trade or quote. However, it is well know that the process generating the times of trades and price movements in tick time are not statistically independent [e.g., Engle and Russell (2006) and Rydberg and Shephard (2000)]. This would seem to rule out the direct application of the methods we use here in tick time, suggesting care is needed in that case.

They show that as $n \to \infty$ so[13]

$$\delta^{-1/2}\left([Y_{\mathcal{G}_n}]_t - [Y]_t\right) = 2\delta^{-1/2} \sum_{j=1}^{t_j \le t} \int_{t_{j-1}}^{t_j} (Y_u - Y_{t_{j-1}})\mathrm{d}Y_u$$

$$\xrightarrow{L} MN\left(0, 2\int_0^t \left(\frac{\partial H_u^{\mathcal{G}}}{\partial u}\right)\sigma_u^4 \mathrm{d}u\right),$$

where

$$H_t^{\mathcal{G}} = \lim_{n\to\infty} H_t^{\mathcal{G}_n}, \quad \text{where} \quad H_t^{\mathcal{G}_n} = \delta^{-1}\sum_{j=0}^{t_j\le t}\left(t_j - t_{j-1}\right)^2,$$

and we have assumed that σ follows a diffusion and $H^{\mathcal{G}}$, which is a bit like a QV process but is scaled by δ^{-1}, is differentiable with respect to time. The $H^{\mathcal{G}}$ function is nondecreasing and runs quickly when the sampling is slower than normal. For regularly space data, $t_j = \delta j$ and so $H_t^{\mathcal{G}} = t$, which reproduces (16).

It is clear that

$$[Y_{\mathcal{G}_n}]_t^{[4]} = \delta^{-1}\sum_{j=1}^{t_j\le t}\left(Y_{t_j} - Y_{t_{j-1}}\right)^4 \xrightarrow{p} 3\int_0^t\left(\frac{\partial H_u^{\mathcal{G}}}{\partial u}\right)\sigma_u^4\mathrm{d}u,$$

which implies the feasible distributional result in (18) and (21) also holds for irregularly spaced data, which was one of the results in Barndorff-Nielsen and Shephard (2006b).

3.4   Multiple grids

Zhang (2004) extended the above analysis to the simultaneous use of multiple grids – allowing the same $[Y]$ to be estimated using a variety of realized QV-type objects based on slightly different spacing between observations. In our exposition we will work with $\mathcal{G}_n(i) = \{0 = t_0^i < t_1^i < \ldots < t_n^i = T\}$ for $i = 0, 1, 2, \ldots, I$ and $\delta_i = T/n_i$. Then define the ith estimated QV process $[Y_{\mathcal{G}_n(i)}]_t = \sum_{j=1}^{t_j^i\le t}(Y_{t_j^i} - Y_{t_{j-1}^i})^2$. Additionally, we need a new cross term for the covariation between the time scales. The appropriate term is

$$H_t^{\mathcal{G}(i)\cup\mathcal{G}(k)} = \lim_{n\to\infty} H_t^{\mathcal{G}_n(i)\cup\mathcal{G}_n(k)}, \quad \text{where}$$

$$H_t^{\mathcal{G}_n(i)\cup\mathcal{G}_n(k)} = (\delta_i\delta_k)^{-1/2}\sum_{j=1}^{t_j^{i,k}\le t}\left(t_j^{i,k} - t_{j-1}^{i,k}\right)^2,$$

---

[13] At an intuitive level, if we ignore the drift then

$$\int_{t_{j-1}}^{t_j}(Y_u - Y_{t_{j-1}})\mathrm{d}Y_u \simeq \sigma_{t_{j-1}}^2\int_{t_{j-1}}^{t_j}(W_u - W_{t_{j-1}})\mathrm{d}W_u,$$

which is a martingale difference sequence in j with zero mean and conditional variance of $\frac{1}{2}\sigma_{t_{j-1}}^2(t_j - t_{j-1})$. Although this suggests the stated result, formalizing it requires a considerable number of additional steps.

where $t_j^{i,k}$ comes from

$$\mathcal{G}_n(i) \cup \mathcal{G}_n(k)$$
$$= \{0 = t_0^{i,k} < t_1^{i,k} < \ldots < t_{2n}^{i,k} = T\}, \quad i, k = 0, 1, 2, \ldots, I.$$

Clearly, for all i,

$$\delta_i^{-1/2} \left([Y_{\mathcal{G}_n(i)}]_t - [Y]_t\right) = 2\delta_i^{-1/2} \sum_{j=1}^{t_j^i \le t} \int_{t_{j-1}^i}^{t_j^i} (Y_u - Y_{t_{j-1}^i}) \mathrm{d}Y_u$$

so the scaled (by $\delta_i^{-1/2}$ and $\delta_k^{-1/2}$, respectively) asymptotic covariance matrix of $[Y_{\mathcal{G}_n(i)}]_t$ and $[Y_{\mathcal{G}_n(k)}]_t$ is

$$2 \begin{pmatrix} \int_0^t \left(\dfrac{\partial H_u^{\mathcal{G}(i)}}{\partial u}\right) \sigma_u^4 \mathrm{d}u & \bullet \\ \int_0^t \left(\dfrac{\partial H_u^{\mathcal{G}(i) \cup \mathcal{G}(k)}}{\partial u}\right) \sigma_u^4 \mathrm{d}u & \int_0^t \left(\dfrac{\partial H_u^{\mathcal{G}(k)}}{\partial u}\right) \sigma_u^4 \mathrm{d}u \end{pmatrix}.$$

Example 1 *Let $t_j^0 = \delta(j + \varepsilon), t_j^1 = \delta(j + \eta)$ where $|\varepsilon - \eta| \in [0, 1]$ are temporal offsets, then $H_t^{\mathcal{G}(0)} = H_t^{\mathcal{G}(1)} = t$,*

$$H_t^{\mathcal{G}(0) \cup \mathcal{G}(1)} = t \left((\eta - \varepsilon)^2 + (1 - |\eta - \varepsilon|)^2\right).$$

Thus

$$\delta^{-1/2} \begin{pmatrix} [Y_{\mathcal{G}_n(0)}]_t - [Y]_t \\ [Y_{\mathcal{G}_n(1)}]_t - [Y]_t \end{pmatrix}$$

$$\xrightarrow{L} MN \left(0, 2 \begin{pmatrix} 1 & \bullet \\ (\eta - \varepsilon)^2 + (1 - |\eta - \varepsilon|)^2 & 1 \end{pmatrix} \int_0^t \sigma_u^4 \mathrm{d}u \right).$$

The correlation between the two measures is minimized at $1/2$ by setting $|\eta - \varepsilon| = 1/2$.

Example 1 extends naturally to when $t_j^k = \delta(j + \frac{k}{K+1}), k = 0, 1, 2, \ldots, K$, which allows many equally spaced realized QV like estimators to be defined based on returns measured over δ periods. The scaled asymptotic covariance of $[Y_{\mathcal{G}_n(i)}]_t$ and $[Y_{\mathcal{G}_n(k)}]_t$ is

$$2 \left\{ \left(\frac{k - i}{K + 1}\right)^2 + \left(1 - \left|\frac{k - i}{K + 1}\right|\right)^2 \right\} \int_0^t \sigma_u^4 \mathrm{d}u.$$

If $K = 1$ or $K = 2$ then the correlation between the estimates is $1/2$ and $5/9$, respectively. As the sampling points become more dense the correlation quickly escalates which means that each new realized QV estimator brings out less and less additional information.

3.5   Subsampling

The multiple grid allows us to create a pooled grid estimator of QV – which is a special case of subsampling a statistic based on a random field, see for example the review of Politis, Romano, and Wolf (1999, Chapter 5). A simple example of this is

$$[Y_{\mathcal{G}_n^+(K)}]_t = \frac{1}{K+1} \sum_{i=0}^{K} [Y_{\mathcal{G}_n(i)}]_t, \tag{22}$$

which was mentioned in this context by Zhou (1996, p. 48). Clearly $[Y_{\mathcal{G}_n^+(K)}]_t \xrightarrow{p}$ $[Y]_t$ as $\delta \downarrow 0$, while the properties of this estimator were first studied when $Y \in \mathcal{BSM}$ by Zhang, Mykland, and Aït-Sahalia (2005b). Zhang (2004) also studies the properties of unequally weighted pooled estimators, while additional insights are provided by Aït-Sahalia, Mykland, and Zhang (2005).

Example 2 Let $t_j^k = \delta(j + \frac{k}{K+1})$, $k = 0, 1, 2, \ldots, K$. Then, for fixed K as $\delta \downarrow 0$ so

$$\delta^{-1/2} \begin{pmatrix} [Y_{\mathcal{G}_n(0)}]_t - [Y]_t \\ [Y_{\mathcal{G}_n(1)}]_t - [Y]_t \end{pmatrix}$$

$$\xrightarrow{L} MN \left(0, \frac{2}{(K+1)^2} \sum_{i=0}^{K} \sum_{k=0}^{K} \left\{ \left(\frac{k-i}{K+1} \right)^2 + \left(1 - \left| \frac{k-i}{K+1} \right| \right)^2 \right\} \int_0^t \sigma_u^4 du \right).$$

This subsampler is based on a sample size $K+1$ times the usual one but returns are still recorded over intervals of length δ. When $K = 1$ then the constant in front of integrated quarticity is 1.5 while when $K = 2$ it drops to 1.4074. The next terms in the sequence are 1.3750, 1.3600, 1.3519, and 1.3469 while it asymptotes to 1.333, a result due to Zhang, Mykland, and Aït-Sahalia (2005b). Hence, the gain from using the entire sample path of Y via multiple grids is modest and almost all the available gains occur by the time K reaches 2. However, we will see later that this subsampler has virtues when there are market frictions.

3.6   Serial Covariances

Suppose we define the notation $\mathcal{G}_\delta(\varepsilon, \eta) = \{\delta(\varepsilon + \eta), \delta(2\varepsilon + \eta), \ldots\}$, then the above theory implies that

$$\begin{pmatrix} \delta^{-1/2} \left([Y_{\mathcal{G}_n(2,0)}]_t - \int_0^t \sigma_u^2 du \right) \\ \delta^{-1/2} \left([Y_{\mathcal{G}_n(2,-1)}]_t - \int_0^t \sigma_u^2 du \right) \\ \delta^{-1/2} \left([Y_{\mathcal{G}_n(1,0)}]_t - \int_0^t \sigma_u^2 du \right) \end{pmatrix} \xrightarrow{L} MN \left(\begin{pmatrix} 0 \\ 0 \\ 0 \end{pmatrix}, \begin{pmatrix} 4 & 2 & 2 \\ 2 & 4 & 2 \\ 2 & 2 & 2 \end{pmatrix} \int_0^t \sigma_u^4 du \right).$$

Define the realized serial covariance as

$$\widehat{\gamma}_s(Y_\delta, X_\delta) = \sum_{j=1}^{\lfloor t/\delta \rfloor} \left(Y_{\delta j} - Y_{\delta(j-1)} \right) \left(X_{\delta(j-s)} - X_{\delta(j-s-1)} \right), \quad s = 0, 1, 2, \dots, S,$$

and say $\widehat{\gamma}_{-s}(Y, X) = \widehat{\gamma}_s(Y, X)$ while $\widehat{\gamma}_s(Y_\delta) = \widehat{\gamma}_s(Y_\delta, Y_\delta)$. Derivatives on such objects have recently been studied by Carr and Lee (2003b). We have that

$$2\widehat{\gamma}_1(Y_\delta) = [Y_{\mathcal{G}_n(2,0)}]_t + [Y_{\mathcal{G}_n(2,-1)}]_t - 2[Y_{\mathcal{G}_n(1,0)}]_t + o_p(\delta^{1/2}).$$

Note that $\widehat{\gamma}_0(Y_\delta) = [Y_{\mathcal{G}_n(1,0)}]_t$. Then, clearly

$$\delta^{-1/2} \begin{pmatrix} \widehat{\gamma}_0(Y_\delta) - \int_0^t \sigma_u^2 du \\ \widehat{\gamma}_1(Y_\delta) \\ \vdots \\ \widehat{\gamma}_S(Y_\delta) \end{pmatrix} \overset{L}{\to} MN \left(\begin{pmatrix} 0 \\ 0 \\ \vdots \\ 0 \end{pmatrix}, \begin{pmatrix} 2 & 0 & \cdots & 0 \\ 0 & 1 & \cdots & 0 \\ \vdots & \vdots & \ddots & \vdots \\ 0 & 0 & \cdots & 1 \end{pmatrix} \int_0^t \sigma_u^4 du \right),$$

(23)

see Barndorff-Nielsen et al. (2004, Theorem 2). Consequently

$$\delta^{-1/2} \begin{pmatrix} \widehat{\gamma}_1(Y_\delta)/\widehat{\gamma}_0(Y_\delta) \\ \vdots \\ \widehat{\gamma}_S(Y_\delta)/\widehat{\gamma}_0(Y_\delta) \end{pmatrix} \overset{L}{\to} MN \left(0, I \frac{\int_0^t \sigma_u^4 du}{\left(\int_0^t \sigma_u^2 du \right)^2} \right),$$

which differs from the result of Bartlett (1946), inflating the usual standard errors as well as making inference multivariate mixed Gaussian. There is some shared characteristics with the familiar Eicker (1967) robust standard errors but the details are, of course, rather different.

3.7   Kernels

Following Bartlett (1950) and Eicker (1967), long-run estimates of variances are often computed using kernels. We will see this idea may be helpful when there are market frictions and so we take some time discussing this here. It was introduced in this context by Zhou (1996) and Hansen and Lunde, (2006b), while a thorough discussion was given by Barndorff-Nielsen et al. (2004, Theorem 2). A kernel takes on the form of

$$RV_w(Y) = w_0[Y_\delta] + 2 \sum_{i=1}^{q} w_i \widehat{\gamma}_i(Y_\delta),$$

(24)

where the weights w_i are nonstochastic. It is clear from (23) that if the estimator is based on δ/K returns, so that it is compatible with (22), then

$$\left\{ \frac{\delta}{K} \left(w_0^2 + 2 \sum_{i=1}^{q} w_i^2 \right) \right\}^{-1/2} \left(RV_w(Y_{\frac{\delta}{K}}) - w_0 \int_0^t \sigma_u^2 du \right)$$

$$\overset{L}{\to} MN \left(0, 2 \int_0^t \sigma_u^4 du \right).$$

(25)

In order for this method to be consistent for integrated variance as $q \to \infty$ we need that $w_0 = 1 + o(1)$ and $\sum_{i=1}^{q} w_i^2 / K = O(1)$ as a function of q.

Example 3 *The Bartlett kernel puts $w_0 = 1$ and $w_i = (q + 1 - i)/(q + 1)$. When $q = 1$ then $w_1 = 1/2$ and the constant in front of integrated quarticity is 3, while when $q = 2$ then $w_1 = 2/3$, $w_2 = 1/3$ and the constant becomes $4 + 2/9$. For moderately large q this is well approximated by $4(q + 1)/3$. This means that we need $q/K \to 0$ for this method to be consistent. This result appears in Barndorff-Nielsen, Hansen, Lunde, and Shephard (2004, Theorem 2).*

3.8   Other Measures

3.8.1   *Realized Range*

Suppose $Y = \sigma W$, a scaled Brownian motion, then

$$E\left(\sup_{0 \le s \le t} Y_s^2 \right) = \varphi_2 \sigma^2 t, \quad \text{where} \quad \varphi_r = E\left(\sup_{0 \le s \le 1} |W_s|^r \right),$$

noting that $\varphi_2 = 4 \log 2$ and $\varphi_4 = 9\zeta(3)$, where ζ is the Riemann function. This observation led Parkinson (1980) to provide a simple estimator of σ^2 based on the highs and lows of asset prices. See also the work of Rogers and Satchell (1991), Alizadeh, Brandt, and Diebold (2002), Ghysels, Santa-Clara, and Valkanov (2006), and Brandt and Diebold (2006). One reason for the interest in ranges is the belief that they are quite informative and somewhat robust to market frictions. The problem with this analysis is that it does not extend readily when $Y \in \mathcal{BSM}$. In independent work, Christensen and Podolskij (2005) and Martens and van Dijk (2006) have studied the realized range process. Christensen and Podolskij (2005) define the process as

$$\backslash Y \backslash_t = \text{p}-\lim_{\delta \downarrow 0} \sum_{j=1}^{\lfloor t/\delta \rfloor} \sup_{s \in [(j-1)\delta, j\delta]} \left(Y_s - Y_{(j-1)\delta} \right)^2, \tag{26}$$

which is estimated by the obvious realized version, written $\backslash Y_\delta \backslash_t$. Christensen and Podolskij (2005) have proved that if $Y \in \mathcal{BSM}$, then $\varphi_2^{-1} \backslash Y \backslash_t = \int_0^t \sigma_u^2 du$. Christensen and Podolskij (2005) also shows that under rather weak conditions

$$\delta^{-1/2} \left(\varphi_2^{-1} \backslash Y_\delta \backslash_t - [Y]_t \right) \overset{L}{\to} MN\left(0, \frac{\varphi_4 - \varphi_2^2}{\varphi_2^2} \int_0^t \sigma_u^4 du \right),$$

where $\varphi' = (\varphi_4 - \varphi_2^2)/\varphi_2^2 \simeq 0.4$. This shows that it is around five time as efficient as the usual realized QV estimator. Christensen and Podolskij (2005) suggest estimating integrated quarticity using

$$\delta^{-1} \varphi_4^{-1} \sum_{j=1}^{\lfloor t/\delta \rfloor} \sup_{s \in [(j-1)\delta, j\delta]} \left(Y_s - Y_{(j-1)\delta} \right)^4,$$

which means this limit theorem is feasible. Martens and van Dijk (2006) have also studied the properties of $\backslash Y_\delta \backslash_t$ using simulation and empirical work.

As far as we know no results are known about estimating $[Y]$ using ranges when there are jumps in Y, although it is relatively easy to see that a bipower-type estimator could be defined using contiguous ranges which would robustly estimate $[Y^{ct}]$.

3.8.2   Discrete Sine Transformation

Curci and Corsi (2003) have argued that before computing realized QV we should prefilter the data using a discrete sine transformation to the returns in order to reduce the impact of market frictions. This is efficient when the data X is a Gaussian random walk Y plus independent Gaussian noise ε model, where we think of the noise as market frictions. The Curci and Corsi (2003) method is equivalent to calculating the realized QV process on the smoother $E(Y|X; \theta)$, where θ are the estimated parameters indexing the Gaussian model. This type of approach was also advocated in Zhou (1996, p. 112) and is related to Hansen, Large, and Lunde (2006).

3.8.3   Fourier and Overlapping Approaches

Motivated by the problem of irregularly spaced data, where the spacing is independent of Y, Malliavin and Mancino (2002) showed that if $Y \in \mathcal{BSM}$ then

$$[Y_J^l, Y_J^k]_{2\pi} = \pi^2 \left[\frac{1}{J} \sum_{j=1}^{J} \left(a_j^l a_j^k + b_j^l b_j^k \right) \right] \xrightarrow{p} [Y^l, Y^k]_{2\pi}, \qquad (27)$$

as $J \to \infty$, where the Fourier coefficients of Y are

$$a_j^l = \frac{1}{\pi} \int_0^{2\pi} \cos(ju) \mathrm{d}Y_u^l, \quad b_j^l = \frac{1}{\pi} \int_0^{2\pi} \sin(ju) \mathrm{d}Y_u^l.$$

The Fourier coefficients are computed by, for example, integration by parts

$$a_j^l = \frac{1}{\pi} \left(Y_{2\pi}^l - Y_0^l \right) + \frac{j}{\pi} \int_0^{2\pi} \sin(ju) Y_u^l \mathrm{d}u$$

$$\simeq \frac{1}{\pi} \left(Y_{2\pi}^l - Y_0^l \right) + \frac{1}{\pi} \sum_{i=0}^{n-1} \{\cos(jt_i) - \cos(jt_{i+1})\} Y_{t_i}^l,$$

$$b_j^l \simeq \frac{1}{\pi} \sum_{i=0}^{n-1} \{\sin(jt_i) - \sin(jt_{i+1})\} Y_{t_i}^l.$$

This means that, in principle, one can use all the available data for all the series, even though prices for different assets appear at different points in time. Indeed each series has its Fourier coefficients computed separately, only performing the multivariate aspect of the analysis at step (27). A similar type of analysis could be based on wavelets, see Hog and Lunde (2003).

The performance of this Fourier estimator of QV is discussed by, for example, Barucci and Reno (2002a, 2002b), Kanatani (2004b), Precup and Iori (2005),

Nielsen and Frederiksen (2005), and Kanatani (2004a) who carry out some extensive simulation and empirical studies of the procedure. Reno (2003) has used a multivariate version of this method to study the Epps effects, while Mancino and Reno (2005) use it to look at dynamic principle components. Kanatani (2004a, p. 22) has shown that in the univariate case the finite J Fourier estimator can be written as a kernel estimator (24). For regularly spaced data he derived the weight function, noting that as J increases, so each of these weights declined and so for fixed δ so $[Y_J]_{2\pi} \to [Y_\delta]_{2\pi}$. An important missing component in this analysis is any CLT for this estimator.

A related approach has been advocated by Corsi (2005, Chapter 5), Martens (2003) and Hayashi and Yoshida (2005, Definition 3.1). They study the estimator

$$\}Y^l, Y^m \left\{_t = \sum_{i=1}^{t_i \leq t} \sum_{j=1}^{t_j \leq t} \left(Y^l_{t_i} - Y^l_{t_{i-1}}\right)\left(Y^m_{t_j} - Y^m_{t_{j-1}}\right) I\left\{(t_{i-1}, t_i) \cap (t_{j-1}, t_j) \neq \oslash\right\}.$$

(28)

This multiplies returns together whenever time intervals of the returns have any component which are overlapping. This artificially includes terms with components which are approximately uncorrelated (inflating the variance of the estimator), but it does not exclude any terms and so does not miss any of the contributions to quadratic covariation. They show under various assumptions that as the times of observations become denser over the interval from time 0 to time t, this estimator converges to the desired quadratic covariation quantity. Recently, Mykland (2006) has shown this estimator is, under some quite weak conditions, the maximum likelihood estimator in the case of irregularly spaced data.

3.8.4   Generalized Bipower Variation

The realized bipower variation process suggests studying generic statistics of the form introduced by Barndorff-Nielsen, Graversen, Jacod, Podolskij, and Shephard (2006) and Barndorff-Nielsen, Graversen, Jacod, and Shephard (2006)

$$Y_\delta(g, h)_t = \delta \sum_{j=1}^{\lfloor t/\delta \rfloor} g\left(\delta^{-1/2}\left(Y_{\delta(j-1)} - Y_{\delta(j-2)}\right)\right) h\left(\delta^{-1/2}\left(Y_{\delta j} - Y_{\delta(j-1)}\right)\right), \quad (29)$$

where the multivariate $Y \in \mathcal{BSM}$ and g, h are conformable matrices with elements which are continuous with at most polynomial growth in their arguments. Both QV and multivariate BPV can be cast in this form by the appropriate choice of g, h. Some of the choices of g, h will deliver statistics which will be robust to jumps.

Barndorff-Nielsen, Graversen, Jacod, Podolskij, and Shephard (2006) have shown that as $\delta \downarrow 0$ the probability limit of this process is always the generalized BPV process

$$\int_0^t \rho_{\sigma_u}(g)\rho_{\sigma_u}(h)\mathrm{d}u,$$

where the convergence is locally uniform, $\rho_\sigma(g) = \mathrm{E}g(X)$ and $X \sim N(0, \sigma\sigma')$. They also provide a central limit theorem for the generalized power variation estimator.

An example of the above framework which we have not covered yet is achieved by selecting $h(y) = |y^l|^r$ for $r > 0$ and $g(y) = 1$, then (29) becomes

$$\delta^{1-r/2} \sum_{j=1}^{\lfloor nt \rfloor} \left| Y_{\delta(j-1)}^l - Y_{\delta(j-2)}^l \right|^r, \tag{30}$$

which is called the realized rth-order power variation. When r is an integer it has been studied from a probabilistic viewpoint by Jacod (1994) while Barndorff-Nielsen and Shephard (2003) look at the econometrics of the case where $r > 0$. The increments of these types of high-frequency volatility measures have been informally used in the financial econometrics literature for some time when $r = 1$, but until recently without a strong understanding of their properties. Examples of their use include Schwert (1990), Andersen and Bollerslev (1998b), and Andersen and Bollerslev (1997), while they have also been abstractly discussed by Shiryaev (1999, pp. 349–350) and Maheswaran and Sims (1993). Following the work by Barndorff-Nielsen and Shephard (2003), Ghysels, Santa-Clara, and Valkanov (2006) and Forsberg and Ghysels (2004) have successfully used realized power variation as an input into volatility forecasting competitions.

It is unclear how the greater flexibility over the choice of g, h will help econometricians in the future to learn about new features of volatility and jumps, perhaps robustly to market frictions. It would also be attractive if one could generalize (29) to allow g and h to be functions of the path of the prices, not just returns.

3.9   Nonparametric Forecasting

3.9.1   Background

We saw in Section 2.4 that if s is small then

$$\mathrm{Cov}\,(Y_{t+s} - Y_t | \mathcal{F}_t) \simeq \mathrm{E}\,([Y]_{t+s} - [Y]_t | \mathcal{F}_t).$$

This suggests:

1. estimating components of the increments of QV;
2. projecting these terms forward using a time series model.

This separates out the task of historical measurement of past volatility (step 1) from the problem of forecasting (step 2).

Suppose we wish to make a sequence of one-step or multi-step ahead predictions of $V_i = [Y]_{hi} - [Y]_{h(i-1)}$ using their proxies $\widehat{V}_i = [Y_\delta]_{hi} - [Y_\delta]_{h(i-1)}$, raw returns $y_i = Y_{hi} - Y_{h(i-1)}$ (to try to deal with leverage effects) and components $\widehat{B}_i = \{Y_\delta\}_{hi} - \{Y_\delta\}_{h(i-1)}$, where $i = 1, 2, \ldots, T$. For simplicity of exposition we set $h = 1$. This setup exploits the high-frequency information set, but is somewhat robust to the presence of complicated intraday effects. Clearly, if $Y \in \mathcal{BSM}$ then the CLT for realized QV implies that as $\delta \downarrow 0$, so long as the moments exist,

$$\mathrm{E}\left(V_i | \mathcal{F}_{i-1}\right) \simeq \mathrm{E}\left(\widehat{V}_i | \mathcal{F}_{i-1}\right) + o(\delta^{1/2}).$$

It is compelling to choose to use the coarser information set, so

$$\mathrm{Cov}\left(Y_i - Y_{i-1} | \widehat{V}_{i-1}, \widehat{V}_{i-2}, \dots, \widehat{V}_1, \widehat{B}_{i-1}, \widehat{B}_{i-2}, \dots, \widehat{B}_1, y_{i-1}, \dots, y_1\right)$$
$$\simeq \mathrm{E}\left(V_i | \widehat{V}_{i-1}, \widehat{V}_{i-2}, \dots, \widehat{V}_1, \widehat{B}_{i-1}, \widehat{B}_{i-2}, \dots, \widehat{B}_1, y_{i-1}, \dots, y_1\right)$$
$$\simeq \mathrm{E}\left(\widehat{V}_i | \widehat{V}_{i-1}, \widehat{V}_{i-2}, \dots, \widehat{V}_1, \widehat{B}_{i-1}, \widehat{B}_{i-2}, \dots, \widehat{B}_1, y_{i-1}, \dots, y_1\right).$$

Forecasting can be carried out using structural or reduced form models. The simplest reduced form approach is to forecast $\widehat{V}_i$ using the past history $\widehat{V}_{i-1}, \widehat{V}_{i-2}, \dots, \widehat{V}_1, y_{i-1}, y_{i-2}, \dots, y_1$ and $\widehat{B}_{i-1}, \widehat{B}_{i-2}, \dots, \widehat{B}_1$ based on standard forecasting methods such as autoregressions. The earliest modeling of this type that we know of was carried out by Rosenberg (1972) who regressed $\widehat{V}_i$ on $\widehat{V}_{i-1}$ to show, for the first time in the academic literature, that volatility was partially forecastable.

This approach to forecasting is convenient but potentially inefficient for it fails to use all the available high-frequency data. In particular, for example, if $Y \in \mathcal{SV}$ then accurately modeled high-frequency data may allow us to accurately estimate the spot covariance $\Sigma_{(i-1)h}$, which would be a more informative indicator than $\widehat{V}_{i-1}$. However, the results in Andersen, Bollerslev, and Meddahi (2004) are reassuring on that front. They indicate that if $Y \in \mathcal{SV}$ there is only a small loss in efficiency by forgoing $\Sigma_{(i-1)h}$ and using $\widehat{V}_{i-1}$ instead. Further, Ghysels, Santa-Clara, and Valkanov (2006) and Forsberg and Ghysels (2004) have forcefully argued that by additionally conditioning on low power variation statistics (30) very significant forecast gains can be achieved.

3.9.2   Illustration

In this subsection we will briefly illustrate some of these suggestions in the univariate case. Much more sophisticated studies are given in, for example, Andersen, Bollerslev, Diebold, and Labys (2001, 2003), Andersen, Bollerslev, Diebold, and Ebens (2001), Bollerslev et al. (2005), and Andersen, Bollerslev, and Meddahi (2004), who look at various functional forms, differing asset types and more involved dynamics. Ghysels, Santa-Clara, and Valkanov (2006) suggest an alternative method, using high-frequency data but exploiting more sophisticated dynamics through so-called MIDAS regressions.

Table 10.3 gives a simple example of this approach for 100 times the returns on the DM/Dollar series. It shows the result of regressing $\widehat{V}_i$ on a constant, and simple lagged versions of $\widehat{V}_i$ and $\widehat{B}_i$. We dropped a priori the use of y_i as regressors for this exchange rate, where leverage effects are usually not thought to be important. The unusual spacing, using 1, 5, 20, and 40 lags, mimics the

Table 10.3. Prediction for 100 times returns on the DM/Dollar series. Dynamic regression, predicting future daily RV $\widehat{V}_i$ using lagged values and lagged values of estimated realised BPV terms $\widehat{B}_i$. Software used was PcGive. Subscripts denote the lag length in this table. Everything is computed using 10 minute returns. Figures in brackets are asymptotic standard errors. Port$_{49}$ denotes the Box-Ljung portmantau statistic computed with 49 lags, while log-L denotes the Gaussian likelihood

Const	Realized QV Terms				Realized BPV Terms				Summary Measures	
	$\widehat{V}_{i-1}$	$\widehat{V}_{i-5}$	$\widehat{V}_{i-20}$	$\widehat{V}_{i-40}$	$\widehat{B}_{i-1}$	$\widehat{B}_{i-5}$	$\widehat{B}_{i-20}$	$\widehat{B}_{i-40}$	log L	Port$_{49}$
0.503									−1751.42	4660
(0.010)										
0.170	0.413	0.153	0.061	0.030					−1393.41	199
(0.016)	(0.018)	(0.018)	(0.018)	(0.017)						
0.139					0.713	0.270	0.091	−0.110	−1336.81	108
(0.017)					(0.075)	(0.074)	(0.074)	(0.073)		
0.139	−0.137	−0.076	−0.017	0.116	0.551	0.180	0.071	0.027	−1342.03	122
(0.017)	(0.059)	(0.059)	(0.058)	(0.058)	(0.023)	(0.023)	(0.022)	(0.021)		

Table 10.4. *Prediction for 100 times returns* $Y_i - Y_{i-1}$ *on the DM/Dollar series. GARCH-type model of the conditional variance* h_i *of daily returns, using lagged squared returns* $(Y_{i-1} - Y_{i-2})^2$, *realized QV* $\widehat{V}_{i-1}$, *realized BPV* $\widehat{B}_{i-1}$ *and lagged conditional variance* h_{i-1}. *Throughout a Gaussian quasi-likelihood is used. Robust standard errors are reported. Carried out using PcGive*

Const	Realized Terms		Standard GARCH Terms		log L
	$\widehat{V}_{i-1}$	$\widehat{B}_{i-1}$	$(Y_{i-1} - Y_{i-2})^2$	h_{i-1}	
0.504					−2636.59
(0.021)					
0.008			0.053	0.930	−2552.10
(0.003)			(0.010)	(0.013)	
0.017	−0.115	0.253	0.019	0.842	−2533.89
(0.009)	(0.039)	(0.076)	(0.019)	(0.052)	
0.011	0.085		0.015	0.876	−2537.49
(0.008)	(0.042)		(0.017)	(0.049)	
0.014		0.120	0.013	0.853	−2535.10
(0.009)		(0.058)	(0.019)	(0.055)	
0.019	−0.104	0.282		0.822	−2534.89
(0.010)	(0.074)	(0.116)		(0.062)	

approach used by Corsi (2003) and Andersen, Bollerslev, and Diebold (2003). The results are quite striking. None of the models have satisfactory Box-Ljung portmanteau tests (this can be fixed by including a moving average error term in the model), but the inclusion of lagged information is massively significant. The lagged realized volatilities seem to do a reasonable job at soaking up the dependence in the data, but the effect of bipower variation is more important. This is in line with the results in Andersen, Bollerslev, and Diebold (2003) who first noted this effect. See also the work of Forsberg and Ghysels (2004) on the effect of inclusion of other power variation statistics in forecasting.

Table 10.4 shows some rather more sophisticated results. Here we model returns directly using a GARCH-type model, but also include lagged explanatory variables in the conditional variance. This is in the spirit of the work of Engle and Gallo (2006). The results above the line show the homoskedastic fit and the improvement resulting from the standard GARCH(1,1) model. Below the line we include a variety of realized variables as explanatory variables; including longer lags of realized variables does not improve the fit. The best combination has a large coefficient on realized BPV and a negative coefficient on realized QV. This means when there is evidence for a jump then the impact of realized volatility is tempered, while when there is no sign of jump the realized variables are seen with full force. What is interesting from these results is that the realized effects are very much more important than the lagged daily returns. In effect the realized quantities have basically tested out the traditional GARCH model.

Overall this tiny empirical study confirms the results in the literature about the predictability of realized volatility. However, we have also seen that it is quite easy to outperform a simple autoregressive model for RV. We can see how useful bipower variation is and that taken together the realized quantities do provide a coherent way of empirically forecasting future volatility.

3.10   Parametric Inference and Forecasting

Throughout we have emphasized the nonparametric nature of the analysis. This is helpful due to the strong and complicated diurnal patterns we see in volatility. These effects tend also to be unstable through time and so are difficult to model parametrically. A literature which mostly avoids this problem is that on estimating parametric SV models from low-frequency data. Much of this is reviewed in Shephard (2005, Chapter 1). Examples include the use of Markov chain Monte Carlo methods (e.g., Kim, Shephard, and Chib, 1998) and efficient method of moments (e.g., Chernov et al. 2003).Both approaches are computationally intensive and intricate to code. Simpler method of moment procedures (e.g., Andersen and Sørensen, 1996) have the difficulty that they are sensitive to the choice of moments and can be rather inefficient.

Recently various researchers have used the time series of realized daily QV to estimate parametric SV models. These models ignore the intraday effects and so are theoretically misspecified. Typically the researchers use various simple types of method of moments estimators, relying on the great increase in information available from realized statistics to overcome the inefficiency caused by the use of relatively crude statistical methods. The first papers to do this were Barndorff-Nielsen and Shephard (2002) and Bollerslev and Zhou (2002), who studied the first two dynamic moments of the time series $\widehat{V}_1$, $\widehat{V}_2$, ... , $\widehat{V}_T$ implied by various common volatility models and used these to estimate the parameters embedded within the SV models. More sophisticated approaches have been developed by Corradi and Distaso (2006) and Phillips and Yu (2005). Barndorff-Nielsen and Shephard (2002) also studied the use of these second-order properties of the realized quantities to estimate V_1, V_2, ... , V_T from the time series of $\widehat{V}_1$, $\widehat{V}_2$, ... , $\widehat{V}_T$ using the Kalman filter. This exploited the asymptotic theory for the measurement error (16). See also the work of Meddahi (2002), Andersen, Bollerslev, and Meddahi (2004, 2005).

3.11   Forecast Evaluation

One of the main early uses of realized volatility was to provide an instrument for measuring the success for various volatility forecasting methods. Andersen and Bollerslev (1998a) studied the correlation between V_i or $\widehat{V}_i$ and h_i, the conditional variance from a GARCH model based on daily returns from time 1 up to time $i - 1$. They used these results to argue that GARCH models were more successful than had been previously understood in the empirical finance literature. Hansen and Lunde (2005a) study a similar type of problem, but look at a wider class of forecasting models and carry out formal testing of the superiority of one modeling approach over another.

Hansen and Lunde (2006a) and Patton (2005) have focused on the delicate implications of the use of different loss functions to discriminate between competing forecasting models, where the object of the forecasting is $\text{Cov}(Y_i - Y_{i-1}|\mathcal{F}_{i-1})$. They use $\widehat{V}_i$ to proxy this unobserved covariance. See also the related work of Koopman, Jungbacker, and Hol (2005).

4 ADDITION OF JUMPS

4.1 Bipower Variation

In this short section we will review some material which nonparametrically identifies the contribution of jumps to the variation of asset prices. A focus will be on using this method for testing for jumps from discrete data. We will also discuss some work by Cecilia Mancini which provides an alternative to BPV for splitting up QV into its continuous and discontinuous components.

Recall $\mu_1^{-2}\{Y\}_t = \int_0^t \Sigma_u du$ when Y is a $\mathcal{BSM}$ plus jump process given in (7). The BPV process is consistently estimated by the $p \times p$ matrix realized BPV process $\{Y_\delta\}$, defined in (10). This means that we can, in theory, consistently estimate $[Y^{ct}]$ and $[Y^d]$ by $\mu_1^{-2}\{Y_\delta\}$ and $[Y_\delta] - \mu_1^{-2}\{Y_\delta\}$, respectively.

One potential use of $\{Y_\delta\}$ is to test for the hypothesis that a set of data is consistent with a null hypothesis of continuous sample paths. We can do this by asking if $[Y_\delta]_t - \mu_1^{-2}\{Y_\delta\}_t$ is statistically significantly bigger than zero – an approach introduced by Barndorff-Nielsen and Shephard (2006a). This demands a distribution theory for realized BPV objects, calculated under the null that $Y \in \mathcal{BSM}$ with $\sigma > 0$.

Building on the earlier CLT of Barndorff-Nielsen and Shephard (2006a), Barndorff-Nielsen, Graversen, Jacod, Podolskij, and Shephard (2006) have established a CLT which covers this situation when $Y \in \mathcal{BSM}$. We will only present the univariate result, which has that as $\delta \downarrow 0$ so

$$\delta^{-1/2}\left(\{Y_\delta\}_t - \{Y\}_t\right) \to \mu_1^2\sqrt{(2+\vartheta)}\int_0^t \sigma_u^2 dB_u, \tag{31}$$

where $B \perp\!\!\!\perp Y$, the convergence is in law stable as a process and

$$\vartheta = \left(\pi^2/4\right) + \pi - 5 \simeq 0.6090.$$

This result, unlike Theorem 1, has some quite technical conditions associated with it in order to control the degree to which the volatility process can jump; however we will not discuss those issues here. Extending the result to cover the joint distribution of the estimators of the QV and the BPV processes, they showed that

$$
\delta^{-1/2}\begin{pmatrix} \mu_1^{-2}\{Y_\delta\}_t - \mu_1^{-2}\{Y\}_t \\ [Y_\delta]_t - [Y]_t \end{pmatrix}
$$
$$
\xrightarrow{L} MN\left(\begin{pmatrix} 0 \\ 0 \end{pmatrix}, \begin{pmatrix} (2+\vartheta) & 2 \\ 2 & 2 \end{pmatrix} \int_0^t \sigma_u^4 du\right),
$$

a Hausman (1978) type result as the estimator of the QV process is, of course, fully asymptotically efficient when $Y \in \mathcal{BSM}$. Consequently

$$
\frac{\delta^{-1/2}\left([Y_\delta]_t - \mu_1^{-2}\{Y_\delta\}_t\right)}{\sqrt{\vartheta \int_0^t \sigma_u^4 du}} \xrightarrow{L} N(0,1), \tag{32}
$$

which can be used as the basis of a test of the null of no jumps.

4.2   Multipower Variation

The "standard" estimator of integrated quarticity, given in (17), is not robust to jumps. One way of overcoming this problem is to use a multipower variation (MPV) measure – introduced by Barndorff-Nielsen and Shephard (2006a). This is defined as

$$
\{Y\}_t^{[\mathbf{r}]} = \text{p}-\lim_{\delta \downarrow 0} \delta^{(1-r_+/2)} \sum_{j=1}^{\lfloor t/\delta \rfloor} \left\{\prod_{i=1}^{I} \left|Y_{\delta(j-i)} - Y_{\delta(j-1-i)}\right|^{r_i}\right\},
$$

where $r_i > 0, r = (r_1, r_2, \ldots, r_I)'$ for all i and $r_+ = \sum_{i=1}^{I} r_i$. The usual BPV process is the special case $\{Y\}_t = \{Y\}_t^{[1,1]}$.

If Y obeys (7) and $r_i < 2$ then

$$
\{Y\}_t^{[\mathbf{r}]} = \left(\prod_{i=1}^{I} \mu_{r_i}\right) \int_0^t \sigma_u^{r_+} du,
$$

This process is approximated by the estimated MPV process

$$
\{Y_\delta\}_t^{[\mathbf{r}]} = \delta^{(1-r_+/2)} \sum_{j=1}^{\lfloor t/\delta \rfloor} \left\{\prod_{i=1}^{I} \left|Y_{\delta(j-i)} - Y_{\delta(j-1-i)}\right|^{r_i}\right\}.
$$

In particular, the scaled realized tri and quadpower variation,

$$
\mu_1^{-4}\{Y_\delta\}_t^{[1,1,1,1]} \quad \text{and} \quad \mu_{4/3}^{-3}\{Y_\delta\}_t^{[4/3,4/3,4/3]},
$$

respectively, both estimate $\int_0^t \sigma_u^4 du$ consistently in the presence of jumps. Hence either of these objects can be used to replace the integrated quarticity in (32), so producing a nonparametric test for the presence of jumps in the interval $[0, t]$. The test is conditionally consistent, meaning if there is a jump, it will detected and has asymptotically the correct size. Extensive small sample studies are reported in Huang and Tauchen (2005), who favor ratio versions of the statistic like

$$\frac{\delta^{-1/2} \left(\dfrac{\mu_1^{-2} \{Y_\delta\}_t}{[Y_\delta]_t} - 1 \right)}{\sqrt{\vartheta \dfrac{\{Y_\delta\}_t^{[1,1,1,1]}}{(\{Y_\delta\}_t)^2}}} \xrightarrow{L} N(0, 1),$$

which has pretty reasonable finite sample properties. They also show that this test tends to under reject the null of no jumps in the presence of some forms of market frictions.

It is clearly possible to carry out jump testing on separate days or weeks. Such tests are asymptotically independent over these nonoverlapping periods under the null hypothesis.

To illustrate this methodology we will apply the jump test to the DM/Dollar rate, asking if the hypothesis of a continuous sample path is consistent with the data we have. Our focus will mostly be on Friday January 15th, 1988, although we will also give results for neighboring days to provide some context. In Figure 10.5 we plot 100 times the change during the week of the discretized Y_δ, so a one unit uptick represents a 1% change, for a variety of values of $n = 1/\delta$, as well as giving the ratio jump statistics $\widehat{B}_i / \widehat{V}_i$ with their corresponding 99% critical values.

In Figure 10.5 there is a large uptick in the D-mark against the Dollar, with a movement of nearly 2% in a 5 minute period. This occurred on the Friday and was a response to the news of a large fall in the U.S. balance of payment deficit, which led to a large strengthening of the Dollar. The data for January 15th had a large $\widehat{V}_i$ but a much smaller $\widehat{B}_i$. Hence the statistics are attributing a large component of $\widehat{V}_i$ to the jump, with the adjusted ratio statistic being larger than the corresponding 99% critical value. When δ is large the statistic is on the borderline of being significant, while the situation becomes much clearer as δ becomes small. This illustration is typical of results presented in Barndorff-Nielsen and Shephard (2006a) which showed that many of the large jumps in this exchange rate correspond to macroeconomic news announcements. This is consistent with the recent economics literature documenting significant intraday announcement effects, for example, Andersen, Bollerslev, Diebold, and Vega (2003).

4.3 Grids

It is clear that the martingale-based CLT for irregularly spaced data for the estimator of the QV process can be extended to cover the BPV case. We define

$$\{Y_{\mathcal{G}_n}\}_t = \sum_{j=1}^{t_j \le t} \left| Y_{t_{j-1}} - Y_{t_{j-2}} \right| \left| Y_{t_j} - Y_{t_{j-1}} \right| \xrightarrow{p} \{Y\}_t.$$

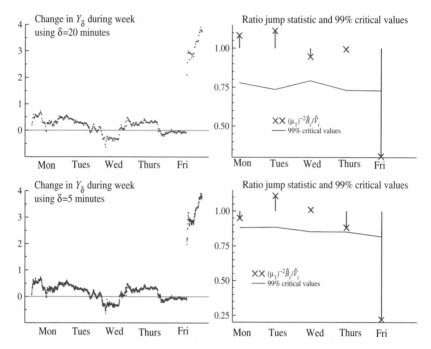

Figure 10.5. Left-hand side: change in Y_δ during a week, centered at 0 on Monday 11th January and running until Friday of that week. Drawn every 20 and 5 minutes. An uptick of 1 indicates strengthening of the Dollar by 1%. Right-hand side shows an index plot of $\widehat{B}_i/\widehat{V}_i$, which should be around 1 if there are no jumps. Test is one sided, with criticial values also drawn as a line.

Using the same notation as before, we would expect the following result to hold, due to the fact that $H^{\mathcal{G}}$ is assumed to be continuous,

$$\delta^{-1/2}\begin{pmatrix} \mu_1^{-2}\{Y_{\mathcal{G}_n}\}_t - \mu_1^{-2}\{Y\}_t \\ [Y_\delta]_t - [Y]_t \end{pmatrix}$$

$$\overset{L}{\to} MN\left(\begin{pmatrix} 0 \\ 0 \end{pmatrix}\begin{pmatrix} (2+\vartheta) & 2 \\ 2 & 2 \end{pmatrix}\int_0^t \left(\frac{\partial H_u^{\mathcal{G}}}{\partial u}\right)\sigma_u^4 du\right).$$

The integrated moderated quarticity can be estimated using $\mu_1^{-4}\{Y_\delta\}_t^{[1,1,1,1]}$, or a grid version, which again implies that the usual feasible CLT continues to hold for irregularly spaced data. This is the expected result from the analysis of power variation provided by Barndorff-Nielsen and Shephard (2006b).

Potentially there are modest efficiency gains to be had by computing the estimators of BPV on multiple grids and then averaging them. The extension along these lines is straightforward and will not be detailed here.

4.4   Infinite Activity Jumps

The probability limit of realized BPV is robust to finite activity jumps. A natural question to ask is: (i) is the CLT also robust to jumps, (ii) is the probability limit also unaffected by infinite activity jumps, that is jump processes with an infinite number of jumps in any finite period of time. Both issues are studied by Barndorff-Nielsen, Shephard, and Winkel (2006) in the case where the jumps are of Lévy type, while Woerner (2006) looks at the probability limit for more general jump processes.

Barndorff-Nielsen, Shephard, and Winkel (2006) find that the CLT for BPV is affected by finite activity jumps, but this is not true of tripower and high-order measures of variation. The reason for the robustness of tripower results is quite technical and we will not discuss it here. However, it potentially means that inference under the assumption of jumps can be carried out using tripower variation, which seems an exciting possibility. Both Barndorff-Nielsen, Shephard, and Winkel (2006) and Woerner (2006) give results which prove that the probability limit of realized BPV is unaffected by some types of infinite activity jump processes. More work is needed on this topic to make these result definitive. It is somewhat related to the parametric study of Aït-Sahalia (2004). He shows that maximum likelihood estimation can disentangle a homoskedastic diffusive component from a purely discontinuous infinite activity Lévy component of prices. Outside the likelihood framework, the paper also studies the optimal combinations of moment functions for the generalized method of moment estimation of homoskedastic jump-diffusions. Further insights can be found by looking at likelihood inference for Lévy processes, which is studied by Aït-Sahalia and Jacod (2005a, 2005b).

4.5   Testing the Null of No Continuous Component

In some stimulating recent papers, Carr et al. (2003) and Carr and Wu (2004), have argued that it is attractive to build SV models out of pure jump processes, with no Brownian aspect. It is clearly important to be able to test this hypothesis, seeing if pure discreteness is consistent with observed prices.

Barndorff-Nielsen, Shephard, and Winkel (2006) showed that

$$\delta^{-1/2} \left(\{Y_\delta\}_t^{[2/3,2/3,2/3]} - [Y^{ct}]_t \right)$$

has a mixed Gaussian limit and is robust to jumps. But this result is only valid if $\sigma > 0$, which rules out its use for testing for pure discreteness. However, we can artificially add a scaled Brownian motion, $U = \sigma B$, to the observed price process and then test if

$$\delta^{-1/2} \left(\{Y_\delta + U_\delta\}_t^{[2/3,2/3,2/3]} - \sigma^2 t \right)$$

is statistically significantly greater than zero. In principle, this would be a consistent nonparametric test of the maintained hypothesis of Peter Carr and his coauthors.

4.6   Alternative Methods for Identifying Jumps

Mancini (2001, 2003, 2004) has developed robust estimators of $\left[Y^{ct}\right]$ in the presence of finite activity jumps. Her approach is to use truncation

$$\sum_{j=1}^{\lfloor t/\delta \rfloor} \left(Y_{j\delta} - Y_{(j-1)\delta}\right)^2 I\left(\left|Y_{j\delta} - Y_{(j-1)\delta}\right| < r_\delta\right),\tag{33}$$

where I (.) is an indicator function. The crucial function r_δ has to have the property that $\sqrt{\delta \log \delta^{-1}} r_\delta^{-1} \downarrow 0$. It is motivated by the modulus of continuity of Brownian motion paths that almost surely

$$\lim_{\delta \downarrow 0} \sup_{\substack{0 \le s, t \le T \\ |t-s| < \delta}} \frac{|W_s - W_t|}{\sqrt{2\delta \log \delta^{-1}}} = 1.$$

This is an elegant theory, which works when $Y \in \mathcal{BSM}$. It is not prescriptive about the tuning function r_δ, which is an advantage and a drawback. Given the threshold in (33) is universal, this method will throw out more returns as jumps during a high volatility period than during a low volatility period.

Aït-Sahalia and Jacod (2005b, Section 7 onwards) provides additional insights into these types of truncation estimators in the case where Y is scaled Brownian motion plus a homogeneous pure jump process. They develop a two-step procedure, which automatically selects the level of truncation. Their analysis is broader still, providing additional insights into a range of power variation-type objects.

5   MITIGATING MARKET FRICTIONS

The semimartingale model of the frictionless, arbitrage-free market is a fiction. When we use high-frequency data to perform inference on either transaction or quote data then various market frictions can become important. O'Hara (1995), Engle, 2000, Hasbrouck (2006), and Engle and Russell (2006) review the detailed modeling of these effects. Inevitably such modeling is quite complicated.

With the exception of subsection 2.9, we have so far mostly ignored frictions by thinking of δ as being only moderately small. This is ad hoc and it is wise to try to more formally identify the impact of frictions. In this context the first econometric work was carried out by Fang (1996) and Andersen et al. (2000) who used so-called signature plots to assess the degree of bias caused byfrictions using a variety of values of δ. The signature plots we draw show the square root of the time series average of estimators of V_i computed over many days, plotting this against δ. If the log-price process was a pure martingale then we would expect the plot to have roughly horizontal lines.

Hansen and Lunde, (2006b) have reviewed the literature on the effect of market frictions on realized QV statistics. Their broad conclusions are that for thickly traded stocks: (i) for returns measured over 10 to 20 minute returns using mid-quotes the central limit theories based on no noise give good approximations to the reality, (ii) for returns measure over 1 to 10 minutes, noise becomes important but it is empirically realistic to view the noise as independent of Y, (iii) for higher frequency data the situation is much more complicated.

Econometricians have recently started to try to use higher frequency data to estimate $[Y]$, taking into account the effect of market frictions. All the work we have seen assumes independence of Y with the frictions. Important approaches are (a) subsampling by Zhou (1996), Zhang, Mykland, and Aït-Sahalia (2005b), Zhang (2004), Aït-Sahalia, Mykland, and Zhang (2005), Zhang, Mykland, and Aït-Sahalia (2005a), and Mykland (2006); (b) point process by Large (2005); (c) kernels by Barndorff-Nielsen et al. (2004). It is unclear how this rapidly evolving literature will settle in the next few years. Particularly important contributions need to be made in the multivariate case where the effects of market frictions are most readily felt. Relevant references include Hayashi and Yoshida (2005), Griffin and Oomen (2006), and Zhang (2005).

6 CONCLUSIONS

This paper has reviewed the literature on the measurement and forecasting of uncertainty through quadratic variation-type objects. The econometrics of this has focused on realized objects, estimating QV and its components. Such an approach has been shown to provide a leap forward in our understanding of time varying volatility and jumps, which are crucial in asset allocation, derivative pricing and risk assessment. A drawback with these types of methods is the potential for market frictions to complicate the analysis. Recent research has been trying to address this issue and has introduced various innovative methods. There is still much work to be carried through in that area.

ACKNOWLEDGMENTS

We are grateful to Tim Bollerslev, Eric Ghysels, Peter Hansen, Jean Jacod, Dmitry Kulikov, Jeremy Large, Asger Lunde, Andrew Patton, Mark Podolskij, Kevin Sheppard, and Jun Yu for comments on an earlier draft. Talks based on this paper were given in 2005 as the Hiemstra Lecture at the 13th Annual conference of the Society of Non-linear Dynamics and Econometrics in London, the keynote address at the 3rd Nordic Econometric Meeting in Helsinki and as a Special Invited Lecture at the 25th European Meeting of Statisticians in Oslo. Ole Barndorff-Nielsen's work is supported by CAF (www.caf.dk), which is funded by the Danish Social Science Research Council. Neil Shephard's research is supported by the UK's ESRC through the grant "High frequency financial econometrics based upon power variation." The calculations made for this paper were carried out using PcGive of Doornik and Hendry (2005) and software written by the authors using the Ox language of Doornik (2001).

References

Aït-Sahalia, Y. (2004): "Disentangling Diffusion from Jumps," *Journal of Financial Economics*, 74, 487–528.

Aït-Sahalia, Y. and J. Jacod (2005a): "Fisher's Information for Discretely Sampled Lévy Processes." Unpublished paper, Department of Economics, Princeton University.

——— (2005b): "Volatility Estimators for Discretely Sampled Lévy Processes." Unpublished paper, Department of Economics, Princeton University.

Aït-Sahalia, Y., P. A. Mykland, and L. Zhang (2005): "Ultra High Frequency Volatility Estimation with Dependent Microstructure Noise," Unpublished paper, Department of Economics, Princeton University.

Alizadeh, S., M. Brandt, and F. Diebold (2002): "Range-Based Estimation of Stochastic Volatility Models," *Journal of Finance*, 57, 1047–1091.

Andersen, T. G. and T. Bollerslev (1997): "Intraday Periodicity and Volatility Persistence in Financial Markets," *Journal of Empirical Finance*, 4, 115–158.

——— (1998a): "Answering the Skeptics: Yes, Standard Volatility Models Do Provide Accurate Forecasts," *International Economic Review,* 39, 885–905.

——— (1998b): "Deutsche Mark-Dollar Volatility: Intraday Activity Patterns, Macroeconomic Announcements, and Longer Run Dependencies," *Journal of Finance* 53, 219–265.

Andersen, T. G., T. Bollerslev, and F. X. Diebold (2003): "Some Like It Smooth, and Some Like It Rough: Untangling Continuous and Jump Components in Measuring, Modeling and Forecasting Asset Return Volatility," Unpublished paper, Economics Dept, Duke University.

Andersen, T. G., T. Bollerslev, F. X. Diebold, and H. Ebens (2001): "The Distribution of Realized Stock Return Volatility," *Journal of Financial Economics*, 61, 43–76.

Andersen, T. G., T. Bollerslev, F. X. Diebold, and P. Labys (2000): "Great Realizations," *Risk,* 13, 105–108.

——— (2001): "The Distribution of Exchange Rate Volatility," *Journal of the American Statistical Association,* 96, 42–55. Correction published in 2003, Vol. 98, p. 501.

——— (2003): "Modeling and Forecasting Realized Volatility," *Econometrica,* 71, 579–625.

Andersen, T. G., T. Bollerslev, F. X. Diebold, and C. Vega (2003): "Micro Effects of Macro Announcements: Real-Time Price Discovery in Foreign Exchange," *American Economic Review*, 93, 38–62.

Andersen, T. G., T. Bollerslev, and N. Meddahi (2004): "Analytic Evaluation of Volatility Forecasts," *International Economic Review*, 45, 1079–1110.

——— (2005): "Correcting the Errors: A Note on Volatility Forecast Evaluation Based on High-Frequency Data and Realized Volatilities," *Econometrica*, 73, 279–296.

Andersen, T. G. and B. Sørensen (1996): "GMM Estimation of a Stochastic Volatility Model: A Monte Carlo study," *Journal of Business and Economic Statistics*, 14, 328–352.

Back, K. (1991): "Asset Pricing for General Processes," *Journal of Mathematical Economics*, 20, 371–395.

Barndorff-Nielsen, O. E., S. E. Graversen, J. Jacod, M. Podolskij, and N. Shephard (2006): "A Central Limit Theorem for Realised Power and Bipower Variations of Continuous Semimartingales," in *From Stochastic Analysis to Mathematical*

Finance, Festschrift for Albert Shiryaev, Edited by Y. Kabanov, R. Lipster, and J. Stoyanov, pp. 33–68, New York: Springer.

BARNDORFF-NIELSEN, O. E., S. E. GRAVERSEN, J. JACOD, AND N. SHEPHARD (2006): "Limit Theorems for Realised Bipower Variation in Econometrics," *Econometric Theory*, 22, 677–719.

BARNDORFF-NIELSEN, O. E., P. R. HANSEN, A. LUNDE, AND N. SHEPHARD (2004): "Designing Realised Kernels to Measure the Ex-Post Variation of Equity Prices in the Presence of Noise," Unpublished Paper, Nuffield College, Oxford.

BARNDORFF-NIELSEN, O. E. AND N. SHEPHARD (2001): "Non-Gaussian Ornstein–Uhlenbeck-Based Models and Some of Their Uses in Financial Economics (with discussion)," *Journal of the Royal Statistical Society, Series B*, 63, 167–241.

———— (2002): "Econometric Analysis of Realised Volatility and Its Use in Estimating Stochastic Volatility Models," *Journal of the Royal Statistical Society, Series B*, 64, 253–280.

———— (2003): "Realised Power Variation and Stochastic Volatility," *Bernoulli*, 9, 243–265. Correction published in pages 1109–1111.

———— (2004): "Econometric Analysis of Realised Covariation: High Frequency Covariance, Regression and Correlation in Financial Economics," *Econometrica*, 72, 885–925.

———— (2005): "How Accurate is the Asymptotic Approximation to the Distribution of Realised Volatility?" in *Identification and Inference for Econometric Models. A Festschrift in Honour of T. J. Rothenberg*, Edited by D. W. K. Andrews and J. H. Stock, pp. 306–331, Cambridge: Cambridge University Press.

———— (2006a): "Econometrics of Testing for Jumps in Financial Economics Using Bipower Variation," *Journal of Financial Econometrics*, 4, 1–30.

———— (2006b): "Power Variation and Time Change," *Theory of Probability and Its Applications*, 50, 1–15.

BARNDORFF-NIELSEN, O. E., N. SHEPHARD, AND M. WINKEL (2006): "Limit Theorems for Multipower Variation in the Presence of Jumps," *Stochastic Processes and Their Applications*, 116, 796–806.

BARTLETT, M. S. (1946): "On the Theoretical Specification of Sampling Properties of Autocorrelated Time Series," *Journal of the Royal Statistical Society, Supplement*, 8, 27–41.

———— (1950): "Periodogram Analysis and Continuous Spectra," *Biometrika*, 37, 1–16.

BARUCCI, E. AND R. RENO (2002a): "On Measuring Volatility and the GARCH Forecasting Performance," *Journal of International Financial Markets, Institutions and Money*, 12, 182–200.

———— (2002b): "On Measuring Volatility of Diffusion Processes with High Frequency Data," *Economic Letters*, 74, 371–378.

BOLLERSLEV, T., U. KRETSCHMER, C. PIGORSCH, AND G. TAUCHEN (2005): "The Dynamics of Bipower Variation, Realized Volatility and Returns," Unpublished paper, Department of Economics, Duke University.

BOLLERSLEV, T. AND H. ZHOU (2002): "Estimating Stochastic Volatility Diffusion Using Conditional Moments of Integrated Volatility," *Journal of Econometrics*, 109, 33–65.

BRANDT, M. W. AND F. X. DIEBOLD (2006): "A No-Arbitrage Approach to Range-Based Estimation of Return Covariances and Correlations," *Journal of Business*, 79, 61–73.

BRANGER, N. AND C. SCHLAG (2005): "An Economic Motivation for Variance Contracts. Unpublished paper, Faculty of Economics and Business Administration, Goethe University.

BROCKHAUS, O. AND D. LONG (1999): "Volatility Swaps Made Simple," *Risk*, 2, 92–95.

CALVET, L. AND A. FISHER (2002): "Multifractality in Asset Returns: Theory and Evidence," *Review of Economics and Statistics*, 84, 381–406.

CARR, P., H. GEMAN, D. B. MADAN, AND M. YOR (2003): "Stochastic Volatility for Lévy Processes," *Mathematical Finance*, 13, 345–382.

———— (2005): "Pricing Options on Realized Variance," *Finance and Stochastics*, 9, 453–475.

CARR, P. AND R. LEE (2003a): "Robust Replication of Volatility Derivatives," Unpublished paper, Courant Institute, NYU.

———— (2003b): "Trading Autocorrelation," Unpublished paper, Courant Institute, NYU.

CARR, P. AND K. LEWIS (2004): "Corridor Variance Swaps," *Risk*, 67–72.

CARR, P. AND D. B. MADAN (1998): "Towards a Theory of Volatility Trading," in *Volatility*, edited by R. Jarrow, pp. 417–427, Risk Publications.

CARR, P. AND L. WU (2004): "Time-Changed Lévy Processes and Option Pricing," *Journal of Financial Economics*, 71, 113–141.

CHERNOV, M., A. R. GALLANT, E. GHYSELS, AND G. TAUCHEN (2003): "Alternative Models of Stock Price Dynamics," *Journal of Econometrics*, 116, 225–257.

CHRISTENSEN, K. AND M. PODOLSKIJ (2005): "Asymptotic Theory for Range-Based Estimation of Integrated Volatility of a Continuous Semi-Martingale. Unpublished paper, Aarhus School of Business.

COMTE, F. AND E. RENAULT (1998): "Long Memory in Continuous-Time Stochastic Volatility Models," *Mathematical Finance*, 8, 291–323.

CORRADI, V. AND W. DISTASO (2006): "Semiparametric Comparison of Stochastic Volatility Models Using Realized Measures," *Review of Economic Studies*, 73, 635–667.

CORSI, F. (2003): "A Simple Long Memory Model of Realized Volatility," Unpublished paper, University of Southern Switzerland.

———— (2005): "Measuring and Modelling Realized Volatility: From Tick-By-Tick to Long Memory," Ph.D. thesis, Department of Economics, University of Lugano.

CURCI, G. AND F. CORSI (2003): "A Discrete Sine Transformation Approach to Realized Volatility Measurement," Unpublished paper.

DACOROGNA, M. M., R. GENCAY, U. A. MÜLLER, R. B. OLSEN, AND O. V. PICTET (2001): *An Introduction to High-Frequency Finance*," San Diego: Academic Press.

DEMETERFI, K., E. DERMAN, M. KAMAL, AND J. ZOU (1999): "A Guide to Volatility and Variance Swaps," *Journal of Derivatives*, 6, 9–32.

DOOB, J. L. (1953): *Stochastic Processes*, New York: John Wiley and Sons.

DOORNIK, J. A. (2001): *Ox: Object Oriented Matrix Programming, 3.0*, London: Timberlake Consultants Press.

DOORNIK, J. A. AND D. F. HENDRY (2005): *PC Give, Version 10.4*, London: Timberlake Consultants Press.

EICKER, F. (1967): "Limit Theorems for Regressions with Unequal and Dependent Errors," in *Proceedings of the Fifth Berkeley Symposium on Mathematical Statistics and Probability*, Volume 1, pp. 59–82, Berkeley: University of California.

ENGLE, R. F. (2000): "The Econometrics of Ultra-High Frequency Data," *Econometrica*, 68, 1–22.

ENGLE, R. F. AND J. P. GALLO (2006): "A Multiple Indicator Model for Volatility Using Intra Daily Data," *Journal of Econometrics*, 131, 3–27.

ENGLE, R. F. AND J. R. RUSSELL (1998): "Forecasting Transaction Rates: The Autoregressive Conditional Duration Model," *Econometrica*, 66, 1127–1162.

——— (2006): "Analysis of High Frequency Data," in *Handbook of Financial Econometrics*, edited by Y. Aït-Sahalia and L. P. Hansen, Amsterdam: North Holland.

EPPS, T. W. (1979): "Comovements in Stock Prices in the Very Short Run," *Journal of the American Statistical Association*, 74, 291–296.

FAN, J., Y. FAN, AND J. LV (2005): "Aggregation of Nonparametric Estimators for Volatility Matrix. Unpublished paper, Princeton University.

FANG, Y. (1996): "Volatility Modeling and Estimation of High-Frequency Data with Gaussian Noise," Unpublished Ph.D. thesis, Sloan School of Management, MIT.

FORSBERG, L. AND E. GHYSELS (2004): "Why Do Absolute Returns Predict Volatility so Well." Unpublished paper, Economics Department, UNC, Chapel Hill.

FOSTER, D. P. AND D. B. NELSON (1996): "Continuous Record Asymptotics for Rolling Sample Variance Estimators," *Econometrica*, 64, 139–174.

FRENCH, K. R., G. W. SCHWERT, AND R. F. STAMBAUGH (1987): "Expected Stock Returns and Volatility," *Journal of Financial Economics*, 19, 3–29.

GENON-CATALOT, V., C. LARÉDO, AND D. PICARD (1992): "Non-Parametric Estimation of the Diffusion Coefficient by Wavelet Methods," *Scandinavian Journal of Statistics*, 19, 317–335.

GHYSELS, E., A. C. HARVEY, AND E. RENAULT (1996): "Stochastic Volatility," in *Statistical Methods in Finance*, edited by C. R. Rao and G. S. Maddala, pp. 119–191, Amsterdam: North-Holland.

GHYSELS, E., P. SANTA-CLARA, AND R. VALKANOV (2006): "Predicting Volatility: Getting the Most Out of Return Data Sampled at Different Frequencies," *Journal of Econometrics*, 131, 59–95.

GONCALVES, S. AND N. MEDDAHI (2004): "Bootstrapping Realized Volatility," Unpublished paper, CIRANO, Montreal.

GRIFFIN, J. E. AND R. C. A. OOMEN (2006): "Covariance Measurement in the Presence of Non-Synchronous Trading and Market Microstructure Noise," Unpublished paper, Department of Statistics, University of Warwick.

HALL, P. AND C. C. HEYDE (1980): *Martingale Limit Theory and its Applications*. San Diego: Academic Press.

HANSEN, P. R., J. LARGE, AND A. LUNDE (2006): "Moving Average-Based Estimators of Integrated Variance," *Econometric Reviews*, forthcoming.

HANSEN, P. R. AND A. LUNDE (2005a): "A Forecast Comparison of Volatility Models: Does Anything Beat a GARCH(1,1)?" *Journal of Applied Econometrics*, 20, 873–889.

——— (2005b): "A Realized Variance for the Whole Day Based on Intermittent High-Frequency Data," *Journal of Financial Econometrics*, 3, 525–554.

——— (2006a): "Consistent Ranking of Volatility Models," *Journal of Econometrics*, forthcoming.

——— (2006b): "Realized Variance and Market Microstructure Noise (with discussion)," *Journal of Business and Economic Statistics*, 24, 127–218.

HASBROUCK, J. (2006): "*Empirical Market Microstructure*. Oxford: Oxford University Press. Forthcoming.

HAUSMAN, J. A. (1978): "Specification Tests in Econometrics," *Econometrica*, 46, 1251–1271.

HAYASHI, T. AND N. YOSHIDA (2005): "On Covariance Estimation of Non-Synchronously Observed Diffusion Processes," *Bernoulli*, 11, 359–379.

HESTON, S. L. (1993): "A Closed-Form Solution for Options with Stochastic Volatility, with Applications to Bond and Currency Options," *Review of Financial Studies*, 6, 327–343.

HOG, E. AND A. LUNDE (2003): "Wavelet Estimation of Integrated Volatility," Unpublished paper, Aarhus School of Business.

HOWISON, S. D., A. RAFAILIDIS, AND H. O. RASMUSSEN (2004): "On the Pricing and Hedging of Volatility Derivatives," *Applied Mathematical Finance*, 11, 317–346.

HUANG, X. AND G. TAUCHEN (2005): "The Relative Contribution of Jumps to Total Price Variation," *Journal of Financial Econometrics*, 3, 456–499.

JACOD, J. (1994): "Limit of Random Measures Associated with the Increments of a Brownian Semimartingale," Preprint number 120, Laboratoire de Probabilitiés, Université Pierre et Marie Curie, Paris.

———— (1997): "On Continuous Conditional Gaussian Martingales and Stable Convergence in Law," in *Séminaire Probability XXXI*, Lecture Notes in Mathematics, Vol. 1655, pp. 232–246, Berlin: Springer-Verlag.

JACOD, J. AND P. PROTTER (1998): "Asymptotic Error Distributions for the Euler Method for Stochastic Differential Equations," *Annals of Probability*, 26, 267–307.

JACOD, J. AND A. N. SHIRYAEV (2003): *"Limit Theorems for Stochastic Processes*, 2nd ed., Berlin: Springer-Verlag.

JAVAHERI, A., P. WILMOTT, AND E. HAUG (2002): "GARCH and Volatility Swaps," Unpublished paper, available at www.wilmott.com.

KANATANI, T. (2004a): "High Frequency Data and Realized Volatility," Ph.D. thesis, Graduate School of Economics, Kyoto University.

———— (2004b): "Integrated Volatility Measuring from Unevenly Sampled Observations," *Economics Bulletin*, 3, 1–8.

KARATZAS, I. AND S. E. SHREVE (1991): *Brownian Motion and Stochastic Calculus*, 2nd ed., *Vol. 113: Graduate Texts in Mathematics*, Berlin: Springer-Verlag.

———— (1998): *"Methods of Mathematical Finance*, New York: Springer-Verlag.

KIM, S., N. SHEPHARD, AND S. CHIB (1998): "Stochastic Volatility: Likelihood Inference and Comparison with ARCH Models," *Review of Economic Studies*, 65, 361–393.

KOOPMAN, S. J., B. JUNGBACKER, AND E. HOL (2005): "Forecasting Daily Variability of the S&P 100 Stock Index Using Historical, Realised and Implied Volatility Measurements," *Journal of Empirical Finance*, 12, 445–475.

LARGE, J. (2005): "Estimating Quadratic Variation When Quoted Prices Jump by a Constant Increment," Unpublished paper, Nuffield College, Oxford.

LÉVY, P. (1937): *"Théories de L'Addition Aléatories*, Paris: Gauthier-Villars.

MAHESWARAN, S. AND C. A. SIMS (1993): "Empirical Implications of Arbitrage-Free Asset Markets," in *Models, Methods and Applications of Econometrics*, edited by P. C. B. Phillips, pp. 301–316, Basil Blackwell.

MALLIAVIN, P. AND M. E. MANCINO (2002): "Fourier Series Method for Measurement of Multivariate Volatilities," *Finance and Stochastics*, 6, 49–61.

MANCINI, C. (2001): "Does Our Favourite Index Jump or Not," Dipartimento di Matematica per le Decisioni, Universita di Firenze.

———— (2003): "Statistics of a Poisson-Gaussian Process," Dipartimento di Matematica per le Decisioni, Universita di Firenze.

———— (2004): "Estimation of the Characteristics of Jump of a General Poisson-Diffusion Process," *Scandinavian Actuarial Journal*, 1, 42–52.

MANCINO, M. AND R. RENO (2005): "Dynamic Principal Component Analysis of Multivariate Volatilites Via Fourier Analysis," *Applied Mathematical Finance*, 12, 187–199.

MARTENS, M. (2003): "Estimating Unbiased and Precise Realized Covariances," Unpublished paper.

MARTENS, M. AND D. VAN DIJK (2006): "Measuring Volatility with the Realized Range," *Journal of Econometrics*, forthcoming.

MEDDAHI, N. (2002): "A Theoretical Comparison Between Integrated and Realized Volatilities," *Journal of Applied Econometrics*, 17, 479–508.

MERTON, R. C. (1980): "On Estimating the Expected Return on the Market: An Exploratory Investigation," *Journal of Financial Economics*, 8, 323–361.

MUNROE, M. E. (1953): *Introduction to Measure and Integration*, Cambridge, MA: Addison-Wesley Publishing Company, Inc.

MYKLAND, P. A. (2006): "A Gaussian Calculus for Inference from High Frequency Data," Unpublished paper, Department of Statistics, University of Chicago.

MYKLAND, P. A. AND L. ZHANG (2002): "Inference for Volatility-Type Objects and Implications for Hedging," Unpublished paper, Department of Statistics, University of Chicago.

——— (2006): "ANOVA for Diffusions and Ito Processes," *Annals of Statistics*, 33, forthcoming.

NEUBERGER, A. (1990): "Volatility Trading," Unpublished paper, London Business School.

NIELSEN, M. O. AND P. H. FREDERIKSEN (2005): "Finite Sample Accuracy of Integrated Volatility Estimators," Unpublished paper, Department of Economics, Cornell University.

OFFICER, R. R. (1973): "The Variability of the Market Factor of the New York Stock Exchange," *Journal of Business*, 46, 434–453.

O'HARA, M. (1995): *Market Microstructure Theory*, Oxford: Blackwell Publishers.

PARKINSON, M. (1980): "The Extreme Value Method for Estimating the Variance of the Rate of Return," *Journal of Business*, 53, 61–66.

PATTON, A. (2005): "Volatility Forecast Evaluation and Comparison Using Imperfect Volatility Proxies," Unpublished paper, Department of Accounting and Finance, LSE.

PHILLIPS, P. C. B. AND S. OULIARIS (1990): "Asymptotic Properties of Residual Based Tests for Cointegration," *Econometrica*, 58, 165–193.

PHILLIPS, P. C. B. AND J. YU (2005): "A Two-Stage Realized Volatility Approach to the Estimation for Diffusion Processes from Discrete Observations," Unpublished paper, Cowles Foundation for Research in Economics, Yale University.

POLITIS, D., J. P. ROMANO, AND M. WOLF (1999): *Subsampling*. New York: Springer.

PRECUP, O. V. AND G. IORI (2005): "Cross-Correlation Measures in High-Frequency Domain," Unpublished paper, Department of Economics, City University.

PROTTER, P. (2004): *Stochastic Integration and Differential Equations*, New York: Springer-Verlag.

RENO, R. (2003): "A Closer Look at the Epps Effect," *International Journal of Theoretical and Applied Finance*, 6, 87–102.

ROGERS, L. C. G. AND S. E. SATCHELL (1991): "Estimating Variance from High, Low, Open and Close Prices," *Annals of Applied Probability*, 1, 504–512.

ROSENBERG, B. (1972): "The Behavior of Random Variables with Nonstationary Variance and the Distribution of Security Prices," Working paper 11, Graduate School of Business Administration, University of California, Berkeley. Reprinted in Shephard (2005).

RYDBERG, T. H. AND N. SHEPHARD (2000): "A Modelling Framework for the Prices and Times of Trades Made on the NYSE," in *Nonlinear and Nonstationary Signal Processing*, edited by W. J. Fitzgerald, R. L. Smith, A. T. Walden, and P. C. Young, pp. 217–246, Cambridge: Isaac Newton Institute and Cambridge University Press.

SCHWERT, G. W. (1989): "Why Does Stock Market Volatility Change Over Time?" *Journal of Finance*, 44, 1115–1153.

———— (1990): "Indexes of U.S. Stock Prices from 1802 to 1987," *Journal of Business*, 63, 399–426.

———— (1998): "Stock Market Volatility: Ten Years after the Crash," *Brookings-Wharton Papers on Financial Services*, 1, 65–114.

SHEPHARD, N. (2005): *Stochastic Volatility: Selected Readings*, Oxford: Oxford University Press.

SHEPPARD, K. (2005): "Measuring Realized Covariance," Unpublished paper, Department of Economics, University of Oxford.

SHIRYAEV, A. N. (1999): *Essentials of Stochastic Finance: Facts, Models and Theory*, Singapore: World Scientific.

WASSERFALLEN, W. AND H. ZIMMERMANN (1985): "The Behavior of Intraday Exchange Rates," *Journal of Banking and Finance*, 9, 55–72.

WIENER, N. (1924): "The Quadratic Variation of a Function and Its Fourier Coefficients," *Journal of Mathematical Physics*, 3, 72–94.

WOERNER, J. (2006): "Power and Multipower Variation: Inference for High Frequency Data," in *Proceedings of the International Conference on Stochastic Finance 2004*, edited by A. N. Shiryaev, M. do Rosario Grossinho, P. Oliviera, and M. Esquivel, pp. 343–364, Berlin: Springer Verlag.

ZHANG, L. (2004): "Efficient Estimation of Stochastic Volatility Using Noisy Observations: A Multi-Scale Approach," Unpublished paper, Department of Statistics, Carnegie Mellon University.

———— (2005): "Estimating Covariation: Epps Effect and Microstructure Noise," Unpublished paper, Department of Finance, University of Illinois, Chicago.

ZHANG, L., P. A. MYKLAND, AND Y. AïT-SAHALIA (2005a): "Edgeworth Expansions for Realized Volatility and Related Estimators," Unpublished paper, University of Illinois at Chicago.

———— (2005b): "A Tale of Two Time Scales: Determining Integrated Volatility with Noisy High-Frequency Data," *Journal of the American Statistical Association*, 100, 1394–1411.

ZHOU, B. (1996): "High-Frequency Data and Volatility in Foreign-Exchange Rates," *Journal of Business and Economic Statistics*, 14, 45–52.

CHAPTER 11

Discussion of Aït-Sahalia and
Barndorff-Nielsen and Shephard

Oliver Linton[*] and Ilze Kalnina[†]

We discuss the issue of estimating quadratic variation of a discretely observed continuous time stochastic price process in the presence of measurement error induced by market microstructure. This issue has come to the forefront in recent months and is part of the research program described in both papers. It builds on the work of Barndorff-Nielsen and Shephard who established distribution theory for quadratic variation estimators without measurement error. We first review the main model and results.

An underlying continuous time log price X_t is observed discretely at times $t_1, \ldots, t_n$ in some fixed interval and is measured with error, that is, one observes only $\{Y_{t_1}, \ldots, Y_{t_n}\}$ with

$$Y_{t_i} = X_{t_i} + \varepsilon_{t_i}, \ i = 1, \ldots, n \tag{1}$$

where ε_{t_i} is an additive measurement error. The spacing of the data $\delta_i = t_{i+1} - t_i$ goes to zero with sample size and in most of the work is assumed to be deterministic and $O(n^{-1})$. In the strongest version of the model, ε_{t_i} are i.i.d. and independent of X_{t_i}. The parameter of interest is the quadratic variation of X on some interval. This is a classical measurement error model without feedback, and the usual realized volatility estimators of quadratic variation are inconsistent. In common with other measurement error models (Robinson, 1986) there has to be some difference between the signal and noise for identification, or some instrument that can purge out the measurement error (Bound, Brown, and Mathiowetz, 2001). In this case it appears to come from the fact that the variance of the signal $\text{var}[\Delta X_t]$ is small, $O(n^{-1})$, compared with the variance of the noise $\text{var}[\Delta \varepsilon_t]$, which is $O(1)$ (where n is the full sample size). What makes this problem difficult is that it is the noise that dominates in the differenced scale. This can be overcome because aggregation over many periods raises the

[*] Department of Economics, London School of Economics, Houghton Street, London WC2A 2AE, United Kingdom. E-mail: o.linton@lse.ac.uk.

[†] Department of Economics, London School of Economics, Houghton Street, London WC2A 2AE, United Kingdom. E-mail: i.kalnina@lse.ac.uk.

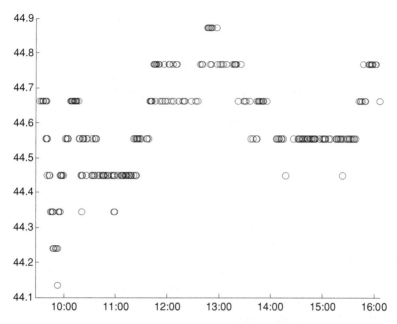

Figure 11.1. Intraday price series for GM (August 3rd 1994).

variance of the signal ΔX_t but has no effect on the variance of the noise $\Delta \varepsilon_t$. The authors have established under quite general conditions a class of estimators with convergence rates of order $n^{-1/4}$ for the MSRV (multiple scale realized volatility) estimators and order $n^{-1/6}$ for the simpler TSRV (two scale realized volatility) class. The estimators are explicitly defined and involve an additive bias correction. The assumptions have now been weakened in various directions to allow specifically for autocorrelated measurement error of quite general geometric mixing type (Aït-Sahalia, Mykland, and Zhang, 2005). However, in the presence of autocorrelation the bias correction part of the estimator must be modified in a nontrivial way.

Note that model (1) only makes sense in the discrete time as a triangular array formulation since there can be no continuous time process $t \mapsto \varepsilon_t$ with ε_t i.i.d. for all t. In addition, there are some rather strong assumptions being made about the error term. The strongest set of assumptions are some subset of:

(A1) ε is independent of X
(A2) ε has constant scale regardless of the size of the observation interval
(A3) ε is homoskedastic and has no variation in mean
(A4) ε is i.i.d.

Figure 11.1 shows the intraday price sequence for General Motors for a typical day in the 1990s; there is evidently a great deal of discreteness, which would appear to be inconsistent with assumptions A1–A4. A common statistical model for this type of discreteness is a rounding model, see for example, Gottlieb and Kalay (1985). Suppose that we observe

$$Y_{t_i} = d[X_{t_i}/d], \qquad (2)$$

where $[x]$ denotes the closest integer to x and d is a parameter that measures the size of the discreteness (for simplicity we consider rounding on log-prices). Then we can write

$$Y_{t_i} = X_{t_i} + \varepsilon_{t_i}, \quad \text{where } \varepsilon_{t_i} = d[X_{t_i}/d] - X_{t_i} \in [-d/2, d/2].$$

Although this is in the form (1), the ε_{t_i} violates some of the assumptions: ε_{t_i} is not independent of X_{t_i} and is also autocorrelated when X_{t_i} is. This model can be viewed as a simple example of a more general class of nonlinear measurement error models.

Errors due to discreteness also have another effect. The minimum price variation increment is always defined in terms of price, but we are modeling log-prices, thus the magnitude of error induced by discreteness varies depending on the level of the efficient price. Regarding (A2), while one might argue that the bid-ask spread does not depend on the frequency of trades, this is much more difficult to justify in the case of adjustment of the price due to a learning process of the market participants. It has also been shown in practice that these assumptions do not hold. For example, Hansen and Lunde (2006) have shown that the noise is correlated with the efficient price, and that the properties of the noise have changed substantially over time.

We discuss a weakening of the main assumptions to allow the measurement error to be small in an explicit pathwise asymptotic sense and only require a sort of local stationarity on the measurement error. We also allow for correlation between returns and the measurement error. The main consistency result holds in this more general setting although the rates of convergence are affected by a scale parameter denoted α.

Suppose that the observation times $t_i = i/n \ i = 1, \ldots n$ are equally spaced in $[0, 1]$ and that

$$\varepsilon_{t_i} = \mu(i/n) + n^{-\alpha/2}\sigma_\epsilon(i/n)\epsilon_{t_i}, \qquad (3)$$

where ϵ_{t_i} are i.i.d. mean zero and variance one, $\alpha \in [0, 1)$, and $\sigma_\epsilon(.)$ and $\mu(.)$ are smooth functions [in fact, they could have a finite number of jump discontinuities]. This is a special case of the more general class of locally stationary processes of Dahlhaus (1997). For pedagogic reasons we suppose that

$$X_{t_{i+1}} = X_{t_i} + u_{t_{i+1}}/\sqrt{n}, \qquad (4)$$

where u_{t_i} is i.i.d. and that $\text{cov}(u_t, \epsilon_s) = \rho_{u\varepsilon}1(s = t)$ [this process converges to a geometric Brownian motion as $n \to \infty$]. The parameter of interest is the quadratic variation of X on $[0, 1]$, denoted QV_X. The usual benchmark measurement error model here has $\alpha = 0$ and $\sigma_\epsilon(.)$ and $\mu(.)$ constant and $\rho_{u\varepsilon} = 0$. The generalization to allowing time varying mean and variance in the measurement error allows one to capture diurnal variation in the measurement error process, which is likely to exist in calendar time. Correlation between u and ε is also plausible due to rounding effects or other reasons (Diebold, 2006; Hansen and Lunde, 2006). In a recent survey of measurement error in microeconometrics models, Bound, Brown, and Mathiowetz (2001) emphasize "mean-reverting" measurement error that is correlated with the signal.

Allowing a nonconstant scaling factor ($\alpha > 0$) seems natural from a statistical point of view since the ε_{t_i} represent outcomes that have happened in the small interval $[(i - 1)/n, i/n]$; the scale of this distribution ought to reduce as the interval shrinks, that is, as $n \to \infty$, at least for some of the components of the market microstructure noise. Many authors argue that measurement error is small; small is what the sampling interval is also argued to be and asymptotics are built off this assumption. Assumption (3) implies that $\text{var}[\Delta\varepsilon_{t_i}] = O(n^{-\alpha})$, and nests both the i.i.d. case ($\alpha = 0$) and the diffusion case ($\alpha = 1$) but allows also for a range of meaningful intermediate cases. Indeed, Zhang, Mykland, and Aït-Sahalia (2005, p. 11) implicitly allow this structure. However, their later work in Theorems 1 and 4 appear to explicitly rule this case out.

In the $\alpha = 0$ case, the measurement error persists at any frequency, so strictly speaking according to the asymptotics the measurement error is of the same magnitude as the true returns at the daily frequency. By taking $\alpha > 0$ we predict measurement error to be smaller magnitude than true returns at daily frequency.

Another advantage with the small measurement error assumption is that it provides a justification for the additivity as an approximation to a more general measurement error model. Suppose that for some function f with $f(0, 0) = 0$, $\partial f(0, 0)/\partial x = 1$ and $\partial f(0, 0)/\partial \varepsilon = 1$,

$$\Delta Y_t = f(\Delta X_t, \Delta\varepsilon_t). \tag{5}$$

This nests the additive model $f(x, z) = x + z$. Furthermore, when both $\Delta X, \Delta\varepsilon$ are "small" $\Delta X + \Delta\varepsilon$ is a valid first-order approximation so that quadratic variation computed from model (5) will behave to first order as if data came from model (1).

We just treat the TSRV estimators. Let

$$[Y, Y]^n = \sum_{i=1}^{n} \left(Y_{t_{i+1}} - Y_{t_i}\right)^2$$

be the realized variation of Y, let $[Y, Y]^{\bar{n}}$ denote the subsample estimator based on a K-spaced subsample of size $\bar{n}$ with $K \times \bar{n} = n$, and let $[Y, Y]^{\bar{n}}_{\text{avg}}$ denote the averaged $\bar{n}$-subsample estimator. It can be shown that

$$[Y, Y]^{\bar{n}} = QV_X + O_p\left(\bar{n}^{-1/2}\right) + 2\bar{n}n^{-\alpha}\sigma_\epsilon^2$$
$$+ 2n^{-(1+\alpha)/2}\bar{n}\sigma_\epsilon\rho_{u\varepsilon} + O_p\left(\bar{n}^{1/2}n^{-\alpha}\right), \tag{6}$$

where $\sigma_\epsilon^2 = \int_0^1 \sigma_\epsilon^2(u)du$ and $\sigma_\epsilon = \int_0^1 \sigma_\epsilon(u)du$. The cross-product term now yields an additional bias term due to the covariance between returns and measurement error. This term is slightly smaller than the main measurement error bias under our conditions that is, $\sum_{i=1}^{n} \Delta X_{t_i} \Delta \varepsilon_{t_i} = n^{-(1+\alpha)/2} n \sigma_\epsilon \rho_{u\varepsilon} + O_p(n^{-\alpha/2})$. The validity of this expansion follows along the lines of Zhang, Mykland, and Aït-Sahalia (2005) with additional steps coming from the Taylor expansions that establish the smallness of $\mu(K(i+1)/n) - \mu(Ki/n)$ and $\sigma_\epsilon^2(K(i+1)/n) - \sigma_\epsilon^2(Ki/n)$ in relative terms for any K with $K/n \to 0$ fast enough. Then, averaging over all similar subsamples induces the usual variance reduction in both of the stochastic terms due to the measurement error. Define the bias corrected estimator (the TSRV)

$$\widehat{QV}_X = \frac{[Y,Y]_{\text{avg}}^{\bar{n}} - \left(\dfrac{\bar{n}}{n}\right)[Y,Y]^n}{1 - \dfrac{\bar{n}}{n}}. \tag{7}$$

This is consistent for QV_X under some conditions on K. Suppose that $K = n^\beta$ and $\bar{n} = n^{1-\beta}$. It can be shown that

$$\widehat{QV}_X \simeq QV_X + O_p\left(n^{-(1-\beta)/2}\right) + O_p\left(n^{(1-2\beta)/2} n^{-\alpha}\right), \tag{8}$$

for which the error is minimized by setting $\beta = (2 - 2\alpha)/3$; this yields $\beta = 2/3$ when $\alpha = 0$ and convergence rate of $n^{-1/6}$. In general the required amount of averaging is less than $O(n^{2/3})$ because the noise is smaller, and the convergence rate is faster and is $n^{-(1+2\alpha)/6}$. As $\alpha \to 1$ the rate of convergence increases to $n^{-1/2}$ (but at $\alpha = 1/2$ lack of identification takes over). With dependent noise one should replace $[Y,Y]^n$ by $[Y,Y]_{\text{avg}}^{\bar{n}}$ for some other $\bar{K}, \bar{n}$ set, but the above results would carry over like in Aït-Sahalia, Mykland, and Zhang (2005).

In conclusion, the TSRV estimator is consistent in this more general setting. Indeed, formulas (58) and (62) of Zhang, Mykland, and Aït-Sahalia (2005) remain valid under the sampling scheme (3) provided $E(\varepsilon^2)$ is interpreted according to our specification as half the integrated variance of ε_{t_i}, $\sigma_\epsilon^2/2n^\alpha$. Thus, a data-based rule derived from their formula can be implemented for selecting the optimal K.

The magnitude of α might be of interest in itself: it measures the relative size of the signal to noise ratio. It also governs the best achievable rates for estimating QV_X. To estimate α we use the asymptotic relation (6) for n large assuming that $\alpha < 1$. Therefore, let

$$\widehat{\alpha} = -\frac{\ln\left(\dfrac{[Y,Y]^n}{n}\right)}{\ln(n)}.$$

This is a consistent estimator of α. Unfortunately, it is badly biased and the direction of the bias depends on whether σ_ϵ^2 is larger or smaller than $1/2$. A bias corrected estimator is

$$\widehat{\alpha}_{bc} = -\frac{\ln\left(\dfrac{[Y,Y]^n}{n}\right) - \ln\left(2\sigma_\epsilon^2\right)}{\ln(n)},$$

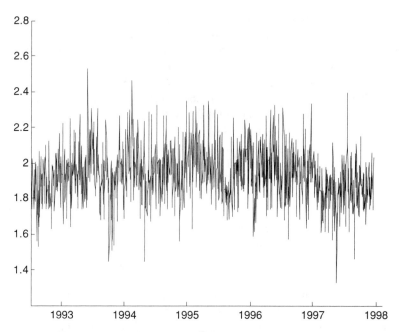

Figure 11.2. Estimated daily $\widehat{\alpha}$ for GM, for every day during period Jan 4, 1993–May 29, 1998.

which performs much better in simulations but is infeasible due to the presence of σ_ϵ^2. Under some conditions one can obtain that

$$\sqrt{n}\log n\,(\widehat{\alpha}_{bc} - \alpha) \Longrightarrow N\left(0, (2 + \kappa_4/2)\sigma_\epsilon^4/(\sigma_\epsilon^2)^2\right),$$

where $\sigma_\epsilon^4 = \int_0^1 \sigma_\epsilon^4(u)du$ and κ_4 is the fourth cumulant of ϵ_{t_i}. In the normal homoskedastic case the limiting distribution is $N(0, 2)$. Note that the consistency of $\widehat{\alpha}$ is robust to serial correlation in ϵ_{t_i} – if there is serial correlation then σ_ϵ^2 in $\widehat{\alpha}_{bc}$ should be replaced by the long-run variance of ϵ_{t_i} and the limiting variance becomes more complicated. In Figure 11.2, we show some estimated α values for daily IBM stock series during the 1990s. The typical values are quite large and greater than one in most cases, although there is a great deal of variation over time. We have tried a number of different implementations including varying $\overline{n}$, replacing $[Y, Y]^n/n$ by $[Y, Y]_{avg}^{\overline{n}}/\overline{n}$ but obtain similar results in all cases.

Is there some way of estimating α better and estimating also σ_ϵ^2 or even $\sigma_\epsilon^2(u)$? The obvious estimator of σ_ϵ^2 doesn't work here because

$$n^{\widehat{\alpha}}\frac{[Y,Y]^n}{2n} = \exp(\log(n^{\widehat{\alpha}}/n^\alpha))n^\alpha\frac{[Y,Y]^n}{2n}$$
$$= \exp((\widehat{\alpha} - \alpha)\log n)n^\alpha\frac{[Y,Y]^n}{2n}$$
$$= \exp\left(-\ln\left(2\sigma_\epsilon^2\right)\right)2\sigma_\epsilon^2 + o_p(1) = 1 + o_p(1).$$

When $\alpha = 0$ it is possible to consistently estimate the function $\sigma_\epsilon^2(u)$ but otherwise not.

We make one final set of remarks about the rounding model. It may well fit into the general framework described after (3) but there is one area of concern. The error term and its difference may not necessarily be geometric mixing. Since the process X_{t_i} is not mixing we can't expect ε_{t_i} to be mixing. Then, although ΔX_{t_i} is mixing there is no guarantee that $\Delta \varepsilon_{t_i}$ is mixing due to the nonlinearity involved (rounding and differencing are not commutable operators). Lack of mixingness would potentially cause the bias correction method not to work since sums like $\sum (\Delta \varepsilon_{t_i})^2/n$ may not converge in probability. However, we have simulated various processes of this type and our simulations suggest better news, specifically, the correlogram of the differenced noise decays rapidly. Furthermore, $\sum (\Delta \varepsilon_{t_i})^2$ diverges in probability but $\sum (\Delta \varepsilon_{t_i})^2/n$ converges to zero in probability. The term $\sum_{i=1}^{n} \Delta X_{t_i} \Delta \varepsilon_{t_i}$ grows very slowly. This suggests that the TSRV and MSRV are consistent under this sampling scheme. It may be that the rounding model has become less significant over time as the NYSE has moved from 1/8ths to 1/100ths as the smallest possible unit of pricing. Nevertheless, this model can be viewed as a representative of a more general class of nonlinear measurement error models so the issues raised in its analysis may carry over to other situations.

In conclusion, the results for TSRV-type estimators of quadratic variation remain valid in quite general settings and without parametric assumptions. This is partly due to the simple explicit structure of the estimator. Estimators like bi-power variation can be similarly analyzed under measurement error but are likely to require stronger assumptions on the distribution of the noise. We think this is an interesting and lively area of research and we congratulate the authors on their work.

References

AïT-SAHALIA, Y., P. MYKLAND, AND L. ZHANG (2005): "Ultra High Frequency Volatility Estimation with Dependent Microstructure Noise," Unpublished paper, Department of Economics, Princeton University.

BOUND, J., C. BROWN, AND N. MATHIOWETZ (2001): "Measurement Error in Survey Data," in *The Handbook of Econometrics*, Edited by J. J. Heckman and E. Leamer, Vol. 5, pp. 3705–3843.

DAHLHAUS, R. (1997): "Fitting Time Series Models to Nonstationary Processes," *Annals of Statistics*, 25, 1–37.

DIEBOLD, F. X. (2006): "On Market Microstructure Noise and Realized Volatility," Discussion of Hansen and Lunde (2006).

GOTTLIEB, G. AND A. KALAY (1985): "Implications of the Discreteness of Observed Stock Prices," *The Journal of Finance*, XL, 135–153.

HANSEN, P. R. AND A. LUNDE (2006): "Realized Variance and Market Microstructure Noise (with discussion)," *Journal of Business and Economic Statistics*, 24, 127–171.

ROBINSON, P. M. (1986): "On the Errors in Variables Problem for Time Series," *Journal of Multivariate Analysis*, 19, 240–250.

ZHANG, L., P. MYKLAND, AND Y. AÏT-SAHALIA (2005): A Tale of Two Time Scales: Determining Integrated Volatility with Noisy High-Frequency Data," *Journal of the American Statistical Association*, 100, 1394–1411.

CHAPTER 12

Understanding Bias in Nonlinear Panel Models: Some Recent Developments*
Manuel Arellano and Jinyong Hahn

1 INTRODUCTION

The purpose of this paper is to review recently developed bias-adjusted methods of estimation of nonlinear panel data models with fixed effects. Standard estimators such as maximum likelihood estimators are usually inconsistent if the number of individuals n goes to infinity while the number of time periods T is held fixed. For some models, like static linear and logit regressions, there exist fixed-T consistent estimators as $n \to \infty$ (see, e.g., Andersen, 1970). Fixed T consistency is a desirable property because for many panels T is much smaller than n. However, these type of estimators are not available in general, and when they are, their properties do not normally extend to estimates of average marginal effects, which are often parameters of interest. Moreover, without auxiliary assumptions, the common parameters of certain nonlinear fixed effects models are simply unidentified in a fixed T setting, so that fixed-T consistent point estimation is not possible (see, e.g., Chamberlain, 1992). In other cases, although identifiable, fixed-T consistent estimation at the standard root-n rate is impossible (see, e.g., Honoré and Kyriazidou, 2000; Hahn, 2001).

The number of periods available for many household, firm-level or country panels is such that it is not less natural to talk of time-series finite sample bias than of fixed-T inconsistency or underidentification. In this light, an alternative reaction to the fact that micro panels are short is to ask for approximately unbiased estimators as opposed to estimators with no bias at all. That is, estimators with biases of order $1/T^2$ as opposed to the standard magnitude of $1/T$. This alternative approach has the potential of overcoming some of the fixed-T identification difficulties and the advantage of generality.

The paper is organized as follows. Section 2 describes fixed effects estimators and the incidental parameters problem. Section 3 explains how to construct analytical bias correction of estimators. Section 4 describes bias correction of

* Prepared for the Econometric Society World Meetings, London, August 2005. We are grateful to Whitney Newey and Tiemen Woutersen for helpful comments on this and related work. The second author gratefully acknowledges financial support from NSF Grant SES-0313651.

the moment equation. Section 5 presents bias corrections for the concentrated likelihood. Section 6 discusses other approaches leading to bias correction, including Cox and Reid's and Lancaster's approaches based on orthogonality, and their extensions. Section 7 describes quasi maximum likelihood estimation for dynamic models. Section 8 considers the estimation of marginal effects. Section 9 discusses automatic methods based on simulation. Section 10 concludes.

2   INCIDENTAL PARAMETERS PROBLEM WITH LARGE T

We first describe fixed effects estimators. Let the data observations be denoted by $z_{it} = \left(y_{it}, x_{it}' \right)'$, $(t = 1, \ldots, T; i = 1, \ldots, n)$, where y_{it} denotes the "dependent" variable, and x_{it} denotes the strictly exogenous "explanatory" variable.[1] Let θ denote a parameter that is common to all i, α_i a scalar individual effect,[2] and $f(y_{i1}, \ldots, y_{iT} \mid \theta_0, \alpha_{i0})$

$$ f(y_{i1}, \ldots, y_{iT} \mid \theta_0, \alpha_{i0}) = f(y_{i1}, \ldots, y_{iT} \mid x_{i1}, \ldots, x_{iT}, \theta_0, \alpha_{i0}) $$

a density function of $y_{i1}, \ldots, y_{iT}$ conditional on the strictly exogenous explanatory variables $x_{i1}, \ldots, x_{iT}$. Assuming that y_{it} are independent across i and t, we obtain the log likelihood

$$ \sum_{i=1}^{n} \sum_{t=1}^{T} \log f_{it}(y_{it} \mid \theta, \alpha_i), $$

where $f_{it}(y_{it} \mid \theta, \alpha_i)$ denotes the density of y_{it} conditional on $x_{i1}, \ldots, x_{iT}$. For notational simplicity, we will write f for f_{it} below. The fixed effects estimator is obtained by doing maximum likelihood treating each α_i as a parameter to be estimated. Concentrating out the α_i leads to the characterization

$$ \widehat{\theta}_T \equiv \operatorname*{argmax}_{\theta} \sum_{i=1}^{n} \sum_{t=1}^{T} \log f(y_{it} \mid \theta, \widehat{\alpha}_i(\theta)), $$

$$ \widehat{\alpha}_i(\theta) \equiv \operatorname*{argmax}_{\alpha} \sum_{t=1}^{T} \log f(y_{it} \mid \theta, \alpha). $$

Here the $\widehat{\alpha}_i(\theta)$ depends on the data only through the ith observation $z_{i1}, \ldots, z_{iT}$. Let

$$ L(\theta) \equiv \lim_{n \to \infty} n^{-1} \sum_{i=1}^{n} E\left[\sum_{t=1}^{T} \log f(y_{it} \mid \theta, \widehat{\alpha}_i(\theta)) \right]. $$

It will follow from the usual extremum estimator properties (e.g., Amemiya, 1985) that as $n \to \infty$ with T fixed, $\widehat{\theta}_T = \theta_T + o_p(1)$, where $\theta_T \equiv \operatorname{argmax}_{\theta}$

---

[1] Throughout most of the paper except in Section 7, we will assume away dynamics or feedback.
[2] Our analysis extends easily, albeit with some notational complication, to the case where there are multiple fixed effects, that is, where α_i is a multidimensional vector.

$L(\theta)$. In general, $\theta_T \neq \theta_0$. This is the incidental parameters problem noted by Neyman and Scott (1948). The source of this problem is the estimation error of $\widehat{\alpha}_i(\theta)$. Because only a finite number T of observations are available to estimate each α_i, the estimation error of $\widehat{\alpha}_i(\theta)$ does not vanish as the sample size n grows, and this error contaminates the estimates of parameters of interest.

Example 1   *Consider a simple model where* $y_{it} \overset{i.i.d.}{\sim} \mathcal{N}(\alpha_{i0}, \sigma_0^2)$, $(t = 1, \dots, T; i = 1, \dots, n)$, *or*

$$
\log f\left(y_{it}; \sigma^2, \alpha_i\right) = C - \frac{1}{2}\log\sigma^2 - \frac{(y_{it} - \alpha_i)^2}{2\sigma^2}.
$$

This is a simpler version of the model considered by Chamberlain (1980). Here, we may write $\theta = \sigma^2$, *and the MLE is such that*

$$
\widehat{\alpha}_i = \frac{1}{T}\sum_{t=1}^{T} y_{it} \equiv \bar{y}_i, \quad \widehat{\theta} = \frac{1}{nT}\sum_{i=1}^{n}\sum_{t=1}^{T}\left(y_{it} - \bar{y}_i\right)^2.
$$

It is straightforward to show that $\widehat{\theta} = \theta_0 - \frac{1}{T}\theta_0 + o_p(1)$ *as* $n \to \infty$ *with* T *fixed. In this example, the bias is easy to fix by equating the denominator with the correct degrees of freedom* $n(T-1)$.

Note that the bias should be small for large enough T, that is, $\lim_{T\to\infty} \theta_T = \theta_0$. Furthermore, for smooth likelihoods we usually have

$$
\theta_T = \theta_0 + \frac{B}{T} + O\left(\frac{1}{T^2}\right) \tag{1}
$$

for some B. In Example 1, $B = -\theta_0$. The fixed effects estimator $\widehat{\theta}$ will in general be asymptotically normal, although it will be centered at θ_T: as $n, T \to \infty$, $\sqrt{nT}(\widehat{\theta} - \theta_T) \overset{d}{\to} N(0, \Omega)$ for some Ω. Under these general conditions the fixed effects estimator is asymptotically biased even if T grows at the same rate as n. For $n/T \to \rho$, say,

$$
\sqrt{nT}\left(\widehat{\theta} - \theta_0\right) = \sqrt{nT}\left(\widehat{\theta} - \theta_T\right) + \sqrt{nT}\frac{B}{T}
$$

$$
+ O\left(\sqrt{\frac{n}{T^3}}\right) \overset{d}{\to} N\left(B\sqrt{\rho}, \Omega\right).
$$

Thus, even when T grows as fast as n, asymptotic confidence intervals based on the fixed effects estimator will be incorrect, due to the limiting distribution of $\sqrt{nT}(\widehat{\theta} - \theta_0)$ not being centered at 0.

Similar to the bias of the fixed effects estimand $\theta_T - \theta_0$, the bias in the expected fixed effects score at θ_0 and the bias in the expected concentrated likelihood at an arbitrary θ can also be expanded in orders of magnitude of T:

$$E\left[\frac{1}{T}\sum_{t=1}^{T}\frac{\partial}{\partial\theta}\log f\left(y_{it}\mid\theta_0,\widehat{\alpha}_i\left(\theta_0\right)\right)\right]=\frac{1}{T}b_i\left(\theta_0\right)+o\left(\frac{1}{T}\right) \tag{2}$$

and

$$E\left[\frac{1}{T}\sum_{t=1}^{T}\log f\left(y_{it}\mid\theta,\widehat{\alpha}_i\left(\theta\right)\right)-\frac{1}{T}\sum_{t=1}^{T}\log f\left(y_{it}\mid\theta,\overline{\alpha}_i\left(\theta\right)\right)\right]$$
$$=\frac{1}{T}\beta_i\left(\theta\right)+o\left(\frac{1}{T}\right) \tag{3}$$

where $\overline{\alpha}_i(\theta)$ maximizes $\lim_{T\to\infty}E[T^{-1}\sum_{t=1}^{T}\log f(y_{it}\mid\theta,\alpha)]$. These expansions motivate alternative approaches to bias correction based on adjusting the estimator, the estimating equation, or the objective function. We next discuss these three approaches in turn. We shall refer to B/T, b_i/T, and β_i/T as the order $1/T$ biases of the fixed effects estimand, expected score, and expected concentrated likelihood, respectively.

3   BIAS CORRECTION OF THE ESTIMATOR

An analytical bias correction is to plug into the formula for B estimators of its unknown components to construct $\widehat{B}$, and then form a bias-corrected estimator

$$\widehat{\theta}^1\equiv\widehat{\theta}-\frac{\widehat{B}}{T}. \tag{4}$$

3.1   Formulae for the Order $1/T$ Bias

To implement this idea, we need to have an explicit formula for B. For this purpose, it is convenient to define

$$u_{it}\left(\theta,\alpha\right)\equiv\frac{\partial}{\partial\theta}\log f\left(y_{it}|\theta,\alpha\right),\quad v_{it}\left(\theta,\alpha\right)\equiv\frac{\partial}{\partial\alpha_i}\log f\left(y_{it}|\theta,\alpha\right),$$

$$V_{2it}\left(\theta,\alpha\right)\equiv v_{it}^2\left(\theta,\alpha\right)+\frac{\partial v_{it}\left(\theta,\alpha\right)}{\partial\alpha_i},$$

$$U_{it}\left(\theta,\alpha\right)\equiv u_{it}\left(\theta,\alpha\right)-v_{it}\left(\theta,\alpha\right)E\left[v_{it}^{\alpha_i}\right]^{-1}E\left[u_{it}^{\alpha_i}\right],$$

$$\mathcal{I}_i\equiv-E\left[\frac{\partial U_{it}\left(\theta_0,\alpha_{i0}\right)}{\partial\theta'}\right].$$

Note that $E\left[U_{it}^{\alpha_i}\right]=0$, which in the MLE case implies that U_{it} and v_{it} are orthogonalized. We will denote the derivative with respect to θ or α_i by appropriate superscripts, for example, $U_{it}^{\alpha_i}\left(\theta,\alpha\right)\equiv\partial U_{it}\left(\theta,\alpha\right)/\partial\alpha_i$, $U_{it}^{\alpha_i\alpha_i}\left(\theta,\alpha\right)\equiv\partial^2 U_{it}\left(\theta,\alpha\right)/\partial\alpha_i^2$. For notational convenience we suppress the arguments when expressions are evaluated at the true values θ_0 and α_{i0}, for example $v_{it}^{\alpha_i} = \partial v_{it}(\theta_0, \alpha_{i0})/\partial \alpha_i$.

It can be shown that

$$B = \left(\lim_{n \to \infty} \frac{1}{n} \sum_{i=1}^{n} \mathcal{I}_i \right)^{-1} \lim_{n \to \infty} \frac{1}{n} \sum_{i=1}^{n} b_i(\theta_0) \tag{5}$$

where $b_i(\theta_0)/T$ is the $1/T$ bias of the score function. It can also be shown that

$$b_i(\theta_0) = -\left(\frac{E\left[v_{it} U_{it}^{\alpha_i}\right]}{E\left[v_{it}^{\alpha_i}\right]} - \frac{E\left[U_{it}^{\alpha_i \alpha_i}\right] E\left[v_{it}^2\right]}{2\left(E\left[v_{it}^{\alpha_i}\right]\right)^2} \right). \tag{6}$$

or

$$b_i(\theta_0) = \left(\frac{-E\left[v_{it}^2\right]}{E\left[v_{it}^{\alpha_i}\right]} \right) \left[-\frac{1}{(-E\left[v_{it}^2\right])} \left(E\left[v_{it} u_{it}^{\alpha_i}\right] - E\left[v_{it} v_{it}^{\alpha_i}\right] \frac{E\left[u_{it}^{\alpha_i}\right]}{E\left[v_{it}^{\alpha_i}\right]} \right) \right.$$
$$\left. - \frac{1}{2E\left[v_{it}^{\alpha_i}\right]} \left(E\left[u_{it}^{\alpha_i \alpha_i}\right] - E\left[v_{it}^{\alpha_i \alpha_i}\right] \frac{E\left[u_{it}^{\alpha_i}\right]}{E\left[v_{it}^{\alpha_i}\right]} \right) \right]. \tag{7}$$

Intuition on the derivation of the bias of the score function is provided in Section 4. See also Hahn and Newey (2004), for example. The bias correction formula (5) does not depend on the likelihood setting, and so would be valid for any fixed effects m-estimator.

However, in the likelihood setting because of the information identity $E[v_{it}^2] = -E[v_{it}^{\alpha_i}]$ and the Bartlett equality

$$E\left[v_{it} U_{it}^{\alpha_i}\right] + \frac{1}{2} E\left[U_{it}^{\alpha_i \alpha_i}\right] = -\frac{1}{2} E\left[V_{2it} U_{it}\right], \tag{8}$$

we can alternatively write

$$B = \frac{1}{2} \left(\lim_{n \to \infty} \frac{1}{n} \sum_{i=1}^{n} \mathcal{I}_i \right)^{-1} \lim_{n \to \infty} \frac{1}{n} \sum_{i=1}^{n} \frac{E\left[U_{it} V_{2it}\right]}{E\left[v_{it}^{\alpha_i}\right]}. \tag{9}$$

In Example 1 with $\theta = \sigma^2$, we can see that

$$u_{it} = -\frac{1}{2\theta_0} + \frac{(y_{it} - \alpha_i)^2}{2\theta_0^2}, \quad v_{it} = \frac{y_{it} - \alpha_{i0}}{\theta_0}, \quad E\left[v_{it}^{\alpha_i}\right] = -\frac{1}{\theta_0}$$

$$E\left[u_{it} v_{it}\right] = 0, \quad U_{it} = u_{it} = -\frac{1}{2\theta_0} + \frac{(y_{it} - \alpha_{i0})^2}{2\theta_0^2},$$

$$E\left[\mathcal{I}_i\right] = \frac{1}{2\theta_0^2}, \quad V_{2it} = \frac{(y_{it} - \alpha_{i0})^2}{\theta_0^2} - \frac{1}{\theta_0},$$

$$E\left[U_{it} V_{2it}\right] = \frac{1}{\theta_0^2}, \quad \frac{E\left[U_{it} V_{2it}\right]}{E\left[v_{it}^{\alpha_i}\right]} = -\frac{1}{\theta_0},$$

$$B = -\frac{1}{2} \left(\frac{1}{2\theta_0^2} \right)^{-1} \frac{1}{\theta_0} = -\theta_0,$$

and we obtain

$$\widehat{\theta}^1 = \widehat{\theta} - \frac{\widehat{B}}{T} = \frac{T+1}{T}\widehat{\theta}.$$

Recall that $\widehat{\theta} = \theta_0 - \frac{1}{T}\theta_0 + o_p(1)$ as $n \to \infty$ with T fixed. It follows that

$$\widehat{\theta}^1 = \theta_0 - \frac{1}{T^2}\theta_0 + o_p(1),$$

which shows that the bias of order T^{-1} is removed.

3.2   Estimators of the Bias

An estimator of the bias term can be formed using a sample counterpart of the previous formulae. One possibility is

$$\widehat{B}(\theta) = \left(\frac{1}{n}\sum_{i=1}^{n}\widehat{\mathcal{I}}_i\right)^{-1}\frac{1}{n}\sum_{i=1}^{n}\widehat{b}_i(\theta) \tag{10}$$

where

$$\widehat{\mathcal{I}}_i = -\left(\widehat{E}_T\left[\widehat{u}_{it}^{\theta}\right] - \widehat{E}_T\left[\widehat{u}_{it}^{\alpha_i}\right]\widehat{E}_T\left[\widehat{v}_{it}^{\alpha_i}\right]^{-1}\widehat{E}_T\left[\widehat{u}_{it}^{\alpha_i\prime}\right]\right) \tag{11}$$

$$\widehat{b}_i(\theta) = \left(\frac{-\widehat{E}_T\left[\widehat{v}_{it}^2\right]}{\widehat{E}_T\left[\widehat{v}_{it}^{\alpha_i}\right]}\right)\left[-\frac{1}{(-\widehat{E}_T\left[\widehat{v}_{it}^2\right])}\left(\widehat{E}_T\left[\widehat{v}_{it}\widehat{u}_{it}^{\alpha_i}\right] - \widehat{E}_T\left[\widehat{v}_{it}\widehat{v}_{it}^{\alpha_i}\right]\frac{\widehat{E}_T\left[\widehat{u}_{it}^{\alpha_i}\right]}{\widehat{E}_T\left[\widehat{v}_{it}^{\alpha_i}\right]}\right)\right.$$
$$\left. -\frac{1}{2\widehat{E}_T\left[\widehat{v}_{it}^{\alpha_i}\right]}\left(\widehat{E}_T\left[\widehat{u}_{it}^{\alpha_i\alpha_i}\right] - \widehat{E}_T\left[\widehat{v}_{it}^{\alpha_i\alpha_i}\right]\frac{\widehat{E}_T\left[\widehat{u}_{it}^{\alpha_i}\right]}{\widehat{E}_T\left[\widehat{v}_{it}^{\alpha_i}\right]}\right)\right] \tag{12}$$

where $\widehat{E}_T(.) = \sum_{t=1}^{T}(.)/T$, $\widehat{u}_{it}^{\theta} = u_{it}^{\theta}(\theta,\widehat{\alpha}_i(\theta))$, $\widehat{u}_{it}^{\alpha_i} = u_{it}^{\alpha_i}(\theta,\widehat{\alpha}_i(\theta))$, etc. The bias corrected estimator can then be formed with $\widehat{B} = \widehat{B}(\widehat{\theta}_T)$.

The other possibility exploits the likelihood setting to replace some derivatives by outer product terms:

$$\widetilde{B}(\theta) = \left(\frac{1}{n}\sum_{i=1}^{n}\widetilde{\mathcal{I}}_i\right)^{-1}\frac{1}{n}\sum_{i=1}^{n}\widetilde{b}_i(\theta) \tag{13}$$

where

$$\widetilde{\mathcal{I}}_i = -\left(\widehat{E}_T\left[\widehat{u}_{it}\widehat{u}_{it}'\right] - \widehat{E}_T\left[\widehat{u}_{it}\widehat{v}_{it}\right]\widehat{E}_T\left[\widehat{v}_{it}^2\right]^{-1}\widehat{E}_T\left[\widehat{v}_{it}\widehat{u}_{it}'\right]\right)$$
$$= -\widehat{E}_T\left(\widehat{U}_{it}\widehat{U}_{it}'\right), \tag{14}$$

$$\widetilde{b}_i(\theta) = \frac{\sum_{t=1}^{T}\widehat{U}_{it}(\theta,\widehat{\alpha}_i(\theta))V_{2it}(\theta,\widehat{\alpha}_i(\theta))}{2\sum_{t=1}^{T}v_{it}^{\alpha_i}(\theta,\widehat{\alpha}_i(\theta))}, \tag{15}$$

and

$$\widehat{U}_{it} \equiv \widehat{U}_{it}\left(\theta, \widehat{\alpha}_i\left(\theta\right)\right) = u_{it}\left(\theta, \widehat{\alpha}_i\left(\theta\right)\right) - \frac{\widehat{E}_T\left[\widehat{u}_{it}\widehat{v}_{it}\right]}{\widehat{E}_T\left[\widehat{v}_{it}^2\right]} v_{it}\left(\theta, \widehat{\alpha}_i\left(\theta\right)\right),$$

(16)

so that an alternative bias correction can be formed with $\widetilde{B} = \widetilde{B}\left(\widehat{\theta}_T\right)$.

3.3 Infinitely Iterated Analytic Bias Correction

If $\widehat{\theta}$ is heavily biased and it is used in the construction of $\widehat{B}$, it may adversely affect the properties of $\widehat{\theta}^1$. One way to deal with this problem is to use $\widehat{\theta}^1$ in the construction of another $\widehat{B}$, and then form a new bias corrected estimator as in equation (4). One could even iterate this procedure, updating $\widehat{B}$ several times using the previous estimator of $\widehat{\theta}$. To be precise, let $\overline{B}(\theta)$ denote an estimator of B depending on θ, and suppose that $\widehat{B} = \overline{B}(\widehat{\theta})$. Then $\widehat{\theta}^1 = \widehat{\theta} - \overline{B}(\widehat{\theta})/T$. Iterating gives $\widehat{\theta}^k = \widehat{\theta} - \overline{B}(\widehat{\theta}^{k-1})/T$, $(k = 2, 3, \ldots)$. If this estimator were iterated to convergence, it would give $\widehat{\theta}^\infty$ solving

$$\widehat{\theta}^\infty = \widehat{\theta} - \overline{B}\left(\widehat{\theta}^\infty\right)/T.$$

(17)

In general this estimator will not have improved asymptotic properties, but may have lower bias for small T. In Example 1 with $\theta_0 = \sigma_0^2$, we can see that

$$\widehat{\theta}^k = \frac{T^k + T^{k-1} + \ldots + 1}{T^k}\widehat{\theta} = \frac{T^{k+1} - 1}{T^k(T-1)}\widehat{\theta} \to \frac{T}{T-1}\widehat{\theta} = \widehat{\theta}^\infty$$

as $k \to \infty$, and the limit $\widehat{\theta}^\infty$ has zero bias.

4 BIAS CORRECTION OF THE MOMENT EQUATION

Another approach to bias correction for fixed effects is to construct the estimator as the solution to a bias-corrected version of the first-order conditions. Recall that the expected fixed effects score has the $1/T$ bias equal to $b_i(\theta_0)$ at the true value, as noted in (2). Let us consider $\widehat{S}(\theta) = \sum_{i=1}^n \sum_{t=1}^T u_{it}(\theta, \widehat{\alpha}_i(\theta))/(nT)$, so that the fixed effects estimator solves $\widehat{S}(\widehat{\theta}_T) = 0$, and let $\widehat{b}_i(\theta)/T$ be an estimator of the $1/T$ bias of the expected score at the true value. A score-corrected estimator is obtained by solving the modified moment equation

$$\widehat{S}(\theta) - \frac{1}{nT}\sum_{i=1}^n \widehat{b}_i(\theta) = 0.$$

(18)

To understand the idea of correcting the moment equation and its connection to estimating B, it is convenient to note that the MLE $\widehat{\theta}$ is a solution to

$$\sum_{i=1}^{n}\sum_{t=1}^{T} u_{it}\left(\widehat{\theta},\widehat{\alpha}_i\right) = 0.$$

Consider an infeasible estimator $\overline{\theta}$ based on $\widehat{\alpha}_i\,(\theta_0)$ rather than $\widehat{\alpha}_i$, where $\overline{\theta}$ solves the first-order condition $0 = \sum_{i=1}^{n}\sum_{t=1}^{T} U_{it}\left(\overline{\theta},\widehat{\alpha}_i\,(\theta_0)\right)$. Standard arguments suggest that

$$\sqrt{nT}\left(\overline{\theta}-\theta_0\right) \approx \left(\frac{1}{n}\sum_{i=1}^{n}\mathcal{I}_i\right)^{-1}\frac{1}{\sqrt{nT}}\sum_{i=1}^{n}\sum_{t=1}^{T} U_{it}\left(\theta_0,\widehat{\alpha}_i\,(\theta_0)\right).$$

Because $E\left[U_{it}\left(\theta_0,\widehat{\alpha}_i\,(\theta_0)\right)\right] \neq 0$, we cannot apply the central limit theorem to the numerator on the right side. We use a second-order Taylor series expansion to approximate $U_{it}\left(\theta_0,\widehat{\alpha}_i\,(\theta_0)\right)$ around α_{i0}:

$$\frac{1}{\sqrt{nT}}\sum_{i=1}^{n}\sum_{t=1}^{T} U_{it}\left(\theta_0,\widehat{\alpha}_i\,(\theta_0)\right) \approx \frac{1}{\sqrt{nT}}\sum_{i=1}^{n}\sum_{t=1}^{T} U_{it}$$

$$+\frac{1}{\sqrt{nT}}\sum_{i=1}^{n}\sum_{t=1}^{T} U_{it}^{\alpha_i}\left(\widehat{\alpha}_i\,(\theta_0)-\alpha_{i0}\right)$$

$$+\frac{1}{2\sqrt{nT}}\sum_{i=1}^{n}\sum_{t=1}^{T} U_{it}^{\alpha_i\alpha_i}\left(\widehat{\alpha}_i\,(\theta_0)-\alpha_{i0}\right)^2.$$

The first term on the right will follow a central limit theorem because $E[U_{it}] = 0$. As for the second and third terms, we note that $\widehat{\alpha}_i(\theta_0) - \alpha_{i0} \approx -T^{-1}\sum_{t=1}^{T} v_{it}(E[v_{it}^{\alpha_i}])^{-1}$, and substituting for $\widehat{\alpha}_i(\theta_0) - \alpha_{i0}$ in the approximation for $U_{it}(\theta_0,\widehat{\alpha}_i(\theta_0))$ leads to

$$\sum_{i=1}^{n}\sum_{t=1}^{T} U_{it}\left(\theta_0,\widehat{\alpha}_i\,(\theta_0)\right) \approx \sum_{i=1}^{n}\sum_{t=1}^{T} U_{it}$$

$$-\sum_{i=1}^{n}\left[\frac{\sum_{t=1}^{T} v_{it}}{\sqrt{T}E\left[v_{it}^{\alpha_i}\right]}\right]\left[\frac{1}{\sqrt{T}}\sum_{t=1}^{T}\left(U_{it}^{\alpha_i}-\frac{E\left[U_{it}^{\alpha_i\alpha_i}\right]}{2E\left[v_{it}^{\alpha_i}\right]}v_{it}\right)\right]. \quad (19)$$

Taking an expectation of the second term on the right and subtracting it from the LHS, we expect that

$$\sum_{i=1}^{n}\sum_{t=1}^{T} U_{it}\left(\theta_0,\widehat{\alpha}_i\,(\theta_0)\right) + \sum_{i=1}^{n}\left(\frac{E\left[v_{it}U_{it}^{\alpha_i}\right]}{E\left[v_{it}^{\alpha_i}\right]}-\frac{E\left[U_{it}^{\alpha_i\alpha_i}\right]E\left[v_{it}^2\right]}{2\left(E\left[v_{it}^{\alpha_i}\right]\right)^2}\right)$$

$$=\sum_{i=1}^{n}\sum_{t=1}^{T} U_{it}\left(\theta_0,\widehat{\alpha}_i\,(\theta_0)\right) - \sum_{i=1}^{n} b_i\,(\theta_0)$$

is more centered at zero than $\sum_{i=1}^{n}\sum_{t=1}^{T} U_{it}(\theta_0,\widehat{\alpha}_i(\theta_0))$.

An estimator of the $1/T$ bias of the moment equation is given by $\widehat{b}_i(\theta)/T$ in (12). We then expect the solution to

$$\sum_{i=1}^{n}\left[\sum_{t=1}^{T}u_{it}(\theta,\widehat{\alpha}_i(\theta))-\widehat{b}_i(\theta)\right]=0 \tag{20}$$

to be less biased than the MLE $\widehat{\theta}_T$. Alternatively, the bias can be estimated using the estimator of the bias in (15) that exploits Bartlett identities, leading to the moment equation

$$\sum_{i=1}^{n}\left[\sum_{t=1}^{T}u_{it}(\theta,\widehat{\alpha}_i(\theta))-\widetilde{b}_i(\theta)\right]=0. \tag{21}$$

The first expression would be valid for any fixed effects m-estimator, whereas the second is appropriate in a likelihood setting. These two versions of bias-corrected moment equation are discussed in Hahn and Newey (2004).

In a likelihood setting it is also possible to form an estimate of $b_i(\theta)$ that uses expected rather than observed quantities, giving rise to alternative score-corrected estimators, such as those considered by Carro (2004) and Fernández-Val (2005) for binary choice models. To see a connection between bias correction of the moment equation and iterated bias correction of the estimator, it is useful to note that $\widehat{\theta}^{\infty}$ solves the equation $\widehat{\theta}-\theta=\overline{B}(\theta)/T$ or

$$\sum_{i=1}^{n}\left[\overline{\mathcal{I}}_i(\theta)\left(\widehat{\theta}-\theta\right)-\frac{1}{T}\overline{b}_i(\theta)\right]=0 \tag{22}$$

where $\overline{B}(\theta)$ is as in (10) or (13). This equation can be regarded as an approximation to the previous corrected moment equations as long as $\overline{\mathcal{I}}_i(\theta)$ is an estimator of $\partial\widehat{E}_T[u_{it}(\theta,\widehat{\alpha}_i(\theta))]/\partial\theta$ and $\overline{b}_i(\theta)/T$ is an estimator of the $1/T$ bias for $\widehat{E}_T[u_{it}(\theta,\widehat{\alpha}_i(\theta))]$. Thus, the bias correction of the moment equation can be loosely understood to be an infinitely iterated bias correction of the estimator.

5 BIAS CORRECTION OF THE CONCENTRATED LIKELIHOOD

Because of the noise of estimating $\widehat{\alpha}_i(\theta)$, the expectation of the concentrated likelihood is not maximized at the true value of the parameter [see (3)]. In this section, we discuss how such problem can be avoided by correcting the concentrated likelihood.

Let $\ell_i(\theta,\alpha)=\sum_{t=1}^{T}\ell_{it}(\theta,\alpha)/T$ where $\ell_{it}(\theta,\alpha)=\log f(y_{it}\mid\theta,\alpha)$ denotes the log likelihood of one observation. Moreover, let $\overline{\alpha}_i(\theta)=\operatorname{argmax}_\alpha\operatorname{plim}_{T\to\infty}\ell_i(\theta,\alpha)$, so that under regularity conditions $\overline{\alpha}_i(\theta_0)=\alpha_{i0}$. Following Severini (2000) and Pace and Salvan (2006), the concentrated log likelihood for unit i

$$\widehat{\ell}_i(\theta)=\ell_i(\theta,\widehat{\alpha}_i(\theta)) \tag{23}$$

can be regarded as an estimate of the unfeasible concentrated log likelihood

$$\bar{\ell}_i(\theta) = \ell_i(\theta, \bar{\alpha}_i(\theta)). \tag{24}$$

The function $\bar{\ell}_i(\theta)$ is a proper log likelihood which assigns data a density of occurrence according to values of θ and values of the effects along the curve $\bar{\alpha}_i(\theta)$. It is a least-favorable target log likelihood in the sense that the expected information for θ calculated from $\bar{\ell}_i(\theta)$ coincides with the partial expected information for θ (c.f. Stein, 1956; Severini and Wong, 1992; and Newey, 1990, for related discussion on semiparametric bounds). $\bar{\ell}_i(\theta)$ has the usual log likelihood properties: it has zero mean expected score, it satisfies the information matrix identity, and is maximized at θ_0.

Now, define

$$H_i(\theta) = -E\left[\frac{\partial v_{it}(\theta, \bar{\alpha}_i(\theta))}{\partial \alpha}\right], \quad \Upsilon_i(\theta) = E\left\{[v_{it}(\theta, \bar{\alpha}_i(\theta))]^2\right\}.$$

A stochastic expansion for an arbitrary fixed θ gives

$$\hat{\alpha}_i(\theta) - \bar{\alpha}_i(\theta) \approx H_i^{-1}(\theta) v_i(\theta, \bar{\alpha}_i(\theta)) \tag{25}$$

where $v_i(\theta, \alpha) = \sum_{t=1}^T v_{it}(\theta, \alpha)/T$. Next, expanding $\ell_i(\theta, \hat{\alpha}_i(\theta))$ around $\bar{\alpha}_i(\theta)$ for fixed θ, we get

$$\ell_i(\theta, \hat{\alpha}_i(\theta)) - \ell_i(\theta, \bar{\alpha}_i(\theta)) \approx v_i(\theta, \bar{\alpha}_i(\theta))[\hat{\alpha}_i(\theta) - \bar{\alpha}_i(\theta)]$$
$$- \frac{1}{2} H_i(\theta)[\hat{\alpha}_i(\theta) - \bar{\alpha}_i(\theta)]^2. \tag{26}$$

Substituting (25) we get

$$\ell_i(\theta, \hat{\alpha}_i(\theta)) - \ell_i(\theta, \bar{\alpha}_i(\theta)) \approx \frac{1}{2} H_i(\theta)[\hat{\alpha}_i(\theta) - \bar{\alpha}_i(\theta)]^2. \tag{27}$$

Taking expectations, we obtain

$$E[\ell_i(\theta, \hat{\alpha}_i(\theta)) - \ell_i(\theta, \bar{\alpha}_i(\theta))] \approx \frac{1}{2} H_i(\theta) Var[\hat{\alpha}_i(\theta)] \approx \frac{\beta_i(\theta)}{T}$$

where

$$\beta_i(\theta) = \frac{1}{2} H_i(\theta) Var\left(\sqrt{T}[\hat{\alpha}_i(\theta) - \bar{\alpha}_i(\theta)]\right) = \frac{1}{2} H_i^{-1}(\theta) \Upsilon_i(\theta). \tag{28}$$

Thus, we expect that

$$\sum_{i=1}^n \sum_{t=1}^T \ell_{it}(\theta, \hat{\alpha}_i(\theta)) - \sum_{i=1}^n \beta_i(\theta)$$

is a closer approximation to the target log likelihood than $\sum_{i=1}^{n} \sum_{t=1}^{T}$ $\ell_{it} (\theta, \widehat{\alpha}_i (\theta))$. Letting $\widehat{\beta}_i (\theta)$ be an estimated bias, we then expect an estimator $\widetilde{\theta}$ that solves

$$\widetilde{\theta} = \arg\max_{\theta} \sum_{i=1}^{n} \left[\sum_{t=1}^{T} \ell_{it} (\theta, \widehat{\alpha}_i (\theta)) - \widehat{\beta}_i (\theta) \right] \tag{29}$$

to be less biased than the MLE $\widehat{\theta}_T$.

We can consistently estimate $\beta_i (\theta)$ by

$$\widehat{\beta}_i (\theta) = \frac{1}{2} \left(-\frac{1}{T} \sum_{t=1}^{T} \frac{\partial v_{it} (\theta, \widehat{\alpha}_i (\theta))}{\partial \alpha} \right)^{-1} \frac{1}{T} \sum_{t=1}^{T} [v_{it} (\theta, \widehat{\alpha}_i (\theta))]^2 . \tag{30}$$

Using this form of $\widehat{\beta}_i (\theta)$ in (29), $\widetilde{\theta}$ solves the first-order conditions

$$\sum_{i=1}^{n} \sum_{t=1}^{T} u_{it} (\theta, \widehat{\alpha}_i (\theta)) - \sum_{i=1}^{n} \frac{\partial \widehat{\beta}_i (\theta)}{\partial \theta} = 0. \tag{31}$$

Because $\widehat{\alpha}_i (\theta)$ satisfies

$$0 = \sum_{t=1}^{T} v_{it} (\theta, \widehat{\alpha}_i (\theta)) , \tag{32}$$

we can obtain

$$\frac{\partial \widehat{\alpha}_i (\theta)}{\partial \theta} = -\frac{\sum_{t=1}^{T} v_{it}^{\theta} (\theta, \widehat{\alpha}_i (\theta))}{\sum_{t=1}^{T} v_{it}^{\alpha_i} (\theta, \widehat{\alpha}_i (\theta))} . \tag{33}$$

Using this equation and the fact $v_{it}^{\theta} = u_{it}^{\alpha_i}$, it follows that

$$\frac{\partial \widehat{\beta}_i (\theta)}{\partial \theta} = \widehat{b}_i (\theta) \tag{34}$$

where $\widehat{b}_i (\theta)$ corresponds to the estimated score bias in (12). Therefore, the first-order conditions from (29) and the bias corrected moment (20) are identical.

Moreover, in the likelihood context, we can consider a local version of the estimated bias constructed as an expansion of $\widehat{\beta}_i (\theta)$ at θ_0 using that at the truth $H_i^{-1} (\theta_0) \Upsilon_i (\theta_0) = 1$ (Pace and Salvan, 2006):

$$\widehat{\beta}_i (\theta) = \widetilde{\beta}_i (\theta) + O \left(\frac{1}{T} \right) \tag{35}$$

where

$$
\widetilde{\beta}_i(\theta) = -\frac{1}{2} \log \left(-\frac{1}{T} \sum_{t=1}^{T} \frac{\partial v_{it}(\theta, \widehat{\alpha}_i(\theta))}{\partial \alpha} \right)
$$

$$
+ \frac{1}{2} \log \left\{ \frac{1}{T} \sum_{t=1}^{T} [v_{it}(\theta, \widehat{\alpha}_i(\theta))]^2 \right\}. \tag{36}
$$

This form of the estimated bias leads to the modified concentrated likelihood

$$
\ell_i(\theta, \widehat{\alpha}_i(\theta)) + \frac{1}{2} \log \left\{ -\frac{1}{T} \sum_{t=1}^{T} \left[\frac{\partial v_{it}(\theta, \widehat{\alpha}_i(\theta))}{\partial \alpha} \right] \right\}
$$

$$
- \frac{1}{2} \log \left\{ \frac{1}{T} \sum_{t=1}^{T} [v_{it}(\theta, \widehat{\alpha}_i(\theta))]^2 \right\}. \tag{37}
$$

This adjustment was considered by DiCiccio and Stern (1993) and DiCiccio et al. (1996). They showed that (37) reduces the bias of the concentrated score to $O(1/T)$ in the likelihood setting. In fact, it can be shown that (37) is maximized at $\frac{1}{n(T-1)} \sum_{i=1}^{n} \sum_{t=1}^{T} (y_{it} - \overline{y}_i)^2$ in Example 1.

It can be easily shown that

$$
\frac{\partial \widetilde{\beta}_i(\theta)}{\partial \theta} = \frac{\widehat{E}_T \left[\widehat{v}_{it}^{\alpha_i} \right]}{\left(-\widehat{E}_T \left[\widehat{v}_{it}^2 \right] \right)} \widehat{b}_i(\theta). \tag{38}
$$

Therefore, the DiCiccio–Stern first-order condition is using a valid estimate of the concentrated score $1/T$ bias as long as the information identity holds, so that in general it will be appropriate in likelihood settings. Note that $\partial \widetilde{\beta}_i(\theta)/\partial \theta$ differs from $\widetilde{b}_i(\theta)$ in (15), which exploits Bartlett identities as well as the information equality.

In the likelihood setting it is also possible to form estimates of $H_i(\theta)$ and $\Upsilon_i(\theta)$ that use expected rather than observed quantities. An estimator of the bias of the form of (36) that uses the observed Hessian but an expectation-based estimate of the outer product term $\Upsilon_i(\theta)$ is closely related to Severini's (1998) approximation to the modified profile likelihood. Severini (2002) extends his earlier results to pseudo-ML estimation problems, and Sartori (2003) considers double asymptotic properties of modified concentrated likelihoods in the context of independent panel or stratified data with fixed effects.

6   OTHER APPROACHES LEADING TO BIAS CORRECTION

The incidental parameters problem in panel data models can be broadly viewed as a problem of inference in the presence of many nuisance parameters. The leading statistical approach under this circumstance has been to search for suitable modification of conditional or marginal likelihoods. The modified profile likelihood of Barndorff-Nielsen (1983) and the approximate conditional likelihood of Cox and Reid (1987) belong to this category [see Reid (1995) for an overview]. However, the Barndorff-Nielsen formula is not generally operational, and the one in Cox and Reid requires the availability of an orthogonal effect.

We begin with discussion of Cox and Reid's (1987) adjustment to the concentrated likelihood followed by Lancaster's (2002) proposal.

6.1   Approaches Based on Orthogonality

6.1.1   Cox and Reid's Adjusted Profile Likelihood Approach

Cox and Reid (1987) considered the general problem of inference for a parameter of interest in the presence of nuisance parameters. They proposed a first-order adjustment to the concentrated likelihood to take account of the estimation of the nuisance parameters.

Their formulation required information orthogonality between the two types of parameters. That is, that the information matrix be block diagonal between the parameters of interest and the nuisance parameters. Suppose that the individual likelihood is given by $\prod_{t=1}^{T} f(y_{it} \mid \theta, \alpha_i)$. In general, the information matrix for (θ, α_i) will not be block-diagonal, although it may be possible to reparameterize α_i as a function of θ and some η_i such that the information matrix for (θ, η_i) is block-diagonal (Cox and Reid explained how to construct orthogonal parameters).

The discussion of orthogonality in the context of panel data models is due to Lancaster (2000, 2002), together with a Bayesian proposal that we consider below. The nature of the adjustment in a fixed effects model and some examples were also discussed in Cox and Reid (1992).

In the panel context, the Cox–Reid (1987) approach maximizes

$$\sum_{i=1}^{n} \sum_{t=1}^{T} \ell_{it}\left(y_{it}; \theta, \widehat{\alpha}_i(\theta)\right) - \frac{1}{2} \sum_{i=1}^{n} \log\left(-\sum_{t=1}^{T} \frac{\partial^2 \ell_{it}\left(y_{it}; \theta, \widehat{\alpha}_i(\theta)\right)}{\partial \alpha_i^2}\right). \tag{39}$$

The adjusted profile likelihood function (39) was derived by Cox and Reid as an approximation to the conditional likelihood given $\widehat{\alpha}_i(\theta)$. Their approach was motivated by the fact that in an exponential family model, it is optimal to condition on sufficient statistics for the nuisance parameters, and these can be regarded as the MLE of nuisance parameters chosen in a form to be orthogonal to the parameters of interest. For more general problems the idea was to derive a concentrated likelihood for θ conditioned on the MLE $\widehat{\alpha}_i(\theta)$, having ensured via orthogonality that $\widehat{\alpha}_i(\theta)$ changes slowly with θ.

6.1.1.1 Relation to Bias Correction of the Moment Equation. It is useful to spell out the first-order condition corresponding to the adjusted profile likelihood:

$$
0 = \sum_{i=1}^{n} \left[\sum_{t=1}^{T} u_{it}\left(\theta, \widehat{\alpha}_i\left(\theta\right)\right) - \frac{1}{2} \frac{\sum_{t=1}^{T} u_{it}^{\alpha_i \alpha_i}\left(\theta, \widehat{\alpha}_i\left(\theta\right)\right)}{\sum_{t=1}^{T} v_{it}^{\alpha_i}\left(\theta, \widehat{\alpha}_i\left(\theta\right)\right)} \right.
$$
$$
\left. - \frac{1}{2} \frac{\sum_{t=1}^{T} v_{it}^{\alpha_i \alpha_i}\left(\theta, \widehat{\alpha}_i\left(\theta\right)\right) \frac{\partial \widehat{\alpha}_i\left(\theta\right)}{\partial \theta}}{\sum_{t=1}^{T} v_{it}^{\alpha_i}\left(\theta, \widehat{\alpha}_i\left(\theta\right)\right)} \right]
\tag{40}
$$

where we used the fact $v_{it}^{\theta} = u_{it}^{\alpha_i}$. Moreover, using equations (32) and (33), we obtain that the moment equation of the adjusted profile likelihood is equal to

$$
\sum_{i=1}^{n} \left[\sum_{t=1}^{T} u_{it}\left(\theta, \widehat{\alpha}_i\left(\theta\right)\right) - \widetilde{b}_i^{CR}\left(\theta\right) \right] = 0
\tag{41}
$$

where

$$
\widetilde{b}_i^{CR}\left(\theta\right) = \frac{1}{2} \frac{\widehat{E}_T\left[\widehat{u}^{\alpha_i \alpha_i}\right]}{\widehat{E}_T\left[\widehat{v}_{it}^{\alpha_i}\right]} - \frac{1}{2} \frac{\widehat{E}_T\left[\widehat{v}_{it}^{\alpha_i \alpha_i}\right] \widehat{E}_T\left[\widehat{u}_{it}^{\alpha_i}\right]}{\left(\widehat{E}_T\left[\widehat{v}_{it}^{\alpha_i}\right]\right)^2}.
\tag{42}
$$

Ferguson, Reid, and Cox (1991) showed that under orthogonality the expected moment equation has a bias of a smaller order of magnitude than the standard expected ML score.

Under information orthogonality $E\left[u_{it}^{\alpha_i}\right] = 0$ and $E\left[v_{it} u_{it}^{\alpha_i}\right] = -E\left[u_{it}^{\alpha_i \alpha_i}\right]$. Using these facts and the information identity, the bias formula (7) becomes

$$
b_i\left(\theta_0\right) = \frac{1}{2} \frac{E\left[u_{it}^{\alpha_i \alpha_i}\right]}{E\left[v_{it}^{\alpha_i}\right]}.
\tag{43}
$$

Comparison with the Cox–Reid moment equation adjustment $\widetilde{b}_i^{CR}\left(\theta\right)$ reveals that the latter has an extra term whose population counterpart is equal to zero under orthogonality. It can in fact be shown that this term does not contribute anything to the asymptotic distribution of the resultant estimator under the large n large T asymptotics.

6.1.1.2 Relation to Bias Correction of the Concentrated Likelihood. To see the connection between the Cox–Reid's adjustment, which requires orthogonalization, and the one derived from the bias-reduction perspective in the previous section, which does not, note that (37) can be written as

$$
\ell_i\left(\theta, \widehat{\alpha}_i\left(\theta\right)\right) - \frac{1}{2} \log\left\{ -\frac{1}{T} \sum_{t=1}^{T} \left[\frac{\partial v_{it}\left(\theta, \widehat{\alpha}_i\left(\theta\right)\right)}{\partial \alpha} \right] \right\}
$$
$$
- \frac{1}{2} \log \widehat{\mathrm{Var}}\left(\sqrt{T}\left(\widehat{\alpha}_i\left(\theta\right) - \bar{\alpha}_i\left(\theta\right)\right)\right)
\tag{44}
$$

where

$$\widehat{\text{Var}}\left(\sqrt{T}\left(\widehat{\alpha}_i\left(\theta\right) - \overline{\alpha}_i\left(\theta\right)\right)\right) = \frac{T\sum_{t=1}^{T}\left[v_{it}\left(\theta, \widehat{\alpha}_i\left(\theta\right)\right)\right]^2}{\left(\sum_{t=1}^{T}\left[v_{it}^{\alpha_i}\left(\theta, \widehat{\alpha}_i\left(\theta\right)\right)\right]\right)^2}. \tag{45}$$

Thus, a criterion of the form (44) can be regarded as a generalized Cox–Reid adjusted likelihood with an extra term given by an estimate of the variance of $\sqrt{T}\left(\widehat{\alpha}_i\left(\theta\right) - \overline{\alpha}_i\left(\theta\right)\right)$, which accounts for nonorthogonality (the discussion of this link is due to Pace and Salvan, 2006). Under orthogonality the extra term is irrelevant because the variance of $\widehat{\alpha}_i\left(\theta\right)$ does not change much with θ.

6.1.1.3 Other Features of Adjusted Likelihood Approach. We note that Cox and Reid's (1987) proposal and other methods in the same literature, were not developed to explicitly address the incidental parameter problem in the panel data context. Rather, they were concerned with inference in models with many nuisance parameters.

We also note that this class of approaches was not developed for the sole purpose of correcting for the bias of the resultant estimator. It was developed with the ambitious goal of making the modified concentrated likelihood behave like a proper likelihood, including the goal of stabilizing the behavior of the likelihood ratio statistic. We can see that it achieves some of these other goals at least in the context of Example 1, where it can be shown that

$$\widehat{\theta} = \frac{1}{n\left(T - 1\right)}\sum_{i=1}^{n}\sum_{t=1}^{T}\left(y_{it} - \overline{y}_i\right)^2$$

maximizes (39), and the second derivative of (39) delivers $\frac{2\theta^2}{n(T-1)}$ as the estimated variance of $\widehat{\theta}$. Because the actual variance of $\widehat{\theta}$ is equal to $\frac{2\theta^2}{n(T-1)}$, we can note that the Cox–Reid approach even takes care of the problem of correctly estimating the variance of the estimator. It is not clear whether such success is specific to the particular example, or not. More complete analysis of other aspects of inference such as variance estimation is beyond the scope of this survey.

6.1.2   Lancaster's (2002) Bayesian Inference

Lancaster (2002) proposed a method of Bayesian inference that is robust to the incidental parameters problem, which like Cox and Reid's method critically hinges on the availability of parameter orthogonality, which may not be feasible in many applications. Sweeting (1987) pointed out that such procedure is in fact approximately Bayesian. These approaches have been later generalized by Woutersen (2002) and Arellano (2003) to situations where orthogonality may not be available. Their generalizations are based on correcting the first-order condition of the adjusted profile likelihood estimator, and will be discussed in the next section.

In a Bayesian setting, fixed effects are integrated out of the likelihood with respect to the prior distribution conditional on the common parameters (and covariates, if present) $\pi\,(\alpha\mid\theta)$. In this way, we get an integrated (or random effects) log likelihood of the form

$$\ell_i^I\,(\theta) = \log\int e^{T\ell_i(\theta,\alpha)}\pi\,(\alpha\mid\theta)\,d\alpha.$$

As is well known, the problem with inferences from $\ell_i^I\,(\theta)$ is that they depend on the choice of prior for the effects and are not in general consistent with T fixed. It can be shown that under regularity conditions the maximizer of $\sum_i \ell_i^I\,(\theta)$ has a bias of order $O\,(1/T)$ regardless of $\pi\,(\alpha\mid\theta)$. However, if α and θ are information orthogonal, the bias can be reduced to $O\,\left(1/T^2\right)$.

Lancaster (2002) proposes to integrate out the fixed effects η_i by using a noninformative prior, say a uniform prior, and use the posterior mode as an estimate of θ. The idea is to rely on prior independence between fixed effects and θ, having chosen an orthogonal reparameterization, say $\alpha_i = \alpha\,(\theta,\eta_i)$, that separates the common parameter θ from the fixed effects η_i in the information matrix sense. In other words, his estimator $\widehat{\theta}_L$ takes the form

$$\widehat{\theta}_L = \underset{\theta}{\mathrm{argmax}}\int\cdots\int\prod_{i=1}^{n}\prod_{t=1}^{T} f\left(y_{it}\mid\theta,\alpha\,(\theta,\eta_i)\right)d\eta_1\cdots d\eta_n. \quad (46)$$

In Example 1 with $\theta = \sigma^2$, we have $E\,[u_{it}v_{it}] = 0$ so the reparameterization is unnecessary. Lancaster's estimator would therefore maximize

$$\int\cdots\int\prod_{i=1}^{n}\prod_{t=1}^{T}\frac{1}{\sqrt{\theta}}\exp\left(-\frac{(y_{it}-\alpha_i)^2}{2\theta}\right)d\alpha_1\cdots d\alpha_n$$

$$\propto\frac{1}{\left(\sqrt{\theta}\right)^{T-1}}\exp\left(-\frac{\sum_{i=1}^{n}\sum_{t=1}^{T}\left(y_{it}-\overline{y}_i\right)^2}{2\theta}\right),$$

and

$$\widehat{\theta}_L = \frac{1}{n\,(T-1)}\sum_{i=1}^{n}\sum_{t=1}^{T}\left(y_{it}-\overline{y}_i\right)^2.$$

Note that $\widehat{\theta}_L$ has a zero bias.

Asymptotic properties of $\widehat{\theta}_L$ are not yet fully worked out except in a small number of specific examples. It is in general expected $\widehat{\theta}_L$ removes bias only up to $O(T^{-1})$, although we can find examples where $\widehat{\theta}_L$ eliminates bias of even higher order.

6.2   Overcoming Infeasibility of Orthogonalization

The Cox–Reid and Lancaster approaches are successful only when the parameter of interest can be orthogonalized with respect to the nuisance parameters. In general, such reparameterization requires solving some partial differential equations, and the solution may not exist. Because parameter orthogonalization is not feasible in general, such approach cannot be implemented for arbitrary models. This problem can be overcome by adjusting the moment equation instead of the concentrated likelihood. We discuss two approaches in this regard, one introduced by Woutersen (2002) and the other by Arellano (2003). We will note that these two approaches result in identical estimators.

6.2.1   Woutersen's (2002) Approximation

Woutersen (2002) provided an insight on the role of Lancaster's posterior calculation in reducing the bias of the fixed effects. Assume for simplicity that the common parameter θ is orthogonal to α_i in the information sense, and no reparameterization is necessary to implement Lancaster's proposal. Given the posterior

$$\prod_{i=1}^{n} \left(\int \prod_{t=1}^{T} f\left(y_{it} \mid \theta, \alpha_i\right) d\alpha_i \right),$$

the first-order condition that characterize the posterior mode can be written as

$$0 = \sum_{i=1}^{n} \frac{\int \left(\sum_{t=1}^{T} u_{it}\left(\theta, \alpha_i\right)\right) \prod_{t=1}^{T} f\left(y_{it} \mid \theta, \alpha_i\right) d\alpha_i}{\int \prod_{t=1}^{T} f\left(y_{it} \mid \theta, \alpha_i\right) d\alpha_i}. \tag{47}$$

Woutersen (2002) pointed out that the ith summand on the right can be approximated by

$$\sum_{t=1}^{T} u_{it}\left(\theta, \widehat{\alpha}_i\left(\theta\right)\right) - \frac{1}{2} \frac{\sum_{t=1}^{T} u_{it}^{\alpha_i \alpha_i}\left(\theta, \widehat{\alpha}_i\left(\theta\right)\right)}{\sum_{t=1}^{T} v_{it}^{\alpha_i}\left(\theta, \widehat{\alpha}_i\left(\theta\right)\right)}$$

$$+ \frac{1}{2} \frac{\left(\sum_{t=1}^{T} v_{it}^{\alpha_i \alpha_i}\left(\theta, \widehat{\alpha}_i\left(\theta\right)\right)\right) \left(\sum_{t=1}^{T} u_{it}^{\alpha_i}\left(\theta, \widehat{\alpha}_i\left(\theta\right)\right)\right)}{\left(\sum_{t=1}^{T} v_{it}^{\alpha_i}\left(\theta, \widehat{\alpha}_i\left(\theta\right)\right)\right)^2},$$

where $\widehat{\alpha}_i\left(\theta\right)$ is a solution to $\sum_{t=1}^{T} v_{it}\left(\theta, \widehat{\alpha}_i\left(\theta\right)\right) = 0$. Therefore, Woutersen's estimator under parameter orthogonality is the solution to

$$0 = \sum_{i=1}^{n} \left[\sum_{t=1}^{T} u_{it}\left(\theta, \widehat{\alpha}_i\left(\theta\right)\right) - \frac{1}{2} \frac{\widehat{E}_T\left[\widehat{u}_{it}^{\alpha_i \alpha_i}\right]}{\widehat{E}_T\left[\widehat{v}_{it}^{\alpha_i}\right]} + \frac{1}{2} \frac{\widehat{E}_T\left[\widehat{v}_{it}^{\alpha_i \alpha_i}\right] \widehat{E}_T\left[\widehat{u}_{it}^{\alpha_i}\right]}{\left(\widehat{E}_T\left[\widehat{v}_{it}^{\alpha_i}\right]\right)^2} \right]. \tag{48}$$

Note that this estimator solves the same moment equation as Cox and Reid's moment equation (41).

Woutersen pointed out that the moment function

$$\bar{u}_{it}\left(\theta, \alpha\right) \equiv u_{it}\left(\theta, \alpha\right) - \rho_i\left(\theta, \alpha\right) v_{it}\left(\theta, \alpha\right) \tag{49}$$

where

$$\rho_i(\theta, \alpha) \equiv \frac{\int u_i^\alpha(y; \theta, \alpha) f_i(y; \theta, \alpha) dy}{\int v_i^\alpha(y; \theta, \alpha) f_i(y; \theta, \alpha) dy} \tag{50}$$

would satisfy the orthogonality requirement in the sense that at true values

$$E\left[\bar{u}_{it}^\alpha(\theta_0, \alpha_{i0})\right] = 0.$$

Recall that $U_{it}(\theta, \alpha_i) \equiv u_{it} - v_{it} E[v_{it}^2]^{-1} E[v_{it} u_{it}]$ defined in Section 3 cannot be used as a basis of estimation because the ratio $E[v_{it}^2]^{-1} E[v_{it} u_{it}]$ is not known in general. It was used only as a theoretical device to understand the asymptotic property of various estimators. On the other hand, $\rho(\theta_0, \alpha_{i0}) = E[v_{it}^\alpha]^{-1} E[u_{it}^\alpha] = E[v_{it}^2]^{-1} E[v_{it} u_{it}]$, so we can consider $\bar{u}_{it}(\theta, \alpha_i)$ as a feasible version of $U_{it}(\theta, \alpha_i)$. Woutersen's moment equation when parameter orthogonality is unavailable is therefore obtained by replacing $u_{it}(\theta, \widehat{\alpha}_i(\theta))$ in (48) by $\bar{u}_{it}(\theta, \widehat{\alpha}_i(\theta))$.

6.2.2   Arellano's (2003) Proposal

An orthogonal transformation is a function $\eta_i = \eta_i(\theta, \alpha)$ such that

$$\frac{\eta_{\theta i}}{\eta_{\alpha i}} = \rho_i(\theta, \alpha)$$

where $\eta_{\theta i} = \partial \eta_i / \partial \theta$, $\eta_{\alpha i} = \partial \eta_i / \partial \alpha$, and $\rho_i(\theta, \alpha)$ is given in (50). Such a function may or may not exist, and if it does it need not be unique.

Arellano (2003) considers a Cox and Reid's (1987) objective function that is written for some transformation of the effects $\eta_i = \eta_i(\theta, \alpha)$ and he rewrites it in terms of the original parameterization. The resulting criterion is given by (39) with the addition of the Jacobian of the transformation:

$$\sum_{t=1}^T \ell_{it}(y_{it}; \theta, \widehat{\alpha}_i(\theta)) - \frac{1}{2} \log\left(-\sum_{t=1}^T \frac{\partial^2 \ell_{it}(y_{it}; \theta, \widehat{\alpha}_i(\theta))}{\partial \alpha_i^2}\right)$$
$$+ \log\left(\widehat{\eta}_{\alpha i}\right)$$

where $\widehat{\eta}_{\alpha i} = \left(\eta_{\alpha i} \mid_{\alpha = \widehat{\alpha}_i(\theta)}\right)$. The corresponding moment equation is

$$\sum_{t=1}^T u_{it}(\theta, \widehat{\alpha}_i(\theta)) - \widetilde{b}_i^{CR}(\theta) + m_i(\theta)$$

where $\widetilde{b}_i^{CR}(\theta)$ is given in (42) and

$$m_i(\theta) = \frac{\partial}{\partial \theta} \log\left(\widehat{\eta}_{\alpha i}\right) = \frac{\widehat{\eta}_{\alpha \theta i}}{\widehat{\eta}_{\alpha i}} + \frac{\widehat{\eta}_{\alpha \alpha i}}{\widehat{\eta}_{\alpha i}} \frac{\partial \widehat{\alpha}_i(\theta)}{\partial \theta}$$
$$= \left(\frac{\partial}{\partial \alpha} \frac{\eta_{\theta i}}{\eta_{\alpha i}}\Big|_{\alpha = \widehat{\alpha}_i(\theta)}\right) - \frac{\widehat{\eta}_{\alpha \alpha i}}{\widehat{\eta}_{\alpha i}} \left(\frac{\widehat{E}_T\left[\widehat{u}_{it}^{\alpha_i}\right]}{\widehat{E}_T\left[\widehat{v}_{it}^{\alpha_i}\right]} - \frac{\widehat{\eta}_{\theta i}}{\widehat{\eta}_{\alpha i}}\right).$$

If $\eta_i(\theta, \alpha)$ is an orthogonal transformation

$$m_i(\theta) = \left.\frac{\partial \rho_i(\theta, \alpha)}{\partial \alpha}\right|_{\alpha=\widehat{\alpha}_i(\theta)} - \frac{\widehat{\eta}_{\alpha\alpha i}}{\widehat{\eta}_{\alpha i}}\left(\frac{\widehat{E}_T\left[\widehat{u}_{it}^{\alpha_i}\right]}{\widehat{E}_T\left[\widehat{v}_{it}^{\alpha_i}\right]} - \rho_i(\theta, \widehat{\alpha}_i(\theta))\right)$$

(51)

so that

$$m_i(\theta_0) = \left.\frac{\partial \rho_i(\theta_0, \alpha)}{\partial \alpha}\right|_{\alpha=\widehat{\alpha}_i(\theta_0)} + O\left(\frac{1}{T}\right).$$

Thus, regardless of the existence of an orthogonal transformation, it is always possible to obtain a locally orthogonal Cox and Reid moment equation. Arellano's moment equation is therefore obtained as

$$0 = \sum_{i=1}^{n}\left[\sum_{t=1}^{T} u_{it}(\theta, \widehat{\alpha}_i(\theta)) - \widetilde{b}_i^{CR}(\theta) + \left.\frac{\partial \rho_i(\theta, \alpha)}{\partial \alpha}\right|_{\alpha=\widehat{\alpha}_i(\theta)}\right], \qquad (52)$$

after supressing the transformation-specific term in (51) that is irrelevant for the purpose of bias reduction. Indeed, Carro (2004) has shown that Arellano's moment equation reduces the order of the score bias regardless of the existence of an information orthogonal reparameterization.

It can be shown that this moment equation is identical to Woutersen's (2002) moment equation. This can be shown in the following way. Now note that Woutersen's (2002) moment equation is equal to

$$0 = \sum_{i=1}^{n}\left[\sum_{t=1}^{T}\overline{u}_{it}(\theta, \widehat{\alpha}_i(\theta)) - \frac{1}{2}\frac{\sum_{t=1}^{T}\overline{u}_{it}^{\alpha_i\alpha_i}(\theta, \widehat{\alpha}_i(\theta))}{\sum_{t=1}^{T}v_{it}^{\alpha_i}(\theta, \widehat{\alpha}_i(\theta))}\right.$$
$$\left.+\frac{1}{2}\frac{\left(\sum_{t=1}^{T}v_{it}^{\alpha_i\alpha_i}(\theta, \widehat{\alpha}_i(\theta))\right)\left(\sum_{t=1}^{T}\overline{u}_{it}^{\alpha_i}(\theta, \widehat{\alpha}_i(\theta))\right)}{\left(\sum_{t=1}^{T}v_{it}^{\alpha_i}(\theta, \widehat{\alpha}_i(\theta))\right)^2}\right]. \qquad (53)$$

Using (32), we can obtain:

$$\sum_{t=1}^{T}\overline{u}_{it}(\theta, \widehat{\alpha}_i(\theta)) = \sum_{t=1}^{T}u_{it}(\theta, \widehat{\alpha}_i(\theta)),$$

$$\sum_{t=1}^{T}\overline{u}_{it}^{\alpha_i}(\theta, \widehat{\alpha}_i(\theta)) = \sum_{t=1}^{T}u_{it}^{\alpha_i}(\theta, \widehat{\alpha}_i(\theta))$$

$$-\left.\left(\sum_{t=1}^{T}v_{it}^{\alpha_i}(\theta, \widehat{\alpha}_i(\theta))\right)\rho_i(\theta, \alpha)\right|_{\alpha=\widehat{\alpha}_i(\theta)}$$

and

$$\sum_{t=1}^{T} \overline{u}_{it}^{\alpha_i \alpha_i} (\theta, \widehat{\alpha}_i (\theta)) = \sum_{t=1}^{T} u_{it}^{\alpha_i \alpha_i} (\theta, \widehat{\alpha}_i (\theta))$$

$$- \left(\sum_{t=1}^{T} v_{it}^{\alpha_i \alpha_i} (\theta, \widehat{\alpha}_i (\theta)) \right) \rho_i (\theta, \alpha)\big|_{\alpha = \widehat{\alpha}_i (\theta)}$$

$$- 2 \left(\sum_{t=1}^{T} v_{it}^{\alpha_i} (\theta, \widehat{\alpha}_i (\theta)) \right) \frac{\partial \rho_i (\theta, \alpha)}{\partial \alpha}\bigg|_{\alpha = \widehat{\alpha}_i (\theta)} .$$

Plugging these expressions to (53), we obtain after some simplification an alternative characterization of Woutersen's (2002) moment equation:

$$0 = \sum_{i=1}^{n} \left[\sum_{t=1}^{T} u_{it} (\theta, \widehat{\alpha}_i (\theta)) - \frac{1}{2} \frac{\sum_{t=1}^{T} u_{it}^{\alpha_i \alpha_i} (\theta, \widehat{\alpha}_i (\theta))}{\sum_{t=1}^{T} v_{it}^{\alpha_i} (\theta, \widehat{\alpha}_i (\theta))} \right.$$

$$\left. + \frac{1}{2} \frac{\left(\sum_{t=1}^{T} v_{it}^{\alpha_i \alpha_i} (\theta, \widehat{\alpha}_i (\theta)) \right) \left(\sum_{t=1}^{T} u_{it}^{\alpha_i} (\theta, \widehat{\alpha}_i (\theta)) \right)}{\left(\sum_{t=1}^{T} v_{it}^{\alpha_i} (\theta, \widehat{\alpha}_i (\theta)) \right)^2} + \frac{\partial \rho_i (\theta, \alpha)}{\partial \alpha}\bigg|_{\alpha = \widehat{\alpha}_i (\theta)} \right],$$

which can be seen to be identical to moment equation (52). We can therefore conclude that Woutesen's (2002) is identical to Arellano's (2003).

6.2.3   *Relation to Bias Correction of the Moment Equation*

The moment equation used by Woutersen, Arellano, and Carro can be written as

$$\sum_{i=1}^{n} \left[\sum_{t=1}^{T} u_{it} (\theta, \widehat{\alpha}_i (\theta)) - \widetilde{b}_i^W (\theta) \right] = 0 \tag{54}$$

where

$$\widetilde{b}_i^W (\theta) = \widetilde{b}_i^{CR} (\theta) - \frac{\partial \rho_i (\theta, \alpha)}{\partial \alpha}\bigg|_{\alpha = \widehat{\alpha}_i (\theta)}, \tag{55}$$

$$\widetilde{b}_i^{CR} (\theta) = \frac{1}{2 \widehat{E}_T \left[\widehat{v}_{it}^{\alpha_i} \right]} \left(\widehat{E}_T \left[\widehat{u}^{\alpha_i \alpha_i} \right] - \widehat{E}_T \left[\widehat{v}_{it}^{\alpha_i \alpha_i} \right] \frac{\widehat{E}_T \left[\widehat{u}_{it}^{\alpha_i} \right]}{\widehat{E}_T \left[\widehat{v}_{it}^{\alpha_i} \right]} \right),$$

and at true values

$$\frac{\partial \rho_i (\theta_0, \alpha_{i0})}{\partial \alpha} = \frac{1}{E \left[v_{it}^{\alpha} \right]} \left(E \left[u_{it}^{\alpha \alpha} \right] - E \left[v_{it}^{\alpha \alpha} \right] \frac{E \left[u_{it}^{\alpha} \right]}{E \left[v_{it}^{\alpha} \right]} \right)$$

$$+ \frac{1}{E \left[v_{it}^{\alpha} \right]} \left(E \left[u_{it}^{\alpha} v_{it} \right] - E \left[v_{it}^{\alpha} v_{it} \right] \frac{E \left[u_{it}^{\alpha} \right]}{E \left[v_{it}^{\alpha} \right]} \right). \tag{56}$$

Comparing the resulting expression with the theoretical bias (7), we note that moment condition (54) is using a valid estimate of the concentrated score $1/T$ bias as long as the information identity holds, so that in general it will be appropriate in likelihood settings. The estimated bias $\widetilde{b}_i^W(\theta)$ uses a combination of observed and expected terms. Note that, contrary to the situation under orthogonality when the theoretical bias reduces to (43), there is no redundant term here.

The term $\partial \rho_i(\theta, \widehat{\alpha}_i(\theta))/\partial\alpha$ in (52) can be interpreted as a measure of how much the variance of $\widehat{\alpha}_i(\theta)$ changes with θ. In this respect, note the equivalence between the derivative of the log variance of $\widehat{\alpha}_i(\theta)$ in (45) and a sample counterpart of (56):

$$
-\frac{\partial}{\partial\theta}\frac{1}{2}\log\widehat{\mathrm{Var}}\left(\sqrt{T}\left(\widehat{\alpha}_i(\theta)-\overline{\alpha}_i(\theta)\right)\right)
$$

$$
=\frac{1}{\widehat{E}_T\left[v_{it}^{\alpha_i}\right]}\left(\widehat{E}_T\left[\widehat{u}_{it}^{\alpha_i\alpha_i}\right]-\widehat{E}_T\left[\widehat{v}_{it}^{\alpha_i\alpha_i}\right]\frac{\widehat{E}_T\left[\widehat{u}_{it}^{\alpha_i}\right]}{\widehat{E}_T\left[\widehat{v}_{it}^{\alpha_i}\right]}\right)
$$

$$
+\frac{1}{\left(-\widehat{E}_T\left[\widehat{v}_{it}^2\right]\right)}\left(\widehat{E}_T\left[\widehat{u}_{it}^{\alpha_i}\widehat{v}_{it}\right]-\widehat{E}_T\left[\widehat{v}_{it}^{\alpha_i}\widehat{v}_{it}\right]\frac{\widehat{E}_T\left[\widehat{u}_{it}^{\alpha_i}\right]}{\widehat{E}_T\left[\widehat{v}_{it}^{\alpha_i}\right]}\right). \quad (57)
$$

7   QMLE FOR DYNAMIC MODELS

The starting point of our discussion so far has been the assumption that the fixed effects estimator actually maximizes the likelihood. When we defined $\widehat{\theta}_T$ to be a maximizer of

$$
\sum_{i=1}^n\sum_{t=1}^T\log f\left(y_{it}\mid\theta,\widehat{\alpha}_i(\theta)\right),
$$

we assumed that (i) xs are strictly exogenous, (ii) ys are independent over t given xs, and (iii) f is the correct (conditional) density of y given x. We noted that some of the bias correction methods did not depend on the likelihood setting, while others, that relied on the information or Bartlett identities, did. However, in all cases assumptions (i) and (ii) were maintained. For example, if the binary response model

$$
y_{it}=1\left(x_{it}'\theta+\alpha_i+e_{it}>0\right), \quad (58)
$$

where the marginal distribution of e_{it} is $\mathcal{N}(0,1)$, is such that e_{it} is independent over t, and if it is estimated by nonlinear least squares, our first bias formula is valid.

In the likelihood setting, assumption (ii) can be relaxed choosing estimates of bias corrections that use expected rather than observed quantities. This is possible because the likelihood fully specifies the dynamics, and it is simple if the required expected quantities have closed form expressions, as in the dynamic probit models in Carro (2004) and Fernández-Val (2005).

In a nonlikelihood setting, our analysis can be generalized to the case when the fixed effects estimator maximizes

$$\sum_{i=1}^{n} \sum_{t=1}^{T} \psi \left(z_{it}; \theta, \widehat{\alpha}_i \left(\theta \right) \right)$$

for an arbitrary ψ under some regularity conditions, thereby relaxing assumptions (i) and (ii). For example, the binary response model (58) can still be analyzed by considering the fixed effects probit MLE even when e_{it} has an arbitrary unknown serial correlation.

The intuition for this more general model can still be obtained from the approximation of the moment equation as in (19), which can be corrected by calculating the approximate expectation of the correction term

$$\sum_{i=1}^{n} \left[\frac{\sum_{t=1}^{T} v_{it}}{\sqrt{T} E \left[v_{it}^{\alpha_i} \right]} \right] \left[\frac{1}{\sqrt{T}} \sum_{t=1}^{T} \left(U_{it}^{\alpha_i} - \frac{E \left[U_{it}^{\alpha_i \alpha_i} \right]}{2 E \left[v_{it}^{\alpha_i} \right]} v_{it} \right) \right].$$

The analysis for this more general model gets to be more complicated because calculation of the expectation should incorporate the serial correlation in v_{it} and $U_{it}^{\alpha_i}$, which was a non-issue in the simpler context. Hahn and Kuersteiner (2004) provide an analysis that incorporate such complication.

8   ESTIMATION OF MARGINAL EFFECTS

It is sometimes of interest to estimate quantities such as

$$\frac{1}{nT} \sum_{i=1}^{n} \sum_{t=1}^{T} m \left(z_{it}; \theta, \alpha_i \right) \tag{59}$$

where $z_{it} = \left(y_{it}, x_{it}' \right)'$. For example, it may be of interest to estimate the mean marginal effects

$$\frac{1}{nT} \sum_{i=1}^{n} \sum_{t=1}^{T} \phi \left(x_{it}' \theta + \alpha_i \right) \theta$$

for the binary response model (58), where ϕ denotes the density of $\mathcal{N}\left(0, 1\right)$. It would be sensible to estimate such quantities by

$$\frac{1}{nT} \sum_{i=1}^{n} \sum_{t=1}^{T} m \left(z_{it}; \widetilde{\theta}, \widehat{\alpha}_i \left(\widetilde{\theta} \right) \right)$$

where $\widetilde{\theta}$ denotes a bias-corrected version of $\widehat{\theta}$ computed by one of the methods discussed before, and $\widehat{\alpha}_i(\widetilde{\theta})$ denotes the estimate of α_i at $\widetilde{\theta}$. Hahn and Newey (2004), Carro (2004), and Fernandez-Val (2005) discuss estimation and bias correction of such quantity.

To relate our discussion with the bias-correction formula developed there, it is useful to think about the quantity (59) as a solution to the (infeasible) moment equation

$$
\sum_{i=1}^{n} \sum_{t=1}^{T} (m\,(z_{it}; \widehat{\alpha}_i\,(\theta_0)) - \widehat{\mu}) = 0, \quad \sum_{t=1}^{T} v\,(z_{it}; \widehat{\alpha}_i\,(\theta_0)) = 0 \tag{60}
$$

where, for simplicity of notation, we suppressed the dependence of m on θ. Let

$$
M\,(z_{it}; \alpha_i) = m\,(z_{it}; \alpha_i) - v\,(z_{it}; \alpha_i) \frac{E\,[m^{\alpha_i}\,(z_{it}; \alpha_i)]}{E\,[v^{\alpha_i}\,(z_{it}; \alpha_i)]}
$$

and note that $\widehat{\mu}$ in (60) solves

$$
0 = \sum_{i=1}^{n} \sum_{t=1}^{T} (M\,(z_{it}; \widehat{\alpha}_i\,(\theta_0)) - \widehat{\mu}). \tag{61}
$$

Assuming that serial correlation can be ignored, we can bias-correct this moment equation using the same intuition as in Section 4. We then obtain a bias-corrected version of the moment equation

$$
0 = \sum_{i=1}^{n} \sum_{t=1}^{T} \left(M\,(z_{it}; \widehat{\alpha}_i\,(\theta_0)) - \widehat{\widehat{\mu}} \right)
$$
$$
+ \sum_{i=1}^{n} \left(\frac{\sum_{t=1}^{T} v_{it} M_{it}^{\alpha_i}}{\sum_{t=1}^{T} v_{it}^{\alpha_i}} + \frac{\sum_{t=1}^{T} M_{it}^{\alpha_i \alpha_i}}{2 \left(\sum_{t=1}^{T} v_{it}^{\alpha_i} \right)} \right) \tag{62}
$$

when the fixed effects estimator is based on a correctly specified likelihood, or

$$
0 = \sum_{i=1}^{n} \sum_{t=1}^{T} \left(M\,(z_{it}; \widehat{\alpha}_i\,(\theta_0)) - \widehat{\widehat{\mu}} \right)
$$
$$
+ \sum_{i=1}^{n} \left(\frac{\sum_{t=1}^{T} v_{it} M_{it}^{\alpha_i}}{\sum_{t=1}^{T} v_{it}^{\alpha_i}} - \frac{\left(\sum_{t=1}^{T} v_{it}^{2} \right) \left(\sum_{t=1}^{T} M_{it}^{\alpha_i \alpha_i} \right)}{2 \left(\sum_{t=1}^{T} v_{it}^{\alpha_i} \right)^{2}} \right) \tag{63}
$$

in general. Replacing $M\,(z_{it}; \theta_0, \widehat{\alpha}_i\,(\theta_0))$ in (62) by the feasible version

$$
m\,(z_{it}; \widetilde{\theta}, \widehat{\alpha}_i\,(\widetilde{\theta})) - v\,(z_{it}; \widetilde{\theta}, \widehat{\alpha}_i\,(\widetilde{\theta})) \frac{\sum_{t=1}^{T} m^{\alpha_i}\,(z_{it}; \widetilde{\theta}, \widehat{\alpha}_i\,(\widetilde{\theta}))}{\sum_{t=1}^{T} v^{\alpha_i}\,(z_{it}; \widetilde{\theta}, \widehat{\alpha}_i\,(\widetilde{\theta}))},
$$

we obtain the same bias-corrected estimator $\widehat{\widehat{\mu}}$ as in Hahn and Newey (2004), and Fernandez-Val (2005).

9 AUTOMATIC METHODS

We have so far discussed methods of bias correction based on some analytic formulae. Depending on applications, we may be able to by-pass such analysis, and rely on numerical methods. We discuss two such procedures here.

9.1   Panel Jackknife

The panel jackknife is an automatic method of bias correction. To describe it, let $\widehat{\theta}_{(t)}$ be the fixed effects estimator based on the subsample excluding the observations of the tth period. The jackknife estimator is

$$\widetilde{\theta} \equiv T\widehat{\theta} - (T - 1)\sum_{t=1}^{T}\widehat{\theta}_{(t)}/T \tag{64}$$

or

$$\widetilde{\theta} \equiv \widehat{\theta} - \frac{\widetilde{B}}{T}, \qquad \frac{\widetilde{B}}{T} = (T - 1)\left(\frac{1}{T}\sum_{t=1}^{T}\widehat{\theta}_{(t)} - \widehat{\theta}\right).$$

To explain the bias correction from this estimator it is helpful to consider a further expansion

$$\theta_T = \theta_0 + \frac{B}{T} + \frac{D}{T^2} + O\left(\frac{1}{T^3}\right). \tag{65}$$

The limit of $\widetilde{\theta}$ for fixed T and how it changes with T shows the effect of the bias correction. The estimator $\widetilde{\theta}$ will converge in probability to

$$T\theta_T - (T - 1)\theta_{T-1} = \theta_0 + \left(\frac{1}{T} - \frac{1}{T-1}\right)D + O\left(\frac{1}{T^2}\right)$$

$$= \theta_0 + O\left(\frac{1}{T^2}\right) \tag{66}$$

or

$$(T - 1)(\theta_{T-1} - \theta_T) = \frac{B}{T} + O\left(\frac{1}{T^2}\right).$$

Thus, we see that the asymptotic bias of the jackknife corrected estimator is of order $1/T^2$. Consequently, this estimator will have an asymptotic distribution centered at 0 when $n/T \to \rho$. Hahn and Newey (2004) formally established that $\sqrt{nT}\,(\widetilde{\theta} - \theta_0)$ has the same asymptotic variance as $\sqrt{nT}\,(\widehat{\theta} - \theta_0)$ when $n/T \to \rho$. This implies that the bias reduction is achieved without any increase in the asymptotic variance. This suggests that, although there may be some small increase in variance as a result of bias reduction, the increase is so small that it is ignored when $n/T \to \rho$.

In Example 1, it is straightforward to show that

$$\widetilde{\theta} = \frac{1}{n(T - 1)}\sum_{i=1}^{n}\sum_{t=1}^{T}(y_{it} - \bar{y}_i)^2, \tag{67}$$

which is the estimator that takes care of the degrees of freedom problem. It is interesting to note that the jackknife bias correction completely removed bias in this example: $E(\widetilde{\theta}) = \theta$. This happens only because the $O(T^{-2})$ term is identically equal to zero in this particular example, which is not expected to happen too often in practice.

It is natural to speculate that a higher-order version of the panel jackknife may correct even higher-order bias. For this purpose, assume that an expansion even higher than (65) is valid:

$$\theta_T = \theta_0 + \frac{B}{T} + \frac{D}{T^2} + \frac{F}{T^3} + \frac{G}{T^4} + O\left(\frac{1}{T^5}\right).$$

Because

$$\frac{1}{2}T^2\theta_T - (T-1)^2\,\theta_{T-1} + \frac{1}{2}\,(T-2)^2\,\theta_{T-2}$$

$$= \theta_0 + \frac{F}{T\,(T-1)\,(T-2)} + \frac{3T^2 - 6T + 2}{T^2\,(T-1)^2\,(T-2)^2}G + O\left(\frac{1}{T^3}\right)$$

$$= \theta + O\left(\frac{1}{T^3}\right),$$

we can conjecture that an estimator of the form

$$\widetilde{\widetilde{\theta}} \equiv \frac{1}{2}T^2\widehat{\theta} - (T-1)^2\,\frac{\sum_{s=1}^{T}\widehat{\theta}_{(s)}}{T} + \frac{1}{2}\,(T-2)^2\,\frac{\sum_{s\neq s'}\widehat{\theta}_{(s,s')}}{T\,(T-1)},$$

where $\widehat{\theta}_{(s,s')}$ denotes the delete-2 estimator, will be centered at zero even at the asymptotics where $n = o\left(T^5\right)$.

The panel jackknife is easiest to understand when y_{it} is independent over time. When it is serially correlated, which is to be expected in many applications, it is not yet clear how it should be modified. To understand the gist of the problem, it is useful to investigate the role of $\sum_{t=1}^{T}\widehat{\theta}_{(t)}/T$ in (64). Note that it is the sample analog of θ_{T-1} in (66). When y_{it} is serially correlated, what should be used as the sample analog? One natural candidate is to use the same formula as in (64), with the understanding that $\widehat{\theta}_{(t)}$ should be the MLE maximizing the likelihood of $(y_{i1}, \ldots, y_{i,t-1}, y_{i,t+1}, \ldots, y_T)\,i = 1, \ldots, n$. We are not aware of any formal result that establishes the asymptotic properties of the panel jackknife estimator, even in the simple dynamic panel model where $y_{it} = \alpha_i + \theta\,y_{i,t-1} + \varepsilon_{it}$ with $\varepsilon_{it} \sim \mathcal{N}\left(0, \sigma^2\right)$. Even if this approach is shown to have a desirable asymptotic property, we should bear in mind that such approach requires complete parametric specification of the distribution of $(y_{i1}, \ldots, y_{iT})$. In many applications, we do not have a complete specification of the likelihood.

Another possibility is to use $\widehat{\theta}_{(T)}$ as the sample analog of θ_{T-1}. Note that $\widehat{\theta}_{(T)}$ is the MLE based on the first $T - 1$ observations. It turns out that such procedure will be accompanied by some large increase in variance. To understand this problem, it is useful to examine Example 1 again. It can be shown that

$$\widehat{\theta}_{(T-1)} = \frac{T}{T-1}\widehat{\theta} - \frac{T}{n\,(T-1)^2}\sum_{i=1}^{n}\left(\bar{y}_i - y_{iT}\right)^2$$

and therefore,

$$T\widehat{\theta} - (T-1)\widehat{\theta}_{(T-1)} = \frac{T}{n(T-1)} \sum_{i=1}^{n} \left(\bar{y}_i - y_{iT}\right)^2.$$

We can write with some abuse of notation that $T\widehat{\theta} - (T-1)\widehat{\theta}_{(T-1)} \sim \frac{\theta_0}{n}\chi_n^2$, whereas $\widetilde{\theta}$ in (67) is distributed as $\frac{\theta_0}{n(T-1)}\chi_{n(T-1)}^2$. This implies that (i) $T\widehat{\theta} - (T-1)\widehat{\theta}_{(T-1)}$ is indeed bias free; and (ii) the variance of $T\widehat{\theta} - (T-1)\widehat{\theta}_{(T-1)}$ is $T-1$ times as large as that of as the jackknife estimator $\widetilde{\theta}$. When T is sufficiently large, this delete-last-observation approach will be unacceptable. We expect a similar problem when y_{it} is subject to serial correlation, and eliminate $T\widehat{\theta} - (T-1)\widehat{\theta}_{(T-1)}$ from our consideration.

We argued that the panel jackknife may not be attractive when serial correlation is suspected. The bootstrap is another way of reducing bias. A time series version of the bootstrap is block-bootstrap, which has been shown in many occasions to have desirable properties. We conjecture that some version of a bootstrap bias correction would also remove the asymptotic bias (e.g., with truncation as in Hahn, Kuersteiner, and Newey, 2002).

9.2   Bootstrap-Adjusted Concentrated Likelihood

Simulation methods can also be used for bias correction of moment equations and objective functions. Pace and Salvan (2006) have suggested a bootstrap approach to adjust the concentrated likelihood.

Consider generating parametric bootstrap samples $\{y_{i1}(r), \ldots, y_{iT}(r)\}_{i=1}^{n}$ $(r = 1, \ldots, R)$ from the models $\{\prod_{t=1}^{T} f(y_t \mid \widehat{\theta}, \widehat{\alpha}_i)\}_{i=1}^{n}$ to obtain $\widehat{\alpha}_i^{[r]}(\theta)$ as the solution to

$$\widehat{\alpha}_i^{[r]}(\theta) = \underset{\alpha}{\mathrm{argmax}} \sum_{t=1}^{T} \log f\left(y_{it}(r) \mid \theta, \alpha\right) \quad (r = 1, \ldots, R).$$

Pace and Salvan's (2006) simulation adjusted log-likelihood for the ith unit is

$$\bar{\ell}_i^S(\theta) = \frac{1}{R} \sum_{r=1}^{R} \sum_{t=1}^{T} \ell_{it}\left(\theta, \widehat{\alpha}_i^{[r]}(\theta)\right). \tag{68}$$

The criterion $\bar{\ell}_i^S(\theta)$ is invariant under one-to-one reparameterizations of α_i that leave θ fixed (invariant under "interest respecting reparameterizations").

Alternatively, Pace and Salvan consider the form in (30), using a bootstrap estimate of $V_i[\widehat{\alpha}_i(\theta)]$ given by

$$\widetilde{V}_i[\widehat{\alpha}_i(\theta)] = \frac{1}{R} \sum_{r=1}^{R} \left[\widehat{\alpha}_i^{[r]}(\theta) - \widehat{\alpha}_i(\theta)\right]^2, \tag{69}$$

which leads to

$$\bar{\ell}_i^{SA}(\theta) = \sum_{t=1}^{T} \ell_{it}(\theta, \widehat{\alpha}_i(\theta)) - \frac{1}{2}\left(-\frac{1}{T}\sum_{t=1}^{T}\frac{\partial v_{it}(\theta, \widehat{\alpha}_i(\theta))}{\partial\alpha}\right)\widetilde{V}_i[\widehat{\alpha}_i(\theta)]. \quad (70)$$

10 CONCLUDING REMARKS

We discussed a variety of methods of estimation of nonlinear fixed effects panel data models with reduced bias properties. Alternative approaches to bias correction based on adjusting the estimator, the moment equation, and the criterion function have been considered. We have also discussed approaches relying on orthogonalization and automatic methods, as well as the connections among the various approaches.

All the approaches that we discuss in the paper are based on an asymptotic approximation where n and T grow to infinity at the same rate. Therefore, they are likely to be useful in applications in which the value of T is not negligible relative to n. Examples of this kind include data sets constructed from country or regional level macropanels, the balance-sheet-based company panels that are available in many countries, or the household incomes panel in the US (PSID). However, for n too large relative to T, the sampling distributions of the $1/T$ bias-corrected estimators will not provide accurate confidence intervals because their standard deviation will be small relative to bias. In those situations, an asymptotic approximation where n/T^3 converges to a constant may be called for, leading to $1/T^2$ bias-corrected estimators. A more general issue is how good are the n and T asymptotic approximations when the objective is to produce confidence intervals, or to test a statistical hypothesis. This is a question beyond the scope of this paper.

Next in the agenda, it is important to find out how well each of these bias correction methods work for specific models and data sets of interest in applied econometrics. In this regard, the Monte Carlo results and empirical estimates obtained by Carro (2004) and Fernández-Val (2005) for binary choice models are very encouraging. For a dynamic logit model, using the same simulation design as in Honoré and Kyriazidou (2000), they find that a score-corrected estimator and two one-step analytical bias-corrected estimators are broadly comparable to the Honoré–Kyriazidou estimator (which is consistent for fixed T) when $T = 8$ and $n = 250$. However, the finite sample properties of the bias correction seem to depend on how they are done. For dynamic logit, Carro's score-corrected estimator and Fernández-Val's bias-corrected estimator, which use expected quantities, are somewhat superior to a bias-corrected estimator using observed quantities, but more results are needed for other models and simulation designs.

We have focused on bias reduction, but other theoretical properties should play a role in narrowing the choice of bias-reducing estimation methods. In the likelihood context it is natural to seek an adjusted concentrated likelihood that behaves like a proper likelihood. In this respect, information bias reduction and invariance to reparameterization are relevant properties in establishing the relative merits of different bias-reducing estimators.

References

AMEMIYA, T. (1985): *Advanced Econometrics*, Oxford: Basil Blackwell.

ANDERSEN, E. (1970): "Asymptotic Properties of Conditional Maximum Likelihood Estimators," *Journal of the Royal Statistical Society, Series B*, 32, 283–301.

ARELLANO, M. (2003): "Discrete Choices with Panel Data," *Investigaciones Económicas*, 27, 423–458.

BARNDORFF-NIELSEN, O. E. (1983): "On a Formula for the Distribution of the Maximum Likelihood Estimator," *Biometrika*, 70, 343–365.

CARRO, J. (2004): "Estimating Dynamic Panel Data Discrete Choice Models with Fixed Effects," Unpublished manuscript.

CHAMBERLAIN, G. (1980): "Analysis of Covariance with Qualitative Data," *Review of Economic Studies*, 47, 225–238.

——— (1992): "Binary Response Models for Panel Data: Identification and Information," Unpublished manuscript.

COX, D. R. AND N. REID (1987): "Parameter Orthogonality and Approximate Conditional Inference" (with discussion), *Journal of the Royal Statistical Society, Series B*, 49, 1–39.

——— (1992): "A Note on the Difference Between Profile and Modified Profile Likelihood," *Biometrika*, 79, 408–411.

DICICCIO, T. J. AND S. E. STERN (1993): "An adjustment to Profile Likelihood Based on Observed Information," Technical Report, Department of Statistics, Stanford University.

DICICCIO, T. J., M. A. MARTIN, S. E. STERN, and G. A. YOUNG (1996): "Information Bias and Adjusted Profile Likelihoods," *Journal of the Royal Statistical Society, Series B*, 58, 189–203.

FERGUSON, H., N. REID, AND D. R. COX (1991): "Estimating Equations from Modified Profile Likelihood," in *Estimating Functions*, edited by V. P. Godambe, Oxford: Oxford University Press.

FERNÁNDEZ-VAL, I. (2005): "Estimation of Structural Parameters and Marginal Effects in Binary Choice Panel Data Models with Fixed Effects," Unpublished manuscript.

HAHN, J. (2001): "The Information Bound of a Dynamic Panel Logit Model with Fixed Effects," *Econometric Theory*, 17, 913–932.

HAHN, J. AND G. KUERSTEINER (2004): "Bias Reduction for Dynamic Nonlinear Panel Models with Fixed effects," Unpublished manuscript.

HAHN, J., G. KUERSTEINER, AND W. K. NEWEY (2002): "Higher Order Properties of Bootstrap and Jackknife Bias Corrected Maximum Likelihood Estimators," Unpublished manuscript.

HAHN, J. AND W. K. NEWEY (2004): "Jackknife and Analytical Bias Reduction for Nonlinear Panel Models," *Econometrica*, 72, 1295–1319.

HONORÉ, B. E. AND E. KYRIAZIDOU (2000): "Panel Data Discrete Choice Models with Lagged Dependent Variables," *Econometrica*, 68, 839–874.

LANCASTER, T. (2000): "The Incidental Parameter Problem Since 1948," *Journal of Econometrics*, 95, 391–413.

——— (2002): "Orthogonal Parameters and Panel Data," *Review of Economic Studies*, 69, 647–666.

NEWEY, W. K. (1990): "Semiparametric Efficiency Bounds," *Journal of Applied Econometrics*, 5, 99–135.

NEYMAN, J. AND E. L. SCOTT (1948): "Consistent Estimates Based on Partially Consistent Observations," *Econometrica*, 16, 1–32.

PACE, L. AND A. SALVAN (2006): "Adjustments of the Profile Likelihood from a New Perspective," *Journal of Statistical Planning and Inference*, 136, 3554–3564.

REID, N. (1995): "The Roles of Conditioning in Inference," *Statistical Science*, 10, 138–199.

SARTORI, N. (2003): "Modified Profile Likelihoods in Models with Stratum Nuisance Parameters," *Biometrika*, 90, 533–549.

SEVERINI, T. A. (1998): "An Approximation to the Modified Profile Likelihood Function," *Biometrika*, 85, 403–411.

——— (2000): *Likelihood Methods in Statistics*, Oxford: Oxford University Press.

——— (2002): "Modified Estimating Functions," *Biometrika*, 89, 333–343.

SEVERINI, T. A. AND W. H. WONG (1992): "Profile Likelihood and Conditionally Parametric Models," *The Annals of Statistics*, 20, 1768–1802.

STEIN, C. (1956): "Efficient Nonparametric Testing and Estimation," in *Proceedings of the Third Berkeley Symposium on Mathematical Statistics and Probability*, University of California Press, Berkeley, Vol. 1.

SWEETING, T. J. (1987): "Discussion of the Paper by Professors Cox and Reid," *Journal of the Royal Statistical Society, Series B*, 49, 20–21.

WOUTERSEN, T. (2002): "Robustness Against Incidental Parameters," Unpublished manuscript.

CHAPTER 13

Fixed and Random Effects in Nonlinear Panel Data Model: A Discussion of a Paper by Manuel Arellano and Jinyong Hahn

Tiemen M. Woutersen*

1 INTRODUCTION

It was a pleasure to serve as the discussant for this session. The authors have played a major role in developing the area under discussion. The paper is very good so that my role is to comment rather than criticize. I will discuss a connection between reducing the estimation bias in a fixed effects model versus reducing misspecification bias in a random effects model. For this discussion, I use the framework of Woutersen (2002).

Woutersen (2002) proposes to use a moment that approximately separates the parameter of interest from the individual parameters. Let z_i denote that data on individual i, let α_i be the individual parameter and let θ be the common parameter. Then, for any likelihood model, a moment function $g(\alpha, \theta) = \sum_i g_i(\alpha, \theta, z_i)/N$ can be constructed with the properties (i) $Eg(\alpha_0, \theta_0) = 0$ where $\{\alpha_0, \theta_0\}$ denote the true parameter values and (ii) $Eg_{\alpha_i}(\alpha_0, \theta_0) = 0$ for all i, that is, the partial derivative of the moment function with respect to α_i is zero for all i. Condition (ii) means that the moment function depends somewhat less on α. The moment function $g(\alpha, \theta)$ is then integrated with respect to the likelihood $L^i(\alpha, \theta)$ and the prior $\pi(\alpha_i; \theta)$,

$$g^{i,I}(\theta) = \frac{\int g^i(\alpha_i, \theta)e^{L^i(\alpha_i, \theta)}\pi(\alpha_i; \theta)d\alpha_i}{\int e^{L^i(\alpha_i, \theta)}\pi(\alpha_i; \theta)d\alpha_i}. \tag{1}$$

Inference is then based on the integrated moment

$$g^I(\theta) = \frac{\sum_i}{NT} g^{i,I}(\theta))$$

by minimizing

$$Q(\theta) = g^I(\theta)'g^I(\theta)$$

with respect to θ. Under conditions given in Woutersen (2002) the asymptotic bias of the resulting estimator for θ is $O(T^{-2})$ in an asymptotic in

* Department of Economics, Johns Hopkins University, 3400 North Charles Street, Baltimor, E-mail: woutersen@jhu.edu.

which N increases as fast or faster than T, where N is the number of individuals and T is the number of observations per individual. Thus, correcting the bias in the moment function reduces the bias in the resulting estimator.

The review paper of Arellano and Hahn is for an important part based on the seminal paper of Hahn and Newey (2004). Hahn and Newey (2004) propose to correct for asymptotic bias. Hahn and Newey (2004) assume that the data are independent and identically distributed and allow for GMM estimators. Thus, compared to Woutersen (2002), Hahn and Newey (2004) allow a more general objective function but for less dependence across time periods. In particular, Woutersen (2002) allows for lagged dependence, general predetermined variables and time dummies, but assumes that expectation of the second derivative of the objective function can be calculated. This expectation can be calculated for likelihood models and some other models but it restricts the number of objective functions. The main difference (if a flat prior, $\pi(\alpha_i; \theta) = 1$ is used in equation (1)) between Hahn and Newey (2004) and Woutersen (2002) is that Hahn and Newey (2004) use an average operator (an average over realizations of an individual) where Woutersen (2002) uses an expectation operator. Subsequent papers have tried to combine the advantages of both papers by proposing to use the average operator for models with lagged dependence. A challenge for these subsequent papers is that one only averages over the realizations of one individual. That is, only over T-dependent realizations where T is small (otherwise, there would not be an "incidental parameter" problem to begin with). Averaging over T-dependent realization may very well work for some models but does not work so well for the simulations that I have done or seen.

In their review, Arellano and Hahn do not discuss models with mixing distributions (often called random effects models). In a model with a mixing distribution, one models the mixing or heterogeneity distribution, see Chamberlain (1984) and Baltagi (1995) for reviews. An advantage of fixed effects models is that one does not need to specify the mixing distribution so one is nonparametric for that aspect of the model. However, introducing many parameters into the objective function usually yields an estimation problem that is usually referred to as the incidental parameter problem of Neyman and Scott (1948). An interesting aspect of mixing models is that the problem of misspecifying the mixing distribution is related to the estimation problem of fixed effects. In particular, choosing the wrong mixing distribution also yields an $O(T^{-1})$ bias under general conditions. Moreover, one can remove the sensitivity to the wrong choice of mixing distribution by using approximate parameter separation. In particular, one can interpret $\pi(\alpha_i; \theta)$ in equation (1) as a mixing distribution (i.e., some parameter of the vector θ govern the mixing distribution). This is algebraically the same as interpreting $\pi(\alpha_i; \theta)$ as a prior so that the same tools can be used and the asymptotic bias can be reduced to $O(T^{-2})$. See Woutersen (2002) for details.

Additional References

BALTAGI, B. H. (1995): *Econometric Analysis of Panel Data*, New York: John Wiley and Sons.

CHAMBERLAIN, G. (1984): "Panel Data," in *Handbook of Econometrics,* Vol. 2, edited by Z. Griliches and M. D. Intriligator, Amsterdam: North-Holland.

Name Index

Other titles in the series *(continued from page iii)*